Forced
Into Glory:
Abraham Lincoln's
White Dream

Forced
Into Glory:
Abraham Lincoln's
White Dream

Lerone Bennett Jr.

 Johnson Publishing Company   Chicago 2000

Library of Congress Cataloging-in-Publication Data

Bennett, Lerone, Jr., 1928-
Forced Into Glory: Abraham Lincoln's White Dream /
By Lerone Bennett Jr.
p.cm.

1. Lincoln, Abraham, 1809-1865—Relations with Afro-Americans.
2. United States. President (1861-1865: Lincoln). Emancipation
Proclamation.
3. Slaves—Emancipation—United States.
4. Afro-Americans—Legal status, laws, etc.—History—19th century.
5. Afro-Americans—Civil rights—History—19th century.
6. United States—Politics and government—1861-1865.
7. Lincoln, Abraham, 1809-1865—Public opinion.
8. Public opinion—United States—History—19th century.
I. Title.

E457.2 .B44 1999
973.7'14—dc21
99-049496

ISBN 0-87485-085-1

For the Real Emancipators

FOR
Frederick Douglass, Harriet Tubman,
Nat Turner, Sojourner Truth,

And the slaves and former slaves
Who freed themselves
And almost freed Abraham Lincoln and America.

FOR
The White Americans who believed it
And tried to do it.

FOR
John Brown,
Wendell Phillips, Charles Sumner,
Thaddeus Stevens, Thaddeus Garrett, Salmon P. Chase,
Zebina Eastman, and *Richard Eells.*

FOR
Sid Ordower, Leon Despres, Lucy Montgomery,
George Powers, Kermit Eby, and George Mackechnie.

FOR
William Walker, the Black sergeant who was executed for
Protesting Lincoln's policies, and *Calvin Fairbanks,* the White
Activist Who spent 17 years in jail for helping slaves to escape.

FOR
The so-called "Radicals,"

FOR
James M. Ashley, Owen Lovejoy, Zachariah Chandler,
George W. Julian, Benjamin Wade, Adam Gurowski,
Joshua Giddings, Lyman Trumbull et al.,

Who Forced Lincoln Into Glory.

Is any man so insane as to suppose that any truth concerning Lincoln, or in relation to his thoughts, acts, and deeds, will be hid and buried out of human view? Pshaw! Folly! The best way is to tell the whole truth, and let it by its very presence and eternity crush and burn up all lies.
—William Henry Herndon

I will say then that I am not, nor ever have been in favor of bringing about in any way the social and political equality of the white and black races, [applause] —that I am not nor ever have been in favor of making voters or jurors of Negroes, nor of qualifying them to hold office, nor to intermarry with white people; and I will say in addition to this that there is a physical difference between the white and black races which I believe will for ever forbid the two races living together on terms of social and political equality. And inasmuch as they cannot so live, while they do remain together there must be the position of superior and inferior, and I as much as any other man am in favor of having the superior position assigned to the white race.
—Abraham Lincoln

PREFACE

I was a child in whitest Mississippi, reading for my life, when I discovered that *everything* I had been told about Abraham Lincoln was a lie. Astounded, unable to believe White media or White textbooks, I embarked on a private study designed not to satisfy course requirements but to save my life.

Was I, to paraphrase Sartre, saved? No, lost.

For I discovered that I lived in an Orwellian world where scholars with all the degrees the schools give could say in all seriousness that a separatist was an integrationist and that a White supremacist was the ultimate symbol of race relations and the American Dream. The proof was the Lincoln Memorial and the fact that dreamers of all races had this strange urge to go there and tell their deepest dreams of an integrated millennium to the cold, white, marble statue of a historical figure whose deepest dream was a land without Native Americans, African-Americans, and Martin Luther Kings.

Thirty or so years after my first encounter with the Abraham Lincoln everybody tries to hide, I suggested that *Ebony* magazine do a story with the title, "Was Abe Lincoln A White Supremacist?" My colleagues said the title wouldn't work because everybody knew that Lincoln was the great emancipator. I said, in response, that I could prove that Lincoln was a White supremacist and that the Emancipation Proclamation freed few if any slaves.

They laughed when I sat down at the typewriter.

But Publisher John H. Johnson said that if I could prove it, he would print it. I had already written a Lincoln book in my mind, never thinking that anybody would print it, and it only required a few weeks to produce a book-sized draft that was reduced to magazine size and published in the February 1968 *Ebony*.

To my surprise, the story triggered a national controversy. The *New York Times* and other newspapers published condemnatory editorials, and varied columnists suggested that the Republic was in danger. To meet this threat, assorted historians and freelance writers were rushed to the front lines to write articles proving that I was a Black Power Militant and that Abraham Lincoln always loved colored people in his own way. In an incredible article in the *New York Times*, called "Was Lincoln A Honky?" Herbert Mitgang said it was racist to say that Lincoln was a racist because he opposed Black citizenship and equal rights and—Lincoln's words—"the niggers and white people . . . marrying together."

This was a smokescreen, for anybody who knew anything about Lincoln knew I was right; and after the shouting died down, there was a quiet reevaluation and a general abandonment of the cruder aspects of the great emancipator myth.

This, however, was not the end of it. For although few newspapers print Great White Emancipator editorials on February 12, and although fewer scholars hold Lincoln up as a model of race relations, there is still a tendency to exaggerate his role in the abortive emancipation of African-Americans and to evade the true meaning and imperatives of the First Reconstruction, imperatives that are remarkably similar to the true meaning and imperatives of the Second Reconstruction of the 1980s and 1990s.

At the same time, almost without popular notice, an increasing number of scholars, hooked beyond redemption on the warm and comforting myths of The Immaculate Emancipation and The Great War Between The Northern and Southern [White] Brothers, are circling the wagons around a new and improved version of the old myth, suggesting that Lincoln was converted at the last moment before his tragic assassination or that he said all those terrible things about separation and Black deportation because he wanted to get elected to office, like any other red-blooded American. Worse, far worse, is the fact that few historians—John Hope Franklin, Vincent Harding, Robert Harris and others excepted—deal with Lincoln and the Civil War historically, that is to say, as an unfolding process and *an open wound* that is still festering and poisoning the body politic.

To paraphrase Dwight Macdonald, then, American literature is divided into three parts: fiction, nonfiction, and biographies of Abraham Lincoln.

This is *not* a biography: this is a political study of the uses and abuses of biography and myth, and it suggests, among other things, that your identity, whatever your color, is based, at least in part, on what you think about Lincoln, the Civil War, and slavery.

Abraham Lincoln or somebody said once that you can't fool all the people all the time. By turning a racist who wanted to deport all Blacks into a national symbol of integration and brotherhood, the Lincoln mythmakers have managed to prove Lincoln or whoever said it wrong.

This is the story of how they fooled all the people all the time, and why.

I have assumed here, in telling this story, that slavery was a crime against humanity and that there is no hope for us until we cross the great equator of our history and confront Lincoln, Lee and all the other participants on that level. I have compared Lincoln here not with twentieth-century leaders but with the White men and women of his own time, and I have suggested that one of the reasons we are in trouble racially in this country is that we have systematically downplayed and suppressed the White men and women who, unlike Lincoln, really believed in the Declaration of Independence.

I have suggested finally that Lincoln is a key, perhaps the key, to the American personality and that what we invest in him, and *hide* in him, is who we are.

In the end, then, *Forced Into Glory* is not so much about Lincoln as it is about race, heroes, leadership, political morality, scholarship, and the American Dream.

I said at the beginning that I was astonished in my childhood by the lies of history, the lies written in books and, more importantly, the lies written in things. I should have said also that in the same period, and later, I discovered another history in the classes of great Black teachers at Lanier High School in Jackson, Mississippi, and Morehouse College in Atlanta, Georgia. Among those teachers were great artists like M. V. Manning, Melvin Dow Kennedy, Robert Brisbane, E. B. Williams and Benjamin Elijah Mays, who turned White American history inside out, like a glove, and made great figures like Frederick Douglass and Harriet Tubman dance on the runway of my mind. And although I follow another path here, I am indebted to John Hope Franklin and Benjamin

Quarles for their pathfinding books on Lincoln, and for their life and work. I am also indebted to two eminent historians, Dr. John B. Duff and Dr. Robert Harris, and the Rev. James W. Mack, a specialist in history and philosophy, who read manuscript copies and made critical suggestions.

I have been working on this book forever, and I owe so much to my wife Gloria and my children, Joy Bennett Kinnon, Constance and Courtney Bennett, Lerone Bennett III, and my publisher, John H. Johnson.

I am particularly indebted to Cathy Reedy for designing the book, Herbert Temple for designing the jacket, and computer specialist Ingrid Larkin for helping to pull the pages together. Phyllis R. Horton, Beverly Coppage, Joyce Parks, Habib Womack, Wallace Best, Paul Nascimento, and Deidre Lucas provided valuable technical assistance, and Carmel Tinkchell and Lillian Terrell helped coordinate the process. Basil Phillips of the Book Division was, as always, extremely helpful and went beyond the call of duty explaining to booksellers year after year why the book would be delayed yet another year.

A book of this kind is always a cooperative project between the author and libraries and librarians. Pamela Cash Menzies and the staff of the Johnson Publishing Company Library provided invaluable assistance; so did Connie Gordon and the staff of the Chicago Public Library, Debbie King and the staff of the Chicago Historical Society, and the staffs of the Newberry Library and the Carter G. Woodson Regional Library. Staff members at the Library of Congress, the Butler Library of Columbia University, the Henry E. Huntington Library, and the Illinois State Historical Library were generous in locating and copying primary sources.

None of these men and women are responsible for the wild things I say from time to time, but if stray beams of light fall on the following pages, they are largely responsible. I alone am responsible for the limitations and the errors.

Two final words:

One: This is not a judgment of a personality; it is an appraisal of a historical role, the role—or is it a calling?—of a principle-loving, principle-spouting leader of a group that is oppressing another group for racial reasons despite its principles and because of its principles.

Two: I have not, to paraphrase what Wendell Phillips said in another connection, judged Lincoln at all except by the words of his own mouth and on facts asserted and admitted by his own eulogists and defenders, including Herndon, Sandburg, Randall, Donald et al. I have not claimed here that he should have been perfect, but I have suggested that he should have been consistent and that if government of the people was good for the White majority of Illinois it was good for the Black majority of South Carolina. I have not criticized him for not rising to the level of the Kings and Mandelas of our time—I have deplored the fact that he didn't rise to the level of the great Black and White leaders of his time.

Lerone Bennett Jr.
Chicago 2000

WORKS FREQUENTLY CITED

AC   *Appletons' Annual Cyclopaedia*, 1861-63

CW   *The Collected Works of Abraham Lincoln*, edited by Roy P. Basler, 11 vols. Rutgers, 1955.

BD   *The Diary of Orville Hickman Browning*, edited by T. C. Pease and J.G. Randall. Vol. 1. Springfield, 1925.

CD   *Inside Lincoln's Cabinet: The Civil War Diaries of Salmon P. Chase*, edited by David Donald. New York, 1954.

CP   *The Salmon P. Chase Papers*, edited by John Niven. Vol. 3. Kent, 1996.

FD   *The Life and Writings of Frederick Douglass*, edited by Philip S. Foner, 4 vols. New York, 1955.

GD   Adam Gurowski. *Diary*, 3 vols. New York, 1862-66.

Gay   Adams S. Hill to Sidney Howard Gay, Sidney Howard Gay Papers, Butler Library, Columbia University.

HH   Emanuel Hertz, *The Hidden Lincoln: From the Letters and Papers of William H. Herndon*. New York, 1938.

HI   *Herndon's Informants*, edited by Douglas L. Wilson and Rodney O. Davis. Urbana, 1998.

HW   *Herndon's Lincoln*, by William H. Herndon and Jesse W. Weik. Cleveland, 1930.

NH   J. G. Nicolay and John Hay, *Abraham Lincoln, A History*, 10 vols. New York, 1890.

PS   Wendell Phillips, *Speeches, Lectures, and Letters. Vol. 1, First Series.* Boston, 1894.

RR   Allen T. Rice, *Reminiscences of Abraham Lincoln by Distinguished Men of His Time.* New York, 1888.

SL   *The Selected Letters of Charles Sumner*, edited by Beverly Wilson Palmer. Vol. 2. Boston, 1990.

WD   Gideon Welles. *Diary of Gideon Welles*, Vol. 1. New York, 1911.

WH   Gideon Welles, "The History of Emancipation," *Galaxy*, Dec. 1872.

CONTENTS

Forced
Into Glory:
Abraham Lincoln's
White Dream

Part One

Mirage

Among other remarks he said "he knew his Proclamation would not make a single Negro free beyond our military reach."
—Memoir of John A. Dahlgren

He then went into a prolonged course of remarks about the Proclamation. He said it was not his intention in the beginning to interfere with Slavery in the States; that he never would have done it, if he had not been compelled by necessity to do it, to maintain the Union . . . that he had hesitated for some time, and had resorted to this measure, only when driven to it by public necessity . . . that he had always himself been in favor of emancipation, but not immediate emancipation, even by the States. Many evils attending this appeared to him.
— Confederate Vice President Alexander H. Stephens

1

The Most Famous Act In U.S. History Never Happened

THE presidential campaign of 1860 was over, and the victor was stretching his legs and shaking off the cares of the world in his temporary office in the state capitol in Springfield, Illinois. Surrounded by the perks of power, at peace with the world, the president-elect was regaling old acquaintances with tall tales about his early days as a politician. One of the visitors interrupted this monologue and remarked that it was a shame that "the vexatious slavery matter" would be the first question of public policy the new president would have to deal with in Washington.

The president-elect's eyes twinkled and he said he was reminded of a story. According to eyewitness Henry Villard, President-elect Abraham Lincoln "told the story of the Kentucky Justice of the Peace whose first case was a criminal prosecution for the abuse of slaves. Unable to find any precedent, he exclaimed angrily: 'I will be damned if I don't feel almost sorry for being elected when the niggers is the first thing I have to attend to'" (29).

This story, shocking as it may sound to Lincoln admirers, was in character. For the president-elect had never shown any undue sympathy for Blacks, and none of his cronies was surprised to hear him suggest that he shared the viewpoint of the reluctant and biased justice of the peace. As for the N-word, everybody knew that old Abe used it all the time, both in public and in private. (Since Lincoln supporters are in a state of constant denial, I have not used elision in reporting his use of the offensive word *n——r*.)

In one of the supreme ironies of history, the man who told this story was forced by circumstances to attend to what he called "the nigger question." And within five years he was enshrined in American mythology as "the great emancipator" who freed Blacks with a stroke of the pen out of the goodness of his heart.

Since that time, the mythology of "the great emancipator" has become a part of the mental landscape of America. Generations of schoolchildren have memorized its cadences. Poets, politicians, and long-suffering Blacks have wept over its imagery and drama.

No other American story is so enduring.

No other American story is so comforting.

No other American story is so false.

Abraham Lincoln was *not* "the great emancipator."

The testimony of sixteen thousand books and monographs to the contrary notwithstanding, Lincoln did *not* emancipate the slaves, greatly or otherwise. As for the Emancipation Proclamation, it was not a real emancipation proclamation at all, and did not liberate African-American slaves. John F. Hume, the Missouri antislavery leader who heard Lincoln speak in Alton and who looked him in the eye in the White House, said the Proclamation "did not . . . whatever it may have otherwise accomplished at the time it was issued, liberate a single slave" (138).

Sources favorable to Lincoln were even more emphatic. Lincoln crony Henry Clay Whitney said the Proclamation was a mirage and that Lincoln knew it was a mirage (133). Secretary of State William Henry Seward, the No. 2 man in the administration, said the Proclamation was an illusion in which "we show our sympathy with the slaves by emancipating the slaves where we cannot reach them and holding them in bondage where we can set them free" (Piatt, 150).

The same points have been made with abundant documentation by twentieth-century scholars like Richard Hofstadter, who said the Proclamation "did not in fact free any slaves" (169). Some of the biggest names in the Lincoln establishment have said the same thing. Roy P. Basler, the editor of the monumental *Collected Works of Abraham Lincoln*, said the Proclamation was "itself only a promise of freedom . . ." (1935, 219-20). J. G. Randall, who has been called "the greatest Lincoln scholar of all time," said the Proclamation itself did not free a single slave (1957, 357). Horace White, the *Chicago Tribune* correspondent who covered Lincoln in Illinois and in Washington, said it is doubtful that the Proclamation "freed anybody anywhere" (222).

There, then, the secret is out! **The most famous act in American political history never happened**.

Sandburg wrote tens of thousands of words about it.

Lindsay wrote a poem about it.

Copland wrote a musical portrait about it.

King had a dream about it.[1]

But the awkward fact is that Abraham Lincoln didn't do it. To paraphrase what Robert McColley said about the abortive emancipating initiative of Thomas Jefferson (125), never did man achieve more fame for what he did not do *and for what he never intended to do*. The best authority, Lincoln himself, told one of his top aides that he knew that the Proclamation in and of itself would not "make a single Negro free beyond our military reach" (Dahlgren 382), thereby proving two critical and conclusive points. The first is that Lincoln himself knew that his most famous act would not of itself free a single Negro. The second and most damaging point is that "the great emancipator" did not intend for it to free a single Negro, for he carefully, deliberately, studiously excluded all Negroes *within* "our military reach."

In what some critics call a hoax and others call a deliberate ploy not to free African-Americans but to keep them in slavery, Lincoln deliberately drafted the document so it wouldn't free a single Negro immediately.

What Lincoln did—and it was so clever that we ought to stop calling him honest Abe—was to "free" slaves in Confederate-held territory where he couldn't free them and to leave them in slavery in Union-held territory where he could have freed them.

Despite what everybody, or almost everybody says, January 1, 1863, was not African-American Emancipation Day. Nor, as Randall and other have said, was it a Day of Jubilee for the slaves, except in certain military venues and Northern cities far removed from the hurt and humiliation of Slave Row. To tell the truth, there has never been a day in the United States of America when all the slaves could join hands and say together, "Free at last!" One of the many reasons why a national apology for slavery is an imperative necessity is that there has never been a day of closure for the slaves or the slavehold-ers—or the sons and daughters of the slaves and slaveholders. The real day of deliverance, December 18, 1865, the day and date nobody remembers, the day the Thirteenth Amendment was ratified, was so formal and was hedged about with so many levels of technicality, that it came and went like the oxygen of the air, giving life without giving notice.

It is in the precise sense scandalous that Americans, Black and White, are so totally misinformed on this subject. Professors, mu-seum curators, media prophets say almost without exception that slavery in America was ended by a presidential edict. And "other writers of what is claimed to be history, almost without number, speak of the President's announcement as if it caused the bulwarks of slavery to fall down very much as the walls of Jericho are said to have done, at one blast, overwhelming the whole institution and setting every bond man free"(136). Nothing has changed in America since John Hume wrote those words in 1905. Despite computers, despite the Internet, despite the proliferation of books and pam-phlets, almost all Blacks and Whites, including a not inconsiderable number of Ph.D.'s, believe that slavery in America ceased on the day and hour that Abraham Lincoln signed a document that dis-solves, like a mirage, the closer one comes to it.

The confusion on this issue is monumental as we are reminded every year when schoolchildren and scholars in Memphis, New

Orleans, Louisville, St. Louis, Norfolk, Baltimore and other cities celebrate a January 1 emancipation that specifically excluded Memphis, New Orleans, and Norfolk and didn't even apply to the Border States of Kentucky, Missouri, Maryland, and Delaware. To add to the confusion, millions have created annual celebrations based on the idea that their ancestors were "freed" on January 1, 1863, but were not informed until months later by mean generals and officials.

If pressed, all or almost all scholars will concede that the Proclamation didn't free the slaves on January 1, 1863, but this information is disseminated, if it is disseminated at all, in footnotes or asides, and there is a tendency, even among the best scholars, to defend or even praise the Proclamation that didn't free anybody.

Will someone say that this was an accident or an oversight? But how can anyone fail to see that it required art, forethought, and design to draft a document that freed everybody when in fact it freed nobody? And how explain the fact that the same accident happened twice? For when Lincoln warned rebels in September that he would sign an emancipation in one hundred days if they didn't lay down their arms, he carefully and precisely said that he would free all slaves "within any state, or *designated part* of a state" in rebellion (CW 5:434, italics added).

This language—we shall return to this—was not in the tentative document he read to his cabinet on July 22, 1862. That document said unambiguously that he intended to free *"all* persons held as slaves within any state or states" in rebellion (CW 5:337, italics added). This means that he decided some time between July 22 and September 22 to play a little game. It means that he knew in September what he intended to do in January. It means that he was planning in September to keep in slavery the slaves he promised to free in January.

A growing body of evidence suggests that the Emancipation Proclamation was a ploy designed not to emancipate the slaves but to keep as many slaves as possible in slavery until Lincoln could mobilize support for his conservative plan to free Blacks gradually and to ship them out of the country. What Lincoln was trying to do, then, from our standpoint, was to outmaneuver the real emancipators and to contain the emancipation tide, which had reached such a dangerous intensity that it threatened his ability to govern and to run the war machinery.

This is no mere theory; there is indisputable evidence on this point in documents and in the testimony of reliable witnesses, including Lincoln himself. The most telling testimony comes not from twentieth-century critics but from cronies and confidants who visited the White House and heard the words from Lincoln's mouth. There is, for example, the testimony of Judge David Davis, the three hundred-plus-pound Lincoln crony who visited the White House in 1862, some two months after Lincoln signed the Preliminary Proclamation, and found him working feverishly to subvert his *announced* plan in favor of his *real* plan. What was Lincoln's real plan? It was the only emancipation plan he ever had: gradual emancipation, the slower the better, with compensation to slaveowners and the deportation of the emancipated. His "whole soul," Davis said, "is absorbed in *his* plan [my italics] of remunerative emancipation, and he thinks that if Congress don't fail him, that the problem is solved. . . ."[2]

Wait a minute! What's going on here? *What* plan of remunerative emancipation? Two months ago, Abraham Lincoln announced to the whole world that he was going to free the slaves of rebels with a stroke of the pen on January 1. He didn't say anything then about Congress not letting him down.

What are we to understand by all this? We are to understand, among other things, that words, especially Lincoln's words, are deceiving and that Lincoln announced his first plan as a mask to cover his real plan and his real end. That at any rate is the testimony of another intimate Lincoln friend, Henry Clay Whitney. What was his real end? The Proclamation, Whitney said, was "not the end designed by him, but only the *means* to the end, the end being the deportation of the slaves and the payment for them to their masters—at least to those who were loyal" (323, italics in original).

There is corroboration on this point from, of all people, Abraham Lincoln, who asked Congress in his second State of the Union Message to approve not the Emancipation Proclamation but an entirely different plan, the real plan he had confided to Judge Davis, a plan that contradicted the Proclamation and called for, among other things, the *deportation*—his word—of Blacks and the racial cleansing of the United States of America (CW 5:518-37).

There he was, then, enclosed in a racial prison of his own making, trying to escape the inescapable, saying words—"*We* cannot escape history"—that would light him and all who afterward endorsed the words without denouncing the proposal—down in dishonor to the latest generation. We shall deal with this in the following chapters, but to understand the mirage of the Proclamation, one must go back to the preceding July and consider three signifying facts:

1. On July 17, 1862, Congress passed the Second Confiscation Act, which was the first emancipation proclamation and the most revolutionary act ever passed by the United States Congress. This act, which was signed into law six months before the signing of the Emancipation Proclamation, provided for the confiscation of the property of rebels, defined in the act as traitors, and the freeing of all slaves of rebels. Lincoln's proclamations, both of them, were historically regressive, not going as far, as Randall noted, "as Congress already had gone in the Second Confiscation Act (1957, 357).

2. On July 25, 1862, Lincoln issued, as required by law, the official warning that the confiscation provisions would go into effect within sixty days (CW 5:341).

3. On September 22, 1862, ONE DAY BEFORE THE EFFECTIVE DATE OF THE REVOLUTIONARY CONFISCATION ACT (CP 3:277), Lincoln signed the Preliminary Emancipation Proclamation, which effectively postponed or nullified the emancipating and confiscating required under that act. The effect of all this, whatever the intention, and the inten-

tion was not too far removed from the effect, was to stop the most sweeping act of emancipation and confiscation in American history.

Thus, in one forked-tongued act, Lincoln outflanked his critics, re-enslaved slaves freed by the Second Confiscation Act and promised to free slaves he could not free.

John Hume, the abolitionist who measured Lincoln in Illinois and in the White House, argued in 1905 that the Proclamation was a brilliant political move that disarmed Lincoln's antislavery critics "without giving them any material advantage or changing the actual situation" (146). Two latter-day scholars—Richard Current and Ralph Korngold— made the same points, arguing that the Proclamation could have been designed not to hasten emancipation but to at least slow it down. Current said it could be argued that "the Proclamation had as its purpose and effect the checking of the Radical program," that is to say, the program of immediate emancipation, and that by declaring a one hundred-day grace period, Lincoln shrewdly gave himself an excuse for ignoring congressional laws on confiscation and the use of Black soldiers. By these tactics, Current suggested, Lincoln could have gained time to work for his own plan to free Blacks gradually and to ship them out of the country (226-7).

Korngold was even more explicit, saying that the Proclamation and other Lincoln maneuvers in this period were attempts to take the rudder out of the hands of the friends of Black freedom and to "steer emancipation into what he considered a safer channel"(182).

Lincoln was playing with the lives of more than a half-million slaves, including some one hundred thousand Blacks in New Orleans and other Union-held areas in Louisiana.[3] Many of these slaves had been freed for all practical purposes when Union forces captured New Orleans and surrounding areas in April 1862. Most, if not all of them, had been freed again, this time legally, by the Second Confiscation Act. But since Lincoln had never enforced that act, the Louisiana slaves existed in a kind of no-man's land between Union generals, treasury agents, and the old slavemasters. On January 1, 1863, Abraham Lincoln, commander in chief of the United States Army and Navy, could have freed these slaves again, perhaps forever, with a stroke of the pen. But instead of using his pen to free them, he used it to reenslave tens of thousands of men, women and children, remanding them to the slavemasters and the antebellum status quo.

Five cabinet members and other officials, including at least one Southern governor, told Abraham Lincoln that this was inefficient, unfair and perhaps illegal, but he insisted on condemning these slaves to additional months and years of unnecessary slavery (WH 849). We are thus left with the strange paradox, a paradox overlooked by all or almost all interpreters, that the Emancipation Proclamation enslaved and/or continued the enslavement of a half-million slaves, more slaves than it ever freed. That's an important point. Let's rephrase it and put it another way: *On January 1, 1863, Abraham Lincoln reenslaved and/or condemned to extended slavery more Blacks than he ever freed.*

Did this cause him anguish and pain? If so, he gave no indications, arguing heatedly and passionately for continued slavery in the exempted areas, giving different reasons at different times, citing on one occasion the Constitution and on another the need to strengthen Southern White loyalists (RR 92-3).

Such an unfeeling dismissal of the anguished hopes of the slaves was common in the Lincoln White House. Another instance of it took place in the spring of 1862 when Lincoln sat on the District of Columbia emancipation bill for two nights. Why did he do that? The answer, believe it or not, is that he had promised an old Kentucky friend that he wouldn't sign the bill until the friend could leave town with two of his slaves. In one of the most startling—and revealing—statements of his presidency, Lincoln said he regretted that District of Columbia slaves had been freed at once, "that it should have been for gradual emancipation," and "that now families would at once be deprived of cooks, stable boys &c and they of their protectors without any provision for them" (BD 541). We shall return to this theme repeatedly in this study, for one of the main reasons Lincoln opposed immediate emancipation was his personal and racist concern about the impact such an act would have on the servant problem of slaveholder families.

It was one of the major deficiencies of this talented man, who must have had something, that he never once deigned to notice how he was personally hurting Blacks, which is surprising since it was the major conceit of his presidency that he had never willingly put a thorn in any man's bosom. It is sad to have to say that he never realized that he never in his whole presidency stopped putting thorns into the bosoms of African-Americans and Native Americans. The consensus among his closest friends and advisors was that he had no particular sympathy or concern for either refugees or slaves. The welfare of Negroes, Whitney said, "didn't enter into his policy at all" (323).

This insensitivity colored Lincoln's whole presidency. General James Samuel Wadsworth, who saw Lincoln almost every day at the height of the crisis and who was with him "frequently for 5 or 6 hours at the War Department," was shocked by the racism in the Lincoln White House, where Lincoln "frequently" spoke of "the nigger question" and debated whether this or that act would "touch the nigger." On a typical occasion, Wadsworth was, he said, "talking against [General George] McClellan with [Postmaster General Montgomery] Blair, in Lincoln's presence," when he was "met by Blair with the remark, 'He'd have been all right if he'd stolen a couple of n——rs.' A general laugh, in which Lincoln laughed, as if it were an argument."[4] General Wadsworth said that Lincoln was contemptuous of abolitionist and spoke of the slaves as cattle.

Other contemporaries corroborated Wadsworth. Donn Piatt said Lincoln expressed "no sympathy for the slave "and no dislike for slaveowners and "laughed at the Abolitionists as a disturbing element easily controlled" (RR 481). Eli Thayer said Lincoln spoke of abolitionists "in terms of contempt and derision" (qtd. in Burlingame 173). Ralph Waldo Emerson said in his *Journal* that Lincoln "thinks Emancipation almost *morally wrong* and resorts to it only as a desperate measure . . . " (452 , italics added). For this reason, among others, Jessie Benton Frémont called Lincoln "the Pontius Pilate of the Slaves "(369).

Most major Lincoln historians, have painted great word pictures of how Lincoln suffered during the war, absorbing every bayonet thrust and bleeding the blood of the White soldiers in blue and gray. There is no evidence that he gave more than a passing thought to the plight of the Blacks in blue, not to mention the slaves condemned to slavery and death by the orders he issued and didn't issue. On the contrary, he seems to have been chillingly blind to the impact his decisions would have on millions of Blacks. *The most troubling finding of this study is that Abraham Lincoln was shockingly indifferent and insensitive to the plight of the slaves in particular and African-Americans in general.* Lincoln's law partner and great and good friend, William Henry Herndon, said that "sometimes Lincoln was great, very great, and sometimes small . . ." (HH 186-7).

Very small.

Harriet Tubman said American slavery was "the next thing to hell," and slaveholder Thomas Jefferson said—on one of his good days—that one hour of American slavery was "fraught with more misery than ages of that" which the White American colonists "rose in rebellion to oppose" (Boyd 10:63).

How can anyone defend, much less praise, a "great emancipator" who regretted the emancipation of a people from that hell because it would, among other things, deprive Southern White families of domestic servants "and they of their protectors?" And how can anyone fail to see that the same insensitivity characterized the man who said coldly in the coldly phrased Proclamation that the areas in which more than five hundred thousand slaves lived "are, for the present, left precisely as if this Proclamation were not issued" (CW 6:29).

Precisely.

Lincoln knew what he was doing. Not only that, he told everybody what he was doing, and everybody, or almost everybody, has refused to read and understand the words he wrote to describe what he was doing. In both the Preliminary Proclamation, and in a quotation in the final Proclamation, Lincoln said in the same sentence that the slaves in designated areas would be free and that the government would do nothing to repress them "in any efforts they may make for their actual freedom" (CW 5:434).

Actual: this is the word that gives the game away. Lincoln said he was giving the slaves freedom, and that the government would not repress them if they decided to run away and *actually* free themselves. Of such nuances of language are Memorials on the Mall made.

In his use of language and in his skill in using words to conceal and confuse, Abraham Lincoln resembles Booker T. Washington more than any other American leader, and it is fascinating—and depressing—to watch him playing with the yawning chasm between the show freedom of the Proclamation and "actual" freedom. He even proposed a constitutional amendment to pay "loyal" "owners" of "slaves who shall have enjoyed *actual* freedom by the chances of the war" (CW 5:530, italics added).

This language provides irrefutable proof that Abraham Lincoln never intended to provide for the actual freedom of the slaves, and it is embarrassing to have to say what almost everybody overlooks, and that is that *the most famous document on slavery in history does not deal with slavery at all, does not in fact use the word* slavery *at all*, pretending, in language any first-year law student could have ripped to shreds, to free certain vaguely defined slaves.

If African-Americans had relied on that document alone, they would still be in slavery in several states and areas. The Proclamation didn't apply to the Border States and Tennessee, and it excepted, as we have seen, certain slaves, a lot of slaves, in other states. If we were relying on the Emancipation Proclamation today, then, Blacks would still be in slavery in Delaware, Kentucky, Maryland, Missouri, Tennessee, part of Virginia and part of Louisiana.

What about the slaves in other areas? Would they be free?

dental factor in that process, for he did everything he could to avoid the end that immortalized him. Even if it turns out that the Proclamation advanced the process, he didn't plan it that way. What he planned, in fact, was the precise opposite of what happened. And if he had been told "when he entered on the Presidency," Hume said, "that before his term of office would expire, he would be hailed as 'The Great Emancipator,' he would have treated the statement as equal to one of his own best jokes" (143).

The task before us is to explain how the joke became history and history myth and nightmare.

And in dealing with that task, one must remember always that the unknown and underrated slaves played a major role in liberating themselves. In fact, as Victor B. Howard and others have said, the slaves made a larger contribution to this process than Lincoln. One sees this clearest perhaps in Kentucky where Lincoln condemned slaves to continued slavery and where the slaves reduced his proslavery Border State policy to shambles, Howard said, by refusing "to play the part of slaves any longer." If "the Blacks themselves had not taken the initiative to abandon slavery," he said, "there would have been no emancipation in 1863 . . . "(30).

What saved these slaves was neither Lincoln nor the Proclamation but the Union Army, the Thirteenth Amendment, and three empowering and liberating provisions of the emancipating Thirty-seventh Congress: 1) a revision of the military code forbidding soldiers to return slaves to slaveowners; 2) the Confiscation Act which freed the slaves of all rebels and 3) an act that freed all slaves and their families who enlisted in the Union Army. In 1864 alone, twenty-five thousand Kentucky slaves freed themselves and their families by enlisting— twenty-five thousand more than were ever freed in Kentucky by Lincoln. By the end of that year, Howard said, the Army and the slaves were well on the way to making emancipation a reality in Kentucky (71) and other states—despite Abraham Lincoln, not because of him. This means, among other things, that the slaves were among the greatest of all emancipators and that they helped emancipate themselves and almost emancipated Lincoln.

2

The Emancipation Proclamation That Wasn't

LTHOUGH the Proclamation was a limited document with limited and arguably devious aims, Lincoln issued it with extreme misgivings, going so far as to ask God, in the words Jesus used in the Garden of Gethsemane, "to let this cup pass from me" (RR 533).

Latter-day historians, viewing the Immaculate Emancipation through the haze of the tragic assassination of the nineteenth century and perhaps the conscious or unconscious need to defend and justify the illegitimate White privileges of the twentieth century, have written all kind of nonsense about the Proclamation. But the men who knew Lincoln best tell us, almost without exception, that the document was the incidental, accidental effort of a man who did everything he possibly could to avoid it.

Herndon, who knew him better perhaps than anyone else, save his wife, said his heart wasn't in it (HW 483). Lamon, who was Lincoln's confidant and aide in Washington, said he signed it "with avowed reluctance" (345).

Whitney said "his policy of emancipation was adopted against both his judgment, desire, and conscience . . . " (12) and that he "abhorred" the Proclamation. We think *abhorred* is too strong a word, but Whitney knew Lincoln personally, and we didn't (515).

It is clear from all this, and will become clearer, that Lincoln didn't want to do it.

Why did he change his mind?

Who said he changed his mind?

The only thing we can say, based on the evidence, is that Lincoln changed in order to remain the same and to slow down the emancipation process in favor of his conservative policy of gradual compensated emancipation and deportation.

To rephrase the question, then, without prejudging the issue, why did Lincoln decide to issue the Emancipation Proclamation?

The answer is easy. He had no alternative. The half-hearted, soft-on-slavery policy he had pursued for some eighteen months had created a disastrous situation, and the Union was on the verge of losing a war that was impossible to lose, given the imbalance in manpower and resources. Many critics of the war, even some of Lincoln's friends, said bluntly that Abraham Lincoln was part of the problem and that his policies were directly responsible for prolonging the war and increasing the number of Union casualties. Senator Benjamin Franklin Wade of Ohio told him to his face that "you are murdering your country by inches in consequence of the inactivity of the military and the want of a distinct policy in regard to slavery" (qtd. in Trefousse 184).

In this climate, with the military situation deteriorating and England and other foreign powers threatening to decide the issue by recognizing Southern independence, Lincoln played what he called his last card, invoking the name of freedom, which ended the threat of foreign intervention, and calling on the slaves, who tilted the scale in favor of the Union.

This act, despite itself, saved the Union and immortalized Lincoln, who was forced to an immortality he resisted with every fiber of his being.

Not wisdom, then, but threats, not compassion but pressure moved him to his date with destiny.

The pressure came from Black and White abolitionists, most notably Frederick Douglass and Wendell Phillips, and from men in high places, like Governor John Albion Andrew of Massachusetts, and major leaders of Congress, like Representative Thaddeus Stevens of Pennsylvania and Senator Charles Sumner of Massachusetts, who threatened to withhold men, matériel and money if Lincoln continued his soft-on-slavery policy.

We can say inversely that Lincoln never would have issued a Proclamation, if he hadn't been, in his word, driven to it. Congressman George W. Julian of Indiana, who served on the Joint Committee for the Conduct of the War, said the "popular current had become irresistible," and Lincoln "feared that enlistments would cease, and that Congress would even refuse the necessary supplies to carry on the war, if he declined any longer to place it on a clearly defined antislavery basis" (RR 62-3). He finally yielded to the popular current, Julian said, and in so doing was forced by irresistible pressure into glory.

Lincoln himself said that pressure made him do it. Speaking to Border State representatives on July 12, 1862, he said the antislavery pressure was "increasing" and was forcing him to change his policies. (CW 5:318). By the end of the year, the pressure, John F. Hume said, was "practically irresistible" (146). Representative John Covode said Lincoln told him in the last week of the year that he was "driven"to it, adding: "*It must be done. I am driven to it.* There is no other way out of our troubles. But although my duty is plain, it is in some respects painful . . . "(qtd. in Sandburg 1939, 2:14).

Why was it "painful" to end one of history's most heinous chapters? Why was it a burden to help end the three hundred-year nightmare of four million of his fellow human beings?

The answer is in the question. Abraham Lincoln feared freedom more than he feared slavery, and it is the virtually unanimous testimony of his contemporaries, friends and foes, that he was literally dragged, protesting every step of the way, to the mountaintop.

Count Adam Gurowski, a Polish exile who was working in the

State Department and who had access to some of the major players of the period, was appalled by Lincoln's indecisiveness and his repeated attempts to end the war without destroying slavery. And as history moved Lincoln—slowly, grudgingly, reluctantly—toward reality, Gurowski told his diary that Lincoln had been "whipped" into glory and that history would not allow him to wear "borrowed plumage" (GD 2:99-100).

The ever-watchful Gurowski was too sanguine.

History, American-style, especially the history of Abraham Lincoln, is a history of borrowed plumage and glory. If you doubt that, consider the fate of Lincoln's contemporary, Senator Lyman Trumbull, who, unlike Lincoln, fought for fugitive slaves in Illinois and who, unlike Lincoln, fought for slaves in Washington, authoring the first Confiscation Act, which started the emancipation process, the Second Confiscation Act, which freed the slaves of all rebels, and co-authoring the Thirteenth Amendment, which actually freed the slaves. Despite all this emancipating, Trumbull is virtually unknown to White Americans who have worked night and day for more than 135 years to perpetuate the memory of a White separatist who wanted to deport all African-Americans and who provides, moreover, the greatest example in all history of the wisdom of standing idly by in a great national crisis like slavery or apartheid or the Third Reich.

Gurowski was wrong.

The only plumage *approved* oppressors can wear in an oppressive history and an oppressive historiography is borrowed plumage.

What Lincoln did before signing the Proclamation is strange.

What he did afterward is stranger.

For to the dismay of congressional leaders, he continued to oppose his own Proclamation, even after he signed it. Almost before the ink was dry on the document, he was using the resources of the White House to mobilize a three-pronged national campaign against his own Proclamation. On one level, Lincoln and his chief lieutenants sent open signals to proslavery forces, including enemy politicians and generals, that all was not lost and that it was still possible for good White men to contain, minimize, divert and even negate the Proclamation.

Simultaneously, and paradoxically, Lincoln attacked the the legal foundations of his own Proclamation, saying repeatedly, publicly and indiscreetly that the Proclamation was of doubtful legal validity and could be diverted, subverted or evaded after the war. One of Lincoln's major academic supporters, Roy P. Basler, noted that Lincoln said in no less than half a dozen letters that the Proclamation was "merely a war measure" (1935, 212).

This was a disturbing approach for the chief executive of the Union to take. Was he not playing legal roulette and risking the future of the Union and the future of the slaves when he said two months before his death that in his opinion "the Proclamation was a *war measure* [italics in original]—and would have effect only from its being an exercise of the war power," and that "so far as he [Lincoln] was concerned, he should leave it to the Courts to decide" (Stephens 611).

Lincoln distanced himself further from the Proclamation by campaigning on a third level for a gradual emancipation program that contradicted and imperilled the Emancipation Proclamation he had signed. Five months after signing the Proclamation, he *announced* that "those who are in favor of *gradual emancipation* represented his views better than those who are in favor of *immediate emancipation*"—represented them better, that is, than those in favor of what Lincoln said he was doing in the Emancipation Proclamation (Raymond 430-1, italics in original).

Throughout 1863 and on into 1864, as misinformed Blacks praised him for fighting for their freedom, the president of the United States pressed that view, using his influence in unsuccessful efforts to get the Border States to adopt gradual emancipation plans that contradicted the fundamental principle of the Proclamation. If his advice had been followed, and if Kentucky or Maryland or Missouri had cemented into law gradual emancipation plans, the Thirteenth

Amendment, Ralph Korngold argued, couldn't have been passed in Congress or ratified by the required number of states (1955, 179).

When—again—did Lincoln change his mind? There is—again—no evidence that he ever changed his mind. It was only when congressional leaders foreclosed his options by forcing radical changes that made Black freedom in America irrevocable that Lincoln declared himself in favor of the Thirteenth Amendment.

As the campaign for the Thirteenth Amendment gained steam, first with the abolitionists and then with sensitive legislators like Sumner, Trumbull, and Congressman James Ashley of Ohio, Lincoln watched from his accustomed perch on the sidelines. In October 1863, when crony Leonard Swett told him that public opinion was solidly behind the issue and that it was to his political and historical interest to take a leadership role (HI 164), he mounted his Beautiful Soul white horse, saying indignantly that he had never done anything for purely political reasons, which was news to Swett, who said Lincoln was a world-class trimmer, and to Herndon, who said that politics were his heaven and that he had seldom if ever done anything for any other reason (HL 427).

Following the rule of his life, a rule defined by his reluctant conversion after passage of the Kansas-Nebraska Act and his reluctant conversion on the Proclamation, Lincoln was converted reluctantly for the third major time after massive Republican opposition developed during his campaign for renomination. Thus, after a Republican convention (the National Union Convention) nominated him for a second term, he finally climbed on the Thirteenth Amendment bandwagon, telling a convention committee that he was now in favor of the amendment (CW 7:380). By this time, a rump Republican convention, led by Lincoln critics, had made the amendment a national issue, and it was a matter of survival for Lincoln to join the procession.

There is a pleasant fiction that Lincoln then became a flaming advocate of the amendment and used the power of his office to buy votes to ensure its passage. There is no evidence, as David H.

Donald has noted (554), to support that fiction, but it is interesting—and refreshing—to note that Lincoln acted, at the last moment, to move the legislative process forward. This was so unLin-
colnlike, especially on matters relating to Blacks, that it is virtually
the only positive note in the Lincoln bank. Phillips said in a speech,
published in the February 10, 1865, *Liberator,* that this and other
Lincoln initiatives were forced and Lincoln had not made a single
step toward Black liberation on his own.

Lincoln moved, but he moved in the typically bland and cautious
way he moved on all matters relating to Black liberation, venturing—
his word—in his last State of the Union Message "to recommend the
reconsideration and passage" of the resolution on the Thirteenth
Amendment. The same House of Representatives, with virtually the
same members, had failed earlier to pass the amendment by the
required two-thirds margin, but Lincoln, always attentive to election
returns, noted in December 1864 that "an intervening election shows,
almost certainly, that the next Congress will pass the measure if this
does not." Thus, it was "only a question of time as to when the proposed amendment will go to the States for their action. And as it is to
so go, at all events, may we not agree that the sooner the better."

The defining words here are "an intervening election." At this critical point, and at every other critical point, Lincoln followed the people instead of leading the people. One reads everywhere, or almost
everywhere, that Lincoln dragged his feet on this or that issue
because the people were not ready. In fact, on the Thirteenth Amendment and the use of Black soldiers, the people marched on before
Lincoln. Did he not say on this occasion that "it is the voice of the
people now, for the first time, heard upon the question" (CW 8:149)?

And when the people, marching on ahead of Lincoln, as usual,
came to the White House on February 1, 1865, to celebrate passage
of the amendment, Lincoln once again violated history—and the
record—saying that "he thought all would bear him witness that he
had never shrunk from doing all that he could to eradicate Slavery
by issuing an emancipation Proclamation." Given the record cited

here and Lincoln's lifelong opposition to immediate emancipation, this public statement is startling; it is even more startling to find Lincoln experts quoting it approvingly, especially since it was contradicted by his next sentence: "But that Proclamation falls far short of what the amendment will be when fully consummated."

Why did the Proclamation fall short? Lincoln listed three major limitations of the document that allegedly emancipated Blacks:

1. "A question might be raised whether the Proclamation was legally valid."

2. "It might be added that it only aided those who came into our lines and that it was inoperative as to those who did not give themselves up, or . . . ."

3. "[T]hat it would have no effect upon the children of the slaves born hereafter."

The next line in this extraordinary confession renders inoperative more than 135 years of emancipation mythology.

"In fact [Abraham Lincoln is talking] it would be urged that it [the Proclamation] did not meet the evil. But this amendment is a King's cure for all the evils (CW 8:254, italics added)."

And a King's contradiction for all the myths.

This little speech, lame as it was, was Lincoln's greatest speech on Black freedom. And the first thing to notice—fourteen months after Gettysburg—is that there is no four-score flourish and no new-birth-of-freedom trumpets. We are talking here about the end of the 74,000 nights of slavery, about the end of history's greatest crime. Under these circumstances, we would have expected even the most hardened conservative to give at least one whoop or holler. But Lincoln, who could talk with the greatest when he was talking about the rights of Whites, always sounded like a chancery clerk when talking about the rights of Blacks. It is hardly surprising therefore that his language on this occasion was leaden, pedestrian, earthbound. He "supposed the passage through Congress of the Constitutional amendment for the abolishment of Slavery throughout the United States, was the occasion to which he was indebted for the honor of this call" and he wanted to "congratulate all present, himself, the country and the whole world upon this great moral victory"(CW 8:254).

The alert reader will have noticed that Lincoln congratulated himself for a victory he had opposed almost as much as anyone, a victory that he confessed, *two days later* at the Hampton Roads conference, that he still feared. Astonishingly, he didn't congratulate the real authors, Trumbull, Ashley and the abolitionists who fought for the amendment while he dragged his feet.

Sumner, who played a major role in every emancipation breakthrough, said he couldn't recall a time when Lincoln had given him any support on the issues of African-American freedom and African-American rights. Lincoln, Sumner said, meant well, but "he does not know how to help or is not moved to help," adding: "I do not remember that I have had any help from him in any of the questions which I have conducted [in the antislavery cause]—although a word from him in certain quarters would have saved me much trouble . . . . But he has no instinct or inspiration" (CS 253).

Or commitment.

For at the last moment, with the Confederate armies disintegrating and the states ratifying the Thirteenth Amendment, Lincoln started backtracking, offering wild and unseemly proposals to soften or delay the impact of emancipation, and saying or seeming to say that he had never made the abolition of slavery a precondition for peace.

So there it is again.

Lincoln didn't want to do it.

He did everything he could to keep from doing it.

And when he did it, he didn't do it.

Far from being "the great emancipator,"he came close to being the great contra-emancipator. When General John Charles Frémont freed Missouri slaves, Lincoln reenslaved them, pleading Kentucky and the need to assuage the fears and interests of slaveholders and supporters of slaveholders. When his friend, Major General David Hunter, freed slaves in Georgia, Florida and South Carolina, Lincoln reenslaved them (CW 5:222-3). When Major General Benjamin Franklin Butler moved too forcefully against slavery in Louisiana, he was sacked and put on Lincoln's white list of troublesome antislavery generals. When John W. Phelps, Donn Piatt and other Union officers threatened the interests of slaveowners, they were either sacked, denied promotion or cashiered out of the service.

One of the great legends of the war tells us that Lincoln was so soft-hearted that he was always pardoning [White] Union soldiers condemned to death for desertion and for running away under fire. The plight of Black soldiers, who had a higher mortality rate and who were repeatedly murdered in cold blood by Confederate soldiers, never seemed to affect Lincoln that way. Even when his conservative and racist attorney general told him it was his constitutional duty to order equal pay for Black soldiers, he did nothing. And when a great and unsung sergeant, William Walker of the Third South Carolina Volunteers, was arrested for protesting this breach of faith, the commander in chief of the Union Army did nothing—we shall return to this—to stay the firing squad that executed him (Berlin 365-6).

But, listen, someone will say, you've forgotten what Lincoln *said* in 1864 about the contributions of Black soldiers without whom, he said, the victory could not have been won (CW 7:506-8)—you've forgotten that he said "there will be some black men who can remember that, with silent tongue, and clenched teeth, and steady eye, and well-poised bayonet, they have helped mankind on to this great consummation; while, I fear, there will be some white ones, unable to forget that, with malignant heart, and deceitful speech, they have strove to hinder it" (CW 6: 409-10). Great *words*, imperishable *words*, *words* that should have been said at Gettysburg and remembered by Lincoln when he created and approved Jim Crow governments that denied the ballot to these Black benefactors.

I haven't forgotten these *words*; the problem is that Lincoln forgot them. And it is precisely these words that define Lincoln and the enormity of his default. For on this level, and on every other level, there is a Grand Canyon between what Lincoln said and what he did. Not only that, Lincoln—and his defenders—are famous for taking credit for racial initiatives he opposed and was forced to take. Nobody, as we shall see still more emphatically in coming chapters, opposed the use of Black soldiers more than Lincoln. Nobody dragged his feet more in providing equal pay and equal assignments and in protecting them from Confederate soldiers who murdered some captured Black soldiers and sold others into slavery. Yet nobody was more forward in claiming credit for the initiatives he opposed more than any one else.

Among the Union soldiers neglected and undervalued by the commander in chief was a young man named George Washington Williams, who later wrote the first major book on Black history, *The History of the Negro Race*. Since almost all White historians criticize the author and other Black historians for using "twentieth-century Black power language" to evaluate Lincoln, it is striking to find the same criticisms in the Williams book, which was published in 1882. Like almost all Black soldiers, Williams was appalled by "the conservative policy" of a commander in chief who paid White soldiers thirteen dollars a month and Black soldiers seven dollars a month and who failed to take decisive action when Confederate generals and soldiers murdered Black troops. As for the Proclamation, he said more than one hundred years ago that it was a timid, hesitant document that "left slaves in many counties and States at the South" (274).

With emancipators like that, the slaves, especially "the Lincoln slaves," the five hundred thousand or so slaves excepted, reenslaved or countermanded into extended slavery by Lincoln, didn't need any Lees or Davises, which was precisely what a large number of Republicans said in 1864 before the capture of Atlanta and the Democratic nomination of proslavery General George McClellan created a Lincoln that had never existed before. Arguing in these years against the renomination of Lincoln, certain Republicans in Davenport, Iowa, said in 1864 that Lincoln was a contra-emancipator who had done more to hinder emancipation than to advance it. Far from being an accelerator, he was, they said, "a brakeman," who had "clogged and impeded the wheels and movements of the revolution." According to resolutions adopted by these Republicans, liberty was "about to be born to light, but Lincoln has not the merit of having promoted the birth."[6]

What about the great Proclamation? Did it not argue in favor of the brakeman? Certainly not, they said, citing the Proclamation as one of the strongest arguments against Lincoln. "The Proclamation of emancipation was urged upon him very strongly, but for a long time he refused to issue the same. Finally he proclaimed freedom, but with unnecessary restrictions, excepting Tennessee and other parts of the rebellious States. And after he had performed this *only* [italics in the original] great act of his administration, wrenched from him by a very strong current of public opinion, and dictated also by the dangerous situation of our foreign affairs, he regretted this good and great act as unwise, if Wendell Phillips is to be believed."

Therefore:

"We think he does not merit the name of liberator."

Frederick Douglass, the only Black leader who knew Lincoln well and the only Black leader who had a chance to study him in his lair, so to speak, didn't think so, either— in 1864. A generation later, mellowed by age and influenced by the transfiguring post-assassination myth, Douglass contributed a memorial to a book of reminiscences by survivors of the Lincoln years, remarking on what he called Lincoln's "entire freedom from popular prejudice against the colored race." According to this reminiscence, developed twenty-four years later by a seventy-one-year-old man, Lincoln was "the first great man that I talked with in the United States freely, who in no single instance reminded me of the difference between himself and myself, of the difference of color . . ."(RR 193).

It is dishonest to use this quote—see the fallacy of isolated quotes on pages 125-7— without confronting it with what Douglass said about Lincoln on almost every other occasion. During the war, when events were fresh in his mind, he said that Lincoln was a racist who revealed, in his colonization proposal, "all his inconsistencies, his pride of race and blood, his contempt for Negroes and his canting hypocrisy." Douglass went further, Philip S. Foner said, and virtually accused Lincoln and his top aides of treason. In a speech on July 4, 1862, Douglass said that "our weak, paltering and incompetent rulers in the Cabinet . . . and our rebel worshipping Generals in the field" were "incomparably more dangerous to the country than dead traitors like former President James Buchanan . . ." (FD 3:250).

This was an unprecedented attack on a president by a Black leader, and it caused an uproar. Instead of backing down, Douglass raised the temperature, saying in the August 1862 edition of *Douglass' Monthly* "that ABRAHAM LINCOLN is no more fit for the place he holds than was JAMES BUCHANAN, and that the latter was no more the miserable tool of traitors and rebels than the former is allowing himself to be."

After visiting the White House, Douglass modified his views but didn't change them. A former slave who had made himself one of the greatest men of the century, Douglass was impressed by his reception by the president of the United States. He said later that he felt "big" there, as well he might, having lifted himself by his own exertions to the top rung of society and having moved in one generation from slaving to advising U.S. presidents (FD 3:383).

It was precisely for that reason, it was precisely because he had known men who smiled and meant well and were still slaveholders, and racists, that he didn't misunderstand Lincoln's personal gestures. He knew what twentieth-century commentators claim not to know, that the question of whether Lincoln treated Douglass kindly or whether an Afrikaner treated a South African kindly or whether a Nazi treated a Jew kindly was irrelevant.

The question was not personal; it was *political*. The question was not whether Lincoln smiled and refrained from telling "darky" jokes;

the question was whether he was going to help free Black people and treat Black soldiers and their families the same way he treated White soldiers and their families.

Since Lincoln didn't seem to be serious about these matters, Douglass came out against his renomination, saying that the so-called emancipation was a fraud and that Lincoln was neither an emancipator nor a great leader. In a letter to an English supporter, dated June 1864, he denounced Lincoln's betrayal of the spirit of emancipation and charged that Lincoln and his hand-picked military commanders were "practically re-establishing" the slave system in Louisiana.

Douglass's bill of indictment against Lincoln was long, and personal: "The treatment of our poor black soldiers—the refusal to pay them anything like equal compensation, though it was promised them when they enlisted; the refusal to insist upon the exchange of colored prisoners when colored prisoners have been slaughtered in cold blood, although the President has repeatedly promised thus to protect the lives of his colored soldiers—have worn my patience threadbare. The President has virtually laid down this as the rule of his statesmen: Do evil by choice, right from necessity" (FD 3:404, 406-7).

Douglass changed his mind after the Democrats nominated General McClellan on a proslavery platform but never retracted his words nor backed away from his wish for a stronger Republican candidate.

When, twelve years later, Douglass spoke at the dedication of the Freedmen's Memorial, he made the same points in more elevated language. In this speech, the greatest oration on Lincoln by any African-American, or European-American for that matter, Douglass told a distinguished audience, including the president of the United States, the cabinet and members of the Supreme Court, that one ought to tell the truth all the time, but that a special duty is laid on one to tell the truth "when speaking of a great public man whose example is likely to be commended for honor and imitation long after his" death.

Having established that premise, he immediately drew the conclusion: "It must be admitted, truth compels me to admit, even here
in the presence of the monument we have erected to his memory,
*Abraham Lincoln was not, in the fullest sense of the word, either our man
or our model."*

Who then was Lincoln?

*"In his interests, in his associations, in his habits of thought, and in his
prejudices, he was a white man. He was preeminently the white man's President, entirely devoted to the welfare of white men."*

During the first years of his administration, Douglass said, Lincoln
was "ready and willing at any time" to "deny, postpone, and sacrifice" the rights of Black people to promote the welfare of White people. Why did he do this? He did it, Douglass said, because of racism
and because Black people were not "the special objects of his consideration."

Who were the special objects of his consideration?

"First, midst, and last," he said, speaking to the president and his
cabinet and Whites everywhere, "you and yours were the objects of
his deepest affection and his most earnest solicitude. You are the
children of Abraham Lincoln. We are at best only his step-children;
children by adoption, children by forces of circumstances and necessity" (FD 4:309-19, italics added).

That's what Douglass said: *at best.*

And even this is saying too much, for given Lincoln's horror of
"amalgamation," who in his crazy-quilt world, and in ours, would
the stepmother be?

This was the considered statement of the only Black leader who
knew Lincoln well, and it was uttered, almost as if under oath, before
a gathering that constituted the highest public tribunal of the Republic. And one notes with surprise that this severe judgment is echoed,
almost word for word, by the man Lincoln called his "particular
friend," Ward Hill Lamon, who said that Lincoln was above all else a
White man and that "none of his public acts, *either before or after he*

became President, exhibits any special tenderness for the African race, or any extraordinary commiseration of their lot. On the contrary, *he invariably, in words and deeds postponed the interests of the blacks to the interests of the whites,* and expressly subordinated the one to the other" (italics added).

Lamon, who was in constant attendance on Lincoln in Washington and who talked to him intimately on different subjects, said Lincoln had no intention of extending to Blacks *"the privilege of governing* [italics in original] him and other white men" and that it was "as a white man, and in the interests of white men" that he opposed the extension of slavery (344-6).

The case against "the great emancipator" myth, then, is clear, and compelling.

As an Illinois citizen, as a lawyer, legislator, congressman and politician, Lincoln supported the enslavement of the four million slaves and opposed abolitionists who wanted to free them.

As an Illinois citizen, as a lawyer, legislator, congressman and politician, he personally supported the infamous Fugitive Slave Law and asked his neighbors to go out into the streets and hunt down fugitive slaves and return them to slavery.

As president, he ordered the return of fugitive slaves to slavemasters, supported proslavery generals who returned slaves to slavemasters, and struggled to keep from destroying the institution of slavery.

In all this time, he didn't "aid, directly or indirectly, the movement to abolish slavery, till the voice of the people was heard demanding it in order that the Union might be saved" (RR xlv).

Even then, he continued to oppose immediate emancipation, going to his death arguing for the proposition that men and women should be judged not by the content of their character but by the color of their skin (CW 8:403).

These are facts, unimpeachable facts.

What then is the argument about? The only argument really, as we shall see in succeeding chapters, is not over what Lincoln did and didn't do—everybody concedes, if only in the footnotes, that he supported the continued enslavement of the four million and voted for Jim Crow laws and championed White supremacy—but over Lincoln's alibi. Why did he support slavery and oppose immediate Black freedom? This has led, to appropriate one of Lincoln's best phrases, to "explanations explanatory of explanations explained" (CW 3:405), and it doesn't matter. For men are defined in history not by their wishes or alibis or good intentions but by their deeds which, Abraham Lincoln said, judging and condemning himself, light them down in honor or dishonor to the latest generation (CW 5:537).

This leads logically to the second of three interlocking questions that define these introductory chapters: If Lincoln didn't emancipate the slaves, as cronies and critics and documents say, then who emancipated them?

The answer is plain, although it has somehow eluded ahistorical historians who still believe that history is made by personalities detached from time, space, and social forces.

Who freed the slaves?

History—the movement and orchestration of the dominant forces of the age—freed the slaves, which is another way of saying that events and forces created the conditions and the men and women who used time and the social forces to make the only history it was possible to make.

Does this mean that Blacks were freed by disembodied social forces? Certainly not. This would be to make the same mistake as the personalists make by advancing what Allan Nevins calls "the ludicrously false premise" (235) that a political Santa Claus, a great White man with a beard, freed Blacks on January 1 with a stroke of the pen.

Blacks were not freed by one individual or one social force. They were freed, to the extent that they were ever freed, by an intersection of individuals and social forces in a climate favorable to social change. That climate was created not only by the development of social forces but also, and most importantly, by the development of individuals who anticipated changes that would only become possible later and who planted seeds and prepared the ground in the 1830s and 1840s, while Lincoln was sleeping, for a crop that could only be harvested in the 1860s. What we reproach Lincolnologists for is that they remove Lincoln, and themselves, from history, from the Black men who fought at Bunker Hill and the Black majority in South Carolina and the Black men and women who were hunted down, like beasts, on the streets of Springfield.

And we shall understand nothing about Abraham Lincoln, or ourselves, if we don't put Lincoln, and ourselves, back into that history within the perspective of two complementary and contradictory facts. First of all, and most important of all, there has never been a real emancipation for African-Americans in the United States. The second fact, which contradicts the first and fulfills it, is that the real emancipation of African-Americans started not with Abraham Lincoln but with the first revolt on slave ships and will not end until somebody signs a document ending the Republic's never-ending, never-dying struggle with the only American question, a question bigger than money or property or sex, the question that defeated Washington, Jefferson, Lincoln, Woodrow Wilson, Roosevelt, Eisenhower, Reagan, not to pursue the matter further, the question of slavery, race, equality, *all*. The poet Vachel Lindsay was wrong (169). That wasn't Abraham Lincoln walking at midnight—that was old John Brown and Harriet Tubman and the ghost of the slaves, who are still rattling their chains in the Republic and demanding the wherewithal, the forty acres of land and [mechanical] mules, that separate freedom Lincoln-style from the *actual* freedom that the document mentioned but nowhere provided for or even defined.

And perhaps I should say here, by way of introduction, that almost all major historians have approached Lincoln and the Civil War from a White perspective. With few exceptions, historians have approached Lincoln from the perspective of how and why the war could have been avoided and how and why the issue of slavery could have compromised. Which means, to be blunt, that almost all historians have approached this story from the standpoint of how and why my ancestors could have been kept in slavery longer—for ten, fifty or even a hundred years longer.

I write unapologetically from a different perspective, which may be the only perspective, truth being, as Jean-Paul Sartre and W.E.B. DuBois said, the perspective of the truly disinherited. Early in the war, while Lincoln and almost all senators and congressmen were operating from a White perspective, Phillips said in a speech published in the August 9, 1861, issue of the *Liberator* that the only perspective from which to view this war and Lincoln and Robert E. Lee was the perspective of the slave.

"To-day," Phillips said, "belongs to the Negro. To-day belongs to the slave. Whatever question we discuss to-day, we should discuss as the slave looks at it—from no other standpoint."

It is from that standpoint that I approach this book, from the standpoint, to be precise, of a conscious and lucid slave, aware of his objective interests, and with enough information to evaluate himself and all others in terms of his immediate demands, which included immediate emancipation, arming of the slaves, the destruction of the political and economic power of the slaveholder class, the redistribution of land for Blacks and Whites and an educational crusade for Blacks and Whites. Everybody who supported these demands, whatever his motives, was his friend. *Everybody who opposed them, then and now, whatever his motives, was his enemy.*

"In the whole of this conflict," Phillips said, "I have looked only at Liberty,—only at the slave" (PS 400).

In the whole of this book, I have looked only at freedom, only at the slave who hastened the war and welcomed it, believing that it was the coming of the Lord of history and that the graves of Gettysburg were the stern and just wages of 200 years of Black slavery.

I have assumed, moreover, that slavery was a crime against humanity, like apartheid in South Africa and the concentration camps in Germany, and that all participants, Lincoln and Lee above all, must be evaluated on the basis of what they did and didn't do to end an American holocaust that raises questions of personal and collective responsibility that have not been raised, much less addressed, in the Republic.

For the slave, then, and for all who speak from his space, that is to say, from Slave Row, and Harlem, and the South Sides of the Land of Lincoln, the Civil War was not an aberration. On the contrary, it was a necessary expression of the prophecies of the ancestors and the drums of History, and if it had continued until every drop of blood shed by slaves had been paid for by a drop of the oppressors' blood, it would have been altogether good and righteous. That's what Sumner said (SL 117, 131), and Lincoln after him. But Lincoln didn't believe it or understand it, not if we judge by his Reconstruction policy which inaugurated a new cycle of blood to be paid for by the continuing Gettysburgs that have claimed more casualties since 1865 than all the battles of the Civil War.

What the slave victims believed and wanted was not Lincoln's concern, and the gravest charge one can place against him is that he betrayed the trust of four million slaves who, not having reliable information, believed Lincoln was their friend because their enemies said Lincoln was their enemy. They thought the bad men in Washington were holding up emancipation and returning the slaves to the slavemasters and mocking their hopes and aspirations. They thought Lincoln was fighting the bad men and trying to set them free. *They didn't know that Lincoln was the bad men,* and they made a mistake comparable to the mistake the movie victim makes when she runs away from her friends and flies into the arms of the one person who seeks her continued enslavement and banishment.

If, despite the record, Lincoln has been misinterpreted, it is not his fault. A conservative Illinois lawyer, cautious and conventional in social matters, Lincoln never pretended to be a racial liberal or a social innovator. He said repeatedly, in public and in private, that he believed in White supremacy. Not only that: Lincoln had profound doubts about the possibility of realizing the rhetoric of the Declaration of Independence and the Gettysburg Address on this soil; and he believed until his death that Blacks and Whites would be much better off separated—preferably with the Atlantic Ocean or some other large and deep body of water between them. If, as Benjamin Quarles said, Lincoln became Lincoln because of the Negro (1962, iii), it can be argued that never before in history did a man give so little and so grudgingly to his historical fathers.

The man's personality, his way with words, and his assassination, together with the psychological needs of a racist society, have obscured these contradictions under a mountain of myths which undoubtedly would have amused Lincoln, who had a wonderful sense of the ironic and ridiculous.

If the Lincoln myths were the harmless fantasies of children at play, it would be possible to ignore them. But when the myths of children become adult daydreams and when the daydreams are used to hide historical reality and obscure deep social problems, it becomes a social duty to confront them. When, at the height of the 1967 rebellion season, President Lyndon B. Johnson said he intended to follow a Lincolnian course, historian Vincent Harding rebuked him, pointing out that Lincoln's racial posture was a prescription for social disaster today. Because, as Dr. Harding suggested, we are environed by dangers and because we need all the light we can get; because Abraham Lincoln is not the light, because he is in fact standing in the light, hiding our way; because a real emancipation proclamation has become a matter of national survival and because no one has ever issued such a document in this country—because, finally, lies enslave and the truth is always seemly and proper, it is a national imperative to reevaluate the Lincoln mythology.

Since I asked *Was Abe Lincoln A White Supremacist?* in the February 1968 *Ebony,* almost all Lincoln scholars have recognized the need for a rethinking of the Lincoln myth. Some have suggested that Lincoln's reputation would be more securely based if it were grounded on something other than the Proclamation.

David Donald said in an earlier book, *Lincoln Reconsidered*, that "perhaps the secret of Lincoln's continuing vogue is his essential ambiguity. He can be cited on all sides of all questions"(18). Donald was wrong. Lincoln can't be cited on the side of equal rights for Blacks, an unfortunate fact that has discomfited more than one Lincoln Day orator.

For 135 years, an army of scholars has been digging in the Lincoln mine, and the fact that no one has returned to the surface with a single positive Lincoln quotation on Black liberation and equal rights is most conclusive proof against Lincoln and the sustainers of the myth. On the contrary, there is overwhelming evidence that Lincoln was a wily and determined foe of equal rights and Black liberation. "Indeed," as Kenneth Stampp said, "it may be said that if it was Lincoln's destiny to go down in history as the Great Emancipator, rarely has a man embraced his destiny with greater reluctance than he" (44). Do I hear someone citing in rebuttal the infamous Wadsworth letter in which Lincoln allegedly called for civil and political equality? But Ludwell H. Johnson, among others, has proved incontestably that this is one of the greatest forgeries in historiography. Even without this proof, it is obvious that the counterfeit words violate every act and assertion of Lincoln's life. [7]

In *The Hero in History*, Sidney Hook identifies two kinds of heroes. The real hero, he says, is an event-making man or woman who deliberately and consciously seeks and shapes a conjunction of events that changes or helps to change history. In sharp contrast to the event-making hero who helps make the event that makes him is the eventful figure who is the beneficiary of events that he neither desires nor shapes and, in Lincoln's case, opposed. (154-83). Most historians focus on the eventful hero, praising him for events that happened on his watch, although in some cases, and in Lincoln's case in particular, the events happened not because of his intervention but despite his intervention. And we can appropriate here the words Lincoln himself used about Stephen A. Douglas and the Kansas-Nebraska Act and say that the slaves were freed not because of the Proclamation and its author but in spite of both.

Perhaps the most brilliant analysis of Lincoln's failure on this level was made by a contemporary, Missouri antislavery leader John F. Hume, who said that the Lincoln story on the level of race is the story of a historical failure. For, in the end, Hume wrote, it was not Lincoln's policy but "the policy of Salmon P. Chase, Charles Sumner, Thaddeus Stevens, Horace Greeley, Henry Ward Beecher, and other advocates of the radical cure, with whom the President was in constant opposition, that prevailed . . . and with a decisiveness that proves it to have been feasible and sound from the beginning."

In sharp and significant contrast, Hume said, *every purely Lincoln initiative on race failed.* His Emancipation Proclamation "was ineffective. If it was intended to eradicate slavery altogether, it was too narrow; if to free the slaves of Rebels only, it was too broad. So with his other propositions. His thirty-seven-year liberation scheme, his 'tinkering off' policy (as he called it) for Missouri, his reconstruction proposals, and his colonization efforts, all failed. Indeed, if we take his official action from first to last, it is a question whether the President, owing to his extreme conservatism, was not more of an obstructionist than a promoter of the Anti-Slavery cause" (148).

That was also the final appraisal of Nathaniel W. Stephenson, a major Lincoln defender who said that "when, at last, he decided to take up emancipation as part of his policy, he did so from necessity, not from choice. A great deal of additional evidence might be piled up, making incontestable the conclusion that Lincoln in the history of emancipation is an incidental, not a controlling figure" (431).

The conclusion is inescapable. Lincoln was at best an incidental, accidental rider of a liberating wave that probably would have crested sooner—and higher—without him.

3

Pharaoh And Moses

L INCOLN never stopped apologizing for the act that immortalized him. Unbelievable as the idea might sound today, the "great emancipator" protested every step up the high road to glory, telling anyone who would listen that the Proclamation was not what he wanted to do and that good White men ought to continue the search for a way to soften the impact of Black emancipation and to spread it over a longer period of time—on, if possible, another continent and in another clime.

Lincoln kept on apologizing, even after the act had made him famous. But there were two Lincolns, even three Lincolns, and the apologetic Lincoln was almost certainly in conflict with the ambitious Lincoln who had wanted all his life, his cronies said, to execute a glory-making act that linked his name forever with mankind. The two men who knew Lincoln best said Lincoln's ambivalence on this issue approached clinical dimensions. Speed said Lincoln was both "anxious to avoid it" (HW 422) and anxious to do it. Herndon said Lincoln didn't want to do it, but wanted "to go down in history as the liberator of the black man" (HW 443).

The ambitious Lincoln would have been less than human, less than Lincoln, if he had not been tempted to appropriate the great emancipator image and integrate it into the self-made, honest Abe, Father Abraham, malice-toward-none image he was already paint-

ing for immortality. So, while he was apologizing to friends and conservatives with one hand, and one tongue, he was at the same time
and with another tongue, and the same one, pressing a different but
complementary line, saying, among other things, that the Emancipation Proclamation he had tried so hard to avoid was the *central act of
my administration, and the great event of the nineteenth century"* (Carpenter 90, italics in the original). And we seem to be witness in his
last days to a herculean struggle in which a president divided against
himself struggled to accept and reject at the same time an act that
bore at the same time his greatest dream and his greatest fear. In a
profound comment, Herndon said that the fame Lincoln "dreamed
of" was "very different from that which he actually obtained as an
anti-slavery leader" (HW 140). And one has to feel a little sorry for
Lincoln, whatever one's political orientation, as we watch him trying
at the same time to swallow and to spit out the hot potato history had
put into his mouth.

We are dealing here, then, with a tragedy almost as wrenching as
the Shakespearean tragedies Lincoln adored, the tragedy of a man
who chose the impossible dream of being both Pharaoh and Moses
at the same time, a difficult feat at best but not an impossible one, as
his metamorphosis proves—and who can argue with success.

One of the defining tragedies of this history is that racism gave
clay feet to America's greatest moral hero and made him a minor-
league player, limiting his vision and stunting his growth. This,
someone will say, is heresy, if not blasphemy. How can you call the
man who said the words at Gettysburg a minor-league player? How
can you call him anything else? Any man who believed in government of the people, by the people, for the people in Illinois because
the majority was White and didn't believe in government of the people, by the people, for the people in South Carolina because the
majority was Black was playing in the minor leagues, whatever he
believed and whatever his press releases say. There is, in fact, no
major league for a man who believes in a limited humanity and the
supremacy of White people and the color white in a world that is

overwhelmingly nonWhite.

The sphinx that guards the door of that history, and the major league of human endeavor, says humans must choose for all or none and that the man who questions the humanity of any part of humanity diminishes his own. Lincoln's tragedy, and it was a Homeric one, worthy of Shakespeare or the Spirituals or the Blues, is that he seems to have glimpsed this truth but that racism and his volcanic ambition pulled him back to the ground of the limited humanity that defined him. Watching him try to soar above the racist undercurrent only to fall back time and time again to the ground of the American curse, one is convinced, on the purely human level, that the tragedy of Abraham Lincoln is that he was, in Langston Hughes's words, a broken-winged bird who couldn't fly because he lacked the ballast of a dream higher than White supremacy (Bontemps 194).

Lincoln was a symptom of a larger and deeper problem that has never been addressed in America. Four score and seven years of private and public lying, of sanctioning genocide and blatant racism, of approving violations of the Constitution and the Declaration of Independence, of winking at violations of democracy and free speech in the South not only for Blacks but also for Whites, had weakened the moral fiber of the Republic and its leading men, including Washington, Jefferson, Madison, and Lincoln. How could it have been otherwise? A generation of blatant racism and genocide sickened the whole of German society. How could American society have avoided the effects of the poison that circulated freely from the 1660s and 1760s to the 1860s?

In a groundbreaking analysis, printed in the January 17, 1862, issue of the *Liberator*, Phillips said that the kind of war Lincoln and his aides fought was a function of the kind of men they had become in the poisoned moral atmosphere of the times. Expressing his disgust in 1862 about Lincoln's vacillations and hesitations, Phillips noted that "abolitionists have said for thirty years, and every thoughtful man on the other side of the water has echoed the sentiment, that it was a grave question whether the public and its leaders in the free States had not been so demoralized, so much weakened in its moral sense, so much dulled in their appreciation of the responsibilities of self-government by the influence of slavery, as to make it impossible for us to survive any great crisis."

America survived, primarily, historian George Bancroft said, because of the strength of the people and because, others said, abolitionists—who had opposed the slavery virus—forced Lincoln to high ground he never would have taken on his own. But the question Phillips raised in 1862 remains, and has never been addressed. Why did it take the North so long with its overwhelming financial, technical and numerical advantages to overcome the undermanned South? Lincoln said in so many words that God was punishing the North for slavery and other sins. Phillips said history was punishing the North for betraying its idea. The South, he said, believed in its idea, slavery, but the North didn't believe in its idea, freedom. Four score and seven years of *not believing* in that idea had produced irresolute men like Lincoln and McClellan who were *not-believing* made flesh. For generations, Phillips said, Lincoln and the not-believers had been held hostage to a Union "in which no man dared to follow out the logical inferences from right to wrong because he ran against a great national institution in the presence of which, if he had any hopes of political advancement, or public favor, he must be silent."

This analysis is exceptionally important not only because it reminds us of the poisonous effect of slavery but also because it throws new light on the tragedy of a potentially great man flawed irredeemably by a poisoned moral atmosphere and by the racist vision he was not big enough to confront. Nor does the tragedy stop there, for Lincoln was secretly allied with the forces that broke his wings and kept him from soaring and becoming a King or a Phillips or a Nelson Mandela.

It is on this level, the level of generations of leaders mortgaged morally and spiritually by their self-confessed commitment to a crime against humanity, that we must situate the tragedy of Lincoln, who seems to have been afflicted at the climax of the drama by the historical tremors that seize individuals, especially individuals standing in the way of history, who are swept off their feet by irresistible historical currents and who find themselves as the great tides recede on strange beaches with strange companions and proclamations, far away from their accustomed haunts and ideas. The men and women who suffer history in this way, especially those who impotently resist a history that can't be resisted, find themselves authors of acts they can neither assume fully nor reject fully.

Such actors, whether in the French Revolution or the Freedom Movement of the 1960s, have a certain family resemblance. They seem to be disoriented or disembodied. They seem to be sleepwalking or running in deep water. That's what they said about the demeanor of Abraham Lincoln in the aftermath of the emancipation tidal wave that rolled over him, a tidal wave propelled by irresistible historical forces—by Confederate troops, Union reverses and the passions of the real friends of Black freedom who raised the stakes every time a Lincoln stratagem backfired. Unable to accept or reject the new baby, which history, in its malevolence, had made him the putative father of, Lincoln zigged and zagged, trying on new language and attitudes he was clearly uncomfortable with. His close friend, Illinois Senator Orville Hickman Browning, and others found him weeping and wringing his hands.

All his life he had opposed immediate emancipation, and now the fence—his metaphor—was tumbling down and people were praising *him* for pulling the fence down and winning a victory he had sought to avoid, and that he still feared (CW 2:230).

Has there ever been a stranger emancipator and a more uncomfortable father? In any case, the truest words he ever said was that he had not controlled events but had been controlled and dominated by events (CW 7:282). Nobody believed him, not even the scholars who say they believe him, but there is too much evidence and from too many years, from 1836 to the morning of April 14, 1865, to permit any other conclusion.

Despite these and other limitations, scholars are virtually unanimous in saying that Lincoln was the strongest American president, an assertion that would have shocked leaders of Lincoln's party, who were virtually unanimous in saying that he was a weak and indecisive man, "led along," as Bancroft said, "by the greatness [of the people's] self-sacrificing example; and, as a child, in a dark night, on a rugged way, catches hold of the hand of its father for guidance and support, he clung fast to the hand of the people and moved calmly through the gloom" (1866, 35).

Most of Lincoln's contemporaries—and a surprisingly large number of scholars—agree that Lincoln played little or no role in the rich legislative history of the period and that he had few if any followers. When, in 1864, a Pennsylvania man asked Thaddeus Stevens to introduce him to "a member of Congress who was friendly to Mr. Lincoln's nomination," Stevens took him to Congressman Isaac N. Arnold of Illinois and said, according to a story related by Arnold himself: "Here is a man who wants to find a Lincoln member of Congress. You are the only one I know and I have come over to introduce my friend to you" (386).

This was not an isolated episode. Congressman John B. Alley of Massachusetts, who knew Lincoln well, said that "many of the most distinguished men of the country, who were in daily intercourse with him, thought but little of his capacity as a statesman. And while entirely true, it is hardly to be believed that those in both houses of Congress who knew him best had so little confidence in his judgment and ability to administer the government that few of the members of the Senate and of the House were in favor of his renomination for the Presidency in 1864" (RR 573-4).

The most persuasive argument against Lincoln's effectiveness as a leader is the total failure of his only two presidential initiatives—gradual and compensated emancipation and colonization—which were so wildly impractical that one has to question the political rationality of the man who advanced them. The best evidence on this point is visual. For if Lincoln had been a strong and effective leader, there would be no Blacks here, not even the Blacks who say he was the strongest and best U.S. president, which is a dangerous point to make since (some?) (many?) (most?) (almost all?)—choose one—Whites will find it necessary to fight down a historically conditioned wish that he had succeeded. At the same time, we ought to remember, if only for perspective, that if Lincoln had succeeded there would be no Broadway, no musical comedy, no American music, no Grammy and Rock 'n' Roll, no Beatles or Gershwin or Copland or Fred Astaire, no American athletics to speak of, no Jim Brown or Michael Jordan or Dr. J., a thin White gruel of pale religion and food, and a Constitution and a democracy lacking the ballast of the Fourteenth and Fifteenth amendments and the singing summons of Thurgood Marshall, Martin Luther King Jr., Earl Warren, and Bill Clinton, an America, in short, without color, rhythm, and soul—Australia with a Mississippi River.

A complicating factor here, as Richard Hofstadter and others have pointed out, is that Lincoln was engaged in this period in painting his own portrait for history. After his tragic assassination, the largest army of mythologists ever mobilized—friends, acquaintances, hawkers, writers, politicians, teachers, scholars, almost all of them, curiously, White—started manufacturing myths about Lincoln. Lincoln's son, Robert Todd Lincoln, started the process by censuring the first major study of Lincoln and by jealously guarding the Lincoln papers, which he obsessively carried around with him when he moved from place to place (HH 16-8). There is a rumor, perhaps apocryphal, that he started to burn the papers and was dissuaded by a friend. There are also reports that documents and papers that run counter to the traditional Lincoln legend have been lost or misplaced.

Robert Todd Lincoln, Nicolay and Hay, Sandburg, Stephenson,

Charnwood, all of the great makers of the Lincoln legend followed the path staked out by A. Lincoln, who was the first and greatest Lincoln mythologist. In a brilliant essay that should be better known, Hofstadter argued that Lincoln was "keenly aware of his role as the exemplar of the self-made man," and that "he played the part with an intense and poignant consistency that gives his performance the quality of a high art." The result was that *the first author of the Lincoln legend and the greatest of the Lincoln dramatists was Lincoln himself*" (119, italics added). Another Lincoln scholar, Charles B. Strozier, said it is not frivolous "to guess" that Lincoln "purposely shaped his heroic image to fit a nation longing for unity and greatness" (233). It's not frivolous, and since the data is inconsistent with any other hypothesis, it is more than a guess. The only problem is to explain why the great playwright-actor stumbled at the height of the drama and committed himself to the former slaveowners, who had been condemned by history, instead of committing himself to the former slaves, who represented the future of the world and who would, as he predicted, light him down in dishonor to the latest generation.

In writing, staging and starring in his original real-life Lincoln drama, Lincoln was not above appropriating the lines and images of others. We see this in its purest form in the use Lincoln and others made of the reverse image of the reverse image Blacks created about Lincoln. The first image in this extremely complicated process was the post-Fort Sumter image Southern Whites and Northern conservatives created of Lincoln, who was, they said, hell-bent on freeing the slaves and giving them the White man's land, jobs and even his women. Confederates and Confederate sympathizers said this quite openly, and the slaves, operating on the maxim that the enemy of their enemy was their friend, started creating a reverse image of this reverse image, pouring all their explosive energy into a reverse-reverse image (read: unreal-unreal fiction) of a strange White man named Abraham, no less, who had come, as was foretold in the Scriptures and by the drums, to end the two hundred-year-old nightmare and free the people and give them land. Nobody knew better than the real Abraham that this was the reverse of the truth, yet we catch him, early in the game, *while he was still trying to save slavery and to send Blacks to Africa,* doubling back on his track, covering over and smoothing out telltale footprints leading away from the Proclamation.

When, in February 1864, artist Francis B. Carpenter went to the White House to paint a picture of Lincoln reading the Proclamation to his cabinet for the first time, Lincoln seized the opportunity to revise history before it was written, giving a heroic ex parte statement of how *he* first decided to free the slaves. This self-serving ex parte statement has been swallowed whole by almost all historians, despite the fact that it is full of errors and is contradicted by hard evidence on what Lincoln did during the summer of 1862. We shall deal at great length in following chapters with the errors and distortions in these attempts to revise history, and the point we want to make here is that Lincoln himself was actively involved in the process, playing himself, as tragedians portrayed his favorite play, *Macbeth.*

As the winds of history shifted in favor of the slaves he had underestimated and downplayed, Lincoln became increasingly adept in appropriating successes that happened despite him. Nobody for example was more opposed to the use of Black troops than Lincoln, who questioned the valor of Black people and who told different groups that if he armed Blacks one day all the guns would soon be in the hands of Confederates (CW 5:423). On this point, Lincoln was adamant, telling one delegation that he would rather resign his office than to put guns in the hands of Black men. Even when Congress authorized the use of Black troops, even when almost all members of his cabinet, including the ultraracists and ultraconservatives, approved the use of Black troops, Lincoln resisted. But when the initiative proved to be a success, and when the two hundred thousand Black soldiers proved to be the difference between the Union saved and the Union dismembered, nobody was more effusive in congratulating himself and others. Astonishingly, Lincoln started posing as a pioneer-of-the-movement, telling himself and others how much *he* had suffered in the struggle for Black rights. The same man who said on September 13, 1862, that he doubted the valor of Blacks and feared the reaction of Kentucky if Blacks were armed was the same man who told General Ulysses S. Grant and his officers in 1864 that when *he* made the decision to use Black troops, men of little insight and vision opposed him. What did he tell the bigots who doubted the courage of Blacks and feared the reaction of Kentucky? "I used to tell them," he said, "that at such times it was just as well to be a little color-blind" (Porter 218-9).

And a little forgetful, as Lincoln demonstrated by telling one of his patented stories. "I think, general," he told Grant, "that we can say of the black boys what a country fellow who was an old-time abolitionist in Illinois said when he went to the theater in Chicago and saw Forrest playing *Othello*. He was not very well up in Shakespeare, and didn't know that the tragedian was a white man who had blacked up for the purpose. After the play was over the folks who had invited him to go to the show wanted to know what he thought of the actors, and he said: 'Waal, layin' aside all sectional prejudices and any partiality I may have for the race, derned ef I don't think the nigger held his own with any on 'em'" (Porter 219).

This is an extraordinary story not only because of the N-word, which was par for the Lincoln course, but also and most importantly because it throws a disturbing light on Lincoln's habit of making an extreme dissociation between his words and his acts. No one had opposed the use of Black soldiers more than the teller of this tale, who was at that very moment the chief culprit in the Union policy of discriminating against Black soldiers in pay and assignments, and yet no one was more willing to take credit for their successes, as the same storyteller also did in the case of the Emancipation Proclamation and the Thirteenth Amendment.

Lincoln went further and appropriated the "Massa Linkum" myth that almost all Lincoln biographers stress. Thus, when the presidential carriage passed a group of Black children, who shouted, according to Noah Brooks, "Hurrah for Massa Linkum!" Mary Todd Lincoln asked her husband to guess how many of "those piccaninnies" had been named Abraham Lincoln. Assuming a mock serious pose, Lincoln considered the matter gravely, factoring in the gestation rate and the rumor rate, and saying: "Let's see; this is April, 1863. I should say that of all those babies under two years of age, perhaps two thirds have been named for me" (56).

He was probably right, and the words of his mouth and the fact that he was trying at that very moment to subordinate these children—and their parents—and to deport them to a foreign country condemn him utterly.

It is that trust that Abraham Lincoln betrayed and that history is now calling him to account for, according to that stern and inflexible rule, a rule he himself quoted, saying, "We cannot escape history," a rule higher than history books and history associations, the rule that men and women (even historians) are responsible in history not only for what they did and didn't do (and write) but also for what the men and forces they used and relied on and supported, even implicitly, did and didn't do (CW 5:537).

We are confronted therefore with a process and a procession, and not a personality. And to see Lincoln whole and in living color, we must focus not on Lincoln but on a multicolored, million-tongued procession, black, yellow, white, amber, red, and burning brown, marching through the ages, all through the seventeenth, eighteenth and nineteenth centuries, three hundred years by the clock, infinitely longer by the lash, a process-procession that encircled the Mount Vernons and Monticellos from the countryside, like a guerrilla movement, retreating when its adversaries advanced, advancing when they retreated, wearing them down with the persistence of its spirit, and its blues, and its soul, which became paradoxically the only original music in the new place, entrapping and defining the black-faced Whites who entrapped and defined the minstrel-loving Lincoln.

Born in the blood of history's greatest crime, the obscenity of the four hundred-year slave trade with its forty-to one hundred-million victims, it was brought forth on this land, as was said, by a revolution of SOME in the name of ALL, a White humanist contradiction that became the American contradiction, producing a fatal flaw in the American psyche and in the being of all Whites, Lincoln and Jefferson above all, who did not confront it and transcend it and expiate it by allying themselves with the only thing that could save them, the procession that contained their identity and their truth.

Starting with isolated acts by individual males and females who threw themselves against the system with suicidal desperation, hacking, bludgeoning and poisoning, the small procession became a larger procession and eventually a movement with an underground network of guerrilla agents, Black and White, who moved escaping slaves from the South to Canada, and an overground network of abolitionist agents who used words and direct action to inflame the climate and to create contempt for a people and a religion and a Constitution that sanctioned the buying, selling, hunting, and defiling of men, women, and children.

Attacked by Lincoln and others who called them incendiaries, and opposed by mainstream leaders like Senators Henry Clay and Daniel Webster, who called, as Lincoln called, for compromise on an issue that could not be compromised, the procession grew by the contradictions it fed on, strengthened rather than weakened by the blood of martyrs.

We have come, the African-American National Anthem says, *treading our path through the blood of the slaughtered.*

That's the way the great procession came, losing more casualties than groaned on the slopes of Gettysburg, Shiloh, *and* Antietam. Among the casualties was Margaret Garner of *Beloved* fame, who killed her daughter to keep the slavecatchers Lincoln supported from returning her to slavery. Dragged before a judge—who can judge when the judges and the Law and its defenders need judging?—Garner reportedly begged the judge to kill her, saying she would "go singing to the gallows " rather than return to slavery, which was, she said, hell for a Black woman [and a Black man] and which was not to be borne for a single hour or a single day (Siebert 302-3).

Lincoln, who wanted to drag emancipation out for thirty or forty or a hundred years, never said a Gettysburg word in celebration of what Margaret Garner and the slaves and friends of slaves did for freedom, but history noticed, especially in the thirties and forties when controversies over fugitive slaves and attacks on White abolitionists inflamed the political climate and foreshadowed the coming struggle. There could hardly be a better example of this than the martyrdom of Elijah Parish Lovejoy, a brave White editor who was shot to death while defending his press from a White mob in Alton, Illinois. Neither Lovejoy's death nor the national furor that followed moved Lincoln, who barely mentioned the event in a speech he made at the time about White freedom. No matter. The White terror in Illinois converted scores of Whites and brought the Abolitionist Movement Wendell Phillips, a greater voice than Lincoln's, and, from the standpoint of the slaves, a greater man.

The tribe of Lincolns stood idly by in the nineteenth century, as it stood idly by in the twentieth, as it has always stood idly by, but the martyrs and those who stood with them attracted new forces and faces almost every week.

In 1836, the year Abraham Lincoln called for a White-only suffrage, a White attorney named Salmon Portland Chase stood in the door of a Cincinnati, Ohio, building and faced down a mob trying to lynch a White abolitionist editor.

In 1838, the year Illinois state legislator Abraham Lincoln voted to tax "slaves and servants of color," an untutored slave named Frederick Douglass escaped from slavery in Baltimore and began the fifty-seven-year career that made him one of the benefactors of the century.

In 1839, members of the Liberty Party joined the antislavery procession along with the heroic slaves who killed the captain and took over the slave ship *Amistad* in one of the slave mutinies that Lincoln feared.

1848 was a good year, bringing with it the Free Soil Party that Lincoln deplored. So was 1849, the year Harriet Tubman, afterward called "the Moses of Her People," escaped from slavery in Maryland, at a time when Congressman Lincoln was pressing a gradual emancipation plan and a fugitive slave law for the District of Columbia.

Lincoln didn't make emancipation; emancipation, which he never understood or supported or approved, made Lincoln. And to see him in red, white and black, we must see him first against the backdrop of this vast procession of Blacks and a saving remnant of Whites marching through the centuries, gaining adherents from every outrage, taking two steps forward and one step and sometimes three steps backward, halting sometimes in the same place for years, even decades, going backward at times to the beginning and starting all over again, oftentimes losing its way and then awakening to itself in a new moment, a new atrocity, a new face.

On and on it came, a great black carpet of moving forms and energies with squares of white and brown and yellow, history's stepchildren at history's door. The Reverend Nat Turner, David Walker and John Brown were among that number. So were Douglass, Tubman, Zebina Eastman and the Illinois activists who fought the battles Lincoln evaded. White and Black, nonviolent and violent, politicians and preachers and guerrillas, all marched in the great procession which was helped even by its enemies, even by Stephen Douglas, who pulled the scab off the gangrenous Missouri Compromise and forced a national crisis—even and especially by Confederate soldiers who vetoed an easy victory and thereby made emancipation necessary and inevitable, no matter who occupied the White House. And don't leave out the White dreamers, the Jeffersons and Lincolns, who said *all*, meaning *some,* who said *human,* meaning White, and played into the hands of the real liberators.

When the marchers locked, like a laser beam, on the central energy of the age, the drive toward industrialization, everything helped, even the equivocations of its opponents. Thus, at a critical juncture, Lincoln, who loathed abolitionists and heaven-stormers and who said John Brown was insane (CW 3:503), found himself in the front ranks of a procession made up of heaven-stormers and men singing songs about John Brown.

Lincoln, who was no friend of John Brown and the Black and White men who died with Brown, tried at first to push the procession back. Failing that, he tried to divert the marchers into the side roads of gradualism and colonization. But when it became necessary to free the slaves to save the Union and to stop the slaughter of husbands, brothers, fathers and friends, conservative White people raised their voices, and the procession became irresistible, pushing a protesting Lincoln on before it into glory. "From first to last," Hume said, "he was more of a follower than leader in the procession" (147).

That's the way it happened, more or less, in the long lens of a history that never forgives and never forgets and is always, as the slaves said, signifying and calling somebody's name. And the spectacle of Abraham Lincoln the Separatist, Colonizationist and Racist marching in the front ranks of the emancipation procession he had opposed all his life causes us to meditate on the irony of a history that conspired in these years to make an Illinois White supremacist the signer of the Emancipation Proclamation, as it had conspired in another time to make a Virginia slaveholder the author of the Declaration of Independence, and with the same results.

Part Two

Mirror

What I would most desire would be the separation of the white and black races.

—Abraham Lincoln

Truth is proper and beautiful at all times and in all places, and it is never more proper and beautiful in any case than when speaking of a great public man whose example is likely to be commended for honor and imitation long after his departure to the solemn shades, the silent continents of eternity. It must be admitted, truth compels me to admit, even here in the presence of the monument we have erected to his memory, Abraham Lincoln was not, in the fullest sense of the word, either our man or our model. In his interests, in his associations, in his habits of thought, and in his prejudices, he was a white man. He was preeminently the white man's president, entirely devoted to the welfare of the white people of this country.

— Abolitionist Frederick Douglass

4

A Fantasy For All Seasons

IF Abraham Lincoln was not the great emancipator, then who was he? Not, mind you, *what* was he. *Not* what did he do or what did he say, but *who* was he? Sixteen thousand books and monographs have been written to answer that question (Peterson 374), but few ask the question, much less answer it, and we can address it here provisionally with the hope that enterprising scholars, Black and White, will follow the provocative leads of the latest scholarship and begin the process of creating a meaningful Lincoln whole out of the volumes of discrete data.

The problem on this level is that most Lincoln biographies, even the so-called classics, are collections of isolated and disconnected data that lead away from Lincoln instead of toward him. In all or almost all standard biographies, we are presented with a series of still frames—Lincoln is sad, Lincoln is telling a joke, Lincoln is supporting slavery, Lincoln is emancipating or, rather, not emancipating—without any sense that Lincoln is a totality and that the Lincoln who told jokes and the Lincoln who fought the Indians and said Negroes were inferior was the same Lincoln.

This totalistic approach defines our inquiry, but before pursuing it, we must say once again that this is a political study, not a biography, and that we are only interested in these phenomena as they point to that unique whole called Abraham Lincoln who was sad and White and conservative in a certain way because he was in his totality and in every act of his life a certain stand about the world, about life, death, Blacks, Whites and the human condition.

From this standpoint, we can offer provisionally three explanatory keys to understanding the whole man who appeared on the first page of this book telling a n——r joke and who presented himself on the last day of his life (pages 623-4) arguing for a Jim Crow government that denied the vote to Blacks, including Black Union veterans who helped save the Union.

Who must Abraham Lincoln have been in order to appear to himself and to us in these different and complementary manifestations?

The answer is clear. He was, as *he* said in 1858, and as Frederick Douglass said in 1874, *a man* who defined himself as a *White* man. By his own definition and by his own words and acts, he was a man who defined himself by the color of his skin, a man who evaluated objects, people, events, slavery, emancipation, the "white-man's" Declaration of Independence, *everything*, from the standpoint of a *White* man. Frederick Douglass, who measured him before and after the assassination, said, "In his interests, in his associations, in his habits of thought, and in his prejudices, he was a white man" (FD 4:312). Ward Hill Lamon, whom Lincoln called his special friend, said it was "as a white man, and in the interests of white men" that he opposed the extension of slavery and the granting of equal rights to Blacks (346).

We must be quite clear on this point, and we must be quite clear about what it means, and, more importantly, about what it does not mean. For we are not saying here that Lincoln was a White man because of the color of his skin; we *are* saying that he was a White man because *he* defined himself as a White man and because he based his philosophy, politics, and ethics on the color of his skin, making whiteness his truth and fundamental being. This means, among other things, that Lincoln chose himself originally and continuously as a White man. It means that he *made* himself *White* by what he did and didn't do and that he *became* a White man by the grace of culture, which assigned him to a group, and by the grace of personal acts of perpetually choosing what had been chosen for him and justifying it by faith, as they say, and works.

On this level, then, whiteness was a cultural or, better, a political pledge that was made in Lincoln's name before he was born, a pledge he internalized after birth and freely reassumed every minute of his life. Having internalized this role or, better, this *calling*, and having learned the gestures and words required, whiteness became his being, and he saw as a White man, spake as a White man, dreamed as a White man, loved and feared as a White man. Above all else, he was a man who pretended to be an emancipator for tactical reasons and was so overwhelmed by the role that he decided to be it without being what he would have had to be in order to be it.

This is neither the time nor the place to provide what is sorely needed, a phenomenology of whiteness, and the point of all this is to emphasize that whiteness was/is a choice and that Abraham Lincoln created Abraham Lincoln by choosing the way he was going to manifest his whiteness.

Can we say, then, that blackness is also a choice? Yes, if we understand that one cannot *not* be in a group, but that there is a qualitative difference between being in a group that defines itself as a mode of historical coexistence and being in a group that defines itself biologically as superior to all other groups and which maintains itself by a White Terror which requires every White, on pain of excommunication or worse, to remain White and to exclude, subordinate or terrorize nonWhites in the name of the White mission.

Because of physical and mental differences, and accidents of birth and place, different Whites relate to the White Terror—defined here as sanctions, even the mild sanctions of frowning or expressing disapproval— in different ways. But whether a White person born into the group accepts the group imperative or rejects it or puts it in brackets, he or she must take a stand on it, especially in a situation where whiteness is oppressing nonwhiteness or where whiteness is struggling nonviolently and violently to keep White superior and NonWhite subordinate. John Brown and Wendell Phillips rejected the White vow in the name of a human vow, proving, among other things, that one doesn't have to be White. Lincoln, who was always talking, even as president, about his "duty" to whiteness, accepted it. The different choices Brown, Phillips and Lincoln made enable us to say that whiteness has many ways of being White, and that to choose to be a White man is to choose to be a particular kind of White man.

What kind of White man was Lincoln?

He was an *American Dilemma* White man, who praised the Declaration and didn't, couldn't, wouldn't do it. He was an "it will take time" White man. He was a Union-above-all White man. He was a colored *boy* and *Aunty* Mary White man. He was *that* kind of White man, and it is precisely for that reason that he is endlessly honored. To say that he was a racist is to understate the case and to divert attention from the fact that racism was the center and circumference of his being and that one cannot say a single true word about him that is not informed by that fact.

To recapitulate, then, Abraham Lincoln was a man who defined himself and chose himself as a White man. Secondly, and more concretely, he was a man who defined himself and chose himself as a racist committed to the subordination of nonWhites. Thirdly, he was a man who defined himself and chose himself as a colonizationist and who was reduced, out of anguish and out of fear of the future and the human condition, to projecting a world without the African-Americans whom he wanted to eliminate, not by actual murder, but by the symbolic murder of banishment.

It is clear from all this, from Lincoln's self-definition and the choices he made, that Abraham Lincoln was a man who defined himself as a White man—but every White man was not Abraham Lincoln. How do we get from the first determination to the ultimate determination? The short answer is that we follow a ladder of *whos*, which should enrich our understanding at every level, and push us *up* to the foundation *who* which bottoms our inquiry.

To return, then, to the question we started with: Who was Lincoln? The answer to that question on a first level of approximation is that he was a tragically flawed figure, marked by Black fear and Indian fear and limited by his commitment to the White supremacy ethic. Socially, he was the archetype of the poor White who makes good and marries the "frivalous" [sic] daughter —that's what her sister called her—of the rich plantation owner and slavemaster (HI 443). Politically, he was the archetype of the sensitive, suffering, ineffectual *fence* figure—in America, in the Third Reich, in Algeria, in South Africa—who is born on a fence and lives and dies on a fence, unable to accept or reject the political evil that defines him objectively.

Reading and re-reading his speeches and private papers, one is struck suddenly by the unexpected fact that down to his last antithesis, down to his last *but,* he is the classic example of the cautious politician, known to every city hall reporter, who assails the extremists on both sides. Is it any wonder then that he is a god to trimmers who have never risked anything for freedom, and that anybody who says he was sad and eloquent and loved the North and the South—not the slave—is immediately given the Pulitzer Prize?

History knows its own, *hides* its own, and selects its own, creating men with needs that meet the needs of the time; and it is an open question whether history chose Lincoln because it was preparing a history of halfness that would end slavery formally without ending slavery in fact or whether Lincoln chose that history because history had given him that halfness and because the halfness was in him and of him and the true expression of his objective being. Whatever: the result was the same. The son of the luckless and virtually illiterate Thomas Lincoln and the doomed Nancy Hanks Lincoln, born in a log cabin, halfway between the rich White slaveowners and the Indians and slaves, and distinguished only by his *dark* White skin, entered the ranks against the slaves and the poor Whites, choosing the party of aristocracy and privilege.

Why was the poor and uneducated Lincoln marching in the front ranks of the big-money crowd? Some of his Sangamon County neighbors and some students say he was mesmerized by the image and speeches of his idol, Whig leader Henry Clay, who said *he* would rather be right *about supporting slavery* than president. Nobody tells us what Clay said he would rather be right about, but Lincoln knew and pulled himself to the top by quoting, paraphrasing and virtually plagiarizing the Kentucky slaveholder (Fredrickson 41).

Another reason Lincoln chose the big-money crowd was that he perceived early in the game that the money people were generally Whigs and that political power sooner or later followed economic power. A number of informants told Herndon that Lincoln started out as a Jacksonian but was converted by his bosses and mentors. From that point onward, he surrounded himself, Herndon excepted, with conservative supporters and partisans of the slave system. Some, like his closest friend, Joshua Fry Speed, and his future wife, Mary Todd, were slaveholders or products of slaveholders. All or almost all believed the Negro was inferior and supported the Illinois Black Laws and the hunting and capturing of fugitive slaves in and around Springfield.

Not only did the Lincoln circle believe in Negro inferiority, but there was a doubt about democracy and the germ plasm of poor Whites. Lincoln himself had, like most Whigs, deeply ingrained doubts about the potential of the [White] masses, and some of his associates in Sangamon County loathed Catholics and the impoverished immigrants from Ireland and other countries. One of their number was Lincoln's legislative associate and future in-law, Ninian Wirt Edwards, who was, Usher Linder said, "naturally and constitutionally an aristocrat [who] hated democracy . . . as the devil is said to hate holy water"(280).

Reinhard H. Luthin, among others, has deplored the systematic attempt to portray Lincoln as "more democratic . . . than he actually was" (127). Lincoln, in fact, as Donald and others have demonstrated, had a decidedly limited view of democracy for White people and his "version of the American dream was in some ways a curiously limited one" (Donald 234). So was his version of human nature. Piatt said he had "a low, but good-natured view of humanity" and "could not understand that men would get up in their wrath and fight for an idea" (RR 480).

They never stop talking in America about Lincoln's vision of government of the people, but as Robert W. Johannsen pointed out accurately, Lincoln was a republican (small *r*) but not a democrat. He believed not in government of the people but government of the "best [White] citizens,"—"men of property and education who had a reverence for (and a stake in) law and order" (91). Lincoln's sympathetic secretaries, John G. Nicolay and John Hay, said in their standard work that "the better sort of people in Sangamon County were Whigs . . . and he preferred through life the better sort to the majority" (NH 1:104-5).

If this was not exactly government of the people, it was at least government of the better sort of people, and Lincoln made the most of it, living it up with his newfound friends, taking the color or pretending to take the color of their conservatism and reaction. It was not by chance, therefore, that he clung to the Whig Party which had, as Phillips said, "no confidence in the people, no trust in the masses . . . did not believe in the conscience or the intelligence of the millions [and] looked . . . upon the whole world as . . . a probate court . . . (529).

The Todd-Stuart-Edwards circle that Lincoln adopted exacted its pound of ideological flesh, setting strict limits beyond which none of its adherents could safely go. Nicolay and Hay said that the Todd-Stuart-Edwards circle and the "Kentucky" crowd were "strongly averse to any discussion of slavery (1:150). Traditional historians who have wondered for so long why it took Lincoln so long to say a coherent word on the extension of slavery need only read the Springfield evidence. Stephen Trigg Logan, Lincoln's second partner, said that during the Kansas-Nebraska crisis Lincoln cleared his new political position with him and perhaps other members of the

Logan-Stuart-Todd circle. "Lincoln was in a fix," Logan recalled. "Lovejoy and others in the Legislature: they wanted Lincoln to say that he would go for the doctrine that there should be no Slavery in the Territories: Lincoln came to me and asked about the matter, Saying to me Knowing my politics, will it tramp your toes—I Said 'No—whatever you do, though I don't agree to the doctrine it won't tread on my toes. Lincoln made the pledge" (HI 467). A family insider said there was a "Todd-Stuart-Edwards family" uproar over Lincoln's "House Divided" speech and that Lincoln "said he would Explain" and "did Explain" in the debate speeches in which he softened and watered down the House Divided doctrine (HI 438).

Lincoln crony David Davis apparently never forgave Lincoln for not supporting him when he ran for judge against a member of the Edwards family. Davis said later that Lincoln "hadn't the manhood to come out for me in preference to Ben Edwards whom he despised—wouldn't do so because Ben was in the family " (HI 349).

It is scarcely surprising, given his ambition and the orientation of his friends and family, that Lincoln dimmed his light and kept silent on so many critical issues. Lincoln himself said that he did not openly oppose the anti-immigrant Know-Nothing Party because in his district "they are mostly my old political and personal friends . . ." (CW 2:316). Former United States Senator Paul Simon has suggested that Lincoln was silent after the Lovejoy murder because so many of his friends and associates, including Linder and gubernatorial candidate Cyrus Edwards, were either in the mob or allies and defenders of the mob (142-5).

By 1840, people, especially political opponents, were charging that "marriage into the aristocracy" had changed Lincoln, who had, according to political charges, sold out to the Todds and their retainers and hangers-on (HI 251), a charge Lincoln heatedly denied.

Even before the game started, even before he met the daughter of the rich slaveowner, Lincoln had given hostages to fate and had signalled his intention by siding with the party of the status quo instead of the party of change. This was a choice not only of the present but also of the past and the future. It was a choice of the men and forces that had destroyed the father he disliked. It was a choice of hard money and high tariffs and generous subsidies for big operators. It was a choice, above all, of the Southern Whigs who owned the big plantations and lived out of the sweat and blood of the slaves.

Two of Lincoln's closest friends, Herndon and Lamon, said Lincoln saw his marriage into the slaveholding Todds as a step up the status ladder. Lamon, following Herndon almost word for word, says "it was natural" that Lincoln, "born into the humblest circumstances, uneducated and poor," should "seek in a matrimonial alliance those social advantages which he felt were necessary to his political advancements . . . . This was, in fact, his own view of the matter" (237-8).

There is no doubt that ambition was involved in Lincoln's marital choice, although we can doubt that Lincoln actually said it, but this choice, like other choices detailed here, was a total choice which expressed at the same time political, sexual, and economic determinants. There survives, for example, an extraordinary passage in which Ninian Edwards's wife, Elizabeth Todd Edwards, recalled the strange courtship of Abraham Lincoln. "I have happened in the room where they were sitting often & often," she said, "and Mary led the Conversation—Lincoln would listen & gaze on her as if drawn by some Superior power, irresistably so . . . " (HI 443).

What do you think he was gazing at? He was gazing at a woman, but he was also gazing, transfixed, at a new world. Perhaps the hell of life at a certain level, as Herndon said, is that Lincoln got what he wanted, and more than he wanted (HH 164-5). Whatever he got, it is worth noting that before Mary Todd Lincoln became a social problem, the Lincolns received slave-begotten subsidies from her slave-owning father. When the father died, the Lincolns received some of the slave-created wealth, and Lincoln himself helped process a will that involved the selling of slaves (Townsend 176-7).

Thus, it came about that Abraham, son of Thomas and grandson of Abraham, who was killed by an Indian, became a conservative, and a supporter of the status quo (read: White supremacy, the Illinois

Black Laws, and slavery) and an opponent of rapid and radical social change (read: social legislation for poor Whites, like his daddy, and immediate emancipation for the slaves). Simon noted in his classic book, *Lincoln's Preparation for Greatness*, that Lincoln's record on education "was not particularly good" and that "he generally voted against legislation which would have moved the schools ahead" (277).

Like so many poor people who pull themselves up by their bootstraps, Lincoln loved the view from the top and had no intention of imperilling his place by ill-advised forays on behalf of poor Blacks or poor Whites. Lord Charnwood said correctly that he "accepted the institutions to which he was born, and he enjoyed them "(455).

In conservatism, as in every other movement studied here, Lincoln lagged behind the leaders of conscience and courage. Some Whigs, unlike Lincoln, were passionate advocates of educational measures in favor of poor Whites. Some Whigs called themselves conscience Whigs and flirted with abolitionism. Abraham, son of Thomas the ne'er-do-well, shunned them, casting his lot with the right wing of his party and siding more often than not with plantation Whigs like Alexander Stephens, with whom he was philosophically and politically attuned.

The testimony on the color of his politics is virtually unanimous. Quarles said Lincoln was "an extreme moderate" (82). Barton said he was a conservative Whig, defined "by his caution and conservatism." He was not "an abolitionist; he was not even a Free-Soiler .... He did not belong to the most progressive element of the Whig Party" (1925, 297). He belonged, in fact, to the right wing of a right-wing party, which meant, among other things, that he would have belonged in contemporary terms, *mutatis mutandis*, to the Reagan-Gingrich right wing of the Republican Party instead of the Kemp-Rockefeller left wing.

There is corroboration on this point from Herndon, who said

Lincoln was "cautious and conservative in his nature, "often "over-cautious, sometimes bordering on the timid" (HH 121). He was, Herndon added, "absolutely conservative . . . ." There was in him "a kind of blind worship of old things, etc." (HH 211).

More than one analyst have expressed amazement that Lincoln clung so long to the doomed Whig Party which died, one wit said, of a vain attempt to swallow the Fugitive Slave Law. Barton couldn't help asking whether Lincoln wouldn't have been "a braver, more capable leader" if he had "entirely abandoned the Whig Party and gone with the Free-Soilers" (1925, 299). The answer is yes and no and maybe, for Lincoln was who he was—a compromising conservative who chose the nearest fence because he was a fence. Better still, he was the Lincoln he chose, and he couldn't have abandoned the blind, "footless," com-promising Whigs without becoming another person, which was theo-retically possible but extremely unlikely. It was no more possible for the prairie Lincoln to take an abolitionist posture in the 1850s than it was for President Lincoln to take an avant-garde emancipation posi-tion in the 1860s. *In fact, it is impossible to conceive of an abolitionist Abraham Lincoln.*

A whole constellation of supporting tendencies and latencies orbited around the conservative Lincoln core. Lincoln specialists tell us in a disjoined sort of way that Lincoln was ambitious, but that is an understatement. According to Herndon, according to Lamon, according to Joseph Gillespie, Lincoln lusted after public office the way some men lust after money and women. Herndon said in a justly famous phrase that "his ambition was a little engine that knew no rest . . ."(HW 304). Herndon said he ran for every legislative office, "from the trusteeship of our then little village to the presi-dency" (HH 88). Lamon, another close friend, said "he struggled incessantly for place. There is no instance where an important office seemed to be within his reach, and he did not try to get it. *Whatever he did in politics, at the bar, in private life, had more or less reference to this great object of his life*" (237, italics added).

This Lincoln, the one everybody tries to hide, was also a

consummate opportunist. Not only was he a trimmer, but he was, Leonard Swett said, "such a trimmer the world has never seen" (HI 165). His tactics, Swett added, "were to get himself in the right place and remain there until events would find him in that place" (162). And when events found him in the wrong place, he changed with the changing flow. Donald W. Riddle said, as we shall see, that Lincoln deliberately chose the extension-of-slavery issue to advance himself.

Herndon and Swett said Lincoln trimmed in his relationship with men but never trimmed principles, as if there is a difference between the two, as if one can be false to men and true to principles. Lincoln's old rival, Stephen Douglas, who was a blatant racist, at least understood that, and he charged that Lincoln changed colors with changing environments, that his principles in abolitionist-oriented northern Illinois were jet black, "in the centre they are in color a decent mulatto, and in lower Egypt they are almost white" (CW 3:176).

Douglas exaggerated for political effect, but he captured a fundamental Lincoln tendency that deepened in the post-Proclamation period. And although Lincoln was never "jet-black," except in his minstrel imagination, he continued to veer from white to off-white, sometimes, as Douglas noted, in the same speech, sometimes in the same paragraph, sometimes in the same sentence.

Lincoln, who was the first Lincoln mythmaker, represented himself and has been represented to the readers of history as a humble man. In his first major campaign, he said, according to the reminiscence of Abner Y. Ellis: "Gentlemen and fellow citizens I presume you all Know who I am [.] I am humble Abraham Lincoln . . . . My politics are short and sweet like the old Womans dance . . . " (HI 171). The word *humble* was always on Lincoln's lips, even in later years. But he protested too much. Herndon and White House secretary John Hay said Lincoln was defined most precisely by "his intellectual arrogance and unconscious assumption of superiority" (HI 332).

One of Lincoln's problems was that his dreams and needs were so vast and grandiose that nothing could satisfy them. Lamon said his mind was filled with "extravagant visions of personal grandeur and power" (475). Lincoln himself said it was his "peculiar misfortune"—and he thought Speed suffered from the same malady—that he tended to "dream dreams of Elysium far exceeding all that any thing earthly can realize" (CW 1:280). After he schemed for years to win a congressional seat, he confessed that "the triumph has not pleased me as much as I expected" (CW 1:391).

All of these determinations—the grandiosity, the voracious ambition, the conservatism—are different ways of saying the same thing. To say that Lincoln was ambitious is to say that he was always on the lookout for the main chance and that he was willing to scheme, plan and trim in order to get what he wanted. To say that he was an ambitious poor man on the make in a society that rewarded ambitious poor men who supported the status quo and slavery and racism is to say that he was a supporter of the status quo and racism and slavery.

For all practical purposes, then, racism equalled ambition, and ambition equalled racism, and racism plus ambition plus grandiosity defined a strategy, a tactic, and a politic. They were expressions of the same whole, and they return us, as we promised, to the foundation *who*, a man who chose himself first as a White man, and as a particular kind of White man, and who became as a consequence of that choice and the necessary sequence of choices it entailed— Henry Clay, the Whigs, the Sangamon Circle, Mary Todd, the Illinois Black Laws, the Fugitive Slave Law, the Slavery Status Quo, Colonization, the Conservative War Policy, the Emancipation Proclamation That Wasn't, the White Reconstruction—the Abraham Lincoln of history.

Of all those who appraised Lincoln in these years and later, perhaps the drafter of the twenty-eighth annual report of the American Anti-Slavery Society understood it best. Lincoln, he said, was "a sort of bland, respectable middle-man, between a very modest Right and the most arrogant and exacting Wrong, a convenient hook whereon to hang appeals at once to a moderate anti-slavery feeling and to a timid conservatism practically pro-slavery, half-way assertions of human rights, and whole-way concessions to a wicked prejudice against dark-colored manhood, arguments against slavery extension, and apologies for continued complicity in slaveholding . . . ."

A poor man on the make, volcanically ambitious, Whiggish and conservative by inclination and by choice, glad to be hobnobbing with rich (and conservative) people, willing to trim and tack to get where he wanted to go, unwilling to jeopardize his hard-won place for social causes opposed by the "better sort" in Illinois and in Georgia, secretly dreaming of glory, Abraham Lincoln was almost a caricature of the "fence" or "bridge" personality we find in almost all situations of oppression. The reason we don't see this is that Lincoln interpreters separate Lincoln from the system that produced him. Their mistake, methodologically, is not that they fail to mention slavery from time to time but that they mention Lincoln *at any time and in any context* without explicitly or implicitly noting that the context and the man, Gettysburg above all, were defined, shaped, and colored by the oppression that defined Lincoln and his era.

The point here—and the point has not, unfortunately, been explored—is that *Lincoln was in and of himself, and in his objective being, an oppressor*, a point that he went out of his way to emphasize by endorsing slavery in the South and the Fugitive Slave Law in the North. More precisely, he was an oppressor in a situation of super-exploitation and super-oppression. For to be a conservative in a time of muted, institutionalized and well-hidden oppression is to be one kind of person, which we can name and classify. To be a conservative at a time of extreme oppression, as in South Africa, as in the Third Reich, as in the Slave South, at a time when to be moderate is to be culpable, and to be a conservative is to be an accomplice, is to be a different kind of person.

From this vantage point, Lincoln was a classic example of a type engendered by the French and American revolutions, which created a demand for sensitive souls who could suffer publicly and dramatically *in their own lives* while explaining to themselves and others why the All-Men-Are-Created-Equal proposition couldn't be extended [immediately?] to nonEuropeans. This was a delicate task which required men who could make a career out of Bad Faith and who could affirm and deny *at the same time* that all men were created equal and who could seem to believe at the same time both the affirmation and the denial. It required, above all else, Beautiful Souls who were too sensitive to accept who they were and the reality they were living and who therefore created a Platonic heaven, high above the slave ships and plantations and Indian massacres, where the beautiful words revolved around in a vacuum and were only beautiful words.

Such men used *pretty* words to hide themselves and others from the ugly reality they were living. (I am using here and elsewhere the word *pretty* to define an academic/political orientation based on the use and misuse of sugar-coated words to hide ugly realities.) Such men acted not to change reality but to whiten their souls. Such men lived a lie and talked the truth. Lincoln was such a man. It was Lincoln, or a man like Lincoln, that Hegel had in mind when he said that "the spirit and substance of their community are, thus, the mutual assurance of their conscientiousness, of their good intentions, the rejoicing over this reciprocal purity of purposes, the quickening and refreshment received from the glorious privilege of knowing and of expressing, of fostering and cherishing, a state so, altogether admirable." Such was Abraham Lincoln, rejoicing over *the purity of his purposes and good intentions* and "the quickening and refreshment" received from the glorious privilege of expressing at Gettysburg and Peoria and other venues words he had no intention of living (664, italics added).

At a still deeper level, it can be argued that Lincoln was one of those men, common to every Western oppression, who are called to the unenviable task of throwing spans over the yawning chasms separating

the Whites and coloreds they were destined, because of superior tech-
nology, to roll over and destroy. In some venues, they were called
White liberals; in others, they were called moderates. Whatever they
were called, they were bridge figures, destined to stand in the middle
of raging battlefields and to suffer and wring their hands and tell the
oppressors that they were better than they were.

Lincoln was the father of all bridges. One reason liberals and others cling to him so desperately, despite clear evidence that he was not
what they say he was, is that they fear that if the bridge collapses,
there will be no way to the other side (of themselves and of humanity). But the defense of indefensible icons, of Lincoln, Churchill, Lee,
Rhodes et al., is part of the problem, for it is impossible to lie oneself
to the other side, especially since Lincoln's defenders have painted
themselves into a corner by deliberately forgetting and downplaying
White Americans who *were* bridges beyond the bridges and who are
today the only hope of communication and interchange between the
two sides.

At this level, we can pose a new question to history: What must
America be to demand this Lincoln? What must American scholarship be, what must we be, in order to make a Separatist an integrationist and a Racist the ultimate American symbol of racial harmony?

Part of the answer to that question is to be found in the contradictions that make Lincoln the ultimate American fantasy figure.
Frederick Douglass said that Lincoln knew the American people
better than they knew themselves (FD 4:318). Douglass didn't mean
that Lincoln knew the American people in the sense of ideas, for
Lincoln frequently and dangerously misjudged public opinion in the
North and in the South, never more so than in the twilight period
between his election and inaugural and the crisis period between
Bull Run and Atlanta. The knowing Douglass alluded to was more
complex. It was a matter of the viscera, not the head. It was a matter
of being, not knowledge—and it was not entirely complimentary. In

his prejudices, Douglass said, in his blind spots, and in his good intentions, Lincoln was the American of Americans, meaning by that that he was the American who made the bargain between slavery and freedom in the Constitution, the American who supported the Fugitive Slave Law, Indian dispossession and the compromises and defaults that gave us Watts, My Lai, and the Emancipation Proclamation, limited as it was, and Head Start and Medicare.

If, as I shall contend, Wendell Phillips, Charles Sumner, and Thaddeus Stevens represented all that is best in the vision of White America, Lincoln represented all that was real in maintaining America, which has always believed the Word in its own way and which has always been able to accommodate itself to "the necessities,"as Lincoln put it, that made it impossible, in his view, to realize the Word. Lincoln defenders never stop telling us that he said that "the central idea" of America was "the equality of man." But they never tell us that he added in the next sentence that he and the White people he knew and loved had "always submitted patiently to whatever of inequality there seemed to be as a matter of actual necessity" (CW 2:385). As for himself, he said: "I have never manifested any impatience with the necessities that spring from the actual presence of black people amongst us, and the actual existence of slavery amongst us where it does already exist . . . " (CW 3: 222).

What were Abraham Lincoln's "necessities"?

There were four. One was the necessity to keep Blacks in slavery. Another was the necessity to keep free Blacks subordinate and segregated. The third was the necessity to prevent amalgamation or Black and White sex. The fourth, flowing with and out of one, two and three, was the necessity to preserve White supremacy.

"*I have never*"—remember the words—"*manifested any impatience with the necessities that spring from the actual presence of black people amongst us . . . .*"

This was Lincoln's strength and his weakness, and in assessing him we must never lose sight of the fact that history selected him precisely because he was a conservative on the race issue and because history and the people *knew* he wasn't a radical or a visionary or a great leader. He was selected as a presidential candidate, Joshua Giddings said, because his "anti-slavery sentiment had been less prominent than that" of other prominent candidates (qtd. in Berwanger 136). He was selected, in other words, not because he was what he was but because he was what he was not, *and he is honored endlessly today for the same nonreason.*

The same reason that made him available in 1860 explains why he failed so disastrously in 1861 and 1862 in meeting the Confederate challenge by issuing a defining call to mobilize the maintaining North. Herndon said he "was not visionary" and "had relatively no imagination, and no fancy . . ." (HH 89). Another crony, Joseph Gillespie, said, "He endeavored to bring back things to the old land marks but he never would have attempted to invent and compose new systems [.] He had boldness enough when he found the building racked and going to decay to restore it to its original design but not to contrive a new & distinct edifice . . ." (HI 184). And it is sacrilege perhaps to say what appears plainly on the record: Abraham Lincoln, America's moral center and vision of visions, lacked vision. He had no vision of a great America transformed by Whites, Blacks, Browns, and Reds. He had no vision of a rainbow America leading a crusade of all the peoples of the world. Abraham Lincoln lacked the vision thing. He was the George Bush of the nineteenth century.

The best thing one can say about Lincoln is that he seemed to be aware of his problem and compensated for it by contradicting himself and by manufacturing excuses. Whatever the reasons and whatever the psychological mechanisms involved, the self-made man who is held up as a model of responsibility by almost everybody is defined precisely by his failure to assume responsibility for his own acts. And if one thinks about it seriously, one is almost forced to recognize that the most unflattering side of his personality was that he was always making excuses, and alibiing, and good-intentioning, and washing his hands in public, like Pontius Pilate, and blaming something or somebody else—God, the Constitution, Kentucky—

for the decisions he freely made about racism and slavery.

The technical name for this failure, which is the abiding disease of the post-Slave Trade world, is bad faith, which we can define here, borrowing Sartre's words, as the art of "hiding a displeasing truth or presenting as truth a pleasing untruth" (49).

On the political level, the only level we are concerned with here, bad faith is a lie, but a special kind of lie, the lie that one tells oneself and that one believes or half-believes. In bad faith, one looks oneself in the eye and tells oneself a lie, as slaveholder Thomas Jefferson did when he wrote the Declaration of Independence, as Jefferson disciple Abraham Lincoln did when he affirmed both the Declaration of Independence and slavery where it existed. One does this so often, as Lincoln did, and as Jefferson did, that it becomes a way of life, a way of seeing and being.

This tendency is threaded throughout Lincoln's whole life. Twentieth-century interpreters have stressed his openness and honesty, but the men who knew him best all stressed his compulsive secrecy, even about minor things. Herndon said he was "the most secretive—reticent—shut-mouthed man that ever existed" (HW xxxix).

Lincoln's bad faith assumed two different but complementary modes. In the first mode, he identified with his function, saying he was only a White politician or he was only a president and couldn't do right because his function required him to do wrong. In this mode, he used the well-known formula: I AM ONLY WHAT I AM. At the same time, and at first sight somewhat paradoxically, he had recourse to the opposite formula, and the same formula: I AM GREATER THAN I AM. How did this work? Watch! President Lincoln is about to send a letter saying, among other things, that he would keep all slaves in slavery, perhaps forever, if it would save the Union. Having written these words, which have been lavishly praised by almost all scholars, he immediately called for his trusty semicolon, which he almost always used to do his dirty work, and added: "I intend no modification of my oft-expressed *personal* wish that all men every where could be free" (CW 5:389, Lincoln's italics).

Isn't that remarkable? One Lincoln, the real Lincoln, says he would condemn all Blacks to eternal slavery and dons with the same gesture the mask and transcendence of the other Lincoln, who is the same Lincoln, and says in the same breath that he, the other Lincoln, the ethereal Lincoln, is greater than the flesh-and-blood Lincoln, and wishes—*personally,* not politically—that all men, including the men and women the bad Lincoln has just condemned to continued slavery, were free. Who's lying here, and who's telling the truth? The "good" Lincoln or the "bad" Lincoln? To answer that question, we have to ask another question: Which Lincoln is real? The answer is both, and neither. The flesh-and-blood Lincoln acts but refuses to accept responsibility for his acts; the Beautiful Soul Lincoln *wishes* but refuses to accept responsibility for his wish. The only difference—and what a difference—is that the acts of the real Lincoln have real and inexpiable consequences—rape, murder, death—whereas the wishes of the Beautiful Soul never come to anything.

It is no accident that Lincoln defined himself and that others define him by the alibi of good intentions, oblivious apparently to the well-known maxim that the road to hell is paved with great emancipators with good intentions. In that sense, Lincoln was Everyman, especially Every-Oppressor in a situation of oppression: "For the good that I would I do not; but the evil which I would not, that I do." Maybe that's why he still speaks to us. As he or somebody else said, God must have loved fence-straddlers—he made so many of them.

In any case, it is not without cause that one spends one's life making excuses, as Lincoln demonstrated, making excuses right up to the end, apologizing in his last speech for the lily-White Reconstruction government in Louisiana and saying, finally, that it was his personal—you know the word, he said it everywhere—*wish* that the franchise could be opened to Black Union veterans and *very intelligent* Negroes.

In his last speech, and in all his speeches going back to Illinois, even and especially the Gettysburg speech, Lincoln showed his countrymen how to affirm and deny at the same time, how *to be* an oppressor and how *not to be* an oppressor at the same time. The question this raises, and the question we will be dealing with in the following chapters, is what is the meaning, what is the phenomenology of a man who embodies in his person the principle and the negation of the principle and who is equally eloquent in defending both and in using the negation to ennoble, and whiten the principle? We can cite any Lincoln speech to illustrate his art, but it can be argued that he never surpassed the sentence in which he said that "in our greedy chase to make profit of the Negro, let us beware, lest we 'cancel and tear to pieces' even the white man's charter of freedom" (CW 2:276).

This is the most remarkable sentence in the whole of political science. In six words—*the white man's charter of freedom*—Lincoln affirms and denies the words *all men are created equal* by making them the exclusive property of *the white man*.

This image of a man affirming "the white man's charter of freedom" and saying a patronizing word for the Negro in the same sentence is historical hutzpa at its highest and required a master to carry it off right. Lincoln had no peer in this area, not even Jefferson. That's why he was elected president. That's why he has been elevated to secular sainthood. He speaks with unparalleled power—and duplicity—to the need to both deny and support a system of oppression while affirming and rejecting it at the same time. Polemics apart, how can anyone fail to understand this fence-straddler who fleshes out all our fears and anxieties and who nevertheless wins in the end not by sticking his neck out but by *not* sticking his neck out?

It's all there, it's all perfectly clear, there is no possibility of misunderstanding: Lincoln in his heart of hearts was an *affirmnial*, a man defined by affirmations that were denials and denials that were affirmations. Wherever we look, in his shuttling from mirth to sadness, in his attacks on slavery and his defense of slavery, in his affirmation of the Declaration and his denials of the Declaration, we find fractures and contradictions. A modern interpreter, George Sinkler, said correctly that he "hated both equality and inequality" (49).

Lincoln defenders say these contradictions make it impossible to define Lincoln. On the contrary, it is the contradictions that define him. He was, as Herndon and others said, a walking contradiction. He was the man who was not what he was and who was what he was not. He was Pharaoh and Moses, minstrel and Macbeth, an oscillator who never stopped oscillating, a clock that said twelve o' clock and six o' clock at the same time.

The issue posed by all this is not the state of the soul of Abraham Lincoln but the state of the soul of the Republic, which finds its deepest moral values in a White supremacist who opposed integration and wanted to deport all Blacks. One can say that the Republic has been unfortunately deluded by scholars who have systematically hidden the truth in one of the most extraordinary episodes in the history of scholarship. But that's too easy. History, as we have said over and over again, knows its own. And history, White history, *knows* Lincoln. At least it knows that Abraham Lincoln was not John Brown or Wendell Phillips, which means that it knows at a level deeper than scholarship, deeper than footnotes and documents, that nothing Lincoln ever said or did, including signing the Emancipation Proclamation, posed any threat to White interests.

Thus, fleetingly, as in the first four bars of a blues, as in the opening theme of a symphony, we begin to catch a glimpse of the hidden Lincoln. We shall develop these themes in the following chapters, but it is clear, even in these introductory chapters, that Lincoln is still a man of unexplored complexes and contradictions. Addicted to abstract principles that he never intended to practice, forever protesting his innocence and trying to keep his distance from the screams of the victims of a system he privately questioned but publicly supported, Abraham Lincoln was history's most famous and most tragic Beautiful Soul.

As Herndon said, as Swett, Davis and even Lamon said, there

was something strange and distant and cold in Lincoln, particularly in his approach to African-Americans. Lord Charnwood, Lincoln's English biographer, said that in appraising Lincoln's attitude toward slavery and the opponents of slavery "we feel with a great American historian that the North would have been depraved indeed if it had not bred abolitionists, and it requires an effort to sympathise with Lincoln's rigidly correct feeling—sometimes harshly expressed and sometimes apparently cold" (126).

The coldness is obvious, but there is no evidence that the feeling was "rigidly correct," since the men he denounced turned out to be historically correct and since Lincoln's racial plans, all of them, colonization and compensated emancipation with the rest, turned out to be not only wrong but weird. It is to be noted also, at least in passing, that Lincoln, like Ronald Reagan, with whom he shared so many traits, including unbridled commitment to the White Dream, could make social and political gaffes of gargantuan proportions. Speaking at Worcester, Massachusetts, in September 1848, he made an impromptu reference to the slain Elijah Lovejoy that shocked some people in the audience: "I have heard you have abolitionists here. We have a few in Illinois and we shot one the other day" (HI 681).

Great care has been taken to hide *this* Lincoln from the American public, which is, all things considered, a pity. For on the personal level, Abraham Lincoln was the strangest and most fascinating of all American presidents. Compared to him, in fact, Richard Nixon was a paragon of normalcy. "Never," John J. Duff wrote, "has a President possessed a more complicated personal character" (141). Lincoln's friend Whitney said he was "one of the most uneven, eccentric and heterogeneous characters, probably, that ever played a part in the great drama of history" (153).

Tragic and comic, humble and arrogant, sensitive and insensitive, humane, bigoted, superstitious, carrying the cross of Black fear and Indian fear and Woman fear, a man's man, never happier than when he was raising cain with the boys on the circuit (HI 349), and never completely comfortable in the presence of the ladies, lewd sometimes and often crude with the boys but eloquent on the stump, a White man's man who loved peace but volunteered three times for the war to ethnically cleanse Illinois of Indians, a lover of equality who told n———r jokes, Pharaoh and Moses, Macbeth and Minstrel, White on the outside and Black on the inside, a funny man, and a sad one, always telling jokes on a high-wire above a personal abyss, trying to laugh away demons that repeatedly drove him to the edge of insanity, this is the Lincoln Nobody Wants To Know but the Lincoln Everybody Must Know if we are to understand the "darkness" he feared and the whiteness that limited him. The real question is why did the "saddest and gloomiest man of his time" want to be a stand-up comedian and why did he tell one visitor that he would willingly give up the office of president for the talent to write dialect jokes?

This, in turn, raises other questions. What is the signification of humor? What does it intend and portend? And what is the connection between the humor and the sadness? We know now—how could we have ever thought anything else?—that humor is a conservative strategy, designed not to tear down but to buttress the status quo. We will not be surprised, at any rate, to discover that one of the defining characteristics of Lincoln biographers is the line they draw between the good guys, the conservatives who laugh at Lincoln's jokes, and the bad guys, the radicals who said he was a fool to stand around telling jokes, some of them dirty, while Union soldiers were bleeding to death and the slaves were suffering a fate worse than death.

Finally, how did all this affect and color the life and politics of Abraham Lincoln, a unique totality who, like everybody else, expressed himself totally in everything he did, who expressed his racism, his fears, his humor and his conception of life, death and human nature in every act of his life, including the joke about "Darky Jim" and the Emancipation Proclamation that didn't emancipate?

All these questions—and others—will be on the agenda once we recapture the beauty and tragedy of our common history and start telling the truth.

5

Prologue In Blackface And Whiteface

BRAHAM Lincoln was fascinated—and horrified—by the color black and couldn't get enough of imitation Whites imitating the imitation Blacks he wanted to banish from his White American Eden.

Attracted and repelled, tempted and threatened, he loved "n——r jokes" and "n——r shows" but feared real Black people, real Black violence and the darkening of White America. It will be said, of course, that Lincoln was "friendly" to Negro servants and suppliants, but "the friendliness of Lincoln toward colored people was," as Lincoln authority J.G. Randall said, "a Southern [White] type of friendliness" (1946, 47), and no one can read the record without realizing that he had an almost obsessional fear of Black violence and slave insurrections.

The threat of blackness, the temptation of blackness, the magic of blackness, the blackness of blackness: Lincoln seemed to have been obsessed by the subject. It was in response to blackness, and as a relation to blackness, that he created his identity, making color the center of his world and making what he considered the opposite of blackness, that is to say, whiteness, his main value. And so while living a double life psychologically, putting on blackface in his imaginary minstrel life and manipulating the mask of whiteness on the political stage, he constructed a personal myth of Black inferiority based on the presence or absence of color.

If there was one notion he was committed to, it was that the Negro race was inferior to the White race because of its color.

If there was one thing he was certain of, it was that he was better than Black people because of the whiteness of his skin.

"Certainly," he said, over and over again, "the Negro is not our equal in color—perhaps not in many other respects . . ." (CW 2:520).

This was, to say the least, astounding. For if we assume, as we must assume, that Lincoln was a relatively intelligent man, then we must assume that he knew that color was a variable that changed with climate and copulation, and that some Blacks, perhaps many Blacks, were whiter than he was, which might have been the problem, or part of the problem. For Abraham Lincoln, the alleged emancipator of Negroes, was so dark-skinned that some people said he was a Negro. On one occasion, a White House visitor pointed to a photograph of a dark-skinned man on the White House wall and said:

"I see a photograph of you there, but it does not appear to have any sun in it."

"No," said Lincoln," with his peculiar smile, "Parson [William G.] Brownlow says I am a nigger, and if he had judged alone from that picture, he would have had some ground for his assertion" (RR 597).

There were split decisions, even in the sunshine. It was even said by some people that Lincoln was a descendant of Africa where he wanted to "return" all Negroes. On April 6, 1840, when he addressed a Whig rally in Carlinville, the Democratic *Register* said he was "the lion of the Tribe of Sangamon . . . and judging from outward appearance, originally from Liberia" (LDD 1:134).

What was the real color of the lion of the tribe of Sangamon?

His law partner said he was "saffron-brown" (HH 198). Lincoln himself said he was of a "dark complexion" (CW 3:512). He also said he was black. Writing to a man who may not have remembered him, he said: "Perhaps you have forgotten me. Don't you remember *a long black fellow* who rode on horseback with you from Tremont to Springfield nearly 10 years ago . . . ?" (CW 1:450, italics added).

It was rumored in Black America for years that Abraham Lincoln was a Negro. I have no information on the subject; I didn't look for information on the subject—my primary interest here is in the never-before-explored phenomenon of a dark-skinned man who believed he was superior to Blacks because of the color of his skin.

What about his family? It has been established that certain of his forefathers and foremothers were free spirits sexually and that Lincoln believed "his mother was a bastard" (HH 59). Herndon said Lincoln told him that his mother's real father was a Virginia aristocrat, a story that cannot be authenticated. Rumors about her paternity and *his* paternity may have played a role in his extreme sensitivity on this point.

Whatever Lincoln's color, whether he was saffron-brown or dark-complexioned or "a long black fellow," and whatever his family background, he had a mountain-sized color problem. George Fredrickson, who does not necessarily agree with my thesis, said that in view of "Lincoln's unequivocal statement that Blacks are inferior in color . . . it seems reasonable to conclude that Lincoln sensed in the attitudes of White Americans, and probably in himself as well, a strong distaste for Negroid physical features and a powerful preference for White pigmentation as the human norm" (47). Concerning which three points can be made. First of all and most important of all, color *in the Western World* is not a physiological characteristic—it is a historical or, better, a *political* characteristic. Secondly, color, however defined, is not the cause of racism—it is the excuse or justification. Thirdly, "a strong distaste for Negroid physical features" didn't bother Thomas Jefferson and other slaveholders who showed, according to all available statistics, "a powerful preference" for nonWhite norms.

Don E. Fehrenbacher questioned Fredrickson's conclusion from another angle, saying "we cannot be certain that he [Lincoln] was not merely expressing an aesthetic judgment or noting the social disadvantages of being Black" (197, 106). Fehrenbacher forgot or overlooked another Lincoln statement that went far beyond aesthetics or even "normal" perception, however defined. Rebutting one of Stephen A. Douglas's arguments on another subject, Lincoln said, in passing: "You can as easily argue the color out of the Negroes' skin. Like the 'bloody hand' you may wash it, and wash it, the red witness of guilt still sticks, and stares horribly at you" (CW 2:276).

In this horrible and horribly revealing statement, which indicated unhealthy obsessions of clinical proportions, Lincoln, or Lincoln's unconscious, said that the color of blackness, like the "bloody hand" of the murderer, was a "witness of guilt"—what did Lincoln think the Black *race* was guilty of?—that "sticks and stares horribly at you."

Anyone reading that statement would say that the man who made it had serious human problems. If he or she were told in addition that the same man was fascinated by blackness and put on black faces in his imagination, there would be no doubt about the conclusion.

Despite or perhaps because of his color complex, Lincoln was always, his cronies said, rendezvousing in the neighborhood of blackness. Ward Lamon, the good-timing lawyer who entertained him in Illinois and in the White House, said "he was fond of Negro melodies" (1895,151). Herndon said he had it on good authority that Lincoln consulted a Negro fortune teller on his 1831 visit to New Orleans, "asking her to give him his history, his end and his fate" (HH 409).

Nothing, we are told, gave Lincoln more pleasure than minstrel shows. Whitney said he "was especially fond of Negro minstrel performances"(161). Author Jesse Weik said "he had an insatiable fondness for Negro minstrelsy and seemed to extract the greatest delight from the crude jokes and harmless [sic] fun of the black-faced and red-lipped performers" (Weik 75).

The implications of this have never been fully appreciated. For it is unusual to say the least for a man who was terrified by the possibility of being overwhelmed by "inferior" Blacks to be so taken by the spectacle of White people with burnt cork on their faces pretending to be Black. Since it was impossible for the minstrel show to succeed if Lincoln and the other spectators didn't identify with the black-faced performers by completing with their own flesh the racial transformation outlined onstage, it can be said that Lincoln had an insatiable fondness for imagining that he was a Negro. "To wear or even enjoy blackface," Eric Lott said, "was literally, for a time, to become black, to inherit the cool, virility, humility, abandon, or *gaite de coeur* that were the prime components of white ideologies of black manhood" (52).

The minstrel shows Lincoln loved were conceived in cupidity and dedicated to the proposition that all Negroes were created unequal, frozen for all time in timeless Jim Crow archetypes of shuffling, mindless buffoons. Cunningly created to give Whites a sense of superiority in their whiteness and a sense of disdain for Blacks, the shows were written by racists, performed by racists and watched by racists. This was not, as Lincoln admirers contend, "harmless" fun. This was sadistic fun with political overtones that poisoned the social atmosphere, fastening the chains of the slaves and providing ideological support for the inhuman Black laws that Lincoln supported.

Form followed function in these shows, which were essentially variety shows for White people presented by White men in Black face, "their painted lips leering," Ken Emerson wrote, "like gashed watermelons as they laughed at their own racist jokes" (97).

Sex defined the postures and presentations, which were based in many cases, Lott said, on phallic and homoerotic images (120-2).

It was a visual art, a voyeur's art, that made it possible for Lincoln and other Whites to visit Slave Row (and Harlem and the South Side) while remaining White and insular and smug.

It was also a sadistic art, which encouraged "murderous fantasies" (Lott 150) about the death and disappearance of Blacks. There was a suspiciously large amount of dying in minstrel shows, and Lincoln and other minstrel fans, including Walt Whitman and Mark Twain, spent a lot of time shedding tears over the untimely end of Old Black

Joes "gone whar de good N——rs go," to that great plantation in the sky (Emerson 107). More than racial cruelty was involved in all this. For this "generic death drive," as Lott said, "was ultimately rooted in the most pressing racial questions of the day." In and through the minstrel drama, minstrel fans "repeatedly wished away the existence of blacks altogether." And it seemed to Lott and others that "what was being symbolically eliminated and put to rest was the whole lamented business of slavery in the United States, by means of the elimination of black people themselves."

On this level, blackface constituted a disguised wish for "the elimination—by extinction, expulsion or magic—of the black race " (Emerson 108), a disguised wish directly linked to the politics of Lincoln and other Whites who favored colonization.

Perhaps the worst example of the "metaphorical murder" (Lott 189) of the genre Lincoln loved is the verse, cited in *Popular Songs of the Nineteenth Century*, in which Stephen Foster joked about a boat that sank, drowning *five hundred* Blacks.

> *I jump'd aboard the telegraph*
> *And trabbled down de ribber,*
> *De lectrick fluid magnified,*
> *And kill'd five hundred Nigga.*
>
> *Oh, Susanna, do not cry for me.*

Or for Amos and Andy, either.

This was not entertainment; this was genocide in blackface, and there was a direct link between this political theatre and the sexual, racial, and economic anxieties of Lincoln and other nineteenth-century Whites. It was, at any rate, no accident that Lincoln and other devotees of the politics of burnt cork made Daddy Rice's "Jim Crow" the biggest hit of the 1830s.

> *Weel a-bout and turn a-bout*
> *and do just so.*
> *Every time I weel a-about*
> *I jump Jim Crow.*

Wheeling about and turning about and jumping just so, Daddy Rice, the White man who was called "the Negro par excellence," shuffled across the stage at New York's Bowery Theatre in 1832 in blackface and gave America its first international song hit. By 1838, as I have pointed out elsewhere (1961, 255-7), Jim Crow was wedged into the language as a synonym for Negro. A noun, an adjective, a "comic" way of life. By the 1850s, when Lincoln launched his campaign to colonize real Blacks, the Jim Crow song, the Jim Crow train, the Black-faced minstrel and the White-faced auditor were so mixed up in the American mind that it was impossible to tell where the lyrics ended and the whips and chains began.

Cultural historians say the minstrel show was the beginning of the American entertainment industry, meaning that it was the beginning of the White entertainment industry, meaning that it was the beginning of the White performer's burden of going to the "neighborhood," however named, and stealing and marketing watered-down and distorted versions of Black songs and rhythms. Lincoln, who was virtually a minstrel show groupie, was there at the beginning. On one occasion, a literary man tried to find out if Lincoln while in St. Louis had attended a lecture by the celebrated English writer William Makepeace Thackeray. One of Lincoln's Springfield, Illinois, friends sent a message back that if Lincoln "was in St. Louis and the wonderful Mr. Thackeray was billed to lecture in one public hall and Campbell's or Rumsey's Negro Minstrels were to hold forth in another hall on the same evening, it would have been folly to look for Lincoln at the lecture. Instead of the latter the 'n——r show' would have caught him every time" (Weik 86-8).

It was a minstrel show or as he and his friends said indelicately "a n——r show" that caught Lincoln on his visit to Chicago two months before he was nominated for president of the United States. Whitney said that when, on March 23, 1860, he was presented three tickets to Rumsey and Newcomb's Minstrels, he "asked him if he would like to go to a 'n——r show' that night. Lincoln "assented rapturously," saying: "Of all things I would rather do to-night that suits me exactly . . . ."

The "piece d'resistance" of the show, Whitney reported, was a performance of a new song, an "Ethiopian 'walk round'" called "Dixie's Land." One of the verses went like this:

> Sugar in de gourd an' stony batter,
> De whites grow fat an' de niggahs fatter;
> Look away—look 'way—away—Dixie's land.

The song, Whitney said, "was then entirely new; and was the most extravagant minstrel performance I ever saw. Lincoln was perfectly 'taken' with it: and clapped his great hands, demanding an *encore*, louder than anyone. I never saw him so enthusiastic" (102-3, 161) .

Whitney may have been mistaken about the date or the name of the show. According to the *Chicago Tribune*, "the renowned Hooley and Campbell's Late George Christy's Minstrels" were at Metropolitan Hall for six nights in March 1860. A *Chicago Tribune* review of March 22, 1860, said "Urusworth was 'Brudder Bones' to perfection." Whatever the details or the names of the performers, it is significant that Lincoln ended what some historians call his "prelude to greatness" by attending what he and his friends called "a n——r show."

During his term as a congressman and during his tenure in the White House, Lincoln frequented "n——r shows." In January 1849, Congressman Lincoln and his wife Mary attended a performance of "the Ethiopian Serenaders" at Carusi's Saloon. Lincoln and his wife found the white-faced crowd as fascinating as the black-faced "Ethiopians." The future president, who is usually pictured as grim-visaged, and his wife watched fascinated as two young women wearing black fur bonnets worked the crowd with evident success. The Lincolns were fascinated by the duo, whom they dubbed "our two girls."

After Mary Todd Lincoln left Washington, Lincoln saw the women at a musical on the Capitol grounds and wrote: "Our two girls, whom you remember seeing first at Carusis, at the exhibition of the Ethiopian Serenaders, and whose peculiarities were the wearing of black fur bonnets, and never being seen in close company with other ladies, were at the music yesterday. One of them was attended by their brother, and the other had a member of Congress in tow. He went home with her; and if I were to guess, I would say, he went away a somewhat altered man—most likely in his pockets, and in some other particular. The fellow looked conscious of guilt, although I believe he was unconscious that every body around knew who it was that had caught him. "

The Lincolns, if this letter is a guide, had a more complex relationship than is generally assumed (CW 1:495-6).

Although minstrel show melodies were not what we would call music to emancipate by, Lincoln patronized minstrel shows during his White House years. On one occasion, during a discussion of theatrical fare, President Lincoln told Leonard Grover of the Grover Theatre, "Do you know, Mr. Grover, I really enjoy a minstrel show." Responding to that broad hint, Grover later told Lincoln—according to a Grover reminiscence in the April 1909 issue of *Century* magazine—that he had booked Hooley's Minstrels for his viewing pleasure (943-50).

Rumsey and Newcomb's Minstrel, Hooley and Campbell's Late George Christy's Minstrels, Barney Williams, the Ethiopian Serenaders, Dombey & Sons, Brudder Bones: Abraham Lincoln knew them all. And the question we have to ask ourselves, once again, is who must Abraham Lincoln have been in order to imagine that he was an Oreo minstrel, black on the outside and white on the inside, chocolated and transformed and pulled out of his whiteness by ersatz Negro melodies and rhythms?

The answer, once again, is that he was in this regard, as in everything else, a quintessential racist, torn apart by his attraction to the Blacks he wanted to subordinate and banish, partly because he had projected his fears and desires and otherness onto them. The historian Benjamin Quarles, who tried to save Lincoln from him-self, said Lincoln"like most Whites . . . believed that the Negro as such was funny (39). Lincoln also believed, as Quarles also noted, that the Negro as such was inferior and was not "on a par with the white man in mental endowment" (36).

Lincoln was as active as any racist of his time in perpetuating Negro stereotypes. The words *n——r, darky* and colored *boy* came eas-ily to his lips. It appears from the admittedly incomplete record that Lincoln used the N-word at least as often as the Mark Fuhrmans of today. He might have used it even more, for unlike Fuhrman, who tried to hide his hand on official occasions, Lincoln used the word openly on public platforms and in the Illinois State House and the White House. Harold Holzer, who edited a collection of the Lincoln-Douglas debates, was surprised that Lincoln used the N-word twice in the first Lincoln-Douglas debate, which was held in the relatively progressive town of Ottawa, Illinois (1993,42). Speaking to some fif-teen thousand Whites, Lincoln denied that he wanted "to set the nig-gers and white people to marrying together" and said, in passing, that there was "no danger that the people of Kentucky will shoulder their muskets, and, with a young nigger stuck on every bayonet, march into Illinois and force them upon us" (CW 3:20, 27).

Since there is a widespread tendency to ignore, excuse and deny testimony from Lincoln's own mouth, we are, as we indicated ear-lier, departing from our usual practice and printing Lincoln's words without elision. It is worth noting in this connection that Carl Sand-burg, who spent decades researching Lincoln's life, denied that Lin-coln used the N-word. In a letter to Paul M. Angle on July 16, 1929, Sandburg said of the Carlinville speech, quoted below, that "the use of the word 'Nigger' was never indulged in by Lincoln unless he was quoting somebody . . . " (1968, 267).

Lincoln wasn't quoting anybody when he denied before some fif-teen thousand people at the sixth Lincoln-Douglas debate that he wanted a "Nigger wife" (Holzer 1993, 318). Nor was he quoting anyone when he told a crowd of some four thousand White Illinois citizens at the last debate in Alton, Illinois, that he supported the notorious Fugitive Slave Law although he personally had "no taste for running and catching niggers" (CW 3:317).

Like Sandburg, Paul Angle, another eminent Lincoln authority, refused to accept the evidence of his eyes and blamed incompetent reporters for putting bad words in Lincoln's mouth (1930, 188). This was clearly insufficient, since different reporters in different states in different years heard the same word. One must also remember that Lincoln himself swore by the accuracy of Robert Roberts Hitt (Sparks 77-8), the shorthand expert who reported the Lincoln-Douglas debates for the *Chicago Tribune* and recorded some of the offending words. Even more persuasive is the fact that Lincoln himself corrected the debate manuscripts before they were published as a collection, changed poorly chosen words and didn't touch or evince any qualms about the N-words Hitt reported. "In my own speeches," he told the editors, "I have corrected only a few small typographical errors" (CW 3:373). The typographical errors didn't include the N-word.

In 1946, Roy Prentice Basler, a supreme Lincoln authority, threw in the towel, conceding that "it seems more likely" that "in extempore speaking, Lincoln sometimes used it [the N-word] as the common and quite natural colloquial term" (1946, 450).

"Quite natural?"

Basler didn't mean that, did he? Whatever he meant, the fact that he wrote it in 1946, and that nobody has called him on it, is a reflection of a serious problem in the lands of Lincoln.

Before, after and during the Lincoln-Douglas debates, in public and in private, Lincoln used and abused the N-word. In the Carlinville, Illinois, speech, he used the word twice, and it is surprising that historians who are always praising Lincoln's skill in opening speeches never mention the Carlinville speech, which started, according to the Carlinville *Democrat*, with this sentence: "He said the question is often asked, why this fuss about niggers?" (CW 3:77).

The answer, Lincoln said, was that the extension of slavery posed a threat to White workers. "Sustain these men and Negro equality will be abundant, as every white laborer will have occasion to regret when he is elbowed from his plow or his anvil by slave niggers" (CW 3:77-8). Sandburg and others, as we have noted, suggested that Lincoln was misquoted, and it is odd that a different reporter heard the same word when Lincoln told a crowd in Elwood, Kansas, a year later, "People often ask, why make such a fuss about a few *niggers*? (CW 3:495).

There was also, to cite another typical example, Lincoln's involved and involving denial that Senator Douglas had invented the concept of popular sovereignty. This led naturally to the question of what was popular sovereignty. "Was it," he asked, " the right of emigrants in Kansas and Nebraska to govern themselves and a gang of niggers, too, if they wanted them?" If so, he said, this was the invention of General Lewis Cass, not Douglas. Cass, according to Lincoln, had said the same thing six years before, but "he had not the *impudence* to say that the *right of people to govern niggers* was the *right of people to govern themselves*. His notions of the fitness of things were not moulded to the brazen degree of calling the right to put a hundred niggers through under the lash in Nebraska, a *'sacred right of self-government.'*" The only thing Douglas did was to invent a new name for General Cass's dogma. "He [Douglas] discovered that the right of the white man to breed and flog niggers in Nebraska was POPULAR SOVEREIGNTY!" (CW 3:94-5, italics and capitals in original).

There are—count them—four N-words in one paragraph of this speech. But Lincolnology being what it is, the number of White scholars who can't see these words and who don't report them is understandably large.

In the same period, Lincoln made it clear that he was opposed not to slavery but to the extension of slavery to the territories. Why was he opposed to slavery in the territories? He didn't want the West, he said, "to become an asylum for slavery and niggers" (CW 3:487).

Basler conceded that Lincoln *said* the word but denied that he *wrote* it, as if saying n——r is less of a sin than writing n——r . But in a letter, dated May 25, 1857, Lincoln told a correspondent that since the Dred Scott decision federal courts "have jurisdiction in all possible cases except such as might redound to the benefit of a 'nigger' in some way" (CW 11:13). In an 1859 letter, he told the editor of the *Central Transcript,* that "the world knows who are alluded to by the mention of stealing niggers and mail-bags" (CW 3:390).

The N-word went to Washington with Lincoln. Lord Charnwood said congressmen and other officials "were puzzled and pained by the free and easy way in which in grave conversation he would allude to 'the nigger question' " (317) or question, others said, whether it was advisable to "touch the nigger." Still others were pained by the free and easy way he interrupted official conferences to tell stories about "darky" preachers or "darky" arithmetic.

People are always saying that Lincoln was a great storyteller, but some of the most revealing stories he told are never told by people who are always talking about the great stories he told.

The main reason for this reticence is that "the great emancipator" loved pre-Amos and Andy stories about the doings of "shuffling" Blacks on the Catfish Rows of his imagination.

"Our colored brother was . . . a conspicuous butt of ridicule," Whitney said, adding that Lincoln was as adept as anyone in poking fun at "the ludicrous element in the Ethiopian mind . . . ." Colleagues told Lincoln that this was cruel, racist and sadistic, but he ignored them and even managed to imply, as almost all modern Lincoln interpreters imply, that there was something wrong with men who didn't like a good "darky" joke. When Ohio Congressman Joshua Reed Giddings wondered out loud "that anybody could be so cruel" as to poke fun at Blacks, then Congressman Lincoln and his colleagues told, in effect, even crueller stories" and many a rig did they run on Uncle Joshua," Whitney said, "by reason of this sympathetic proclivity" (195).

Even before Lincoln went to Washington, he was renowned for stories like the one he told at a Chicago banquet about "the darky who, when a bear had put its head into the hole and shut out the daylight, cried out, 'What was darkening de hole?' 'Ah,' cried the other darky, who was on to the tail of the animal, 'if de tail breaks you'll find out" (CW 2:384).

By this time, as Charnwood says perceptively, Lincoln was "almost a professional humorist" (70), and we can say here what no Lincolnian has said, that Abraham Lincoln was the first comedian elected president of the United States. Basler, like Charnwood, pointed out that the passion for well-turned jokes was central to Lincoln's identity. There was "a deep-seated comic urge" in Lincoln, Basler said, and an "eternal craving to entertain people" (1946, 12, 16). Herndon describes Lincoln in terms that are all too familiar to anyone who has known a great comedian, saying that he was always on the lookout for a chance to seize the spotlight, and that "his great anxiety to tell a story" made him a poor conversationalist (HH 178).

Not only did Lincoln perform nonstop for his legal colleagues and the in-crowd in Springfield, but he was also called upon to tell tales publicly. When, in 1842, former President Martin Van Buren visited the area, Lincoln was pressed into service to entertain "the visitor and the company" (HW 208). Joseph Gillespie, who served in the legislature with Lincoln, said, "It was as a humorist that he towered above all other men it was ever my lot to meet. When Mr. Lincoln was about I never knew a man who would pretend to vie with him in entertaining a crowd" (HI 508). Another close friend, T. G. Onstot, said that "in the role of story teller, I never knew his equal" (Thomas 1934, 146).

Joke upon joke, link upon link, evasion upon evasion, the connection between the prewar Lincoln and the post-Sumter Lincoln was forged in a direct line. Don E. Fehrenbacher saw this period as "a prelude to greatness" (1962). Paul Simon saw it as "a preparation for greatness." Victor Searcher saw it as "a journey to greatness." Herndon, who was there, saw it best perhaps, saying that Lincoln was also preparing himself for an intensification of the contradictions that defined his life. "Amid such surroundings," he wrote, " a leading figure in such society, alternatively reciting the latest effusion of the bar-room or mimicking the clownish antics of the Negro minstrel, he who was destined to be an immortal emancipator was steadily and unconsciously nearing the great trials of his life" (HW 251).

When the trials came, Lincoln was unusually adroit in playing two contradictory roles: the role of head of state *and* stand-up comedian. It was believed at first, in fact, that the electorate had made a mistake and that "by some 'irony of Fate,' a low comedian had got into the presidential chair and that the nation was being delivered over to the conflagration while this modern Nero fiddled upon its ruins ... " (Whitney 153).

Twentieth-century historians have created an extremely sympathetic portrait of the jokester president, but contemporaries, even sympathetic contemporaries, repeatedly criticized his joke-making, particularly in periods of national mourning over massive Union reverses and disasters. Stephenson says that "Lincoln's choice of fables was often a deadly offense" (131). Randall noted, in passing, that his humor often"miscarried" or "backfired" (1957, 223-6). When, shortly after the national disaster of the first Bull Run, the president interrupted state business to tell a visiting crony the latest jokes, a high-ranking general who specialized in making cannons stormed out of the White House, "declaring that Lincoln was a fool and had got closeted with a damned old hoosier from Ills. and was telling dirty stories while the country was going to hell" (HI 405). On another occasion, shortly after another disaster, Congressman James M. Ashley interrupted a Lincoln story, saying, "Mr. President, I did not come here this morning to hear stories; it is too serious a time." Lincoln told Ashley and other critics that comedy lightened his burdens and that "were it not for this occasional *vent*, I should die" (Carpenter 152, italics in original).

Cabinet members and congressmen sympathetic to the slave cause generally gave Lincoln the comedian bad reviews. When, in

November 1864, Lincoln halted a War Department meeting on the election returns to read from the writings of Petroleum V. Nasby, Secretary of War Stanton could barely contain himself (Wilson 578). "God damn it to hell," he told Charles A. Dana, "was there ever such nonsense! Was there ever such inability to appreciate what is going on in an awful crisis? Here is the fate of this whole republic at stake, and here is the man around whom it all centers, on whom it all depends, turning aside from this momentous issue, to read the God damned trash of a silly mountebank!"

The *Nasby Papers*, featuring the crude, dialect jokes of Petroleum V. Nasby, were Lincoln favorites. So taken was he with the Nasby jokes that he told Sumner and others that "for the genius to write these things I would gladly give up my office" (SW 15:66). "I'm going to write to 'Petroleum,'" he told a high-level group, "to come down here, and I intend to tell him if he will communicate his talent to me, I will 'swap' places with him" (Carpenter 151).

Why did Lincoln invest so much time and energy in telling jokes? Why did he say, even in jest, if it was in jest, that he would rather be funny than president?

This critical question, like other critical Lincoln questions, has never been answered. Some students say that jokes were vents that made it possible for him to endure sadness and the horror of war. Others say he used jokes as a diversion or a strategy. His closest friend, Joshua Speed, said telling jokes was "necessary to his very existence" (HI 499). None of this, of course, addresses the real question, which is *why* jokes were necessary to his existence. This is not the place to answer that question in detail, and the main point we want to make here is that humor was a weapon that Lincoln deliberately chose to deal with the world and to keep the world at bay in the same way that Jack Benny and Mark Twain used humor to enlarge themselves and to triumph over the world and the devil.

Whether humor was a vent or a diversion or, as seems most likely, a life-defining way of dealing with the world, President Lincoln joked his way through his term, telling stories on, among other things, "darky" arithmetic and "darky" theology. There was the time, for instance, that the president of the United States, to the dismay of Senator Henry Wilson of Massachusetts, interrupted a White House discussion on the tragically high Union mortality rate to tell a group of English visitors a story about "darky" arithmetic (RR 286-8).

The "dignified representatives of the learning and higher thought of Great Britain and her American dominion" were shocked.

"I did not know, Mr. President," one said, "that you have two systems of arithmetic.

"Oh, yes," said the president. "I will illustrate that point by a little story: Two young contraband, as we have learned to call them, were seated together, when one said, 'Jim, do you know 'rithmetic?'"

"Jim answered, 'No; what is 'rithmetic?'

'Well,' said the other, 'it's when you add up things. When you have one and one, and you put them together, they makes two. And when you substracts things. When if you have two things, and you takes one away, only one remains.'

'Is dat 'rithmetic?'

'Yes.'

'Well, 'tain't true den; it's no good.'

"Here a dispute arose, when Jim said:

'Now, you s'spose three pigeons sit on that fence, and somebody shoot one of dem, do t'other two stay dar? I guess not, dey flies away quicker'n odder feller falls . . . ."

Wilson said that if he had known a thousand stories he wouldn't have told that one to Professor [Godwin] Smith "and his grave-looking English friends [who seemed to enjoy the performance] and he was mortified that the President . . . should so inopportunely indulge in such frivolity."

Inopportunely or not, the president of the United States indulged in such frivolities at cabinet meetings. During a discussion on Spain and Santo Domingo on February 2, 1864, thirteen months after he signed the Emancipation Proclamation, the president said he was reminded, Secretary of Navy Gideon Welles noted in his diary, "of an interview between two Negroes, one of whom was a preacher endeavoring to admonish and enlighten the other. 'There are,' said Josh, the preacher, 'two roads for you, Joe. Be careful which you take. One ob dem leads straight to hell, de odder go right to damnation.' Joe opened his eyes under the impressive eloquence and awful future and exclaimed, 'Josh, take which road you please; I go, troo de wood.' I am not disposed to take any new trouble," said the President, "just at this time, and shall neither go for Spain nor the Negro in this matter, but shall take to the woods" (WD 519-20).

This apparently was one of Lincoln's favorite stories, for he changed the characters and locale in a White House conference with Cassius Clay of Kentucky, who said he was with Lincoln "when a report came that one of our unionists was caught in Virginia by the rebels and condemned to death, the choice being left him to be hung or shot. I saw a trace of humor pass over his sad face when he said he was reminded of a camp-meeting of colored Methodists in his earlier days. There was a brother who responded often to the preacher with 'Amen,' 'Bless the Lord," etc. The preacher drew a strong line, sweeping the sinners on both sides into the devil's net: "All those who thus are in the downward *path* to ruin, and all those who so act, including about the whole human race, are on the sure *road* to hell.' The unctuous brother, bewildered, cried out: 'Bless the Lord, this nigger takes to the woods" (RR 305-6, italics in original).

Lincoln mimicked the language, gait and rhythm of his imaginary Negroes, lending his whole body to the telling, becoming, so to speak, the imaginary Negroes in the story. Needless to say, almost all of *his* Negroes were Amos and Andy stereotypes.

Lincoln knew next to nothing about Black people and had never been in a Negro church in his life. Yet, he, like so many Whites of his day, and this one, considered himself an expert on Blacks, especially Black preachers "floundering in the deep water of theology." One of his favorites was "a colored preacher who worked here [at the White

House] on the grounds through the week, and who loved the deep waters of theology in which he floundered daily. One evening I asked him why he did not laugh on Sunday, and when he said it was because it was 'suthin' frivlus,' I told him that the Bible said God laughed. The old man came to the door several days after that and said, 'Marse Linkum, I've been totin' dat yar Bible saying "God larfed," and I've 'cluded dat it mus' jes' tak' a joke as big as der universe ter mak God larf. Dar ain't no sech jokes roun' dis yere White House on Sunday'" (Zall 147-8).

Then there was the story of the balloonist—stop me if you've heard this one—who, according to Lincoln, was forced down in New Orleans "befo' de wa." The "aeronaut," arrayed "in silks and spangles like a circus performer," came down, according to the story Lincoln told, "in a cotton field, where a gang of slaves were at work." Lincoln said "the frightened Negroes took to the woods—all but one venerable darkey, who was rheumatic and could not run, and who, as the resplendent aeronaut approached, having apparently just dropped from heaven, said: "Good mawning, Massa Jesus; how's your Pa?" (Zall 136).

Lincoln, sad to say, was not above "Massa Lincoln" jokes. When Alexander W. Randall and Joseph T. Mills visited the White House in August 1864, they were entertained with jokes about the Lincoln-Douglas debates. Lincoln was reminded especially of a Democratic opponent who, Lincoln said, told his audience that "if these republicans get into power, the darkies will be allowed to come to the polls & vote. Here comes forward a white man, & you ask him who will you vote for. I will vote for S A Douglas. Next comes up a sleek pampered Negro. Well Sambo, who do you vote for. I vote for Massa Lincoln. Now asked the orator, what do you think of that. Some old farmer cried out, I think the darkey showed a damd sight of more sense than the white man" (CW 7:508). And "a damd sight" more sense than Lincoln, who overlooked the fact that he had opposed Black suffrage and Black citizenship in the same debates.

"And so," Lincoln critic Adam Gurowski said at the height of the

Civil War conflict,"[Jefferson] Davis is making history and Lincoln is telling stories" (qtd. in Fischer 99).

If Lincoln didn't see anything wrong with dialect jokes and epithets, others did. During a White House conference with the Committee for Recruiting Colored Troops in 1864, a spirited young man named Henry Samuels corrected the president when he used the epithet *Cuffie*. According to Samuels, the president listened quietly as the committee members asked the government to pay Black workers employed by the Army the same salary paid White workers. He then replied, according to Samuels, "Well, gentlemen, you wish the pay of 'Cuffie' raised." Samuels interrupted him, saying: "Excuse me, Mr. Lincoln the term 'Cuffie' is not in our vernacular. What we want is that the wages of the American Colored Laborer be equalized with those of the American White Laborer."

Lincoln accepted the correction gracefully, saying: "I stand corrected, young man, but you know I am by birth a Southerner and in our section that term is applied without any idea of an offensive nature. I will, however, at the earliest possible moment do all in my power to accede to your request" (Randall 1957, 370).

We know this game, Americans played it during the days of segregation. What Lincoln, with Randall's support, is saying here is what White segregationists used to say in the Old South: *We* Southerners *know* Negroes, and what to call them, and how to treat them. What he is doing is claiming *jurisdiction*. In the process, he is expressing the verbal aggression and violence that underlay the whole racism/slave system. For the linguistic determinations— *Cuffie, darky, n——r, boy*—were integral parts of a verbal milieu that identified, designated, defamed, de-manned, de-womaned the objects of oppression and prepared the way for acts of violence against them.

Like almost all Whites who "knew" Negroes and what to call them, Lincoln was fascinated by myths about Negro sexuality. On March 30,

1849, one of Lincoln's fellow congressman wrote him and asked: "Do you remember the story of the old Virginian stropping his razor on a certain *member* of a young Negro's body which you told and connected with my mission to Brazil . . ." (Mearns 169, italics in original). There is no need to point out what no one has pointed out before, that Lincoln expressed in this story the ultimate castration fantasy.

Three years later, in 1852, Lincoln recalled a song about Miss Sally Brown in a public address at the Springfield Scott Club.

> *Sally is a bright Mulatter,*
> *Oh, Sally Brown—*
> *Pretty gal, but can't get at her,*
> *Oh, Sally Brown. (CW 2:157)*

This song is significant not only because it proves that Lincoln *knew* that there was no real difference, physically or otherwise, between Blacks and Whites but also because it brings out of the shadows the unexpurgated Lincoln who had, his friends say, an unexpected fondness for sexual matters.

Most Lincoln defenders have denied that Lincoln told dirty stories, but the evidence is against them. The men who heard him tell stories, in contrast to scholars who read the stories in libraries, said he loved to tell stories that today's Supreme Court would define as obscene.

Most of Lincoln's favorite songs contained sexual metaphors, N-words and/or disparaging references to Blacks. Some like "Zip Coon" poked fun at the pretensions of "larned" Black "skolars" who dared to study and read.

> *O ole Zip Coon he is a larned skolar,*
> *O ole Zip Coon he is a larned skolar . . .*
> *Sings possum up a gum tree and coony in a holler.*

In addition to "Jim Crow, " the Beatle-sized hit that gave its name to an institution and a way of life, Lincoln loved and applauded the lubricious "Miss Lucey Long," a famous "wench" song with sexual and racial overtones. The zenith of the minstrel art, the song usually featured a White man in drag pretending simultaneously to be a Negro and a woman. The *New York Tribune* noted in 1853 that "'Lucey Long'" was sung by a white Negro as a male female danced" (qtd. in Lott 49).

> *Miss Lucey, she is handsome,*
> *And Miss Lucey, she is tall;*
> *To see her dance Cachucha,*
> *Is death to N———rs all.*
> *Oh! take your time, Miss Lucey,*
> *Take your time, Miss Lucey Long.*

During the bloodiest days of the Civil War, Lincoln relaxed by listening to the songs of his bigoted, banjo-playing, liquor-swigging crony, Ward Hill Lamon of Illinois, who said Lincoln loved and always asked for a "favorite," "The Blue-tailed Fly," a song about stinging flies who pestered "ole massa" and eventually caused his death," related from the standpoint of a slave who didn't seem overly distressed by his decease:

> *When I was young I used to wait*
> *On Massa and hand him de plate;*
> *Pass down de bottle when he git dry,*
> *An bresh away de blue-tail fly.*
>
> *Jim crack corn I don't care,*
> *Jim crack corn I don't care*
> *Ole Massa gone away.*
>
> *Den arter dinner massa sleep,*
> *He bid dis n———r vigil keep;*
> *An' when he gwine to shut his eye,*
> *He tell me watch de blue tail fly.*
>
> *Jim crack corn I don't care,*
> *Jim crack corn I don't care*
> *Ole Massa gone away.*

There is no more revealing—or disturbing—image in the whole Lincoln encyclopedia than this image of the great emancipator listening with teary eyes to the passing of "de bottle" at "massa's table" while Black and White Union troops and Southern White Rebel troops danced the bloody dance that would decide the fate of history's last official "massas."

Lincoln defenders say that whatever his political and musical limitations, his personal relations with Negroes "were almost models of democratic correctness and friendly courtesy," which raises large questions about their definition of "democratic correctness." For although Lincoln, as James G. Randall concedes, "was careful" in "the presence of his Negro visitors . . . not to use expressions or tell stories which might offend them" (1957, 370), he routinely used the term *boy* to refer to Black men of all ages and made racial distinctions in listing White House employees, giving Whites the standard courtesy titles and calling Black women *aunt.* On November 9, 1862, he sent the following note to his wife: "Mrs. Cuthbert & Aunt Mary want to move to the White House, because it has grown so cold at Soldiers Home. Shall they?" (CW 5:492). Is there a scholar anywhere in the world who doesn't know the racial identity of *Mrs.* Cuthbert and *Aunt* Mary?

This was not a social lapse caused by inattention or the press of business—this was Lincoln's habitual address to Blacks. He apparently made an exception for Frederick Douglass, although Lincoln's secretary, John Hay, called Douglass "Frederick" (79). Neither Hay nor Lincoln made an exception for Sojourner Truth. And it tells you a lot about the current state of historiography when contemporary White historians don't find it strange or offensive that the autograph Lincoln gave to that great and gracious lady in 1864 was to "Aunty Sojourner Truth". The most recent Lincoln biography gives a glowing account of this interview but neglects somehow to tell us what Lincoln wrote in the book.

Will it be said that Sojourner Truth didn't object? But how do we know she didn't have better manners than Lincoln and that she didn't know the difference between White men who called Black women *Mrs.* and White men who called them "aunty"? And who are these people who maintain that it is socially acceptable to call minorities derogatory names if they don't object immediately? In any case, we are reminded of the deliciously witty reply Mary McLeod Bethune made to a White man who made the mistake of calling *her* aunty: "And which one of my sister's boys are you?"

There's no secret about any of this. Randall, Sandburg, Stephenson, Thomas—everybody who has studied Lincoln has read the dialect stories and "darky" jokes, and almost everybody who has studied him has suppressed them or explained them away by blaming Lincoln's melancholia—"He was so sad he had to tell jokes or die"—or his crushing war duties or the nagging of his wife. None of this explains why Lincoln's anguish sought release in anti-Negro stories or why he was telling "darky" stories before he became commander in chief and even before he met Mary Todd Lincoln.

N-words, N-shows, N-jokes, Cuffie, Sambo, aunty, colored *boy:* these phenomena have a name and a meaning.

No interpretation of Lincoln that fails to take them into account by *naming* them and him is valid.

Part Three

Myth

None of his public acts, either before or after he became President, exhibits any special tenderness for the African race, or any extraordinary commiseration of their lot. On the contrary, he invariably, in words and deeds, postponed the interests of the blacks to the interests of the whites, and expressly subordinated the one to the other. When he was compelled, by what he deemed an overruling necessity, founded on both military and political considerations, to declare the freedom of the public enemy's slaves, he did so with avowed reluctance, and took pains to have it understood that his resolution was in no wise affected by sentiment.

—Lincoln crony Ward Hill Lamon

History is not history unless it is the truth.

—Abraham Lincoln

6

Fooling All The People All The Time

B Y omissions and evasions, by half-truths and quarter-truths and lies, by selective quotations and suppressed quotations, by begging the question and forgetting the question and ignoring the question, by committing all the logical fallacies in the book, and by inventing new ones, by all these methods, and others, and by the biggest attempt in recorded history to hide a man, Lincoln defenders have managed to turn a separatist into an integrationist and to fool all the Black people and all the White people, save one or two, all the time.

In the process, they have not only hidden Lincoln, but they have also managed to prove him wrong. He said once, according to the myth, that "you can fool all the people some of the time and some of the people all the time, but you cannot fool all the people all the time."[8] Lincoln or whoever said that was wrong, for his apotheosis proves that it is possible to fool enough of them long enough to make a racist a national symbol of brotherhood and racial understanding.

Lincoln said repeatedly in private and public, in Springfield and in the White House, that he was a White supremacist and that he wanted to deny Blacks equal rights because of their race and deport them to a tropical clime with people of their own color and kind.

How do you hide such a man, and how do you make him a symbol of twentieth-century community? More importantly, and more dangerously, why would you want to make such a man a symbol of integration and the American Dream?

The answer, in part, is that Lincoln is theology, not historiology. He is a faith, he is a church, he is a religion, and he has his own priests and acolytes, most of whom have a vested interest in "the great emancipator" and who are passionately opposed to anybody telling the truth about him.

Not only is Lincoln a church, he is also an industry. Hundreds, perhaps thousands, of men and women earn their living feeding the Lincoln machine, turning out the Lincoln slogans, hailing the proclamation that never was.

Over and above this, the mythological Lincoln is a defining structure in the identity system of most Americans, who are hooked on Lincoln, as on a drug, and who need periodic fixes to reaffirm their sense of reality. Adlai Stevenson said once that "a man in public life can find no surer guide than Lincoln" (qtd. in Peterson 325). It is a condemnation of the American educational system that an intelligent man like Stevenson could make such an uninformed statement. What did Stevenson hope to learn from Lincoln? How to deny Blacks equal rights, or how to ship them to Africa?

For all these reasons, and for others as well, Lincoln transcends the rules of logic and evidence, even in the academy. Barbara Burns Petrick said in the *New York Times* on February 9, 1986, that Lincoln is such a god that the rules of evidence do not apply to him. She might have added that things have reached such a pass that it is considered permissible to lie and to hide evidence in order to protect the Republic. "It might be said of Lincoln," Petrick said, "what Voltaire said of God: If there had been no Lincoln, it would have been necessary to invent him." It is no accident that Petrick compared Lincoln to God and that she failed to note that the evidence she and others cite indicate that there was no Lincoln or at least no great emancipator and that it *was* necessary to invent him.

The fascinating question here is not how people have managed to hide Lincoln, but how they have managed to hide him while writing thousands of books about him. Whatever the answer, they never stop talking about Abraham Lincoln in America, and they never stop hiding him. And with rare exceptions, you can't believe what any major Lincoln scholar tells you about Abraham Lincoln and race.

To cite two striking examples, as a sort of introduction and background, there is a mammoth scholarly work, *Lincoln Day By Day,* which purports to tell us where Lincoln was on almost every day of his life. "Nothing in the annals of biography," Merrill D. Peterson says, equals *Lincoln Day By Day* (265).

If you want to know what Lincoln was doing on, say, January 5, 1836, you only have to turn to that date in the great Lincoln book— and it is great on every level except race—and discover that he was voting with the majority in the Illinois House to pass the Vermillion Saline bill and was casting a nay vote on a resolution condemning the Whig Party (LDD 1:53).

This, however, does not begin to capture the color of Lincoln's interesting day. If you consult the *House Journal* of the Ninth General Assembly, which can be found in the Chicago Public Library, you will discover that shortly after 2 p.m. on the day in question Abraham Lincoln voted on the following resolution:[9]

> "*Resolved,* That the price of the public lands ought to be reduced.
> *Resolved,* That all white male citizens of the age of 21 years upwards, are entitled to the privilege of voting whether they own real estate or not.
> *Resolved,* That the elective franchise should be kept pure from contamination by the admission of colored votes.
> *Resolved,* That we approve of the granting of pre-emption rights to settlers on the public lands."
> Mr. Hughes moved the previous question.
> The question was taken on the amendment of Mr. Webb to the amendment.
> And decided in the affirmative. —Yeas 35.—Nays 16.

One of the thirty-five White men who voted on Tuesday, January

5, 1836, to keep the Illinois franchise pure from contamination by Black voters was the twenty-six-year-old representative from Sangamon County, the Honorable Abraham Lincoln.

How did the authors of *Lincoln Day By Day* miss that fact? Perhaps, someone will say, this was a meaningless oversight, which happens all the time in historical research, even we assume in *Forced Into Glory*. Fair enough, let's continue our search, keeping in mind that *Lincoln Day by Day* is one of the few sources to tell us that Lincoln voted on December 10, 1840, for the White Illinois school system. What was Abraham Lincoln doing on May 2, 1840? *Lincoln Day By Day* says he was speaking in Tremont, Illinois, in favor of presidential candidate William Henry Harrison, the hero of Tippecanoe, and that he related "many amusing anecdotes which convulse [d] the house with laughter" (136).

What was all the laughing about?

Lincoln Day By Day doesn't tell us, but if we turn to the *Sangamo Journal* of May 15, 1840, we will discover that some of the laughing was triggered by Lincoln's demagogic attack on presidential candidate Martin Van Buren, "and especially his votes in the New York Convention in allowing Free Negroes the right of suffrage, and his Janus-faced policy in relation to the war." According to a dispatch to the newspaper from Tremont, dated May 4, Lincoln, "in this part of his speech," was "particularly felicitous, and the frequent and spontaneous bursts of applause from the People, gave evidence that their hearts were with him."

What shall we conclude from all this? Shall we conclude that the author is such a brilliant researcher that he can discover Lincoln facts that have eluded the greatest academic posse ever mobilized? I would encourage that conclusion if I were not certain that the answer lies in another direction. For the fact that facts pointing to the racist Lincoln are not generally available is no accident. Why aren't they available? In some cases, they have been deliberately overlooked and suppressed. In other cases, they have been overlooked by men and women who have developed a trained blindness and simply can't see certain things. The best example of that, as we have seen, is that generations of Lincoln scholars have been unable to see or read the N-words that can be found throughout the Lincoln record.

To make things even more interesting, there are—despite the greatest academic search in history—jarring potholes in the record. In 1853 and again in 1855, Lincoln spoke to the Springfield Colonization Society, which was organized to send African-Americans "back" to Africa. The speeches, *both* speeches, have disappeared, and there is no record of what Lincoln said. There is no evidence that the speeches were deliberately lost, and there is no evidence that they were not deliberately lost. It is relevant to note, however, that the disappearance of the speeches serves the interest of Lincoln mythmakers, for if we had a record of what he said it would only add to the growing body of evidence on his anti-Black activities. "The accident of their failure to survive,"Mark Neely Jr. said, "has probably helped Lincoln's reputation in modern times" (1993, 41).

Lincoln, who was his own mythmaker and who was as jealous of his reputation as John F. Kennedy, helped muddy the water. Compulsively secretive, he tried to censor his own record, especially during the first years of the war when he and his top aides tried to operate under the radar beam of history. "No more was put upon paper," Secretary of Navy Welles said, "than was necessary" and "verbal instructions were given to commanders not to entice slaves to come to them . . ." (WH 839).

But that's only the beginning of the problem. For the Lincoln record has been distorted at the source by the defining sin of Lincoln studies, post-assassination *reversus*. Appalled by the deed and afflicted by varying degrees of remorse and guilt, almost all public men changed their perceptions and, in some cases, their records after 1865. Before the assassination, Lincoln had few disciples and thousands of critics. After the assassination, he had few critics and thousands of disciples, and it became a duty, it became a public necessity, to get right with Mr. Lincoln and the myth.

Depending on their metabolism and their public needs, different men responded to this exigency in different ways. Some restated their pre-assassination views and said that history—the words they actually used and what Lincoln did and didn't do—was wrong. Illinois wartime governor Richard Yates prepared a mea culpa eulogy, which, interestingly, he never delivered. The undelivered eulogy said: "I thought he was too slow in calling out men, too slow in arming the freedmen, too slow in issuing his Proclamation of Emancipation, but in his own time came, in succession, all these important measures, and the whole world now plainly sees and acknowledges that Abraham Lincoln always did the right thing in the right way, at the right time, and at the right place" (Neely 1982, 341).

Another wartime governor, and another Lincoln critic, John A. Andrew of Massachusetts, responded, as so many men of that period responded, by trying to change his record or, at least, the meaning of his record. During the war, as we shall see, Andrew repeatedly denounced Lincoln in critical letters to Adam Gurowski. After the assassination, Gurowski biographer LeRoy H. Fischer says, Andrew, who played a major role in support of Black soldiers, had second thoughts and "was hesitant about giving his consent to a postwar effort to publish the letters." Some of the originals of the letters to Gurowski have apparently disappeared. Fischer says, "Andrew's letters to the Count, which should be in the Gurowski Papers, are not known to be extant" (91).

There are different ways to change a record or to change the meaning of a record, and whether the anti-Lincoln record is extant or restricted or lost, the effect is the same. To cite a provocative example, media icon Joseph Medill was, after Gurowski and Phillips, perhaps the most sulphurous Lincoln critic, but that information is not generally disseminated in Chicago, not even at the Medill School of Journalism, where Elmer Gertz's *Joe Medill's War* is an untold and unknown story.

The longer the men who knew Lincoln lived, the more their reminiscences and records changed. This is a natural process, which happens on a smaller scale in our recollections of friends and relatives. What we find deplorable, in examining the Lincoln record, is how often investigators forget that the best evidence is the evidence of what witnesses said, thought and did during and immediately after the event.

Post-assassination *reversus* affected almost everyone, including Frederick Douglass, who said eleven years after the assassination that Lincoln was a racist but who softened his view in a collection of reminiscences published twenty-three years after the event. Wendell Phillips stood his ground. "I think now exactly as I did then—A.L. had merits but he had spots & large ones on his disk " (HI 704).

Like Phillips, Senator Trumbull refused to change his record, even in the state of Illinois. Trumbull said that "as President during a great civil war, Lincoln "lacked executive ability, and that resolution and prompt action essential to bring the war to a speedy and successful close" (qtd. in White 430).

Even crusty old Thaddeus Stevens said a good word about Lincoln, although he said it with tongue in cheek, telling Congress on March 19, 1867, that "that good man," unlike his successor, had never "willingly infringed upon the rights of" Congress. Having said that much, Stevens pulled up and looked the legend in the face: "It is not to be denied that his anxiety for the admission of members from Louisiana . . . gave uneasiness to the Country. The people had begun to fear that he was misled, and was about to fall into error. If he would have fallen into that course, it is well for his reputation that he did not live to execute it."

Stevens didn't want to be misunderstood. He hadn't changed his views. And he wanted the House to understand that "what we say at the graves of admired friends or statesmen or heroes is not biography. The stern pen of history will strip such eulogies of their meretricious ornaments."[10]

How was he to know that history would become meretriciousness and meretriciousness history?

This was not entirely the fault of individual historians, for in history, as in Las Vegas casinos, the odds are always stacked in favor of the house, in favor, that is, of men and women who fear or oppose radical or fundamental social change. More than a hundred years ago, a lot of people, including a lot of White radicals, feared the enfranchising of the former slaves in states like South Carolina, where they were the majority of the people. Even today, more than one hundred years later, most major Lincoln biographers still seem to be terrified by the idea of giving the Black majority of South Carolina the vote more than one hundred and thirty-five years ago.

The bias in favor of the house is supplemented from another direction by the exclusion on principle of the testimony of conscious slaves, Black and White abolitionists, and Republican leaders who believed that Abraham Lincoln was a disaster as president.

Almost all Lincoln specialists maintain a full-court press against Whites who called for the immediate emancipation of slaves and the use of Black soldiers. The usual practice is to dismiss Lincoln critics with adjectives like "extreme," or "shrill" or "hysterical." In the generally excellent *Abraham Lincoln Encyclopedia*, Neely calls media icon Joseph Medill "shrill," primarily because of his attacks on Lincoln for his failure to free the slaves and use Black soldiers. Illinois wartime Governor Richard Yates, who attacked Lincoln for the same reasons, was called "somewhat hysterical" (208-9, 340-1).

In the end, then, oppression becomes its own proof, condemning us to see the slaves and Lincoln and the Civil War through the eyes of the enemies of the slaves or, worse, through the eyes of "moderates" like Nicolay and Hay, who meant well perhaps but who were terrified by the rising Black tide and who called Native Americans *savages.*

The result is that historiography becomes the accomplice and the alibi of the oppression it records. How could it be otherwise? For, to paraphrase the brilliant analysis of Maurice Merleau-Ponty, people record the horrors of slavery and the inhumanity of the slaveholding founding fathers and are no less racist and inhumane for it. They notice in passing the passion of John Brown and Phillips and the great yea-sayers of the White tradition and are no less conservative for it. The story of the slaves and of how they were robbed of their humanity and resources is not inscribed in history as they lived it. The screams of the victims and the cracks of the whips are quieter, and the blood is whiter. "History takes still more from those who have lost everything," Merleau-Ponty said, "and gives yet more to those who have taken everything. For its sweeping judgments acquit the unjust and dismiss the pleas of their victims. History never *confesses*" (4).

And never watches the house.

Since the odds in this game are always stacked in favor of the house, it would be prudent to watch the hands of the dealers and defenders of the Lincoln faith, who are grouped into schools according to their principal organs of defense and offense.

The most widely used defense, of course, is evasion, coupled with the hiding of all "darky" and "n——r" stories. Faced with overwhelming evidence on the life and times of the racist Lincoln, the practitioners of the dominant school refuse all discussion about facts and content themselves with calling testimony as to character. Lincoln had, they say, so many private virtues, and he was sad and had a nagging wife, which is true but irrelevant to the point at issue, which is not the appraisal of a personality but of a historical role. On this level, and every other level, Lincoln defenders beg the question, assuming the truth of the point at issue and relying on arguments from tradition, personality, and so forth. In deep denial, terrified by new disclosures on the depth of Lincoln's racism, they tell you in all seriousness that Lincoln was good because he was Lincoln and that he was Lincoln because he was good.

The dominant Lincoln school is the See-No-Racism, Hear-No-Racism, Report-No-Racism school. Ignoring the N-words and the Jim Crow votes and statements, and paying no attention at all to the frequent calls for racial cleansing, the practitioners of the pedagogy of silence create an idea-tight submarine bulkhead between Lincoln and racial reality, pretending in book after book and symposium after symposium that they can discuss Lincoln and the Declaration or Lincoln and democracy without reference to Negroes and slaves, a practice that reminds us that scholars are paid not only for what they see and say but also for what they don't see and say.

If pressed, members of this school will discuss Lincoln's racism in a segregated academic preserve called "Lincoln and the Negro." This compartmentalization quarantines race and the critics, relegating the whole issue to a few lines in the footnotes or in the conference summary.

Another and allied school, the Auteur School, substitutes a cardboard or ventriloquist Lincoln for the real-life Lincoln. Before letting Lincoln speak or act, members of this school set the scene and tell us that Lincoln is going to say or do something he doesn't really mean. "On July 4," a Lincoln biographer tells us, ". . . Sumner called again and urged 'the reconsecration of the day by a decree of emancipation . . . . Lincoln *pretended* [my emphasis] to disagree with him . . . . (Since we are dealing with a collective default, I have deliberately omitted the names of individual scholars.)

The summit of this art is what I call anticipatory absolution. Anticipating an antiBlack or anti-emancipation move by Lincoln, Lincoln interpreters rush in and give him absolution before the act, telling the reader that Lincoln is going to act like a racist but not to worry because he is only responding to the racism of his constituents or the balance of forces. Thus, before telling us that Lincoln asked Black people to leave America, another biographer gives him scholarly absolution, saying: "*Because one of the chief objections to emancipation was the widespread belief that whites and blacks could never live together harmoniously*, he revived his long-cherished idea of colonizing free blacks outside the United States."

Two absolutions, one before the act and one afterward, are better than one, so a biographer tells us first that "Lincoln wouldn't *force* Negro suffrage on Louisiana" and adds afterward that Lincoln was "sympathetic to the Negroes" he had just denied the suffrage by his failure to ask for equal rights.

This is a double-edged process. For in order to give Lincoln scholarly absolution, historians must recognize and approve the sin before giving absolution. Thus, when they tell us, as they are always telling us, that Lincoln, endowed now with divine omniscience, "knew" or was "aware" or "recognized" that he had to do certain things, they are telling us what they know. Lincoln *knew*, a biographer says, that Negro suffrage was "political dynamite." "He was aware," we are told, "that when as President he should issue an emancipation proclamation, there would be thousands of deserters...."

Aware: it is a big word in Lincoln circles. "Aware," a biographer says, "that emancipation sentiment in a slave state had to be carefully nurtured, he repeatedly warned against those who urged radical steps."

It is no accident that what Lincoln and his biographers are *aware of* or what they *know* is almost always an argument in favor of slavery or racism, or both. "As a man of Southern origins," a Lincolnian said, "Lincoln understood that racial adjustments would take time and careful planning." As a Black man of Southern origins, and as a survivor of the segregation era when almost all Whites said it would take time, I know what he and Lincoln meant.

The usual practice is to drop the absolution into the text casually to indicate that Lincoln's racism and his support of violent and inhumane acts against Blacks were natural. *Naturally*, we are told, Lincoln used the word n———r. *Naturally*, he voted for Jim Crow legislation and supported the Black laws, "like most Whites of his time."A major Lincoln scholar tells us that "so far as it is possible to ascertain today, not one word of condemnation was spoken publicly" by Lincoln and Springfield citizens when a White mob murdered abolitionist editor Elijah P. Lovejoy, adding: "In the light of the southern origin of most of them, the attitude of the townspeople on abolition was a *natural* one."

More important than what Lincoln biographers tell us is what they don't tell us.

Benjamin Thomas, the author of what most experts call the "best one-volume biography" of Lincoln, doesn't tell us that Lincoln used the N-word.

He doesn't tell us that Lincoln loved n——r jokes.

He doesn't tell us that Lincoln voted for Jim Crow legislation in the Illinois legislature.

He doesn't tell us that Lincoln said there was "a natural disgust in the minds of nearly all White people" about Black and White sex.

He doesn't tell us that Lincoln supported the Illinois Black Laws.

He doesn't tell us that President Lincoln personally ordered Union officers to return runaway slaves to slavemasters.

He doesn't tell us that President Lincoln tried for "nearly a year and a half," in his own words, to save slavery in the United States.

If the "best one-volume biography on Lincoln," according to the specialists, neglects to tell us all that, either the specialists or the one-volume book or the Lincoln methodology or all of the above are in trouble.

Thomas is a symptom of a larger problem. He is praised and quoted by almost all Lincolnians because he expressed the hidden values and assumptions of all Lincoln schools, including the Isolated Quote School, which makes its way by quoting isolated feel-good statements and ignoring surrounding statements and acts that negate the statements. A Lincoln biographer tells us that Lincoln said in Springfield on June 26, 1857, that he [Lincoln] thought the Declaration of Independence "contemplated the progressive improvement in the condition of all men everywhere." He doesn't tell us that Lincoln said on the same page that he and Stephen A. Douglas were "horrified at the thought of the mixing blood by the white and black races" (CW 2:407).

Members of the Feelgood School tell us that Lincoln said at Cincinnati that "there is room enough for us all to be free" (CW 3:446). They don't tell us that he said in the same speech that there was no room at all for slaves in the South to be free and that it was necessary to provide "an efficient fugitive slave law" to return to slavery fugitive slaves who believed there was room for us all to be free (CW 3:460).

Everybody, or almost everybody, tells us that Lincoln said in Chicago in July 1858 that we should stop all this quibbling about this race or that race and get on with the business of realizing the Declaration of Independence, which Lincoln called the "white man's" Declaration of Independence. Almost nobody tells us that he said in the same speech that the interests of White people made it necessary to keep Blacks in slavery and that God himself was a fellow White conspirator, having, as Lincoln put it, "made us separate" (2:498-501).

Nearly all scholars note that Lincoln said in New Haven, Connecticut, in 1860 that "I want every man to have the chance— and I believe a black man is entitled to it—in which he can better his condition" (CW 4:24), but no scholar tells us that Lincoln said in the same speech that it was necessary to leave slavery in the South alone (CW 4:29) and that if the slave system had not existed in 1860, it would have been necessary to invent it (CW 4:17-8) and keep the four million slaves from bettering their condition.

There is finally the Mother Of All Lincoln Quotes—the Last Best Hope of Earth quotation from the We Cannot Escape History peroration of the 1862 Annual Message to Congress. Everybody uses these quotes in which Lincoln, according to historian Basler, reached "peaks of eloquence unsurpassed in the annals of history" (1946, 38). Neither Basler nor any other major Lincoln specialist tells us that Lincoln used the words in a futile attempt to persuade Congress to pass constitutional amendments calling for, among other things, the ethnic cleansing of the United States of America.

Composer Aaron Copland is paradigmatic on this point, telling us in his universally celebrated *Lincoln Portrait* that Lincoln said— "This is what he said/This is what Abraham Lincoln said"—that we cannot escape history .

That's what Lincoln said all right, but Copland doesn't tell us what he said before and after he said what he said.

Before he said what he said, he said that the fiery trials would light "this Congress and this administration" down in honor or dishonor to the latest generation, down to 2000 in fact, if they didn't do what Lincoln wanted them to do.

What did Lincoln want them to do?

He wanted them to try to escape history. He wanted them to ethnically cleanse the United States of America by buying the slaves over a thirty-seven-year period and sending them "back" to Africa. And that included incidentally the ancestors of the distinguished African-Americans who are always recruited to recite the expurgated Copland words that call for the deportation of their great-great-grandmothers and great-great-grandfathers.

Thus, quotation doth make cowards and oppressors of us all.

In the same spirit, Copland tells us what Lincoln said on page 315 of his Alton speech but does not tell us what Lincoln said on page 317 of the same speech.

This is what he said on page 315 of *The Collected Works:*

> It is the eternal struggle between these two principles—right and wrong—throughout the world . . . . It is the same spirit that says, "You work and toil and earn bread, and I'll eat it." No matter in what shape it comes, whether from the mouth of a king who seeks to bestride the people of his own nation and live by the fruit of their labor, or from one race of men as an apology for enslaving another race, it is the same tyrannical principle.

Tell it like it is, Abe.

That's what I thought the first time I heard a great Black American recite what Lincoln said on page 315 in a Copland concert at Chicago's Orchestra Hall. And I was shocked when I consulted the document and discovered that neither Copland nor the reader turned to page 317 where Lincoln endorsed "the same tyrannical principle," saying that it was necessary to maintain the divine right of slaveholders in the South and to join with them in "running and catching niggers" who escaped from people who believed in the divine right of kings and slaveholders (CW 3:317).

Finally, and definitively, Copland tells us, as everybody tells us, that Lincoln said that "as I would not be a *slave*, so I would not be a *master*" (CW 2:532). He doesn't tell us that the same man made hundreds of thousands of slaves, and that William E. Channing was closer to the truth when he said that "there is something worse than to be a slave. It is to make other men slaves" (qtd. in PS 207).

These are not, let us emphasize once again, isolated examples, for in practically all major historical exhibitions and Lincoln biographies, Lincoln's words are systematically wrenched out of context to make him say the precise opposite of what he really said.

The fallacy of the isolated quote is linked in spirit and intent with the fallacy of detached data, which wrenches Lincoln out of his social and historical context and presents a lifeless abstraction who tells jokes and loves everybody, except the slaves, but has no connection with the violent and racist system of slavery and Jim Crow that stained his soul and the soul of the nation. Here was a man who supported, voted for and helped manage the worst system of slavery and racism in human history, but scholars routinely write six hundred-page books without mentioning these facts in context. If someone forces them to confront a racist fact, they excuse it in a one-liner or, better, in a footnote and proceed with the hagiography. The summit of this art is to move the whole discussion to a footnote or a special conference session on Lincoln and race, thereby segregating the man from the system that defined him and gave him clay feet.

Another Lincoln school, which we will call the Logos School, maintains that the Lincoln word *is* reality. The theology is questionable, of course, but that doesn't seem to bother the true believers who assume that the Lincoln word, like the word of God, creates reality.

Thus, we find scholars everywhere making the Lincoln leap from unsupported assertion to conclusion, telling us, first, *as every Lincoln scholar tells us*, that Lincoln *said* he had always hated slavery. Then, using the first part of that statement without telling us that Lincoln qualified it, they tell us that Lincoln always hated slavery. Isn't that marvelous? They go from *he said* to *he did*, making the word the reality and eliminating the need for verification and evidence.

In the beginning was the Lincoln word.

Given this faith, it is no wonder that Lincolnians contend that Lincoln's anti-Black words were true until the Freedom Movement of the 1960s made them false and that the real problem is not Lincoln's racism but the zealousness of Black Power militants.

What shall we call these technique? Misdirection? Misinformation? Mystification? In any case, they are designed to intimidate. For the Lincoln myth is sustained not only by inertia and mystification but also by terror and by an implicit and explicit understanding that sanctions will be invoked and pressure brought to bear to keep people from telling the truth or even thinking the truth about Abraham Lincoln in America.

To tell the truth, it is dangerous to tell the truth about Abraham Lincoln in America, and it is remarkable how many gatekeepers tell students and researchers that it is neither wise nor safe to pursue certain lines of inquiry. I have been astonished, on the personal level, by the number of Blacks who have said with a sense of real concern and fear that it is dangerous to say that Lincoln was a racist, especially if what you say is likely to be heard by a significant number of people.

Nothing has changed in this regard since poor William Herndon was forced to run a gauntlet of timidity and Pharisaism more than one hundred years ago. Herndon, who refused to back down and who "contributed more than any other individual to our knowledge of Lincoln" (HW xxxvii), never ceased to attack the timidity of orthodox Lincolnians who tried to hide themselves and Lincoln from history. "Mr. Lincoln," he said, "must stand on truth or not stand at all" (HH 38). As for the terror, Herndon asked in 1866, "Is any man so *insane* as to suppose that any truth concerning Lincoln, or in relation to his thoughts, acts, and deeds, will be hid and buried out of human view? Pshaw! Folly! The best way is to tell the whole truth, and let it by its very presence and eternity crush and burn up all lies" (HH 40-1). Because the academy did not heed Herndon, "a definitive Life of Lincoln is still a dream unfulfilled," Hertz said in 1938, "and a natural hesitation in revealing certain aspects of Lincoln's life has hardened into a policy of secrecy" (HH 4).

The struggle Herndon and others initiated continues on several levels, and there are indications that young scholars and graduate students have been pressured to preserve the party line. Young scholars are naturally reluctant to talk about this pressure since a hint or a word from a high priest of the guild could kill an application or a research grant or a publishing proposal. In the July 1952 issue of the *Journal of Negro History,* Paul J. Scheips made a penetrating observation about the continuing effort to discredit Benjamin F. Butler and his report of Lincoln's last-minute attempt to deport African-Americans. Scheips noted that another researcher devoted "some attention" to the Butler account in his master's thesis but failed to mention it in a later article which concluded that "perhaps" John Hay's view that Lincoln gave up the idea of colonization in 1864 "'best depicts Lincoln's changed attitude.'"

Why did the researcher change his mind?

In a provocative footnote, Scheips said the researcher "explained in a letter to the writer (Jan. 16, 1951) that [an eminent Lincoln scholar] persuaded him prior to publication of his article to reconsider his manuscript conclusion that Lincoln never really gave up the idea of colonization on the grounds that such a view . . . 'ran counter to the established scholarly opinion on the subject.'"[11]

The best place to sample "established scholarly opinion" is in works of the Bogart School, which bogarts its way by unsupported assertions that turn facts and history upside down. In fact, the more damning the evidence against Lincoln, the more passionate is the defense. Did Lincoln say he was opposed to Negro citizenship and

"the niggers and white people . . . marrying together" (CW 3:20)?
The Bogart School says he virtually invented the American Dream.
Did Lincoln say that Blacks and Mexicans were inferior and that he
as much as any other White man believed in White supremacy? The
Bogart School says he went up to the mountaintop of Gettysburg
and virtually invented a new America with 272 words.

Perhaps the best representative of the Bogart style is Gabor S.
Boritt, who says in *Lincoln and the Economics of the American Dream*,
one of "the 10 Best Books On His Life,"[12] that Lincoln made the
American Dream the central idea of America "in one of the most
important metamorphoses of an idea in American history" (158).
Not only that, Lincoln, "in one of the supreme creative acts in the
making of American ideology," insisted "on its [the Dream's] reality
persistently, and [get this] lived it fully" (160).

Is Boritt serious? Has he forgotten that Lincoln tried to ethnically
cleanse America and create a lily-White democracy? Has he forgotten
that the only dream Lincoln lived fully was the apartheid system of
Illinois that he supported and voted for?

Boritt knows that.

All Lincoln scholars know that, whether they tell us or not, and
Boritt, believe it or not, tells us, saying fourteen pages later, that
"Lincoln's arguments about the American Dream were addressed
[not to Black people or Native Americans but] to the white people of
Illinois and of the North, people whose votes were necessary to
uphold his views. He probably [note that word] also shared *to some
extent* [my emphasis] the confusions and prejudices of his people [he
meant *White* people] about the black man. . . " (172).

Continuing on the next page, Boritt says that Lincoln "tempered
his views by disclaiming any desire for the social and political
equality of blacks. He also suggested that they, 'perhaps,' were not
the equal of whites 'in moral or intellectual endowment.' He
suggested that God may have given 'little' to them and thus their
achievements were likely to be little."

That is, all things considered, a strange way to invent the American Dream. Is the man who wrote the lines on pages 158 and 160 the same man who wrote the lines on pages 172 and 173?

And is he talking about the same man?

Boritt's high-wire tightrope walk across the widening chasm between what Lincoln said and what others want to believe are symptoms of a major crisis in Lincoln historiography, which was afflicted in the 1960s and 1970s by what Merrill D. Peterson called "scholarly anxiety to preserve the image of the Great Emancipator." In the wake of widespread attacks on the traditional Lincoln myth, historians, Peterson said, "proved resourceful in finding new explanations to acquit the President of fault or blame in race relations. Thus if he had been slow to back limited Black suffrage in Louisiana, it was because he was waiting for public opinion to catch up with him. Thus if he adhered too long to the chimera of colonization, the reason was psychological: colonization served as a defense mechanism against thinking about the tough problems of racial accommodations under conditions of freedom" (384).

Since I said in a February 1968 article in *Ebony* magazine that the great emancipator was naked or, at least, was wearing borrowed clothes, Lincoln experts have circled the wagons. Surveying the post-sixties reevaluation—"Much of the recent debate," Vorenberg said (24), "was set off by" by the *Ebony* article—Professor Arthur Zilversmit said in a *Chicago Sun-Times* analysis (February 12, 1980):

> Bennett's article struck a nerve. He had not only called into question the reputation of a beloved hero, but he had challenged the American picture of our history as the story of measured progress toward liberal goals.
>
> Several historians and journalists argued with his version of the facts, but his charges could not be easily dismissed by other historians, several of whom began a comprehensive re-evaluation of Lincoln's racial views.

The latest reevaluation appears in the endnotes of David H. Donald's book, *Lincoln*. Summarizing the views of the leading members of the Lincoln establishment, Donald said correctly that it is an error to try to excuse Lincoln's racial views by saying that he grew up in a racist society and that everybody was a racist. He added, however, that Lincoln "fortunately escaped the more virulent strains of racism." What is the evidence for this? The evidence is that Lincoln didn't say hideous things about Blacks—can anyone say anything more hideous than that a whole race of people is inferior and should be denied equal rights and deported because of its race?—and that Lincoln's racist views were "*nearly* [my italics] *always* expressed tentatively." Donald cited approvingly Don E. Fehrenbacher's statement that Lincoln "conceded that the Negro *might not* be his equal, or he said that the Negro *was not* his equal *in certain respects*" (italics in original).[13]

This is a direct issue not between Lincoln and me but between the Lincoln establishment and Lincoln. Fehrenbacher says with Donald's approval that Lincoln conceded—note that word—that the Negro might not be his equal. Where did that word *might* come from? That's not what Lincoln said. "Certainly," Lincoln said, "the Negro is not our equal in color—perhaps not in many other respects" (CW 2:520). Is *certainly* a tentative word? Lincoln didn't think so, for he used it repeatedly: "I agree with Judge Douglas he is not my equal in *many* respects—certainly not in color, perhaps not in moral or intellectual endowment" (CW 3:16, italics added). On at least fourteen occasions between 1854 and 1860, Lincoln said unambiguously that he believed the Negro race was inferior to the White race. In Galesburg, he referred to "the inferior races" (CW 3:222). Who were "the inferior races?" African-Americans, he said, Mexicans, whom he called "mongrels" (CW 3:235), and probably all colored people.

In addition to all this, Lincoln said repeatedly that there was a *physical* difference between the Black and White races. What did he mean by the word *physical*? He meant bodily, corporeally, somatically, biologically, *in accordance with the laws of nature*. He meant that the difference was more than skin deep. He meant that the difference was immutable and was, he believed, going to last forever and would *forever* forbid Blacks and Whites living in equality. *For-*

ever, even *probably forever*, does not come within the bounds of tentativeness.

The Lincoln defenders are eminent, they are eloquent—and they are wrong. Lincoln did say—repeatedly—that the Negro race was *physically* inferior to the White race. He repeatedly poked fun at Blacks in "darky" jokes and used the N-word at least as often as Mark Fuhrman.

Nor can we agree with the defense of Lincoln's tentative embrace of inequality. If Lincoln said on one occasion that the Negro—that is to say, a whole race of people—was not his equal biologically in *some* respects, he said on other occasions that the Negro race was not his equal in "many" respects. But what are we arguing about here? What is the difference between *many* and *some* and *forever* and *probably forever*? If, as the defenders concede, Lincoln said that the Negro, that is to say, the Negro *race*, was not his equal in certain respects or in any respect and should be denied equal rights *because of its race*, he was a racist and it is a waste of time to try to quantify the degree of racism or to argue over whether he was a biological, social, or empirical racist.

But we see what is involved here. The proponents of this argument would have us believe that Abraham Lincoln was a *good* racist. He was, God help us, a *tentative* racist. How, after the Third Reich and the First and Second American South and South Africa, can anyone say that? A man who condemns a whole race and excludes it from the basic rules of the social contract—the right to vote and to sit on juries and attend schools—is not a good racist, and if he were not Abraham Lincoln, we would say he is not a good man. If additionally such a man proposes concretely—not vaguely or tentatively—to ethnically cleanse a country by deporting a whole people because of its race, we would say he doesn't even share our sense of humanity.

Conor Cruise O'Brien makes an extremely perceptive comment, saying that the worst racists are the counting racists, the men and women who are always counting the reasons the oppressed group is inferior to the oppressing group (315). George Washington, who was a racist on other levels, was not, O'Brien says, a counting racist.

Thomas Jefferson and Abraham Lincoln were. They had, to appropriate the words he used about Jefferson, "the classical racist itch to identify characteristics [color, intellect, morality, aesthetics] that could be interpreted as indications of genetic inferiority (315)" and as reasons why Blacks should be oppressed.

Most of Lincoln's information on Blacks came from minstrel shows and stag sessions with the boys, and he never really got over the idea that the stock minstrel show figure—loud, funny, dumb, loquacious—was the typical Negro. The men who observed him every day and heard him talk publicly and privately said he had a low opinion of Blacks and that he poked fun at them and ridiculed them. Donald said that Lincoln "never described them [Blacks] as indolent or incapable of sustained work (633)," but Lamon, who was there and heard the words from Lincoln's mouth, said the sixteenth president "claimed that those who were incidentally liberated by the Federal arms were poor-spirited, lazy, and slothful" and "as docile in the service of the Rebellion as the mules that ploughed the fields or drew the baggage trains." It is no wonder, then, Lamon said, that "with such views honestly formed . . . that he longed to see them transported to Hayti, Central America, Africa, or anywhere, so that they might in no event, and in no way, participate in the government of *his* country" (345, italics added).

So much for the tentative school.

No less censurable is the Everybody Was A Racist School, which says that everybody or almost everybody in the nineteenth century was a racist and that it is unnatural and, some say, racist to expect Lincoln to be anything else. Ignoring Whites like Zebina Eastman and Wendell Phillips, this school says Lincoln was a man of the nineteenth century and should be judged by nineteenth century standards, as if freedom is defined by dates, as if equality was invented by Thurgood Marshall, as if the N-word was invented by Mark Fuhrman. Ignoring White men like Trumbull who got elected without totally supporting slavery in the South and man-hunting in the North, they say, in so many words, that if Lincoln hadn't talked like a racist in the nineteenth century, we wouldn't have this warm, comforting integration symbol to worship in the twentieth.

This defense concedes the essential point and forces Lincoln defenders like Oates to defend Lincoln in words that indict him. Explaining and explaining away a Lincoln vote in the Illinois legislature against Negro suffrage, Oates says that "public opinion was almost universally against political rights for black people, and young Lincoln, who had elected to work within the system, was not about to ruin his career by supporting Negro suffrage" (38).

The psychology is apt, and the description of Lincoln's opportunism is devastatingly accurate. The only question is whether Oates is defending Lincoln or attacking him. For you can't say anything more derogatory about a man than that he had elected to work within a system that condemned four million people to slavery and made it a crime for a Black person to settle in his state.

It's remarkable that people who say Lincoln lied and pretended to be a racist to get elected don't realize that the apology is worse than the accusation. For it is not all clear that it is better to lie in order to get elected than to honestly confess racism. The defense, moreover, is clearly insufficient, since Lincoln said the same thing in Ohio when he was not running for office and in Washington after he had been elected president. And Strozier is correct when he says that "it would be naive to ignore the essential racism that informed Lincoln's thoughts wherever he spoke" (174).

It's not that easy being a Lincoln defender as Fehrenbacher proved unwittingly when he crafted the most ingenious defense in the whole Lincoln catalog. Faced with the Charleston Confession (CW 3:145-6) in which Lincoln said he opposed Negro citizenship and equal rights, Fehrenbacher said that "if he [Lincoln] had responded differently at Charleston and elsewhere, the Lincoln of history simply would not exist" (1987, 105-6), meaning, if words have any meaning, that if Lincoln had not come out for White supremacy and racial separation in the nineteenth century, he would not be a national symbol of brotherhood and integration in the twentieth, meaning, if words have any meaning, that racism is historically defensible if a tragic assassination and myths make you into the opposite of what you were.

Beyond all that, the argument, though ingenious, is insufficient. There is no evidence and there will never be enough evidence to prove that Lincoln *had* to say the specific things he said in the Charleston Confession and elsewhere in order to get elected. What he said, in fact, lost the election and was at best of marginal importance to the presidential power brokers who wanted a conservative candidate with a public image to the right of Chase and Seward and who were more impressed by the tone of his Cooper Institute address than his Charleston Confession. We can say inversely that what Lincoln said at Charleston and elsewhere went further than the situation required, even for realpolitik, and that history, despite the default of historians, will never let him forget it. The same thing can be said about Lincoln's gratuitous statements about the "natural disgust" about Black and White sex, his references to Mexican "mongrels" and n——rs, and his quixotic campaign for colonization. But it doesn't matter. For a man who race-baits in order to get elected and who supports man-hunting, woman-hunting, and children-hunting because of his ambition has nothing to say to us, no matter how many historians sing his praises.

If we examine these defenses closer, we realize that the inarticulate major premise of all Lincoln schools is a defense of *contemporary* racial policies by a defense of Lincoln's conservatism and his anti-Black opposition to immediate, general and real freedom for Blacks. Benjamin Thomas puts himself in Lincoln's place and writes, "One must be realistic about this slavery issue, Lincoln thought" (112). Where have we heard this before? My God, yes, that's what segregationists and their White liberal allies said in the days of segregation. That's what segregationists and their White liberal allies have always said. Lord Charnwood, Lincoln's English biographer, denounced "the cold pedantry" of Secretary of the Treasury Salmon P. Chase and others who criticized Lincoln "on the ground of some natural right of all men to the suffrage." The true policy, Charnwood said, thinking about the South Africa of his day, was "doubtless that which [Cecil] Rhodes and other statesmen adopted in the Cape Colony [in South Africa] and which Lincoln had advocated in the case of Louisiana" (334-5).

By drawing this strange and just parallel between what Lincoln was trying to do in Louisiana and what Rhodes was trying to do in South Africa and by invoking the inarticulate premises of his class, Lord Charnwood reminds us that all or almost all major Lincoln interpreters write from the perspective of that Abraham Lincoln who supported slavery in the South and the Black Laws in Illinois and who defined himself as a White man. Writing from that perspective, that is to say, from the perspective of a cautious, conservative politician, most major Lincoln scholars—comfortable, conservative, cautious males—make themselves academic accomplices of the oppression and the slavery Lincoln supported.

But let us be clear once again that when I say *White* on this level, I am referring to a political or, better, an epistemological category based not on birth but on a conscious or unconscious commitment to an illegitimately privileged political space and an illegitimately privileged collectivity *whose historical being is a function of certain irreversible historical events*—the African Slave Trade, American Slavery, the Indian Holocaust, Segregation.

People are always saying, as we have seen, that they were not living *then*, whenever the *then*, and that they are not responsible for slavery. But that's a complete misreading of history and time. For the history we are examining here is written in things, buildings, notions and concepts, and we cannot, no matter what we do, as Lincoln said, in a saying that he didn't understand, escape the history that we inherited and the history that we are. The responsibility, from this vantage point, is personal. It is the conscious, deliberate and continuing identification with that history by living men and women who practically and effectively assume responsibility for that history by saying WE in that history, thereby linking past and present oppression and the necessity—Lincoln's word and notion—of future oppression.

Oppression, in other words, is hell, and requires everyone connected with oppression to examine his or her choices every moment, particularly his or her choices in the Civil War, for nothing more accurately reveals the choice he or she has made in today's world than the choice he or she makes in Lincoln's world.

Someone will say, exposing his card, that this is absurd. How can a White person choose any other perspective? Well, let's see. Abraham Lincoln said that in a choice between the White race and justice, he would choose the White race (CW 2:256; 3:145-6). Wendell Phillips said that in a choice between the white race and justice, he would choose right (PS 385-6).

Lincoln said in a speech nobody quotes that when a house is on fire, there "can be but two parties": a party for letting the fire burn, and a party for putting out the fire (CW 3:503). Lincoln forgot that truth, as he forgot so many other truths, but there is no reason we should forget it.

Many, perhaps most, contemporary scholars view Lincoln, Robert E. Lee, and General George B. McClellan through a moderate-to-conservative lens with an automatic and preprogrammed bias against "extremists on both sides" and sudden and revolutionary social changes.

It is distressing, in any case, that so many experts flaunt their biases in books that win major prizes and are even praised by some Blacks. The authors of at least three of the top ten Lincoln books (Nicolay and Hay, Herndon, Thomas) call Indians "savages" and one (Thomas) calls Black men "savages": "What haunted everyone [he meant everyone White in the South in the election of 1860] was the specter of savage black men roaming the country uncontrolled. . ." (223).

In *Conversations with Lincoln*, Charles M. Segal notes without a disclaimer that "liberated 'darkies' were proving a problem in Federal military districts. . ." (187). Ellis P. Oberholtzer tells us outright that "the Negroes were an inferior race of people" (171).

In a major lecture and in a much-quoted book, J. G. Randall, who has been called "the greatest Lincoln scholar of all time" (Neely 1982, 255), recommended the wisdom of an "old darky" (1946, 81). In his universally praised four-volume study, the same scholar tells us that to understand the "long-standing loyalties" of the slaves and "their faithful records in servitude," they must be viewed "in association with *their* [my italics] white folk" and in relation to "their prideful habit of identifying themselves with their white families." It's impossible, he says, to understand "these people" at all except in their Southern—he meant *White* Southern—locale (1945-55, 95). Where did the word *their* come from? Did the slaves belong to the White families, or did the White families belong to the slaves? And, biggest question of all, who did James Garfield Randall belong to, not to mention the scores of scholars who have read and praised these words without disclaiming them?

Not only do some Lincoln scholars defend slaveholders but they implicitly or explicitly defend slavery. Oberholtzer introduces us to what he calls "the better side of" of slavery (388), and Sandburg of all people tells us that enslaved Blacks were better off than free poor Whites. The poor Whites, he said, "*lacked* [my italics] slaves, land, and the decent creature comforts of the Negro house servant . . . . " They were even worse off than enslaved field hands who had better "quantities of food, clothing, shelter, and *employment* . . ." (1939, 1:11).

The point here is that almost—strike that word *almost*—everything scholars say about Lincoln is political. For by choosing our Lincoln—and our slavery—we choose ourself, and our today. The reverse is also true. By choosing our today, and the racial status quo of our today, and by choosing ourselves in that racial status quo, we choose the racial status quo of yesterday.

These considerations bring us a step closer to understanding the wider implications of the Abraham Lincoln salvage society, which never stops talking about Blacks and slaves, and which seldom if ever shows us real Blacks or real slaves. The Abraham Lincoln morality play is, in fact, a White morality play which is concerned primarily not with the emancipation of Blacks but with the salvation of the White soul. This explains why Blacks don't have speaking roles in the drama. Apart from two or three adoring members of the *chorus*, who come on from time to time to say, "Bress you, Massa Linkum," or, as in Oates, "I'se contraband (240)," there is nothing in these accounts to indicate that Blacks were on the scene and acting.

Neither Frederick Douglass nor H. Ford Douglass nor John Jones is identified or questioned about his views on emancipation and civil rights. To be sure, Frederick Douglass is quoted from time to time but only episodically and never in connection with an independent analysis of the main action, and never on that Lincoln who, he said, was preeminently the white man's president. Even so, most White scholars are clearly uncomfortable in Douglass's presence. One scholar, who shall remain nameless here, denounces Douglass for his effrontery in criticizing Lincoln. Sandburg refers to Douglass repeatedly as "a mulatto" and goes out of his way to comment on his "pompadoured head" (2:410), which was, at best, selective reporting since Douglass, as contemporary photos show, generally wore his hair in an early "natural."

Black personalities apart, there is no coverage in these biographies of the human dimensions of a mass movement that changed the color of the war. As a Southerner, I find it appalling that from 1865 to the latest PBS special, historians and televangelists identify the South with the White cause and Southerners with White Southerners, to the exclusion of all those old Southern Black families who constituted the majority in several Southern states, including South Carolina and Mississippi, and an overwhelming presence in others. It's traditional to assume in 2000—as John Calhoun and Abraham Lincoln assumed in 1849— that the White South *is* the South.

Not only do major Lincoln scholars ignore Black slaves and

activists, but they also ignore Black scholars like W.E.B. DuBois and Black soldier-scholars like George Washington Williams. DuBois almost singlehandedly reconstructed Reconstruction history, but there is not one quote from him in the ten top Lincoln books. Until my essay appeared in 1968, White Lincoln scholars didn't deign to notice major contemporary scholars like Benjamin Quarles or John Hope Franklin. I discovered all this the hard way when as a member of the board of a major historical organization, I protested unsuccessfully against a Lincoln exhibition booklet which didn't even list Quarles or Franklin or DuBois in the works cited.

Even today, Black scholars are quoted sparingly and usually on some tangential issue. It is de rigueur now to quote every available Black to counter my argument, and almost every Lincoln book published since 1968 tells us approvingly that Douglass and Sojourner Truth said, according to these authors, that Lincoln was a good White man who didn't have a prejudiced bone in his body, proving once again that history *never* confesses and takes still more from the people from whom it has taken everything.

It is only fair to add that the defenders of the faith are equal opportunity deniers. They don't as a rule notice Blacks who spoke from a Black perspective, and they don't as a rule—Sandburg and Donald are notable exceptions—notice Whites who spoke from a Black perspective. Great American leaders like Wendell Phillips and Charles Sumner, who were right when Lincoln was wrong, are not mentioned often, and when they are mentioned, they are put down for being in favor of Black emancipation and the use of Black soldiers. This POLITICAL position defines the defenders of the faith, who define themselves by defining Lincoln and who choose themselves in and through their choice of Lincoln.

There is finally the school of historians who defend Lincoln's support of slavery on the basis of a consent theory of government. Lincoln, in the view of this school, was exemplary because he opposed the efforts of people to end slavery and the slave trade in the District of Columbia without the consent, Donald says, of "the inhabitants [he means the *White* inhabitants] of Washington" (136).

Harry V. Jaffa said approvingly that Lincoln made District emancipation "dependent upon a vote of the citizens of the District," meaning the same thing since there were no Black citizens in Washington in 1849. Thus Lincoln, unlike the abolitionists, understood, Jaffa writes, "the element of consent required for the *just* acts of government."[14] This means, if words have any meaning, that it would have been *unjust* to stop slaveowners from enslaving slaves without giving slaveowners the *right* to vote on whether they wanted to give up "their" slaves.

This is an ingenious and disturbing theory. Where is it written that people have a right to vote for or against slavery or concentration camps? How would the doctrine of consent apply to apartheid in South Africa and the internment of Gypsies, Jews, and Communists in the Third Reich? And how could Lincoln, or any person, defend "the right to consent" of slaveholders without noticing that the slaveholder's existence and the existence of the slave state and the United States were based on a denial of the consent of the (slave) (and African-American) governed.

To sum up, then, we are confronted with an academic default based on five factors: 1) the de facto acceptance (and approval) of slavery; 2) the de facto acceptance (and approval) of Black Laws and inequality; 3) the deification of an inhuman status quo based on the violent oppression of some four million people; and 4) the defining fallacy of the pedagogy of oppression, the fallacy of detached data and the separation of the man from the context, and the context from history, and the history from yesterday and today.

It is clear from all this, and will become clearer in subsequent chapters, that Lincoln is indefensible on the level of race and that the only way to defend him leads to the concentration camps of the Indians, slaves and Jews and the forty to one hundred million victims of the African Slave Trade and American slavery.

There is thus nothing we can learn from Abraham Lincoln about race relations, except what not to say or do.

Because we have not confronted Lincoln, or ourselves, on that level, because we have not confronted him on the level of the racism that informed everything he said and did, including the Gettysburg Address, because we have not asked him why he said pretty words he didn't believe and had no intention of living, because we have not asked him why he wanted to deport Black people and make this a White man's country, because we have not asked him why he excluded the Black minority of Illinois and the Black majority of South Carolina from his government of the people, because, to come right out with it, we have not paid him the honor of taking him seriously, because we have not evaluated him from the mountaintop he defined and devalued and because almost everybody, authors, scholars , presidents, composers, museum curators, preachers have been engaged for more than a century in a massive effort to hide a man and a history, no one operating in the traditional structure says or writes a whole or relevant word about Abraham Lincoln today.

How explain this? How, to paraphrase the philosopher, do you hide the most celebrated man in American history?

All ways are good, including Pulitzer Prizes and Memorials on the Mall.

Part Four

"The Last Best [White] Hope"

In the course of his reply, Senator Douglas remarked, in substance, that he had always considered this government was made for the white people and not for the Negroes. Why, in point of mere fact, I think so too.

—Abraham Lincoln

Now irrespective of the moral aspect of this question as to whether there is a right or wrong in enslaving a Negro, I am still in favor of our new Territories being in such a condition that white men may find a home . . . . I am in favor of this not merely . . . for our own people who are born amongst us, but as an outlet for free white people everywhere, *the world over . . . .*

—Abraham Lincoln

7

"The Last Best [White] Hope"

BRAHAM Lincoln had a dream. His dream, like Martin Luther King Jr.'s dream, was deeply rooted in Thomas Jefferson's dream. But Lincoln's dream, like Jefferson's dream, was a dream of a lily-White America without Negroes, Native Americans, and Martin Luther Kings.

Lincoln called his dream "the last best, hope of earth" in a universally praised presidential message, which called, among other things, for a constitutional amendment "as permanent constitutional law" to deport Blacks and ethnically cleanse the United States (CW 5:518-37).

Unlike King, unlike Phillips, unlike Douglass, and like Jefferson, Lincoln dreamed of an all-White nation, governed by White people for White people.

When, in 1858, Senator Douglas told him and applauding crowds that *he* believed this government was made by Whites for Whites, Lincoln said: "In the course of his reply, Senator Douglas remarked, in substance, that he had always considered this government was made for the white people and not for the Negroes. Why, in point of mere fact, I think so too" (CW 2:281).

In point of mere fact, Lincoln thought America was a God-given Eden for free White people all over the world, and when he came, on Friday, October 15, 1858, in Alton, Illinois, to give *his* "I Have A Dream" speech, he said he was in favor of the new territories "being in such a condition that white men may find a home." He was in favor of "this not merely . . . for our own people who are born amongst us, but as an outlet for *free white people everywhere* the world over—in which Hans and Baptiste and Patrick, and all other men from all the world, may find new homes and better their conditions in life." [Loud and long continued applause.] (CW 3:312, Lincoln's italics).

This was his dream, and his faith.

"His democracy," Oscar Sherwin said, "was a White man's democracy. It did not contain Negroes" (453).

Nor did it contain Native Americans or even Mexicans, whom Lincoln considered "mongrels" (CW 3:234-5).

Someone will say, as Lincoln apologists are always saying, that this was the nineteenth century, for goodness' sake. How could you expect the man to match Martin Luther King's magnificent exhortation of the twentieth century? The answer to that question is another question: What's time got to do with it? At least two of Lincoln's contemporaries, abolitionists Frederick Douglass and Wendell Phillips, matched King word for word and dream for dream, saying the same thing in the 1860s that King said in the 1960s.

Unlike Lincoln, who looked backward to the old Union, Douglass looked forward to a new Union in which there would be neither Black nor White. Like Douglass, and unlike Lincoln, Phillips saw the Civil War as a decisive struggle to create a common American nationality embracing "under our banner all tongues, all creeds, all races—one brotherhood . . ." (PS 414). And when, on the eve of the Civil War, he made his "I Have A Dream" speech, he climbed to the mountaintop reserved for Kings and Mandelas, saying that the task before America was "to found a Capitol whose corner-stone is Justice, and whose top-stone is Liberty; within the sacred precincts of whose Holy of Holies dwelleth One who is no respecter of persons, but hath made of one blood all nations of the earth to serve him."

Ninety-four years before King, 133 years before Mandela, he saw crowding into the shelter of its rainbow arch, "old and young, learned and ignorant, rich and poor, native and foreign, Pagan,

Christian, and Jew, black and white, in one glad, harmonious, triumphant procession" (PS 318).

Unlike Phillips, Douglass, Sumner, Tubman who saw, more than one hundred years ago, this "glad, harmonious, triumphant procession" of Blacks, Whites, Indians, Asians, and Hispanics, holding hands and marching into a rainbow future with bells ringing on Stone Mountain and a rainbow choir of angels singing over the Alleghenies, Lincoln saw a procession of Whites, stretching as far as the eye could see, gathered perhaps on the Mall, without the grace of color except possibly on the outer edges and in a decidedly inferior position.

Along with most of the White fathers, Jefferson and Madison above all, Lincoln extolled the virtues of white on whiteness and associated land and climate with blood and color. Springfield, Chicago, Los Angeles, Atlanta, New Orleans, Harlem, the whole of America, even the acres around what is now the Lincoln Memorial, had been set aside for exclusive settlement by White settlers and future White immigrants from Europe and other "White"lands (CW 2:268, 499-500; CW 3:311-2).

Set aside by whom?

By God, of course. Who else?

There was no secret about what Abraham Lincoln wanted. He wanted all Blacks out, slave and free, educated and uneducated, black-skinned, brown-skinned, yellow-skinned, white-skinned, Christians and Moslems, Frederick Douglass as well as William de Fleurville, who shaved him and who thought he was Lincoln's friend. He wanted them in Africa, in South America, in the Caribbean, anywhere except in Springfield and Chicago and Washington.

Lincoln outlined his colonization dream in speeches contemporary scholars never stop praising, and what he said on the public platform is corroborated by close friends who heard the words from his mouth. And when, as president, he proposed a final solution to the race problem, he asked Congress to pass constitutional amendments providing for, among other things, "colonizing free colored persons, with their own consent, at any place or places without the United States" (CW 5:530).

What was the alternative? What would happen if Congress refused to heed his plea for an all-White asylum. You know the words, *everybody* knows the words: "We shall nobly save, or meanly lose, the last best, hope of earth" (CW 5:529-37).

People who prefer quotations to truth are always quoting those words to say something that was totally different from what Lincoln had in mind when he said them. A Lincoln specialist wrote a whole book on "the last best, hope" without telling us what the phrase meant and why Lincoln said it, and one notes with astonishment that Black schoolchildren were shepherded to a 1996 museum exhibit on *The Last Best Hope Of Earth*, blissfully unaware that Lincoln said the words in a vain attempt to deport their ancestors and create an all-White nation.

Here as so often in Lincoln, we find soaring rhetoric masking a sordid reality. *And we can construct a rule: the higher the octane of Lincoln's rhetoric, as in the Gettysburg Address, as in the Second Inaugural, the lower the level of concrete freedom for African-Americans.*

Lincoln's White Dream has been hidden from the American people for more than 135 years, and it is one of the greatest ironies of our history that Black, Brown, and Red people are always marching to the Lincoln Memorial to tell their dream to the statue of a man who dreamed of a world without Blacks, Browns, and Reds.

Why did Lincoln dream of endless White cities on the prairie?

Why did he believe that an all-White America was "the last best, hope" of an earth that is overwhelmingly Black, Brown, Red, and Yellow?

These questions can't be understood or answered without a prior understanding of the mediating forces that produced Lincoln and the White dream. The most subtle and perhaps far-reaching of these forces was the White (and racist) humanism of the French and

American revolutions. Both revolutions projected a White Utopia in which all White men or, at least, all White men with property were equal. Both revolutions defined Blacks and Reds as subhumans who were not entitled to the full rights of the Declaration of Man and the Declaration of Independence. Both managed to live with history's greatest crime, the African Slave Trade, and the second great root of the Lincoln tradition, the genocidal destruction of the Indian cultures and peoples of the West. Lincoln's forefathers were among the pioneers in the dispossession of the Indians, and Lincoln himself was directly involved in the ethnic cleansing of the state of Illinois.

Lincoln inherited the contradictions of the declarations and carried them to new heights of fantasy at Gettysburg. But it was clear, long before Gettysburg, that the Declaration of Independence could not be realized without a confrontation with the third defining root of Lincoln's life, African-American slaves and the descendants of slaves, whose very existence raised questions that could not be evaded.

What did *all* mean?

The African-American survivors of the Slave Trade were the living, pulsating, accusing embodiment of that question. If the Declaration Dream could be made real for them, it could be made real for everybody. If it couldn't be made real for them and for the wretched of the American earth, it could not be made real for anybody, and the Declaration was a Utopia or a White hoax.

By simply breathing, and by weighing as heavily as possible on their chains, the slaves turned the Declaration of Independence inside out, like a glove, revealing it to be the opposite of what it pretended to be. So long as they lived and breathed, it was a lie, a nonentity, a nonstarter. "In the presence of slavery," Congressman George S. Boutwell said, "the Declaration of Independence had lost its power; practically, it had become a lie. In the presence of slavery we were to the rest of mankind and to ourselves a nation of hypocrites. The gift of freedom to four million Negroes was not more valuable to us than to the friends of liberty in other parts of the world" (RR 134).

From this standpoint, then, the slaves, not Jefferson, were the truth of the Declaration, not because they spoke the truth but because they *were* the truth, because their very existence was a negation and a practical critique of the document. By the same token, the slaves, not Lincoln, were the truth of the Proclamation, which they defined in their being.

There is a tendency in all media to play down this gift of the slave quarters and the Harlems of America. But it is impossible to tell how much, and how little, Abraham Lincoln means if we don't situate him first in relationship to this Black gift, which was one of the fertilizing foundations of Lincoln, who tried to ignore it and ended up becoming Abraham Lincoln because of it.

Not only did African-Americans force consideration of this contradiction but they also—in another great gift that has never been adequately recognized or repaid—cleared the land and created the take-off wealth of America, thereby setting the stage for the fourth element in the quadriad of Lincoln roots, the dispossession and forced migration of the White wretched of Europe. For hundreds of years, ships packed with unfree laborers crossed the Atlantic. Most of these ships came from the West Coast of Africa, but some came from the coasts of England, bearing poverty-stricken Whites, many of whom became indentured servants. Some of these unfree and quasi-free immigrants were named Garrison. Some were called Kwame. Some were called Lincoln.

The Lincoln line has been traced back to one Samuel Lincoln, an English weaver who migrated to Massachusetts in 1637.

Let the record show: This was eighteen years after the arrival of the twenty Black seeds of Jamestown, Virginia, whose descendants Lincoln wanted to send "back" to Africa.

Whatever they were called, and whatever their status, the unfree laborers came seeking their dream, which did not in their beginning exclude anybody. In the beginning, in fact, as I have shown elsewhere (1975, 5-35), Black and White indentured servants, male and female, worked side by side in the fields and shops, ran away together, mated and married. Some, Black and White, worked their way out of indentured servitude and accumulated pounds and plantations. That dream, the first dream, died for the first time—was it the last?—in the 1660s when the White founding fathers violently separated Black and White workers and started the slave regime which led, like a lighted wick, to the explosion of the Civil War and the graves at Gettysburg. To make the new dispensation work, the men who controlled Colonial America created a system of violence, subordination, and control, based on an ideology of racism, which is not an individual idea but an institutionalized ideology that commits the focal institutions of a society to the destruction of a people because of race.

This system gave poor Whites preference over Blacks and Indians, thereby giving them an economic stake in the color of their skin. This process, which Lincoln actively and personally supported—he supported the Illinois Black Laws and argued for differential advantages for White immigrants in the territories—was institutionalized in Lincoln's time and peaked in the twentieth century.

Between 1830 and 1860, some five million White immigrants came to America. Most of these immigrants, poor, illiterate and willing to accept almost any job at almost any wage, settled in the cities, depressing wages and driving Blacks out of traditional Black preserves. The struggle between Irish workers and Black workers was particularly acrimonious, and was reflected in the riots and anti-Black propaganda in major Northern cities during the Civil War. At that time and for several decades thereafter, the Irish were considered "White n——rs" and were subject to discrimination and denial.

The results were curious and tragic. Instead of linking up with Black workers, White ethnics became the loudest champions of White supremacy. The grand outcome was not only the disappearance of traditional Black jobs but also the strengthening of White workers at the expense of Black workers. Year by year, decade by decade, Black workers were forced out of occupation after occupation—and the process is still going on. The traditional image of wave after wave of White immigrants rolling to relative security over the bruised and battered backs of Blacks is rooted in fact and history, although their descendants continue to say, with the approval of the Supreme Court, that *they were not here then* and had nothing to do with it. They *were* here then in the oath of the generations—whiteness today, whiteness tomorrow, whiteness forever— sworn in their name by their parents, an oath they reaffirmed after birth by accepting the illegitimate gains and privileges—and debts—and which they reassume every day by saying WE to what Whites have done (the slave trade, slavery, segregation, Indian massacres, John Wayne), what they are doing, and what they will do in the future. There are no innocents in history. We are what we said yes to and what we didn't say no to.

In recent years, Black nationalists and White nationalists have debated whether this group or that group was involved in the centuries-long assault on African-American men and women. In fact, every White group was involved in it. The enslavement and subordination of Blacks was an ecumenical project which continued for three centuries, and continues. Abraham Lincoln and his kin, all of them, were directly and indirectly involved in the process, not only as slavemasters and members of the slave patrol but as maintainers of a system of violence they inherited and reinvented every day in their words and gestures.

Thus, the fourth defining root of Lincoln's life, the vast, silent, noisy, inarticulate, ignored, unknown and always explosive poor Whites of America, who have always been ready to listen to any demagogue who would tell them that Blacks or some other scapegoats are the reasons for their misery. In Abraham Lincoln's day, and in ours, the dominant-characteristics of this group were fear-envy of rich Whites and fear-hatred of Blacks. Unable to compete against the rich Whites who owned most of the slaves, they hated not the rich

Whites and the institution of slavery, which was the source of their problem, but poor slaves, who were their fellow victims.

If poor Whites hated Blacks, they didn't on that account love slaveholders. They knew that planters looked down on them as "White n——rs," and they realized dimly that they were paying in the flesh for planter ease and power. Even Lincoln had intermittent flashes of poor White consciousness, telling fellow legislator Joseph Gillespie on one occasion that the class dynamics of slavery were destroying the fabric of Kentucky and other states (HI 183). The resentment was there, but poor Whites didn't know what to do about it, for they never developed or found a leadership of their own—and Abraham Lincoln was definitely not *their* leader.

Certain of Lincoln's contemporaries, Major General David Hunter and Union officer Donn Piatt in particular, suggested that the poor White syndrome is a key to an understanding of Lincoln's character. "Descended from the poor whites of a slave state, through many generations," Piatt said, "he inherited the contempt, if not the hatred, held by that class for the Negro and could no more feel sympathy for that wretched race [Blacks] than he could for the horse he worked or the hog he killed" (RR 481-2). Piatt may have overstated the case, but the same point was made with different emphases by Lamon and other cronies and intimates. Major General David Hunter, an old friend who saw Lincoln often during the war, said he was an irresolute man "of honest intentions—born a poor White in a Slave State, and, of course, among aristocrats—kind in spirit and not envious, but anxious for approval, especially of those to whom he has been accustomed to look up—hence solicitous of support of the Slaveholders in the Border States, and unwilling to offend them—without the large mind necessary to grasp great questions—uncertain of himself, and in many things ready to lean too much on others" (CD 172).

William H. Herndon, that discerning observer of Lincoln and his times, seems to have agreed with parts of that analysis. At any rate, he left an unusually vivid portrait of the class dynamics of Lincoln's

Springfield: "The established families were mainly from Kentucky. They reechoed the sentiments and reflected the arrogance and elegance of a slave-holding aristocracy. 'The Todds [Lincoln's future in-laws], Stuarts, and Edwardses were there, with priests, dogs, and servants;' there also were the Mathers, Lambs, Opdykes, Forquers, and Fords. Amid all 'the flourishing about in carriages' and the pretentious elegance of that early day was Lincoln. Of origin, doubtful if not unknown; 'poor,' without the means of hiding his poverty, he represented yet another importation from Kentucky which is significantly comprehended by the term, 'the poor whites'" (HL 146).

Scholars have generally ignored the poor White stratum, which is critical to an understanding of slavery, segregation, Lincoln and contemporary America. This doesn't mean, as so many people have suggested, that poor Whites were responsible for racism in America. The problem then and now was not poor Whites—the problem was rich Whites. Poor Whites, then and now, owned few slaves [or workers] and made no major political or economic decisions. Rich Whites, then and now, owned most of the slaves (and workers) and waved the red flag of racism, like skilled bullfighters, to keep poor Whites in line and to make them jailers, overseers, and constables of themselves as well as Negroes.

It is wrong therefore to suggest that the poor White milieu automatically engendered Lincoln's racism, and it is worth remembering that one of Lincoln's greatest protagonists and one of the greatest leaders of the antislavery movement—William Lloyd Garrison—was a poor White who, unlike Lincoln, chose poor whiteness over Whigness and freedom over slavery. Garrison, to be sure, copped out at the defining tip point, which I call "the Garrison Fault," that moment in every freedom struggle when Blacks threaten to break through to real power and real freedom, thereby separating the sheep and the paternalists—the Camuses, the Garrisons—from the radical humanitarian, the John Browns and the Wendell Phillipses.

The name was accurate. Poor Whites were poor people who called themselves White. In Lincoln's time, the category included at the very least the five million Whites who had never owned a slave and who blamed both the slave and the slaveowner for their plight. Unable to compete with the big planters for the rich bottom land, they had retreated to the hills and Piedmont areas where they eked out a scrubby existence on land no one else wanted.

Lincoln was a poor White. More to the point, he was a poor White Southerner. He was born, as is endlessly said, in a Border State, but the distinction was purely formal. For when, on February 12, 1809, Lincoln was born in Hardin County, Kentucky, the county and the state were dominated by [White] Southern institutions, Southern values and Southern preconceptions, especially about Negroes and poor Whites; and one of Lincoln's most unattractive qualities was that he never really got over habit of calling big slaveholders and rich Whites *gentlemen.*

As we have seen, Lincoln defined himself as a Southerner, saying that "we Southerners" were accustomed to calling Blacks *Cuffie* and other derogatory words. He was accustomed, too, if we can judge by the reports of associates and friends, to other Southern practices, especially in race relations. An Illinois contemporary, *Chicago Tribune* editor Charles H. Ray, believed Lincoln's conservatism on race was directly linked to his Southern birth and Southern orientation. "I must confess," he said in an 1854 letter to Elihu B. Washburne, "I am afraid of 'Abe.' He is Southern by birth, Southern in his association and Southern, if I mistake not, in his sympathies." Ray added in an amazingly accurate prediction that he thought Lincoln "would not come squarely up to the mark in a hand to hand fight with Southern influence and dictation."[15] This was also the view of Wendell Phillips, who said in a speech reported in the *Liberator*, May 5, 1963, that Lincoln was "emphatically a Southern man," and that this made it impossible for him to look at Blacks the same way he looked at Whites.

We don't believe that being born anywhere makes it impossible for anyone to see or think anything, but we know what Ray and Phillips meant. For Lincoln ever afterward gravitated to Southern men, Southern milieu and Southern values. We agree with Phillips and others, including cronies like Lamon, that the direction of his orientation is significant, but we see in it not a determinism but a choice. Lincoln, like every other person in this drama, and like every scholar interpreting this drama, chose himself. He was what he was not because he was born where he was but because he chose himself wherever he was as a man who had been born where he was. That's what Randall meant, more or less, when he said "the state of his childhood never ceased to hold a special place in his thought and feeling. Ties to Kentucky held strong and sure; they would later give the key to much of his presidential policy" (1945-55, 1:6).

Indisputably; but the problem here, once again, was not Southern people or Northern people. The problem rather—and this is the main point—was a system, created by the actions of millions of Southern and Northern people who made certain choices and who were ultimately overwhelmed by their own choices, which became imbedded in a process that assumed a life of its own and dictated to its human creators, carrying them step by step to the cannons and corpses and sawed-off legs and arms of Gettysburg.

This system, with its economic infrastructures and its racist ideology and its inevitable corollaries of oppression and paternalism, was a variant of the system Europeans and descendants of Europeans set up all over the world. Like the system the French created in Haiti, mouthing all the time the Declaration of Man, and the system the English created in Jamaica, mouthing all the time the doctrine of natural law, the system created by Americans, mouthing all the time the Declaration of Independence, created different structures and different names (Slavery, Black Laws, Indian Removal, Segregation) to accomplish the same end, the subordination of people on the basis of race and the appropriation of their resources. In order to do this, in order to push people down and to keep them down and steal their labor and hope and enrich Whites and create the White Dream, it was necessary to kill a certain number of Blacks and to crush the skulls and hopes of others. Millions died during the process—estimates vary from forty million to one hundred million—and tens of thousands died during the Lincoln years.

None of this is mentioned in context in standard Lincoln biographies. There is, in fact, no prewar violence in books about Abraham Lincoln. In a story conceived in violence and defined by violence, almost nobody talks about the violence of slavery and the violence of the Illinois Black Laws. We are given the forced removal of Indian leader Black Hawk without the violence of Lincoln and his fellow volunteers. We are given the oratory of John Calhoun without the whips and chains and blood that constituted his being. We are given *Gone With The Wind* without the Whites who were whipped and violated in prisons and public squares because they dared to carry banned books and banned ideas to Scarlett O'Hara's land.

There is no prewar violence in South Carolina and Springfield in standard Lincoln biographies. The violence started, they say, at Fort Sumter—but they are wrong. The violence that made Fort Sumter, Shiloh, and Gettysburg inevitable started at least 400 years before Fort Sumter and was perpetuated by Lincoln and his contemporaries who woke up every day and went out into the world and re-invented the violence they had inherited from the people Lincoln called "the fathers."

A child of the objective violence of a system of slavery, Indian Removal, and Black Laws, Lincoln came into the world branded in his skin by a cycle of violence that began before he was born and continued in the tragedy of his death and the birth and death of the Black freedom he feared and helped deliver to its enemies.

The violence he inherited and renewed was total. It was in things, words, principles, declarations, skin color, and it, too, continues in the social Gettysburgs he bequeathed to us as part of his legacy and in the historical and ideological defenses of the slavery, Indian Removal, and Black Laws that defined him, and us.

8

In The Red, White And Black Beginning

IT is no accident that the Lincoln saga begins with a killing. The victim, astonishingly, was Abraham Lincoln, not *that* Abraham Lincoln but his grandfather, the *first* Abraham Lincoln, who came through the Cumberland Gap seeking the White Dream and ran smack into Indians defending *their* land and their dream.

This slaying and another violent event involving Blacks probably played a role in shaping Lincoln's pervasive fear of Black and Indian violence and his conservative position on race relations. Both incidents bring out the worst in Lincoln specialists, who talk about "thieving Negroes," "skulking Indians," and "savages."

There is no hard evidence on the Indian attack or the Black confrontation, and secondary sources are so confusing and contradictory as to be worthless. Lincoln, relying on family tradition, recalled some seventy-three years later that his grandfather and namesake, Abraham Lincoln, was killed by Indians, "not in battle, but by stealth, when he was laboring to open a farm in the forest" (CW 3:511).

Based on suggestive but uninformative scraps of memory, scholars have created a John Wayne scenario of cowboys and Indians.[16] Benjamin Thomas says the grandfather was killed from ambush by "a skulking Indian." Sandburg says the ambush was witnessed by Abraham's three sons, including Thomas, who would later father Abraham the younger. When Abraham fell to the ground, Sandburg says, the three sons shouted, "Indians!" just like in the movies, and scattered, Mordecai running for the cabin, Josiah running to the fort for help, and Thomas running to his father.

Benjamin Thomas, author of what has been called "the best one-volume biography of Lincoln," says "the savage" picked up Thomas Lincoln and was "making off into the forest." Sandburg says it didn't happen that way. According to him, the Indian approached Thomas and his mortally wounded father and when the son looked up, the Indian was standing over him. Suddenly, as if in a movie, as if in a book, the Indian clutched his body and fell to the ground, shot to death by Mordecai from his perch in the cabin.

Certain informants say the Indian was smeared with "war-paint" and that Mordecai aimed "at a white ornament on the breast of the savage [sic] and brought him down." Other historians say Mordecai aimed at "a silver half moon trinket" the Indian wore.

The historians, who, after all this time, seem to be more excited than the Indians and the Lincolns, offer different versions of what happened next, wildly and improbably increasing the number of Indians. Nicolay and Hay say "savages" poured out of the thickets, firing and shouting. Herndon says help came from the fort and that the "savages were easily dispersed, leaving behind one dead and one wounded."

That's not all the Native American or Native Americans left behind. "This tragedy," Nicolay and Hay wrote, "made an indelible impression on the mind of Mordecai. Either a spirit of revenge for his murdered father, or a sportsmanlike pleasure in his successful shot, made him a determined Indian-stalker, and he rarely stopped to inquire whether the red man who came within range of his rifle was friendly or hostile" (NH 1:21). Herndon says "the tragic death of his father filled Mordecai with an intense hatred of the Indians—a feeling from which he never recovered. It was ever with him like an avenging spirit" (HW 11).

When a few Indians passed through his town, a resident said, "old Mordecai heard of them passing through mounted on his horse and took his Rifle gun on his Shoulder and followed on after the

Indians and was gone Two days when he returned he said he left one Lying in a sink hole for the Indians had killed his farther [sic] and he was determined to have satisfaction" (HI 220).

Violence in the field, violence on the roads, violence in the mind: the infection entered the nation's bloodstream, poisoning the body politic, becoming a part of family legends, passed on from generation to generation. Thomas Lincoln used to gather his children, young Abraham among them, around the fire and tell the story of how Mordecai brought down the Indian with one shot. Lincoln said later that "the story of his [grandfather's] death by the Indians, and of Uncle Mordecai, then fourteen years old, killing one of the Indians, is the legend more strongly than all others . . . imprinted upon my mind and memory"(CW 2:217].

This raises acute questions. *What* was so deeply imprinted upon Lincoln's mind? And what really happened? Was the first Abraham Lincoln killed by one Indian or a band of Indians? Was the Indian defending what he considered his land? Dennis F. Hanks said the Indians were "irritated by the encroachment of the whites" (HI 27). Was the Indian counterattacking or seeking vengeance for a prior wrong? What in the world was happening on that isolated Kentucky farm, some twenty miles from Louisville, on that day in 1786 when the first Abraham Lincoln died?

We don't know, and we will never know. Nor, to fast-forward to the second violent incident, will we ever know what happened on the dark—for literary and moral reasons, it had to be a "dark"— night when, J.G. Holland says, "seven Negroes attacked the life of the future liberator of their race . . . ."[17] Nine persons, we are told, were involved in this brawl in 1828, and only one left an account. "When he was nineteen, still residing in Indiana," Abraham Lincoln wrote, referring to himself in the third person, "he made his first trip upon a flat-boat to New Orleans. He was a hired hand merely; and he and a son of the owner, without other assistance, made the trip.

The nature of part of the cargo-load, as it was called—made it necessary for them to linger and trade along the Sugar coast—and one night they were attacked by seven Negroes with intent to kill and rob them. They were hurt some in the melee, but succeeded in driving the Negroes from the boat, and then 'cut cable' 'weighed anchor' and left" (CW 4:62). Lincoln's companion, Allen Gentry, left no report. Years later, Gentry got drunk on a boat and fell into the river and drowned. Since the Black or Blacks didn't leave accounts, we are left with the Lincoln version, which again raises more questions than it answers. What was the nature of "part of the cargo-load," as it was called? What was "the future emancipator" doing peddling goods on the Louisiana slave coast? More to the point, what was he selling? And to whom? Slaves, slavemasters, or poor Whites? And who were these seven Blacks—the precision of the number is suspicious—roaming around free and militant in the hysterical armed camp of antebellum Louisiana, looking for some White to kill and rob?

Neither slaves nor free Blacks could roam freely, especially on the riverfront, and Lincoln's version raises other questions. Were the Blacks slaves or free men? Were they guerrillas based in the woods or, as seems most likely, were they fugitive slaves trying to find a boat to take them to freedom? Finally, had there been a prior altercation between Lincoln and Gentry and the Blacks? Lincoln's language is suggestive. He says "they were attacked by seven Negroes with intent to kill and rob them." Notice the sequence of words: to kill *and* rob them. Why was Lincoln so certain that these Blacks wanted to kill Abraham Lincoln and his friend?

Additional questions are raised by latter-day historians, who tell us in great and contradictory detail that Lincoln and Gentry were attacked by "a Negro," or "a band of thieving Negroes," or "a lawless band of Negroes,"or "a party of marauding Negroes." The attack occurred, they say, on the sugar coast of Louisiana "somewhere between Natchez and New Orleans" or a few miles below Baton Rouge by a group who either came on board or threatened from the shore. J.G. Holland says Lincoln and his friend were awakened by "a noise on *shore*" (my italics) and that Lincoln saw seven Negroes and "guessed . . . at once" that they were thieves and started flailing away. Lamon says they heard "footsteps on *board*" (my italics) and "knew instantly that it was a gang of Negroes come to rob, and, perhaps to murder them." Nicolay and Hay tell us that they heard "shuffling footsteps" (1:44) on board. (How do *shuffling* footsteps sound?) The assailants, armed, Beveridge says, with hickory clubs, were repulsed by an aroused Lincoln, wielding either a handspike (Holland), a crab-tree club (Sandburg) or a huge bludgeon (Lamon). Beveridge and Herndon tell us that Lincoln and Gentry pursued the invaders and then hastily departed, "fearing," Lamon said, "lest they should return in greater numbers to take revenge."

None of the authorities quote the detailed account by Gentry's widow, Anna Caroline Gentry, who said her husband and Lincoln survived because of a ruse. "When my husband & L went down the river," she said, "they were attacked by Negroes—Some say Wade Hamptons Negroes, but I think not; the place was below that called *Mdme Bushams Plantation* 6 M below Baton Rouche—Abe fought the Negroes—got them off the boat—pretended to have guns—had none—the Negroes had hickory Clubs—my husband said 'Lincoln get the guns and Shoot'—the Negroes took alarm and left" (HI 131).

Sandburg tells us that both men were bleeding and that Lincoln had a gash over his right eye—some informants say it was over the right ear—that left a scar for life.

By nearly all accounts, then, Lincoln's confrontation with Blacks and his grandfather's confrontation with Native Americans left physical and probably emotional scars. Did these scars play a role in Lincoln's views on race relations, especially his obsession with Black violence? Since Lincoln himself said that the first incident was the legend more strongly imprinted on his mind than any other, and since he, according to confidants, returned to the second incident several times, displaying the scar like an old war wound, the answer is almost certainly yes. On the following pages, we shall deal at length with Lincoln and African-Americans, and we can note here in passing that his subsequent relations with Indians were equally questionable. Lincoln, for instance, was uncharacteristically hard-hearted in his review of the sentences handed down to the Sioux Indians who killed some four hundred Whites in a Minnesota rebellion in 1862. Union commanders recommended death sentences for three hundred Sioux. The original list was headed, George Sinkler noted, by an African-American with Indian connections. But Lincoln, prodded by members of his staff, most notably Secretary of the Navy Gideon Welles, reduced the number to thirty-eight. Asked by Congress how he came to that decision, Lincoln made a surprising admission, saying: "I caused a careful examination of the records . . . to be made in view of first ordering the execution of such as had been proved guilty of violating females." The president was surprised. "*Contrary to my expectation* [italics added] only two of this class were found."

Although Lincoln was famous for halting the execution of Union soldiers, he approved one of the largest mass executions in military history. "*Thirty-eight Indians were hanged,*" George Sinkler wrote in *The Racial Attitudes of American Presidents,* "*while after the Civil War not one rebel swung for rebellion.* While the President expressed no attitude toward the Indian other than to remember that one sneaked up behind his grandfather and killed him while he was working in a field, a double standard of race value might have had something to do with his treatment of the Sioux" (66-8, italics added).

"The motive," Lincoln said, "is born before the man" (HW 345).

He could have been talking about the slaying of the first Abraham, a tragedy that leapfrogged a generation and gave Abraham the younger a one-room cabin and a problematic family as destiny. The funeral of the first Abraham was scarcely over when the chain of motives started working, changing the fortunes of Lincoln's father who, as the youngest son, wasn't in the line of succession and who was forced to earn his keep as a day worker and a carpenter. Thomas Lincoln managed somehow to get enough money to buy a farm, but the farms available to a poor White in the slave-dominated Kentucky economy were marginal.

There is thus a kind of bitter economic poetry in the fact that Lincoln's personal story opens with his father, the luckless Thomas Lincoln, marooned on hard and unpromising land in Hardin County, Kentucky, waiting for the birth of a son, whom he would call Abraham. When on Sunday, February 12, 1809, Abraham Lincoln was born, Thomas Jefferson was sixty-five, John Brown was eight, Nat Turner was eight, the American Revolution was one score and thirteen years old, and the African Slave Trade was more than three hundred years old.

The son was born under the mark of the slave—and the slaveholder. By 1811, two years after his birth, there were 1,007 slaves in Hardin County and only 1,627 White males over sixteen.

The White people of Hardin County and other communities where the Lincolns lived in Kentucky and Indiana were hard-working, hard-drinking, hard-praying poor Whites whose "habitation," Nicolay and Hay said, "were hardly superior to those of the savages [sic] with whom they waged constant war" (NH 1:18) The only thing that distinguished them from the Indians and Blacks surrounding them was the color of their skin, and it was on that rock, so to speak, that they built their church, and their economics.

They were, almost all commentators say, a superstitious people, hooked on White witchcraft from "old and New England," "touched with a peculiar tinge of African magic" (NH 1:41). If we can believe Herndon and others, Lincoln was "superstitious, believed more or less in dreams, consulted Negro oracles . . ." (HH 199). Lincoln himself said later that he "always was superstitious" (CW 1:289).

As in Egypt, as in all venues of oppression, the oppressors demanded that the oppressed sing them a song. By the rivers of the Mississippi and the Ohio, as by the rivers of Babylon, the people who held Blacks captive, *Abraham Lincoln's people*, demanded a song.

Bumbry B. Lloyd told Herndon that Kentucky Whites "had lots of whisky—had suppers—hoe downs—dances old fashion—old n——r would play—pat juba—Sing "Juba"—you old dog Juba" No n——r Could stand Still at this . . . (HI 533).

Nor could any White.

Even before Lincoln was born, he was spoken for by his forefathers, the ones who owned slaves and the ones who didn't, who swore an oath of whiteness in his name, an oath that Lincoln later confirmed and reconfirmed in his own name. This oath, whether spoken or not, was a real oath in the world and required Thomas Lincoln and his son, Abraham, to defend the fortress of whiteness with their lives if necessary but certainly by their lives. Having internalized this oath in his own name, Lincoln, from the beginning, saw the world through white-colored glasses and evaluated all events, people and things from the standpoint of whether they threatened or maintained White supremacy.

Before Lincoln was born, his father, like almost all White males in Kentucky, was pressed into service to defend the system that penalized him. On at least one occasion, the father had served a term with the county slave patrol, riding the dark and deserted roads to keep the slaves in their quarters and to preserve the White peace. Under the laws of the state, the paddy-rollers, as the slaves called them, could summarily punish on the spot slaves found "strolling" without permission of slavemasters or attending unlawful meetings or carrying unauthorized articles of property. For these and other "crimes," Abraham Lincoln's father and other patrollers were authorized to punish slaves by lashing them up to ten times on their bare backs. Nor did the mark of violence and slavery stop there. For after the death of Abraham Lincoln's mother, Thomas Lincoln married the widow of the Hardin county jailer. There was no use fighting it: the poor Whites of Hardin County were condemned by their own choices and the choices written in things to serve the slavery machine that destroyed them.

A lot of ink and paper have been wasted trying to provide an antislavery background for Lincoln. It is said, for example, that there was a great deal of antislavery agitation in Hardin County churches in the first decades of the century. Thomas Lincoln, according to these writers, "could" have heard some of this agitation. This, of course, is worse than useless, and no one has provided one scrap of information linking Thomas or his son to antislavery activity. People who knew the Lincolns in these early years are contemptuous of these retrospective alibis. Herndon said there was no truth to these stories and that Thomas Lincoln "never in later years manifested any especial aversion to it [slavery]" (HW 20).

Nor did his son.

Dennis F. Hanks, who had a better chance than any other informant to observe the Lincolns in this period, noted that "it is said in the Biographies that Mr. Lincoln left the State of Ky because and only because Slavery was there. This is untrue. He movd [sic] off to better his Condition . . . . Slavery did not operate on him" (HI 36).

Or on his son, either.

The son said later that the whole story of his family could be summed up in the well-known phrase, "the short and simple annals of the poor"(HI 57), but there's more to it than that. For although all poor Whites (and poor Blacks) are alike in some ways, every poor White, and every poor Black, is poor and White or poor and Black in his own way. The challenge to the interpreter is to find the peculiar points where family and personal history intersect history—the history of the group or the collectivity—and the burning points that mark an individual in such a way that he meets a historical need. Most of these burning points occur in the first years of life where, in most cases, objective testimonies are lacking. In these cases, as in practically all others, we have to work backwards, defining the qualities that made Lincoln available, and floating hypotheses to identify possible determinations. So, to begin with, Lincoln, as we have established, was insatiably ambitious. But ambition is not a thing; it is transcendence, choice, a man inventing himself, desiring, grasping, struggling for place and position everywhere and on every level.

Herndon said in a famous phrase that Lincoln's "ambition was a little engine that knew no rest" (HW 146). Precisely. And we shall understand nothing about Lincoln if we don't hear the clack, clack, clack of that engine not here nor there but everywhere—in his marriage to the socially prominent Mary Todd, in his challenge to Stephen Douglas in the Lincoln-Douglas debates, and in the Emancipation Proclamation he issued and, more importantly, the emancipation proclamation he didn't issue.

Can we say, then, that Lincoln was motivated by ambition and not principle? The answer is yes, no and maybe. In truth, the question is badly formulated. For if Lincoln, as we have said, was a whole who expressed himself totally in every act of his life, then ambition and principle were different but complementary facets of the same reality. Herndon, who was more perceptive than almost all twentieth-century interpreters, said the qualities of "this terribly reticent, secretive, shut-mouth man" (HW 204) were connected and defined a worldview. More modern than almost all Lincoln interpreters, Herndon said over and over again that Lincoln's characteristics were members and expressions of each other. "I have often said to you," he wrote Jesse W. Weik, "that Lincoln was terribly ambitious and to that extent he was egoistic, selfish, cold" (HH 129-30).

This analysis brings us to the biggest and most explosive question in the Lincoln historiography, a question no biography can ignore although almost all Lincoln biographies have managed to ignore it. The question is simple, and explosive: *What was wrong with Abraham Lincoln?* What were the demons that repeatedly drove him to the edge of madness and suicide?

Everybody who knew Lincoln well grappled with these questions; and Lincoln cronies never tired of saying to themselves and others that something was seriously amiss in Lincoln's emotional economy. Herndon said to anyone who would listen that Lincoln was a very peculiar man. "Lincoln I say again and again," Judge Davis wrote, "was a peculiar man." Leonard Swett, who rode with Lincoln on the Eighth Circuit, asked Herndon, a year after the assassination, to tell him, if he knew, what was wrong with Lincoln. "I would like to have you write me what the skeleton was with Lincoln? What gave him that peculiar melancholy? What cancer had he inside?" (HI 214).

That was the question.

What was the cancer inside the sixteenth president of the United States? What was the malady that never stopped hemorrhaging inside him, the malady that led Herndon and others to say that he seemed at times "to be a little off . . ." (HH 214).

Herndon, Davis, Swett, Whitney, Lamon, Stuart, practically all his close friends said there seemed to be a human vacuum in the man who tended, they said, to manipulate and use friends and acquaintances like tools, discarding them after they served their purposes.

In one of the great scenes of the *Death of a Salesman*, Willy Loman deplored the morals of corporate leaders who sucked all the juice out of men and then threw them away like orange peelings. Arthur Miller may have gotten the line from Herndon who said in a chilling phrase that *nobody* quotes that ambition "eclipsed his [Lincoln's] better nature, and when he used a man and sucked all the uses out of him, he would throw away the thing as an old orange peeling" (HH 134-5). To make his meaning clearer, Herndon changed the metaphor and said, "He was a remorseless trimmer with men. They were his tools, and when they were used up, he threw them aside as old iron and took up new tools" (HH 208).

We are only interested in these phenomena as they provide light on Lincoln's strange career as an "emancipator." From that standpoint, it is relevant to note, as Herndon and other cronies noted, that the future "emancipator" had volcanic emotional problems that pushed him more than once to the edge of suicide.

Whitney tells a story that in a brief illuminating flash seems to capture the strangeness and anguish of the man. It was common, Whitney said, for lawyers riding the Eighth Judicial Circuit in Illinois to sleep in the same room and in the same bed. "One morning," Whitney said, "I was awakened early—before daybreak—by my companion sitting up in bed, his figure dimly visible by the ghostly firelight, and talking the wildest and most incoherent nonsense all to himself. A stranger to Lincoln would have supposed he had suddenly gone insane. Of course I knew Lincoln and his idiosyncrasies, and felt no alarm, so I listened and laughed. After he had gone on in this way for say, five minutes, while I was awake, and I know not how long *before* I was awake, he sprang out of bed, hurriedly washed, and jumped into his clothes, put some wood on the fire, and then sat in front of it, moodily, dejectedly, in a most sombre and gloomy spell, till the breakfast bell rang, when he started, as if from sleep, and went with us to breakfast. Neither [David] Davis nor I spoke to him; we knew this trait; it was not remarkable for Lincoln . . . ." This was, Whitney said, quoting, "a proof" that "true wit to madness, sure, is oft allied" (68).

It was at least allied to odd behavior. Sometimes, without warning, Herndon said, [Lincoln would] burst out in a loud laugh or quickly spring up and run downstairs as if his house were on fire saying nothing" (HH 263).

The two men who knew more about Lincoln than anyone else — Herndon and Speed—say he had a serious breakdown in 1841, probably because of a broken engagement with Mary Todd. Speed said "Lincoln went crazy—had to remove razors from his room— take away all Knives and other such dangerous things—&c—it was terrible" (HI 475). Herndon said Lincoln was "crazy as a loon" and that his friends "forcibly arrested him" and removed "all razors, knives, pistols, etc., from his room and presence, that he might not commit suicide" (HH 37).

The "crazed spells" were only the tip of an emotional iceberg that extended to unfathomable depths in Lincoln, who had problems, according to most of his cronies, in expressing love and affection. It was a common refrain among Abraham Lincoln cronies: Abraham Lincoln rewarded his enemies, even in picking Union generals, and forgot his friends. His first law partner, John T. Stuart, said "L did forget his friends . . . there was no part of his nature which drew him, to do acts of gratitude to his friends."

If there's one thing twentieth-century schoolchildren know about Lincoln, it is that he was a warm-hearted man who felt the pain of the people.

If there's one thing most of his cronies are agreed on, it was that he was a cold, calculating, selfish man who never probably, in Herndon's view, loved anyone except himself. Herndon said, "Lincoln was not a social man, loved no man much, was more or less selfish . . . ." Lincoln's sister-in-law, Elizabeth Edwards, said he was "a cold man" who had "no heart" (HI 443, 446).

The consensus among Lincoln's friends was that there was a deadness or, better still, a flatness in his psychic economy. John Todd Stuart, who had a good opportunity to observe him, deplored "his want of passion—Emotion—imagination . . ." (HI 63). Judge Davis, who was the ring leader of the Eighth Judicial Circuit group, said the same thing in stronger language: "Lincoln had no spontaneity—nor Emotional Nature—no strong Emotional feelings for any person— Mankind or thing" (HI 348).

Former Congressman Isaac N. Arnold was one of Lincoln's most passionate supporters, but when Herndon told him, "I don't think Mr. Lincoln had a broad & *Universal* affection for men," Arnold agreed, saying only that he would change "the word '*universal*' to *generous* (HI 592, italics in original).

This may explain why Lincoln seemed to have no understanding or sympathy with the slaves. Herndon said he "was tender-hearted *when in the presence* of suffering or when it was enthusiastically or poetically described to him . . . [but] he had no imagination to invoke, through the distances, suffering, nor fancy to paint it" (HH 121).

But listen, someone will say in objection, everyone knows that Lincoln was a gregarious man who was always telling funny stories. But who cannot see that Lincoln, like all great comics, used comedy as an offense and a defense and laughed, as he said repeatedly, to keep from crying? Judge Davis said, "Mr Lincoln was not a social man by any means; his Stories—jokes &c. which were done to whistle off sadness are no evidences of sociality . . ." (HI 348). Robert L. Wilson, who served in the legislature with Lincoln, said that he told him the same thing. "In a conversation with him . . . he told me that although he appeared to enjoy life rapturously, Still he was the victim of terrible melancholy. He Sought company, and indulged in fun and hilarity without restraint, or Stint as to time [.] Still when by himself, he told me that he was so overcome with mental depression, that he never dare [sic] carry a knife in his pocket." (HI 205).

That's what Herndon meant, more or less, when he said, "A peculiar man, this Abraham was" (HH 170).

If, as these testimonies indicate, there were negative qualities, there were also positive qualities, oftentimes growing out of the same root. Perhaps one required the other. At any rate, it was almost certainly ambition, a driving determination to better himself and perhaps to outdo his father and live like the uppity slaveowners and their lawyers, that made it possible for Lincoln to educate himself and rise to the top of the pile.

Like Frederick Douglass, like William Lloyd Garrison, young Abraham Lincoln escaped from his prison on a ladder of words, reading in the fields, in the forest, everywhere. Almost everything else they say about him is dross; but the self-made story is pure gold. Some deplored his humble beginnings, but Herndon celebrated them, saying: "So far as I am concerned I don't care how Lincoln came into the world; the lower he was created, the higher and grander . . . to me he is" (HH 53).

All of this—the ambition, the "crazed spells," the melancholy and especially the mirth—can be explained as a desperate and creative attempt by a deprived youth to save his life and repair a damaged self-esteem. And it is fascinating to note something that has never been, to my knowledge, adequately explored, and that is that Lincoln's humor, like Jack Benny's humor, like Bob Hope's humor, was linked to his ambition and was another strategy he used to elevate himself. At an early age, he learned the power of words when other children and even grown men gathered around him, entranced by his imitation of a preacher's sermon or his recital of the latest jokes, not all of which could be told in mixed company. He later used that power to make men stop working and gather around him.

Reading the reminiscences of the men who knew him as a child and as a young man, we are struck by a fact that most biographers have ignored or glossed over: Lincoln—why hasn't somebody said this before?— was a showman who loved to hog the spotlight. His stepmother, Sarah Bush Johnson, said, "he would hear sermons preached—come home—take the children out—get on a stump or log and almost repeat it word for word . . . . His father had to make him quit sometimes as he quit his own work to speak & made the other children as well as the men quit their work" (HI 107). His childhood friend, Dennis F. Hanks, said "sometimes when he went to log-house raising, corn shucking, and suchlike things he would say to himself and sometimes to others: 'I don't want these fellows to work any more,' and instantly he would commence his pranks, tricks, jokes, stories, and sure enough all would stop, gather around Abe, and listen, sometimes crying and sometimes bursting their sides with laughter" (HH 282).

There was more than a little hostility in this, for Lincoln, who lacked the social graces, delighted in breaking up dances and social affairs by gathering all the men in a secluded corner to hear his jokes. He would, Herndon said, "annoy the women dancers, because the men dancers would stop in the dance to hear the story," which Lincoln told *"just* loud enough for the ladies to hear . . . ." Lincoln, Herndon said, "would enjoy to the ends of his toenails his social cruelty" (HH 215).

From that time until his death, humor was a major *weapon* in the Lincoln armory, used sometimes as an offense, sometimes as a defense, and always as "a vent" for what his cronies called with no sense of irony the "black fits" that drove him to the edge of suicide.

The two states—hilarity and sadness—were joined in Lincoln, and he was always shuttling from one to the other, sometimes in the same conversation, sometimes in the same sentence.

In his melancholy moods, "Whitney wrote, "the exuberant fountains of his pleasantry and mimicry were completely sealed and frozen up, but when the black [sic] fit passed by, he could range from grave to gay, from lively to severe, with the greatest facility."

Whitney was struck by the rapid changes Lincoln made from dignity to "freaks of frivolity and inanity" and "the most ridiculous buffoonery" (135, 154).

Most students have assumed that sadness happened to Lincoln and that he chose laughter. In fact, Lincoln chose both. He made himself sad, as he made himself glad. The proof is that when he was not sad, he asked Ward Hill Lamon to sing a sad song so that he could be sad. The proof is that he collected long, lugubrious poems that he read to make himself sad.

Whatever "was suggestive of death, the grave, the sorrows of man's days on earth," Lamon said, "*charmed* his disconsolate spirit, and captivated his sympathetic heart." Sad music, he said, *enchanted* Lincoln (478, italics added).

Why did Lincoln want to be sad?

Three tentative explanations have been offered, one of which we can dismiss immediately, the idea advanced by Whitney and others that "his digestive apparatus [failed] to work normally" (147). The second is that he suffered some sort of brain damage in his tenth year when he was kicked in the head by a horse and remained in a coma for several hours. The other theory suggests that the bad blood between Lincoln and his father was a function of still unexplained disturbances in his family relations. Sartre said once that glory is a family relation, meaning that one seeks glory not to win the love and applause of one's contemporaries but to win the love and applause of family members, parents especially, and especially dead parents, and to make them realize that they blew it by not recognizing what a great son or daughter they had.

Thus, the future emancipator, a strange, ambitious, conservative, *driven* man, living on the edge, between hilarity and tears. Whitney said he presented the appearance "of being at once the most melancholy and the most jocund of men," combining within himself "the strangely diverse *roles* of head of the state in the agony of civil war, but he was likewise the court jester . . . " (118). There was a theatrical dimension to all this, a dimension Lincoln himself played with, emphasizing the minstrel/Macbeth aspects of his life, calling attention repeatedly to the grandiosity of his suffering—"I am the most miserable man in the world"—and the centrality of his comedic self.

Who must Lincoln have been in order to blend these disparate roles into one functioning whole? And what burning points, especially in his formative years, made him what he was?

The objective testimonies that could help us answer these questions do not exist, but it doesn't matter. For the qualities we have cited almost certainly represent some tension or malfunction in the early years between the mother and son and/or the father and son, or both. And it is hardly surprising to discover that Lincoln had an Oedipal problem and that he seemed to have loathed his father who was not invited to his wedding and who never visited him in his home after his wedding to the socially prominent Mary Todd. The story of his life at any rate is the story of a quest for substitute fathers, including the founding fathers he ambivalently praised and tried to outdo the rest of his life.

As for his mother, the much-abused and much-discussed Nancy Hanks, the evidence is ambiguous. People say he adored her, but on at least one occasion he described her in withering terms, telling a woman acquaintance that a former love interest reminded him unpleasantly of his mother. "[W]hen I beheld her," he wrote, "I could not for my life avoid thinking of my mother; and this, not from withered features, for her skin was too full of fat, to permit its contracting in to wrinkles; but from her want of teeth, weather-beaten appearance in general, and from a kind of notion that ran in my head, that *nothing* could have commenced at the size of infancy and reached her present bulk in less than thirtyfive [sic] or forty years; and, in short, I was not all pleased with her . . . " (CW 1:118).

I was not pleased with her.

With whom? His former love interest? His mother? Or both? The answers to these questions, and the answer to part of the mystery of the Emancipation Proclamation that was not an emancipation procla-mation, are almost certainly to be found in the short and mysterious history of Nancy Hanks Lincoln. Herndon says Lincoln told him that his mother "was a bastard, was the daughter of a nobleman so called of Virginia" (HH 73). There is no evidence to confirm this story, but there is plenty of evidence to show that people gossiped about Nancy Hanks and her mother, Lucy Hanks, who was something of a free spirit and who had, gossips said, a checkered sexual past.

The rumors may or may not have been true, but it is undeniably true that young Lincoln went through a series of childhood traumas that could have given complexes to anyone. In the first place, Nancy Hanks Lincoln contracted the dread "milk sickness" and died dra-matically and horribly, her body contorting and levitating in "jacti-tation" in the one-room Lincoln shack where everything happened, eating, sleeping, cooking, loving, dying. Then for several days, until carpenter Thomas Lincoln could cut the green wood and make her coffin, the body lay in the same room where the Lincolns ate and slept, and one can imagine the horror that meant to at least some members of the family.

As if that wasn't enough, Thomas Lincoln left the two children to fend for themselves and went back to Kentucky to find a wife. During his long absence, we are told, the children, terrified perhaps out of their mind, almost returned to nature. Years later, and perhaps for the rest of his life, Lincoln heard in his mind's ear, "the panther's scream," filling the "night with fear" (CW 1:386). When the new Mrs. Lincoln returned to Indiana with Thomas Lincoln, she "was astonished to find that there was no floor or Door to the House of her Husband, no furniture of any Kind, no Beds or Bedding or scarcely any" (HI 99).

After Sarah Johnson Lincoln cleaned the children up and smoothed over the rough places, the family of Thomas Lincoln, augmented now by relatives and stepchildren, continued its losing fight against the big slaveholders, moving finally to Illinois, a Southerner-oriented Northern state with a harsh Black Code and widespread sympathy for slavery. No one will be surprised, social conditioning being what it is, to learn that both the father and son, having escaped the turbulent embrace of big slaveholders, spent most of the rest of their lives trying to make life easier for big slaveholders.

Lincoln's White House secretaries, Nicolay and Hay, said he was deeply, perhaps irremediably, afflicted by the taint of slavery that colored the perceptions of the White people of Illinois. "The taint of slavery," they wrote, "the contagion of a plague they had not quite escaped, was on the people of Illinois. They were strong enough to rise once in their might and say they would not have slavery among them. But in the petty details of every day, in their ordinary talk, and in their routine legislation, their sympathies were still with the slave-holders. They would not enlist with them, but they would fight their battles in their own way" (NH 1:146).

Out of this long apprenticeship, and the long journey from Massachusetts to Virginia to Kentucky, by way of the White Dream of the Declarations and the violence against Indians and Blacks, out of all this, and out of the ambiguous relationships with the mother and the estranged father and the adopted aristocrats of his social teething came Abraham Lincoln, who never enlisted with the slave-holders but who fought their battles in his own way.

Part Five

The Jim Crow Lincoln

Judge Douglas has said to you that he has not been able to get from me an answer to the question whether I am in favor of Negro citizenship. So far as I know, the Judge never asked me the question before. He shall have no occasion to ever ask it again, for I tell him very frankly that I am not in favor of Negro citizenship.

—Abraham Lincoln

I have all the while maintained that inasmuch as there is a physical inequality between the white and black, that the blacks must remain inferior . . . .

—Abraham Lincoln

9

Backing The Black Laws

ABRAHAM Lincoln's Illinois was a schizophrenic state, characterized by Negrophobia and a Black Code "that would have been a disgrace to a slave state." Neither Southern nor Northern, neither a free state nor a slave state, the Land of Lincoln, as Illinois is called today, was overdetermined and underdetermined, cleft between the past and the future, between slavery and freedom, between the New England and European immigrants in the lake counties and the slavery-loving good old boys in the river counties.

Robert P. Howard said Illinois was "almost a slave state" and had "'a slave code that was harsher and wider in scope than some of those in the South" (129, 131).

Former United States Senator Paul Simon said Illinois "was not as 'free' a state as many imagine during the period when Lincoln served in the legislature . . ." (121).

The secret of Illinois was the secret of its birth. It came into the Union as a free state but was admitted under fine-print provisions that "permitted," among other things, indentured servants to "freely" sell themselves into extended periods of servitude. From the time Lincoln settled in New Salem in 1831 until he left Illinois in 1861 to assume the presidency, slaves and quasi-slaves were held, whipped, hunted, litigated and terrorized in the state of Illinois.

Although there were few Blacks in the state—there were 747

slaves and 1,637 free Blacks in 1830—Illinois Whites seemed to be obsessed by the subject of race and returned to it time and time again in paroxysms of legislation fueled by fear, loathing, and desire. After adopting a comprehensive Black Code in 1819, Illinois legislators returned to the subject in 1825, 1831, 1833, 1841 and 1845.[18]

The man Lincoln called his special friend, Ward Hill Lamon, had no particular sympathy for Blacks, but even he decried the laws of the state, saying that the Illinois Black Code was "of the most preposterous and cruel severity, —a code that would have been a disgrace to a Slave state, and was simply an infamy in a free one. It borrowed the provisions of the most revolting laws known among men, for exiling, selling, beating, bedeviling, and torturing Negroes, whether bond or free " (206).

The "revolting" Illinois Black Laws didn't seem to bother Lamon while he was living there. Nor did they bother Lincoln, who never said a word against the Black Laws, although they were enforced in Illinois every year he lived there and were not repealed until 1865.

Under provisions of this code, one of the severest in a Northern state, Illinois Blacks had no legal rights White people were bound to respect. It was a crime for them to settle in Illinois unless they could prove their freedom and post a $1,000 bond. John Jones, the most prominent Black in Illinois in Lincoln's day, pointed out that these provisions were in violation of the Illinois constitution, which declared "that *all* men are born free and independent and have an indefeasible right to enjoy liberty and pursue their own happiness." It was also, Jones noted, "a gross violation" of the United States Constitution which said "that the citizens of each State shall be entitled to all the privileges and immunities of citizens of the several States" (4).

None of this disturbed Lincoln, who lived, without audible distress, with a Black Code, commonly called Black Laws, which said that any Black found without a certificate of freedom was considered a runaway slave and could be apprehended by any White and auctioned off by the sheriff to pay the cost of his confinement.

If a Black had a certificate of freedom, he and his family were required to meet reporting and registration procedures reminiscent of a totalitarian state. The head of the family had to register all family members and provide detailed descriptions to the supervisor of the poor, who could expel the whole family at any moment.

Blacks who met these requirements were under constant surveillance and could be disciplined or arrested by any White. They could not vote, sue, or testify in court.

No Negro was safe.

No Negro was secure.

Any Negro without certified freedom papers on his person was a legitimate prey of kidnappers who roamed the streets of Lincoln's Springfield and other Illinois cities and towns. By the 1850s, and especially after passage of the Compromise of 1850, which Lincoln supported, kidnapping Negroes, with the aid and support of the state and the White population, had become a profitable business.

The way it worked, N. Dwight Harris said, was that two or three White men would form a Black-hunting gang. "One would establish himself at St. Louis, or at one of the other border towns, and work up a reputation as a seller of slaves. The others would move about the Illinois counties on the lookout for Negroes—slave or free. The freebooters never stopped to inquire whether a colored person was free or not. The question simply was, could he be carried off in safety."

If the kidnappers didn't get him, the state would.

With Lincoln's active and passive support, the state used violence to keep Blacks poor. Most trades and occupations were closed to them, and laws and customs made it difficult for them to acquire real estate.

With Lincoln's active and passive support, the state used violence to keep Blacks ignorant. Schools and colleges were for the most part closed to Blacks. A law on the apprenticeship of children said "that the master or mistress to whom such child shall be bound as aforesaid shall cause such child to be taught to read and write and the ground rules of arithmetic . . . except when such apprentice is a *negro* or *mulatto*."

To make matters worse, the state taxed Blacks to support public schools that were closed by law—and by the vote of Abraham Lincoln—to Black children. The law, which Lincoln supported, specified that the school fund should be distributed on the basis of "the number of white persons under 20 years of age." This disturbed a number of very conservative Illinois White people. In 1853, a year before Lincoln's Peoria Declaration, the *Alton Telegraph* praised Ohio for establishing schools for Black children and criticized Illinois for taking money from Blacks to educate White children. No one in the legislature paid any attention to this criticism, and Lincoln, the state's most powerful Whig politician, said nothing.

During all the years of what some historians call Lincoln's rehearsal for greatness, indentured servants, "a polite phrase," Elmer Gertz said, "for the northern brand of slaves" (467), were hemmed in by laws and restrictions similar to the ones in Southern states. They could be whipped for being lazy, disorderly or disrespectful to the "master, or master's family."

As for the pursuit of happiness, which Lincoln occasionally paid tribute to, Blacks could not play percussion instruments, and any White could apprehend any slave or servant for "riots, routs, unlawful assemblies, trespasses and seditious speeches." It was a crime for any person to permit "any slave or slaves, servant or servants of color, to the number of three or more, to assemble in his, her or their house, out house, yard or shed for the purpose of dancing or revelling, either by night or by day . . . ."

What did Abraham Lincoln say about these violations of government of the people, et cetera, et cetera?

He said he was in favor of the violations—that's what he said. Not only did he back the Black Laws, but he voted to keep the suffrage lily-White and to tax Blacks to support White schools Black children couldn't, in general, attend.

In 1848 Illinois adopted a new constitution that denied Blacks the right to vote and to serve in the state militia. To make sure everyone got the message, the constitution authorized the state legislature to pass legislation barring slaves and free Negroes from settling in the state. Article XIV of the new constitution read:

> The General Assembly shall at its first session under the amended constitution pass such laws as will effectually prohibit free persons of color from immigrating to and settling in this state, and to effectually prevent the owners of slaves from bringing them into this state, for the purpose of setting them free.

In February 1853, one year before Abraham Lincoln praised the "White man's" Declaration of Independence at Peoria, the legislature made it a high crime punishable by a fine for a Black to settle in the state. If a Black violator couldn't pay the fine, he or she could be sold by the sheriff to pay court costs, making some Whites fear that the new law would bring back slavery.

The architect of this Negro Exclusion Law, which was, Eugene H. Berwanger said, "undoubtedly the most severe anti-Negro measure passed by a free state," was John A. Logan, who introduced the measure "solely to improve his political stature" (49). During debate on the issue, Logan attacked White critics of his bill, which was called "An Act To Prevent the Immigration of Free Negroes into the State." Logan said he could not understand "how it is that men can become so fanatical in their notions as to forget that they are white. Forget that sympathy over the white man and have his bosom heaving with it for those persons of color. " Logan looked around the hall and said words that many of his compatriots would say in the 1990s: "It has almost become an offense to be a white man" (J. Jones 17-9).

Neither this speech nor his Negro Exclusion Law hurt the reputation of "Black Jack" Logan, who was later named a major general by Abraham Lincoln and who is celebrated today all over Chicago as a Civil War icon.

Most Illinois Whites supported the provisions of Logan's Negro Exclusion Law, but twenty-two legislators, eleven Whigs and eleven Democrats, voted against it in the lower house. There was also strong opposition in fourteen Northern counties, particularly from Quakers, Presbyterians, Congregationalists, and New England immigrants.

The severity of the Negro Exclusion Law shocked antislavery forces. Frederick Douglass was outraged by the "enormity" of an act that "coolly" proposed to "sell the bodies and souls of the blacks to increase the intelligence and refinement of the whites [and] to rob every black stranger who ventures among them to increase their literary fund." It seemed to Douglass that "the men who enacted that law had not only banished from their minds all sense of justice, but all sense of shame" (FD 2:248-9). Another editor who felt that way was Horace Greeley, who said in the *New York Tribune* that it was "punishment enough" for Blacks "to live among such cruel, inhospitable beings"as the White residents of Illinois, not to mention the additional burden of having to live under such a law (qtd. in Berwanger 50). The *New Orleans Bee* said the law was "an act of special and savage ruthlessness." The *Jonesboro Gazette* in the land of Lincoln asked: "How long will the people of this hitherto 'Free State' suffer this shameful enaction to disgrace their statute book?" (Cole 225, 226).

What did Lincoln say?

He didn't say a mumblin' word.

Despite his Jim Crow votes and Jim Crow style, Lincoln got up on platforms and said he believed that the Declaration of Independence gave Blacks the right to *some* of the rights enumerated in that document, including life, liberty and the pursuit of happiness. If he believed this—and the evidence goes the other way—it was news to Illinois Blacks, who were denied the right to pursue anything in Lincoln's Illinois, except poor-paying jobs that Whites shunned until economic crises lowered the color of their expectations.

Most Illinois Blacks—Illinois reported a total Black population of 7,628 in 1860—were poor laborers who lived in besieged pockets in Chicago and other towns. In spite of the handicaps under which they lived, they were—then and now—a contentious lot with their own churches and meeting halls and a not inconsiderable number of prototypical Jesse Jacksons. Even then, Black Chicagoans had a certain style. The *Cairo Weekly Times* said "they [Chicagoans] are undoubtedly the most riotous people in the state. Mention Negro and slave together in the same breath and they are up in arms."[19] Black and White Chicagoans repeatedly rescued slaves from slavecatchers and even police, and Blacks organized a Black police force to patrol their areas.

Although Chicago had a reputation as a hotbed of abolitionism, the city, like the state, was a civil war of warring worlds, split between the slavery-hating German and New England immigrants, and the poor White immigrants, largely Irish, who competed with Blacks for the lowest-paying jobs and who generally supported slavery and racially restrictive legislation. The upper hand in the Civil War era was held by the German immigrants and New England Protestants, some of whom called the Irish "White n——rs," but the Democratic proslavery forces made themselves felt by constant verbal and physical attacks on abolitionists and Blacks.

The Black population at that point was relatively small, numbering some 300 out of 29,000 in 1850 and some 1,000 out of 109,000 in 1860. Certain Chicago Blacks, most notably John Jones, who became the city's leading tailor, and H.O. Wagoner, a hominy manufacturer, beat the system, but they, too, were subject to the Black Laws that limited the aspirations of all Blacks.

Jones is generally ignored in standard Lincoln texts—he is not mentioned at all in what the Lincoln establishment calls the ten best books on Lincoln. This is unfortunate, for it is impossible to see Lincoln whole if we do not see him in the reflected black light of the John Joneses of Illinois. Even a little John Jones would go a long way in correcting the extravagant and preposterous inferences scholars have drawn from Lincoln's so-called prelude to greatness.[20]

Born free in North Carolina, Jones learned the trade of tailoring and moved to Illinois in 1841, settling first in Alton and then going on in 1845 to Chicago, the center of the state's abolitionist movement, where he opened a tailoring business and allied himself with White abolitionists, who helped him learn how to read and write. The enterprising businessman, who was twenty-nine years old when he settled in Chicago, later constructed one of the first office buildings in Chicago's Loop and branched out as a leader of men, denouncing the Black Laws and the silence of White men like Abraham Lincoln. Tall, gaunt, "with piercing eyes and a flame touched beard," he was associated with John Brown and Frederick Douglass in the national movement to end the slavery and Black Laws Lincoln supported. In 1847, the year Lincoln paid his first visit to Chicago, Jones wrote a series of articles for Chicago's *Western Citizen* on the rights of Blacks. In 1848, the year the Illinois constitution banned Black immigration, he was a delegate to a national Black convention in Cleveland. In 1864, the year Lincoln gave his blessings to a lily-White Reconstruction government in Louisiana, he wrote a pamphlet, *The Black Laws of Illinois and A Few Reasons Why They Should Be Repealed.* During these years and later, Jones made a lot of money, but he also made a lot of freedom, befriending John Brown and Frederick Douglass and maintaining an Underground Railway station in his business.

No less talented, but less militant, was Springfield's William de Fleurville.[21] It has been said that de Fleurville, who was called "Billy the Barber," was Lincoln's friend. This was not the case; de Fleurville was at best a Lincoln acquaintance and a colored acquaintance at that. He cut Lincoln's hair and shaved him, and his barber shop was a favorite gathering place for Lincoln and other White males. Although Lincoln looked out for his legal interests, there were definite racial limitations on the relationship. Lincoln, for example, never excluded de Fleurville from his general view that Blacks were inferior racially and should be denied equal rights.

The clearest indication of the limitations of "racial" friendships is the story of their different responses to the peculiar Illinois law that taxed de Fleurville and other Blacks to pay for the schooling of White children while denying educational funds to Black children. Lincoln the legislator voted for the white-only language, which was a major bone of contention to de Fleurville and other Blacks. Did the two men ever discuss that issue? Apparently not, for Lincoln never changed his position publicly and was silent when other Whites, responding to Black and White protests, changed the law so Black tax dollars could be used for the education of Black children. After the passage of this law in 1855, de Fleurville, without any public or visible help from his "friend," led a movement to start a Black school in Springfield.

This episode is interesting not only because it illuminates Lincoln's insensitivity to the plight of Black Illinoisans but also because it underscores the obvious fact that Lincoln's (and any other oppressor's) relation with individual Negroes was irrelevant to the main issue since those relations were based on and assumed a continuation of a structure of White domination and Black subordination.

Lincoln the lawyer represented several Black clients. In 1841, he filed a divorce case for Mary Shelby. Six years later, the Lincoln and Herndon law firm appeared in the case of "Negro Bob."

There was little or no real communication in any of these cases or relationships, which were defined by the language of "Negro Bob" and the etiquette of racial subordination. Lincoln couldn't resist a sly Amos and Andy dig in his divorce petition, noting that Shelby and her husband, identified whimsically as "a gentleman of color," had lived together for several years but "not in the highest state of connubial felicity" (Frank 37). Lincoln, as they say, was a riot: even in court, he played a minstrel hand.

Lincoln said he had never been in a meeting of Negroes, but a number of his White contemporaries went to nineteenth-century "neighborhoods" and entered into a dialogue with Blacks. Zebina Eastman, for example, visited Chicago Black churches, addressed Black audiences and listened to Black petitioners. On March 3, 1853, Eastman spoke at an AME church fair in Chicago.

Eastman and other abolitionists also shared public platforms with Blacks. In 1844, Ichabod Codding, one of the major speakers of the Illinois Antislavery Society, toured Lake County with William

Jones, a free Black who told the crowd how he had been robbed and kidnapped in Chicago. Indiana Congressman George Julian even appeared on a platform with Frederick Douglass (Clarke 123).

Although Lincoln was a powerful figure in state politics for almost two decades, and although he spoke on many legislative subjects, he never uttered one word in favor of these men and movements. On the contrary, he repeatedly criticized abolitionists who attacked slavery in the South and asked for a repeal of the Illinois Black Laws. Whitney said he abhorred abolitionists (317). Lamon said he was "the steady though quiet opponent" of abolitionists like Owen Lovejoy (210). Contemporary news reports say he "scathingly" attacked the abolitionists on the stump and went to great lengths to dissociate himself from their name and program (CW 2:14).

During this period, Lincoln pressed his lifelong campaign against Black suffrage. It can be said, in fact, that he started and ended his political career supporting discrimination against Black voters. In January 1836, during his first term in the Illinois legislature, he voted, as we have indicated, to keep the franchise pure from Black contamination. Twenty-nine years later, he supported a Louisiana government which denied Blacks, including Black Union veterans, the right to vote. There is a direct line, straight as the columns on the Lincoln Memorial, from Lincoln's 1836 vote against Black suffrage to his last public speech, which endorsed invidious distinctions between Black and White voters.

Some investigators say the difference between the prairie Lincoln and the presidential Lincoln is so great that they seem to be dealing with two different men. They *are* dealing with two different men, comparing a mythical prairie Lincoln and a mythical presidential Lincoln. If they put the real Lincoln back into real history with real Negroes, real slaves and real abolitionists, Black and White, they will discover that the DNA of the prairie Lincoln and the DNA of the presidential Lincoln match perfectly. The Lincoln who voted against

Black suffrage in the Illinois legislature is the same Lincoln who proposed invidious distinctions between Black and White voters in his last public speech. The Lincoln who called for the deportation of Blacks in 1852 is the same Lincoln who drafted a constitutional amendment for the deportation of Blacks in 1862. The Lincoln who said in 1852 that freeing all slaves immediately would create a greater evil than slavery is the same Lincoln who opposed immediate emancipation until his death and who wrote a Proclamation that freed few if any slaves.

The same language. The same acts. The same excuses. The same man.

The fight to ban Black voters was apparently a major Lincoln obsession, one he returned to repeatedly. Six months after he voted to keep the suffrage pure and White, he opened his campaign for reelection to the legislature with a letter in favor of a lily-White suffrage:

NEW SALEM, JUNE 13, 1836.

To the Editor of the Journal:

In your paper of last Saturday, I see a communication over the signature of "Many voters," in which the candidates who are announced in the Journal, are called upon to "show their hands." Agreed. Here's mine.

I go for all sharing the privileges of the government, who assist in bearing its burthens. Consequently *I go for admitting all whites to the right of suffrage,* who pay taxes or bear arms, (by no means excluding females). (CW 1:48, italics added)

This was a backwards step, even for Whites, since the franchise was open then to all White males, whether they paid taxes or not. As for White females, Lincoln, as Donald and others have said, was probably making a joke since he and all his constituents knew that White women didn't pay taxes or bear arms.

Reelected to the legislature, partly because of this racist appeal, Lincoln repeatedly voted for measures denying Blacks basic rights, according to Paul Simon, whose excellent *Preparation for Greatness* I am following here, with the understanding that it is not clear to me from this record what Lincoln was preparing himself for. In the 1838-39 legislative session, for example, he voted to tax "slaves and servants of color." On December 30, 1840, he voted for a resolution instructing "the committee on Education . . . to report a bill distributing the State School Fund among the several counties, in proportion to the number of white inhabitants under twenty years of age. . . ." [22]

This opens a fascinating subject which has never been adequately explored. What did it mean to be Black in "the Land of Lincoln" in Lincoln's time? What did it mean to walk the streets of Springfield and Chicago and Alton with the man who was preparing, his defenders say, to be the great emancipator? It meant, if we can credit contemporary observers, degradation and humiliation on a world-class scale with the active support of Abraham Lincoln, who backed—by his votes, by his speeches, by his silence—a system that violently placed all Blacks outside the bonds of community and violently condemned them to subhuman status.

To be Black in Lincoln's time and in Lincoln's city, Black leaders said, was to be a legal outcast (Foner, Walker 65). To be Black in the Land of Lincoln in the 1830s, 1840s, and 1850s, in the heyday of Lincoln, was, the *Chicago Tribune* said, to be a pariah (McGaul 9). To be Black in that time, John Jones said, was to be treated "as strangers in the land of our birth, and as enemies, by those who should have been our friends" (15).

Lincoln would make his mark nationally by talking to Stephen A. Douglas about the Declaration of Independence, which neither one of them believed. Both should have been debating the Declaration with the only people in the state of Illinois who believed it, the Black Illinoisans (and their White allies) Lincoln and Douglas had helped make legal outcasts by their votes, speeches and acts of omissions and commission.

Since neither Douglas nor Lincoln paid any attention to the pleas of their victims, and since neither Sandburg nor Thomas nor any other major White Lincoln scholar deals with them in detail, it is only fair to complete the historical record by comparing what Lincoln said and believed with what his victims said and believed.

Lincoln said the Declaration of Independence didn't require equal rights and that he was in favor of denying political and civil rights to Blacks in Illinois and other states.

The representatives of Black Illinoisans said at state conventions in 1853 and 1856 "that all men are born free and equal, possessing certain inalienable rights, that can neither be conferred or taken away . . . " (Foner, Walker 52-67).

Lincoln said he was opposed to Negro citizenship.

The representatives of Black Illinoisans said "we claim to be citizens of Illinois . . . and are of right entitled to all the immunities of other citizens of the commonwealth; that we believe with the fathers of 'Seventy Six,' that taxation and representation should go together . . . ."

Lincoln said he was opposed to Black people serving as jurors and holding public office.

The representatives of Black Illinoisans said in Lincoln's time and within Lincoln's public earshot that "we are denied the right of giving our testimony in like manner with that of our white fellow-countrymen, in the courts of the State by which our persons and property, are subject to every species of violence, insult, and fraud, without any redress, even from the common law. We are also, by law, not only denied the right of citizenship, the inestimable right of voting for those who rule over us in the land of our birth, but, by the so-called 'Black Laws,' we are denied the right enjoyed by the meanest rebel that treads the surface of the earth, the right to live and possess a peaceful home on the broad and beautiful prairies of this noble State."

Lincoln supported and voted for Illinois laws that taxed Blacks for the support of schools for "white" citizens.

The representatives of Black Illinoisans, including Black representatives from Lincoln's Springfield, asked "for the removal of such positive obstructions and disabilities as past legislators [including Representative Abraham Lincoln of Sangamon County] have seen fit to throw in our way, and heap upon us," including the white-only laws that "practically excluded

[Blacks] from the schools of the State, (notwithstanding we are tax-payers), thereby denying our children the most sacred right of a national being . . . the cultivation of that intellect which the Creator has endowed them.

Lincoln said there was a physical difference between Blacks and Whites that would make it impossible to ever achieve integration in Illinois—what *would* he have thought about a Black mayor of Chicago and a Black woman United States senator who won a statewide office that he failed to win—and that it was necessary to send Blacks "back" to Africa.

The representatives of the Black Illinoisans of Lincoln's day said that "we regard all schemes for colonizing the free colored people of the United States in Africa, or in any other foreign land, originating in whatever motive, as directly calculated to increase pro-slavery prejudice, to depress our moral energies, to unsettle all our plans for improvement, and finally to perpetuate the wicked and horrible system of slavery."

Lincoln invited Whites from everywhere to settle in Illinois but never said a word against the infamous Illinois law that made it a crime for Blacks from anywhere to settle in Illinois.

"We would particularly remind you," the First Convention of the Colored Citizens of Illinois said, "of the late enactment of your Legislature, which was an attempt to strike down at a single blow, the rights of all persons having African blood in their veins, who shall come into the State to seek a peaceful home, and an honorable employment. And yet you invite all others to come freely into the State and possess it, and they shall be protected by your Republican laws. But if any colored person shall come into the State, for the very same purpose which you commend as praiseworthy in others, your Legislators have seen fit to condemn such colored persons as having committed a high crime against the State for which they shall be punished, not with death, but with that which Patrick Henry declared to be worse than death, namely, SLAVERY."

The delicate but essential point here, a point that has been overlooked or glossed over by Lincoln defenders, is that Lincoln was not only a supporter of oppression, but he was also in and of himself an oppressor, who consistently and in his own name acted to make the system of racial exploitation and violence work to keep Blacks poor, ignorant, subordinate, and exploitable.

The proof is that he consistently supported—as a private citizen, as a legislator, as a congressman, as president—one of the most violent and racist systems ever contrived by man, saying repeatedly in his own name that slaveowners had the right to do whatever they pleased with "their" slaves (CW 2:493; CW 3:116, 277).

The proof is that he consistently supported the most violent and racist act ever passed by Congress, the odious Fugitive Slave Law.

The proof is that he consistently voted for and supported the Illinois Black Code which required and/or permitted the state and private White citizens to use violence to deny Blacks the right to settle in the state and to exclude them from the common good.

All this made Lincoln in the precise sense of the word a man of violence but not necessarily a violent man, though the distinction was purely formal to the real Indians and real Blacks who were murdered, maimed or caused irreparable and irremediable harm by the measures Lincoln proposed, approved or passively accepted.

Based on this evidence, the evidence of what he said and did over a twenty-nine-year period extending from his Jim Crow vote in the Illinois legislature in 1836 to his defense of the Jim Crow Louisiana constitution in 1865, we can say that every relation between Abraham Lincoln [and any other White supporter of the System] and a Black was a relation of violence, not because it happened by violence but because it happened *in* violence and because Lincoln was a willing agent and beneficiary of a two hundred-year-old system of violence and racial extortion that defined him and other Whites as superhuman and used violence and force, with Lincoln's active consent and approval, to define all Blacks as subhuman and to exclude them from the commonwealths for racial reasons.

It is irrelevant, then, whether Lincoln said facile words or was "nice" to William de Fleurville, for the truth of the situation—which was a truth of violence and domination and dehumanization— defined Lincoln and "Billy the Barber" and continued to distort, deform and dehumanize their lives despite or—better—because of the pretty words Lincoln used to justify the situation. And perhaps we should say again that we are using the word *pretty* in a technical sense to signify sugary rhetoric that hides, masks, cloaks, veils, shrouds bitter oppression.

To the extent, then, that he made himself an instrument of the White peace, to the extent that he personally manipulated the levers of the system in order to keep four million human beings in slavery, to the extent that he personally ordered generals to return Blacks to slavery, to the extent that he personally denied Blacks equal rights, to the extent that he personally poked fun at Negroes, calling them lazy, contented, irresponsible, to the extent that he called them n——r and aunty and boy, to the extent that he spread the libel that they were unassimilable aliens who had to be segregated and denied and deported, to the extent that he said this and did this for more than twenty-nine years, *for whatever reasons,* Abraham Lincoln chose himself and practically identified himself as the common enemy of the slave and the ally, not to go further, of their torturers and murderers.

One reads everywhere or almost everywhere that Lincoln had to talk like a racist and vote like a racist because of the racist atmosphere of the time. This apology overlooks the relatively large number of White politicians who acted and voted for freedom despite racism.[23]

In Pennsylvania, Thaddeus Stevens, the future leader of the wartime House of Representatives, singlehandedly defeated an attempt to bar Black immigration and refused to sign a constitution that limited voting to White males. (Woodley, 108-12).

In Massachusetts, in 1849, Charles Sumner inaugurated the century-long public school struggle, arguing in *Roberts vs. the City of Boston* against segregated schools.

In New York, Senator Seward, Lincoln's secretary of state, spoke out for Negro suffrage.

Will someone say that these men lived in the liberal East and that they didn't face the problems White politicians faced in the Midwest? What then are we to say about the great Ohio trio—future senator and Secretary of the Treasury Salmon P. Chase, future Senator Benjamin Wade, and Congressmen Joshua Giddings—and their brilliant campaigns in the 1840s and 1850s for Negro suffrage and repeal of the Black Laws that Lincoln supported in Illinois. In 1845, Chase called for equal suffrage and denounced "the whole policy of our legislature in relation to the colored population." Four years later, in 1849, the year Congressman Abraham Lincoln opposed an anti-slave trade resolution, Chase drafted a bill to repeal Ohio's Black Laws.

Nor was he alone.

In Michigan, Civil War Governor Austin Blair backed Negro suffrage. In the same state, DeWitt Leach, a future congressman, supported Negro suffrage at the constitutional convention of 1850.

Indiana and Illinois were in a dead heat in the contest for the worst Northern state, but three delegates who later became congressmen, Schuyler Colfax, William Dunn, and David Kilgore, opposed Negro exclusion at the Indiana constitutional convention of 1850, and another future congressman, George W. Julian, led the fight against Black Laws.

There was even some action in Illinois where John M. Palmer, Jesse O. Norton, James Knox and even Lincoln's conservative friends, David Davis and James Matheny, opposed the Negro Exclusion Act at the constitutional convention of 1847.

Year by year, while Lincoln remained silent, deprecating their efforts, sensitive Illinois representatives presented petitions calling for integrated schools, repeal of the Black Laws, and an end to taxation without representation.

With the election of the first abolitionist state representative, Owen Lovejoy, brother of the martyred Elijah Parish Lovejoy, "a new sound," Edward Magdol said, "was heard in the House" and "a new spirit breathed into the language and precepts of Jefferson and Paine," a new spirit, one might add, that was never heard in the legislature in Lincoln's day and was certainly never heard from Abraham Lincoln (121).

Elected in 1854, Lovejoy lost no time in raising the banner of freedom, introducing a bill to repeal the Black Laws that denied Blacks the right to testify in courts. The bill was tabled, but Lovejoy, undaunted, continued to raise the issue, and people came from all over on February 6, 1855, one month after Lincoln called for the colonization of Blacks, to hear him make *the first abolitionist speech* in the Illinois General Assembly in support of three resolutions that would have instructed Illinois representatives and senators in Congress to oppose the extension of slavery and to vote for a repeal of the Fugitive Slave Law. Lovejoy said the new Republican Party had opened a new era in American life. It "had stepped forth like Minerva from the head of Jupiter, full grown, and fully equipped for the battle, and has already indeed gained no inconsiderable victories."

Lovejoy went on to say that the Fugitive Slave Law, which Lincoln supported, was degrading to all Americans and that he, an elected official of the state of Illinois, would not obey that law, even if it cost him imprisonment or death.

When Lovejoy finished, there was resounding applause, and some people cried. A boundary of sorts had been crossed in the state of Illinois, and the Springfield correspondent of the *Chicago Tribune* wrote: "This has been a great day for the state and the cause of Humanity. *For the first time in the history of Illinois*, a regular Abolitionist, in his place in the Hall of the House of Representatives, has made a speech in defense of his principles, and hundreds of persons heard for the first time, the enunciation of such principles from one whose history and character are a guaranty that he would nothing extenuate." People said later that "Lovejoy . . . made the greatest speech ever made in the State House. . . " (Magdol 121-6, italics added).

One would have expected someone to say that about one of Lincoln's speeches to the legislature if the Abraham Lincoln of mythology had been real and if he had lived in Illinois in those days.

But, *unhappily, there was no Abraham Lincoln in Illinois in Abraham Lincoln's time.*

While the flesh-and-blood Lincoln, a very different person from the mythical Lincoln, was keeping the suffrage pure and White and voting for a White school system, other Whites were mobilizing to end the slave system. The decade of the thirties began with the revolt of the Reverend Nathaniel Turner and the founding of William Lloyd's Garrison's *Liberator* and ended with the escape of Black abolitionist Frederick Douglass and the national mobilization of political abolitionists like James Birney and Salmon P. Chase. All over the country now, on every level, men and women, Black and White, were laying the foundations of the antislavery campaign that triumphed two decades later in the Thirteenth Amendment. Instead of joining these men and women, Lincoln ran away from them (HW 299). Instead of helping them, Lincoln hindered them, saying in a mildly worded 1837 "protest" that slavery in the abstract was bad but that abolitionism was probably worse (CW 1:75).

In the beginning, then, as in the middle and end of the antislavery crusade, Lincoln was more of a hindrance than a help. If there is any doubt on that score, one need only examine his nonrole in a defining event of the period, the martyrdom of Owen Lovejoy's brother, abolitionist editor Elijah Parish Lovejoy. When, in Alton, Illinois, on November 7, 1837, a White mob murdered Lovejoy and threw his press into the Mississippi River, Lincoln was characteristically silent. Worse, when, some three months later, he made a big speech to the Young Men's Lyceum of Springfield about "The Perpetuation of Our Political Institutions," he didn't mention Lovejoy by name or deal with the Alton lynching, except to say, in passing, seven vague words about the impropriety of shooting editors and throwing printing presses into the river (CW 1:111).

How explain Lincoln's silence at this turning point of morals and worlds? The answer is plain, and troubling. The "better sort" of people were either in the mob or associated with the mob, and Lincoln, to borrow a phrase Oates used in another connection (38), "was not about to ruin his career" by speaking out for an "extremist" whose methods and *goals* he deplored. A second and probably more pressing reason for his silence was that at least three of his friends and associates—Alton businessman John Hogan, Alton's state senator Cyrus Edwards, who was widely touted as the next governor, and Illinois Attorney General Usher F. Linder—were directly or indirectly implicated in the Lovejoy murder. Linder, in fact, egged the mob on and tried to imprison the men who helped Lovejoy.

Linder and other people in the mob or on the fringes of the mob, and the vast number of silent people in Springfield, could do a lot to help a young legislator, and it is a reasonable surmise, Simon said, that Lincoln remained silent in part to advance his career. Whatever the reason, Simon—a former United States senator whose racial standards were higher than Lincoln's—said "the silence of Lincoln on the Lovejoy incident is not Lincoln's most shining hour" (125).

Unquestionably; the problem, however, is that Lincoln didn't have any shining hours on Black freedom before the Proclamation, and the moonlight of that event came from the sun of militants and slaves.

If Lincoln didn't mention Lovejoy by name in the Lyceum speech, he named himself, leaving all kinds of footprints leading to the real Lincoln. It was in this speech, as almost everybody has noted since Edmund Wilson's essay in *Patriotic Gore,* that Lincoln unwittingly and unconsciously revealed his grandiosity and "the field of glory" he hoped to occupy (CW 1:108-15), warning the nation against men of talent and ambition seeking new new fields of glory—"This field of glory is harvested, and the crop is already appropriated. But new reapers will arise, and *they,* too, will seek a field."

What fields would the glory-seekers seek? "Towering genius," he replied, "disdains a beaten path. It seeks regions hitherto unexplored. It sees no *distinction* in adding story to story, upon the monuments of fame, erected to the memory of others. It *denies* that it is glory enough to serve under any chief. It *scorns* to tread in the footsteps of *any* predecessor, however illustrious. It thirsts and burns for distinction; and, if possible, it will have it, whether at the expense of emancipating slaves, or enslaving freemen." Or, I would add, reenslaving freedmen, as President Lincoln did.

Lincoln was contemptuous of men who aspired to "nothing beyond a seat in Congress, a gubernatorial or a presidential chair." Such men, Lincoln said—and it is hard to believe that he didn't know he was revealing himself—*"belong not to the family of the lion, or the tribe of the eagle"* (CW 1:108-15).

If Lincoln didn't know what he was saying, his unconscious did, and it or perhaps the conscious Lincoln italicized the phrase. In any event, there is a broad consensus on this point: Abraham Lincoln was describing himself and "the field of glory" of his dreams.

It was in this speech incidentally that Lincoln said that bad laws "should be religiously observed"—an alarming observation in view of Stalin's Russia and Hitler's Germany, not to mention the Slave South of his day or the segregated South of our own (CW 1:112). Phillips was clearer and more prophetic, saying: "The best use of good laws is to teach men to trample bad laws under their feet" (PS 91). This was also the opinion of Salmon P. Chase, who told a Black group in Cincinnati that every unjust law "tends to the overthrow of all law, by separating in the minds of the people, the idea of law from the idea of right" (Niven 85).

Once again, unmistakably, we are confronted with one of the defining structures of Lincoln's life: his commitment to the status quo, to any status quo, as long as it was status and quo. One of Lincoln's weaknesses, Herndon said, was "a kind of blind worship of old things . . ." (HH 211). The corollary of this was a fear of social disorder—a point that has been noted by several commentators, although it has not been given, to my knowledge, the significance it deserves. For in all situations of total disorder, in apartheid South Africa, in the American South and North, and in the big cities of today, men and women of the oppressing group have used the fear of social disorder as a distraction to hide themselves from themselves and to keep from dealing with the total disorder that defines them and their situation. It was characteristic of Lincoln, whose policy was based on a fear of the disorder emancipation would bring, and perhaps a fear of the personal disorder that threatened his sanity, that he invested so much energy as a private citizen and as president in fruitless moves to prevent immediate emancipation, which he defined as social disorder.

The demagogue who uses racism to get elected and to keep his opponent from getting elected, the demagogue who calls his opponent a Negro-lover, the demagogue who says his opponent is endangering the power of White men and the virtue of White women, is a stock American figure, older than the Capitol, more American than firecrackers on the Fourth. From Monticello to the subtle and not-so-subtle attacks on the Kennedys and Clintons, the prairies and hills have reverberated with the sound of men shouting Whiter Than Thou. Some of the voices have been brazen and shameless; some have been discreet and shameless—"In Your Heart You Know He's Right"—but all have used racism to get ahead and to keep their opponents—and Negroes—down and out. Stephen A. Douglas, Andrew Johnson, Theodore Bilbo, Cotton Ed Smith, Eugene Talmadge, George Wallace—call the roll, the names and styles are endless and includes, shocking as it may sound, the name and style of Abraham Lincoln, who demonstrated an unsuspected talent for low racial demagoguery. In a typical instance in 1840, Lincoln organized and led a smear campaign against Democratic presidential candidate Martin Van Buren. What was Van Buren's offense? Lamon said Lincoln "imputed to Van Buren the great sin of having voted in the New York State Convention for Negro suffrage with a property qualification" (436).

In his zeal to expose that "sin," Lincoln violated the standards of even cynical politicians by personally involving himself in a search for racially inflammatory material to use against his opponents. In a

March letter to John T. Stuart, who was visiting New York City, he said "you must not fail to send us the New York journal . . ." (CW 1:206). The next month he wrote to a Chicagoan visiting New York: "Do not fail to procure a copy of the *Journal* of the New York Convention of 1821" (CW 1:209).

Why was Lincoln so excited about the New York Convention?

It was in this convention, Lincoln contended, that Van Buren committed the "sin" of voting for the idea that the same standards should apply to Black voters and White voters.

In a speech at Tremont, Illinois, on May 2, 1840, Lincoln opposed this idea, criticizing "the political course of Mr. Van Buren, and especially his votes in the New York Convention in allowing Free Negroes the right of suffrage . . ."(CW 1:210). Debating his perennial opponent, Stephen A. Douglas, Lincoln, according to James H. Matheny and William Herndon, asserted that "Van Buren had voted for Negro suffrage under certain limitations. Douglas said it was a forgery. Lincoln then [produced documentary proof]. Douglas got mad—snatched up the book and Slung it into the crowd—saying "d——n such a book" (HI 471).

Lincoln wasn't ashamed of his demagoguery. He reveled in his triumph and told the story far and wide. "Lincoln told me this story too," Herndon said (HH 380-1).

Someone will say that this sounds bad but at least Lincoln didn't stoop to the level of calling his political opponent a Negro-lover. Whoever says that hasn't read the record. For as one of the editors of a Whig campaign paper called *The Old Soldier*, Lincoln implied, as all demagogues imply, that Van Buren was a Negro-lover with dangerous ideas about Negro suffrage. Lincoln and his coeditors left no doubt about their views in the July 28, 1840, edition, which was full of inflammatory racial appeals.

One headline said:

MARTIN VAN BUREN FOR FREE NEGRO SUFFRAGE.

Another headline and story said the Democratic presidential candidate was the Black candidate:

"Hung be the Heavens with Black."

A recent manifestation of Mr. Van Buren's love for Free Negroes.

In a late trial of Lieut. Hooe of the United States Navy, before a Court Martial, two NEGROES were permitted to be witnesses against him. Lt. Hooe protested against receiving their evidence. It WAS received, however; and Mr. Van Buren has given his OFFI-CIALSANCTION [SIC] TO THE MEASURE—*thus showing that Martin Van Buren* is in favor of allowing *FREE NEGROES and SLAVES* to swear in Courts against *WHITE MEN!!*

Lincoln and his coeditors were shocked and asked:

"Should not Mr. Van Buren be called the 'NEGRO WITNESS' candidate!"

We don't know what to call Van Buren, but there's no doubt about what to call Lincoln and his coeditors.

Shall we say, as all good Lincolnians say, that this was an unfortunate detour by the young Lincoln—he was thirty-one—who immediately returned to the malice-toward-none mode. We can say that, but it wouldn't be true, for twelve years later, Lincoln dug deeper into the demagoguery pile by suggesting that Douglas, if triumphant, would "hie away to the African church in Richmond, Virginia, and make a great speech" in which he would "thrill, and electrify, and throw into spasms of ecstasy his African church auditors . . ." (CW 2:141).

In the same campaign, Lincoln implied all kinds of dirty things because another Democratic presidential candidate, Franklin Pierce, had *reportedly* said that he loathed the Fugitive Slave Law. It was not an accident, Lincoln said, that Pierce was casting aspersions on the Fugitive Slave Law, for what the Democrats wanted to do was to hold their Southern base and attract Free Soil votes. The issue, Lincoln said, mixing sexual and political metaphors, was political amalgamation. For "should Pierce ever be President, he will, politically speaking, not only be a mulatto; but he will be a good deal darker one than Sally Brown" (CW 2:157).

Whatever others may have since believed about the matter, a Lincoln contemporary, abolitionist H. Ford Douglass, had no doubts about the color of Lincoln's convictions. Addressing a Fourth of July mass meeting in Massachusetts in 1860, Douglass said, "I know Abraham Lincoln," adding that he had personal knowledge of Lincoln's "pro-slavery character and principles," especially his support of the Fugitive Slave Law, his equivocal record as a congressman and his support of the Black Laws of Illinois. "In the State of Illinois, where I live," Douglass said, ". . . we have a code of black laws that would disgrace any Barbary State . . . . Men of my complexion are not allowed to testify in a court of justice, where a white man is a party. If a white man happens to owe me anything, unless I can prove it by the testimony of a white man, I cannot collect the debt" (Zilversmit 65-7).

Some people said then—and some people say now—that it was not fair to blame Lincoln for this situation. Maybe he didn't know about the Black Laws. Maybe he didn't know what kind of state he was living in. These alibis, which are automatically put forward to explain the silence and apathy of the "good people," are of little value to hard-pressed Lincoln defenders. For not only did Lincoln know about the laws, he voted for them in the legislature and supported them on the stump and in other public forums.

In 1858—the year Lincoln historians say he spoke so eloquently about his love for the Declaration of Independence—H. Ford Douglass said he, Douglass, "went through the State of Illinois for the purpose of getting signers to a petition, asking the Legislature to repeal the 'Testimony Law,' so as to permit colored men to testify against white men. I went to prominent Republicans, and among others, to Abraham Lincoln and Lyman Trumbull, and neither of them dared to sign that petition, to give me the right to testify in a court of justice!"

Nor was this all.

In Lincoln's Illinois, he said, "they tax the Negro's property to support schools for the education of the white man's children, but the colored people are not permitted to enjoy any of the benefits resulting from that taxation. We are compelled to impose upon ourselves additional taxes, in order to educate our children. The State lays its iron hand upon the Negro, holds him down, and puts the other hand into his pocket and steals his hard earnings, to educate the children of white men; and if we sent our children to school, Abraham Lincoln would kick them out, in the name of Republicanism and anti-slavery!"

Douglass was a little too harsh on Lincoln. Lincoln wouldn't have kicked Black children out of school, but he wouldn't have said a word to get them in and he wouldn't have said a word to keep others from kicking them out.

To the dismay of his biographers and Lincoln Day Orators everywhere, Lincoln was indiscreet enough to say on public platforms that he believed in the Illinois Black Laws that Douglass and other Blacks deplored. It was in Charleston, Illinois, on Saturday, September 18, 1858, a day that will live in infamy to all those condemned to the unenviable task of denying the undeniable, that Lincoln defined himself for the ages, announcing:

> I will say then that I am not, nor ever have been in favor of bringing about in any way the social and political equality of the white and black races, [applause]—that I am not nor ever have been in favor of making voters or jurors of Negroes, nor of qualifying them to hold office, nor to intermarry with white people; and I will say in addition to this that there is a physical difference between the white and black races which I believe will for ever forbid the two races living together on terms of social and political equality. And inasmuch as they cannot so live, while they do remain together there must be the position of superior and inferior, and I as much as any other man am in favor of having the superior position assigned to the white race. (CW 3:145-6)

So there he is, then, everybody's, or almost everybody's, favorite President, confessing his racial faith and giving unimpeachable testimony before some fifteen thousand Whites that he was opposed to equal rights and that he believed there was a physical difference between the Black and White races that would FOR EVER forbid them living together on terms of political and social equality.

The Charleston speech in which Lincoln said these terrible things is not in a foreign language. It is not in Latin or Swahili or Greek—it is in short, blunt Anglo-Saxon words, and no literate person can misunderstand the man or his meaning. Who was he? He was, he said, a racist who believed, as much as any other White man, in White supremacy and the subordination of Blacks.

How do the defenders of the faith deal with this smoking-gun evidence? They deny, first of all, that the gun is smoking or that it is even a gun. Few Lincoln defender, for example, quote that paragraph in its entirety *or in context*. The usual practice is to paraphrase the offending paragraph without telling us what Lincoln said.

Another technique is to give us the paragraph or parts of the paragraph, en passant, and to smother the harsh words with great Mahlerian choruses of affirmation. Neely, in fact, praises Lincoln for his restraint, saying that in this statement Lincoln went as far as he was going to go in denying Black rights (1993, 53). But a man who denies Blacks equality because of their race, and who denies them the right to vote, sit on juries or hold office, couldn't have gone much further.

All who report the statement in whole or in part give Lincoln instant absolution (see page 122-3). Fehrenbacher and Donald say Lincoln was *forced* to make the statement. "The whole texture of American life," Fehrenbacher says, "*compelled* such a pronouncement in 1858, and the Lincoln of history would not exist if he had failed to comply" (1962, 111, italics added). Fehrenbacher, a sophisticated scholar who has added to our knowledge of the nineteenth century, didn't mean that, for he knows that sticks and stones can break bones but that a *texture* can't compel a grown man to say anything.

Donald, like Fehrenbacher, said it was politically expedient and perhaps "a necessary thing" for Lincoln to say he was a racist in a state where most Whites were racist, adding, to his credit, that the statement "also represented Lincoln's deeply held personal views." Having conceded the main point, Donald says paradoxically that it was not Lincoln's true feeling and that Lincoln was not "personally hostile to blacks" (221). But here, once again, an attempt to prove that Lincoln was not a racist backfires and ends up proving the opposite. For what could be more hostile than an attempt by any man to deny a whole race of people equal rights because of race?

Almost all Lincoln specialists blame not Lincoln but Stephen Douglas who, they say, made Lincoln say it. According to this theory, Lincoln, pressured by Douglas, said he was a racist because he, wanted to get elected to office. The proof, they say, is that he was ashamed of what he said at Charleston and didn't say it again.

If Lincoln was ashamed, he had a strange way of showing it. For he traveled all over Illinois and the Midwest, proudly quoting the Charleston Confession, even to people who couldn't vote for him. Nineteen days after the Charleston speech, he quoted the same words to an even larger crowd at Galesburg. A month later, he prepared an extract of *his best* speeches on the subject and listed the Charleston Confession (CW 3:326-8). A year later, in Columbus, Ohio, he was still quoting the Charleston speech to prove that he was opposed to equal rights.

The most ingenious—and startling—explanation of what Lincoln said at Charleston comes from the Bogart School (see page 211), which praises the aesthetics of the Charleston Confession while deploring its sentiments. At least one interpreter, Pulitzer Prize-winner Garry Wills, said there was poetry or potential poetry in the passage, which he scanned:

> I will say then/that I am not/nor ever have been/in favor of bringing about/in any way/ the social and political equality/of the white and black races . . . .

In a triumph of style over content, Wills said that what Lincoln said was indefensible but that he said it "in prose as clear, balanced, and precise as anything he ever wrote,"a view that depends, of course, on one's perspective and one's understanding of prose and clarity (92).

What shall we call the scanned Lincoln lines? The poetics of racism or the racism of any poetic that subordinates any man or woman to any other man or woman because of race, color, or religion?

And to understand the truth of Lincoln's poetic, and how one racism invokes and includes all racisms, one must make another transposition and ask what Lincoln's words would sound like in another language and another color:

> *I will say then . . .*
> *that I am not*
> *nor ever have been*
> *in favor of*
> *making voters*
> *or jurors*
> *of Irishmen*
> *or Italians*
> *or Albanians.*

It's the same principle, and Lincoln pressed that principle from one end of the state to the other from the 1830s to the 1860s.

Between 1854 and 1860, Lincoln said publicly at least two times that America was made for the White people and "not for the Negroes."

At least eight times, he said publicly that he was in favor of White supremacy.

At least twenty-one times, he said publicly that he was opposed to equal rights for Blacks.

He said it at Ottawa:

> I have no purpose to introduce political and social equality between the white and black races. There is a physical difference between the two, which in my judgment will probably forever forbid their living

together upon the footing of perfect equality, and inasmuch as it becomes a necessity that there must be a difference, I, as well as Judge Douglas, am in favor of the race to which I belong, having the superior position. (CW 3:16)

He said it at Galesburg:

I have all the while maintained that inasmuch as there is a physical inequality between the white and black, that the blacks must remain inferior . . . . (Holzer 1993, 254)

He said it in Ohio. He said it in Wisconsin. He said it in Indiana. He said it everywhere:

We can not, then, make them equals. (CW 2:256)

Why couldn't "we" make "them" equals?

There was, Lincoln said, a strong feeling in White America against Black equality, and "MY OWN FEELINGS," he said, capitalizing the words, "WILL NOT ADMIT OF THIS . . ." (CW 3:79).

Is that a prelude to greatness, or what?

If we examine Lincoln's two-year prelude as a congressman from Illinois, we find the same record of equivocation and racism. A number of young politicians—Chase, Giddings, Sumner, Stevens, even William Seward of New York—distinguished themselves by antislavery efforts in pre-Civil War Congresses. In sharp and revealing contrast, Lincoln straddled the fence, voting for and against slavery.

Lincoln said later that he voted at least forty times against the Wilmot antislavery amendment, but this, as almost all Lincoln scholars concede, was campaign oratory. The consensus is that he voted in general for bills banning slavery in the territories, but did not attack slavery where it existed. Nor did he associate himself with congressmen who were digging the institution's grave. Donald W. Riddle, the authority on Lincoln the congressman, said "he did not make any attempt to advocate or support antislavery or abolitionist measures" (178).

During this period, Illinois sent several talented men to Congress, and almost all of them were more creative and more daring in opposing slavery than Lincoln. "Long John" Wentworth, for example, did something in Illinois that would have been unthinkable for Lincoln: he signed a petition asking for a repeal of the law barring testimony by Blacks.

Looking back later, Wentworth said the Lincoln of history is a myth. "Lincoln was elected to the House . . . " he wrote. "What did he say? What did he do? Who knew him?" Look at the record dispassionately, Wentworth said. "Look at his official acts in the Legislature & then read the Globe very carefully. His motions were few & his speeches were few . . . . Born & educated a whig, a notoriously conservative party, called a fossil or old fogy party, wherein did he show himself radical? What new measures did he start? Where did he show progress?" (HI 194-5).

Riddle said "the most conspicuous feature" of Lincoln's congressional career on the slavery issue was his "discreet silence." There were, he noted, thirty-six full-length speeches on slavery in the short session, but none by Lincoln. This was in marked contrast to Lincoln's Illinois contemporaries. Wentworth, Riddle says,"was much more aggressive than Lincoln. Even Lincoln's colleagues [Thomas] Turner and [Orlando] Ficklin were among the thirty-six speakers on slavery . . . . But Lincoln remained silent" (179).

From all this, from Lincoln's silence on slavery in Congress, his Jim Crow votes in the legislature, his demagoguery on the stump and his Charleston Confession, it is clear that Lincoln's equivocal, equivocating prairie years were a dress rehearsal for his equivocal, equivocating performance as president. Based on this résumé, a reasonably intelligent riverboat gambler would have given odds that this man as president would support slavery where it existed and oppose sudden and general changes in the status quo of slaves *and* Blacks. That's precisely what Lincoln did, and it is curious that most Lincoln experts, with the benefit of 135 years of hindsight *and the record of what he actually did,* can't tell us what role the Illinois Lincoln was rehearsing for.

Two authorities on Lincoln's congressional career, Riddle and Reinhard H. Luthin, were justifiably severe in their appraisal of this phase of Lincoln's career, expressing from different perspectives the findings of this study. Riddle said Lincoln was an opportunist who used the slavery issue "to advance his own political standing" (249). Luthin said Lincoln "had drifted with the tide, and up to his election as President in 1860 he had left no record of achievement, except the quest for office" (242).

10

Toward The Ethnic Cleansing
Of America

IF Lincoln had had his way, there would be no Blacks in America. None. Harlem would be a white way, the South Sides would be pale sides and there would be a deafening silence and holes the size of the Grand Canyon where Bojangles and Louis and Duke and Martin Luther King and Michael Jordan and Toni Morrison would be.

If this social, political and cultural disaster didn't happen, Lincoln deserves no credit, for he did everything he could to deport Blacks and to make America a Great White Place.

Lincoln's "long," "dismal," and "pathetic" campaign to ship Blacks to Africa or some other tropical clime surfaced in the 1850s in seven major addresses and a flurry of organizational activity in support of the national push for a final solution to the "race" problem.[24]

The first address, a eulogy delivered in the Hall of Representatives in Springfield, Illinois, on Tuesday, July 6, 1852, in honor of his mentor, Henry Clay, brought together the two dominant themes of his life, the grandeur of "the white man's" Declaration of Independence and the need to defend it and keep it White and pure by banishing all Blacks—by deportation, colonization, emigration—from what he considered a White Eden.

Lincoln inherited *both* ideas from Clay and Thomas Jefferson, both of whom said the words *all men* et cetera with great eloquence and kept their slaves and never stopped apologizing and asking others to repent before it was too late by sending *their* slaves —not the capital derived from the slaves—"back" to Africa. Lincoln was especially indebted to Clay who, he said, taught him all he knew about slavery. I think the word *all* is too strong, but that's the word Lincoln used, and he was in a position to know what he was talking about. Did he not tell a crowd of White people at Carlinville, "I can express all my views on the slavery question by quotations from Henry Clay. Doesn't this look like we are akin?" (CW 3:79).

It does indeed, and it explains why Lincoln mourned and celebrated slaveholder Henry Clay from the vantage point of the plantation houses of the world. There was a vast and unbridgeable chasm between Lincoln and a man like Phillips, who evaluated Clay from the vantage point of the slave shacks and who said in *his* eulogy that he and the slaves were glad God had removed another obstacle from their path.

"When we think of such a man as Henry Clay," Phillips said, "his long life, his mighty influence cast always into the scale against the slave,—of that irresistible fascination with which he moulded every one to his will; when we remember that, his conscience acknowledging the justice of our cause, and his heart open on every other side to the gentlest impulses, he could sacrifice so remorsely his convictions and the welfare of millions to his low ambition; when we think how the slave trembled at the sound of his voice, and that, from a multitude of breaking hearts there went up nothing but gratitude to God when it pleased him to call that great sinner from this world,—we cannot find it in our hearts, we could not shape our lips to ask any man to do him honor" (PS 113-4).

Another man who spoke from the vantage point of the slaves in this season was Frederick Douglass, who by a striking coincidence delivered his great Fourth of July Address in the same season and on almost the same day as Lincoln's paean of praise for the Kentucky slaveowner. It was Lincoln and Clay, or people like Lincoln and Clay, that Douglass had in mind—we shall return to this—when he said on July 5 at Rochester, New York, that the Fourth of July was a fraud and America was conceived in blood and hypocrisy.

Speaking the next day from the vantage point of *that* nation, which he seemed to think was almost perfect, Lincoln praised "the great sinner" Phillips had deplored and the "white-man's" Declaration of Independence that Douglass had denounced, reminding the White crowd in the Hall of Representatives in Springfield of the first American Fourth of July and the good fight "for the maintainance" of the Declaration, a fight that Henry Clay had continued, Lincoln said, in his own way (CW 2:121).

How could a slaveholder lead a movement in favor of the idea that all men are created equal?

Lincoln anticipated that question, saying that although Clay owned slaves he "ever was, on principle and in feeling, opposed to slavery" (CW 2:130). The key words here are *on principle and in feeling*. Everybody knew that Clay was one of the biggest slaveowners in Kentucky and the major architect of the series of compromises that had saved slavery in America, perhaps forever. Lincoln's fellow Illinoisan, H. Ford Douglass, said that Clay "did as much to perpetuate Negro slavery in this country as any other man who has ever lived" (Zilversmit 65). That elementary fact, known to everybody and most especially to Clay's slaves, who slaved and bled and died not in principle but in fact, was unimportant in the Lincoln ledger. What was important, Lincoln said, was that Clay was opposed to slavery "on principle."

By this linguistic maneuver, which Lincoln used everywhere, one could make night day and a Kentucky slaveowner "a friend of freedom, "for almost everybody, including hard-hearted slavedrivers, was in favor of the Sermon On The Mount on principle. And we shall understand nothing about Lincoln or the Emancipation Proclamation or the Gettysburg Address if we don't understand first that everything he said, especially on the subjects of race and slavery, has to be translated from *on principle* to *in fact* and from *abstract* to *concrete*. Thus, when Lincoln said *he* was opposed to slavery, he meant he was opposed to slavery not in the slave South but on principle. The same thing was true of the statements he made about the "white man's" Declaration.

Almost all Lincoln experts have accepted these statements at face value, which is incredible in view of the fact that Lincoln said everywhere that he believed in that document *in principle* but did not believe that it gave any Negro in fact any concrete right that any White man was bound to respect in Illinois or in Georgia, except possibly life, though nobody who believed, as Lincoln believed, that he had a *duty* to return fugitive slaves to slavery and torture and possibly death believed in fact that any Negro had any concrete rights slaveholders were bound to respect.

Must we go further? Must we say once again that Lincoln, like Jefferson, like Clay, had an Orwellian relationship with words, and that he always spoke with a forked tongue when he was talking about Blacks, slaves, and freedom? That's why he said in the much-praised Clay eulogy, with no sense of shame, that "Mr. Clay's predominant sentiment, from first to last, was a deep devotion to the cause of human liberty—a strong sympathy with the oppressed every where, and an ardent wish for their elevation" (CW 2:126).

There is an iron link between such language and the racism that made slavery and the Illinois Black Laws possible and profitable. For politicians who say stones are bread and that a slaveholder is a freedom fighter are distorting reality and preparing the way for slavery, whatever their intentions and whatever their name. The linguistic maneuver that made it possible for Lincoln to call a Kentucky slaveholder who bought and sold men and women and whipped them, or had them whipped, a friend of liberty and of the *oppressed everywhere* was one of the most notable auguries of the social and political confusion that led to Fort Sumter and the graves at Gettysburg.

The proof of these words was in the practice. For Lincoln praised the Kentucky slaveholder not in defense of the oppressed everywhere but in defense of slavery in America in 1852. He praised Clay, in other words, not for Clay's sake but for the sake of underlining and emphasizing the six major articles in the Lincoln Doctrine he had inherited from Clay.

The first article in the Lincoln Doctrine was that it was necessary for all good White men to support the Missouri Compromise and to stop arguing over "that unfortunate source of discord—Negro slavery" (CW 2:127). The Missouri Compromise, which Clay helped craft and which was, Lincoln said, a testimonial to Clay's "inventive genius," had temporarily stayed the gathering battle lines by dividing the country geographically between slave and free states. This was a delicate agreement that required, Lincoln said, a spirit of compromise in both the South and the North—he meant the *White* South and the *White* North.

Above all else, it required, as Lincoln said elsewhere and almost everywhere, Northern Whites to defend the "right" of slaveholders to hold Blacks in slavery and to carry out their "duty" of returning fugitive slaves to their "rightful owners" to be whipped and rechained. To be fair, Lincoln never said the slaves should be whipped, but he had seen the Negro jails and whipping posts in the South and he knew—he had to know—that a runaway slave who was returned to Clay or almost any other slaveholder was punished. Some, in fact, were tortured; some were shipped farther South to be whipped and broken; some were murdered.

In support of the Missouri Compromise, Lincoln quoted not Clay but Jefferson, who had said, from retirement, that the Missouri Compromise controversy over the extension of slavery awakened him from his long sleep "like a fire bell in the night . . . and filled me with terror" (Ford 10:157-8). Certain writers have managed to suggest that Jefferson was awakened suddenly, after a lifetime of backsliding and holding slaves and defending slavery, to the horror of slavery. But it wasn't slavery that awakened the principal author of the Declaration of Independence—he *never* awakened from that deep sleep—but the controversy over the *compromise* that guaranteed the existence of slavery. As that controversy spread, Jefferson realized with alarm that the issue was far from settled. The controversy, he said, "is hushed, indeed, for the moment" but "this is a reprieve only, not a final sentence. A geographical line, coinciding with a marked principle, moral and political, once conceived and held up to the angry passions of men, will never be obliterated; and every irritation will mark it deeper and deeper."

What Jefferson omitted to say was that he himself had made the crisis inevitable by the line he himself had drawn in the dust of the American soul and by his failure to lead either by words or example. In quoting him, Lincoln failed to note that Jefferson wrote these eloquent words, as he wrote all his eloquent words, surrounded in fact or in spirit, by the more than 180 slaves he never emancipated, not even in his will, the more than 180 slaves who created and defined Thomas Jefferson and his world, including the words he wrote to deny them, and exclude them.

Lincoln, like Jefferson, kept the words and denied the slaves. Thus, the second major article of the Lincoln Doctrine was that slavery was so "complex" and involved racial problems so deep and explosive that it was insoluble in White terms. It was Jefferson, Lincoln noted approvingly, who said that the words of the Declaration of Independence were one thing but White "necessity"—Lincoln's term—was another. Did not the sainted Jefferson say of the Declaration and slaves: "We have the wolf by the ears, and we can neither hold him, nor safely let him go. . . . " (CW 2:128-9)? Which is, I suppose, good strategy if you are dealing with wolves instead of human beings.

That distinction didn't deter Lincoln who agreed with Jefferson—this was the third article of the Lincoln Doctrine—that holding the wolf [slave] by the ears was better than letting him go at once. Lincoln was reminded that Clay "did not perceive, as I think no wise man has perceived, how it [slavery] could be at *once* eradicated, without producing a greater evil, even to the cause of human liberty itself." To make sure there would be no mistake about his meaning,

Lincoln himself underlined the words at *once* (CW 2:130).

Like all "wise" men who believed this, like Clay and Jefferson and Madison, and like all the "wise" men who believed it and were too wise to say it, Lincoln believed that freedom was worse than slavery. Someone will say that this is a shocking charge and that Lincoln only—*only*— believed that freedom for Blacks was worse than slavery. But freedom, like slavery, is indivisible; and a man who defines freedom by color and who believes that freeing four million people *immediately* is a greater evil than keeping four million people in slavery indefinitely believes freedom is worse than slavery, however he defines it and however his apologists defend it.

In any event, one thing is certain: Lincoln believed that freeing all slaves immediately by an Emancipation Proclamation or even a Thirteenth Amendment would produce a greater evil than the continuation of a nation half slave and half free.

The fourth point followed from this as night follows the day: The proponents of freedom were as bad as the proponents of slavery. In fact, they were—in the Lincoln Doctrine and in the doctrine of the Lincoln guild—worse, a point that Lincoln emphasized by harshly attacking the abolitionists, whom he loathed, while rapping the knuckles of slaveholders, whom he admired and whom he called his "brethren."

This, of course, was a variation on the extremists on both sides of the issue, and one of the secrets of Lincoln's continuing vogue is that he was history's greatest master in refusing to choose sides in a struggle between freedom and the other side. Anyone who doubts this need only read the words he used to denounce the extremists on both sides of the slavery issue. Noting, as we have noted, that he and Clay believed that immediate freedom would produce a greater evil than slavery, Lincoln said in the next sentence—notice the *therefore*—that Clay's "feeling and his judgment, therefore, ever led him to oppose both extremes of opinion on the subject." What were the extremes? On the one hand, there were "those who would shiver into fragments the Union of these States; tear to tatters its now venerated constitution; and even burn the last copy of the Bible, rather than slavery should continue a single hour, together with all their more halting sympathisers . . ." (CW 2:130).

Who were the extremists on the other side? They were, Lincoln said, changing the tone and temperature, "a few, but an increasing number of men, who, for the sake of perpetuating slavery, are beginning to assail and to ridicule *the white-man's charter of freedom*—the declaration that 'all men are created free and equal'" (CW 2:130, italics added). We shall deal in greater detail with Lincoln's astounding views on the "white man's" Declaration of Independence in a later chapter, and the point we want to emphasize here is the emotional and linguistic differences in his attacks on the "extremists for freedom" and the "extremists for slavery." Lincoln didn't like the "extremists for freedom": no one could miss that point. But it was not clear from his speech who the "extremists for slavery" were or even if they were extremists.

The most important point, however, is a point that has never been adequately analyzed. The "extremists for slavery" were not the men and women who held slaves and whipped them. Nor were they the eminent men, Lincoln's idol, Alexander Stephens among them, who said slavery was the natural state for Negroes and should last forever. Neither these men nor the slavemasters who held slaves and kept their mouths shut were extremists. *The only extremists for slavery, in Lincoln's speech, were "a few, but increasing number of men" who were attacking the* WORDS *of the Declaration of Independence* (CW 2:130).

Owning slaves, in other words, was no sin, but owning slaves and attacking the WORDS of the Declaration of Independence was, and Lincoln contrasted this position with the example of Clay, "that truly national man" who owned slaves *and* praised the words of the Declaration. It was from Clay that Lincoln got the fifth article of his doctrine, the idea that the Declaration of Independence was an abstract document that didn't require concrete slaveowners or concrete White men to do anything concrete about slavery, Negro equality, or anything else.

The sixth article of the Lincoln Doctrine—the notion that the only solution for the slave problem and the Negro (read: White) problem was to free the slaves gradually and deport them immediately—came from Clay by way of Jefferson and Madison. The only instrument capable of dealing with this exigency, Lincoln said, was the American Colonization Society, which Clay had headed for a number of years. In a strange and disconnected peroration, which suggested that Lincoln was primarily concerned about the destination of the live slaves, not the destination of the recently departed Clay, Lincoln recommended the wisdom and example of the deceased, quoting at length from a speech Clay had given to the society *twenty-five years* before. The length of this quotation and its position at the climax of the speech suggest that the whole point of the speech was to elicit public support for the colonization society's goal of getting rid of freedmen and free Blacks.

Whatever his point, the quotation Lincoln chose made him an apologist and an accomplice of the society which, Lincoln said, quoting Clay, helped rather than hindered slavery. The American Colonization Society "goes into no household to disturb its domestic tranquility," Lincoln said, quoting Clay, and meaning with Clay the "domestic" tranquility of a White household *violently* holding Blacks in slavery. "It addresses itself to no slaves *to weaken their obligations of obedience,*" Lincoln said, quoting Clay and making himself responsible for that slaveholder's sentiment. "It seeks to affect no man's property," meaning by that no man's slaves. People who said the society was threatening the institution of slavery were wrong, for "the execution of its scheme [of colonization] would *augment instead of diminishing* the value of the property [read: slaves] left behind" (CW 2:131, italics added).

Who's talking here? Clay or Lincoln?

Both.

What are they saying?

They are saying, both of them, that the American Colonization Society, which was organized to send Blacks "back" to Africa or some other hot place, was the slaveholders' best friend. Lincoln appropriated this idea by quoting it approvingly and went on to defend the society against charges that it was a racist feel-good organization that objectively solidified slavery by relieving the slaveholders of the pressure, presence and constant reproach of free Blacks. At this point, Lincoln said, in his own voice that Clay—and Lincoln—"considered it no demerit in the society, that it tended to relieve slaveholders from the troublesome presence of the free Negroes" (CW 2:132).

The troublesome presence of free Negroes.

That's what the future "emancipator" said, and he said it in a context that made it clear that he shared the slaveholder's belief that the real problem was not the enslaved Negroes but the free Negroes, who were, Clay said, "of all classes of our population, the most vicious . . . . (*Papers* 6: 92).

Shall we call this racism? Obviously. What else? And it is encouraging to note that almost everybody, including some of Lincoln's most ardent supporters, concede that the American Colonization Society and its offshoots were racist institutions based on racist premises. *The Abraham Lincoln Encyclopedia* said "colonization was a profoundly racist movement which, whatever the degree of humanitarianism or paternalism motivating its adherents, could not envision America as anything but an all-white country in the future" (63).

Dwight Dumond said the colonization society "was nourished and kept alive, not by pride in its achievements, but by blind devotion to their doctrine of racial inferiority" (127). The key to an understanding of the American Colonization Society and of the history of race relations, Dumond added, was "acceptance of the immutability of Negro inferiority"(130). This was also the key to an understanding of Abraham Lincoln, who believed that an immutable physical difference between the Black and White races made it impossible *forever* for them to live together in equality (CW 3:16, 145-6).

Since, according to Lincoln, Blacks were condemned forever to a state of inferiority by their color *and their physical constitution,* since White Americans were determined because of their color and their *natural* feelings to never treat Blacks as equals, and since this combination of circumstances created a human barrier that Blacks could never transcend, whatever they did, the only solution to the slave question, and the race question, was to send all Blacks "to their native clime"—"and this too, so gradually, that neither races nor individuals shall have suffered by the change" (CW 2:132).

There was no logic or science in this strange and strained mixture of racism, magic and non sequiturs, but the idea lifted Lincoln to the realm of poetry—the idea of the banishment of Blacks always lifted him to poetry (see page 460). Negro removal, he said, would be "a glorious consummation" of history's greatest crime and he quoted with approval the words of the Kentucky slaveowner who made God his—and Abraham Lincoln's—accomplice, saying: "May it not be one of the great designs of the Ruler of the universe, (whose ways are often inscrutable by short-sighted mortals,) thus to transform an original crime, into a signal blessing to that most unfortunate portion of the globe."[25]

Clay's theology—and Lincoln's theology—was questionable. For whatever the final outcome, the original crime will still be a crime and the original criminals will still be criminals. This is what Frederick Douglass meant when he said to Clay, and by implication to Lincoln, that this was "the most revolting blasphemy . . . . You would charge upon God the responsibility of your own crimes, and would seek a solace from the pangs of a guilty conscience by sacrilegiously assuming that in robbing Africa of her children, you acted in obedience to the great purposes, and were but fulfilling the decrees of the most high God" (FD 1: 289).

Scripture was not Henry Clay's forte, but Clay's word games impressed Abraham Lincoln, who enlisted for reasons of his own in the struggle to make Springfield safe for White people. And it was at this juncture, with colonizationists all over America mobilizing for the final solution of "the Negro question," that James Mitchell, a new and provocative character in the unfolding Lincoln drama, introduced himself. Mitchell was a fast-talking true believer and Methodist minister who visited Springfield in July 1853 "to promote the cause of colonization and to organize the state of Illinois in its interest as [he] had already organized Indiana."

Looking back later, Rev. Mitchell said, according to an interview published in the *St. Louis Daily Globe-Democrat*, August 26, 1894, that he asked a Presbyterian pastor to recommend a local man who could help him organize Illinois for the American Colonization Society. The pastor recommended Lincoln, who didn't, Mitchell said, look like much but who had a firm grasp of the politics of colonization and what Mitchell had done in Indiana. Lincoln was thirty-four years old when he met Mitchell. What did he believe? He "earnestly believed in and advocated colonization as a means of solving 'the race problem,'" Mitchell said. The two men became friends or at least associates, and Lincoln later named Mitchell commissioner of [Black] emigration in the Lincoln administration.

Mitchell's arrival—whether by design or accident—marked an intensification of Lincoln's personal colonization crusade. On August 30, 1853, the *Illinois State Register* said that "the Hon. Abram Lincoln" would speak that night on "Colonization" at the First Presbyterian Church.

"The subject," the *Register* said, "is of deep interest and growing magnitude and well worthy of consideration on the part of all good patriots and well-wishers of humanity. . . ."

We don't know what Lincoln told the "good patriots" and "well-wishers of humanity," for this speech and a later speech to the colonization society on January 4, 1855, have been unaccountably "lost." No matter. We know that Lincoln said here what he said in New York and Washington and everywhere, that failing to deport Blacks would endanger "the last best, [White] hope of earth."

Lincoln was scheduled to speak on January 12, 1854, to the annual meeting of the Illinois State Colonization Society, "organized," *Lincoln Day By Day* notes (2:114), "for purchasing freedom of slaves and 'colonizing' them in Africa. " An illness in the family prevented him from speaking to the "patriots" on that occasion, but he returned to the colonization theme in the Peoria speech, which *all* Lincoln scholars praise, saying that if he had his way he would solve the slave and race problem by sending all Blacks "to Liberia.—to their own native land." [Lincoln seemed to have believed that all Blacks came from Liberia.] But a moment's reflection would convince me," he added, that this was an impossible dream for if "they were all landed there in a day, they would all perish in the next ten days, and *there are not surplus shipping and surplus money enough in the world to carry them there in many times ten days*" (CW 2: 255, italics added).

The 1850s were perhaps the peak years for believers in the White Dream. Following passage of the Compromise of 1850, there was a national surge to enact Negro exclusion acts and to persuade free Blacks that they should leave America. The states of Indiana and Illinois were in the vanguard of this movement. In 1851, Indiana banned Black settlers and officially endorsed the colonization movement. In 1853, Illinois banned Black settlers.

Although Lincoln shunned social movements and took no part in the ferment that changed America and prepared the way for emancipation, he was front and center in the movement to mobilize American Whites for the deportation of Blacks. The official Lincoln record obscures this fact, but we can see what is involved if we follow events in Springfield in the first days of 1855. On the first day of that year, Governor J.A. Matteson said in his special message to the legislature that "the friends of the colored people" have been making a special effort to organize colonization societies on a permanent basis and to raise funds to colonize Blacks and "thereby separate the blacks from the whites, and send them to the land of their fathers."

Matteson said a special effort would be made in that session of the legislature to "have you charter such a society, and aid in its efforts." Matteson supported the initiative and urged the Illinois legislature to pass legislation in favor of the deportation of Blacks.

Three days later, a resolution was introduced in the House asking the Rev. James Mitchell to answer a number of colonization questions, including the key question of whether the state of Illinois should establish a settlement on the coast of Africa for "the accommodation of the colored people." That night, Monday, January 4, 1855, Lincoln addressed the African Colonization Society. We don't know what he said—the speech has been lost—but can anyone doubt that he followed the script outlined by Governor Matteson and the House resolution in contradiction to the fanciful official theory that he wanted the society to call for an amendment to the Kansas-Nebraska Act (CW 2:298-301). The *Chicago Daily Democratic Press* report of January 8, 1855, emphasized Lincoln's tendency to talk out of both sides of his mouth. He "labored very ingeniously," the paper said, "against occupying a portion [position?] obnoxious to anybody" and "provided a kind of loop-hole for escape if anything he said should not satisfy all kinds of views."

As one of the eleven managers of the Illinois State Colonization Society, Lincoln was involved on other levels in the colonization movement. The historian Eugene H. Berwanger says "Lincoln in 1857 urged the Illinois legislature to appropriate money for colonization in order to remove free Negroes from the state and prevent miscegenation" (4-5).

In the same year, in a speech at Springfield on the Dred Scott decision, Lincoln became unusually agitated over the question of amalgamation, that is to say, Black and White sex. On this subject, Lincoln had to admit that there was something wrong with his theory. He contended that there was "a physical difference" between Blacks and Whites that would always keep them apart. Yet census figures indicated, to Lincoln's dismay, that wherever Blacks and Whites lived together they got together, despite laws, despite lynching, despite violence, and made babies. Lincoln concluded therefore that "the only perfect preventive" of amalgamation was separation.

Such separation, Lincoln said, "if ever effected at all, must be effected by colonization," and it distressed him that no political party was doing anything concrete about it. Almost all Lincoln apologists say Lincoln championed colonization as a political tactic to fool White racists and to smooth the way for emancipation; but Lincoln, contradicting the apologists, tells us in 1857 that he was a voice crying in the White wilderness, and that he was almost alone in recognizing the way to the White promised land. The enterprise, he said, was "a difficult one" but "when there is a will there is a way" and what colonization needed most, he said, was "a hearty will," which springs, he said, from "*moral* sense and self-interest."

The key word here is *moral*. Lincoln believed that deporting Blacks and creating an all-White country was a *moral* imperative.

"Let us be brought to believe it is *morally* right," he said, "and, at the same time, favorable to, or, at least, not against, our interest, to transfer the African to his native clime, and we shall find a way to do it, however great the task may be. The children of Israel, to such numbers as to include four hundred thousand fighting men, went out of Egyptian bondage in a body" (CW 2:408-9, italics added).

The relevance of the example was questionable, since it was extremely unlikely that the Atlantic Ocean was going to part, like the Red Sea, but Lincoln continued to his last days to try to form "a will—a public sentiment"—for colonization. On July 17, 1858, he talked about almost everything in a long speech at Springfield, mentioning the Declaration of Independence, the extension of slavery, the "inferiority" of Black people, and the complicity of the presumably White God, who had given Black people "but little." It was only in the last few minutes that he mentioned apropos of nothing and apropos of everything: "What I would most desire would be the separation of the white and black races" (CW 2:521).

When, on Monday, February 27, 1860, Lincoln moved onto the national stage with a speech at Cooper Institute, he returned to the same theme, saying "in the language of Mr. Jefferson, uttered many years ago, 'It is still in our power to direct the process of emancipation, and *deportation* [my italics], peaceably, and in such slow degrees, as that the evil will wear off insensibly; and their places be, *pari passu*, filled up by free white laborers'" (CW 3:541).

That was his dream. It never changed.

Part Six

"White Man's Charter"

He ignored the greatest moral question of the time.
                              —Historian Ralph G. Newman

I have said a hundred times, and I have now no inclination to take it back, that I believe there is no right, and ought to be no inclination, in the people of the free States to enter into the slave States, and interfere with the question of slavery at all.
                              —Abraham Lincoln

11

How To Emancipate
Without Emancipating

TO understand Lincoln's last emancipation decree, one must understand his first emancipation decree. To understand what he was trying to do on January 1, 1863, one must understand what he was trying to do on January 10, 1849, when he unveiled his first emancipation plan.

The first plan, which Congressman Abraham Lincoln announced to a skeptical House of Representatives but never really introduced, was a bill for the gradual and compensated emancipation of slaves in the District of Columbia. This was the first of five emancipation documents that he personally announced. Two of these decrees were preliminary drafts of the final proclamation, but the District of Columbia bill and his proposed constitutional amendment for gradual and compensated emancipation were independent efforts that give us rare and revealing insights into the mind and motives of one of history's strangest phenomena, "a great emancipator" who didn't want to emancipate anybody immediately, and certainly not greatly.

What is striking, in considering these acts, is that Lincoln's first emancipation plan, like his last one, like all the others, was a rebound effort, offered as a diversion to deflect a more radical emancipation effort. In 1862 it was a coalition of liberal Republicans and radical abolitionists who drove the reluctant Lincoln to glory. In 1849, the same forces under the banner of the emerging Free Soil Party forced

Lincoln's hand. In 1849, as in 1862, he moved not to defend the principles of the Declaration of Independence nor to turn back a threat to slaves but to deflect what he considered a radical threat to the interests of slaveholders.

The embodiment of that threat in 1848 and 1849 was a New York congressman named Daniel Gott, who offered on Thursday, December 21, 1848, a resolution requiring the appropriate House committee to report a bill banning the slave trade in the nation's capital. This was a red flag to proslavery sentinels, who stood like armed guards across every avenue leading to liberty and justice for all. For more than fifty years, these forces had fought a brilliant political war, beating back or compromising every legislative challenge to slavery and dominating or neutralizing every federal structure, including the army and the office of the president. Some of their greatest triumphs had been won in Congress, which they dominated not only because of their political skills but also because they believed in slavery passionately while their opponents believed in freedom moderately and were compromised, moreover, by their belief that the Constitution and the rules of the game favored slavery.

The White congressional groups were defined by their style. Southerners swaggered; Northerners sauntered. Southerners blustered; Northerners apologized. Southerners threatened; Northerners compromised. Southerners attacked; Northerners defended. The result was the inevitable result: Southerners won and Northerners lost.

This went on for decade after decade with elegant, aristocratic Southern congressmen and senators arrogantly beating back challenges from apologetic Northern representatives, who were generally called doughfaces. The term was accurate; it referred to Northern congressmen who supported and voted with the proslavery Southern bloc and who didn't oppose slavery in the South.

With the institutionalization of the Abolitionist Movement and the founding of the Liberty and Free Soil parties in the thirties and forties, the political climate changed. This was one of the great forking points that led to the North-South confrontation, and it brought to the fore the unsung political fathers of emancipation, men like Salmon Portland Chase and Joshua R. Giddings of Ohio. Abraham Lincoln was neither a founding father *nor a follower* of the movement that later made him famous. In the 1830s and 1840s, and later, in Illinois and Washington, D.C., he doughfaced or fellow-traveled for doughfaces in support of slavery in the South and "efficient" procedures for capturing and returning fugitive slaves.

These developments, especially the founding of the Liberty and Free Soil parties, created a window of opportunity in Congress for a new breed of Northerners who believed "in human liberty," Thomas F. Woodley said, "just as zealously and perhaps just as fanatically as any Southerner believed in slavery" (212).

Abraham Lincoln was not one of these men, but Thaddeus Stevens of Pennsylvania was, and he told Southern congressmen in one of the defining speeches of the period that the free ride was over. "How often," he said in a House speech, have "these walls been profaned and the North insulted by the insolent threat, that if Congress legislate [d] against southern will, it should be disregarded, resisted to extremity, and the Union destroyed." More than once, he said, we have been told "that if we dared to legislate in a certain way the South would teach the North a lesson!" That phase of American history, Stevens said, was over. "You have too often intimidated Congress. You have more than once frightened the tame North from its propriety, and found 'doughfaces' enough to be your tools . . . . " But the race of doughfaces was dying out. "They were an unmanly, unvirile race, incapable, according to the laws of nature, of reproduction . . . . The old ones are deep in political graves. For them I am sure there is no resurrection, for they were soulless."[26]

Stevens had soul.

So did Joshua Reed Giddings of Ohio, who was the leader of the emerging antislavery forces in the House during Lincoln's one term. Unlike Lincoln and other conservative Northern congressmen, Giddings and his supporters didn't run away from a fight. On the contrary, they seemed to love a good legislative fight and were not above going out of their way to pick one.

When the House censured Giddings for advocating slave escapes, he resigned his seat and went home to his Western Reserve constituents, who promptly reelected him and sent him back to Washington in triumph. Like Stevens, and unlike Lincoln, Giddings gloried in the fight, telling his wife that during one of his antislavery speeches, he was "full of the Spirit, and you may judge of my effort when I say that I had not spoken ten minutes before the sweat rolled down my face, and my underclothes [were] as wet as though I had been in a river . . . . Doughfaces actually turned pale. Those who were never known to vote for freedom before came over and voted with us" (qtd. in Riddle 168).

Abraham Lincoln was not one of them. Donald W. Riddle, whose *Congressman Abraham Lincoln* I am following here, said Giddings converted a number of doughfaces but "got no help from Lincoln." He got a lot of help, however, from Gott who became, Giddings noted in his diary, a passionate free soil supporter. And it was Gott who forced the issue that forced Lincoln's hand, offering on December 21, 1848, a resolution calling for a bill to ban the slave trade in the nation's capital. More and more Whites, some of them quite conservative, were saying that it was obscene to march shackled men, women and children down Pennsylvania Avenue and sell them in sight of the Capitol. Gott spoke for these Whites in a preamble, which sought legislative relief because "the traffic now prosecuted in this metropolis of the Republic in human beings, as chattels, is contrary to natural justice and the fundamental principles of our political system, and is notoriously a reproach to our country throughout Christendom, and a serious hindrance to the progress of republican liberty among the nations of the earth."[27]

The proslavery forces responded by offering a motion to lay Gott's resolution on the table. This, in plain English, was a motion to kill the resolution and to let Gott know who ran the House. But to the consternation of proslavery forces, the House rejected the motion, with eighty-five congressmen, including the entire Giddings antislavery contingent voting nay, and eighty-one congressmen, including the whole Southern contingent, voting aye. How did Abraham Lincoln of Illinois vote? Did he side with the proslavery Southerners or the antislavery Northerners? He sided with the proslavery Southerners and voted aye.

After the House voted overwhelmingly to take up the main question with Lincoln and the Southerners voting nay, Gott's resolution was adopted by a vote of ninety-eight to eighty-eight. Abraham Lincoln of Illinois voted nay with the eighty-eight Southerners and their Northern supporters, publicly opposing the call for a bill banning the slave trade in the District of Columbia .

This was not the end of the struggle, which continued for several days, inflaming the climate and triggering intense campaigning by proslavery and antislavery forces. After calling in IOU's and deploying heavy artillery like Senator John Calhoun of South Carolina and President James K. Polk, White Southerners renewed the battle on the same terrain on December 27, offering a series of motions that defined the issue and the contesting forces. The first resolution was a pending motion to reconsider the House vote directing the Committee on the District of Columbia to report a bill prohibiting the slave trade in the District. The antislavery contingent countered with a motion to kill that motion by laying it on the table.

Thus, the issue was joined and members arrayed themselves on one side or the other.

A vote to lay the motion on the table was, as everybody understood, a vote for the Gott amendment and against the slave trade.

A vote against the motion to table was a vote against the Gott amendment and for slavery and the slave trade.

All White Southerners, whatever their party, and all their allies and supporters, whatever their motives, voted against the motion to table, thereby asking for a reconsideration of the decision to ask for a bill banning the slave trade in the District. All antislavery members voted for the motion to table, which was defeated.

How did Abraham Lincoln of Illinois vote? He voted with the proslavery contingent, which prevailed with his help and the help of
other Northerners.[28]

When the main issue was brought before the House, a lot of
doughfaces pleaded illness or fled the chambers, but Abraham Lincoln stood up and voted with all White Southerners for a reconsideration of the vote on the original Gott resolution. A contemporary,
Congressman George Washington Julian of Indiana, was surprised
by Lincoln's vote. "To vote [with the proslavery side, as Lincoln did]
would have been regarded as a direct support of the slave trade.
This, few northerners were willing to do . . . . Unlike several of his
northern brethren, he [Lincoln] showed no disposition to dodge the
question, but placed himself squarely on the side of the South" (qtd.
in Riddle 170).

In the midst of all this skirmishing, on Wednesday, January 10,
1849, Lincoln made a strange move, pushing himself to the front
ranks of the contending forces by announcing that he intended to
offer a bill for the gradual and compensated emancipation of slaves
in the District of Columbia. This was almost certainly a diversionary
movement, designed as a compromise and a face-saving gesture for
the South. In any case, Lincoln offered it as a *substitute* motion, saying
that his proposed measure had the support of some fifteen White citizens of the District. Whereupon there were shouts all over the chamber. "Who are they? Name them! Name them!" Lincoln refused to
name his White backers, and the proslavery contingent, sensing a
losing proposition, returned to its ultimately successful effort to sidetrack the Gott amendment.[29] What happened to Lincoln's bill? He
never introduced it. Years later, he said that his White backers
deserted him and that he saw no reason to pursue a losing cause (CW
2:22). Whatever the reasons, Lincoln's retreat was a victory for District of Columbia slaves, who were freed outright by Congress in
1862 and who would have remained in slavery until the 1890s or
even the twentieth century under the conservative document Lincoln

drafted. Based on that fact and the emancipation proclamations he actually drafted, we can say that, other things being equal, Lincoln was one of the last men in the United States a conscious slave would have asked to draft an emancipation proclamation.

Apart from saying that his White backers abandoned him, Lincoln never explained his erratic course on slavery in the Thirtieth Congress. The leading experts on his congressional career, Beveridge, Riddle and Quarles, say his votes on slavery were confusing at best and confused and opportunistic at worst. The major exception to this chorus of criticism is Donald, who said, as we have seen, that Lincoln voted for slavery and the slave trade because he loved free speech so much and thought it was wrong to abolish slavery without the consent of "the [White] inhabitants of Washington," not, mind you, the consent of the slaves (136). This, of course, was a variant of the infamous popular sovereignty doctrine. When Stephen Douglas advanced the same idea, Lincoln said it was morally repugnant and worse to suggest that people had the right to vote to do wrong.

The most damaging evidence against Donald's theory, however, is Lincoln himself, who voted to table a Giddings bill, which called for a referendum by the people of the District on the question of slavery. There was, to be fair, a slight difference between Giddings's understanding of government of the people and Lincoln's understanding of government of the people. Giddings called for a referendum of *all* the people of the District, including the White *and* Black residents; Lincoln's bill called for *a referendum of the free White residents* of the District. Since Lincoln opposed a referendum of *all* the people, his problem wasn't the absence of a referendum—his problem, as always, and as his bill proves, was race. Furthermore, and at a deeper level, it can be argued that Lincoln or any other person who believed that the *only* way to end slavery was to ask slaveholders to voluntarily commit suicide by free ballots either didn't understand the situation or was a de facto supporter of slavery as it existed.

Nowhere was this more clearly visible than in Lincoln's first emancipation initiative, which did not prevail but which is a privileged document that throws new light on his mental processes. Here for the first time "the future emancipator" tells us what he thinks about emancipation and how he would go about it, and it is astonishing that this privileged evidence is seldom quoted and never analyzed by Lincoln biographers, who seem to be discomfited or embarrassed by it, as well they should, since it prefigured Lincoln the none-mancipator and reveals with startling clarity the hidden springs of his mind.

There is, to begin with, the title that Lincoln wrote with his own hands, "A bill for an act to abolish slavery in the District of Columbia, by the consent of the free white people of said District, and with compensation to owners." Lincoln wanted no misunderstanding. He wanted it understood from the outset that he, unlike Giddings and Gott, was acting in the interest of and at the behest of "free white people," especially free White people who owned slaves. In the process, he made it unmistakably clear for the third but not the last time that he was unalterably opposed to Black people voting, whether in Illinois or in the District of Columbia (CW 2:20).

Perhaps the most significant fact is the one most often over-looked: Lincoln's first emancipation act, like his last emancipation act, didn't emancipate a single slave. This was not a technicality, hidden in the fine print. This was the intent of the act, stated openly and boldly in Section 4: "That all persons now within said District lawfully held as slaves, or now owned by any person or persons now resident within said District, *shall remain such*" (CW 2:21, italics added). Here, unbelievably, is one of the great novelties of the eman-cipation business, an emancipation act which said not that all slaves would be free but that all slaves would remain slaves.

What did this mean to a slave living in the District in January 1849? It meant that Abraham Lincoln had given him a life sentence and that the slaveowner could hold and whip him or her for seventy or eighty years, or could at his, the slaveowner's discretion, free him at the peak of the market and receive his "full value" (CW 2:21).

It was not by chance that neither the District act nor Lincoln's congressional proposal nor the Emancipation Proclamation freed any slaves immediately. Although the District act said all children born to slave mothers after January 1, 1850, would be free, the fine print—and Lincoln was a master of emancipation fine print—said something completely different, that children born free were to be apprenticed to slavemasters for a number of years (CW 2:21).

This was another Lincoln DNA. Wherever and whenever he was forced to address the question of emancipation, he proposed a twilight period of apprenticeship or quasi slavery so that slaves could slowly end their slavery and slavemasters could slowly end their slavemastership. How many years of apprenticeship did Lincoln call for in his first emancipation?

Lincoln left the number of years blank in the District act, but in the two secret drafts he made for the state of Delaware, the apprenticeship could have extended for twenty-one years for males, and eighteen years for females.

This meant, among other things, that Lincoln wanted slavery to last for a long time. The Delaware drafts specified two different timetables, one ending in 1893 and the other ending later. Which one do you think Lincoln favored? The second one, of course—it was a Lincoln DNA: the longer slavery lasted the better. Under his favorite Delaware plan, slavery in the United States would have ended in 1914 at the beginning of World War I (CW 5:29-31).

Another Lincoln DNA was a curious concern about the servant problem and "the inconveniences public and private" sudden emancipation would cause slaveholders and other Whites (CW 5:223). Section 2 of his 1849 draft said that U.S. government officials "coming into said District on public business, and remaining only so long as may be reasonably necessary for that object, may be attended into, and out of, said District, and while there, by the necessary servants of themselves and their families, without their right to hold such servants in service, being thereby impaired" (CW 2:20).

Once again Lincoln betrays himself, going out of his way to make sure slaveholders and their families would have "the necessary servants" to take care of their needs. This was, as we have seen, one of the enduring anxieties of his life, and we will leave it to the Lincoln legions to explain why a man reputed to have such decent instincts spent so much time worrying about whether slavemasters would have the necessary slaves to fetch their drinks and make their beds. We will also leave to them the task of explaining why honest Abraham Lincoln dishonestly used the words necessary *servants* instead of necessary *slaves*.

There is more, however, and worse, for the Lincoln draft crossed over into a no-man's land of immorality and inhumanity by calling for the extension of the infamous fugitive slave law to Washington, D. C. For fifty-six years, ever since George Washington signed the first bill authorizing the hunting and capturing of human beings in the United States, the nation's capital had been sacrosanct territory, respected by slaveowners and the opponents of slaveowners. But Lincoln wanted to extend this legal crime to the District and to legalize the hunting and capturing of humans within sight of the Capitol.

Section 5 of Lincoln's draft said municipal authorities "are hereby *empowered and required* to provide *active and efficient means* to arrest, and deliver up to their owners, all fugitive slaves escaping into said District" (CW 2:21, italics added).

This was a political and moral blunder, which followed Lincoln to the White House. Eleven years later, during the 1860 presidential campaign, Illinois abolitionist H. Ford Douglass said it was well known "that the [Fugitive Slave] law of 1793 did not apply to the District, and it was necessary, in order that slaveholders might catch their slaves who sought safety under the shadow of the capitol, that a special law should be passed for the District of Columbia; and so Mr. Lincoln went down deeper into the pro-slavery pool than even Mr. [James] Mason did in the Fugitive Slave Law of 1850" (Zilversmit 66).

Wendell Phillips said Lincoln went down deeper than that. In the sharpest prewar criticism of Lincoln, Phillips said in a scathing *Liberator* editorial of July 13, 1860, that Lincoln was guilty of immorality:

ABRAHAM LINCOLN, THE SLAVE HOUND OF ILLINOIS

We gibbet a Northern hound today side by side with the infamous Mason of Virginia. Mason's Slave Bill is based on that clause of the United States Constitution, which provides for the surrender of slaves escaping from one State into another State of the Union.

The Supreme Court of the United States has decided that the District of Columbia is not a State within the meaning of the Constitution . . . . The District of Columbia is not, therefore, included in the terms of the Fugitive Slave clause. Whoever tries to extend the dominion of that clause over the District of Columbia exhibits only his own voluntary baseness, can have no pretence of constitutional obligation, out Masons Mason, and stamps himself a hound of special "alacrity."

This deed Abraham Lincoln, Republican candidate for President, has done.

Lincoln defenders said this was unfair, that Lincoln was merely offering a compromise gambit to make the bill more palatable to slaveholders and conservatives. Phillips said that was precisely the point, that it was "the nature of the compromise with which I find fault." After all, he said, compromise was only trading. "We give so much for so much." But what Lincoln proposed, Phillips said, was to trade so many concrete Black men, women and children for the favor of slaveholders and the friends of slaveholder.

This, from Phillips's standpoint and from the standpoint of the slaves, was insufferable. Some things, he said, are too sacred to be traded away. Among these things are "the life, liberty, and happiness of ourselves, or of others," which are too priceless "to be compromised away for any seeming good . . . . My charge is, that in 1849, Mr. Lincoln did not know that slavehunting was one of these."

Phillips went on to say in a sentence that even liberals censor that had Lincoln offered "to sell his wife or daughter for the same purpose he would have been no more infamous or dishonored in my view."

The worst thing one can say about Lincoln is that he didn't know in 1849 or 1858 or 1861 that selling anybody's wife or daughter was one of the things that could not be compromised for "any seeming good."

Although Lincoln drafted his emancipation bills at different times to meet different situations, they share four features that throw new light on Lincoln and the Emancipation Proclamation.

1. None of the documents he issued or announced publicly, not even the famous Proclamation, emancipated a single slave outright.

2. With the exception of the Emancipation Proclamation, all required the government or the state to buy the slaves and compensate the slaveholders. This flew in the face of the principles of abolitionists, who said that if it was wrong for slaveholders to buy men and women, it was wrong for the government to buy men and women, especially since such an act conceded the vital point, that men could hold property interest in other human beings and could profit from that interest. The fact that the Proclamation departed from this basic Lincoln principle in the beginning—Lincoln tried until the end to get his cabinet to approve a $400,000,000 compensation plan for slaveowners—is one of the strongest arguments against Lincoln's investment in it.

3. All required a period of apprenticeship controlled by the former slaveholders during which time, as Lincoln was fond of saying, the slaves and slaveholders could work themselves out of their old relationship—on the slaves' time and at their expense. It will be said, of course, that the Emancipation Proclamation didn't provide for apprenticeship. Anybody who says that has not read the implementing provisions in Lincoln's Reconstruction plans, which provided for a period of apprenticeship (CW 6:49; CW 7:1-2, 55). Secretary of the Treasury Chase and abolitionists denounced the inhumane apprenticeship provisions which Lincoln defended until the last speech of his life.

4. All were rebound emancipations, designed to provide a safer,

more conservative alternative to emancipation plans that called for immediate emancipation or other moves Lincoln feared. The first emancipation was designed to supplant the Gott amendment and to defuse the explosive situation caused by its introduction. The Delaware bills were designed to outflank congressional critics and to defuse the situation created by Lincoln's revocation of General John Charles Frémont's emancipation decree. The last emancipation act was designed to neutralize the Second Confiscation Act and to outflank congressional critics who were calling for the use of Black soldiers and the immediate emancipation of the slaves of rebels in rebel states and so-called loyal states.

There is a straight line from the emancipation document of January 10, 1849, which didn't free anybody, to the Emancipation Proclamation of January 1, 1863, which didn't free anybody immediately. And what we learn from the first emancipation, and all the emancipation decrees in between, is that the limitations of the last emancipation were generic expressions of the character and orientation of Abraham Lincoln, who seems to have had a vocation for emancipating slaves without emancipating them.

12

A Politician Divided Against Himself

LINCOLN said America could not endure half slave and half free, but he did everything he could for fifty-four of his fifty-six years to ensure that it remained half slave and half free. If this statement seems shocking, I would present as evidence the chief witness, Abraham Lincoln, who said in 1852 in his forty-third year that ending slavery at *once*—his italics— would produce "a greater evil"—we shall return to that paradox— than a country half slave and half free.

From that day—July 6, 1852—to 1863 and beyond, Abraham Lincoln—the main witness against Abraham Lincoln or, to be more precise, the main witness against the mythical Abraham Lincoln—made more than a thousand statements, by his own count, in support of the institution of human slavery in the United States.

To be sure, Lincoln did say from time to time that slavery was wrong in an *abstract*—remember that word—moral sense and that he hoped it would end sometime in the future, in the far distant future, but he never said it without adding that he and "the people of the free States" had no right and ought to have no *inclination* to keep slaveowners from doing exactly as they pleased for as long as they pleased—I'm quoting Abraham Lincoln—with *their* slaves (CW 2:493, 277; CW 3:96, 116-7, 277).

If no one had a right to interfere with slavery, and if Lincoln had no inclination to disturb slaveowners in their lair, how in the world did he think the country was going to cease being half slave and half free? Stephen Douglas and others asked Lincoln that question, but he never answered it, saying in effect that God would solve the problem in his own good time.

Strangely, and significantly, Lincoln seemed to think that the satan of slavery was so strong and wise that it would take God a century or so to whip him. When he was forty-nine years old, he said that perhaps the best way for slavery to end peaceably was for it to last a long time, which was another way of saying that the best way for slavery to end peaceably was for America to remain half slave and half free for a long time. How long? One hundred years at least, he said in 1858 (CW 3:181). In the same year, he conceded with no sense of especial concern that slavery in America might never end, saying that "whether it should ever become extinct or not, he was in favor of living up to all the guarantees of the Constitution" (CW 3:96).

If Lincoln had had his way, in fact, the Civil War would have ended with slavery intact and slaveowners triumphant, at least on their plantations.

How, it will be asked, do you know all this? The answer is that *I* read Lincoln, who had such a horror of the sudden ending of slavery that he said out loud for all to hear and read that he feared success—Black freedom—more than he feared failure—Black slavery.

Here, as everywhere, there has been a major misunderstanding. Lincoln was no emancipationist; Lincoln was scared to death of emancipation. What was he scared of? He was scared—we shall return to this—of Black economic competition, Black and White voters and officeholders, and Black and White sex—I'm quoting Abraham Lincoln, and if you don't believe me, read pages 405, 407-9 and 541 of volume 2 and pages 146 and 234-5 of volume 3 of *The Collected Works of Abraham Lincoln*.

Will someone say that Lincoln also believed that slavery was protected by the Constitution? But who cannot see that this answer is insufficient since he was opposed to sudden emancipation in the District of Columbia, for example, which was not protected by the Constitution.

What then was the problem? *You* know what the problem was. The problem—he tells us so a thousand times—was race. Abraham Lincoln supported slavery in the South because he saw the slaves through the lenses of a White man, and because the institution of slavery contained and postponed racial problems that threatened his White dream.

If someone asks, condemning himself, how else could Lincoln have seen the slaves, the answer is that he could have seen the slaves through the lenses of a human being, as, say, Wendell Phillips saw the slaves. But, to repeat, one of the tragedies of American history—and American historiography—is that racism made it impossible for America's greatest icon to leap over the barrier of his skin and make a human connection.

The evidence on this point is overwhelming, and the main witness—Abraham Lincoln—is unimpeachable.

Let us, forsaking all others, follow the evidence and the principal witness, wherever they lead.

When, in 1855, Lincoln's best friend, Joshua Speed, asked him to clarify his position on slavery, he said frankly, "I now do no more than oppose the *extension* of slavery" (CW 2:323, Lincoln's italics). Lincoln said this so often and so loud that it is astounding that some people, even some historians, claim to misunderstand him.

He said it in CAPITALS at Peoria, Illinois, on October 16, 1854:

> I wish to MAKE and to KEEP the distinction between the EXISTING institution, and the EXTENSION of it, so broad, and so clear, that no honest man can misunderstand me, and no dishonest one, successfully misrepresent me. (CW 2:248)

That didn't deter honest and dishonest men—then or now—and he said it again at Bloomington, Illinois, on September 4, 1858:

We have no right to interfere with slavery in the States. We only want to restrict it to where it is. (CW 3:87)

He said it at Ottawa, Illinois, on August 21, 1858, at the first Lincoln-Douglas debate:

I will say here, while upon this subject, that I have no purpose *directly or indirectly* to interfere with the institution of slavery in the States where it exists. I believe I have no lawful right to do so, and I have no inclination to do so. (CW 3:16, italics added)

He said at the second Lincoln-Douglas debate and the third, fourth, fifth, and sixth debate:

I expressly declared in my opening speech, that I had neither the inclination to exercise, nor the belief in the existence of the right to interfere with the States of Kentucky or Virginia in doing as they pleased with slavery or any other existing institution. (CW 3:277)

Challenged again at the seventh and final debate, he said again:

Now I have upon all occasions declared as strongly as Judge [Stephen] Douglas against the disposition to interfere with the existing institution of slavery. (CW 3:300)

He said it in Illinois.

He said it in Michigan.

He said it in Wisconsin, Kansas, Michigan, Connecticut, Ohio, and New York.

He said it everywhere.

We must not disturb slavery in the states where it exists, because the constitution, and the peace of the country, both forbid us. (CW 3:435)

One has to feel sorry for Lincoln retrospectively and prospectively. For he declared it and, to use his word, "re-declared" it. He quoted himself and "re-quoted" himself. Yet honest and dishonest men—then and now—continued to misrepresent him, despite the fact that he said it a hundred times:

I have said a hundred times and I have now no inclination to take it back, that *I believe there is no right, and ought to be no inclination* in the people of the free States to enter into the slave States, and interfere with the question of slavery at all. *I have said that always* (CW 2:492, italics added).

If he said it a hundred times, he said it a thousand times:

I have declared a thousand times, and now repeat that, in my opinion, neither the General Government, nor any other power outside of the slave states, can constitutionally or rightfully interfere with slaves or slavery where it already exists. (CW 2:471)

Not only did he say it but he cited evidence to prove it.

He asserted positively, and proved conclusively by his former acts and speeches that he was not in favor of interfering with slavery in the States where it exists, nor ever had been. (CW 3:96)

Let us re-read that passage together. Abraham Lincoln, the main witness, *proved conclusively by his former acts and speeches* that he was not in favor of interfering with slavery where it existed, *nor ever had been.* This statement covers every act and speech of Lincoln's life from his birth in 1809 to the speech he delivered in Greenville, Illinois, on September 13, 1858, in his forty-ninth year and provides most conclusive proof that he had never been in favor of interfering with slavery in the slave states.

Shall we go further?

Shall we quote what Lincoln said at Alton, Atlanta, Bath, Beardstown, Belleville, Bloomington, Carlinville, Charleston, Edwardsville, Freeport, Greenville, Havana, Jacksonville, Jonesboro, Lewistown, Monticello, Petersburg, Peoria, Princeton, Shelbyville, Springfield, Quincy, and Vandalia?

In all these Illinois towns and in New Haven, Connecticut, and New York City, and Columbus, Ohio, and Leavenworth, Kansas, and in letters and editorials and private and public acts, the future "emancipator" made it unmistakably clear: He was *not* opposed to slavery in Alabama, Georgia, South Carolina, Louisiana, Arkansas, Texas, Maryland, Missouri, Florida, Delaware, Tennessee, North Carolina, Virginia, and Kentucky. What was he opposed to, then? He was *only* opposed to the extension of slavery to the territories, to places, Frederick Douglass said, where it was not likely to go.

This is a pivotal point, one that has been masked by rhetoric and imperfect analysis. For to say, as Lincoln said a thousand times, that one is *only* opposed to the extension of slavery is to say a thousand times that one is *not* opposed to slavery where it existed. Based on this record and the words of his own mouth, we can say that the "great emancipator" was one of the major supporters of slavery in the United States for at least fifty-four of his fifty-six years.

It is fashionable for Carl Sandburg wannabees to intone deeply and talk about "the mysterious and unknown Lincoln."

Lincoln is not unknown; Lincoln is not quoted—or read.

As we read the record of what Lincoln said and did, we are struck not only by the contradiction between his words and deeds but also by the contradiction between his premises and conclusions. For it was no more possible for him to be for slavery and against its extension than it is to be for cancer and against its growth.

There was, thus, a deeper and more ominous reason for Lincoln's difficulty on this issue—a reason that reflects the strategic weakness of his whole position on slavery. He was committed—out of racism, out of fear of the unknown—to the cancer itself, believing, as he said publicly, that the cure was worse than the disease and that the enslavement of Blacks was a White "necessity."

To come right out with it, Lincoln didn't want slavery to end if it meant free Negroes in the United States. Until somebody came up with a magic wand that would make slaves *and* Negroes disappear, he was content to support the Missouri Compromise, which served as a fence—his metaphor—to contain slaves and Negroes in the slave states.

One is always being told, as unarguable proof of Lincoln's virtue, that he said he hated slavery, as if to profess were to practice. Didn't he say in that famous 1864 letter to A.G. Hodges, "I am naturally anti-slavery. If slavery is not wrong, nothing is wrong. I can not remember when I did not so think, and feel" (CW 7:281)? Didn't he say even earlier, in a Chicago speech of 1858, "I have always hated slavery, I think as much as any Abolitionist" (CW 2:492)?

That's what he said all right, but it's not all he said or the most important thing he said; for this is a case, to quote what Lincoln also said, where "the repetition of half a truth . . . produces the effect of a whole falsehood" (Sandburg 1939, 1:570). One of the defining fallacies of Lincoln historiography and museumography is the failure to report Lincoln's *but*—and there is always a *but* in a Lincoln statement on slavery or Blacks. Take, for example, that eloquent and categorical statement, "If slavery is not wrong, nothing is wrong." Great statement, right? Right, until you discover that it was followed immediately by the weasel-worded sentence: "And yet I have never understood that the Presidency conferred upon me an unrestricted right to act officially upon this judgment and feeling."

The presidency had nothing to do with it, for the sentence that followed the 1858 declaration of private citizen Abraham Lincoln was: "I have always hated it [slavery], but I have always been quiet about it until this new era of the introduction of the Nebraska Bill began."

It was a technique. Lincoln practiced it to perfection. What the left hand gave rhetorically, the right tongue took away practically.

The problem, however, was deeper than that. For the difference between what a person says he believes and what he in fact believes is the difference, as Lincoln said, between a horse-chestnut and a chestnut horse (CW 3:16). This is elementary in law and love affairs, and it is surprising that so many Lincoln enthusiasts forget that a self-serving statement from a person must be tested not only by the statements of other witnesses but also, and more importantly, by what the person does. Almost all Lincoln defenders violate this rule by making a rhetorical leap from assertion to conclusion. Lincoln, we are told, *said* he hated slavery. *Therefore*, he hated slavery.

This leap from saying to doing and from wish to fulfillment without the sayer or the wisher doing anything to make the saying and the wishing real is another defining fallacy of Lincoln studies, hiding both the studiers and the studied. Lincoln said he hated slavery; he may even have believed that he hated slavery—but there is no evidence that he always hated slavery or that he even had *strong* feelings about Negro slavery. No one understood this better than John Hume, who heard Lincoln speak during the Lincoln-Douglas debate and who said that Lincoln "was sentimentally opposed to slavery, but . . . was afraid of freedom . . . . He was opposed to slavery more because it was a public nuisance than because of its injustice to the oppressed black man, whose condition, he did not believe, would be greatly, if at all, benefitted by freedom" (145).

Beyond all this, it is necessary to restore some dignity to language. John Brown *hated* slavery. He hated slavery so much his body vibrated like the strings of a violin when he heard the word. Wendell Phillips *hated* slavery. He hated slavery so much that he seceded from the United States, refusing to practice law or exercise any other function under a government that sanctioned slavery. Harriet Tubman *hated* slavery. She hated slavery so much that she risked her life repeatedly in guerrilla strikes in slavery land. Lincoln was not in their league, either as a hater or lover, and it is a debasement of language and logic to compare his yea-nay to their nay. After all, he was forty-five-years old when he made his first public statement against [the extension of] slavery in October 1854.

Four years later, in his forty-ninth year, Lincoln said that slavery had always been "a minor question" to him until the passage of the Kansas-Nebraska Act (CW 2:514).

Astonishing.

A grown man actually said that.

A grown man actually said in the United States of America on July 17, 1858, that the question of slavery had been a *minor* issue to him and that he thought it was in the "course of ultimate extinction" in the years of Nat Turner, in the years of the escape of some twenty thousand slaves, in the years of the *Amistad*, in the years of the fight over the right to petition in Congress and the right to deliver the mail in South Carolina, in the years when thousands of Black men and women were tortured and lashed and murdered in the South and Illinois and scores of White men and women were jailed in the South for distributing books and saying that all men were created equal.

Astonishing.

Even more astonishing is that none of Lincoln's major interpreters has found it astonishing that he said it and that almost all Americans believe that the man who said it was the wisest voice in the United States at that time—or this one.

These observations press home the heretofore unrevealed magnitude of Lincoln's commitment to slavery and enable us to explain why evidence that purports to prove that Lincoln was antislavery almost always backfires and proves the opposite. In fact, the most conclusive evidence against Lincoln can be found in three events Lincoln defenders cite to prove that he always hated slavery.

Exhibit I for the defense is the famous statement Lincoln made when he saw slavery for the first time in New Orleans: As every schoolchild knows, the future emancipator said, "If I ever get a chance to hit that thing, I will hit it hard."

There are two problems with this statement.

The first is that Lincoln distinguished himself as a private citizen and as president by a decided reluctance to hit slavery at all.

The second problem is that only one person said he heard Lincoln make the statement and he couldn't have heard it because he didn't go to New Orleans with Lincoln.

Strike One.

Exhibit II for the Lincoln defense is that famous incident in which young Lincoln, then an Illinois legislator, "endangered" his career by standing up "almost alone" and protesting slavery. This alleged act of conscience, unfortunately, proves the opposite of what Lincoln defenders say it proves. What Lincoln and his colleague, Dan Stone, did was to take the safe position of denouncing the extremists for slavery and the extremists for freedom, saying in the same sentence "that the institution of slavery is founded on both injustice and bad policy; but that the promulgation of abolition doctrines tends rather to increase than to abate its evil."

To make sure that no one misunderstood their meaning, Lincoln and Stone said in the next sentence that they supported slavery where it existed: "They believe that the Congress of the United States has no power, under the constitution, to interfere with the institution of slavery in the different States" (CW 1:74-5). Having gone that far, they went another mile and said what private citizen Abraham Lincoln never stopped saying: that they were opposed to people interfering with slavery in the District of Columbia, where there was no constitutional prohibition.

Lincoln's law partner, William H. Herndon, contemptuously dismissed people who cited this incident as proof of the antislavery orientation of Lincoln. A careful reading of this "mild and carefully worded" statement, "cautiously framed to suit the temper of the times," provides, Herndon said, "an unqualified and overwhelming refutation of the charge" that Lincoln was an abolitionist. (HW 143-4).

Strike Two.

What about Exhibit III, the famous letter Lincoln wrote in 1855 recalling his anguish at the sight of shackled slaves during a steamboat trip in 1841? "You may remember, as I well do," he wrote to his intimate friend Joshua Speed fourteen years after the event, "that from Louisville to the mouth of the Ohio there were, on board, ten or a dozen slaves, shackled together with irons. That sight was a continual torment to me; and I see something like it every time I touch the Ohio, or any other slave-border" (CW 2:320). This is strong testimony, indicating what seems to be repugnance over "a thing which has, and continually exercises, the power of making me miserable."

But:

In a letter Lincoln wrote to Speed's sister Mary immediately after the event he expressed neither repugnance nor anguish. On the contrary, he invoked the usual racist argument about happy slaves, saying that "nothing of interest happened during the passage" except "vexatious" delays. Almost as an afterthought, he wrote in the next sentence: "By the way, a fine example was presented on board the boat for contemplating the effect of *condition* [his emphasis] upon human happiness. A gentleman [sic] had purchased twelve Negroes in different parts of Kentucky and was taking them to a farm in the South. They were chained six and six together . . . . In this condition they were being separated forever from the scenes of their childhood, their friends, their fathers and mothers, and brothers and sisters, and many of them, from their wives and children, and going into perpetual slavery where the lash of the master is proverbially more ruthless and unrelenting than any other where; and yet amid all these distressing circumstances, as we would think them, they were the most cheerful and apparantly [sic] happy creatures on board . . . . How true it is that 'God tempers the wind to the shorn lamb,' or in other words, that He renders the worst of human conditions tolerable, while He permits the best, to be nothing better than tolerable. To return to the narrative . . . " (CW I:259-60).

Here, to borrow Lincoln's language, is a fine example for contemplating the effect of racial conditioning on perception. And one should note, before passing on quickly, Lincoln's revealing slip in referring to the slavedriver as a *gentleman.* As we have indicated, and as we shall see repeatedly in the following pages, Lincoln never got over the poor White reflex of genuflecting mentally to "gentlemen" who separated mothers and fathers from children and deposited them in the Deep South where the lash of the *gentleman* and his overseer was heard all day and all night long. Notice also the direction of Lincoln's concern. He was moved to speculate on the moral condition of the slaves; he was not moved to speculate on the moral condition of *gentlemen* who bought and sold men, women, and children.

To return to the narrative:

Strike Three, and the mythologists are out. And to get at Lincoln's true position, one must situate him first in a historical space in relation to his principal protagonists—not the slaveholders nor even the Confederates, but the slaves. Lincoln was fond of saying, as we have seen, that he had no right and no inclination to keep slavemasters from doing exactly what they pleased with "their" slaves?

What did this mean in human terms? What did Lincoln's moral default mean to a runaway slave captured and tortured at the stake or a woman raped by an overseer or a grown man being lashed by another man who called himself a slavemaster and who was backed up by the state of South Carolina, the United States of America and politicians like Abraham Lincoln?

The meaning, not to mince words, was that Abraham Lincoln was, by his own words, the de facto enemy of the slave. For by repeatedly endorsing the "right" of slaveowners to do what they pleased with their slaves, Lincoln was personally and unambiguously endorsing one of the most racist and violent social systems in human history.

The key word here and elsewhere is system. The slave system Lincoln supported was a totalitarian system that controlled and conditioned Blacks and Whites, making men and women in its own image.

That system banished freedom of speech, freedom of assembly and freedom of association for Blacks and Whites in slave states.

It "suppressed," Dumond said, "free enquiry and discussion, denying by law and by violence in the slave states the right to express other than support for slavery, in private conversations, in print, in the pulpit, and in courts of justice" (357).

The system searched ships, invaded the mail, banned books and newspapers with sections critical of slavery, raped Black women, whipped Black men, silenced or exiled White preachers, murdered and tortured Black and White resisters.

This was the system that Lincoln supported. This was the system he wanted to last for a long time; and what we are concerned to emphasize here is the internal logic of the slave/racism System, how it had to create Jeffersons and Lincolns in its own image, and how it had to lead to the rotting bones on the slopes of Gettysburg.

Behind the cotton curtain of this system, four million of Abraham Lincoln's fellow human beings were systematically violated and robbed of their labor and the meaning of their lives. Every one of the four million slaves was, as Phillips told Lincoln, a human being, a father like Lincoln, a mother like Mary Todd Lincoln, a child like Robert Todd Lincoln. Every slave was a member of a family, like the families of the people who defend Lincoln's moral default, and every one of them was being violently and systematically destroyed by a system Lincoln was supporting.

To awe these slaves, to beat them into submission and steal their labor and the meaning of their lives, the slave South turned itself into a police state with slave patrols, pass systems, and guards at key installations. Behind this inhuman violence stood the power of the United States government, the massed might of the church and the university, and of all the presidents from Washington to Lincoln.

Let us understand each other.

We are talking here about the attempted destruction of a whole people for racial reasons.

We are talking about *genocide*, which is precisely by United Nations definition the attempted destruction of a whole people or a part of a people because of its race.

We are talking—let there be no misunderstanding—about a crime against humanity.

To be fair, one should say that Lincoln, like Jefferson, like Clay, like all their prototypes and aftertypes in Algeria, South Africa, and Germany, frowned on the atrocities of the system. But to single out isolated atrocities is a trick and a trap, for the system itself was an atrocity, and it engendered, mandated, demanded violence wherever it existed, producing and reproducing violent men. To be sure, overt violence was not always visible, but every relationship between a slave and a slavemaster or a White representing or supporting slave-masters was an act of violence, not because it was accompanied by force but because it unfolded in a historicity (violence past requiring violence present and violence future) of violence that defined them both, a violence that was written in words, things, institutions, whips, chains, plantations, roads, dogs and even principles, especially the principles articulated by Lincoln, who was always quoting principles, not to free the existing slaves but to justify the violence that kept Blacks in slavery. The overt violence of the system was, thus, only a reflection of a fundamental violence that defined everything and corrupted everything, even and especially the Declaration of Independence.

It is this original violence that gives meaning to the carnival of violence reported in every slave state and even in free states like Illinois. Solomon Northup, a free Black who was kidnapped and sold into slavery, said "the crack of the lash, and the shrieking of the slaves [could] be heard from dark till bedtime . . . any day almost during the entire period of the cotton-picking season" (179).

Did Lincoln know this?

Did he know what kind of system he was supporting?

Be serious.

How could a grown man, born in a slave state, not know, especially if he was active in public life and traveled in slave states and marketed goods in slave states? Having been born in the slave state of Kentucky and having been raised in the proslavery environs of Indiana and Illinois, Lincoln knew what slavery required and what it did to Black and White people. He even vacationed on the Kentucky slave plantations of his dear friend, Joshua Speed, and his slaveholding in-laws. On these visits, a personal slave servant was almost certainly assigned to him, and he learned that the Todds, like so many other slaveowners, used and abused female slaves and that some of his new in-laws were Black. Townsend tells us that a scion of the Todd family had fallen in love with a slave woman and the pair had been hurriedly dispatched to Liberia. Lincoln was also involved, as we have seen, in processing the will of his father-in-law and was personally involved in the sale and disposition of some of the Todd slaves (Townsend 179-85, 204-5).

Albert J. Beveridge, a proslavery, anti-Black Lincoln biographer, said "Lincoln was in Kentucky several times after his marriage and saw the condition, treatment, and life of the Negro bondmen in that State. He also witnessed the same things in Washington when he was in Congress, and, unless he went about the capital blindfolded, he saw gangs of slaves plodding in chains along the street" (2:31).

Lincoln didn't wear a blindfold, and there is no secret about what he knew. Does he not tell us himself in letters and speeches that he heard or imagined the pistol-shot sound of the lash striking the slave's back and the cry of the slave in pain? Speaking in Hartford, Connecticut, in 1860, he denied that he or his fellow Republicans were responsible for slave unrest. "If a slave runs away," he said, "they [White Southerners] overlook the natural causes which impelled him to the act; do not remember the oppression or the lashes he received, but charge us with instigating him to flight. If he screams when whipped, they say it is not caused by the pains he suffers, but he screams because we instigate him to outcrying" (CW 4:8).

Lincoln *knew*.

Yet—unbelievably—he was loath to see the lashing, screaming, and "outcrying" end. Worse, he was prepared to see it go on for another one hundred years. (CW 3:370).

Shall we say, as almost every major White historian says, that Lincoln supported this evil—his word—system because of his love for the Constitution? But how can anyone, even eminent historians, fail to see that this explanation is insufficient. The Constitution, as even Lincoln conceded, was/is marks on pieces of paper. The words in that document are susceptible to a thousand interpretations and cannot make anybody do anything. Eminent lawyers, with more credentials and training than Lincoln, disagreed with Lincoln on what the Constitution required of White men. Some argued plausibly that the habeas corpus provision in the Constitution covered fugitive slaves. Some argued plausibly that it was unconstitutional to deny alleged fugitives a jury trial. Still others, the brilliant Salmon Portland Chase, for example, argued ingeniously that the compact the White founding fathers made on slavery was a compact between the individual states and not a compact between the individual states and the United States.

The point here is not whether these arguments or others were sound; the point is that it is a poor lawyer who can't find some law somewhere to support his morals. The Constitution didn't interpret itself. In the end, as even Lincoln himself said, it was up to each person to interpret the Constitution according to his/her own lights. "General [Andrew] Jackson once said," Lincoln recalled, "each man was bound to support the Constitution 'as he understood it.' Now Judge [Stephen] Douglas understands the Constitution according to the Dred Scott decision, and he is bound to support it as he understands it. I understand it another way, and therefore I am bound to support it in the way in which I understand it " (CW 3:278).

Unquestionably; and the only question is why in *every* disputed case—in the case of fugitive slaves, emancipation, Black soldiers, civil rights—Lincoln understood the Constitution to be against Black people, rather than for Black people. Lawyers trained at Harvard, lawyers trained at the best and biggest law schools in the country argued in courts at every level that the Constitution could be interpreted in favor of slaves and fugitive slaves. But Lincoln, who read law for a short time in the office of a country lawyer, *never* found a constitutional provision against Black people that he didn't like. Nor did he ever find a constitutional provision that kept him from doing what he *really* wanted to do. John J. Duff, the authority on Lincoln the lawyer, said "the plain fact is that Lincoln flouted the Constitution [during the Civil War]; he flouted the Supreme Court; he countenanced the disregard of legal amenities and the invasion of due process of law—at times indefensibly, even on the ground of the exigency of a great national emergency" (145-6). The point here is not the rightness or wrongness of his actions (I think he was right); the point is that he ignored the Constitution when he wanted to and hid behind it when he wanted to.

For the hard of hearing and those with reading difficulties, Lincoln dotted the *i's* and crossed the *t's*, saying he would have supported the enslavement of the four million Blacks even if there had been no Constitutional provisions supporting slavery. He held himself, he said, under constitutional obligations to allow the people in all the states "without interference, direct or indirect, to do exactly as they please [about their domestic institutions, including slavery] "and I deny that I have any inclination to interfere with them *even if there were no such Constitutional obligation* [CW 3:116, italics added).

Lincoln went further than that: he supported the evil in places where the Constitution didn't protect slavery, in the nation's capital, for instance. "I suppose," he said, "that in reference both to its actual existence in the nation, and to our constitutional obligations, we have no right at all to disturb it in the States where it exists, and we profess that we have no more inclination to disturb it than we have the right to do it. We go further than that; we don't propose to disturb it where, in one instance [the nation's capital], we think the Constitution would permit us . . ." (CW 3:254-5).

So now you see the problem. The problem wasn't the Constitution; the problem was the man. Better still: the problem was racism in the man. Who said so? Lincoln said so, conceding at least a thousand times that he had no *inclination* to interfere with slavery. What does the word *inclination* mean? It means in dictionary terms that Lincoln had, according to his own words, no disposition, no preference, no *liking* for interfering with or changing or ending slavery in the Southern states.

Was there no limit to what Abraham Lincoln was prepared to do in order to protect slavery?

Apparently not, for one notes with surprise that he even went to the extreme of expressing support for the infamous interstate slave trade, saying that even "if I should be of opinion that Congress does possess the Constitutional power to abolish the slave trade among the different States, I should still not be in favor of the exercise of that power unless upon some *conservative* principle, akin to what I have said in relation to the abolition of slavery in the District of Columbia" (CW 3:42, italics added).

In considering these points, one must never forget that Lincoln always spoke in tongues or in a private code when he was talking about slavery or Negroes. And although he said or seemed to say that slavery was wrong, he always qualified the assertion in the same speech or a succeeding speech, saying either that slavery was wrong in an abstract sense or that it was wrong in so far as it sought to spread itself. Even that was saying too much, for Lincoln maintained that slavery was not wrong where it existed but where it did not exist. In his worldview, slavery was wrong with [1] "due regard for its *actual* existence among us, and [2] the difficulties of getting rid of it in any satisfactory way and [3]. . . all the constitutional obligations thrown about it" (CW 3:312-3, italics added).

The operational word here is *actual*. Like the word *gradual* and the words *the fathers* and *ultimate extinction*, the word *actual* was a mantra that soothed Lincoln's—and the audience's anxieties— making it possible for him to say something without saying anything. On this level, as on practically every other level, especially the Gettysburg level, words, especially words relating to slaves, Negroes, nonWhites, and the Declaration of Independence, had meaning for him, not because they pointed to things but because they pointed to themselves and sounded good in and of themselves.

The word *actual* functioned on that level in his poetic economy. Saying it changed the temperature and the meaning of sentences, giving them at the same time more density, and less. Thus, the Declaration of Independence was good but could not be implemented in Illinois or Georgia because of the *actual* presence of Negroes in Illinois and Georgia. Inversely, slavery was evil with due regard to its actual presence. The word *actual* in these assertions is a code word and a sign, saying that whenever Lincoln said bad things about slavery and good things about the Declaration he wanted everybody to understand that the fact that Blacks were actually there in slavery in Georgia and in subordination in Illinois cancelled, annulled, repealed, revoked, rescinded, abrogated, overrode, suspended, negated whatever the Constitution or the Declaration or the Bible said about human beings and the human condition. All this was as clear as anything needed to be to untutored voters who stood for hours in the hot sun listening to Lincoln, and the only problem is why twentieth-century scholars find it so difficult to decipher the Lincoln code in the white silence of their libraries.

The code was designed to hide Lincoln and his listeners—and his interpreters—from the realities of race. It was designed to keep the pretty words and to hide the ugly reality. Above all else, it was the linguistic equivalent of slavery. I don't mean this in an idealistic sense; I mean that the use of code words to make slavery and the Declaration of Independence compatible and to exclude Blacks and Indians from the common good was slavery itself, with its cotton and whips and chains, invading the intellectual and moral realms. It was the actual existence of slavery in the law, in the morals, in the being of Abraham Lincoln and the supporters of slavery.

The code word *gradual*, for instance, was the system thinking itself, reproducing itself, and defending itself. Unlike the word *actual*, which was a lineblocker word designed to turn back the offense on fourth and one, the word *gradual* was a fullback word seeking not a touchdown or even a long gain but a short, safe probe with minimum risks. Even that is saying too much. For the word *gradual* as Lincoln used it was not designed to change anything or anybody immediately—it was designed to outflank people who wanted to do something immediately by holding out the prospect of a slow and gradual change a long time in the future. It was, as Lincoln's first emancipation plan proves, a nonword designed to hide a nonact. In this instance, anyway, the word was the man, slow, cautious, conservative, *gradual*, an eloquent nonword designed to stave off a real act.

There is still another word that must be taken into consideration in explaining the divided politician, and that is the word *fence*. Time and time again, Lincoln used that word as a metaphor to define his policy on slavery. The way he put it, the Missouri Compromise, which institutionalized a half-slave, half-free America, was a good fence that contained the starving and famished animals—Lincoln's metaphor—that threatened White America and its fine meadows. In overturning the key provisions of the Missouri Compromise, Senator Douglas and others, Lincoln said, were tearing down the fence that protected the free and the White.

Will someone say that I am putting the case too strongly? Listen then to the chief witness, who illustrated his position by asking audiences to suppose that "Abraham Lincoln has a fine meadow, containing beautiful springs of water, and well fenced, which John Calhoun had agreed with Abraham (originally owning the land in common) should be his, and the agreement had been consummated in the most solemn manner, regarded by both as *sacred*." But in the course of time, John Calhoun falls on bad times and looks covetously "on Lincoln's meadow, and goes to it and throws down the fences, and exposes it to the ravages of his starving and famishing cattle . . ." (CW:2:230).

Lincoln gives us the truth unwittingly and in spite of himself—as he often does—in this revealing story. Notice the animal metaphor he uses to describe Black human beings, and notice that he says that the agreement to put up the fence and to make America half slave and half free was "sacred." One has to be a little disoriented to believe that the man who revealed himself in this revealing story was itching to let the ravishing hogs and cattles he described into the fine white meadow of his dreams.

Lincoln told this story all over Illinois. A month later, in a speech at Springfield, Illinois, he returned to the theme, saying: "If I have a field . . . around which the cattle or the hogs linger and crave to pass the fence, and I go and tear down the fence, will it be supposed that I do not by that act encourage them to enter. *Even the hogs would know better*—Much more *men*, who are a higher order of the animal world" (CW 2:242, Lincoln's italics).

Two years later, in 1856, Lincoln was still telling his parable, and it was getting boring. This, at any rate, was the suggestion of a story in the *Illinois State Register*, which said that Lincoln "told his old story about the fence (meaning Missouri restriction) being torn down and the cattle eating up the crops . . ."(CW 2:340).

Nothing could be clearer: Lincoln wanted to fence the slaves— and Negroes—in, and he wanted to fence them out. The Missouri Compromise or the Constitution or whatever arrangement that fenced slaves and Negroes *in*, in the slave South and fenced them *out* of the fine white meadows of the North was good, even sacred. Lincoln had no intention of trying to tear down that fence and free the individuals concentrated there. On the contrary, he looked with disfavor, with horror even, on anyone who wanted to tear down that fence and let the excluded individuals in.

Of all the incredible statements Lincoln made on slavery, the wildest perhaps was the assertion he made in New Haven, Connecticut, two months before he was nominated for president. Warning once again against any effort to interfere with slavery where it existed, he said that if a half-slave, half-free government had not existed in 1860, it would have been necessary to form the same government with the same protection for slavery that "our blessed fathers" formed in 1787. Even at that late date, it would have been necessary, he said, to create the half-slave, half-free government that he said could not endure (CW 4:17).

So much for houses and politicians divided against themselves.

But, listen, someone will say, what about the great notes Lincoln wrote to himself about slavery? And what about the great line the professors and museum curators are always quoting, "As I would not be a *slave*, so I would not be a master" (CW 2:532)? The answer is in the questions, for Lincoln was talking to himself; and *the proof of my thesis is that even when he was talking to himself he* never *said a single word hostile to slavery where it existed or in favor of equal rights for Blacks.*

As for the famous quotation, it is meaningless politically, for it didn't require Lincoln or slaveholders to do anything. So, to take the first and the last questions together, Lincoln was talking about abstract slavery, not real slavery or real Blacks, and he was talking to himself. The clincher is that the words he wrote didn't improve his eyesight or his morality. On the contrary, they soothed his conscience and justified his support of slavery where it existed. Here again I'm not saying anything new. The same contradictions, oftentimes masked and always explained away, can be found in the works of Lincoln defenders. "In 1861," Mark E. Neely Jr. wrote, "he more than once actually forced others who were trying to free slaves to cease doing so."

Actually.

This much is clear: What Lincoln said was one thing, and what he did was another. From first to last, in war and in peace, his approach to slavery was based on five paradoxes, and all the problems of his interpreters can be traced to their attempts to ignore one or more of these paradoxes.

The first paradox—to repeat—is that the man who said that America could not endure half slave and half free did everything he could for fifty-four of his fifty-six years to ensure that America remained half slave and half free.

The second paradox is that Lincoln believed White freedom was a function of Black unfreedom and that the continued freedom and prosperity of Whites in the South and the North depended on the continued enslavement and debasement of Blacks in the South.

Lincoln didn't hide it; he didn't whisper it; he said out loud that the constitutional compromise of 1787 between White freedom and Black slavery ensured the White Constitution and White liberty and that enslaving Blacks and keeping them subordinate was a White necessity. "We had slavery among us," Lincoln said, "we could not get *our* constitution unless we permitted *them* to remain in slavery, we could not secure the good we did secure if we grasped for more . . ." (CW 2:501, italics added).

Never before had the truth appeared so clearly:

White good was a function of Black bad.

Whites were up because Blacks were down.

Whites were rich because Blacks were poor.

Whites were free because Blacks were slaves.

By announcing that shameful secret, without shame, Lincoln embraced it and made himself responsible for it.

"We could not get our *Constitution unless we permitted* them *to remain in slavery . . . ."*

It followed from this that the paradox of White freedom was that it had *a paramount duty* to defend Black slavery.

"I hold it to be a paramount duty of us in the free states," Lincoln said, "due to the Union of the states, and perhaps to liberty itself (paradox though it may seem), to let the slavery of the other states alone . . . "(CW 1:348).

What Lincoln said here is almost as astounding as what he said above. For what does this mean if not that the paradox of Lincoln liberty was that its first duty was to defend slavery.

So saying, Lincoln endorsed—without a dissenting voice from any of his interpreters to date—the peculiarly Western idea that you can sacrifice some people in order to enrich others. It never seemed to occur to him until the Second Inaugural Address, which he immediately forgot, that everyone who makes that bargain makes or finds his own Gettysburg and ends up meditating on the terrible and self-enforcing imperatives that humans must choose for ALL or for none and that you can't question the humanity of others without losing your own.

Flowing with and out of this was an even greater paradox. For Lincoln didn't believe, as we have seen, that slavery "could be at *once* eradicated, without producing a greater evil, even to the cause of human liberty itself "(CW 2:130, Lincoln's italics).

What an extraordinary thing to say! What could possibly be a greater evil to the cause of human liberty than slavery? Freeing all slaves at once, Lincoln said, knocking down all the fences at once—Lincoln's metaphor—and producing the specter of racial mixing and racial conflict over jobs and other values.

The fifth paradox is that Lincoln opposed the extension of slavery not out of the interest of the slaves but out of the interests of Whites. When he made all those brave speeches about keeping slavery out of Kansas and California, he was not thinking about Black people at all—he was thinking about an endless vista of White settlements on the prairie. Speaking in Peoria, Illinois, in 1854, he said that he, like Thomas Jefferson, wanted the territories to be the "the happy home of teeming millions of free, white, prosperous people, and no slave among them" (CW 2:249). In 1856 in Kalamazoo, Michigan, he said the territories "should be kept open for the homes of free white people" (CW 2:363).

It was a litany: "We want them [the territories] for the homes of free white people." When Senator Douglas argued that Lincoln and his supporters had no direct interest in what happened in the territories, Lincoln replied, "I think we have some interest. I think that as white men we have. Do we not wish for an outlet for our surplus population, if I may so express myself?" (CW 3:311).

Lincoln went on to charge in this and other speeches that the extension of slavery posed a direct threat to the economic position of White men. He stressed in particular the threat to White labor and was not above the demagoguery of warning White labor of the threat of *all* Black labor, slave and free. If Northerners permitted slavery to spread to the territories, he said, "Negro equality will be abundant, as every White laborer will have occasion to regret when he is elbowed from his plow or his anvil by slave niggers" (CW 3:78).

What was the best way to prevent this? The best thing to do, he said, was to keep the territories free of all Negroes, slave and free, whatever the spelling. "Is it not rather our *duty* to make labor more respectable by preventing *all* black competition, especially in the territories?" (CW 3:79, italics added). Notice that word: *duty*. We shall return to it again and again. Abraham Lincoln believed it was his duty to White people, that it was *his obligation as a White man*, to keep Black people in slavery and in subordinate positions.

Not the emancipation of the slaves, not the building of a rainbow nation, but the way to the White Dream was his main concern.

13

Ignoring America's Greatest Moral Crisis

NEVER having opposed slavery where it existed and never having assisted the Abolitionist Movement in *any* way Abraham Lincoln came late to the battle, his trumpet giving an uncertain sound.

All through the 1830s and 1840s, in the midst of the greatest moral crisis in the history of America, he remained silent and inactive.

Evaluating Lincoln's "first considerable literary effort," the Lyceum address of 1838, Roy P. Basler, one of the pillars of the Lincoln Establishment, chided Lincoln for "completely ignoring the greatest moral issue of the day—the abolition of slavery" (1946, 8).

Evaluating the Gettysburg Address of 1863, Garry Wills, another one of Lincoln's warm admirers, noted that this universally admired effort, "for all its artistry and eloquence, does not directly address the prickliest issues of its historic moment" (90).

Evaluating Lincoln's whole approach to the slavery issue, historian Ralph G. Newman said in *Ebony* magazine in February 1959 that he "ignored the greatest moral question of the time."

There's no way around it.

From 1836 to 1863 and beyond, the man called America's "Moral Pope" made a career out of evading the greatest moral issues of his time. If, as Dante and Martin Luther King Jr. said, the hottest places in hell are reserved for people who stand on the sidelines in moments of great moral crisis, Lincoln's sideline posture should at least give us pause if not a reason for not standing on the sidelines in the great moral crises his moral default has bequeathed us.

While Lincoln slept, thousands of Black and White Americans rose in rebellion and risked stiff fines and prison terms in order to oppose slavery and help runaway slaves. In the beginning of this crusade and for a long time afterward, as I have indicated elsewhere (1975, 129-32), pioneer Black abolitionists like Samuel E. Cornish and James Forten educated themselves and their White colleagues, most of whom were stuck in reformist-gradualist holes. Building on that platform in the 1830s, in the wake of the slave rebellion of Nat Turner and the founding of William Lloyd Garrison's *Liberator* and the American Anti-Slavery Society, Black and White activists created a militant abolitionist movement which goaded and provoked a slumbering people into facing the greatest moral issue of the day.

The abolitionists accomplished this feat by creating a mass movement remarkably similar to the Freedom Movement of the 1960s. Like the demonstrators of the sixties, the militant abolitionists pioneered in nonviolent direct action, staging sit-ins and freedom rides. They, like their modern counterparts, marched, demonstrated, and picketed. In the end, the militant abolitionists discovered that the issue of Black freedom is a total issue that raises total questions about the meaning of America. The end result was that the Freedom Movement of the 1860s, like the Freedom Movement of the 1960s, branched out into the issues of women's rights, sexual freedom, and economic democracy.

The White wing of this movement was composed largely of middle-income people, ministers, lawyers, teachers, with strong representation from New England and New England-influenced communities and Quakers, Presbyterians, and Congregationalists.

These men and women were arguably the greatest collection of White folks ever assembled on the North American continent, not because they found *the* answer to the race question but because they posed the right questions, putting a parenthesis around everything people have said and thought in this land, including and most especially everything thought and said at Independence Hall and Gettysburg.

All across the North now, as the future Gettysburg orator stuck his head in the sand along with other Whigs, men and women mobilized against the American government. And it is impossible to take his measure if we don't compare him directly with White men who demonstrated more vision, more courage, and more morality in his own times and on his own terrain.

In Ohio in these years, Salmon P. Chase defended fugitive slaves, attended Black meetings, and created the ideological infrastructure of the political antislavery movement.

In Massachusetts, Charles Sumner helped inaugurate the struggle for integrated education.

In Illinois, Owen Lovejoy defied the state and the federal government and assisted every slave who came to his door. In a House speech, he told the nation: "Owen Lovejoy lives at Princeton, Illinois, three quarters of a mile east of the village; and he aids every fugitive that comes to his door and asks it . . . . Thou invisible demon of slavery . . . *I bid you defiance in the name of my God"* (Magdol 51).

What was the future emancipator doing all this time?

He was, as usual, sitting on the fence, telling everybody how much he loved the Declaration of Independence and expressing regrets that it was not unfortunately applicable to the real world or real Blacks in Illinois or South Carolina.

While Lincoln was explaining why his love for the Declaration of Independence and the Constitution made it impossible for him to do anything concrete for concrete slaves, some of his White neighbors were hiding refugees in cellars and barns and moving them from station to station on the Underground Railroad leading to Chicago and Canada. Wilbur H. Siebert, the authority on the Underground Railroad, said White citizens in Illinois "took Negroes to Chicago concealed in wagons loaded with sacks of bran." A certain

Mr. Van Doren of Quincy, he said, personally assisted "some two or three hundred fugitives." Philo Carpenter of Chicago reportedly "escorted 200 fugitives to vessels bound for Canada"(61, 88). No less courageous were Calvin DeWolf, J. H. Collins, Ichabod Codding, and especially Zebina Eastman and Dr. C. V. Dyer, who frequently helped slaves to escape, "sometimes secreting them in their own residences" (Harris 61).

These men and women were by any reckoning more courageous and more moral than Lincoln. Who were they? Were they superheroes or a superelite? Not at all, says N. Dwight Harris, who is very good on this point and whose treatment in *The History of Negro Servitude in Illinois* I am following here. "Many," he says, "were well-to-do farmers, brave, rough-handed men, simple in their lives and creeds. Some were honest tradesfolk and prominent citizens in the towns."

The cost of courage, then and now, was high. Some Underground Railroad operators were shunned by their neighbors; others were physically attacked; still others were ruined economically by court suits and exorbitant fines. But nothing, neither fines nor violence nor ostracism, stopped these Whites, who were strengthened rather than weakened by persecution and who displayed everywhere, Harris says, "an indomitable courage backed by a will not to be balked or thwarted" (58).

We are talking here—let us repeat—about White men and women who risked their careers and their lives by opposing the Fugitive Slave Law in the state of Illinois while Abraham Lincoln was doing everything he could to uphold that law and the institution of slavery in the South. Exclusive and diversionary attention on Abraham Lincoln, who was anti-antislavery, has diverted attention from the only antislavery leaders who mattered, men and women like Dr. Richard Eells, who organized a statewide abolitionist movement and created the Liberty Party and Free Soil Party constituencies that Lincoln latched on to when he awakened from his long sleep.

The crucial point here is not that that some Whites succumbed to racist and economic conditioning but that so many with so few resources defied the times and unjust laws and gave their support to Black fugitives. Some went to prison and paid stiff fines for moving slaves from station to station on the Underground Railroad. Nobody remembers them, of course, which is why they are always in the minority and the Lincolns are always in the majority.

Of the men and women who created these foundations, none was more persistent and creative than a group of virtually forgotten editors who began the long and still unfinished task of giving concrete content to the Declaration of Independence Lincoln only talked about. Benjamin Lundy, editor of the *Genius of Universal Emancipation*, was the great pioneer of this group, followed by Zebina Eastman, who edited the *Western Citizen* and the *Free West*.

Undeterred by persecution and undaunted by criticism from conservatives like Lincoln, these men and others kept the community agitated by publicizing major fugitive slave cases, petitioning for repeal of the Illinois Black Laws and urging "the right and justice of assisting all Negroes to escape from bondage."

Zebina Eastman, editor of the *Western Citizen*, urged defiance of the Fugitive Slave Law. Unlike Lincoln, Eastman opposed compensation to slaveholders "because the title to slaves originated in robbery and kidnapping." He also opposed colonizationists like Lincoln, who wanted to deport Blacks and create a White republic. Blacks, he said, were native-born Americans and had as much right to live in America as Whites.[30]

The Black and White leaders of this first wave of political abolitionists prepared the arguments that Lincoln appropriated when he awakened from his long sleep. The leader of the first major antislavery political wave was not Lincoln but Salmon P. Chase of Ohio, who, the *New York Times* said later, did more than any other person to create the ideological foundations of the political antislavery movement. In an 1850 letter to Charles Sumner, Chase himself listed the three principal Chase ideas that Lincoln and others echoed after passage of the Kansas-Nebraska Act (1903, 205):

> 1. That the original policy of the Government was that of slavery restriction. 2. That under the Constitution Congress cannot establish or maintain slavery in the territories. 3. That the original policy of the Government has been subverted and the Constitution violated for the extension of slavery, and the establishment of the political supremacy of the Slave Power.

Year by year, all through the thirties, forties and fifties, Chase and other abolitionists pressed these and other antislavery ideas. For all this time, for a whole generation, Lincoln did nothing or said nothing in defense of the four million slaves. For all this time, for 10,950 days, he ran with the hunters of human beings and not with the hunted human beings.

While Lincoln slept, thousands of Negroes, slave and free, were tracked down, like beasts of the field, and shipped South for resale at auctions and in slave markets. To cite a single chilling example from the early years of this peculiarly American "business," a woman named Matilda who had lived in Cincinnati for some time was claimed by professional kidnappers allegedly representing a slaveholder named Larkin. Although the evidence indicated clearly that she was not a fugitive within the terms of the act, the judge turned her over to the slavecatcher, who hurriedly put the terrified woman on the next boat to St. Louis. The slavemaster, we are told, never saw her again. Like thousands of other Blacks, Matilda X—the record, which is itself racist, does not list her last name—disappeared into the white hole of history, probably after sale at an auction or a slave mart (Niven 50-4).

During the whole of this period, fugitive slave notices were published in Illinois newspapers, but no one in authority, least of all state Representative Abraham Lincoln, protested. Simon says that Lincoln probably saw ads like the following one (131), which appeared in the *Vandalia Register,* a paper he generally read:

> $100 Reward. Runaway from the subscriber, in Washington County, Mo., on the night of the 3d of October, a Negro man named
>
> # BILL
>
> about five feet, eight or nine inches high, of a black complexion, bowlegged, a small scar near one of his ears, beard light, and down cast when spoken to. Bill is about twenty-nine years old, and had on when he left home a brown cassinet coat, dark pantaloons and vest and took with him a shot gun, and butcher knife. I will give one hundred Dollars to any person that will apprehend said negro and deliver him to me at my residence, near Potosi, or secure him in some jail in this State, so that I may get him again.
>
> JACOB BOAS

Although fugitive slave ads were conspicuous in Illinois newspapers and appeared throughout Lincoln's legislative career, neither Lincoln nor any other legislator, Beveridge said, "did or said anything about the matter" (1:182).

"Running and catching n——rs," to use Lincoln's indelicate phrase, was so abhorrent to some lawyers that they voluntarily defended runaways. Many of the greatest names of the period put their careers and reputations on the line in this effort. Some, like Salmon Chase and Thaddeus Stevens, earned the title of "attorney-general of the slaves." Besides Chase, the honor roll of attorneys general of the slaves included John Andrew of Massachusetts, John P. Hale of New Hampshire, and George W. Julian of Indiana.

Abraham Lincoln's name was not on that honor roll. His law partner, William H. Herndon, accepted fugitive slave cases, but Lincoln didn't, primarily, John W. Bunn said, "because of his unwillingness to be a party to a violation of the Fugitive Slave Law" (Weik 198).

Traditional historians usually cite the *Bailey* v. *Cromwell* case in

Lincoln's defense. But Lincoln didn't represent "the Negro girl" or freedom in that case. He represented David Bailey, who bought a Black woman—the record is again racist and must itself be corrected—giving a promissory note pending authenticated papers proving the woman was a slave. Bailey later refused to pay the note, saying the seller had not produced the necessary papers. Lincoln, in character, represented the man who bought a Black woman and who refused to pay for her because of a defect in the papers, establishing thereby, among other things, that it was wrong to sell a Black woman if you couldn't produce papers proving that she was a slave.

Although Lincoln didn't represent fugitive slaves, he represented at least one "fugitive slaveowner." The case grew out of the peculiar Illinois law which said, in effect, that a slaveowner could work slaves in Illinois if they were clearly identified as seasonal workers and were not kept in the state permanently. Among the slaveowners who took advantage of this law was a swinging bachelor named Robert Matson, who commuted, so to speak, with his slaves between his plantation in Bourbon County, Kentucky, and his plantation in Coles County, Illinois. To get around the Illinois law, he brought slaves to Illinois in the spring and returned them to Kentucky in the fall.[31]

Everything worked so smoothly that Matson got careless, letting his foreman, a formidable slave preacher named Anthony Bryant, stay in Illinois year after year, which made him a free man in fact. In 1847, probably as a favor to Bryant, Matson brought in Bryant's wife, Jane, "a Bright Mulatto 40 years old,"and their four children: Mary Catherine, fourteen; Sally Ann, twelve; Mary Jane, five; and a young son, Robert Noah Bryant. The mother was so fair-skinned that she could pass for White, and it was rumored that she was the daughter of Matson's brother.

As in so many cases of this sort, sex proved to be Matson's downfall. The live-in girlfriend at his Coles County plantation was a woman named Mary Corbin, who developed an intense dislike for Jane Bryant, partly, one can imagine, because of her beauty, partly, no doubt, because Jane Bryant refused to act like *her* slave.

We know what happened next. There were scenes, tantrums, and Mary Corbin played her trump card, telling the Bryants that she was going to ask the slaveowner to ship the whole family back to Kentucky and sell them to the Deep South.

Alarmed, the Bryants ran away to the nearby town of Oakland, where they were aided by a group of abolitionists, led by innkeeper Gideon M. Ashmore, a native of Tennessee, and a young doctor named Hiram Rutherford.

Matson swore out affidavits, and Jane Bryant and her children were jailed and charged with being runaway slaves. The abolitionists, led by Dr. Hiram Rutherford and Gideon Ashmore, two of the Illinois Whites Lincoln biographers always ignore, counterattacked, filing a writ of habeas corpus. In a separate suit, they attacked the morals of Matson, who was subsequently convicted of living in sin, not because he was holding human beings in slavery but because he was "living in open state of fornication with one Mary Corbin."

This was, as can be imagined, enormously entertaining to the bored farmers, who watched, bemused, as the two sides jockeyed for position in the selection of the equivalent of a Coles County legal dream team. In the midst of the wrangling and suing, Lincoln, who had just been elected to Congress but who had not been sworn in, showed up at the county seat. John Duff, an expert on Lincoln the lawyer, said he couldn't fight "down a suspicion that despite Lincoln's fairly numerous court appearances in Coles County from 1841 to 1846, he went to Charleston in October of 1847 solely because of the Matson case, and in anticipation of being retained in the matter" (134).

Dr. Rutherford was delighted to see him. Having known Lincoln for years and having heard him talk about "the wrongs" of slavery, it was only natural that he would ask Lincoln to represent the slaves in the habeas corpus proceeding. When Lincoln told him that he had already been retained by the slaveowners, the shocked doctor denounced him in no uncertain terms. Lincoln, Dr. Rutherford said later, seemed to be ashamed of himself, and tried to get out of his commitment. By that time, however, the doctor's dander was up and he hired another lawyer.

Why did Lincoln accept the case of this disreputable slaveowner, who had been convicted of living in sin and who was suspected of forcing himself on Jane Bryant and other slave women? Was he down on his luck? Did he need ready cash? Or was he blinded by his own racism and the dissembling rhetoric he used to rationalize it? Certain members of the Lincoln fraternity say, curiously, that he accepted the case because a lawyer is a gun for hire, and that it doesn't matter whether he shoots for freedom or slavery. Lincoln's "business," Donald said, "was law, not morality" (104).

Whatever his business, or his morality, Lincoln's insensitivity shocked even his friends. Henry Whitney, one of the lawyers who rode the Eighth Circuit with Lincoln, said "the Matson case was one of the strangest episodes in Lincoln's career at the bar" (315). What made it even stranger is that Lincoln's cocounsel in the case was the infamous Usher F. Linder, a former attorney general of the state who had egged the mob on in the murder of Elijah Parish Lovejoy.

The Matson case was called on Saturday night, October 16, in the courthouse at the county seat of Charleston, where Lincoln would later make the most racist appeal of the Lincoln-Douglas debates. Lincoln argued that the slaveowner had a right to transfer slaves from his Kentucky plantation to his Illinois plantation. Jane Bryant and her children, he said, were *in transitu* and were not permanently domiciled on the Coles County plantation. State Senator Charles H. Constable and Orlando B. Ficklen, arguing for the defendants, said the Bryants were free under the Ordinance of 1787 and Illinois law, and the court agreed. The next morning, after a big breakfast, Lincoln, an eyewitness said, "mounted on his old gray mare, ruefully set out for the next county on the circuit. As he threw across the animal's back his saddle-bags, filled with soiled linen and crumpled court papers, and struck out across the 'measureless prairie,' he gave no further sign, if he experienced it, of any regret because, as a lawyer, he had upheld the cause of the strong against the weak" (Weik 1897, 757).

The Bryants migrated to Liberia. Before leaving the country, they made a victory tour, appealing for funds in Springfield and other towns. One of the contributors to the fund was Lincoln's law partner, William H. Herndon.

Lincoln's role in this case is all the more discreditable in view of the established practices of the day. A slave who publicly challenged a master and who exposed him to public ridicule took a fateful step, fraught with unimaginable consequences. For if he lost and was returned to his master, he faced a future of nightmarish consequences.

Lincoln knew the rules of the game. He knew, he had to know, that he was asking the court to sentence Jane Bryant and her three daughters and son to cruel and unusual punishment and, possibly, death. For if he had been successful and if the Bryants had been returned to Matson, two things would have almost certainly happened. First, Jane Bryant would have been whipped and probably tortured. Secondly, the Bryant family would have been broken up and sold to different slavemasters in the Deep South. The wild cards in all this were Jane Bryant and her older daughters, who would have in all likelihood brought a premium price and probably, almost certainly, would have ended up as mistresses or, worse, prostitutes in what was called the "fancy" trade.

Lincoln partisans would say later that Lincoln's heart wasn't in it and that he virtually threw the case. "Hogwash," said John J. Duff, citing evidence from opposing counsel that Lincoln argued "plausibly, ingeniously and forcibly" in favor of returning Jane Bryant and her children to slavery (139). The "attempt to gloss over Lincoln's acceptance of the case by having it appear that he was halfhearted in protecting the interests of a slaveholder, even though his own client," Duff wrote, "is pure hogwash—another instance of the fantastic length to which some authors have gone to render immune from any slight dispraise the name of Abraham Lincoln. Abounding in the field of Lincoln literature, as in the case of no other historical figure, are the myths so assiduously propagated by the Lincoln sanctifiers, who regard as almost indecent anything short of adulation of one whom they would present as a candidate for sainthood" (141).

It can be argued on this level that Lincoln's continuing vogue is a function not of moral triumph but of moral failure. In any case, it is disquieting to note that the moral imperatives Lincoln evaded are the same moral imperatives his prototypes evaded in colonial Africa, the antebellum and postbellum South and North, the Third Reich, French Algeria, South Africa, wherever and whenever men and women have created situations of oppression based on the subordination of people because of race, religion, or ethnicity.

Lincoln's failure to respond to the defining moral crisis of his age foreshadowed one of the most agonizing questions of the modern world: What is the duty of an oppressor or a member of an oppressing group when his group is responsible for a situation of total oppression? What should an oppressor or a person identified with the oppressing group do in a situation of collective evil sanctioned by the violence of the state. Since there is no possibility of acting morally short of a destruction of the situation which makes him or her illegitimately privileged, no matter what he or she does, where should the oppressor or the person identified with the oppressing group stand? Should he or she, abandoning all others, stand with the oppressed, as Wendell Phillips and John Brown did, or should he or she stand with his group, whatever the evil. Abraham Lincoln said slavery was evil, perhaps the greatest of all evils. Yet he consciously and deliberately chose whiteness, slavery, man-hunting, and evil. What does that tell us about his morals, and ours?

American moralists, who are famous for choosing their victims— and their morals—and who have 20-20 vision in Germany, Russia, and China but are struck blind and dumb in the face of the moral failure of Lincoln or Robert E. Lee, never get around to posing these questions. One reads their books in vain for some light on the moral dilemmas four hundred years of the Slave Trade and two hundred years of slavery, concentration camps, and apartheid prisons have bequeathed to us.

None of the major or minor Lincoln lyricists raise these questions. Is it wrong, for example, for human beings to hold other human beings in slavery? The inarticulate major premise of almost all Lincoln lyricists is that it was right or at least understandable to hold *colored* people in slavery in the nineteenth century but wrong to hold White people in slavery in the twentieth century or any century. Why do learned men and women think that? What makes them think that the century or the color changes the scale of values?

Abraham Lincoln said there was no difference morally between White slaveholders and White nonslaveholders (CW 2:230). He believed or said he believed that it was wrong to hold human beings in slavery in the territories and right and legal to hold them in slavery in Virginia. Don E. Fehrenbacher noted correctly, to his credit, that Lincoln never seems to have suspected "that systematic racial discrimination might be, like slavery, a stain on the national honor and a crime against mankind" (1987, 112). Fehrenbacher understates the case, for Lincoln never, not even in 1865, suspected that slavery where it existed was a crime against mankind. The proof is that he supported slavery where it existed until at least 1863 and opposed all efforts to impose sanctions on the people responsible for that crime.

What shall we say about a man wallowing in that moral confusion, and what shall we say about twentieth-century interpreters who—after Auschwitz and Sharpeville and My Lai—not only ignore the confusion but praise it.

Here, once more, Lincoln personally foreshadowed the most agonizing issues of the twentieth century, posing in his life and politics a question of incalculable importance and danger.

When is it right to do wrong?

When is it right to disobey a law that dehumanizes and attempts to destroy a whole people for reasons of race? And when is it wrong to do right, i.e, to support and accept such a law because it is inscribed in

the Constitution or endorsed by your race and most of your neighbors? And since the costar of the Lincoln morality play is Robert E.
Lee, when and if and under what circumstances is it appropriate to
commit treason? Thaddeus Stevens and other liberal Republicans are
endlessly abused today because they thought war criminals should
have been punished, but it is worth noting that some of Lincoln's
biggest supporters, including secretary John Hay and Attorney General James Speed, a Kentuckian, expressed similar ideas.

As much as the Russian and German concentration camps, as
much as the apartheid prison, slavery was a collective crime, and
everybody who supported it, then and now, and everybody who
inherits its fruits and accepts them and justifies them is personally
responsible for it.

What should a moral man or woman do in an immoral situation?

He or she tries first—if he is moral—to destroy by whatever means
possible an evil system that makes morality and ethics impossible.
In the interim, he tries to increase marginally the amount of good in
the world by acting in the direction of the more human and against
the less human. Lincoln, to his discredit, did precisely the opposite,
acting—in his support of the Illinois Black Laws, the Fugitive Slave
Law and the Slave System, and in his personal attempt, as an attorney, to send a mother and her four children back to slavery—in the
direction of the less human.

Why did Lincoln do it?

Lincoln said he was only obeying the law.

Where have we heard this before?

Of course: That's what the good German said and the good
Frenchman (in Algeria) and the good American (in Springfield and
Birmingham and Charleston).

Like "good" people everywhere who are always doing bad things
because bad is defined as good, Lincoln said he regretted what he was
doing, but, hey, he asked in Alton what was a man to do. The Constitution said, according to his reading, that slaves who escaped were to
be returned to their "owners." This was, Lincoln said, a "right," and

a right was "barren" without legislation to make it "efficient."

We see where this is heading: To be for the end is to be for whatever is required—robbery, murder, kidnapping—to reach the end. Lincoln didn't believe that—did he? But that's what he said. Long before the horrors of our century, he embraced the means-end argument, saying that morality was what supported the Union and the political structures of a slave state (CW 3:317).

In a letter to Speed, Lincoln said, "I confess I hate to see the poor creatures hunted down, and caught, and carried back to their stripes, and unrewarded toils, but I bite my lip and keep quiet" (CW 2:320).

In this image of Lincoln biting his lip and remaining silent in the face of the stripes and screams of the victims of the law he supported, we have the whole history of liberalism in the United States of America, the Third Reich, and the Union of South Africa.

Like Rip Van Winkle, America's greatest moral authority slept through the gravest moral crisis in American history.

14

Supporting The Great American Slave Hunt

ONGRESS passed the Fugitive Slave Law on Wednesday, September 18, 1850. What happened next was a national crime, never expiated, seldom if ever discussed. A *Liberator* dispatch from Pittsburgh, published on October 4, 1850, said, "Nearly all the waiters in the hotels have fled to Canada. Sunday, thirty fled; on Monday, forty; on Tuesday, fifty; on Wednesday, thirty . . . . They went in large bodies armed with pistols and bowie knives, determined to die rather than be captured."

The same thing happened in Illinois, where Lincoln and others urged citizens to go out into the street and help marshals capture men, women and children and return them to slavery. Appalled by the moral myopia of Whites like Lincoln and terrified by the increasing boldness of slavecatchers backed by the power of the United States government, abolitionists, Black and White, told Blacks without authenticated papers to flee for their lives because there was not enough virtue in the United States to keep men from capturing them and returning them to slavery.

They fled to Canada from all over, some three thousand of them, in the first three months after passage of the Fugitive Slave Law. In Chicago, on the day after passage of the act, Black refugees boarded railroad cars chartered by Zebina Eastman and two Blacks, John

Jones and Louis Isabell, to take them to Canada. Harriet Tubman spoke for slaves all over America when she said that she "wouldn't trust Uncle Sam with [her] people no longer" and that the Fugitive Slave Law made it necessary to take fugitive slaves directly to Canada without stopping in the United States (Bradford 39).

Unquestionably the high/low point of official U.S. racism, the law denied runaway slaves the right of trial by jury. Under its provisions, a Black person charged with the "crime" of escaping from slavery could not even testify on his own behalf in star chamber proceedings which gave the judge ten dollars if he ruled against the accused Black and five dollars if he ruled in his/her favor. This was a legal obscenity and a personal threat to every Black, slave or free; for any Black, even a Black who had lived in a Northern community for years, could be accused, tried and hustled off to slavery or the auction block before his family or friends could intervene.

Viewed from the vantage point of the slave, the Fugitive Slave Law was a hysterical response that doomed the system it was designed to defend by, first, nationalizing slavery and, secondly, by personalizing slavery, forcing every White, under pain of severe penalties, to choose between being an accomplice of slaveholders and slavecatchers or a rebel against the Constitution and the United States government. Lincoln readily accommodated himself to this dilemma, choosing slaveholders and slavecatchers in beautiful language that is still admired by people who have already decided in their own lives for or against fugitives, Black or White. Other Whites, some more conservative than Lincoln, said nothing could make them dirty their hands by complying with this law.

Nowhere was this more apparent perhaps than in the city of Chicago, where the Common Council declared the Fugitive Slave Act unconstitutional. According to Charles W. Mann, whose account I am following here, the council adopted on Monday night, October 21, by a vote of nine to two, a resolution which said that the act violated the Constitution by suspending the right of habeas corpus and abolishing trial by jury, endangering not only slaves but White indentured servants. For these reasons, and others, the council said the "free States" senators and representatives who helped pass the law were to be ranked "with the traitors Benedict Arnold and Judas Iscariot" and resolved that "the citizens, officers and police of this city be and they are hereby requested to abstain from any and all interference in the capture and delivering up of the fugitives of unrighteous oppression of whatever nation, name or color."

Some historians have suggested that the council reversed itself after Senator Douglas, one of the "traitors" referred to in the resolution, pleaded for compromise, saying in a three-and-one-half-hour Chicago speech that the council action was "unmitigated nullification." A meeting of Douglas's proslavery supporters "passed without a dissenting vote a series of resolutions drawn up by his own hand," but the Council refused on November 29 by a vote of nine to three to rescind its vote. "Thus," Mann said, "were the co-ordinate powers of the Common Council of Chicago established and its independence maintained." He could have said that never before or since has the Chicago City Council—which was criticized later for subservience to the Democratic machine—spoken so eloquently for freedom in America.

Heartened perhaps by the action of the council, antislavery forces rallied and repulsed Southerners seeking fugitives in Chicago. The leading wedge in the Chicago counterattack was the relatively small Black community, which organized "a colored police system" in "seven divisions, with six persons in each division" to "'patrol the city each night and keep an eye out for interlopers.'"

For the next eleven years, up to and including the inauguration of President-elect Abraham Lincoln, who pledged to enforce the Fugitive Slave Act better than any other Southern White man, America reverberated from sea to shining sea with the sound of White men and dogs hunting fugitive slaves.

In this effort, which dwarfed the Berlin Wall in immorality and inhumanity, Lincoln distinguished himself by publicly and repeatedly supporting the men and the dogs who were trying to capture the men, women and children who were trying to climb over the American Berlin Wall between slavery and Canada. He went further and made support for this law a precondition for serving in his cabinet.

Nothing in this whole record is more disturbing than Lincoln's serene support of this law, which raised—and raises—moral issues as pointed and pressing as the laws of the Nazi regime.

Not only the Chicago Common Council but "political conventions, abolition meetings, ministers' conferences, secret societies" poured forth "a deluge of resolutions and petitions protesting against the law." The *Milwaukee Free Democrat* said on October 2 that "this slave-catching law . . . is not only unconstitutional, but diabolical and damnable . . . . We are under no more obligation to obey such a law than we would be to obey a law requiring us to commit theft, burglary or highway robbery."

What about the personal culpability of leaders who supported an evil law—the issue American prosecutors stressed at Nuremberg.

Lincoln said repeatedly that it was the duty of a public official in such a situation to do evil, but Wendell Phillips said that a person who consented actively "to aid in hunting slaves here and now" showed "a hardness of heart, a merciless spirit, a moral blindness, an utter spiritual death" which totally unfitted him for a judicial office or any other office (205). Lincoln's law partner, William H. Herndon, told him to his face that the law was "a *thing* engendered in hell" (HH 232). Lincoln either had a different definition of hell or believed that a detour by way of hell was politically expedient. In any case, there is "abundant evidence," as Weik said, "for the belief expressed by the late Horace White that there was a certain degree of moral obtuseness in Abraham Lincoln which the public does not recognize and will refuse to believe in the present generation" (216).

The long white years from slavery to the segregated South to the Third Reich to South Africa have taught us that it is one thing to accept personal responsibility for an evil that one can't change but another and more dangerous act to persuade others to support evil. Lincoln crossed that line repeatedly in the fifties, acting as a cheerleader for slavecatchers in public speeches in which he urged Illinois citizens to go out into the streets and woods and help capture runaway slaves and return them to slavery.

This was a sharp departure for Lincoln, who usually led by following. It was his habit as a private citizen and as president to hide his hands and to talk out of both sides of his mouth and straddle both sides of the fence. But on two issues—compensated emancipation/colonization and fugitive slaves—he abandoned his usual caution and went out into the streets and fields to mobilize forces and change minds. He was particularly active in the fifties in support of the Fugitive Slave Law.

Most Lincoln specialists say Lincoln "never believed private persons should be required to assist in executing the law," but they forgot or overlooked the fact that Lincoln repeatedly asked private citizens to obey the law and repeatedly opposed people who wanted to repeal the act that required private citizens to assist in executing it. Speaking in Bloomington on September 23, 1854, Lincoln recommended "that the people should unite energetically for the restoration of the Missouri Compromise, but enjoined upon them not to oppose the Fugitive Slave Law, which would be repelling wrong with wrong." The law, he said, "was a compromise, and *as citizens we were bound to stand up to it, and enforce it*" (CW 2:233, italics added). Lincoln even joked about it, adding: "I own, if I were called upon by a Marshal, to assist in catching a fugitive slave, I should suggest to him that others could run a great deal faster than I could . . . " (CW 2:233).

It wasn't funny, certainly not to slaves who were returned to slavery, torture, and even death. A White man in the crowd wrote to the Bloomington *Weekly Pantagraph* and complained about Lincoln's morals (2:233). This didn't faze Lincoln, who returned to the same theme and the same fence during the Lincoln-Douglas debates, telling a crowd at Alton, Illinois, "We profess to have no taste for running and catching niggers—at least, I profess no taste for that job at all. Why then do I yield support to a Fugitive Slave Law? Because I do not understand that the Constitution, which guarantees that right, can be supported without it" (CW 3:317).

Lincoln said this in speeches all over the country.

At least twenty times between 1854 and 1860, he publicly supported the Fugitive Slave Law.

On August 28, 1854, in Carrollton, Illinois, he spoke "against the repeal of the fugitive slave law" (CW 2:227).

On October 16, 1854, in the defining Peoria speech, he denied that he had asked for "a repeal, or *modification* of the fugitive slave law" (CW 2:260, italics added).

At Freeport, in the second Lincoln-Douglas debate, he told the crowd "I have never hesitated to say, and I do not now hesitate to say, that I think, under the Constitution of the United States, the people of the Southern States are entitled to a Congressional Fugitive Slave Law. Having said that, I have had nothing to say in regard to the existing Fugitive Slave Law further than that I think it should have been framed so as to be free from some of the objections that pertain to it, *without lessening its efficiency*" (CW 3:41, italics added).

Someone will say, as people are always saying, that Lincoln said this in order to get elected. But the defense is worse than the offense and does not come to grips with the fact that Lincoln said the same thing in private letters to citizens who lived in other states and couldn't vote for him.

In 1859, for instance, Lincoln tried to organize a national campaign in support of the Fugitive Slave Law, telling leading Republicans in Ohio and Indiana and elsewhere that the burgeoning national movement for a repeal of the Fugitive Slave Law was hurting the Republican Party in Illinois and would have an adverse effect on the next Republican convention. On June 9, 1859, he told Ohio leader Salmon P. Chase that a plank in the Ohio Republican convention calling for "a repeal of the atrocious Fugitive Slave Law" is "already damaging us here and would divide the next national convention" (CW 3:384, 386). A month later, he told Indiana Congressman Schuyler Colfax that New Hampshire and Ohio Republicans "should forbear tilting against the Fugitive Slave law in such a way as [to] utterly overwhelm us in Illinois with the charge of enmity to the constitution" (CW 3:391). In the same month, he told another Ohio leader that he "very much regretted" the Ohio plank and the repudiation of a Ohio judge who had upheld the Fugitive Slave Law (CW 3:394-5).

What was going on here?

Why was the virtually unknown Lincoln writing letters in support of the Fugitive Slave Law to state leaders who had never met him and who barely knew his name?

The answer is that he was campaigning, trying to attract national attention and to position himself for the next Republican convention. Lincoln's tactics in pursuing the nomination have been endlessly analyzed and praised, but no one, to my knowledge, has given proper attention to the fact that Lincoln climbed to the top over the bruised and battered backs of the Black victims of one of the worst laws ever passed by Congress.

Let us be clear here and say, whatever the price, that a sensitive man wouldn't have supported this law.

Let us say here, whatever the outcry, that a sensitive man would have found some excuse—Christianity, the Constitution, *cowardice*— to refuse assent to a law that required every American citizen to help hunt down and return to slavery men, women and children. And if defiance was not his style, he wouldn't have criticized and opposed other men who asked for a repeal of a law that legalized the hunting and capturing of human beings in the United States of America.

Thousands of men and women, including conservative lawyers and ambitious politicians, risked prison terms and their careers in order to defend fugitive slaves in court or to pass them on from station to station on the Underground Railroad. Some spent years in prison; some paid the ultimate price. One of the most heroic figures in this effort was Calvin Fairbanks, a White activist who spent seventeen years and four months in the Kentucky penitentiary for helping slaves to escape. Fairbanks said he received at least thirty-five thousand stripes before he was released in 1864 (Siebert 157-60).

No less dramatic, and no less accusing, is the case of Margaret Garner, the nineteenth-century inspiration for Oprah Winfrey's *Beloved*. In 1856, Garner, in company with her four children, and her husband, Simon Garner Jr., and his father, fled from Boone County, Kentucky, to Cincinnati and took refuge in the home of a free Black man. When slavecatchers and their allies surrounded the house, Simon Garner opened fire, wounding at least one member of the posse. Before the legal mob closed in on them, Margaret Garner cut the throat of her beloved ten-year-old daughter and tried to kill other children to keep them from being returned to slavery. The daughter died and the Garners were carried to court where she reportedly begged the judge to kill her, saying that slavery was worse than death for a Black woman. With unseemly haste, the Garners were returned to Kentucky and dispatched to the New Orleans slave markets where they disappeared into a white hole of history.

Lincoln never lifted a finger to help the Fairbankses and Garners. On the contrary: he was conspicuous in defending the Fugitive Slave Law and in criticizing men and women who openly violated it or who participated in a passive resistance movement against it.

Forget race.

Forget color.

We are saying that a man who finds it normal and legal *to go out of his way* to support a law calling for the capture and return of human beings to slavery or stalags or concentration camps crosses a line no one can keep silent about without imperilling his own soul.

We are saying further that every historian would say the same thing if we were talking about the hunting and capturing of Chinese in Tiananmen Square, Germans on the Berlin Wall or Jews in Nazi concentration camps.

Looking back later, Nathaniel Stephenson said that "to Lincoln,

the preservation of a great democratic state was a vastly more significant matter than even the breaking of the bonds of all the slaves in
the world."

You read it correctly; he said *"all* the slaves in the world," adding:

"When we recall his extreme personal sensitiveness to suffering,
when we remember how profoundly unhappy he was rendered by
every suggestion of the misery of the slaves, nothing could be more
striking than his whole-hearted, one might even say, serene, support
of the Fugitive Slave Law" (438).

When we recall Lincoln's *serene* and whole-hearted support of a
reprehensible law that returned thousands of slaves to slavery, torture and even death, we are forced, once again, to raise ultimate
questions about the insensitivity of any man who supported for any
reason in any century the hunting and capturing of human beings.

Will it be said that Lincoln serenely supported slavery and violence
against Blacks because of his love for the law? But law has a thousand
faces and colors, and it is a poor lawyer who can only argue on the
side of the oppressor and the status quo. It is, in any case, interesting
to learn that Illinois lawyers with a higher sense of the law and a
higher sense of morality were among leaders of the the fight against
the Fugitive Slave Law that Lincoln the lawyer supported. N. Dwight
Harris, the authority on Negro servitude in Illinois, said "the period
of greatest struggle" in Illinois was between 1840 and 1845, a period
when state legislator Abraham Lincoln was unusually silent. The contest during these years, Harris says, "was serious and stubbornly carried on. It involved talent, ingenuity, determination, and perseverance on both sides . . . ." [and] the brunt of the struggle was carried on
by "a few able and devoted lawyers" (122).

Among "the friends of the Negro," Harris said "were W.T.M. Davis
of Alton, Nathaniel Niles of Belleville, Gustav Koerner of Belleville . . .
Lyman Trumbull," and James H. Collins of Chicago. "They were the
most powerful friends of the Negro, and lived where their assistance

could be readily secured. They told the Negroes repeatedly that they were free, urged them to leave their masters, and fought their cases in the lower courts time and time again, often without fees or remuneration. Chief among them was Lyman Trumbull, whose name should be written large in antislavery annals."

Three obvious and striking points can be made about this list. The first is that Abraham Lincoln's name is not on it. The second is that this is a list of more or less ordinary White professionals who lived and prospered in the state of Illinois in Lincoln's time despite their opposition to slavery and the Fugitive Slave Law. Third, and regrettably, all of these antislavery advocates have been forgotten while Abraham Lincoln, who opposed them and supported slavery and the Fugitive Slave Law, has been elevated to secular sainthood.

And in assessing Lincoln's moral default, and the apologia of his apologists, we must never lose sight of the fact that the Illinois fight against the Fugitive Slave Law was waged not only by lawyers but also by Illinois politicians who were elected to major offices despite or, in some cases, because of their principled advocacy of the rights of slaves. Some of these politicians circulated petitions asking for the repeal of the Fugitive Slave Law and the abolition of slavery in Washington, D.C. Mark Krug, a major Lincoln supporter, said that politician Lyman Trumbull, unlike Lincoln, "took an active part in anti-slavery agitation and late in 1837 traveled from place to place in southern Illinois to deliver talks against slavery." An eyewitness said that after one of these talks, he saw "a number of persons kicking a man by the name of Trumbull" in front of his hotel (62).

Lincoln's record on human rights pales—the precise word—in comparison with the record of Trumbull, who campaigned for justice for "the Negro in Illinois," although he practiced law and ran for office in the proslavery environs of a typical Illinois town, Belleville. Although Trumbull was not an abolitionist, at least not in these years, he was, Harris said, the next best thing, a man with "an honest desire to see justice done to the Negro in Illinois" (123). This did not seem to affect his prestige and esteem. Even his proslavery neighbors in Belleville and surrounding counties, Krug said, "were impressed with the high standards of integrity, personal austerity, and courage of this Yankee lawyer." The slavery-hating Germans in St. Clair, Madison and Cook counties adored him, and he gained "wide support and acclaim" in Lincoln's Springfield and in northern Illinois. Although his mentor and patron was a leader of the proslavery forces, Trumbull, who shared some of the prejudices of his contemporaries, "did not compromise his opposition to slavery" (Krug 65-6).

What we learn from Trumbull, and not from Lincoln, is that no daring is fatal and that every refusal to bend a knee or to bow down in the face of totalitarianism, as Robert Kennedy said, brings out the best in men and women and releases answering echoes of energy. And it is on this high level that Lincoln and Trumbull must be evaluated. For a great politician does not stoop to the level of the crowd: he raises the crowd to his level. A great politician does not put on a mask to cover his face: he banishes all masks, including his own, and shows the people their true face.

In these years, and later, Trumbull, unlike Lincoln, rose to the level of a great politician, despite his racial limitations. It is interesting, at any rate, to note that "this disinterested and able effort, made in all sincerity of purpose, and void of all appearance of self-elevation, rendered him justly popular throughout the State, as well as in the region of his home. The people of his district showed their approval of his work and their confidence in his integrity by electing him Judge of the Supreme Court in 1848, and Congressman from the Eighth District of Illinois by a handsome majority in 1854, when it was well known that he was opposed to the Kansas-Nebraska Bill" (Harris 123).

Will anybody maintain after all this that Lincoln *had* to use racism and compromise his principles in order to get elected? If so, there are two additional facts to be considered. First and foremost, Trumbull defeated Lincoln in the 1855 election for the U.S. Senate, which was, based on Trumbull's later record, and Lincoln's later record, a big plus for the slaves. Second, and definitively, Lincoln lost this race not because he was too radical on the race issue but because he was too conservative on the race issue. Certified antislavery leaders felt so strongly on this issue that they advised antislavery legislators to vote against Lincoln. "We would not advise the Republicans," the *Free West* said on November 30, 1854, "to support for this station Lincoln or any of the moderate men of this stamp. He is only a Whig, and this people's movement is no Whig triumph . . . . Let a man of the people be elected Senator" (qtd. in Harris 195).

In the end, five anti-Nebraska Democrats refused to vote for Lincoln, and he was forced to withdraw in favor of Trumbull, who may not have been a man of all the Illinois people but who was at least not a man of Illinois White people alone.

15

Prelude To Halfness

AFTER forty-five years of silence and yea and nay, Abraham Lincoln, who would go down in history as the greatest antislavery fighter of all time, finally found his voice and stood up in public and made a speech about slavery. This was an extreme act for Lincoln; and in 1854, as in 1863, he was pushed and pulled into glory. The triggering mechanism in 1854 was passage of the Kansas-Nebraska Act, which not only reopened the question of the extension of slavery to the territories of the West but also, and more importantly on a personal level, made it possible for Lincoln to revive a political career that was in terminal arrest.

By a paradoxical act of political poetry, the architect of this act, which virtually repealed the Missouri Compromise, ending the age of compromises, was Lincoln's old nemesis, Senator Stephen Arnold Douglas of the state of Illinois.

Douglas was a racist, and a virulent racist at that, but one should give the devil his due and say at once before passing on that the friends of freedom owe him almost as much as they owe Lincoln. For by ripping the bandage off the festering sore of slavery and by opening or threatening to open the West and perhaps even the North to slavery, Douglas and the forces allied with him unwittingly made it impossible to ignore the question everybody had been trying to ignore since slaveowner Thomas Jefferson, attended by a favorite slave—Robert Hemings, the brother of his future Black mistress, Sally Hemings—sat down in a room in Philadelphia and wrote a document that said all men were created equal.

From that day in 1776 until 1853, the domestic politics of America had revolved around a series of compromises—the Compromise of 1787, the Compromise of 1820, the Compromise of 1850—that tried to settle a problem that could not be settled with words, the problem of the huge and growing gap between the words Jefferson wrote and the reality America lived.

Following Jefferson, Clay, John Calhoun, and Daniel Webster, all of whom "solved" the problem forever, Douglas came forward in 1854 with a tricky formula that proposed once again to solve the problem forever. Douglas called his magic wand "popular sovereignty." Under its provisions, White settlers in a new territory could decide whether they wanted slavery by voting it up or down in a referendum.

If Douglas hoped by this to solve the White problem, he was mistaken. For popular sovereignty made almost everybody mad and set in motion forces that led directly to the Civil War.

Future consequences apart, Douglas's folly had immediate consequences, destroying the foundations of Lincoln's beloved Whig Party and forcing the political realignment that gave birth to the Republican Party. Lincoln's party, the only party really that he ever had, died because it tried to evade the biggest problem of the day, and the fact that Lincoln supported it so long and never really left it is additional evidence, if additional evidence is needed, of his limited historical vision.

Beyond its effect on social forces, the Kansas-Nebraska Act had enormous personal consequences, awakening Abraham Lincoln from his long sleep and reactivating the feud between him and Stephen A. Douglas. For eighteen years, ever since they sparred for the first time in the Illinois legislature, the two men had been circling each other warily, like boxers, bobbing and weaving. During these years, they had competed for offices, honors and the hands of at least one woman. Mrs. Lincoln apart, Douglas had taken almost every match, outdistancing his less charismatic rival and going on to Washington where he became one of the leading men of the nation. He was on his way to the presidency when hubris and the hope of political and economic gain led him into the dead-end trap of the Kansas-Nebraska Act, which made it possible for antislavery forces, led by Senator Chase and Senator Sumner, to frighten and inflame the North.

Antislavery leaders had been trying unsuccessfully since the Compromise of 1850 and passage of the Fugitive Slave Law to arouse the North by stressing the threats to Negro rights and the basic guarantees of the Constitution. But the vast majority of Northern Whites, Lincoln above all, remained remarkably unconcerned about Negro rights and the threats to the Constitution until Douglas came forward with a double-edged gift that seemed to be a direct threat not to Blacks but to White farmers lusting after Western land and big entrepreneurs chafing under the restrictions of the slave power.

It was at this precise moment that a new phenomenon in world history, the antislavery Abraham Lincoln, made his debut, coming, as usual, late to the struggle and talking, as usual, on both sides of the issue. Lincoln was a down-on-his-luck Illinois politician who had blown his one big political chance in Congress and who was widely believed to be in the rigor mortis stage of a once promising political career (HW 47-8). For five years, ever since he left Congress in disfavor, he had been sniffing around the edges of the arena, trying to find or manufacture an issue that would get him back in the game. By 1853, it was clear to him, Donald W. Riddle says, that there was only one issue that could help him recoup his political fortunes (246-7). That issue was the antislavery issue, which was churning up constituencies all over the country. The only problem was that Lincoln had never been identified with that issue. No matter. Riddle and others, including the author, believe that Lincoln deliberately used the antislavery issue to get back into the game and to salvage his personal career. "Never before [the Kansas-Nebraska Act] had Lincoln run for office on the slavery issue," Riddle says, "but never afterward would he run on any other" (252).

The Kansas-Nebraska Act passed Congress on May 30, 1854. Four months later, after a signature period of indecision, Lincoln picked up the high card his old rival had unexpectedly presented him. In the process, he reinvented himself and gave birth to the Lincoln of history. Herndon, who was there, said "Lincoln saw his opportunity and Douglas's downfall . . . " and "rode to glory on the popular waves" (HH 96, 173). Herndon added a startlingly frank analysis that nobody, or almost nobody, quotes. Lincoln, he said, "was *envious* and he manifested it in many of his speeches; he wanted Douglas's position, and his envy, free from hate, made him struggle for it, and that struggle gave him not only Douglas's position, but a higher one, and satisfied his *wants* and gratified his *ambition*" (HH 236, italics in original).

This, then, was the genesis of the first great conversion of Lincoln's life, and it, like the the July and September 1862 conversions to the emancipation policy, was a halfway gesture defined by political expediency.

The new Lincoln announced himself in the Springfield, Illinois, speech of October 4, 1854, which was repeated twelve days later at Peoria and is generally known as the Peoria speech (CW 2:247-83). Lincoln was then forty-five years old. Sympathetic historians say this was his first unambiguous statement against slavery, but they are not entirely correct. For although Lincoln said slavery was wrong in principle, he said in capital letters in the opening paragraphs that he was only opposed "to the EXTENSION of it," and not "the EXISTING institution" (CW 2:248).

Before taking up the subject, Lincoln disclaimed any "prejudice against the Southern people"—he meant the Southern *White* people—saying they were just what Northern White people would be, just what Abraham Lincoln would be, in fact, if they were in the same situation. He came therefore not to criticize Southern Caesars but to confirm them in their constitutional rights and to acknowledge "not grudgingly, but fully, and fairly" their legitimate "right" to keep the slaves they had in the South and to hunt down any slave who escaped in the North. What he asked was not the ending of slavery but the restoration of the Missouri Compromise which sanctioned and confirmed slavery within certain boundaries (CW:2:253).

Wasn't this inconsistent? If he fully and fairly acknowledged the right of a slaveowner to hold and whip a Black man in Georgia and to hunt him down anywhere in Illinois and other states if he tried to escape, why was he opposed to the same slaveowner holding and whipping the same Black man in California? Lincoln wrestled with that question for the next nine years, and never fully answered it. His problem, and it was acute, was that he had, as he said, little or no interest in slavery in the South or the slaves slaving in the South.

What then was his real interest?

His real interest was, as always, the interest of free White labor and free White capital—and free White politicians, Abraham Lincoln above all. What he wanted to do was to take Stephen Douglas's Senate seat and make the West safe for White settlement. But—and this was the delicious irony of the situation—he could not defend the White interest and advance his interest without addressing the main argument of the slaveowners and their supporters, Douglas above all, who said the slaves were either men or property.

Either/or.

If slaves were property, slaveowners had the right, proslavery forces said, to take them anywhere they carried other property, including California. If, on the other hand, they were men, it was a violation of humanity to hold them in slavery anywhere.

Some White men met that argument head-on, but Lincoln did not belong to their tribe, then or ever, and he adopted the yes-no, go-stop strategy of his whole life.

The slave was a man *but*.

Slavery was wrong *but*.

Freedom was right *but*.

The Negro was included in the Declaration of Independence *but*.

After the Peoria Declaration, Lincoln chased Douglas for six years. Was he motivated by ambition? Yes, but with a difference. For this was one of those privileged moments when history uses a man's passions to advance the cause of history. Lincoln hungered and thirsted after Douglas's place. No doubt about that. But he was also energized by what he considered a threat to free White men and what he called "the white-man's charter of freedom."

That's not a paraphrase; that's what Abraham Lincoln called the Declaration of Independence. Two years before the Kansas-Nebraska controversy erupted, he warned in his Henry Clay eulogy against "an increasing number of men, who, for the sake of perpetuating slavery, are beginning to assail and to ridicule the white-man's charter of freedom—the declaration that 'all men are created free and equal'" (CW 2:130).

This was not a slip of the tongue. Lincoln used the same phrase in the Peoria speech, telling the audience that "in our greedy chase to make profit of the Negro, let us beware, lest we 'cancel and tear to pieces' even the white man's charter of freedom" (CW 2:276).

The White man's charter of freedom.

Isn't that remarkable? How can a universal declaration about the rights of *all* men be called a charter for some (*White*) men? Was this the same man who talked at Gettysburg about a nation conceived in liberty and dedicated to the proposition that all men are created equal? Was there any connection between what he said in 1863 and what he said in 1854? Which Declaration of Independence was he talking about? The Declaration he praised at Peoria or the Declaration he praised at Gettysburg?

What did Lincoln mean? And when did he mean it?

Let us go into this matter more deeply.

The first phase of the Lincoln-Douglas debate lasted from 1854 to 1855 and ended with the Illinois legislature electing Lyman Trumbull to the United States Senate over Abraham Lincoln, primarily because

Lincoln was perceived as a trimmer on the slavery issue. The second phase of the debates, including the seven formal debates, lasted from 1858 to 1860 and ended with the election of Lincoln to the presidency. In both phases, Lincoln was given to saying in the same speech, in the same paragraph, in the same sentence, that he believed in White supremacy as a practical matter and in the Declaration of Independence as an abstract matter of principle. Notice, for example, his fence straddling in his Peoria reply (October 16, 1854) to Douglas: "What I do say is, that no man is good enough to govern another man, *without that other's consent*" (CW 2:266, Lincoln's italics).

Indisputably; but why did he add in almost the same breath: "Let it not be said I am contending for the establishment of political and social equality between the whites and blacks. I have already said the contrary."

You see Lincoln's art? First, he says that he doesn't mean it. Then he says it. Then he tells you that he already said in the beginning that he doesn't mean it.

Lincoln returned to the same themes—and the same fence—in a speech in reply to Douglas (July 17, 1858) at Springfield, where he was again eloquent on both sides of the issue.

"I adhere to the Declaration of Independence," he said. "If Judge Douglas and his friends are not willing to stand by it, let them come up and amend it. Let them make it read that all men are created equal, except Negroes" (CW 2:520).

Excellent. Nothing better. But why did he spoil it by adding his own "except Negroes": "I have said that I do not understand the Declaration to mean that all men were created equal in all respects . . . . Certainly the Negro is not our equal in color—perhaps not in many other respects; still, in the right to put into his mouth the bread that his own hands have earned, he is the equal of every other man, white or black" (CW 2:520).

Lincoln defenders fall all over themselves in their effort to praise this statement. None of them seem to realize that this is one of the most damning assertions ever made by a major American political figure. For what does this oft-repeated and often-praised formulation mean if not that Lincoln was creating separate-but-unequal sections of the Declaration of Independence, giving Whites equal political and civil rights and Blacks the inalienable right to put whatever bread they could find in their mouths?

What rights were specified in the "colored" section of the Declaration of Independence? Did this separate-but-unequal section define colored people as citizens? And if it didn't, was Lincoln prepared to fight for African-American citizenship?

Senator Douglas posed these embarrassing questions in the debate at Charleston, Illinois, and Lincoln replied:

> Judge Douglas has said to you that he has not been able to get from me an answer to the question whether I am in favor of Negro citizenship. So far as I know, the Judge never asked me the question before. [Applause.] He shall have no occasion to ever ask it again, for I tell him very frankly that I am not in favor of Negro citizenship. [Renewed applause.]

Did Lincoln believe that the state of Illinois could make an African-American a citizen?

> Now, my opinion is [he said] that the different States have the power to make a Negro a citizen under the Constitution of the United States, if they choose. The Dred Scott decision decides that they have not that power. If the State of Illinois had that power, I should be opposed to the exercise of it. [Cries of "Good," "good," and applause.] (CW 3:179)

What are we to make of all this? What are we to say about a man who says in the same speech that Blacks are *in* and *out* of the Declaration of Independence at the same time? We are to say, among other things, that we are dealing with a very clever man who will end up with a Memorial on the Mall to which people who believe Blacks are in the Declaration and people who believe they are not in the Declaration will come in increasing numbers.

A common impression to the contrary notwithstanding, there

was little or no practical difference between Lincoln and Douglas on the key issues. Both men believed in White supremacy. Both believed Blacks were inferior. Both supported slavery in the South. Both supported segregation and discrimination in Illinois. Douglas denied the humanity of Blacks on principle, Lincoln denied the humanity of Blacks in fact, and it is hard to tell which was more dangerous or devious.

Douglas said this country was made by White people for White people; Lincoln said "why, in point of mere fact, I think so too"(CW 2:281). Douglas said he was against Black people voting and serving on juries; Lincoln said he was against the same things. Douglas said he was against intermarriage; Lincoln said it was wrong to suggest that he was for "the niggers and white people . . . marrying together" (CW 3:20). Douglas said he was in favor of Black slavery where it existed; Lincoln said he supported slavery where it existed and was for the Fugitive Slave Law to boot.

What then was left? Nothing really except the extension of slavery and the language to be used to justify racism. Douglas was an agnostic on the extension of slavery issue, saying that White people in the territories had the right to vote slavery up or down. Lincoln was opposed to the extension. But even here they were together in their difference, for the only real issue between them was whether the extension of slavery would help or hurt White folks. Lincoln thought it would hurt poor Whites and have a negative impact on the White collectivity. Douglas said in so many words that the question was irrelevant, since geography would exclude slavery in certain areas. Neither he nor Lincoln mentioned the real issue, whether it would hurt or help Northern industrialists and their allies.

What then was the debate about?

The debate was over whether White supremacy would be best served by excluding slavery from the territories or by permitting slaveowners to take their slaves wherever they wanted. The question Lincoln and Douglas were trying to answer, above all else, was, who was the White man's best friend, Stephen Arnold Douglas or

Abraham Lincoln?

This led ironically and unexpectedly to a metaphysical argument over whether Blacks were included in the Declaration of Independence. This was the 1858 equivalent of the medieval argument over how many angels can dance on the head of a pin, for to pretend as Lincoln and all his men pretend that it is possible to determine the meaning of a document by examining the words in isolation from the motives, interests, conflicts and material foundations of the originators and animators of the document is sheer sophistry. The Declaration had no meaning then or now apart from living people, apart from the slaves of Mount Vernon and Monticello, and the operations and activities men performed—voting, sharing power, holding office, etc.—to define the Declaration and the Declaration-sayers.

In the beginning, as I have shown elsewhere, some Americans tried to make the Declaration real by emancipating their slaves and calling for a rainbow nation (1961, 70-7). But virtue was as always in the minority in the Republic; and by the 1780s, when Richard Allen and the free Blacks of Philadelphia walked out of the White church and Haitian Blacks revolted and the cotton gin intensified White Southern and Northern greed, the Revolution had been hopelessly betrayed.

From that time forward, American White people defined themselves and the Declaration not by the words of the document but by the speech of their daily life. There was no mystery about what the words of the Declaration meant in Jefferson's Virginia or Lincoln's Illinois. George Washington's Declaration of Independence was defined by his attempt to recover the slaves who escaped from Mount Vernon and left America with the English soldiers. Jefferson's Declaration was defined by Sally Hemings and the slaves who paid for the books and the fine wines of Monticello. Lincoln's Declaration was defined by what he did and didn't do in Jim Crow Illinois and by his opposition to Negroes voting and serving as jurors. To pretend as Lincoln and his defenders pretend that the words had some meaning apart from what Jefferson, Washington and Madison did in relation to Negroes, White indentured servants and Indians is academic voodoo, except that voodoo, as Chicago Mayor Harold Washington used to say, is a more rigorous discipline and has a better track record.

From the beginning, then, and at least until the 1960s when African-Americans wrote their own Declaration and Emancipation Proclamation in the streets, the great *We* statements of American life —"*We* the people" and "*We* hold these truths to be self-evident"— didn't include the slaves or the overwhelming majority of the American people, Blacks, women, poor Whites, Indians, and the White indentured servants of George Washington and other founding fathers. To put it another way, the Declaration was defined operationally, not rhetorically, which means, among other things, that a country's Declaration is not the Declaration it writes but the Declaration it lives.

Douglas, who at least understood that, offered the debate crowds a choice between racism and hypocrisy. Lincoln, who recognized the same thing, offered the crowds a choice between racism and pretty words. The debate crowds, more sophisticated and more devious than both Lincoln and Douglas, chose all of the above, racism, hypocrisy, and the pretty words.

Douglas said that it was absurd to say that the *words, all men are created equal*, included Negroes and that Jefferson and Washington intended to make their slaves their equal. Lincoln was horrified not by Douglas's assertion that Blacks were inferior and should be denied equality in fact—he agreed with that—but by Douglas's statement that Negroes were not included in the metaphysical *words* of the Declaration.

This was not an argument about rights and realities; it was an argument about words. Lincoln had no intention of insisting on equal rights for Negroes in Illinois or the slave states, but he was in love with the sound of the words, and he wanted to keep on saying them, irrespective of the status of Blacks. At Monticello, Illinois, of all places, "he asserted that he did not desire *Negro equality* in all things, *he only wanted that the words* of the Declaration of Independence should be applied . . . " (CW 2:527, italics added).

Read that sentence again: Lincoln didn't desire Negro equality in all things, he only wanted the *words* to apply. He approached the Declaration not as a moralist, not as a politician, but as a poet. He was in love not with *the notion of men being created equal* but with *the sound of words about men being created equal.* He had no intention of doing anything about the words anywhere, and certainly not in Jim Crow Illinois, but he was entranced by the sound and the taste of the vocables. He loved to handle them with his hot mind and roll them around on his tongue: All Men Are Created Equal—*Beautiful.* It was Lincoln, or a man like Lincoln, that the French philosopher Maurice Merleau-Ponty had in mind when he said, in so many words, that oppressed people ought to start cleaning their weapons when oppressors start praising the word *freedom* instead of free people.

The most provocative part of the debate was not what Lincoln said and didn't say but why he was saying it. He was forty-five years old when he fired the first salvo, and he had never before said anything substantial or relevant about the plight of Blacks. How then did it happen that he was up on a platform on the Illinois prairie defending the humanity of Blacks? The answer is to be found in part by a consideration of the exigencies of politics. His arch enemy, Senator Douglas, had taken an advanced and exposed position based on the idea that slaves were property and could be transported across state lines like any other property. In order to attack Douglas, which had become a *personal* and political imperative, Lincoln had to say that Negroes were men "in some respects." For if Negroes were not men, slaveowners, according to proslavery theorists, had as much right to take them to the territory as to take hogs or any other form of property.

The whole argument—and Lincoln's and Douglas's fate—revolved around the being of the Negro, not because Lincoln or Douglas had any particular interest in the Negro but because neither could defend his personal or political interests without defending or attacking Negroes. That point has somehow eluded modern interpreters, but Lincoln understood it clearly, and said it clearly:

> If we admit that a Negro is not a man . . . it is right to allow the South to take their peculiar institution with them and plant it upon the virgin soil of Kansas and Nebraska. If the Negro is not a man, it is consistent to apply the sacred right of popular sovereignty to the question as to whether the people of the territories shall or shall not have slavery; but if the Negro, upon soil where slavery is not legalized by law and sanctioned by custom, *is* a man, then there is not even the shadow of popular sovereignty in allowing the first settlers upon such soil to decide whether it shall be right in all future time to hold men in bondage there. (CW 2:239, Lincoln's italics)

The point of the play, in other words, was to preserve and extend the rights of the teeming millions of free Whites. If you doubt that, go back—pay attention now—and read the second part of the second sentence above, the part following the semicolon that Lincoln almost always used to do his dirty work, the part where he says— you were not paying attention—that the Negro is *not* a man where slavery is legalized by law and sanctioned by custom.

You still don't see it? Let's go over it slowly together, word by word, paying particular attention to the word *not*. Lincoln said "if the Negro, *upon soil where slavery is* NOT *legalized by law and sanctioned by custom*, is a man," which means, if words have any meaning, that the Negro upon soil where slavery *is* legalized by law and sanctioned by custom, is NOT a man.

Lincoln's card-up-the-sleeve routine befuddled Douglas, who couldn't understand why Whites applauded Lincoln when he said in the same paragraph that he believed in White supremacy and the Declaration of Independence. That was the gist of Douglas's complaint in Galesburg, Illinois, on October 7, 1858:

Mr. Lincoln asserts to-day, as he did in Chicago, that the Negro was included in that clause of the Declaration of Independence which says that all men were created equal and endowed by the Creator with certain inalienable rights, among which are life, liberty and the pursuit of happiness. (Ain't that so?) If the Negro was made his equal and mine, if that equality was established by Divine Law, and was the Negro's inalienable right, how came he to say at Charleston to the Kentuckians residing in that section of our State, that the Negro was physically inferior to the white man, belonged to an inferior race, and he was for keeping him in that inferior condition? (Good.) I wish you to bear these things in mind. At Charleston he said that the Negro belongs to an inferior race, and that he was for keeping him in that inferior condition. There he gave the people to understand that there was no moral question involved, because the inferiority being established, it was only a question of degree and not a question of right; here, to-day, instead of making it a question of degree, he makes it a moral question, says that it is a great crime to hold the Negro in that inferior condition. (He's right.) Is he right now, or was he right in Charleston? (Both.) He is right then, sir, in your estimation, not because he is consistent, but because he can trim his principles any way in any section, so as to secure votes. (CW 3:238)

Poor, deluded, racist Stephen Douglas. What he failed to understand, with all his cunning, was that millions of Whites believed and believe, as the crowd said, in *both* White Supremacy and the Declaration of Independence. His failure to understand that point cost him the presidency and may have sent him to an early grave.

Lincoln's verbal dexterity has been highly praised by historians, who have made him the patron saint of the Declaration of Independence. J.G. Randall said "the Declaration of Independence was his platform, his confession of faith." Roy P. Basler said "democracy was to Lincoln a religion . . . ." Horace White said "the Declaration was to him as Holy Writ."[32]

If so, it was a Jim Crow religion with a separate-but-unequal Holy

Writ. For Lincoln never believed that the *all* in question included Blacks, Hispanics, and Native Americans in fact. To be sure, he said that Blacks had a share in what he called "the white-man's charter of freedom," the Declaration of Independence, "humble though it may be"—but the words *white-man's charter* and the *humble* phrase disqualify him utterly.

Most of the new Lincoln defenders stake their case on Lincoln's dissembling discovery of a heretofore unknown *colored* inalienable right, "the right to eat the bread without the leave of anybody else, which his own hand earns" (CW 3:16). Why is it dissembling? It is dissembling because Lincoln's alimentary intuition, based on the inalienable right to put bread into one's mouth, was a mirage and had no meaning apart from *the right to earn bread* to put into one's mouth. Lincoln knew this for when he made this statement he was supporting a slave system in the South which made it a crime, punishable by death, for a slave to arrogate to himself the right to earn his bread. At the same time, he was supporting Black Laws in Illinois which made it a crime for a Black to settle in the state with the intention of earning bread to put into his mouth.

Since Lincoln was opposed to Black citizenship and equal rights for Blacks, since he believed that White men had a "right" to hold Blacks in slavery and to hunt them down anywhere in the United States, and since he believed, inversely, that White men from Europe were entitled to all the privileges of the Declaration simply by being born White, it is obvious, if words have any meaning, that he, like Douglas, identified the *all* of the "white man's charter" with all White men.

In a clever maneuver that apparently fooled modern Lincoln specialists but didn't fool that wily old racist, Stephen Douglas, Lincoln shifted ground and created an absolute division between the abstract rights of an abstract Declaration of Independence that was to be kept in mind when forming new states and "the necessities" that nullified the right of "the inferior races"—Lincoln's words—to equal rights in existing states (read Illinois) and areas (read: the slave states).

To hide that fact, even perhaps from himself, Lincoln performed radical surgery on the Declaration, creating at least four different Declarations which he pulled out from time to time, depending on the audience, like cards from a marked deck.

Lincoln created the first Declaration, which we will call Declaration A, by elevating the real Declaration to a heaven high above the real world where it was not affected by slavery or Indian massacres or by anything White people did and did not do. Declaration A, the Declaration Lincoln never stopped praising and idolizing from afar, was pure, white, undefiled. It was, in Lincoln's words, "an abstract principle" about abstract, that is to say, unreal rights.

It was a perfect Declaration, like Plato's perfect circle, an idea existing in perfection in a realm outside the world.

This was, Lincoln said approvingly, a counsel of perfection that removed the whole Declaration to a level realistic men could deal with. It reminded him of the words of Jesus, "As your Father in Heaven is perfect, be ye also perfect" (CW 2:501). Since it was extremely unlikely that the White people of Lincoln's time—or ours—were going to become as perfect as God in their treatment of Negroes and Indians, there was no use talking about the real Declaration, except on special occasions, like church services or open-air events like Gettysburg.

The real Declaration, then, the Declaration to keep in mind when determining duties to subhumans who were not entitled to all the rights extended to the fully human Whites in the perfect Declaration, was Declaration B, which participated in the real, profane world of slaves and nonWhites. Declaration B contained the same guarantees as the ethereal Declaration but could not be carried out because of the actual presence—Lincoln's words—of slaves and Negroes and the Necessity—Lincoln's word—of keeping them in their place and ensuring the interests of the fully human Whites.

The words *abstract, concrete, actual, necessities* had, as we have seen, the same meaning in Lincoln's linguistics. They meant, as we have said, that whatever else he said in the sentence was not real.

Declaration B—are you still with me?—was, in turn, divided into two declarations, Declaration C, based on the meaning of the words, and Declaration D, based on the venue. Declaration C said that the original Declaration created two classes of rights, certain unspecified nonnatural rights and the "natural" rights enumerated, i.e., the right to life, liberty and the pursuit of happiness. In Lincoln's specious reading, and in the specious reading of all his defenders—we shall return to this—Declaration C extended all rights, natural and non-natural, to all Whites, whenever they came to America and however they came to America. What about Blacks? Because they were non-White and because they didn't come from Europe or a "white" land, they were only entitled, Lincoln said, to the "natural" rights and were excluded from equal political and social rights. This was a factitious reading of the document, which does not specify two classes of rights, saying simply that all men are endowed with certain inalienable rights and that *among these* are the right to life, liberty and the pursuit of happiness.

In Declaration C, Lincoln created separate but unequal sections of the Declaration of Independence, and it is appalling that almost all scholars, all exceptions freely admitted, have, until this date, enthusiastically endorsed the concept.

Even here, however, we are dealing with a stacked deck. For although Lincoln's Declaration C gave Negroes and other "subhumans" certain natural rights in theory and in the abstract, it didn't in fact give any concrete Negro, as opposed to any abstract Negro, any concrete right in Illinois, where the Black Laws, with Lincoln's support, defined Blacks as subhumans, or in the slave states, where Lincoln's "necessities" nullified the provisions. It was only in new societies and in the creation of new states that this could be done. Hence, the fourth Declaration of Independence, Declaration D, the one that operated imperfectly in new states.

Even so, Lincoln was deceiving himself, and others, for he said in a statement that nobody quotes that *Negroes had no rights, natural or otherwise, that they could exercise anywhere in America.* This statement is so shocking that the best thing for us to do is to get out of the way and let Lincoln speak:

> *Negroes have natural rights, however, as other men have, although they cannot enjoy them here,* and even [Chief Justice Roger] Taney once said that "the Declaration of Independence was broad enough for all men." But though it does not declare that all men are equal in their attainments or social position, yet no sane man will attempt to deny that the African upon his own soil has all the natural rights that instrument vouchsafes to all mankind. (CW 3:79, italics added)

Here, then, ominously, is the White man's Declaration of Independence as defined by Abraham Lincoln, a Declaration defined by race and geography and blood, a Declaration that agreed practically with Roger Taney that Negroes had no civil and political rights in America that White men were bound to respect.

Not the least of the ironies of this story is that the roots of Lincoln's political philosophy are to be found in the vulgar idealism Henry Clay devised to explain why he continued to hold slaves and to believe in the Declaration of Independence. In fact, large chunks of Lincoln's debate speeches—Edgar DeWitt Jones counted forty-one references—are taken bodily from Clay's mouth (21). Following Clay, Lincoln said he had never tried to apply the principles of the Declaration of Independence to slavery or the political rights of Blacks in America. On at least fifteen occasions, he said publicly that the principles of the Declaration didn't require him or anybody else to do anything about slavery in the South and Jim Crow in the North.

How in the world did the Lincoln patrol miss these statements? How in the world did they overlook the repeated assertions (CW 2:266, 274, 385, 501, 520; CW 3:16, 222, 249, 255, 276, 300) in which Lincoln said publicly that the "necessities" of whiteness negated any and all eloquent statements he made about the Declaration of

Independence and made it necessary to enslave Blacks in the South and to subordinate them in the North?

How is it that I am the only one to read these words?

How is it that I am the only one to report in this context that Lincoln said—you read the words— "Negroes have natural rights . . . although they cannot enjoy them here."

To answer that question, and to clear up remaining complexities, let us question Lincoln, history, and the Lincoln party.

Q: Why did Lincoln call the Declaration of Independence "the white man's charter of freedom"?

A: He believed—if words have any meaning—that the Declaration was the peculiar if not exclusive charter of White men and that it was of White men, by White men and for White men.

Q: Most people in the world—then and now—were colored. Wasn't it irrational to call a universal declaration a White man's charter?

A: Yes. Lincoln was irrational on the subject of race. So was slave-owner Thomas Jefferson, who wrote the Declaration. So, to tell the truth, are most of their modern-day interpreters.

Q: Did Lincoln believe Black men were included in the statement, "All men are created equal"?

A: Yes and no.

Q: What does that mean?

A: It means that he believed they were included in the statement and that they were *not* included in the statement.

Q: But isn't that irrational?

A: Lincoln was irrational on the subject of race.

Q: To take the first part first then, what did he mean when he said they were included in the statement *all men are created equal.*

A: He meant that Black men had a "humble share" in the *words* of the Declaration.

Q: That sounds sinister and racist. Did White men also have a "humble share" in the *words* of Declaration?

A: No. They had a full share, as White *men, as subjects,* in the actuality of the Declaration.

Q: That *is* sinister. Why do almost all modern Lincoln interpreters praise Lincoln for saying that Black men had a share, "humble though it may be, " in the Declaration?

A: They are either irrational on the subject of race or they haven't read the documents.

Q. What did Whites have to do to be included in the Declaration?

A: The only thing they had to do was to be born White or to migrate to America from Europe or some other White land.

Q: From a *White* land?

A: Yes. Land had a color in Lincoln's cosmology. So did blood. Lincoln explained in great detail in his much-praised Chicago speech that the fully human Whites became eligible for the host of the Declaration as soon as they arrived from Europe (he later added the "White" land of Russia). They were not limited to the Lincoln right of putting bread into their mouths, if they could find any. Because they were White, they could, unlike the subhuman Blacks, vote, sit on juries, etc. Because they were White, they found, when they arrived in America, that they, by some strange alchemy, had "a right" to claim the Declaration "as though they were blood of the blood, and flesh of the flesh, of the men who wrote that Declaration, and so they are."

Q: Did colored men from Africa and Asia become "blood of the blood, and flesh of the flesh" as soon as they got off the boat?

A: Of course not. Neither Lincoln nor Clay nor Jefferson said one word about the rights of immigrants from Africa or even Asia, and Lincoln specifically excluded "the mongrels" of Mexico.

Q: Does this mean that there were separate sections in Lincoln's Declaration of Independence?

A: Yes. Lincoln created separate-but-unequal sections in his Declaration.

Q: What rights if any were specified in the "colored" section of Lincoln's Declaration?

A: Lincoln said colored people were entitled to the "natural" rights enumerated in the document, the right, he said, to life, liberty and the pursuit of happiness.

Q: Did Lincoln believe that?

A: No. Pressed by critics, he could only think of one "colored right," the right to put bread in their mouth.

Q. Did Lincoln believe Blacks had a right to *earn* bread and put it into their mouths in Illinois, which barred Black immigration, or in the slave states, where it was a crime for Blacks to appropriate the fruits of their labor?

A: No.

Q: Did he believe Blacks were entitled to life, liberty and the pursuit of happiness in the slave states?

A: No.

Q: Did he believe Blacks were entitled to life, liberty and the pursuit of happiness in Illinois, which barred Black immigration and denied Blacks the right to vote and testify in court?

A: No.

Q: How did he reconcile these contradictions?

A: He said there were two Declarations, an abstract Declaration containing abstract principles which should be kept in mind, and a real Declaration which could not be practically enforced in existing states because of racism, custom, and constitutional commitments.

Q: Did Lincoln believe the Declaration stated a principle that White men were bound to observe in their social and political relations with nonWhite people?

A: No.

Q: Did Lincoln believe the Declaration stated a principle that he was bound to observe in his relations with African-Americans, Hispanic Americans, or Native Americans?

A: No.

Q: Did Lincoln believe the Declaration required him, or any other White man, to do anything about Jim Crow legislation in Illinois and other states?

A: No.

Q: Did Lincoln believe the Declaration required him or any other

White to do anything about slavery in the states where it existed?

A: No.

Q: What did Lincoln believe the Declaration required him to do except talk?

A: He believed it required him to support verbally and politically the enslavement of the four million Blacks in the South and to oppose verbally and politically the extension of slavery to the West.

Q: Did Lincoln believe all men were created equal?

A: No. He believed Whites were created more equal than Blacks who were, he said, inferior to Whites "in many respects."

Q: Lincoln said at Gettysburg that America was conceived in liberty and dedicated to the proposition that all men were created equal. Did he believe that?

A: No.

Q: Did he believe Thomas Jefferson and George Washington believed it?

A: No.

Q. All scholars praise Lincoln for saying at Independence Hall that he "never had a feeling politically that did not spring from the sentiments embodied in the Declaration of Independence." Who's right, Lincoln or the scholars ?

A. None of the above, as we can see clearly if we ask Lincoln, and the scholars, a few simple questions:

When Lincoln voted on January 5, 1836, in his twenty-sixth year, to keep the Illinois franchise pure from contamination by Black voters, did that feeling spring from the Declaration of Independence?

When Lincoln said at Peoria, in his forty-fifth year, that he believed America was made for White people, and not Negroes, did that feeling spring from the Declaration of Independence?

When Lincoln said at Charleston, in his forty-ninth year, that he was opposed to Negroes voting and holding office, did that feeling spring from the Declaration of Independence?

When Lincoln said on the last day of his life, in his fifty-sixth year, that he supported a Louisiana government that barred Black voters, including Black Union veterans, did that feeling spring from the words "all men are created equal?"

Q. Why hasn't anyone asked Lincoln these questions before?

A. That's a good question.

Lincoln's position, at the beginning of his political career, and at the tragic end, was based on the cornerstone of the American Analytic, the idea that a person born into an oppressing group can escape guilt and responsibility by telling the world how pure and white his soul is and by making high-sounding speeches about his principles. This maneuver didn't save the oppressors (and their supporters) and the oppressed in slavery or segregation or South Africa or the Third Reich. On the contrary, it strengthened the oppression and extended its scope and life, especially in the careers of two of its greatest exponents, Henry Clay and his pupil, Abraham Lincoln. How could it have been otherwise? For if principles are not lived, if they are merely mouthed and brought out on ceremonial occasions, they are not principles—they are alibis and mystifications and instruments of violence and oppression.

It is not enough then to choose principles, for, to vary Merleau-Ponty's words, as long as you have not decided on the people for whom liberty or justice is demanded and with whom Union is to be made, slaves or slavemasters, you have done nothing (221).

Lincoln made book with slaveowners and supporters of slaveowners, and his choice reminds us that there are only two kinds of humanism, the classic, White, racist humanism of Jefferson and Lincoln, who supported slavery and the Slave Trade and man-hunting, and the universal humanism of Frederick Douglass, John Brown, and Frantz Fanon, which embraces all humanity, and especially the wretched of the earth, here and now, with no *ifs*, *ands* and *buts*.

We can see this clearly if we compare Lincoln's vision of the Declaration with the vision of Illinois Whites who believed in a real Declaration that required Whites to struggle in the here and now for equal rights for all men and women. All meant ALL to them, and all meant NOW. This was certainly the understanding of the great and neglected Illinois editor, Zebina Eastman, whose newspaper, the *Western Citizen,* carried the motto: "The Supremacy of God and the Equality of Man."

Eastman, unlike Lincoln, acted on his words, opposing the Illinois Black Laws and the Fugitive Slave Law that Lincoln supported with no sense of visible moral strain. Unlike Lincoln who supported slavery in the South because, he said, it was a social necessity and a political imperative, Eastman said that a moral wrong like the "unspeakable" evil of slavery could never be politically right. Like other Black and White abolitionists, he maintained that the Constitution had perverted the Dream of the Declaration and that it was necessary to return to the principles of that document.

But when Eastman talked about principles, he was not talking about the abstract principles of Lincoln—he was talking about living principles that included living men and women. Unlike Lincoln, who asked White people to obey the infamous Fugitive Slave Law, Eastman worked in the underground, moving slaves from southern Illinois to Chicago and Canada. The Declaration of Independence didn't keep Lincoln from supporting movements for the deportation of Blacks, but it told Eastman that the earth, even the "white" earth of Lincoln's Dream, belonged to everyone.

Eastman's life and the campaign he waged in Illinois flowed from his perception of a Declaration based on the fatherhood of God and the brotherhood of man. This was a dangerous notion, and a dangerous metaphor, to Abraham Lincoln, who was not comfortable, even symbolically, with the notion of a Black and White family.[33]

It will be said in Lincoln's defense that Eastman was a militant working outside the electoral arena and that it was impossible for an elected official to take an advanced position on the Declaration in Lincoln's time. This retrospective alibi overlooks major White politicians, notably Chase, Sumner, and Stevens, who tested the limits of the possible and provided exemplary examples of what a politician can do in a situation of oppression.

Among their number in the state of Illinois was Congressman Owen Lovejoy, who established the curve for an Illinois antislavery politician. Lincoln said over and over, as we have seen, that it was his duty as a White man to keep Blacks subordinate. Lovejoy, the brother of the Illinois martyr, Elijah Parish Lovejoy, said the "duty, destiny and true glory" of the United States was not "to hunt down fugitive slaves and take them back, manacled, to bondage" but "to maintain and illustrate" the truths of the Declaration (Magdol 151-2, 179). Not to talk about the principles, you understand, not to celebrate them on holidays, but to illustrate them day by day in the sense of making them illustrious in Springfield, Chicago, and Washington, D. C.

None of the White Americans who illustrated the Declaration in Lincoln's time was more passionate and more eloquent than abolitionist leader Wendell Phillips, who said in 1852, the same year that Lincoln praised the "white-man's charter," that the Declaration of Independence and other rocks of the American faith were worth nothing if they could not be made to deal with the question of slavery and equality in fact.

"I am willing to confess my faith," he said. "It is this: that the Christianity of this country is worth nothing, except it is or can be made capable of dealing with the question of slavery. I am willing to confess another article of my faith: that the Constitution and government of this country is worth nothing, except it is or can be made capable of grappling with the great question of slavery" (PS 91).

So saying, and acting, Phillips, along with Sumner and Stevens, projected the largest vision of the Declaration of Independence ever elaborated by White men in power in the United States. Since then, give or take a Eugene Debs or two, there has been no major White figure in power or in a major leadership position to speak for the Declaration of Independence from the standpoint of the slaves and the least of these, which is the only standpoint from which to appraise that document.

The defenders of the faith say Lincoln couldn't do any better because all or almost all Whites were racists in the nineteenth century. What would, could, should these historians say about White men who were more advanced racially than almost all Whites living in America in the twenty-first century?

The Lincoln-Douglas debates, like everything else associated with Lincoln, like the Emancipation Proclamation and the First Inaugural, are more often praised than analyzed. And although some teachers and scholars recommend the debates to schoolchildren, they were, in fact, classic examples of the racist style in American politics, as contemporary viewers discovered when they tuned in to the 1994 reenactment of the debates on C-SPAN, the cable public affairs network. Summarizing the first reenactment in Ottawa, Illinois, the Associated Press said in a dispatch, printed in the *Chicago Tribune* on August 21, 1994, "Lincoln and Douglas took up slavery—its expansion and the rights of states to regulate it—and each emphasized that Blacks were not the equals of Whites." The racist tone of the debates shocked some spectators, who had been grossly misled by their teachers and public media. One of the spectators said Lincoln and Douglas "were fighting for the middle ground, and the middle ground was very, very racist."

So was the low ground and the high ground.

And if we view the debates from the perspective of the slave, we can see clearly that Lincoln and Douglas were opposing but complementary facets of the same reality, two markers on the same road, two pincers of the same claw, two immensely talented White men playing good-cop racist and bad-cop racist with the lives of four million human beings.

It was assumed for more than a hundred years that Lincoln was an easy winner in this contest. A closer examination suggests that the contest was at least a draw and that Douglas, the whole-hearted racist, was perhaps ahead on points.

Lincoln's weakness in these debates and in the first years of his administration was his halfness, a weakness that defined and crippled his children in the American South, the Third Reich, and South Africa. A halfhearted racist opposing a wholehearted racist, a halfhearted friend of freedom opposing a wholehearted friend of slavery, he never believed in freedom as much as his opponent believed in slavery, and he was vulnerable precisely because he more than half believed in the racism and unfreedom he said was fighting.

Douglas set the tone of the debates in his opening speech at the first debate before some fifteen thousand in the town square at Ottawa, asking the crowd: "Are you in favor of conferring upon the Negro the rights and privileges of citizenship? ('No, no.') Do you desire to strike out of our State Constitution that clause which keeps slaves and free Negroes out of the State, and allow the free Negroes to flow in, ('never') and cover your prairies with black settlements?" Anticipating one of Lincoln's phrases, Douglas said "this government was made on the white basis" by "white men, for the benefit of white men and their posterity for ever . . . ." He was contemptuous of people who said or implied that God had created all men, including Negroes, equal. He didn't believe "the Almighty ever intended the Negro to be the equal of the white man. ('Never, never.') If he did, he has been a long time demonstrating the fact. (Cheers)" (CW 3:9-10).

There were two ways for Lincoln to respond to this. He could either endorse Douglas's call for White supremacy or he could climb to the Gettysburg mountaintop and do his new-birth-of-freedom routine.

What did Lincoln do?

He did what he did at every other fork of his life: he chose inequality *and* equality, saying he agreed with Douglas on the issue of White supremacy and that the only thing he wanted to do was to ensure that Blacks were included in "the words" of the Declaration in an abstract sense. Douglas said Lincoln was speaking with a forked tongue and that he couldn't believe any sane man would say that Jefferson or the founding fathers intended to include any Negro, abstract or otherwise, in the Declaration. He reminded Lincoln that "when Jefferson wrote that document he was the owner, and so continued until his death, of a large number of slaves. Did he intend to say in that Declaration that his Negro slaves, which he held and treated as property, were created his equals by Divine law, and that he was violating the law of God every day of his life by holding them as slaves? ('No, no.')." Not only Jefferson but every man who signed the Declaration represented a slaveholding constituency and "no one of them emancipated his slaves, much less put them on an equality with himself, after he signed the Declaration." Did Lincoln mean to say that "every man who signed the Declaration of Independence declared the Negro his equal, and then was hypocrite enough to continue to hold him as a slave, in violation of what he believed to be the divine law? ('No, no.')"(CW 3:216).

Rarely if ever before had the question been better posed.

Were the White founding fathers who brought forth on this land a new nation, conceived, Lincoln said, in liberty, consummate hypocrites who violated their principles, if not God's law, every day by holding fellow humans in slavery?

Instead of answering that question, Lincoln shifted ground and said lamely that until five years ago no one had ever heard anyone *say* the Negro was not included in the Declaration of Independence.

No one had ever heard Abraham Lincoln or any other White man outside abolitionists circle say they were included in the Declaration in fact, but that was another story, which didn't interest Douglas, who was concerned not about abstract Negroes but with concrete Negroes taking jobs from concrete White men and making love to concrete White women.

To emphasize that point, Douglas told his set piece about one of Lincoln's "advisers," abolitionist Frederick Douglass, and two White women. Lincoln had never met Douglass, but that was besides the point to Douglas, who told a story, probably apocryphal, about the last time he made a speech in Freeport: "I saw a carriage and a magnificent one it was, drive up and take a position on the outside of the crowd; a beautiful young lady was sitting on the box seat, whilst Fred. Douglass and her mother reclined inside, and the owner of the carriage acted as a driver." The next time he told the story in Jonesboro, "the Negro was sitting inside with the white lady and her daughter" and the husband was outside driving (CW: 3:55-6, 105).

Lincoln retaliated in kind, proving that Douglas had no monopoly on demagoguery. He denied in one speech that he wanted "a Nigger wife" (Holzer 1993, 318) and said in another speech that he had "never seen to my knowledge a man, woman or child who was in favor of producing a perfect equality, social and political, between Negroes and white men." The only exception he could think of was "Judge Douglas' old friend Col. Richard M. Johnson." It was common knowledge that Johnson, a former vice president, lived openly near Lexington, Kentucky, with his mistress, Julia Chinn, and Lincoln titillated the prejudices of the crowd, saying:

"[I] have never had the least apprehension that I or my friends would marry Negroes if there was no law to keep them from it, [laughter] but as Judge Douglas and his friends seem to be in great apprehension that they might, if there were no law to keep them from it, I give him the most solemn pledge that I will to the very last stand by the law of this State, which forbids the marrying of white people with Negroes."(CW 3:145-6).

The tone of the debate went down from that point and reached one of its many lows with Douglas's declaration in the last debate that "I care more for the great principle of self-government—the right of the people to rule themselves—than I do for all the n——rs in Christendom. (Cheers). I would not dissolve this Union; I would not endanger its perpetuity; I would not blot out the great inalienable rights of the white man for all the n——rs that ever existed" (Holzer 1993, 367).

What a difference a vowel makes!

For what Douglas said here was not all that different from what Lincoln said in his celebrated reply to Horace Greeley. And if Douglas could have rephrased that statement and changed his vowels, if he could have said that what he did for Negroes he did because of the Union and that he wouldn't have endangered the perpetuity of the Union for all the Negroes in the world, he would have a Memorial on the Mall, too.

So much, then, for the level of discourse in what has been called the greatest political debate in American history. Even if we discount the sexual demagoguery, the debate was low-grade political theater that contains not one word of wisdom on the major social and political problems of that day, or this one. The only thing a contemporary politician, or a contemporary student, can learn from what Lincoln and Douglas said in that encounter is what not to say about racism in America.

In most of his replies to the ranting of Douglas, Lincoln maintained what some scholars call a "moderate" racist tone. But there are no degrees of racism; there are only racists who express their racism in different degrees. Nothing attests to this more forcefully than the Lincoln-Douglas debates. For although Douglas was mean and racist, and although Lincoln was diffident and racist, they both ended up in the same place. There was, in fact, no essential difference between them on the main issues, although Lincoln was generally more circumspect and apologetic in his support of White supremacy. Even this difference disappeared on the question of racial mixing. For there is a passion in Lincoln's response to Douglas's denunciation of racial mixing that is not evident elsewhere. "There is," he said at Springfield in 1857, "a natural disgust in the minds of nearly all white people, to the idea of an indiscriminate amalgamation of the white and black races . . . " (CW 2:405). Noting that Douglas was "especially horrified at the thought of the mixing blood by the white and black races," Lincoln said: "agreed for once—a thousand times agreed . . . . On this point we fully agree with the Judge; and when he shall show that his policy is better adapted to prevent amalgamation than ours we shall drop ours, and adopt his" (CW 2:407-8).

Lincoln also agreed with Douglas on the immutable, irremediable inferiority of Black people, saying repeatedly during the debates that there was a physical difference between the Black and White race that would *forever* forbid equality. What exactly did Lincoln mean by "the physical difference" between Blacks and Whites? Was it color alone or was it something indefinable and indescribable that entered the genes and bloodstream and determined the intellectual and moral endowments of African-Americans and other "inferior races"?

To Lincoln, who repeatedly defined the phrase in a totalistic context that included the Negro's morals, intellect, courage, working habits, "and funny bones " the difference was biological. Not only that, God was involved in it. This was the theology of a little-noticed section of his July 10, 1858, speech in Chicago. Responding as usual to Douglas, he said: "I protest, now and forever, against that counterfeit logic which presumes that because I do not want a Negro woman for a slave, I do necessarily want her for a wife. [Laughter and cheers.] My understanding is that I need not have her for either, *but as God made us separate*, we can leave one another alone and do one another much good thereby . . . " (CW 2:498, italics added).

If we hadn't read that statement with our own eyes, we wouldn't believe it.

As God made us separate.

Did God also make Blacks subordinate?

Who else?

Having established a premise, the conclusion followed automatically and was self-confirming. For if there were what Lincoln called "inferior races" (CW 3:322-3), based on the natural physical differences ordained by God, it followed logically, semantically and theologically that there were also superior races, descended from the mystical and blessed White fathers, who reflected the pure White father of us all, who stood behind the natural order. Lincoln was considerate and understanding about the matter, telling a crowd in Springfield, "If God gave him ["the Negro"] but little, that little let him enjoy" (CW 2:520).

What shall we call a man who believes the world is run by a White God who for racial reasons gives a small minority of mankind a lot and the overwhelming majority of men and women a little? The answer is obvious. For all of this—the threat and temptation of blackness, the natural and subordinating physical differences and God the coconspirator—corresponded ideologically to a decision about human nature and the role God had assigned to White people and what Lincoln called "the inferior races." And it allows us once again to see that Lincoln's racism was a total phenomenon that defined a global attitude not only toward Blacks but also toward Whites, life, sex, death, and a world in which a White God made the overwhelming majority of human beings inferior to the God-chosen White elite.

Who were the "inferior races" that Lincoln referred to at Galesburg (CW 3:222-3) and other places, saying "we cannot make them equal?"

Well, to begin with, Africans-Americans, Native Americans, Mexicans and by implications all nonWhites. This, at any rate, is the impression one gets from the political-theological statement he made when he warned Douglas that his policy of expansionism would lead to contradictions:

> If Judge Douglas's policy upon this question succeeds, and gets fairly settled down . . . the next thing will be a grab for the territory of poor Mexico, an invasion of the rich lands of South America, then the adjoining islands will follow, each one of which promises additional slave fields. And this question is to be left to the people of those countries for settlement. When we shall get Mexico, I don't know whether the Judge will be in favor of the Mexican people that we get with it settling that question for themselves and all others; because we know the Judge has a great horror for mongrels, [laughter,] and I understand that the people of Mexico are most decidedly a race of mongrels. [Renewed laughter.] I understand that there is not more than one person

there out of eight who is pure white, and I suppose from the Judge's previous declaration that when we get Mexico or any considerable portion of it, that he will be in favor of these mongrels settling the question, which would bring him somewhat into collision with his horror of an inferior race. (CW 3:235)

Did Abraham Lincoln, who was by almost all accounts a rational man when he wasn't talking about race, believe this foolishness? We don't know, and it doesn't matter. The important point is that he talked like he believed it and acted like he believed. In major speeches all over the Midwest, in letters and public documents, and in private gatherings and meetings in Springfield and Washington, D.C., he said there was "a physical difference" between Blacks and Whites that would forever forbid them living together on a basis of equality. And that phrase, which was always on his lips and in his mind, was the foundation of his domestic and foreign policy, molding and shaping everything he did and didn't do during the Civil War.

Although Lincoln believed that Blacks were inferior and actively opposed equal rights, some commentators, even some Black commentators, say he was not anti-Negro. Conceding his bias, these analysts say Lincoln was not a vicious or malevolent man and that he was personally decent. The argument, in other words, is that he was a moderate and that he was only a little bit prejudiced.

Does this change the equation? Certainly not, for one can't be a little bit prejudiced, any more than one can be a little bit pregnant. And you can't say that a person is a supporter of the White Supremacy ethic but that he is not all that bad because he doesn't lynch Black men and take bread out of the mouths of Black children and women; for these virtualities, to paraphrase Fanon, are already on the horizon and are implicit in active commitment to a system of White Supremacy that requires the harming and liquidation of a certain number of Blacks and the appropriation of their bread and resources.

Given this record, it is no wonder that abolitionists were less than enthusiastic about Lincoln's election in November 1860. Frederick Douglass said the Republican victory was a step in the right direction but that the president-elect, based on his White dress rehearsal in Illinois, was questionable. "With the single exception of the question of slavery extension," Frederick Douglass said, "Mr. Lincoln proposes no measure which can bring him into antagonistic collision with the traffickers in human flesh, either in the States or in the District of Columbia . . . . Slavery will be as safe, and safer, in the Union under such a President, than it can be under any President of a Southern Confederacy" (FD 2:527). Phillips agreed, saying Lincoln was "not an Abolitionist, hardly an anti-slavery man."

To emphasize that point, Phillips questioned an imaginary Lincoln in a public speech:

"Do you believe, Mr. Abraham Lincoln, that the Negro is your political and social equal, or ought to be? Not a bit of it.

"Do you believe he should sit on juries? Never.

"Do you think he should vote? Certainly not.

"Should be be considered a citizen? I tell you frankly, no.

"Do you think that when the Declaration of Independence says, 'All men are created equal,' it intends the political equality of blacks and whites? No, sir'" (PS 302).

The real importance of Lincoln, Phillips added, was that he was "a pawn on the political chessboard, his value is in his position; with fair effort, we may soon change him for knight, bishop, or queen, and sweep the board . . . ."

Looking ahead to the Lincoln hosannas of today, Phillips added prophetically: "In 1760 what rebels felt, James Otis spoke, George Washington achieved, and Everett praises today." The same routine, he predicted with amazing accuracy, would go on. What the abolitionists felt, he said in effect, a Lincoln would be forced to achieve, and at the safe distance of eight decades, a Sandburg would "embalm in matchless panegyrics."

Anticipating this process, Phillips said "you see exactly what my hopes rest upon. Growth! The Republican party have undertaken a problem, the solution of which will force them to our position" (PS 314).

It has been said that the election changed Lincoln and that he went to Washington with a new set of racial ideas and attitudes. But this is a retrospective alibi that overlooks the whole orientation of the man's life. Once again the best authority on the racial views of Abraham Lincoln at that stage in his life is Abraham Lincoln, who interrupted his packing in December 1860 to reply to a letter from editor Henry J. Raymond. Raymond had enclosed a letter from a Mississippi legislator named William Smedes, who contended on the basis of erroneous reports that Lincoln was a wild-eyed abolitionist who had made an equal rights speech to a meeting of Negroes. "What a very mad-man your correspondent, Smedes is," Lincoln replied on December 18. "Mr. Lincoln is not pledged to the ultimate extinctinction [sic] of slavery; does not hold the black man to be the equal of the white, unqualifiedly as Mr. S. states it; and never did stigmatize their white people [in other words, slaveholders] as immoral & unchristian . . . ."

As for the speech to Negroes, Lincoln said:

"I was never in a meeting of Negroes in my life . . . "(CW 4:156).

Thus, A. Lincoln, at the end of his "prelude to greatness." And to understand where he was, and where he was tending, we can do no better than to consult his Peoria Declaration, which pointed both to his past and his future (CW 2:247-83). The gist of the speech, from our perspective and from the perspective of Lincoln, who quoted it repeatedly, was in a paragraph (255-6) that begins with a bow to the sensibilities of Southern Whites and an acknowledgment of how hard it was to get rid of slavery "in any satisfactory way":

"When southern people tell us they are no more responsible for the origin of slavery, than we; I acknowledge the fact. When it is said that the institution exists; and that it is very difficult to get rid of it, in any satisfactory way, I can understand and appreciate the saying. *I surely will not blame them for not doing what I should not know how to do myself* (my italics). If all earthly power were given to me, I should not know what to do, as to the existing institution."

Having made that extraordinary confession, Lincoln conceded that he had a few unsystematic ideas:

"My *first impulse* would be to free all the slaves, and send them to Liberia,—to their own native land. But a moment's reflection would convince me, that whatever of high hope, (as I think there is) there may be in this, in the long run, its sudden execution is impossible. If they were all landed there in a day, they would all perish in the next ten days; and there are not surplus shipping and surplus money enough in the world to carry them there in many times ten days" (italics added).

What then should be done?

"Free them all, and keep them among us as underlings? Is it quite certain that this betters their condition? *I think I would not hold one in slavery, at any rate; yet the point is not clear enough for me to denounce people upon.*" [My italics and my remembrance of the very different sentence, "As I would not be a slave, so [I think?] I would not be a master."]

What next?

"Free them, and make them politically and socially, our equals? *My own feelings will not admit of this;* and if mine would, we well know that those of the great mass of white people will not."

Was this fair?

Was this just?

Did this accord with the Declaration of Independence, the Constitution, and the Bible?

All that, Lincoln said, was irrelevant.

"Whether this feeling accords with justice and sound judgment, is not the sole question, if indeed, it is any part of it. A universal feeling, whether well or ill-founded, can not be safely disregarded. *We can not, then, make them equals.* It does seem to me that systems of gradual emancipation might be adopted; but for their tardiness in this, *I will not undertake to judge our brethren of the South*" (CW 2:255-6, italics added).

The fundamental racial and political characteristics of Abraham Lincoln are clearly defined in this passage: his sympathetic identification with the White "brethren" of the South, not the Black people of the South; his support of slavery where it existed; his opposition to equal rights for Blacks; his belief in gradualism and colonization; and his lack of faith in the ability of African-Americans.

The next eleven years accented some of these characteristics and threw different shades of light on others. But the Lincoln who made this speech on October 16, 1854, was the same Lincoln who went to glory on April 15,1865. If you doubt this, go back and read the often-overlooked sentence in the above Declaration:

If all earthly power were given to me, I should not know what to do, as to the existing institution.

What an extraordinary thing to say!

If all earthly power had been given to the average person, Black or White, conservative or militant, he or she would probably have freed the slaves, if only in the imagination. If all earthly power had been given to me, I would have freed the slaves immediately and provided forty acres of land and a mule to each head of household. I would have additionally used all earthly power and any means necessary to create conditions to ensure that the sons and daughters of former slaves and the sons and daughters of former slaveowners lived together equally and peaceably.

That's what I would have done.

What would you have done? What would the Lincoln biographer, who always overlook that sentence, have done?

Abraham Lincoln said that if all earthly power had been given to him, he wouldn't have known what to do.

Let the record show that he was telling the truth. All earthly power, or what passed for all earthly power, was given to him—and he didn't know what to do.

Part Seven

"White Man's War"

After the commencement of hostilities I struggled nearly a year and a half to get along without touching the "institution" . . . .
—Abraham Lincoln

The President went on almost angrily . . . . the General should never have dragged the Negro into the war. It is a war for a great national object and the Negro has nothing to do with it.
— Jessie Benton Frémont

16

"The Negro Has Nothing To Do With It"

L INCOLN grew during the war—but he didn't grow much. On every issue vital to Blacks—on emancipation, confiscation, suffrage, and the use of Black soldiers—he was the essence of the White supremacist with good intentions.

Long before Fort Sumter, and even long before his inauguration, he told White Southerners that he had been misunderstood and that he would execute the Fugitive Slave Law "with more fidelity than any Southern [White] man they could possibly find" (Segal 86).

To prove (to slaveholders) his good faith, he demanded that potential cabinet members abandon their moral scruples and pledge allegiance to the Fugitive Slave Law and other exigencies of the Southern White code. To his shame, he went further, asking Attorney General-designate Edward Bates to violate the Constitution by going slow on enforcing freedom of speech and the press in the South. Under previous administrations, White Southerners had examined and burned United States mail and had whipped and jailed White men and women for expressing "dangerous" ideas.

"It was well understood by intelligent men," Bates said after conferring with Lincoln in Springfield on Saturday, December 15, 1860, "that the perfect and unrestrained freedom of speech and the press which exists at the north was practically incompatible with the existing institutions at the South, and he [Lincoln] feared that Radical Republicans at the North might claim at the hands of the new administration the enforcement of the right, and endeavor to make the mail the means of thrusting upon the South matter which even their conservative and well-meaning men might deem inimical and dangerous." Bates, who "foresaw the practical difficulty of enforcing the law at every crossroad," promised to "carefully look" into the matter, and was later nominated and confirmed (Segal 51-2).

Seven days later, Lincoln wrote a letter to an old friend, Alexander Stephens of Georgia, asking: "Do the people of the South really entertain fears that a Republican administration would, *directly*, or *indirectly*, interfere with their slaves, or with them, about their slaves? If they do, I wish to assure you, as once a friend, and still, I hope, not an enemy, that there is no cause for such fears." In fact, he said, "the South would be in no more danger in this respect, than it was in the days of Washington" (CW 4:160, italics added).

By saying that he would enforce the Fugitive Slave Law better than "it has ever been under . . . my predecessors" (Hertz 181), and by saying that slavery would be as safe in his administration as it was under George Washington, Lincoln again defined himself as an enemy of the slave, a point he underlined in "private & confidential" instructions to Secretary of State-designate William H. Seward on February 1, 1861:

"As to fugitive slaves, District of Columbia, slave trade among the slave states, and whatever springs of necessity from the fact that the institution is amongst us, I care but little, so that what is done be comely, and not altogether outrageous" (CW 4:183).

Here, once again, Lincoln telegraphs his moral myopia and his insensitivity to Black pain, saying he cared "but little" about the capture and return of fugitive slaves to torture and even death so long as what was done was not done too publicly and too outrageously.

As if that wasn't enough, he told a group of officials from Kentucky and Virginia that "he was willing to give a constitutional guarantee that slavery *should not be molested in any way directly or indirectly* in the States; that he was willing to go further, and give a guarantee that it should not be molested in the District of Columbia; that he would go still further, and say that it should not be disturbed in the docks, arsenals, forts, and other places within the slave-holding states; but as for slavery in the territories, that his whole life was dedicated in opposition to its extension there . . . " (Segal 86-7, italics added).

Taking their cue from Lincoln, who said "all opposition, real and apparant [sic] to the fugitive slave [clause] of the constitution ought to be withdrawn" (CW 4:154), Northern leaders inaugurated one of the worst sieges in the history of African-Americans. In Boston, in Chicago, in Cincinnati, in cities all over the North, business and political leaders competed with each other in devising more stringent plans for hunting and capturing Negroes.

What this meant on a human level was manifested most clearly in the Land of Lincoln where during the first week of April the Black community of Chicago was convulsed by rumors that federal marshals were going to sweep the city in search of fugitive slaves. On Sunday, April 7, less than a week before the firing on Fort Sumter, there occurred in Chicago "an exodus such as no city in the United States had ever witnessed." Scores of Blacks, some borne on mattresses, went to the Michigan Southern Depot, where a large crowd assembled to wish them godspeed on their trip to Canada. "Don't forget us, ran the refrain of those on the platform, when you reach 'the other side of Jordan'"(Quarles 1962, 61-2).

Lincoln continued the appeasement theme in his Inaugural Address, saying he had neither the power nor the desire to interfere with slavery in the Southern states. To doubters and naysayers of that day, and of this one, he provided what he called "the most ample evidence," saying:

Apprehension seems to exist among the people of the Southern States, that by the accession of a Republican Administration, their property [he meant their slaves], and their peace, and personal security, are to be endangered. There has never been any reasonable cause for such apprehension. Indeed, the most ample evidence to the contrary has all the while existed, and been open to their inspection. It is found in nearly all the published speeches of him who now addresses you. I do but quote from one of those speeches when I declare that "I have no purpose, directly or indirectly, to interfere with the institution of slavery in the States where it exists. I believe I have no lawful right to do so, and I have no inclination to do so. (CW 4:262-3)

Frederick Douglass, among others, objected to the word *inclination*, which indicated once again that Lincoln had no disposition or desire to strike at slavery. Criticizing the "inhuman coldness," of the "double-tongued" address, and speaking for the slave, Douglass said Lincoln "has avowed himself ready to catch [slaves] if they run away, to shoot them down if they rise against their oppressors, and to prohibit the Federal Government *irrevocably* from interfering for their deliverance" (FD 2:78, italics in original).

Underlining that point, the man who gained some fame by saying that a half-slave, half-free nation could not endure permanently announced to the world that he was in favor of a proposed thirteenth amendment that would have made America permanently half slave and half free:

I understand a proposed amendment to the Constitution . . . . has passed Congress, to the effect that the federal government, shall never interfere with the domestic institutions of the States, including that of persons held to service. To avoid misconstruction of what I have said, I depart from my purpose not to speak of particular amendments, so far as to say that, holding such a provision to now be implied constitutional law, I have no objection to its being made express, and irrevocable (CW 4:270).

This amendment, the *first* thirteenth amendment, was passed by Congress and sent to the states for ratification. Two states—Ohio and Maryland—actually ratified the amendment before the firing on Fort Sumter short-circuited the process. (The *second* thirteenth amendment, never approved by Congress, was the first of three amendments Lincoln proposed for buying and deporting native-born African-Americans.)

If there was any doubt, then and now, about the policy of the administration with no policy, Secretary Seward set the record straight, telling the United States ambassador to France in an official communique that "the condition of slavery in the several States would remain just the same whether it [the rebellion] succeeds or fails" and that it "was hardly necessary to add to this incontrovertible statement the further fact that the new President has always repudiated all designs, whenever and wherever imputed to him, of disturbing the system of slavery as it has existed under the constitution and laws."

How did the Confederacy respond to the appeasement of the Lincoln administration?

On Thursday, March 21, 1861, seventeen days after Lincoln's Inaugural Address, Alexander H. Stephens, now vice president of the Confederacy, sent an answer of sorts to his old friend, defining the Confederacy as the first state founded on a racist-fascist foundation of racial supremacy. In a speech delivered at Savannah, Georgia, on March 21, 1861, Stephens, a contemporary report said, "avowed, in very explicit terms, not only that slavery was the cause of the revolt, but that the insurgents had taken their position of armed hostility to the government in direct opposition to the opinions and the purposes of the founders of the republic, the framers of the Constitution, including those from the slave states" (AC 121).

Stephens was contemptuous of men like Lincoln who wanted to finesse the issue by not talking about Blacks and the Declaration of Independence. It was clear to him that "the immediate cause of the late rupture and present revolution" was a fundamental argument over the role and status of the African-American in American society, and that the Confederacy, unlike the North, had faced that issue honestly. The "corner-stone" of the Confederacy was the idea that "African slavery as it exists among us" is "the proper status of the Negro in our form of civilization." This was in contrast to the ideas of the White founding fathers, who said the same thing in fact while saying rhetorically that all men were created equal. Stephens and the people he represented were tired of Jefferson and Lincoln and their word games:

> Our new government is founded upon exactly the opposite ideas; its foundations are laid, its corner-stone rests, upon the great truth that the Negro is not equal to the white man; that slavery, subordination to the superior race, is his natural and moral condition. This, our new government, is the first in the history of the world based upon this great physical, philosophical, and moral truth.

It might have been the first, but it certainly wasn't the last. One reason it was not the last was that so many people who were horrified by the Third Reich were silent about the first incarnation of a government founded on the cornerstone of racial superiority. None of the "top 10 Lincoln books" quotes Stephens's defining paragraph in full or in context. Few modern scholars notice the similarities between the Third Reich and the Confederacy, and almost no one arraigns it or its leaders for crimes against humanity.

What did Lincoln think about the wild ideas of the man he revered and praised almost everywhere?

What did he think about this new and *evil* thing in the world?

Lincoln was silent, giving no hint publicly of his views on his friend's speech, which was strange for a man reputed to have loved the Declaration more than any other mortal. Abolitionist and liberal Republicans asked him to speak up. Now, they said, was the time for him to tell his Whig idol that the difference between the North and the South was that the North was fighting to complete the Declaration and provide equality for slaves and all men. Lincoln didn't say that then and he didn't say it later at Gettysburg. He never, in fact, confronted Stephens's cornerstone declaration by defining America concretely in terms of the doctrine of equality, which required any honest man, as Stephens implied, to talk about "the proper status of the Negro in our form of civilization."

Gettysburg to the contrary notwithstanding, the last thing in the world the new president wanted was a war for a new birth of freedom. What was he fighting for then? He was fighting for the old Union, for the Constitution as it was, *with its slave clauses*, for South Carolina as it was, with mint juleps, cotton and slaves, and for Illinois as it was, with Black Laws and a constitution barring Black settlers.

Abolitionists and liberal congressmen told Lincoln that the first shot at Fort Sumter had destroyed all that. But he wouldn't listen. He was trying, as T. Harry Williams noted, to do the impossible, to mend broken eggs, to use his phrase, by waging a war "for the preservation of the status quo which had produced the war" (17-8).

The firing on Fort Sumter changed all plans and pleas, and we ought to pause for a moment to adjust to the new climate. Abraham Lincoln was fifty-two years old in this month, Frederick Douglass was forty-four, Wendell Phillips was fifty, Thaddeus Stevens was sixty-nine, and Charles Sumner was fifty. There were 27,000,000 Whites in America, according to the 1860 census, and 4,441,830 Blacks. The overwhelmingly majority of Blacks were slaves, 3,953,760, compared to 488,070 free Blacks. Blacks were in the majority in South Carolina, Mississippi and probably Louisiana. The largest Black populations in the free States were in Pennsylvania (56,949), New York (49,005), and Ohio (36,673). There were only 7,628 Blacks in Illinois, and about one thousand in Chicago, which has an African-American population of more than one million today.

If Lincoln didn't know the difference between an old birth of freedom and a new birth of freedom, Blacks did. In Philadelphia, in New York, in Boston, in cities all over the North, free Blacks thronged the recruiting stations, demanding uniforms and guns and the right to fight for Black freedom and a new and improved—and transformed—Union. The Lincoln administration thanked the Black volunteers and sent them home with the understanding that this was "a White man's war."

The same message was relayed to fugitive slaves, who ignored it and swarmed to Union lines, proving again what almost everyone knew, that the only real Unionists in the South were African-Americans. Many of these fugitives—in one of the heinous crimes of the war—were turned away or returned to the slavemasters. Some were abused and badly treated.

If Lincoln was confused, Benjamin Franklin Butler wasn't, and it was Butler, a new major general from Massachusetts, who began the formal emancipation process on Friday, May 24, 1861, by welcoming three slaves into his lines and grandly dubbing them "contraband of war." The word *contraband* caught on, opening a wedge for freedom, but it required an act of Congress to make Lincoln and his top generals stop returning slaves to slavemasters.

On May 26, 1861, two days after Butler's rhetorical coup, General George Brinton McClellan, whom Lincoln later named commander in chief of the army, gave Colonel B.F. Kelley the following marching orders: [34]

> See that the rights and property of the people are respected and repress all attempts at Negro insurrection.

On the same day, with almost the same breath, General McClellan issued the following proclamation to the people of West Virginia:

> Notwithstanding all that has been said by the traitors to induce you to believe that our advent among you will be signalized by interference with your slaves understand one thing clearly—not only will we abstain from all such interferences, but we will, on the contrary, with an iron hand crush insurrection on their part.

Another proslavery general, Henry W. Halleck, issued on November 20, 1861, the infamous General Order No. 3, directing that no fugitive slave would be permitted "to enter the lines of any camp or of any forces on the march and that any now within such lines be immediately excluded therefrom."[35]

This was, as I have said elsewhere (1995,190-1), a novel way to fight a war. Liberal Republicans, Black and White abolitionists and "hard-war" Unionists asked Lincoln to stop the military slave hunt and hit the South where it would hurt most by freeing the slaves and giving them guns. What kind of war was the president fighting anyway? What was he trying to do? Lincoln said he was trying to save the old Union. What then was to be done with slaves who were abandoning their plantations in droves and flocking to Union lines? Lincoln said his policy was to have no policy.

In this famous statement, beloved by schoolchildren and PBS commentators, honest Abraham told a lie, as he himself admitted later. For he had a policy, and that policy was to win the war without touching slavery. His goal in the first phase of the war was the restoration of the old Union, what he repeatedly called "the Union as of old," with slavery. Lincoln himself provided irrefutable proof on this point, saying publicly and officially that he struggled "nearly a year and a half" to keep from touching slavery. When he was forced by events and public pressure to, as he said, "conditionally" touch slavery, he changed his rhetoric but not his goal, pressing the same old policy with a new component of gradual and compensated emancipation linked to the deportation of the freed slaves.

Almost all interpreters say Lincoln's policy was the ad hoc fumbling of a good man who meant well. Lincoln himself had a different view of the matter. More than a year later, he told one of his conservative Democratic friends that his policy was deliberate and that everything he had done in Washington, the Emancipation Proclamation excepted, followed a blueprint that he had drawn up before he left Springfield. Democratic mole T.J. Barnett said he told him in November 1862 that "the acts of the Administration & all of its responsibilities belong to that unhappy wretch called Abraham Lincoln'—that he has acted on a deliberate policy checked out before he left Springfield with the single exception of the act of Emancipation—which he regards as . . . thwarting servile Insurrection and, to a great extent, a brutem fulmen, as, in its essence, conservative toward the slave owners, who else might have suffered horrors as the price of the freedom . . . which the war has forced on the slaves . . . ."[36] Put a pin in that word *forced.* Lincoln retailed here, and elsewhere, Southern White propaganda which said that the war and outsider agitators had forced a freedom on the slaves that they didn't really want.

What is usually overlooked in evaluating Lincoln's "policy of no policy" is that his struggle to keep from touching slavery required a daily struggle to preserve slavery. Lincoln led the way in this effort, secretly ordering generals to round up escaped slaves and return them to slavery. On Tuesday, July 16, 1861, five days before Bull Run, General Irvin McDowell of the Washington Military Headquarters received an urgent communication from "the general-in-chief": [37]

CONFIDENTIAL.]				HEADQUARTERS OF THE ARMY,
						Washington, July 16, 1861.

Brigadier-General MCDOWELL, *Commanding, &c.*

SIR: The general-in-chief desires me to communicate to you that he has received from the President of the United States a second note dated to-day on the subject of fugitive slaves in which he asks: "Would it not be well to allow owners to bring back those which have crossed" the Potomac with our troops? The general earnestly invites your attention to this subject knowing that you with himself enter fully into His Excellency's desire to carry out to the fullest all constitutional obligations. Of course it is the general's wish that the name of the President should not at this time be brought before the public in connection with this delicate subject.

Entering fully into Lincoln's desire to return fugitive slaves to slavemasters, the general-in-chief instructed the commanding general of the Department of Washington to take "stringent measures" to keep fugitive slaves from "passing over the river" with Union troops. The next day, in accordance with the desires of the future emancipator, the following general order was issued from headquarters, Department of Washington :

GENERAL ORDERS,} HDQRS. DEPARTMENT OF WASHINGTON,
    No. 33.   }   *Washington, July 17, 1861.*
    Fugitive slaves will under no pretext whatever be permitted to reside or be in any way harbored in the quarters and camps of the troops serving in this department. Neither will such slaves be allowed to accompany troops on the march.
    Commanders of troops will be held responsible for a strict observance of this order.
    By command of Brigadier-General Mansfield.

Closer to home, and with Lincoln's knowledge and approval, Lincoln's crony, District of Columbia Marshal Ward Hill Lamon, was capturing fugitive slaves and holding them in the Washington jail for their alleged owners. When Congress demanded to know why the president's special friend was capturing and holding slaves for slavemasters, Lincoln himself drafted a conciliatory letter, disclaiming any proslavery intent. "Lincoln's bland tone," Quarles said, "was typical of his handling of Congress; if he had to quicken his step in order to keep time to a tune called by the men on Capitol Hill, he would give them the old softshoe" (79).

Lincoln said in 1964 that "so long as I have been here I have not willingly planted a thorn in any man's bosom" (CW 8:101). He meant, of course, any *White man's* bosom. For he entered the White House putting thorns into the bosoms of Black men, women and children, and he never, so long as he lived there, stopped. If you're running a tab, you can add the fugitive slaves he personally ordered returned to slavery and the tens of thousands returned to slavery by generals and aides under his command. To this long and mournful procession, one can also add, as we shall see, the 115,000 Missouri

Blacks, who were condemned to four additional years of slavery when Lincoln revoked the Frémont emancipation proclamation, the 926,000 persons in Georgia, Florida, and South Carolina, who were condemned to three additional years of slavery when Lincoln revoked the Hunter emancipation proclamation, and the half-million or so condemned to two more years of slavery by *his* Emancipation Proclamation.

None of this was accidental. This was Lincoln's policy. It was his desire.

"It is the desire of the President," Secretary of War Simon Cameron told a general on August 8, 1861, "that all existing rights in all the States be fully respected and maintained. The war now prosecuted on the part of the Federal Government *is a war for the Union and for the preservation of all constitutional rights of States and the citizens of the States in the Union.*"[38]

Is that a policy, or what?

The addressee, General Benjamin F. Butler, thought it was a policy, and a despicable one at that. "This is too ridiculous," he said, "to be laughed at " (Lester 358).

Ridiculous or not, it was the policy of the president of the United States and almost all his men.

To carry out this policy, Lincoln surrounded himself with an overwhelmingly conservative (and racist) cabinet with only two liberal or moderate members: Secretary of the Treasury Chase and Secretary of War Simon Cameron, who was replaced almost immediately because he was too liberal in advocating the use of Black soldiers. Cameron's replacement was Edwin McMasters Stanton, a Democrat who surprised some people by becoming a major supporter of the hard-war faction.

The other members of the cabinet were different shades of reaction. Attorney General Edward Bates of Missouri was an ultraconservative colonizationist who feared a "social and servile war" and who believed in ethnic cleansing and the forcible deportation of Blacks. Secretary of the Interior Caleb Blood Smith of Indiana was a passionate advocate of colonization who opposed the use of Black soldiers. Postmaster General Montgomery Blair of Maryland had close social connection with Mary Todd Lincoln's slaveholding relatives in Kentucky. A West Pointer and a lawyer like everybody else in the cabinet except editor Welles, he was, like Lincoln, Jefferson, Bates, and Smith, a separatist and a colonizationist who didn't believe Blacks and Whites could live together in the same country. Like Bates, he favored deportation. Like Lincoln, he opposed race mixing. If, as they say, to choose your advisors is to choose your policy, this bizarre collection of ultraconservatives, deportationists and racists defined Lincoln and his chosen policy. And it should be noted, at least in passing, that at this critical juncture, *as at every other critical juncture of his life, Lincoln bonded with the right, and the racist.*

The leading member of the cabinet and Lincoln's chief advisor was Secretary of State William Henry Seward, a New York liberal who moved to the right after inauguration and kept on moving to the right. Abolitionists and liberal Republicans said Seward was a major factor in the administration's soft-on-slavery policy.

That this policy was changed at all was due not to Lincoln's humanitarianism but to rebel battlefield brilliance and the compassion and perseverance of a small band of abolitionists and far-seeing Republicans. Foremost among these men and women were Charles Sumner, the senator from Massachusetts; Frederick Douglass, the bearded Black abolitionist; Harriet Tubman, the courageous Black scout who was perhaps the first woman to lead U.S. troops in battle; Thaddeus Stevens, the Pennsylvania congressman who virtually supplanted Lincoln as head of the Republican Party; and Wendell Phillips, who was generally conceded to be the greatest White orator of the day.

"I never did believe," Phillips told cheering crowds," in the capacity of Abraham Lincoln, but I do believe in the pride of [Jefferson] Davis, in the vanity of the South, in the desperate determination of those fourteen States; and I believe in a sunny future, because God has driven them mad; and their madness is our safety. They will never consent to anything that the North can grant; and you must whip them, because, unless you do, they will grind you to powder " (PS 455).

All of which reminds me, as it reminded Abraham Lincoln, of a story. According to the story, Lincoln was complaining to a visitor that three Republican leaders—Senators Sumner and Wilson and Congressman Stevens —were pestering him night and day, coming sometimes alone, sometimes in twos, sometimes all three together, demanding the freedom of Blacks. As he said that, Lincoln walked to the window and, to his consternation, the same three Republican leaders were approaching the White House. Lincoln called his visitor, Senator John B. Henderson of Missouri, to the window, pointed at the approaching trio, and told a story about a "field school" he attended.

"You know," he said, "we had no reading books, and we read out of the Bible. The class would stand up in a row, the teacher in front of them, and read verses, turn about. This day we were reading about the Hebrew children. As none of us were very good readers, we were in the habit of counting ahead and each one practicing on his particular verse. Standing next to me was a red-headed, freckled-face boy, who was the poorest reader in the class. It so fell out that the names of the Hebrew children appeared in his verse. He managed to work through Shadrach, fell down at Meschach, and went all to pieces at Abednego. The teacher spanked the boy until he cried and then started all over, each boy reading verses and passing the Bible on. The reading went on, and in due course of time came round again, but when the turn came near enough for the boy to see his verse, he pointed to it in great consternation, and whispered to me, 'Look there! Look! There comes them same damn three fellers again.'"[39]

As the war continued and as Northern casualties mounted, the same damn three fellows and their allies put events to use and mobilized a public pressure Lincoln couldn't ignore. Delegation after delegation waited on the president and demanded that he free the slaves and arm them. Lincoln parried the pressure with heat and conviction, citing constitutional, political, and military reasons to justify his anti-emancipation stand.

Lincoln usually expressed his opposition to emancipation in a troubled but polite tone, but he could be pushed across the border of politeness. When Edward L. Pierce urged the president to adopt a more enlightened policy, Lincoln, according to Pierce, exploded and denounced "the itching to get niggers into our lives."[40] Other White House visitors reported that the mere mention of the word *slave* made Lincoln nervous.

The traditional image of Lincoln is of a harried and large-hearted man fending off "extremists of the left and right" only to emerge at the precise psychological moment to do what he had always wanted to do. This image clashes, unfortunately, with incontrovertible evidence that sudden and general emancipation was never Lincoln's policy and that he feared Black freedom for social and racial reasons.

It was not fear of emancipation but the fear of what would happen afterward that palsied Lincoln's hands. He was terrified by the implications of turning loose four million Blacks in White America, and he said repeatedly that it was his considered judgment that "gradual, and not sudden, emancipation, is better for all" (CW 5:145).

Why did Lincoln believe that? Critics said he feared amalgamation, Black and White competition over jobs, and Black violence. Hofstadter said he was always thinking "primarily" of the interests of White workers, and not the interests of Black workers. But in this case, as in others, the personal and the political, as Hofstadter also said, intersected in Lincoln, who shared and magnified the fears he projected onto poor Whites. This explains in part the intensity of his feeling about deporting Blacks, a "fantastic idea," Hofstadter said, that "grew logically out of a caste psychology in a competitive labor market . . . " (167).

Logically or not, it also grew out of a deep-seated fear of Black violence. Even as a young politician, Lincoln had keen anxiety about a slave revolt and suggested that he would stop opposing the extension of slavery and support the violence of slaveowners if the slaves rebelled. In 1845, when he was thirty-six years old, he told a correspondent that "[W]e should never knowingly lend ourselves, directly or indirectly, to prevent . . . slavery from dying a natural death," adding significantly: "Of course I am not now considering what would be our *duty*, in cases of insurrection among the slaves" (CW 1:348, italics added).

Duty: what an extraordinary word to find in this context. Who— White people? White people organized as the state of South Carolina, White people organized as the United States?—gave Lincoln that duty? Who gave him the moral right and the moral obligation to violently put down a slave insurrection and keep Blacks in slavery? And why did Lincoln believe or seem to believe that if it came to a shooting war between [Black] slaves and [White] slaveowners, it would be his duty to shoot the slaves? The answer of course is that Lincoln gave himself that rights-duty-obligation structure by choosing to be White and by establishing an untranscendable limit of whiteness within himself and his world.

To gain some perspective on this phenomenon, which is passed over in silence by almost all historians, one has to confront Lincoln with the diametrically opposite view of his contemporaries, David Walker, Nat Turner, Henry Highland Garnet and Wendell Phillips, who anticipated modern analysts like Jean-Paul Sartre and Frantz Fanon, saying that there never was any other violence, except slaveholder violence, and that slave violence against slaveholder violence not only advanced humanity but was itself an expression of the highest octave of humanity.

"I do not shrink," Phillips said in Boston's Music Hall on February 17, 1861, "from the toast with which Dr. Johnson flavored his Oxford Port,—'Success to the first insurrection of the blacks in Jamaica!'" Phillips said his support of slave violence was dictated by "the highest humanity," adding:

" I know what anarchy is. I know what civil war is. I can imagine the scenes of blood through which a rebellious slave population must march to their rights. They are dreadful. And yet, I do not know, that, to an enlightened mind, a scene of civil war is any more sickening that the thought of a hundred and fifty years of slavery. Take the broken hearts; the bereaved mothers; the infant, wrung from the hands of its parents; the husband and wife torn asunder; every right trodden under foot, the blighted hopes, the imbruted souls, the darkened and degraded millions, sunk below the level of intellectual life, melted in sensuality, herded with beasts, who have walked over the burning marl of Southern slavery to their graves; and where is the battle-field, however ghastly, that is not white, —compared with the blackness of that darkness which has brooded over the Carolinas for two hundred years?" (PS 383-4).

What appalled Phillips was not the possibility of Black violence but the continuation, to change Phillips's palette, of the legalized insurrection of slavery and the white violence of slave states like South Carolina.

The difference between Lincoln and Phillips on this issue was fundamental. Phillips said he preferred a Black insurrection "which frees the slave in ten years to slavery for a century" (PS 383); Lincoln preferred slavery for a century or even forever to a Black insurrection that would have freed the slaves in ten. This fear played a major role in the formation of his war policy, especially his opposition to immediate emancipation and the use of Black soldiers.

Not a few visitors to the White House found Lincoln wringing his hands over the possibility of a Nat Turner-like uprising behind the enemy's lines. What, he wondered, was he going to do if the slaves rebelled behind enemy lines and started burning, pillaging and . . . .

When historian George Bancroft visited the White House on December 16, 1861, he found "the President . . . turning in his thoughts the question of his duty [there is that word again] in the event of a slave insurrection" (1908, 147). There is no mystery about how Lincoln would have answered that question. It is certain that he and Northern and Southern generals would have stopped fighting one another in order to jointly fight Blacks.

If one unreality governed one part of Lincoln's anti-emancipation strategy, another and equally insubstantial unreality governed his Border State strategy, which was based on the idea of appeasing slaveholders and slaveholder interests in the four Border States that remained loyal to the Union, Delaware, Kentucky, Missouri, and Maryland.

BORDER SLAVE STATES

	Free Blacks	Slaves	Whites
Delaware	1,798	19, 829	90, 589
Kentucky	10,684	225, 483	919,484
Maryland	83,942	87,189	515,918
Missouri	3,572	114,931	1,063, 489

SLAVE STATES

	Free Blacks	Slaves	Whites
Alabama	2,690	435,080	526,271
Arkansas	144	111,115	324,143
Florida	932	61,745	77,746
Georgia	3,500	462,198	591.550
Louisiana	**18,647**	**331,726**	**357,456**
Mississippi	**773**	**436, 631**	**353, 899**
North Carolina	30,463	331,059	629,942
South Carolina	**9,914**	**402,406**	**291,300**
Tennessee	7,300	275,719	826,722
Texas	355	182,566	420,891
Virginia	58,042	490,865	1,047,299

There were 447,432 slaves in the Border States, and traditional historians say Lincoln's war policy was based on the idea of separating these states from the Confederacy by inducing them to adopt a gradual emancipation plan extending over thirty or forty years.

How did he propose to do this?

By using the carrot and the stick, by offering government funds to buy the slaves at a cost of $400 or $500 a slave and by warning "loyal slaveholders"—what a phrase—that the bad abolitionists were going to emancipate their slaves immediately and without compensation if they turned down his plan.

Lincoln's supporters say that almost everything he did during the Civil War was colored by his sensitivity to the fears of Kentucky, Missouri, Delaware, and Maryland slaveholders, and their Southern sympathizers in the North. Were these fears real? Yes, but they couldn't be narcotized or wished away by words and gestures. Border State slaveholders and their Southern sympathizers in the North were, as Cassius Marcellus Clay of Kentucky and other close observers told Lincoln, objective traitors. The slaveholders in particular were defined by their economic interests as slaveholders. Slavery was their being, and they couldn't give it up without committing suicide socially. They and the commercial and white ethnic Copperheads in the North were won over finally not by Lincoln's words and maneuvers but by violence—the distribution of rifles and other *armed* appeals as well as by midnight arrests and detention—and the increasing support for the Union cause.

Lincoln's friend, correspondent Noah Brooks, and others said Lincoln's Border State policy was based on bad psychology and bad politics. Lincoln thought, Brooks said, "that the border states must be conciliated and kept in the Union by pleasant promises. The hyena was fed with sugar plumbs, and it snapped at the hand which caressed it." The Border State conservatives and conservative Democrats, Brooks said, "looked upon the President's policy of conciliation as an evidence of weakness and treated his concessions not as grateful acts of mercy and condescension but as surrenders to their just demands, and, consequently, deputations of borderers, impudent in their exactions, have visited the White House, presuming upon the conciliatory policy of the President, to secure their growing demands." Brooks, who was close to the president and his wife, concluded in February 1863 that "the 'border state policy' has proved a failure, and *those states which it was designed to conserve to the Union are, possibly, more dangerous and more difficult to deal with for the reason that they are out of the Union while they profess to be in it*" (1967, 96-7, italics added).

The *New York Tribune*, the *Chicago Tribune* and major congressional leaders said Lincoln's mistaken idea that he could persuade Border State slaveholders and "moderate" slave state slaveholders to sell their slaves to the government in return for virtually unrestricted control over them during an interim apprenticeship period leading to their ultimate deportation was one of the biggest political miscalculations of the war. Congressman Julian called it "a cruel and fatal mistake" (222-3) that almost lost a war that was impossible to lose. In 1862, Border State slaveholders decisively rejected that idea. By 1865, Maryland and Missouri had repudiated the Lincoln plan and had adopted immediate emancipation plans without compensation. What about Kentucky? Kentucky, despite all Lincoln's pleas and compromises, was adamant to the end, and even rejected the Thirteenth Amendment. If Blacks and their allies had depended on Lincoln's overpraised Border State strategy, there would have been no emancipation in 1865 and probably in the nineteenth century.

Beyond all this, it must be said—in contradiction to the whole Lincoln encyclopedia—that Lincoln's end defined his obstacles and his means, not the reverse. For contrary to the popular view (and the dominant American academic view), means, obstacles, allies and enemies are defined not in and of themselves but to the extent, and only to the extent, that they help achieve an end that preexisted them and conferred value on them. It was precisely because Lincoln's fundamental end was saving what he called "the Union as of old" with slavery in Kentucky and South Carolina that Kentucky and the Border States were central to him and *his* war. If he had had another end, if he had desired freedom above all or as a means to a different end, perhaps the economic supremacy of the North or the political supremacy of the Republican Party, then Kentucky would have been a manageable problem and not the foundation of his policy. The point here, and the point is key in defining Lincoln and the war he fought and, more importantly, the war he didn't fight, is that Kentucky and the Border States had no meaning in and of themselves and that Lincoln defined himself and his end by defining his Kentucky.

Nobody was buying the Kentucky "sugar plums" program, but Lincoln, like an obsessive and out-of-phase Willy Loman, continued to sell new and improved versions of the compensated emancipation/colonization plans that he had been trying to market since the 1850s. Nothing came of these proposals, primarily because they were based on the unrealities that governed Lincoln's actions in the first phase of the war.

Of these unrealities, none was more absurd or more costly in terms of men and matériel than the idea that the Civil War was a misunderstanding between White gentlemen, a misunderstanding that had nothing at all to do with Blacks or slavery. Thus, for almost two years, the Union, under Lincoln's leadership, fought the strangest war in military history, calling its friend its enemy, and its enemy its friend, letting what Brooks called "half-confessed traitors" define and delimit its strategy, refusing *as a matter of policy* to utilize its strongest weapons and denying itself the only terrain that promised certain victory over a foe who was brilliantly and brutally slaughtering a whole generation of its young men.

The blood was real, but the strategy was surreal, based on one of history's greatest illusions, an illusion shared not only by the people but also and most importantly by the leaders, who feared the darkness, in the literal sense, so much that they blinded themselves to keep from seeing the light. How else explain the words that the commander in chief spoke to Jessie Benton Frémont in opposition to her husband's order freeing Missouri slaves. "The President," she said, "went on almost angrily. . . . the General should never have dragged the Negro into the war. It is a war for a great national object and the Negro has nothing to do with it" (266).

This was not an isolated statement, made in anger. Lincoln said the same thing privately and publicly. And it was this idea—the idea of preserving government of White people for White people—that Lincoln was arguing for at Gettysburg.

Nothing to do with it . . . .

He might as well have said that cotton had nothing to do with it.

He might as well have said that railroads, oil, gold, John Calhoun, John Brown, Stephen Douglas, Daniel Webster, Nat Turner, the Missouri Compromise, and greed for Black bodies and Indian land had nothing to do with it. For the slave, more than anyone else, more even than the slaveholders, *was* the war, and nobody was going to get out of it without dealing with that fact.

If Lincoln couldn't or wouldn't see that, Wendell Phillips could, and he crisscrossed the North, telling thousands of listeners that the Negro was the key to the situation (PS 434), and that the best way for Lincoln to save lives and money was to strike at the root, slavery. Not only were slaves the key to the war but they were also the key to the American future. "Hitherto," he said, "the Negro has been a hated question. The Union moved majestic on its path, and shut him out, eclipsing him from the sun of equality and happiness. He has changed his position to-day. He now stands between us and the sun of our safety and prosperity . . ." (PS 445). Lincoln, Phillips said, knew this. "He [Lincoln] knows as well as . . . as every man this side of a lunatic hospital knows, that, if we want to save lives and money, the way to end this war is to strike at slavery" (PS 448).

Why didn't Lincoln see this? Why was he equivocating and making absurd statements to Jessie Benton Frémont? The answer, as always, as Phillips and Douglass and others said, was racism, not only the racism of Abraham Lincoln but the racism of most Northern Whites. For it will not do to blame Lincoln alone for his failure to rise above the racist environment that made him an apostle of a limited humanity. The blighting of the vision and reach of "America's greatest moral leader" was, to be sure, one of the greatest tragedies of American racism, but Lincoln's racism was persuasive because it grew out of and amplified the racism of millions of other Americans, who by opposing emancipation and equal rights made themselves responsible for the results and the consequences.

The failure was collective, and the failure was almost total, as General John W. Phelps said in a letter to Sumner: "The President tries to hide himself behind Congress; Congress tries to hide itself behind the people, and the people still want to worship the calf of their own cunning—like a simple girl they want to be a whore and virtuous too; they want slavery and liberty both" (qtd. in Sandburg 1939, 2:256).

It was an old American failure. Jefferson started it, and it was the duty of Lincoln, it was the duty of a great leader, Phelps said, to tell the people that they couldn't be a whore and a virgin at the same time and love slavery and liberty at the same time. But Lincoln was no more persuasive on this level than on any other level. For he was many things, including a great user of the English language, when he was talking about White folks, but he was not by most reckonings, not by the reckoning of most members of his cabinet or most members of Congress or most of his cronies, a great leader. All who knew him well said it was his nature to equivocate and "drift," to use Herndon's word. Gurowski said, in a pungent phrase, that Lincoln acts only "when the gases of public exasperation rise powerfully and strike his nose" (GD 180). He acted, Phillips said, and Stevens said, and Douglass said, and Herndon said, by following. Donn Piatt, a journalist and Union officer who observed Lincoln closely during the war, said that he never tried to lead the people, "save in the direction they sought to follow" (RR 482).

Unlike a statesman who realizes all the possibilities of a historical situation by showing the people their true face and pulling them up the mountaintop to the dream they wanted but couldn't name or visualize, Lincoln, Phillips said, using the most contemptible word in his vocabulary, was a *politician* who was always looking over his shoulders "to see how far the people will support him."

Stevens, like Phillips, was contemptuous of politicians who cut their conscience to fit the prejudices of the people. For he knew "that the limit of their advance would be determined only by the lengths to which he could lead them" (Woodley 360).

It was Lincoln's art to lag behind until most marchers had passed him by so that he would have to run to catch up, giving himself and others the impression that he had been running all the time. Woodley said that "in every single stand he took, which superficially might appear to be an original attitude, either substantial or major groups had passed that point before him, and it was only the support that they had gathered and their potential strength that enticed Lincoln to the position" (298-9).

The irony of all this is that Lincoln was elected not to lead but to do what he had always done, to temporize, and that the qualities that elected him were the precise opposite of the qualities he needed as a war leader. Congressman Joshua Giddings said he was nominated not because he was antislavery but because "his anti-slavery sentiment had been less prominent" than William H. Seward and other front-runners (Berwanger 136). Congressman George W. Julian said "his nomination . . . had been secured through the diplomacy of conservative Republicans, whose morbid dread of abolitionism unfitted them, as I believe, for leadership in the battle with slavery which had now become inevitable . . ." (RR 47-8). Julian was not a Lincoln fan, but Herndon was, and he tells us that Lincoln was a follower, not a leader, and that he "never ran in advance of his age" (HH 82).

It is one of the anomalies of the American Analytic—the academic and media lens through which American reality is filtered—that almost all historians honor Lincoln not for leading but for *not* leading. Although almost all historians believe he is the greatest presidential leader in our history, he is celebrated by the same historians not for leading public opinion but for following it. This, of course, is a *political* position based on a conservative reading of leadership. What the analysts who say this mean is that it is the duty of a leader, *especially in a situation of oppression* (read segregation, read apartheid), to follow the prejudices of the people.

This is a false dichotomy that ensures a faulty reading of Lincoln's politics and contemporary politics. For leadership is not a matter of slavishly following the people nor of running ahead of them. What is required is the ability to read a situation and to tell what is possible and what is necessary. Beyond all that, it is simply a matter of inventing what later events will show was demanded by the time.

The public and the public opinion that Lincoln was called on to create was not given.That public, the public that approved and even demanded emancipation and the Thirteenth Amendment, the public that the abolitionists, congressional leaders, and Civil War victories created, did not exist before Fort Sumter. It had to be created, and it could not be created by men who followed the public opinion of "the Union as it was" and would never be again.

The great educator Benjamin E. Mays said that not failure but low aim is sin. Lincoln, especially in the first years of his administration, aimed low, and from all sides, from antislavery advocates and proslavery advocates came a recurring refrain: there was no purpose, no backbone, no "stiffness" in him. Lincoln specialists, who manage somehow to make a virtue out of every Lincoln vice, say he must have been doing something right if everybody, or almost everybody, thought what he was doing was wrong. This argument assumes that there is no moral difference between being moderately in favor of slavery or moderately in favor of freedom. It ignores, moreover, the fact that the criticism came from cabinet members, conservatives, abolitionists, cronies, and congressional leaders.

Illinois Senator Lyman Trumbull said Lincoln lacked "the will necessary in this great emergency" (White 171). A conservative Louisiana White man told Lincoln that "trying to please everybody . . . will satisfy nobody" (CW 5:350). Lincoln crony Orville

Browning said Lincoln was "a failure" as a leader and that he had always doubted whether Lincoln was "big enough for his position" (Baxter 158). Assistant Secretary of War Peter H. Watson told A. S. Hill, according to a letter of October 1862, that Lincoln was "the worst possible ruler" (Gay). Another Lincoln administration leader, Attorney General Edward Bates, said during the war that the president lacked "*will* and *purpose,* and, I greatly fear he has not *the power to command*" (1: 676).

Unbelievable as it may seem now, most Republican leaders as late as the summer of 1864 believed Lincoln was a disaster as a leader. Senator Wilson asked Sumner, who liked Lincoln but who believed he was "utterly unfit to be President," the classical question: If not Lincoln, who? Sumner replied without a beat that he could name at least twenty men in the Senate who were more qualified to be president of the United States than Abraham Lincoln (Nicolay 84). After thinking about it awhile, he told a correspondent that he could name at least one hundred people who could do a better job than President Lincoln (SL 253).

Lincoln would be virtually canonized later in the state of Illinois, which is known today as "The Land of Lincoln." But during the war, a significantly large number of Illinoisans said Lincoln was a weak-willed leader with little or no understanding of the war or the social forces of his time. Religious leaders in the state sent volleys of petitions and pleas for emancipation, and political leaders like Governor Richard Yates scolded him publicly. The *Chicago Tribune* and its editors, Charles Ray and Joseph Medill, were as passionate as Horace Greeley and the *New York Tribune* in attacking Lincoln's conservative posture on freeing and arming Blacks. The legendary Medill, for whom the Northwestern University School of Journalism is named, was especially caustic, telling Lincoln in a February 9, 1862, letter: "Mr. Lincoln, for God's sake and your country's sake rise to the realization of our awful national peril. I, you and the County know that this is a Slave holders rebellion."[41]

Since Lincoln seemed to be confused about the nature of the conflict, Medill stressed that point over and over again to Lincoln and others. "Slavery," he told Secretary Chase, "is at the bottom of the whole trouble. The revolt was inaugurated to expand and strengthen the system, to give the oligarchy more domain, more slaves and the unrestricted powers of Government to defend and foster the institution . . . . And until the Administration sees the contest in its true light the blood of loyal men will be shed in vain and the war will come to naught" (CL 97). Medill never really changed his mind about Lincoln and his "d——d do-nothings." In 1864, he supported the national movement to postpone the presidential contest in order to find an alternative presidential candidate. Lincoln, he said, had exhibited "some very weak and foolish traits of character."[42]

Reading the letters and newspapers of that day, one is struck by the unanimity of opinion and by the withering terms friends and foes used to describe Lincoln. Garrison said he was "a wet rag." Phillips said he was " a tortoise." Douglass and others said he was "a slow coach." Iowa Republicans said he reminded them of Phillip II of Spain, "who did not understand his time any better than Lincoln does." The consensus comparison was Louis XVI, the inept French king who lost his head in the French Revolution. Chase said Lincoln "may be the Louis 16th . . . of America". Gurowski said Lincoln reminded him somewhat of Louis XVI, "similar goodness, honesty, good intentions; but the size of events seems to be too much for him." [43]

Almost all liberal Republicans said Lincoln's policies prolonged the war and increased the cost and casualties. "It is hard," Sumner said, "to read of all this blood & sacrifice, & to think that it might have been averted—which I most solemnly believe" (SL 124). Sumner said Lincoln's "delays tended to prolong the war" and "if ever the account is impartially balanced he [Lincoln] & the Secy of State must answer for much treasure & bloodshed" (SL 306). Trumbull agreed, saying a better man and a better president might have won the war "in half the time, and with half the loss of blood and treasure" (qtd. in White 428).

Critics differed in their emphasis and focus but agreed on five recurring complaints. First and foremost, Lincoln permitted slave-holders and supporters of slaveholders, in the Border States and in the Slave States, to define his policy on slavery and his overall strat-egy, giving them a veto over his war policy. Lincoln defenders take this anomaly for granted, and even praise it, but ask yourself what this would have meant if the Athenians had let the Spartans define their policy, and if the Allies had let the Axis define theirs.

Secondly, and astoundingly, Lincoln violated the first rule of war by refusing, because of racism, because of conservatism, because of a mistaken conception of the struggle, to hit the enemy where it would hurt most by freeing the slaves and arming them. Critics said if Lin-coln had moved with vigor on this level in the first phase of the war, and even later, he could have added four hundred thousand fighting men to the Union ranks and ended the conflict expeditiously.

Thirdly, and regrettably, Lincoln compounded his other mistakes by putting proslavery Democrats in command of military forces charged with defeating the defenders of slavery. In the first years of the war, most of the leading generals were Democrats who hated slaves and Negroes and loved or admired slaveholders. Senator Wil-son said in a Senate speech in 1861 that eighty of the one hundred and ten brigadier generals were Democrats. Congressman Julian said that four out of every five brigadier and major generals were Democrats. Worse, most of the *commanding* generals in the first phase of the war, McClellan, Don Carlos Buell and Halleck, were Democrats who were more than half convinced of the truth of the Confederate idea. Secretary Chase said Lincoln entrusted the direction of the war "almost exclusively to his political opponents" (Williams 15-6).

Medill said the principal reason for the major disasters of the first two years of the war was Lincoln's policy of promoting "quasi loyal" proslavery generals. "The reason the war has made such slow progress," he told Chase, "is because our anti slavery soldiers have been placed under the command of proslavery Generals—Look at the list, McClellan, Halleck, Buell; the Shermans, McCook, Nelson Lockwood, Hooker, McDowell Sturgis &c&c" (CP 208).

Medill, Sumner, Stevens, Douglass, Tubman, Chase, Stanton, Gurowski— almost all Republican leaders criticized Lincoln on this score, pointing out, as Medill pointed out, that "a pro-slavery revolt can not be put down by conducting the war on pro-slavery principles . . . " (CP 97).

Nor could it be put down by admitting "its enemies to the inner circles of its counsels." General Carl Schurz, who liked Lincoln and who wished him well, told him in the middle of the war that he was his own worst enemy and that his administration had strengthened the enemies of the Union by admitting "its professed opponents to its counsels" and by placing the army "into the hands of its enemies." Lincoln had, he said, created a situation unique in politics and war, for "in all personal questions to be hostile to the party of the government seemed to be as title to consideration." In a personal letter, Schurz told Lincoln that he had forgotten "the great rule, that if you are true to your friends, your friends will be true to you, and that you make your enemies stronger by placing them upon equality with your friends."[44]

He had also forgotten, it seems, that soldiers need a burning idea to march for and to die for. And it is extraordinary that Lincoln, who reportedly lived by and for the Declaration of Independence, failed to seize the moral initiative and define the Union and freedom in terms that would generate the same moral fervor in Union soldiers as Alexander Stephens and others generated in Confederate soldiers in their defense of anti-freedom.

The real question, Phillips said, indeed, "the only question is, In the service of which political idea shall the war be waged,—in the service of saving the Union as it was, or the Union as it ought to be? Mr. Lincoln dare not choose between these two phrases. *He is waging a war which he dare not describe, in the service of a political idea that he dare not shape into words*" (PS 450, italics added).

Most Lincoln critics deplored the fact that Lincoln didn't understand the primacy of "the idea." In a major speech published in the *Liberator*, January 17, 1862, Phillips said that the White South, unlike Lincoln and the White North, "is true to her idea, slavery." But Lincoln and the White North "dare not whisper the idea on which it rests." The same criticism was made by Medill, who said "this war has been prosecuted for an *idea* and that idea the Administration would thrust out of sight" (CP 98).

What was the *idea* on which the North rested? And why was Lincoln hiding the light of that idea under the bushel of his fears?

The answer to the first question, Phillips said, was the idea of equality, born of the Declaration of Independence. The reason so many in the White North, Lincoln foremost among them, dared not whisper that idea is that they didn't believe in it and were terrified by its implications. For a war for freedom and equality in 1861, he said, was necessarily a war for the freedom of the slaves and a confrontation with the long-delayed imperative of the Declaration of Independence—equality.

This returns us to a point that recurs repeatedly in this study—Lincoln's failure to give more than lip service to the Declaration of Independence. Nothing at any rate is more telling than his failure to invoke the Declaration as a fighting faith in the Civil War, even after Gettysburg, and his refusal to make a connection between the Declaration and Black (or Red or Brown) freedom. Lincoln never made that connection and never put the two live wires—the Declaration of Independence and Black freedom—together, not even at Gettysburg, which was based on his Jessie Benton Frémont thesis. But Lincoln, like everybody else, like Phillips, Douglass, Tubman, the unknown slave and the known McClellan, was caught up in a process that transcended him and controlled him. It was clear, before Shiloh, before Gettysburg, that the pedagogy of events had decided that this war would be powered by the dialectic of slavery and freedom, even imperfect freedom, and that the energy of the North could not be liberated until it was hooked up to the electric current of its idea.

Since Lincoln was silent, since he didn't see any connection between Fort Sumter and Bunker Hill, and Thomas Jefferson and the slaves of

Monticello, it was left to Republican congressional leaders and abolitionists to lift the war to a level that men could fight for and sing for and go up to Gettysburg and make speeches for—the level of a war for freedom to complete and make more perfect the unfinished American Revolution, which, according to the abolitionist critique, had been distorted beyond recognition by slaveholders and friends of slaveholders, Thomas Jefferson above all. There was poetry in that idea, and the war had scarcely begun and the first White soldiers were still learning the new fight song, "John Brown's Body lies a-mouldering in the grave but his soul goes marching on," when abolitionist William Goodell defined the "The Second American Revolution," saying:

"It has begun. It is in progress . . . . The Revolution must go on, to its completion—a National Abolition of Slavery . . . . What but the insanity of moral blindness can long delay the proclamation, inviting [African-Americans] to a share in the glorious second American Revolution" (qtd. in J. McPherson 65).

The same theme was echoed by mainstream journals like the *Chicago Tribune*, which called the first Sunday after Fort Sumter "the first Sunday of the second American Revolution" (qtd. in Kinsley 185).

Phillips said that 1861 was "the most glorious [year] of the Republic since '76" (PS 418-9). "I know," he said, "no sublimer hour in history" (PS 379). What about the Revolutionary War? The Revolutionary War, he said, "was a holy war," a war for independence. But "this [the Civil War] is a holier" war, a war "for LIBERTY" (PS 408).

The task before America, therefore, was more than military victory. What was needed now, Douglass said, was "a radical revolution in all the modes of thought which had flourished under the blighted slave system." As for Lincoln's attempt to bring back the old Union, Douglass said the old Union was dead. "We are fighting for something incomparably better than the old Union. We are fighting for unity; unity of idea, unity of sentiment, unity of object, unity of institutions, in which there shall be no North, no South, no East, no West, no black, no white, but a solidarity of the nation, making every slave free, and every free man a voter" (FD 3: 386).

Far in advance of Lincoln, far in advance of everybody, Douglass, Phillips, Sumner, and Stevens sounded the first public call for an authentic American nationality, saying that the Civil War was a God-given opportunity, more than a hundred years before Mandela's South Africa, to achieve for the first time in the history of mankind a rainbow nation with a common nationality.

This meant, among other things, that everything was up for grabs and that it was time, as Phillips said, to create for the first time a "true nationhood." Unlike Lincoln, who worshiped the old slave Union, Phillips "embraced a vision of a union socially and morally transformed, instead of militarily restored, a union made tangible by an egalitarian national culture of republican freedom rather than by parties, race hierarchies, frozen class structures, and discriminatory laws" (Steward 222-4).

The difference between Lincoln and Phillips was a difference of being, not tactics. Lincoln's "last best hope" formulation was based on the idea of the last best hope of an American Dream of whiteness today, whiteness tomorrow, whiteness forever. Phillips's "idea of American nationality" was based on "the last best growth of the thoughtful mind of the century, treading under foot sex and race, caste and condition, and collecting . . . under the shelter of noble, just, and equal laws, all races, all customs, all religions, all languages, all literature, and all ideas" . . . and saying to African-Americans and women, "'Take your place among the teachers of American Democracy'"(PS 243-4).

Phillips's demand and Douglass's demand and the demands of Sumner, Stevens and Tubman were based on the breathtakingly revolutionary idea that the United States of America had not yet been created—*it still hasn't been created*—and that the Civil War was a once-in-a-millennium opportunity to recognize for the first time the Red/Black/Brown rainbow reality that existed in contradiction of the White reality Jefferson, Madison, and Lincoln projected.

"Nationality!" Phillips said in a speech, reported in the *Liberator* on January 1, 1863. "It is built on races. The despised Negro . . . comes in with the sound of trumpets, an army with banners, in the terror of the conflict, to insure us success."

Over and over again, like a great jazz musician, Phillips improvised on this theme, saying that his American Dream, unlike Lincoln's American Dream, was "broad enough for all races and colors, all sects, creeds, and parties, for heads and hearts too; broad enough to help the poor, teach the ignorant, shield the weak, raise the fallen, and lift the high higher . . . " (PS 250).

Phillips said that 137 years ago. Since that time, no other White American leader, certainly no other White Americans in power or in a leading position in a national organization, has come near his mountaintop vision of a new American personality based not on Europe alone nor on Asia or Africa alone but on the blending of the highest truths of these different and yet complementary realities. Lincoln and McClellan were still fighting a White Man's War, returning slaves to slaveholders and refusing to accept Black volunteers, when Phillips sounded a new and multicolored theme:

"Some men say they would view this war as white men. I condescend to no such narrowness. I view it as an American citizen, proud to be the citizen of an empire that knows neither black nor white, neither Saxon nor Indian, but holds an equal sceptre over all" (PS 419). Never, he said, "until we welcome the Negro, the foreigner, all races as equal, and, melted together in a common nationality, hurl them all at despotism, will the North deserve triumph or earn it at the hands of a just God." So saying and so believing, he heard "in the dim distances the first notes of the jubilee rising from the hearts of the millions. Soon, very soon, you [too] shall hear it at the gates of the citadel, and the Stars and Stripes shall guarantee liberty forever from the Lakes to the Gulf" (PS 562).

Soon, very soon . . . .

The words still warm hearts. But, alas, the good Phillips was *too* soon. And he, like Douglass, like Stevens (see pages 608-9), was forced to concede that there was not enough virtue in the Republic to make the Declaration of Independence real. Before that happened, Phillips and his colleagues, Black and White, male and female, created a miracle in America, establishing Black or at least off-White states in South Carolina, Louisiana, and Mississippi, and writing civil rights laws that were stronger than the civil rights laws passed in the 1960s.

It was fashionable in later years to debate the question of which White leader made the largest contribution to the emancipation of the slaves. Many contemporaries, Douglass among them, divided the honors between Senator Sumner and Congressman Stevens. Others held out for Phillips. Senator Henry Wilson of Massachusetts said in an April 19, 1870, letter to Sumner that "it was [due] to Wendell Phillips, more than to any other, more than to all others," that Blacks were not cheated out of their citizenship after Emancipation." John F. Hume said that if he were "asked to name the man to whom the colored people of this country, who were slaves, or who were liable to become slaves, are under the greatest obligation for their freedom, I would unhesitatingly say Salmon Portland Chase" (59).

We are, of course, as we have said repeatedly, comparing Lincoln with other Whites, but we should never lose sight of the fact that Douglass and other Black leaders played major roles and that the unknown slave made perhaps the largest contribution—as a fugitive, soldier, and definer—to his own emancipation.

Few contemporaries put Lincoln on the list of great emancipators. To the contrary, many said he was one of the major obstacles to emancipation. Some historians say in defense that Lincoln held back emancipation until public opinion was prepared for it, a specious theory contradicted by Lincoln who said that he "struggled for nearly a year and a half" to save slavery (CW 6:48-9) and that immediate emancipation had never been his policy. During this period and later, antislavery critics said he inadvertently or advertently, directly and indirectly, reduced antislavery morale and potential and revived and stimulated proslavery morale and anti-Negro morale. Sumner said that "the President himself has played the part of the farmer in the fable, who warmed the frozen snake [of conservatism and Copperheadism] at his fire" (SL 127-8).

17

The Bull Run Blues

NOBODY pauses and reflects on July 21, which is a pity. For that day—the day of the Union's stunning defeat at Bull Run in 1861—is at least as important as the January 1 it heralded and made inevitable.

Before Bull Run, which was witnessed by scores of Washingtonians, who sauntered out to Manassas Junction with whiskey bottles and picnic baskets to view the fun, many White Northerners, including Lincoln and key members of his conservative cabinet, were hallucinating about a quick and easy war that would bring the humbled White Southern brethren back into the fold with their slaves.

If that scenario had prevailed, and if the White North had routed the White South and marched on to Richmond on Sunday, July 21, 1861, there would have been no emancipation in 1865 or probably in the nineteenth century. But Bull Run I (and II) changed all calculations, forcing a long, bloody, bitter war that made the freeing of the slaves inevitable, no matter who was president. To tell the truth, emancipation would have almost certainly come sooner with better preparation if someone other than Lincoln, with his deep-seated racial fears, had occupied the president's office.

The significance of Bull Run I was that it bracketed or at least put on hold political fantasies about the White Man's War. The smoke of battle had scarcely cleared and the images of White Union soldiers throwing down their rifles and running back to Washington were still circulating in the public mind when Senator Sumner told himself and others that all bets were off and that the North was in for a long and bitter struggle out of which would come a new nation and the emancipation of the slaves. So enamored was Sumner of this idea that he committed the political faux pas of sharing it with Lincoln, who was, one can imagine, horrified. "I told the Presdt," he wrote Wendell Phillips on August 3, 1861, "that our defeat was the worst event & the best event in our history; the worst, as it was the greatest present calamity & shame,—the best, as it made the extinction of Slavery inevitable" (SL 74).

The Thirty-seventh Congress, meeting in a special session, made Sumner a prophet by enacting a Confiscation Act that proclaimed freedom to all slaves used by Confederates in the rebellion. This was the first, small, legalistic, provisional step toward emancipation, and it was a direct response to the arrogance of Southerners, who brazenly and openly used slave laborers to move equipment and build Confederate fortifications and defenses at Bull Run.

Before Bull Run, and after Bull Run, Lincoln contended that he couldn't act against slavery because of constitutional prohibitions. Early in this emergency session, on August 2, Congressman Stevens attacked that theory and by implication Lincoln, saying: "We are told that because the Constitution does not allow us to confiscate a certain species of property, therefore we cannot liberate slaves. Mr. Speaker, I thought the time had come when the laws of war were to govern our action; when constitutions, if they stood in the way of the laws of war in dealing with the enemy, had no right to intervene."[45]

Stevens paused and looked around the House menacingly with a real or rhetorical glance in the direction of the White House and asked:

"Who pleads the Constitution against our proposed action? It is the advocates of rebels, of rebels who have sought to overthrow the Constitution and trample it in the dust; who repudiate the Constitution. Sir, these rebels, who have disregarded and set at defiance that instrument, are, by every rule of municipal and international law, estopped from pleading it against our action . . . ."

Having made that point, Stevens at once deduced its consequence: "When a country is in open war with an enemy, every publicist agrees that you have the right to use every means which will weaken him. Every measure which will enable you sooner to subdue him and triumph over him, is justified on your part." He was shocked to hear some people, some in high places, say that "when you have rescued an oppressed people from the oppression of the enemy," they should be returned to bondage. "By what principle of philanthropy," he asked, "can you return them to the bondage from which you have delivered them, and rivet again the chains you have once broken?"

This was disgraceful, Stevens said.

"It is a disgrace to the party which advocates it. It is against the principle of the law of nations. It is against every principle of philanthropy. I, for one, shall never shrink from saying, when these slaves are once conquered by us, 'Go and be free.' God forbid that I should ever agree that they should be returned again to their masters! . . ."

Stevens conceded that he was, like a true leader, a step or two ahead of the people. But he predicted that "if this war is continued long, and is bloody," the Whites of the North would not "stand by and see their sons and brothers and neighbors slaughtered by thousands and tens of thousands by rebels, with arms in their hands, and forbear to call upon their enemies to be our friends, and to help us in subduing them . . . ."

Who were, to use Stevens's words, "the enemies of our enemies?" They were the slaves, and the only viable war policy was the emancipation and arming of the slaves. "One of the most glorious consequences of victory," he said, quoting Vattel, the Swiss-born jurist, "is giving freedom to those who are oppressed."

Even in August 1861, Stevens didn't shrink from that doctrine, and he predicted that it "will be the doctrine of the whole free people of the North before two years roll round."

Before two years rolled around, the whole free people of the North, including Abraham Lincoln, had adopted the Stevens doctrine. Bull

Run and its necessary sequence of events was the beginning of that process, and the Bull Run syndrome—a Union military disaster and astronomical casualties followed by rising calls for a hard war against those traitorous White Southerners who were using slave laborers and killing our boys—is the key to understanding emancipation and the Civil War.

After Bull Run, for example, almost every ambivalent move—a congressional resolution saying that the war was not being fought to destroy slavery, and the appointment of a proslavery commander in chief, General McClellan—played into the hands of antislavery forces, dangerously (from the proslavery point of view) defining the issues and forcing more men and women to choose between freedom and slavery and reality and fantasy. This dialectic, which made proslavery advocates unwitting allies of Black freedom, explains so much that is unexplainable in the Civil War and requires some clarification and elaboration.

By some alchemy no person can understand, history (read: the dominant historical forces) selects actors, especially at historical crossroads, who condense in their own personality the strength and weaknesses of the contending parties. McClellan was a textbook example of Union halfness and demoralization. A spit-and-polish West Pointer, openly tempted by the protofascism of Southern aristocrats and their virulent racism, "McNapoleon, " as he was called, was gifted in training and drilling soldiers but was irresolute in leading them into battle, tending to see an ambush behind every tree and to believe that he was outnumbered, even when he held the high ground and the larger forces.

There were at least two moments in this war when McClellan held Lincoln, the North, and the slave in his hand. The first one was in the Peninsular Campaign when he was, by some reports, four miles from Richmond, and the city lay open and waiting. The second was in the Antietam struggle when a Union officer found a copy of Lee's battle plans *before* the battle. On both occasions, McClellan procrastinated, saving the South and ensuring a longer war and the emancipation of the slaves. He may not have intended it that way, but he couldn't have been more helpful to the slaves objectively if he had subjectively decided to let Lee cross the river with his battered troops.

By all this we must understand that history knew what it was doing when it made Lincoln put the first phase of the Civil War, the White Man's War to save slavery, into the hands of the erratic McClellan, who accomplished the opposite of what he intended. Since he so clearly favored Southern aristocrats, and since he oftentimes dawdled and let Confederate armies escape, some people accused McClellan of treason. His defenders, and not a few historians, have contended that McClellan was always loyal to the Union and White Northerners *in his own way*, a defense that completely misses the point. For, as Phillips and Douglass astutely pointed out, whatever McClellan intended in his heart he couldn't have done more to help the South—and paradoxically the slave—if he had followed battle plans prepared by Jefferson Davis.

On this level, McClellan was the perfect representative of the central dynamic of the war, the dialectic that made the wrath of man praise the slaves, turning minuses into pluses and ostensible proslavery moves into positives for the antislavery cause. The same thing can be said about Lincoln, who was as irresolute politically as McClellan was militarily, and who was secretly tempted by the aristocratic ethos of the Kentucky of his youth. Phillips said in a Boston speech, printed in the *Liberator* on May 29, 1864, that Lincoln was the McClellan of politics. "What McClellan was on the battlefield—"Do as little hurt as possible!"— that Lincoln is in civil affairs—'Make as little change as possible! . . .'"

Anticipating McClellan, President Lincoln spoke in his usual abstract White spirit when he defined the war. What kind of war was it? Lincoln's friend, Alexander Stephens, contended, as we have noted, that it was a war to establish a government based on the cornerstone of human slavery and to clear up any misunderstanding about what the statement "all men are created equal" really meant. Lincoln, in reply, avoided that dangerous ground and told Congress in his first message that it was "a People's contest" to maintain a government "whose leading object is, to elevate the condition of men—to lift artificial weights from all shoulders—to clear the paths of laudable pursuit for all—to afford all, an unfettered start, and a fair chance, in the race of life " (CW 4:438).

Almost all historians enthusiastically applaud that vague formulation without asking Lincoln what kind of people he was talking about.

Let us correct that oversight by interrogating him and them.

Was Lincoln talking about *all* people or was he, as usual, talking about *all* White people? Was he talking about a Black/White/Brown people's contest or was he talking about a White people's contest? Did he intend to lift artificial weights from the shoulders of slaves in South Carolina and Blacks in Illinois? Did he intend then, or in the future, to afford all Black children in Washington, D.C., or New Orleans, Louisiana, or Chicago, Illinois, "an unfettered start, and a fair chance, in the race of life"?

To ask these questions is to answer them, for nobody believes that Abraham Lincoln believed in 1861 that the Civil War was a Black/White/Brown/Red people's contest to create a new birth of freedom and to elevate the condition of the slaves or the free Blacks of Illinois. Did not Lincoln say repeatedly that the war was a White people's contest, that the Negro had nothing to do with it, and that the central object of the war was to restore the old Union with slavery in the South and Jim Crow laws in Illinois and other Northern States?

What about the Declaration of Independence?

Lincoln didn't say a word about the Declaration in his State of the Union message in December 1861 and only mentioned it in passing in his special message of July 1861. In the special message, which was the first opportunity to speak to the people and the elected representatives of the people, he didn't even mention slavery.

Nothing, in fact, infuriated the new president more than confused people who mixed up the White man's grand crusade to save White self-government with the struggles of Blacks for freedom. Told on May 7, 1861, that his daily correspondence was "thickly interspersed by such suggestions" (Hay 19), Lincoln said that some Northerners seemed to have been "bewildered and dazzled by the excitement of the hour." One man, "a venerable and most respected gentleman," had told him in all seriousness that he should enlist Black soldiers. Another man, Lincoln said, seemed inclined to believe that the war was to "result in the entire abolition of slavery."

Lincoln pooh-poohed these wild ideas.

"For my part," he said, "I consider the central idea pervading this struggle is the necessity that is upon us, of proving that popular government [for White people] is not an absurdity." We shall return to this point later in greater detail, and the point we want to emphasize here is that it was this idea, the idea of government of White people, by White people, for White people, that Lincoln championed from May 1861 to April 1865 and talked about at Gettysburg.

Lincoln, like McClellan, repeatedly played into the hands of anti-slavery advocates by acts that backfired and cleared away the intervening foliage, bringing the real antagonists face to face and forcing men and women to choose for or against slavery. The first and most dramatic boomerang acts occurred shortly after Bull Run when the charismatic John Charles Frémont freed the slaves of Missouri rebels. This unexpected act, coming after a long series of Union reverses, startled and thrilled the North, and was applauded by conservatives and liberals alike. There was even applause from Lincoln's friends and advisors, who urged Lincoln to approve the act. But Lincoln, McClellan-like, countermanded the Missouri emancipation proclamation, condemning Missouri slaves to four more years of slavery, and giving new impetus to the antislavery movement. The *Tribune's* Medill said revocation of the Frémont order was a Bull Run disaster on the political level. "The President's letter to Gen[.] Frémont," he wrote Chase, "has cast a funeral gloom over our patriotic city [Chicago]. We are stricken with a heavier calamity than the battle of Bull Run. It comes upon us like a killing June frost—which destroys the [coming] harvest" (CP 97-8).

From all over, from abolitionists who wanted a hard war and from hardened conservatives who cared nothing about slaves but who wanted the administration to do something, even if it was wrong, came letters of denunciation and disapproval. Some said Lincoln was guilty of a "dereliction of duty"; others called him "President of Kentucky" and said he had demonstrated his subservience to slavery and the Border States; still others said he had demonstrated once again his lack of leadership ability. Even Lincoln partisans were offended. Lincoln's old law partner, William Herndon, said "Frémont's proclamation was right. Lincoln's modification of it was wrong."

   Lincoln's conservative crony, Senator Orville H. Browning, wrote "13 pages of foolscap," telling Lincoln that Frémont's proclamation embodied "a true and important principle" (BD 503). Horace White, a *Chicago Tribune* editor, said in a private letter to Lincoln's old Eighth Circuit crony, Judge David Davis: "Dear Judge. Our President has broken his own neck if he has not destroyed the country. The public rage here, caused by his order countermanding Frémont's proclamation, *is fearful*, & my own indignation, I confess, is too deep for words. Accursed be the day that I ever voted for such cowards & blacklegs."[46]

If we dig deeper into all this, we will find that Lincoln's emancipation policy was defined by what we will call The Bull Run Dance: 1) a military disaster or a proslavery faux pas, followed by 2) public outrage and demands for a hard war, followed by 3) a Lincoln Rebound designed to undercut or to take the steam out of 2). Keeping this dynamic in mind, we will not be surprised to find that 2) is almost always followed by 3), by what historian Benjamin Quarles called a Lincoln "softshoe "(79), a Lincoln feint or flanking action in the direction of emancipation.

Thus, as the pro-Frémont chorus swelled and as Republican leaders returned to Washington for what would almost certainly be an antislavery Congress, Lincoln started playing to the antislavery gallery, telling senators and congressmen that *he* was planning antislavery action and that he was only weeks or, in some cases, months behind the most advanced antislavery voices. While saying this in private conferences, he was pushing an entirely different policy in public, calling in his first Annual Message to Congress, comparable to our State of the Union Address, for a war for an old birth of freedom and warning against letting the contest degenerate into "a violent and remorseless revolutionary struggle" to create a new birth of freedom. (CW 5:49). Lincoln didn't hide it; he said out loud for all to hear, that his "People's contest"was designed to restore the status quo that defined Blacks as subhumans and to ensure that self-government by White men for White men would not perish from this earth.

Charles Sumner, among others, argued that God and history forced Lincoln's hand, providing "delay and disaster" to soften hard hearts and to open the eyes of the blind, Lincoln's among them. "There is this consolation even in our disasters," he said in November 1862, "that they have brought the Presdt to a true policy. A wise, courageous & humane statesman, with proper forecast might from the beginning have directed this whole war to the suppression of Slavery, & have ended it by this time . . . . But with Lincoln as Presdt, & Seward as Secretary this was impossible. Another agency was necessary & Providence has interposed delay & disaster, which have done for us more than argt. or persuasion" (SL 131).

Everything or almost everything advanced the cause, even McClellan, who had been the "author of the delays." Even so, Sumner said, "we must be grateful to him, for only in this way has the Presdt. been overcome."

Lincoln has been praised for saying or seeming to say in the Second Inaugural Address that the Civil War was God's way of punishing the United States for the sin of slavery. But there is no evidence that he believed it since he proposed a Reconstruction program that would have continued to pile up wealth on the Black man's back and would have continued the blood-letting at the expense of Blacks. The most telling evidence against him is that he refused to listen to Black and White messengers who quoted the same message against him, and others, before the Second Inaugural. Even as Lincoln maneuvered desperately in 1862 to save slavery and the old Union, Sumner was telling a correspondent that "our reverses have been misconstrued. They have been the chastisement and expiation imposed by Providence for our crime towards a long-suffering race. Had we succeeded early, we should not have suffered according to our deserts. We must lose other battles, and bury more children; but the results will be attained" (SM 132-3).

It is scarcely possible to understand Lincoln or the Civil War if we don't keep that dialectic in mind and remember, as C. C. Hazewell said presciently in the *Atlantic Monthly* in November 1862, that "the American people are capable of conquering their prejudices, provided that their schooling shall be sufficiently severe and costly."

18

"Linconia": The Fantasy Plan
For Banishing Blacks

T HE new president's racial policy was based on the wildest idea ever presented to the American people by an American president. What Lincoln proposed officially and publicly was that the United States government buy the slaves and deport them to Africa or some other hot place. This was not a passing whim. In five major policy declarations, including two State of the Union addresses and the Preliminary Emancipation Proclamation, the sixteenth president of the United States publicly and officially called for the deportation of Blacks. On countless other occasions, in conferences with cronies, Democratic and Republican leaders, and high government officials, he called for colonization of Blacks or aggressively promoted colonization by private and official acts.

If Lincoln had completed his second term, his friend Henry Whitney said, he would "have made still more heroic [sic] efforts, looking to that end" (12).

Colonization, Whitney said, was close to the heart of Lincoln's policy, for "he was not only of the opinion that this nation could not remain partly free and partly a slave nation; but he was equally pronounced in his belief that the white and colored races could not occupy the same nation in peace" (306).

In 1862, largely at President Lincoln's urging, Congress appropriated $600,000, a sum desperately needed, Hume said, to prosecute the war, to begin the colonization process but balked at the hundreds of millions of dollars Lincoln officially requested in his 1862 State of the Union Address, which ended with the famous words, "We cannot escape history."

Nobody tried harder than Lincoln to escape the history he couldn't escape. For he never gave up this wildly impractical idea—*it was, in fact, the only racial solution he ever had*—and under his leadership, almost without notice, certainly without the notice of latter-day historians, racial cleansing became, 72 years before the Third Reich, 133 years before Bosnia, the official policy of the United States of America.

"Almost from the commencement of this administration," Secretary of the Navy Gideon Welles said, "the subject of deporting the colored race has been discussed" (WD 150). On Wednesday, April 10, two days before the firing on Fort Sumter, Lincoln interrupted his war gaming to confer with Ambrose W. Thompson, a shady character who would play a major role in the administration's colonization efforts (LDD 3:34).

At this conference or at a later conference, Thompson outlined a plan for transporting Blacks to a Panamanian isthmus where his Chiriqui Improvement Company had a contract, he said, to mine coal. Welles and others told Lincoln that Thompson was a hustler and that the contract was questionable at best, but Lincoln bought the idea and asked Secretary Welles to follow up.

"As early as May 1861," Welles told his diary, "a great pressure was made upon me to enter into a coal contract with this company. The President was in earnest in the matter, *wished to send the negroes out of the country"* (WD 150, italics added*)*.

Welles investigated and told Lincoln that Chiriqui—which the bemused media called "Linconia"—was "a swindling speculation," but Lincoln, desperate for a place to send Blacks, referred the matter to a cabinet ally, Secretary of Interior Caleb Blood Smith, who favored deportation of Blacks and who was certain to return a favorable report. Smith as expected "made a skillful and taking report, embracing both coal and Negroes. Each was to assist the other. The Negroes were to be transported to Chiriqui to mine coal, for the Navy, and the Secretary of the Navy was to make an immediate advance of $50,000 for coal not yet mined,—nor laborers obtained to mine it, nor any satisfactory information or proof that there was decent coal to be mined." Welles and other cabinet ministers argued against the proposal, but "the President and Smith were persistent" (WD 151).

The same message, with the same or even greater persistence, was communicated to other cabinet members and insiders. On Monday, July 8, 1861, Lincoln and his close friend, Senator Orville Browning of Illinois, discussed for two-and-a-half hours "all matters relating to our present troubles . . . . We also discussed the Negro question, and agreed upon this as upon other things that the government neither should, nor would send back to bondage such as come to our armies, but that we could not have them in camp, and that they must take care of themselves till the war is over, and then, colonize &c"(BD 478).

Colonize &c:

That, in a phrase, was the racial policy of the sixteenth president of the United States. We don't know, and will probably never know, what that ominous "&c" meant, but at least one thing was clear: To the extent that Lincoln had an emancipation policy, it was to get rid of slaves and Negroes by his dual program of compensated emancipation and colonization.

There was an iron link in Lincoln's mind between compensated emancipation and colonization, and whenever he mentioned one, he was talking about the other. The two programs were part of what Lincoln authority J. G. Randall called his "grand concept" for ending slavery and creating a White nation, and he pressed it with the tenacity and enthusiasm of a true believer. Lincoln himself said that his whole soul was involved in compensated emancipation and colonization. "On no other matter," Randall said, "did he so far extend his presidential leadership in attempted legislation, adding: "One can hardly find any subject on which Lincoln argued and pleaded more earnestly than on this" (1945-55: 142,145). Whitney, who heard the words from Lincoln's mouth, said "there was nothing except the restoration of the Union about which he felt such great anxiety" (318). There is corroboration on this point from Lamon, who was there, and who said that President Lincoln "zealously and persistently devised schemes for the deportation of the Negroes, which the latter deemed cruel and atrocious in the extreme . . ." (345).

This was not an ad hoc political tactic or a hastily devised response to the pressure of events—this was, Lincoln's emigration aide Rev. James Mitchell told the *St. Louis Daily Globe-Democrat* on August 26, 1894, the foundation of Lincoln's private and public policy. It was "his honest conviction that it was better for both races to separate. *This was the central point of his policy, around which hung all his private views, and as far as others would let him, his public acts"* (italics added). Lincoln was "fully convinced" that "the republic was already dangerously encumbered with African blood that would not legally mix with the American [sic]. . . . He regarded a mixed race as eminently anti-republican, because of the heterogeneous character it gives the population where it exists, and for similar reasons he did not favor the annexation of tropical lands encumbered with mixed races . . . ."

On all other issues relating to Blacks, on emancipation and the use of Black soldiers, Lincoln was slow, tardy, hesitant, but on the issues of separation and Black deportation he was passionate and impetuous, brushing aside all objections, conferring with questionable characters, sending aides abroad and messages to the foreign offices of colonial powers. In December 1861, he discussed the possibility of sending a high-level mission to Chiriqui, and it was evident from the instructions he prepared, Scheips says, that "the President was motivated by a sense of extreme urgency" (421).

As one examines the record, and reviews the comments of men who worked with Lincoln day by day, one is struck by the repetition of the same phrases: The president "was in earnest." "He was persistent." He was "motivated by a sense of extreme urgency." He "wished to send the Negroes away."

The orchestrated campaign to send Negroes away moved into high gear in November and December 1861 with a flurry of proposals, including one for paying Delaware, Maryland, Kentucky, and Missouri $500 apiece for each slave, providing they adopted gradual emancipation plans. Lincoln told his friend Browning that the plan was linked "to a scheme of colonizing the blacks some where on the American Continent . . ." (512).

In his first State of the Union Message, Lincoln didn't mention emancipation, but he mentioned Negro removal and urged that steps be taken for colonizing Blacks freed by Congress or acts of war "at some place, or places, in a climate congenial to them."

Like most nineteenth-century racists, Lincoln pretended to believe that Blacks had to live in tropical climes, although he knew it required marshals and the massed White population to keep slaves from running away to the arctic zone of Chicago, which was founded by a free Black man, Jean Baptiste Pointe DuSable, more than fifty years before the Lincolns arrived in Illinois.

Not only freed slaves but also free Black citizens were scheduled for removal under Lincoln's plan. It "might be well to consider, too," he said in his first State of the Union Address, "whether the free colored people already in the United States could not, so far as individuals may desire, be included in such colonization" (CW 5:48). Whenever Lincoln remembered or whenever he was prompted, he always added the phrase, "so far as individuals may desire." But he knew—he had to know—that his official announcements in favor of Negro removal played into the hands of racist forces who were prepared to do anything to destroy African-Americans.

It does no good to say, as apologists are always saying, that this was not what Lincoln intended, which is interesting if true but irrelevant whether true or false. For a man is responsible in history for the consequences of his acts, especially when those consequences were predictable. Not only that, a man is responsible for the forces he relies on and the forces he uses and unleashes. After the first year of the war, and the rise of antislavery forces in the North and in the U.S. Congress, the only forces the conservative Lincoln could rely on—in the North and in Congress—were conservatives and slaveholding interests in Border States. All or almost all of these forces, and especially the White ethnic forces in anti-Negro strongholds like New York City, and Charleston, Illinois, were organized around racist fears. From Sumter to Appomattox and beyond, most teetered on the edge of treason. And we can say again that by choosing his audience, Lincoln chose his program, or, what amounts to the same thing, by choosing his program, he chose his audience. For in a country divided by civil war, there were only two real audiences, and anyone who rallied against the Union mobilized the forces in favor of the Confederacy. By relying on these dubious forces and by stoking the fires of their fears, Lincoln made himself—objectively—their choreographer and accomplice.

The implications of all this were shrewdly weighed by Adam Gurowski, the expatriate Polish count who was fired from his State Department position primarily because of his sulphurous views on the leadership of Abraham Lincoln. "Those colonizers," he wrote in his diary, "forget that if they should export 100,000 persons a year, an equal number will be yearly born at home, not to speak of other impossibilities. If carried on on a small scale, this scheme amounts to nothing; and on a grand scale it is altogether impossible, besides being as stupid as it is recklessly cruel. Only those persons insist on colonization who hate or dread emancipation"(187). Gurowski said that colonization was harmful to the best interests of Blacks and Whites, Northerners and Southerners, for "exportation of the four millions of slaves [would deprive] the country of laborers, which a century of emigration cannot fill again. All these fools ought to be sent to a lunatic asylum. To export the emancipated would be equivalent to devastation of the South, to its transformation into a wilderness" (129-30).

Another man who believed colonizationists belonged in an insane asylum was Wendell Phillips, who said: "Colonize the blacks! A man might as well colonize his hands; or when the robber enters his house, he might as well colonize his revolver . . . ." Phillips added: "We are none of us, as a nation, fit for the lunatic asylum, and until we are, we never shall colonize four million of workers . . . " (PS 545-7).

Both Phillips and Douglass said that the Union needed Blacks not only for the war but also and, perhaps more importantly, for the peace. "The Negro," Phillips said, "for fifty, or thirty, years has been the basis of our commerce, the root of our politics, the pivot of our pulpit, the inspiration of almost all that is destined to live in our literature" (PS 320). Over and above that, he said, the destiny of America was linked to the destiny of the Negro, who was the only democratic force in the South and the only base for building a democracy in that section.

Although a handful of Blacks supported colonization for reasons markedly different from the reasons advanced by Lincoln, the overwhelming majority of Blacks repudiated Lincoln's vision. Most agreed with Frederick Douglass, who said "the destiny of the colored American . . . is the destiny of America . . . . The allotments of Providence seem to make the black man of America the open book out of which the American people are to learn lessons of wisdom, power and goodness—more sublime and glorious than any yet attained by the nations of the old or the new world."

So:

"We are here, and here we are likely to be. To imagine that we should ever be eradicated is absurd and ridiculous . . . . We shall neither die out, nor be driven out; but shall go with this people, either as a testimony against them, or as an evidence in their favor throughout their generations . . . " (FD 225).

Part Eight

The Emancipators Nobody Knows

[T]his second session of the Thirty-seventh Congress perfected and enacted a series of antislavery measures which amounted to a complete reversal of the policy of the General Government.
— White House secretaries John G. Nicolay and John Hay

But for your race among us there could not be war . . . . [W]ithout the institution of Slavery and the colored race as a basis, the war could not have an existence. It is better for us both, therefore, to be separated.

—Abraham Lincoln

19

The Emancipating Congress

IT began, if processes of this magnitude can be said to have a beginning, on Monday, December 2, 1861, with the opening of the second session of the Thirty-seventh Congress, which was the second milestone, after Bull Run, on the road to emancipation, and the beginning of the end of slavery in the United States.

"At this session," a contemporary report said, "the legislation of Congress assumed a new aspect. Two positions were taken, which became the basis of the action of the controlling majority in that body on all subjects relating to the troubles of the country."

The first position was that slavery was the cause of the troubles of the country. The second was that "the Government was engaged in a struggle for its existence, and could, therefore, resort to any measure which a case of self-defense would justify" (AC 1862, 275).

What all this meant as a practical matter was that the Thirty-seventh Congress, pushed by the Bull Run dialectic and pulled by the demands of constituents, had moved to the hard-war position defined earlier by antislavery leaders. Because the Thirty-seventh Congress saw further than Lincoln, and because it probed deeper, it became the emancipating Congress and the leader of the Republican Party, Abraham Lincoln, and the American people.

Allan Nevins said the Thirty-seventh Congress opened "a new chapter of national affairs . . ." (189).

Leonard P. Curry said the Thirty-seventh Congress, "far more than the President" (6), created "the blueprint for a new America" (9).

Nicolay and Hay, Lincoln's secretaries, were partial to their boss but said frankly that "the Thirty-seventh Congress perfected and enacted a series of antislavery measures which amounted to a complete reversal of the policy of the General Government," meaning by that, the policy of Abraham Lincoln (NH 6:97).

Adam Gurowski said the Thirty-seventh Congress destroyed the foundations of slavery in the United States, changed the direction of the country and whipped Lincoln into glory (GD 2:99-100).

Sumner went further, saying that the Thirty-seventh was one of the greatest legislative assemblies in world history. "I doubt if any legislative body," he wrote, "ever did more memorable work; certainly none except, perhaps, the Long Parliament & the Constituent Assembly of France" (SL 148).

Based on these testimonies, we can say that although Lincoln was a Republican president, Republican congressional policy between 1861 and 1865, as others have noted, was the policy not of Abraham Lincoln but of an extraordinary group of congressional rebels who made a legislative revolution against Lincoln and created a new America.

One of the pivotal figures in that revolution was Senator Lyman Trumbull, a singularly neglected politician who was the author of the First and Second Confiscation acts and a major architect of the Thirteenth Amendment. Not the least of the things that astonish us in this revolution is that Trumbull and Lincoln were products of the same political and social forces. Both came out of the decidedly conservative and racist Illinois political environment, but Trumbull, unlike Lincoln, sought and found the hidden crevices that empowered him and his constituents. Attorney Trumbull, unlike Attorney Lincoln, distinguished himself in the legal struggle against the Fugitive Slave Law, and it is hardly surprising that Senator Trumbull played a decisive role in turning the war against slavery while President Lincoln was trying to save slavery.

It was Trumbull who moved the debate to a new level by giving notice immediately after the organization of the Senate "of his intention to introduce a bill for the confiscation of the property of rebels and giving freedom to the persons they hold in slavery." This bill, a milestone in the history of emancipation, was announced on Monday, December 2, 1861, and dominated debate in Congress until its passage in July 1862 pushed Lincoln to the brink of reality.

In the House, on the same day, Congressman Stevens offered a resolution requesting the president "to declare free, and to direct all of our generals and officers in command to offer freedom to all slaves who shall leave their masters, or who shall aid in quelling this rebellion."

Two other signs showing still more clearly which way the wind was blowing were the introduction of a bill by Senator Henry Wilson for the emancipation of the slaves of Washington, D.C., and the creation of a supercommittee to watch Lincoln and the struggle, the Joint Committee on the Conduct of the War.

Before the administration could recover from these blows, the House decisively repudiated Lincoln's policy by backtracking on the Crittenden resolution. Four months before, Congress had overwhelmingly adopted this resolution, which said that the war was not being fought to destroy slavery. But when the same resolution was offered to the same body in December, it was tabled by a vote of 71 to 65.

The feeling was growing that slavery and a lot of other things were going to be destroyed before this conflict was settled.

It was on this note that Congress and the Union crossed over into 1862, marching to the sound of different drummers. Lincoln was deaf to the new music, but Congressman Stevens heard it and announced it, rising in the House on the 22nd day of the New Year to speak in favor of his Joint Resolution.[47] The burden of his speech was simple: "The black man . . . is really the mainstay of the war" and "must be made our allies" by a policy of "universal emancipation." Prejudice "may be shocked," he said, "weak minds startled, weak nerves may tremble, but they must hear and adopt it. Those who now furnish the means of the war, but who are the natural enemies of slaveholders, must be made our allies. Universal emancipation must be proclaimed to all."

Part of the problem was that the Lincoln administration lacked "that determined and invincible courage that was inspired in the Revolution by the grand idea of liberty, equality and the rights of man."

Like Sumner in the Senate, like Douglass and Phillips on the stump, like Garrison in the *Liberator,* like men and women all over, like Harriet Tubman, George Washington Williams, Sojourner Truth and the great men of the state of Illinois, John Jones, Joseph Medill, and Governor Yates, all of whom demanded a new birth of freedom, Stevens said the basic issue of the hour was the issue Alexander Stephens had defined, the issue Lincoln was trying to avoid, the issue of the concrete meaning of the Declaration. The Confederates, Stevens said, had "rebelled for no redress of grievances, but to establish a slave oligarchy which would repudiate the odious doctrine of the Declaration of Independence, and justify the establishment of an empire admitting the principle of king, lords and slaves."

Stevens was shocked by the failure of Lincoln to address that issue. "Our statesmen, unlike the men of the Revolution, do not seem to know how to touch the hearts of freemen and rouse them to battle. No declaration of the great objects of Government, no glorious sound of universal liberty has gone forth from the capital . . . . " Worse, Stevens said, Union generals were hunting and capturing men and and women and returning them to slavery. "We have put a sword into one hand of our generals and shackles into the other," he said, adding:

"Freemen are not inspired by such mingled music."

Stevens was talking, lest we forget, about a moral vacuum in the heart of Abraham Lincoln. The problem, he was saying, without naming Lincoln, was a president who was pursuing a mistaken policy of trying to save the old Union instead of fighting for a new birth of freedom.

"Oh," Stevens said, "for six months' resurrection in the flesh of stern old Jackson! . . . He would abolish slavery as the cause and support of the insurrection; he would arm the free people of color, as he did at New Orleans; he would march into the heart of slavedom to put weapons into every freed man's hands. . . . [and] end the war by a wholesale hanging of the leaders."

The only solution, Stevens said, was a struggle to give new meaning to the Declaration of Independence: "Let the people know that this Government is fighting not only to enforce a sacred compact, but to carry out to final perfection the principles of the Declaration of Independence, which its framers expected would long since have been fulfilled on this continent, and the blood of every freeman, would boil with enthusiasm, and his nerves be strengthened for holy warfare."

The war, in other words, was an unparalleled "invitation to "strike the chains from four million human beings, to create them MEN; to extinguish slavery on this whole continent; to wipe out . . . the most hateful and infernal blot that ever disgraced the escutcheon of man . . . ."

By resurrecting the principles of the Declaration of Independence, Stevens posed a direct challenge to Lincoln, who believed that "the white man's Charter" was an abstract document that didn't apply to any concrete situation involving Blacks and Whites. Who was right? Insofar as that question relates to Stevens's statement about what the framers, Jefferson in particular, expected "would have long since have been fulfilled on this continent," I believe Lincoln was right, for Jefferson and Lincoln shared the same dream of deporting Negroes and creating a White Eden. But since words have their own logic, the leaders of the Thirty-seventh Congress were right above Lincoln in calling for the redemption of a compact which bonded all men [and all women] and which could not be repudiated except by adopting the racist formula that tempted Lincoln, the formula that only White men are full men.

All this was as clear as anything needed to be to abolitionist leader Wendell Phillips, who went up and down the North, denouncing Lincoln and his generals and calling for total war. Unquestionably the greatest White orator of his time and perhaps of any time, the abolitionist leader became a force above the government and did more as a private citizen to mobilize people for emancipation, observers said, than anyone in government, including Abraham Lincoln. The *Daily Dispatch* of St. Louis said he "exercised a greater influence on the destinies of the country as a private man than any public man, or men, of his age" (Martyn 358). It has been estimated that Phillips commanded one of the largest media audiences of the age. Greeley said he spoke to at least fifty thousand people in the crucial winter of 1861-62 and that his speeches, read by some five million, helped turn the country against Lincoln's pro-slavery policy.

From the beginning, Phillips linked 1861 and 1776, the Civil War and the Revolutionary War, the struggle for Black freedom and the struggle for White freedom. From the beginning, he identified the slave with John Hancock, emancipation with July Fourth.

Unlike Lincoln, who celebrated a successful revolution, Phillips recalled a botched revolution. Unlike Lincoln, who celebrated the triumph of the fathers, Phillips said the Civil War was "the inevitable fruit of our fathers' faithless compromise in 1787" (355). The central meaning of the Civil War, he said, was the struggle to fulfill and complete the abortive revolution of 1776.

Responding to the central dynamic of his leadership, Lincoln started sending up trial balloons, based on his formula of gradual emancipation. The Lincoln initiatives had little or no chance of being accepted by the Border States or Congress and were designed primarily as tactical moves to thwart or sidetrack the mushrooming Emancipation movement and to gain time for a big victory or a political maneuver that would either save slavery or limit the impact of emancipation by limiting the number of slaves freed and by spreading the liberation process over thirty or forty years. As the Thirty-seventh Congress moved to almost certain passage of the District of Columbia emancipation bill, and as more newspapers joined the emancipation bandwagon, Lincoln created diversionary headlines by conferring with Border State representatives and asking Congress, in a special message of March 6, 1862, to adopt the following Joint Resolution:

> "Resolved that the United States ought to co-operate with any state which may adopt gradual abolishment of slavery, giving to such state pecuniary aid, to be used by such state in it's [sic] discretion, to compensate for the inconveniences public and private, produced by such change of system." (CW 5:144-5)

Did you catch the defining phrase? "To compensate for the *inconveniences* public and private, produced by" the change from slavery to freedom. That phrase originally read "to compensate for the *evils* public and private" produced by emancipating Blacks. At the last moment, Lincoln scratched out the word *evils*, a word that he almost always associated with Black freedom, and inserted *inconveniences*. Whatever he called it, it is, once again, shocking that he spent so much time bemoaning the fact that immediate emancipation would force slavemasters to give up slavemaster perks like waiters and cooks and stable boys.

To prevent these and other private and public "evils," Lincoln drafted his gradual emancipation plan so that it didn't require slaveowners to do anything. "The point," he told Congress, "is not that all the states tolerating slavery would very soon, *if at all*, initiate emancipation; but that, while the offer is equally made to all, the more Northern shall, by such initiation, make it certain to the more Southern, that in no event, will the former ever join the latter, in their proposed confederacy. *I say 'initiation' because, in my judgment, gradual, and not sudden emancipation, is better for all*" (CW 5:145, italics added).

Did you catch the qualifying phrase? The man who would be hailed later as the great emancipator said in an official document in 1862 that he was not asking the slave states to emancipate slaves soon *if at all.*

This was typical Lincolnese, a lot of words, some for freedom, some for slavery, but none dealing with the pressing questions raised by congressional advocates of emancipation. Lincoln went out of his way to emphasize that he had no intention—*in March 1862*—of "interfering" with slavery. "Such a proposition," he said, "on the part of the general government, sets up no claim of a right, by federal authority, to interfere with slavery within state limits, referring, as it does, *the absolute control* of the subject, in each case, to the state and it's [sic] people, immediately interested" (CW 5:145, italics added).

To drum up support for the proposal, Lincoln met with Border State representatives, disclaiming "any intent to injure the interests or wound the sensibilities of the slave States" and affirming that his "purpose was to protect the one and respect the other . . . ." Pressed to say that publicly, Lincoln demurred for political reasons but added that "unless he was expelled by the act of God or the Confederate armies, he should occupy that house for three years, and as long as he remained there Maryland had nothing to fear, either for her institutions or her interests . . . (E. McPherson 210-1).

Congress later passed Lincoln's resolution, but Stevens objected, saying he couldn't understand "what made one side so anxious to pass it and the other so anxious to defeat it." The Lincoln resolution, he told the House on March 11, 1862, was "the most diluted milk-and-water-gruel proposition" ever presented to the American nation.

The Lincoln resolution was both the high-water mark and the watery grave of Lincoln's hobbyhorse of compensated gradual emancipation. Although Lincoln submitted other compensated emancipation plans, and although he proposed a $400 million giveaway on the eve of his death, Congress never again played the pay game in the slave states. One reason was the rising tide of antislavery feeling. Another grew out of an idea Lincoln never grasped, the idea that although it might be necessary to pay ransom money to free the slaves, it was unwise and immoral for anybody, and especially the United States government, to concede that individuals could own other individuals.

Lincoln never did learn that lesson. To the consternation of anti-slavery advocates, he continued to call for compensation to rebel slaveholders, who had already cost the country hundreds of millions of dollars. Among the people appalled by this logic were Charles Ray and Joseph Medill of the *Chicago Tribune,* who repeatedly expressed misgivings about the performance of Illinois's favorite son in the big leagues of Washington. The newspaper was especially critical of the dominant myth of the Lincoln establishment, the idea that Lincoln couldn't do any better because he couldn't go faster than the people. "The people," the *Tribune* said, "are a long way ahead of the Government, the Press and the Pulpit in knowledge of the causes of the War. The march of human development sweeps grandly over the worst obstacles of venerable ignorance and wickedness. They who seek to oppose it, do but build sand hillocks on the sea shore, which the next wave shall level" (Monaghan 254).

As the waves of discontent rose higher and higher, and as millions of dollars and tens of thousands of Northern youths disappeared into the bottomless pit of the Virginia peninsula, the Thirty-seventh Congress rejected the idea of compensating rebels and passed a series of laws that destroyed the foundations of slavery in America.

The first act, an additional Article of War proposed by Charles Sumner, forbade Union officers to return fugitive slaves "to any such persons to whom such service or labor is claimed to be due." There then followed the landmark District of Columbia emancipation act, which Sumner called "the first installment of that great debt which we all owe to an enslaved race." Lincoln opposed what Sumner called "the first practical triumph of freedom" and refused to sign the bill until an old friend could leave the city with his slaves. When Senator Orville Browning of Illinois visited the White House on Monday night, April 14, Lincoln told him that:

> He regretted the [D.C.Emancipation] bill had been passed in its
> present form—that it should have been for gradual emancipa-
> tion—that now families would at once be deprived of cooks, sta-
> ble boys &c and they of their protectors without any provision for
> them. He further told me that he would not sign the bill before
> Wednesday—That old Gov Wickliffe had two family servants
> with him who were sickly, and who would not be benefitted by
> freedom, and wanted time to remove them, but could not get
> them out of the City until Wednesday, and that the Gov had come
> frankly to him and asked for time. (BD 541)

Once more we are brought face to face with the Lincoln everybody tries to hide, the Lincoln who had reactionary ideas about who
would be "benefitted by freedom" and who wanted to save slavery,
or as much slavery as he could, because he didn't want to deprive
families—he meant *White* families, he meant well-to-do White families—of their "cooks, stable boys &c" and "they of their protectors
without any provision for them."

While Lincoln held the District bill, "poor slaves were in conceal-
ment," Sumner said, "waiting for the day of Freedom to come out
from their hiding places." While they waited, Sumner went to the
White House to urge speed, astonished "that the President could
postpone the approval a single night" (SW 8:255). Another visitor
was Bishop Daniel A. Payne of the African Methodist Episcopal
Church, who may have been the first African-American to confer
with a president on a matter of public policy. "I am here," Payne told
Lincoln," to learn whether or not you intend to sign the bill of emancipation. . . "(146). Lincoln didn't tell him, but he finally signed the
bill on April 16. By that time, Wickliffe and other slaveholders with
"family servants" who "would not be benefitted by freedom" had
apparently escaped. If you're running a thorn-in-the-bosom tab, you
can add the two "sickly" Wickliffe "servants" and the scores and
perhaps hundreds of slaves who were hurriedly removed from

Washington and who spent three more years in slavery, courtesy of Abraham Lincoln.

Among those who hailed the first dawn of freedom was Frederick Douglass, who told Charles Sumner: "If slavery is really dead in the District of Columbia . . . to you, more than to any other American statesman, belongs the honor of this great triumph of Justice, Liberty, and Sound Policy"(FD 3:233-4).

The act incidentally contained provisions for the voluntary colonization of the freedmen "according to the wish of the President" (SM 69). Lincoln reportedly said that "I am so far behind the Sumner lighthouse, that I will stick to my old colonization hobby" (Lester 386).

When Lincoln signed the bill, he equivocated, declining to say whether there were "matters within and about this act, which might have taken a course or shape, more satisfactory to my jud[g]ment," but expressing gratification that "the two principles of compensation, and colonization" were recognized (CW 5:192).

He could have noted that the act proved what has been abundantly established: that he was a poor prophet. A little over a year before, he had "guaranteed" a group of proslavery leaders that slavery would not be "molested" in the District as long as he was president (Segal 86). For all that, Lincoln came out better than his mentor, Henry Clay, who told the Senate once that "the actual abolition of slavery in the District is about as likely to occur as the abolition of the Christian religion" (Rimini 508).

Christianity survived, but slavery didn't, primarily because of the Thirty-seventh Congress, which also banned slavery in the territories and authorized the use of Black soldiers. Lincoln followed Congress's lead slowly and grudgingly, signing these acts with evident displeasure.

To salvage Lincoln's reputation, Lincoln specialists have of late developed the collaboration theory, saying that Lincoln and Congress collaborated in freeing Blacks. In fact, as we have seen, and as we shall see, Lincoln opposed the major emancipating acts of this Congress.

Before the emancipating carnival of the Thirty-seventh ended, the great emancipators nobody knows had, as Williams said, virtually smashed Lincoln's conservative war policy, making emancipation one of the war aims, mandating the use of Black soldiers and weakening the influence of proslavery generals and conservative cabinet members (18). These and other acts forced a profound political transformation, and it is singular that so few people know the names of the men who made this revolution, and who made it against Lincoln.

"Negroes whose sense of honoring their benefactors exceeded their knowledge of history might name their sons after Lincoln," Benjamin Quarles wrote, "but [Frederick] Douglass, with a truer appreciation, knew that if Negroes wish to honor the greatest friend they ever had in public life they should place wreaths on the tomb of Charles Sumner" (1948, 274). And the tombs of Thaddeus Stevens, Owen Lovejoy, Lyman Trumbull—call the roll—George Washington Julian, James M. Ashley, Henry Wilson and on and on. For if the Civil War ended in the nominal freedom of Blacks with a legislative infrastructure that has never been redeemed or even understood, it is in due in large part to the leaders of the Thirty-seventh Congress.

Some of these men, especially Sumner and Owen Lovejoy, were leaders of vision and of the word. "I am in morals," Sumner used to say, "not politics." Others, like Stevens, were in politics but a rainbow politics that has never been dreamed or sung or taught in the Republic. Still others, Trumbull and Wade and Chandler, came to the cause from quadrants of their own.

It is fashionable today to defend Abraham Lincoln by saying that the men who demanded Black freedom didn't love Black people for themselves, whatever that means, which is regrettable if true but irrelevant to the *political* question posed here, if true or false, for three reasons. First of all and most important of all, few if any of the people posing that question have earned the right to ask it. The second reason, flowing with and out of the first, is that to decry the limitations of men who demanded Black freedom is no defense of Lincoln, who opposed Black freedom and who didn't like Black people either, except perhaps as servants or subordinates.

One must also note, thirdly, that in defining *public* rights, love is and was irrelevant. Whether a man *really* "loved" Negroes or Irish people or Italians is an interesting question for his psychiatrist or confessor but is irrelevant in weighing his public acts if those public acts were exemplary and reflected a public demand for equal rights in all areas.

T. Harry Williams, who said he was concerned because the congressional liberators allegedly didn't love the Negro "for himself," was on better grounds when he said that these men stood for four things: "instant emancipation," the confiscation of the land of rebels, the use of Black soldiers and "civil, and, when it should become expedient, political equality for the Negro" (6). And we are authorized, on the basis of these four propositions, to return to the point I made in the beginning: anybody who supported these propositions, *for any reason*, was the slave's friend. Anybody who opposed them—then and now—*for any reason*, was the slave's enemy.

There is another point here that is extremely important in understanding the limitations and possibilities of White leadership on Black issues: The congressional emancipators were friends of the cause not because they *said* they were friends but because they used their power to befriend. Sumner, who was not a traditional politician, was chairman of the Senate Foreign Relations Committee and raised the question of Black freedom almost every day in the Senate and in the White House. Senator Willard Saulsbury of Delaware asked him once to give the Senate "one day without the n——r."

No less vigilant in the House was Thaddeus Stevens, who was chairman of Ways and Means and who controlled the ways and means—the money—of the war. Other friends of the Black cause— the ultraconservative attorney general called them *Les amis des noirs*— controlled the Senate Military Affairs Committee (Henry Wilson), the

Senate Finance Committee (William Pitt Fessenden) and the Senate Judiciary Committee (Lyman Trumbull of Illinois). Overlooking all and overarching all was that unique Civil War institution, similar in many respects to a revolutionary committee of the French Revolution, the Joint Committee on the Conduct of the War, which was chaired by Senator Wade of Ohio and led by, among others, Senator Chandler of Michigan, Congressmen Julian of Indiana and Covode of Pennsylvania.

Two of these men, Sumner and Stevens, were, as I said elsewhere (1968, 183-94), the best White friends Black Americans have ever had in public power. Together and separately, alone and with like-minded colleagues, they made Congress and the American people take the longest stride of soul in the history of the commonwealth. The Thirteenth, Fourteenth, and Fifteenth amendments are permanent testimonials to their vision and devotion, and the most daring proposals of contemporary legislators are only pale reflections of the civil rights bills they offered in the 1860s and 1870s. It was Stevens who captured the imagination of freedmen with a proposal that became the "forty acres and a mule" of Black legend. It was Sumner who proposed a civil rights bill that would have banned segregation in schools, churches, cemeteries, public conveyances, and places of public accommodation *in the 1870s.*

Both Sumner and Stevens were White, but both, unlike Lincoln, publicly repudiated the claims of White supremacy. Both were politicians, but both, unlike Lincoln, disdained the low art of speaking with forked tongues and tickling the prejudices of the people. Both were lawyers, but both, unlike Lincoln, believed that laws were made for men and not men for laws. Lincoln said that nothing against slavery where it existed was constitutional; Sumner said nothing against slavery was unconstitutional.

Because they believed Blacks were human beings and because they called for a new birth of freedom before and after Gettysburg,

Sumner and Stevens have been systematically vilified by a whole generation of historians, who say they forced Black suffrage and equal rights on the White South, thereby precipitating the "horrors" of Reconstruction. The truth is that the failure of Reconstruction and America's current racial crisis are direct results of the disastrous Reconstruction plans of Lincoln and Andrew Johnson and the failure to adopt the comprehensive plan articulated by Sumner, Stevens, Douglass, Phillips, and others.

This opens up a provocative vein of thought. For if Sumner and Stevens and their allies were so advanced in their racial views, if they said in the nineteenth century what almost no White politicians say today, why aren't they better known? Why aren't they held up as models for White (and Black) youths instead of the vacillating, equivocating Lincoln?

The answer is a function of the question.

It is precisely because they believed in equality that they are vilified.

It is precisely because Lincoln didn't believe in equality that he is deified.

Certain of these men tried to transcend Whiteness, which is perhaps impossible in a situation that makes blackness a crime and whiteness a privilege, no matter what Black people or White people do. Stevens refused to be buried in a White cemetery, and Phillips and Garrison—until he defaulted at the climax—never stopped apologizing for the crimes of oppression. "I never rise to address a colored audience," Garrison told a colored audience in 1831, "without feeling ashamed of my own color; ashamed of being identified with a race of men who have done you so much injustice, and who yet retain so large a portion of your brethren in servile chains" (1831). Phillips said in a speech published in the *Anti-Slavery Standard* on October, 28, 1865, "I can never forget—I never wish to forget, the long years I have been permitted to serve the Negro race. The poor, poor Negro, who never yet leaned on the word of a white man with out finding it a broken reed . . . ."

That's why Phillips and his White colleagues are still dangerous. That's why they are still on the Civil War index.

Will it be said in rebuttal that they are still on the Civil War index because they demanded "revenge"? That's a strange position for people who demanded—properly—*a political and moral accounting* after World War II. All Stevens, Phillips, Wade, and Chandler asked was a just peace, which required compensation to the victims, *assignment and acceptance of responsibility* and the destruction of the conditions that created the war. All they asked was punishment for men who committed crimes against humanity and who unleashed, for racial reasons, a human holocaust that cost the lives of some 600,000 people. To be shocked by what Phillips and Stevens asked in the nineteenth century and to applaud what we asked in the twentieth, one must define crimes against White humanity and crimes against Black humanity in different ways.

Stevens and Phillips and their associates embarked, of course, on "a fool's errand," the errand White Reconstruction politician Albion Tourgee defined as the attempt in any age to prove that there is no safety for all except in all. Their only consolation perhaps is that truth and time are not their enemies and that people will not have to say of them, as they have to say of Lincoln, that they were White and couldn't do any better because they lived in the nineteenth century. *It may be, in fact, that their* real *crime was proving that White people can do better, even in the twenty-first century.*

Americans have forgiven almost everybody associated with the Civil War.

They have forgiven Lee, who resigned his commission and violated his oath to wage war on his country.

They have forgiven Jefferson Davis.

They have forgiven Ku Klux Klan Grand Wizard Nathan Bedford Forrest, who was responsible for the Fort Pillow atrocity and who was never called to account by the Lincoln administration.

They have forgiven almost everything, murder, genocide, treason. But they have not forgiven Sumner, Stevens, Phillips and other White men who fought for and with Blacks for American freedom in the Civil War and Reconstruction.

What was their crime? Did they also commit treason? Obviously, or worse, for the people who committed treason are hailed as heroes, and the men who demanded freedom for the slaves and equality for Black people have never been forgiven by historians who never stop assassinating them with adjectives.

They were, we are told, "doctrinaire." They were "ideologues." They were "extremists." They were "zealots," and they were, above all else, "humorless."

One of the most celebrated Lincoln biographers pursues these men with a violence that raises personal questions. Senator Wade was, he said, "bellicose," "profane," "crude," and "sardonic." Senator Chandler was "gruff" and "hard-drinking." Another Lincoln heavyweight deplored Wade's "insolence, coarseness of method, and vulgarity."

One observes with concern how often some Lincoln specialists use animal metaphors to express their loathing for the friends of Black freedom. One historian says Wade had "mastiff like jaws" and that Chandler had "a long horse-like face." Another deplores Wade's "bulldog tenacity" and his "bulldog obduracy." Still another protests "Chandler's savagery" and says Wade and Chandler were "rabid" for control of the government.

Lincoln specialists are partial to the same terms or at least they read one another and borrow from one another. All or almost all— Oates is an exception—play the game of "flogging the vindictives," striving with one another to come up with the most repulsive "vindictive" combination. The White men who demanded Black freedom had, we are told, a "vindictive spirit" and were "mercilessly vindictive" in criticizing Lincoln's policy.

The good guys in Lincoln books, Lincoln and Company, support slavery where it existed and oppose Black emancipation for the best of motives. They have principles and high ideals. The bad guys support emancipation and equal rights for the worst of motives. They are motivated not by a love of freedom but by hatred of the South and "personality conflicts." Lincoln, who was a Super Bowl of personality conflicts, is never mentioned or analyzed on that level.

You can tell the good guys from the bad guys by the adjectives preceding their names. Chandler is "grim" in almost all texts, Sumner is "pompous" and "pontifical," Julian is "impetuous." Generals John Charles Frémont and David Hunter electrified the nation by issuing proclamations freeing the slaves in their jurisdictions at a time when Lincoln was doing everything he could to save slavery in their jurisdictions. A major historian dismissed them with a throwaway phrase: "the noisy Frémont and Hunter."

Most American historians are grossly insensitive in their continuing attacks on Stevens, who was born with a clubfoot and who burned with a passion for the wretched and the handicapped and the put-upon. Like so many people in the nineteenth century, who associated a clubfoot with the devil, many, too many, Lincoln defenders say or imply that Stevens's physical handicap was the outer sign of an inner deformity. In any case, it is depressing to read the constant association of Stevens's *physical* handicap with his *political* position. One historian gives us a "black-wigged, clubfooted Stevens." Another warns against "caustic, terrifying, clubfooted old Thaddeus Stevens." Still another said Stevens's "dour countenance, protruding lower lip, limping clubfoot, and sarcastic invective made him the perfect type of vindictive ugliness."

Thus, History 101 in the two hundred and thirteenth year of the Republic.

Someone will say that this is a meaningless argument over words. After all, what other adjectives are there? Well, to begin with, there is "the *magnanimous* Lincoln" and—you better believe it—"the *noble* Lee."

Generations of American historians have systematically vilified and libeled Stevens, painting over his original portrait with layers and layers of "vindictive" prose. In order to get some idea of what the real man was like, one must go back in time to a contemporary like Noah Brooks, who was a Lincoln man but who recognized real talent when he saw it. Who was Stevens? "He was, "Brooks said in 1863, "the oldest and ablest man in congressional life" (1895, 17), adding in another place: "The redoubtable Republican leader is undoubtedly the foremost man in the House. Whatever he opposes is well-nigh predestined to die, and whatever he supports is almost certain to go through" (1967, 103-4).

What was Stevens's secret? His secret, Brooks said, lay "in his indomitable will, his energy of purpose, and the dominant character of his mind. He is never tender, winning, or conciliatory, but always argumentative, harsh, ironical, grim, and resolute. He sits at the left of the Speaker in the center of the Republican side of the House, and when he rises to make a speech all of the members of that side cluster around to hear, hanging on the desks like boys listening to the instructions of a father, while the Opposition, as if half-ashamed to concede so much, hover on the outside, filling up the area in front of the Speaker's desk, to listen to the irony, the gall, the polished wit, and the rough denunciation of the master of satire . . . ."

Brooks said Stevens was "about sixty-five years old, wears a dark brown, wavy-haired wig, is thick-set, has a high and massive forehead and deep set, dull, gray blue eyes almost hidden under his enormous brows. When he rises to speak he locks his hands loosely before him, and never makes a gesture, but calmly, slowly, and ponderously drops his sentences as though each one weighed a ton . . . ." Brooks added, "Nothing can terrify him, nothing can turn him from his purpose."

An additional and perhaps even more threatening reason for the endless vilification of Stevens and his associates is that they represented a new phenomenon in American politics. Unlike Jefferson and Lincoln, who talked about principles but never did anything about them in their private lives or in their politics, Stevens and the militant Republicans of the war years suggested, to the horror of Lincoln and his interpreters, that a serious and responsible leader should not only make Gettysburg speeches but should also live a Gettysburg life. Unlike Lincoln, Stevens was contemptuous of politicians who catered to the prejudices of the people in order to gain temporary political triumphs that "must prove disastrous to our country" in the end. The duty of a politician, he said, was not to wallow in the prejudices of the people but "instead of prophesying smooth things, and flattering the people with the belief of their present perfection, and thus retarding the mind in its onward progress, to create and sustain such laws and institutions as shall teach us our wants, foster our cravings after knowledge, and urge us forward in the march of intellect" (qtd. in Woodley 160-4).

This cuts across the grain of American politics and American scholarship, which is based on the idea that a politician in a situation of oppression, a Lincoln in Illinois or a Jefferson in Virginia, must respect the racism of his constituents and forego the dangerous idea that a man's principles ought to be reflected in his politics. This explains why almost all Lincoln defenders still profess horror at the proposals of the more militant Republicans and call them "doctrinaire" "ideologues." It also explains why some of these men, notably Trumbull and Phillips, discovered near the end of their careers that race and labor were different words for the same thing. Trumbull volunteered for the Eugene Debs case, which was conducted by Clarence Darrow, who said later that "the socialistic trend of the venerable statesman's opinions in his later years sprang from his deep sympathies with all unfortunates; that sympathy made him an anti-slavery Democrat in his early years, and afterwards a Republican. He became convinced that the poor who toil for a living in this world were not getting a fair chance. His heart was with them" (qtd. in White 425-6).

Gurowski noted, as LeRoy H. Fischer pointed out, that the Trumbulls, Stevenses, and Phillipses shared common denominators and characteristics. "The search for precedents, which generally plagued the American mind," did not, he said, hamper these men, who could and did act in crises without examples. Another trait which separated them from Lincoln and the conservatives was "a sense of righteous indignation combined with intense wrath and *joy* . . . ." Not wrath alone, you understand, nor joy alone but wrath *and* joy *and* righteous indignation gave them a weight, Gurowski said, unprecedented in American history (94, italics added).

If the "magnanimous" Lincoln and the "noble" Lee didn't succeed in their different and yet complementary efforts to preserve the Union as it was, it was due in large part to two groups, 1) the maligned Thirty-seventh Congress, which changed the emancipation agenda, and 2) African-American slaves, who broke into the war, like burglars, and imposed their own rhythm on events. Abandoning plantations in the thousands and tens of thousands, shouting Jubilee songs and demanding a piece of the Civil War action, they helped emancipate themselves—and Lincoln.

"We have entered Virginia," Secretary of State Seward said in February 1862, "and already five thousand slaves, emancipated simply by the appearance of our forces, are upon the hands of the Federal government there. We have landed upon the coast of South Carolina, and already nine thousand . . . hang upon our camps . Although the war has not been waged against slavery, yet the army acts . . . as an emancipating crusade. To proclaim the crusade is unnecessary" (qtd. in Randall 1945-55, 2:131-2).

Seward didn't want the crusade proclaimed because he was opposed to the crusade. That, however, does not negate two facts, abundantly documented elsewhere, that he saw clearly. One is that the word, as always, followed the fact. The second is that Lincoln, as usual, was one of the last, perhaps the last, to hear it.

One could see this plainly in New Orleans and the areas around Beaufort, South Carolina, where early Union advances brought new opportunities and dramatized Lincoln's lack of policy. Watching Lincoln's hesitant response to the rising pressure of thousands of Black refugees seeking freedom and demanding arms and land, Gurowski told his diary that what Lincoln feared most of all was not failure but success. "Again," he wrote, "Lincoln is frightened with the success in

South Carolina, as in his opinion this success will complicate the question of slavery" (GD 1:121). Gurowski told Massachusetts Governor John A. Andrew in May 1862 that Lincoln believed that "emancipation will smother the Free States. Such are his precise words." A month later, "on the occasion of the organization of slaves at Beaufort [South Carolina]," Gurowski said Lincoln exclaimed, 'Slavery is a big job, and will smother us!' It will [Gurowski replied] if dealt with in your way, Mr. President" (GD 1:223).

If Lincoln feared Black freedom, other men, more daring perhaps, certainly more sensitive, welcomed it and moved to give it wings. Among their number was an old Lincoln friend, General David Hunter, who on May 9, 1862, declared all slaves in South Carolina, Georgia, and Florida "forever free" (CW 5:222). Ten days later, Lincoln returned these men, women and children to slavery—and if you're keeping a thorn-in-the-bosom tally, add another million or so.

In a simultaneous rebound action, Lincoln asked the Border States to accept his offer of gradual and compensated emancipation. "I do not argue," he said, "I beseech you to make the arguments for yourselves. You can not if you would, be blind to the signs of the times." What were the signs of the times? The growing demand for emancipation, as evidenced by the Hunter proclamation, and the growing power of antislavery adherents. There was also, he said, in a strange sentence he deleted before publication, a "strong tendency to a total disruption of society in the South," meaning, of course, a total disruption of slave society, which he feared.

What was the solution? The solution was not the general emancipation of Hunter, Frémont, and the congressional militants. The solution was his gradual, compensated "abolishment," which, he said, "makes common cause for a common object, casting no reproaches upon any. It acts not the pharisee. The change it contemplates would come gently as the dews of heaven, not rending or wrecking anything" (CW 5:223).

If we examine this overly pretty and overly praised sentence more closely—who believes that the liberation of slaves and concentration camp inmates should come as slowly and as gently as the dew?—we find that it repeats two of the recurring refrains in the Lincoln apologia. The first is that Lincoln didn't want to reproach anybody for holding people in slavery. The other is that Lincoln was looking for a way to end slavery so gradually and so gently (for the slaveholders) that the slaveholders would never notice. In the best of all possible worlds, as he said in his second State of the Union Address, most living slaveholders (and slaves) would be dead before the slaves were emancipated and deported, which was, of course, charity for living slaveholders and malice for the slaves (CW 5:531).

While Lincoln worried about "the public and private inconveniences of emancipation," ordinary citizens assumed the burden of leadership, going in ones and twos and tens to the White House to urge action and emancipation. The Lincoln administration, in fact, created a new form of political theater, attracting a constant stream of delegations with petitions and arguments in favor of the emancipation of Black Americans. From all over America, from New England and the Midwest, from Republicans, Democrats, preachers, businessmen, and abolitionists came petitions for the freeing of the slaves. There were even petitions from schoolchildren trying to improve the moral vision of the president of the United States. So many petitions came from so many White people that it is hard to understand why so many historians say that Lincoln was waiting for the people to catch up with him.

When a delegation of Quakers, including great names like Thomas Garrett and Dinah Mendenhall, came to the White House on Friday, June 20, and told Lincoln that God wanted him to free the slaves, he said that he "had sometime thought that perhaps he might be an instrument in God's hands of accomplishing a great work . . . . " He was not convinced, however, that the time was ripe or that God favored a decree of emancipation. Perhaps, he said, "God's way of accomplishing the end which the memorialists have in view may be different from theirs " (CW 5:278-9).

Since the Quakers believed that God's way was an emancipation proclamation and since Lincoln and apparently Lincoln's God had another way in mind, the question naturally arises of what other way was available. The answer to this question, as to so many others that arose during this period, was apparently McClellan. At that point, in June of 1862, McClellan and his troops were aimed like a dagger at the heart of the Confederacy, and Lincoln was feverishly awaiting news of the triumphant Union march into Richmond. Count Gurowski told his diary that Secretary of State Seward believes "that July 4th will be celebrated by us in Richmond" (226).

Just in case the Richmond hope failed again, Lincoln continued to press his favorite plan of gradual compensated emancipation and sudden deportation. Conferring with Congressman John W. Crisfield of Maryland, a member of a congressional committee charged with drafting a report on his favorite plan of compensated emancipation, he asked:

"Well, Crisfield, how are you getting along with your report, have you written it yet?"

Crisfield said no.

"You had better come to an agreement," Lincoln replied. "Niggers will never be higher" (Lamon 1911, 290).

It was at this juncture, at the low point of his campaign to buy the slaves and send them away, that Lincoln was forced by events and pressure to change his language and his style, if not his mind.

When did Lincoln change?

Why did he change?

More importantly, *did* he change?

These questions pose no problem for traditionalists, who, as usual, favor variants of the spontaneous generation theory, with some saying that Lincoln, like Saul, was converted suddenly on the road to Richmond and others contending that the deteriorating military and political situation, especially the hardening of the hearts of Northern Whites, appalled by the slaughter of sons, brothers, and fathers, forced the change.

Almost all Lincoln scholars say the big change came in July 1862, but, as we shall see, Lincoln made so many contradictory statements and did so many contradictory things in that month, that this thesis—the thesis of almost all Lincoln historians—is untenable. To see this clearly, one need only revisit that famous July with Lincoln, keeping in mind five indispensable rules for anyone tracking Lincoln on the road to emancipation:

Rule One: The Emancipation Proclamation was *never* Lincoln's plan. The Proclamation was forced on him by events and the pressure of Black and White activists.

Rule Two: Lincoln wanted to end the war without touching slavery. For at least eighteen months, by his own admission, he did everything he could to ensure that America remained half slave and half free.

Rule Three: When Southern tenacity and mounting war casualties and his own policies, including the appointment of bumbling proslavery generals, doomed that policy, he changed in order to remain the same, proposing the only emancipation plan he ever believed in, gradual, compensated emancipation linked to the sudden deportation of Blacks.

Rule Four: Lincoln was tenacious and even devious in supporting *his* plan of gradual emancipation and deportation and in opposing the idea of an *immediate* emancipation proclamation, which he feared more than slavery. He never changed his mind on that point and continued to fight for gradual emancipation and deportation, even after Republican leaders forced him to adopt a different language. If that meant saying emancipation words and issuing emancipation documents, without following through with emancipation acts, the better to blind his adversaries and to prepare the way for the triumph of his plan, Lincoln was up to it. It was the essence of his art to yield without yielding and to change while remaining the same.

Rule Five: Lincoln's actions in support of emancipation were *rebound* actions made in response to the initiatives of the real supporters of Black freedom or the overwhelming pressure of events and were designed, at least in part, to counter, sidetrack and even thwart the movement for real emancipation.

Before dealing with these rules in some detail, let me emphasize that Lincoln scholars have been saying the same thing for years without integrating their comments into an analysis and without realizing, I think, what they were saying. J. G. Randall, for instance, tells us at great length that the Emancipation Proclamation was of *minor* importance to Lincoln because it was never *his* plan (1945-55, 2:141). Cronies, critics, and latter-day historians say "his whole soul" was involved not in the Proclamation but in *his* plan.

What was Lincoln's plan? His plan, according to Randall, Sumner, Julian and cronies David B. Davis and Henry C. Whitney, to name a few, was gradual, compensated emancipation linked to immediate deportation. And we can say once more that any Lincoln emancipation initiative that was not a compensation/colonization plan was not a Lincoln plan. Ward Hill Lamon, Lincoln's close friend and aide, said "'compensated' and 'voluntary emancipation,' on the one hand, and 'colonization' of the freedmen on the other, were essential parts of every 'plan,' which sprung out of his own individual mind" (340). In one of the great sentences of the Lincoln literature, Sandburg said, "Two plans the President struggled with incessantly, like an engineer wrestling to put bridges over a swollen river during a flood rush. One of these was to make practical the colonization of Negroes to be freed. The other was gradual compensated abolishment" (1:578).

As for the second rule, Lincoln is a witness for my side. "After the commencement of hostilities," he said, "I struggled nearly a year and half to get along without touching the 'institution' . . ." (CW 6:48). Lincoln's arithmetic was off; it usually was when he was computing in color. He struggled longer than that and never really stopped struggling, using every weapon at his command to slow down, sidetrack or stop the emancipation flow. When all else failed, he changed in order to remain the same, making emancipation *promises* to kill emancipation *acts*, offering *mild* emancipation measures to counter *strong* emancipation measures. *The Emancipation Proclamation itself was, as we have seen and as we shall see, the high point of a brilliant campaign in favor of slavery not freedom,* and was designed not to emancipate all slaves immediately but to prevent the emancipation of all slaves immediately and to contain the emancipation pressures until conservatives could, as Lincoln said, help themselves (CW 5:345).

All or almost all Lincoln scholars concede that point without, I think, understanding what they are conceding. Oates tells us that Lincoln's compensated emancipation resolution was designed "to *forestall a more revolutionary move against slavery*" (324). Thomas tells us that Lincoln proposed recognition of Haiti and Liberia "*to mollify the antislavery faction of his party,*" enraged "*as Lincoln faithfully enforced the Fugitive Slave Law, and Washington jails filled up with runaway slaves waiting to be claimed by masters*" (311, italics added).

The Lincoln literature is full of these half-insights. Here are two more from Thomas: Foreseeing "*that he could not resist the antislavery pressure much longer,*" Lincoln recommended that Congress pass a joint resolution offering financial aid to any state undertaking gradual emancipation (311, italics added). *Knowing that "he could not much longer stay his hand against slavery,*" he appealed to congressmen representing Border slave states for the third time (313, italics added).

This evidence is overpoweringly persuasive, especially since it is incidental testimony, and especially since it comes from pillars of the Lincoln establishment. Williams said that Lincoln proposed a gradual, compensated emancipation scheme to Congress "largely for the purpose of conciliating the rising antislavery spirit which the radicals were whipping up in the country." (157). Stephenson, who virtually invented the "vindictive" maneuver, says that "*as a compromise, to cut the ground from under the Vindictives, he . . . urged the loyal Slave States to endorse a program of compensated emancipation*" (250, italics added).

As for the Emancipation Proclamation, Donald says that it was a response to the Second Confiscation Act. Lincoln was opposed to the Confiscation Act, Donald says, "but rather than confront Congress over the abstract issue, *Lincoln decided to accept the bill—and to undercut the congressional initiative for emancipation by acting first*" (365, italics added).

Here, unmistakably, is the secret of the Lincoln dialectic:

Antislavery *action*, Lincoln *reaction*.

Strong antislavery pressure, *mild* antislavery response.

An *act* for freedom and a *gesture* in *the direction of freedom.*

No one can read the record attentively without noticing this dialectic, which is the deeper meaning of the five explanatory keys we outlined above.

Let us test these explanatory keys, seeing how many Lincoln doors they will unlock, starting with that strange and almost totally neglected conference Lincoln held with his friend Orville Browning immediately after breakfast on the first day of his month of decision. During the conversation on Tuesday, July 1, 1862, Lincoln, according to a Browning diary entry of the same day, read a paper he had prepared for his cabinet, which embodied "his views of the objects of the war, and the proper mode of conducting it in its relations to slavery. " The paper was based on four propositions:

1. "No Negroes necessarily taken and escaping during the war are ever to be returned to slavery."

2. "No inducements are to be held out to them [slaves] to come into our lines for they come now faster than we can provide for them and are becoming an embarrassment to the government."

3. "At present none are to be armed."

4. "Congress has no power over slavery in the states, and *so much of it as remains after the war is over will be in precisely the same condition that it was before the war began,* and must be left to the exclusive control of the states where it may exist" (BD 555, italics added).

If we can credit this contemporary diary entry, the "great emancipator" on Tuesday, July 1, 1862, was still fighting to preserve the Old

Union. He didn't intend to return freed or escaped slaves to their masters. He was embarrassed by the large number of slaves escaping to Union lines and didn't want any inducements to be held out to them. He was opposed to arming Blacks. He didn't believe Congress had any power over slavery in the states. He believed that "so much of [slavery]" as remained after the war was over would be "in the same condition that it was before the war began" and would have to be left "to the exclusive control" of the states where it existed.

If words are to have any meaning, this diary entry means that Lincoln, on July 1, 1862, on the eve of his so-called conversion, was still waging an anti-emancipation war to save as much slavery as he could.

Four, possibly five, events changed his public posture if not his mind. The first and possibly most significant event, the collapse of General McClellan's Virginia campaign, forced Lincoln to give up his fantasy of Union troops marching into Richmond, ending the war and saving the institution where it existed. On July 2, he telegraphed McClellan: "If you think you are not strong enough to take Richmond just now, I do not ask you to try just now" (CW 5:301).

This was a confirmation at a higher level of desperation of the Bull Run dialectic, and it is worth emphasizing that almost all contemporaries and scholars concede that the failure of the Peninsular Campaign stimulated the antislavery movement and hastened emancipation. The president's secretaries, Nicolay and Hay, say "it was doubtless the sudden collapse of McClellan's Richmond campaign which brought President Lincoln to the determination to adopt his policy of general military emancipation much sooner than he would otherwise have done" (NH 6:120). Navy Secretary Welles said "the reverses before Richmond undoubtedly hastened the movement of emancipation." Until then, Welles said, Lincoln had hoped to end the war without "disturbing" slavery (WH 842).

The reverses on the Virginia peninsula were a severe blow to Lincoln's plan to save the Union without touching the institution of slavery, and it left him virtually defenseless against the rising tide of emancipation. Even as he read the whining dispatches from McClellan, he was besieged by demands for new political and military measures against slavery. On Friday, July 4, Senator Sumner called on Lincoln twice to urge him to issue an emancipation decree, which would make the Fourth, he said, "more sacred, and more historic, and do for it better than the Continental Congress." The first time he called, the president, Sumner said, "seemed not disinclined to do it for Eastern Virginia [but] objected to a general decree, as being 'too big a lick,'" an observation that did not go down well with Secretary of War Stanton, who said 'we wanted big licks now'" (Gay). When, two hours later, Sumner returned with the same suggestion, Lincoln changed his mind again, saying "there were two objections: 1. That half the army would lay down its arms, if emancipation were declared: 2 That three more States would rise, Ky. Md. Mo." Sumner told him he was "plainly mistaken."[48]

Sumner's critique was echoed by military leaders like General Lew Wallace, who told a Washington crowd in an impromptu balcony speech, that it was "crazy" from a military standpoint for an army not to use every available resource, including Black soldiers. There was, the *New York Tribune* report of July 11 said, "loud and continuing cheering at that point," and the general added, looking no doubt in the direction of the White House, "Oh, if I could get a little backbone into those who are governing us."

This was followed, two days later, by a landmark event that changed the boundaries and the goal lines for all the participants. And to understand what Lincoln did next, and why, we must return to the congressional emancipators nobody knows. For almost six months, week after acrimonious week, while Lincoln backed and filed, congressional leaders had bitterly debated Trumbull's confiscation bill. To minimize the war of words, and to advance the process, Republican leaders had turned the whole matter over to a Conference Committee, which seemed to have been hopelessly deadlocked. Then, without warning, on Friday, July 11, as the *New York Tribune* reported on July 12, "the Confiscation bills, after apparently a deadlock, were suddenly resuscitated by the Conference Committees and a report was agreed upon, made to the House, and passed that body by a vote of 82 to 42, the Republicans almost without exception [including three members from Slave States] voting for it." The next day, Saturday, July 12, the Senate followed suit, with all Republicans voting yes except Lincoln's friend and spokesman, Orville Browning of Illinois, and Edgar Cowan of Pennsylvania.

This was a pivotal event that marked a turning point in the Civil War and the beginning of the end of slavery in the United States. It can be said, in fact, without exaggeration, that it was the first and only real emancipation proclamation before the Thirteenth Amendment. Anyone who doubts this need only read Section 9 of the bill, which said "that all slaves of persons who shall hereafter be engaged in rebellion against the Government of the United States, or who shall in any way give aid or comfort thereto, escaping from such persons and taking refuge within the lines of the Army, and all slaves captured from such persons, or deserting from them, and coming under the control of the Government of the United States, and all slaves of such persons found or being within any place occupied by Rebel forces, and afterward occupied by the force of the United States, shall be deemed captives of war, and shall be forever free of their servitude, and not again held as slaves."

Here at long last was a real emancipation proclamation, liberating millions of slaves immediately and declaring them "forever free." This language, as Randall and others noted, went further than the Emancipation Proclamation and was not limited by a one hundred-day warning or "the very considerable territorial exceptions of the President's decree" (1947, 27). The *Chicago Tribune,* the *New York Tribune* and leading Republicans contended that this act freed the slaves of all rebels and all slaveholders aiding the rebellion from the date of its passage on July 17.

How did Lincoln respond to all this? He responded the way we said he would respond (see page 416), sending up flares and smoke screens in a frantic effort to contain or deflect the radical initiative of congressional leaders. On Saturday, July 12, the day after the congressional deadlock was broken, Lincoln called representatives of Border States to the White House and renewed his plea for his gradual emancipation plan. Lincoln told the legislators that they were friends and allies, not enemies, and that they shared the same goal. *"You prefer that the constitutional relation of the states to the nation shall be practically restored,* without disturbance of the institution; *and if this were done, my whole duty, in this respect, under the constitution, and my oath of office, would be performed"* (CW 5:318, italics added).

Lincoln talked to the congressmen like a financial advisor or an insurance agent, showing them how they could improve their financial position and provide for their families and their old age. "If the war continue long, as it must, if the object be not sooner attained, the institution in your states will be extinguished by mere friction and abrasion—by the mere incidents of the war. It will be gone and you will have nothing valuable in lieu of it . . . . How much better for you, and for your people, to take the step which, at once, shortens the war, and secures substantial compensation for that which is sure to be wholly lost in any other event" (CW 5:318).

This was a powerful if immoral argument, and it's hard to see why the Border State representatives kept turning it down, especially since Lincoln was not asking them to do anything immediately. "I do not speak of emancipation *at once,* but of a *decision* at once to emancipate *gradually."* He spoke also of a decision at once to remove the freed slaves. "Room in South America for colonization, can be obtained cheaply, and in abundance; and when numbers shall be large enough to be company and encouragement for one another, the freed people will not be so reluctant to go" (CW 5:318, Lincoln's italics).

Lincoln begged the representatives to relieve him of the rising pressure for immediate and general emancipation. The pressure from that direction, he told them, was growing, and threatening "division among those who, united are none too strong." A case in point, he said, was General Hunter, who had issued a proclamation freeing all slaves in three Southern states. Lincoln had repudiated the proclamation, thereby, he said, giving "dissatisfaction, if not offence, to many whose support the country can not afford to lose. And this is not the end of it. *The pressure in this direction, is still upon me, and is increasing.* By conceding what I now ask, you can relieve me, and, much more, can relieve the country in this important point" (CW 5:318, italics added).

This confirms once again the explanatory rebound schema outlined above. For Lincoln says here as plainly as a man can say that his initiative was a rebound initiative designed to relieve him of the pressure for immediate and general emancipation.

To see this clearly, one need only read what Lincoln said the next day—the day after the Senate overwhelmingly passed a bill freeing the slaves of *all* rebels—when he rode in a carriage with Secretary Welles, Secretary Seward, and Seward's daughter-in-law, Mrs. Frederick Seward, to the funeral of Stanton's infant child.

"It was on this occasion," Welles said, "and on this ride that he first mentioned to Mr. Seward and myself the subject of emancipating the slaves by proclamation in case the Rebels did not cease to persist in their war on the Government and the Union, of which he saw no evidence. He dwelt earnestly on the gravity, importance, and delicacy of the movement, said he had given it much thought and had about come to the conclusion that it was a military necessity absolutely essential for the salvation of the Union, that we must free the slaves or be ourselves subdued, etc., etc."

The cabinet members, Welles said, were surprised and even shocked. "It was a new departure for the President," Welles added, "for until this time, in all our previous interviews, whenever the question of emancipation or the mitigation of slavery had been in any way alluded to, he had been prompt and emphatic in denouncing any interference by the General Government with the subject" (WD 70-1).

What caused this new departure?

Lincoln said, according to Welles, that the emancipation policy "was forced upon him as a necessity," "was thrust at him from various quarters" and had been "driven home to him by the conference of the preceding day . . ." (WH 843). Lincoln was disingenuous, and so was Welles. There was nothing new in the conference with the Border State representatives, who didn't, in fact, give their answer until the next day. The major problem on Lincoln's mind on Sunday, July 13 and the major political reality of Washington and the North on Sunday, July 13, was that the United States Senate had passed on July 12 a Confiscation bill freeing the slaves of all rebels, and that legislators were meeting to reconcile the House and Senate versions. The strongest argument against Welles's account, and Lincoln's alleged statement, is that neither man, according to this account, discussed the biggest and most pressing political reality of July 13, 1862.

Lincoln, according to Welles, did not mention the Senate vote, but he did say that he had tried everything to keep from emancipating the slaves and that "his reluctance to meddle with this question, around which there were thrown constitutional safeguards, and on which the whole Southern mind [read: White Southern mind] was sensitive, was great" (WH 842).

The diary entry in which Welles relates all of this is not a regular diary entry and is somewhat suspect. It is also difficult to imagine the secretive and woman-shy Lincoln discussing such a delicate matter so openly and fully in a carriage that also contained Mrs. Frederick Seward, a noncabinet member. And in considering this report and all other post-assassination reminiscences, it is important to remember that Lincoln apparently made a habit of telling different persons that he had decided to emancipate and that the person he was talking to was the first person he had shared that information with. In May, when he was pushing his compensated emancipation plan and arguing passionately against immediate emancipation, he reportedly went through this ritual with Secretary of War Stanton. In June, when he was mobilizing all his resources to block the emancipation provisions of the projected Second Confiscation Act, and when he was expecting General McClellan to march into Richmond at any moment, he reportedly gave Vice President Hannibal Hamlin the treatment. In July, it was Welles's and Seward's turn, if we can believe Welles's delayed report. During the same period, Sumner and others claimed to have heard the word.

What are we to make of all this? Were these diversionary gestures, designed to take the steam out of the growing demand for emancipation, or were they the sincere and confused gestures of a sincere and confused leader who repeatedly stuck his toe into the water and repeatedly scurried back to the safety of the shore?

Perhaps they were all of these, and more, for subsequent events—Lincoln's assassination, the Union victory and the actual freeing of the slaves—gave these incoherent gestures a meaning that they didn't have at the time, particularly to post-assassination romantics who wanted to claim special information about the emancipation or a special relation to an icon on his way to glory. In any case, nobody, not even Abraham Lincoln, seems to have taken his pre-Proclamation words seriously at the time. The evidence for this is that the participants, including Lincoln, Seward and even Welles, neglected to make a note of these events at the time and had extreme difficulty later remembering who said what, where and on what day.

What Lincoln did the day after the carriage ride raises large doubts about what he allegedly said during the carriage ride. For after telling Welles and Seward, according to Welles, that he had "about" decided to emancipate the slaves immediately, he made a 180-degree turn and asked Congress to compensate any state that abolished slavery. Since he submitted the bill only three days before the end of the session, thereby ensuring that it would not be seriously considered, this was obviously a public relations gesture, designed to take some of the steam out of the mushrooming emancipation movement.

On the same day—Monday, July 14—Lincoln conferred behind closed doors with Browning, who rushed to the White House with a copy of the proposed Confiscation Act. Browning, enraged, wanted Lincoln to veto the bill. The administration, he said, had reached the "culminating point," and how Lincoln dealt with this crisis would determine "whether he was to control the abolitionists and radicals, or whether they were to control him" (BD 558).

Lincoln, Browning says, was noncommittal. When Browning saw him the next day—Tuesday, July 15—he looked "weary, care-worn and troubled. . . ." Browning told Lincoln that he was concerned about him and "regretted that troubles crowded so heavily upon him, and feared his health was suffering." The president, Browning said, "held me by the hand, pressed it, and said in a very tender and touching tone—"Browning I must die sometime . . . ." He looked very sad, and there was a cadence of deep sadness in his voice. We parted I believe both of us with tears in our eyes" (BD 559-60).

This was a strange scene. Why did Lincoln start talking about dying? And why were there tears in his eyes? The only political threat before him on this day was the Confiscation Act, which called for the freeing of the slaves of all rebels and the confiscation of their property. Why was Lincoln so overwhelmed by these possibilities, and why did Browning believe that the pressure for emancipation was threatening his health and triggering untimely tears?

Whatever caused the tears, one thing was clear on Tuesday, July 15, 1862: pressure for a hard-war policy, including emancipation, was growing and had become almost irresistible. One of Lincoln's few devoted supporters in Congress, Representative Isaac N. Arnold of Illinois, said, according to an A.S. Hill letter of July 18, that "within the last two or three days the President has been subjected to the greatest pressure in favor of vigorous war measures that was ever brought to bear upon him" (Gay).

Some of this pressure came from senators like Joseph A. Wright of Indiana, who told the Senate on July 15, according to a *New York Tribune* report of July 16, that although he was a conservative Democrat from Indiana, he was in favor of the president using Negroes "in any way feasible." He said he would have the president order his generals to stop protecting rebel property and start enforcing the Confiscation Act everywhere.

How would Wright fight the war?

"He would concentrate our armies and hurl them into the Cotton

States, and there subsist them upon the enemy."

Senator John B. Henderson of Missouri said in the same debate that "our sin . . . had been in taking too much pains to protect the Border States . . . . He would have the armies of the United States march out of the Border States and leave them to protect themselves, and march into the Cotton States in columns that could not be withstood."

The next day, the point of no return was reached when the House and the Senate agreed on the Second Confiscation Act, which freed the slaves of all rebels. The headline of a *Chicago Tribune story*, dated July 18, said: **THE SLAVES OF REBELS [ARE] FREEMEN.**

This revolutionary act, which carried the official and, to Lincoln, portentous title of "An Act To Suppress Insurrection, to Punish Treason and Rebellion, To Seize and Confiscate the Property of Rebels, and For Other Purposes," authorized and directed the president to use Black soldiers and to seize for the benefit of the United States "all the estate and property, money, stocks, credit and effects of officers of the army and navy, administrative officers, national, state or municipal, of the so-called confederate States of America." The *Chicago Tribune* accurately called it "the Confiscation and Emancipation Bill."

Alarmed by this direct threat to his policy and power, Lincoln threatened a veto, saying that the section that divested slaveowners of their title forever was unconstitutional. This seemingly small disagreement over fee simple and divestiture nevertheless reflected a matter of the gravest importance. For *Lincoln's action ended Reconstruction before it began* and made it impossible to achieve real democracy in the South in the Reconstruction period or in the long white days of segregation and sorrow.

Lincoln's intervention on behalf of big Southern slaveholders was bitterly denounced by members of his party. Congressman Julian said "Congress was obliged to make the modification required as the only means of securing the important advantages of other features of the measure; but the action of the President was inexpressibly provoking to a large majority of Congress. It was bitterly denounced as an anti-Republican discrimination between real and personal property, when the nation was struggling for its life against a rebellious aristocracy founded on the monopoly of land and the ownership of Negroes.

Congressman Julians said *"the President was charged with thus prolonging the war and aggravating its cost by paralyzing one of the most potent means of putting down the rebellion,* and purposely leaving the owners of large estates in full possession of their lands . . . *He was arraigned as the deliberate betrayer of the freedmen and poor whites,* who had been friendly to the Union . . ." (RR 58, italics added).

The threatened veto caught congressional leaders off guard, and a joint resolution was passed to meet Lincoln's objections. When, on Thursday, July 17, Lincoln returned the signed bill, he unwisely sent along the veto message he had prepared, precipitating a congressional explosion that showed clearly how exposed he was politically.

Many members refused to listen to the message, and when the question was called on printing the message in the House, "no Republican was found to urge it," and it was left to "peace" Democrats to move the printing, which was blocked by Republicans. "The Democrats," a *Chicago Tribune* report of July 18 said, "all clamored and voted for printing, and assumed to be the president's special champion."

Thus, at the end of the second session of the Thirty-seventh Congress, the president of the United States was in the dangerous position of being virtually a man without a party, depending on the charity of conservative Democrats who opposed the war he was leading.

This was revolution, some said, or the prelude to revolution, and there was a great deal of talk on this day about the similarities between Washington in 1862 and Paris during the French Revolution.

Looking back later, Congressman Julian said, "No one at a distance could have formed any adequate conception of the hostility of the Republican members toward Lincoln at the final adjournment, while it was the belief of many that our last session of Congress had been held in Washington. Mr. Wade said the country was going to Hell, and that the scenes witnessed in the French Revolution were nothing in comparison with what we should see here" (1884, 220).

20

The "Conversion" Of Abraham Lincoln

WITH the passage of the Second Confiscation Act, a door slammed shut on one of history's greatest conceits, a Confederacy founded on the rock of Negro inferiority and designed, like other conceits of its kind, to last forever. The Second Confiscation Act didn't end the Confederacy, but it cut off one of its last avenues of escape and forced the beginning of America's confrontation with slavery, slaves, and African-Americans, with implications that are still reverberating in the land.

Seen whole, then, and in proper perspective, the Second Confiscation Act was one of the great hinges of our history. More sweeping than the Lincoln proclamations, more threatening to the slave interests than anything that came out of the Lincoln White House, this act freed the slaves of all rebels and struck at the roots of the slave system by confiscating the property and plantations of slaveowners, an unheard-of American revolution that Abraham Lincoln thwarted at the last moment by a threatened veto in favor of the Southern plantation system.

The act also marked the public debut of the Lincoln Opposition Party, a self-conscious but loosely structured tendency within and without the Republican Party. Never adequately identified in the literature, this party included the principal congressional leaders, major editors like Medill of the *Chicago Tribune* and Greeley of the *New York Tribune*, militant abolitionist leaders like Phillips and Douglass, industrialists like John Murray Forbes, and fellow travelers like Union General James S. Wadsworth and Assistant Secretary of War Peter Watson. Not only New England ministers and intellectuals but also, surprisingly, Midwestern preachers and laymen, especially in Illinois, supported the party. So did fathers, mothers, relatives, and friends of Union soldiers, who complained that Lincoln was not doing enough to hurt the rebels who were killing and maiming tens of thousands of Northerners.

The leading members of this group knew one another and communicated with one another—Medill to Chase, Sedgwick to Forbes, Andrew to Gurowski, Phillips and Douglass to Sumner, and Sumner to everybody. They attended the same meetings, patronized the same salons and discussed the latest Lincoln outrage with *Chicago Tribune* correspondent Horace White and *New York Tribune* correspondent Adams S. Hill. At crucial moments, they acted as a unit and mobilized pressure to push Lincoln forward. In the critical days before the signing of the Preliminary Proclamation, the *New York Tribune and* the *Chicago Tribune* mobilized and focused grass-roots pressure. In the critical days before the signing of the Emancipation Proclamation, capitalist John Murray Forbes coordinated a campaign designed to strengthen Lincoln's resolve.

It is customary to count the Lincoln Opposition Party in the Lincoln ranks, but the group had an anti-Lincoln style (hard, passionate, angry) and an anti-Lincoln agenda Lincoln never accepted: a hard-war policy based on hitting the Confederacy where it would hurt most by freeing the slaves, using Black soldiers and confiscating the land and property of the leading rebels.

The group was also united by a new and, shall we say, un-American, idea of politics. Unlike Jefferson (and Lincoln), who loved ideas (and principles) in the abstract but who would have been horrified if anyone had suggested that they try to make their principles real in the politics of Virginia or Illinois, the Lincoln Opposition Party believed that ideas, especially the Declaration of Independence idea that Jefferson authored but disowned, should be realized in concrete propositions for concrete men and women. This was a new thing in American politics, never before seen, and Lincoln defenders have never stopped denouncing the "wild" idea that the art of politics is not, as Stevens said, the art of fostering and flattering ignorance and prejudice but the art of creating and sustaining "such laws and institutions as shall teach us our wants, foster our cravings after knowledge, and urge us forward in the march of the intellect" (qtd. in Woodley 160-1, 164).

To make sure Lincoln got that message, leading senators and congressmen took the revolutionary step of going over the president's head and issuing in the *New York Tribune*, on Saturday, July 19, the "Address of the Republican Members of Congress to the Loyal People of the United States." Among the seven senators who signed this revolutionary document were Wade (Ohio), Wilson (Massachusetts), James Lane (Kansas), and Samuel Pomeroy (Kansas). The House advocates included Stevens (Pennsylvania), Julian (Indiana), Ashley (Ohio), William Cutler (Ohio), and Lovejoy (Illinois).

Calling on all loyal Americans to support the war effort, Republican congressional leaders asked Lincoln to strike at the strength of the rebels by freeing and arming the slaves.

"An imperilled country," they said, "is entitled to the service of all her children. The slave who comes in the hour of her trial to the rescue of his Country that forgot him in his bonds, is surely entitled to higher consideration than the traitor who, while he enslaves him, strikes also at the liberty and life of his country."

Like almost everybody appealing to the people in those days, the Republican legislators invoked the names of the White founding fathers. But the White founding father the liberal Republicans appealed to was not Jefferson who, like Lincoln, spoke of liberty in the abstract but Madison, who spoke of power and interests in the concrete and who had warned in another crisis that the slaves were "an unhappy species of population abounding in SOME OF THE STATES who, during the calm of regular government, are sunk below the level of men, but who, in the tempestuous scenes of civil violence, may emerge into the human character and give a superiority of strength to any party with which they may associate themselves."

Madison's (and David Walker's and Fanon's and Sartre's) idea of slaves—and oppressed people—emerging into their human character in and through violence was never quoted by Lincoln, who worshiped, we are told, the White founding fathers, but it was cited and approved by the Republican Members of Congress, who ended with a felicitous quote that should have been in Lincoln's repertoire but wasn't, a quote from the address to the people by the Congress of 1783:

"The people of the United States are responsible for the greatest trust ever committed to a political society . . . . If the great cause which we have engaged to vindicate shall be dishonored or destroyed, the last and fairest experiment in favor of the rules of human nature will be turned against them, and their patrons and friends exposed to be insulted and silenced by the votaries of tyranny and oppression."

On the day this address was published, a group of Republican senators stepped up the pressure by attending a cabinet meeting and urging a hard-war policy. Led by Senator Trumbull of Illinois, they asked for a new policy of letting Union soldiers subsist on the land in hostile areas, a policy Lincoln obligingly announced three days later at his July 22 cabinet meeting.

The crucial point here, a point overlooked by many commentators, is that Lincoln was virtually a man without a party until Sherman's victory at Atlanta and McClellan's victory at the Democratic convention created a new war and a new Republican Party. For all that time, from Fort Sumter to Atlanta and beyond, Lincoln tried vainly to create a new conservative Union party of conservative

Democrats and conservative Republicans. Nothing dramatized this more clearly than the Second Confiscation Act, which was bitterly opposed by Lincoln, and which passed both houses of Congress by a two-to-one margin with only two Republican senators and three Republican representatives voting nay.

It was in this volatile atmosphere, which several witnesses called revolutionary or prerevolutionary, that Lincoln embraced or seemed to embrace the idea of an emancipation proclamation, an idea that suggested or seemed to suggest immediate or general emancipation with one stroke of the pen. But after broaching the idea on July 13, Lincoln said nothing else about it, giving the impression that he had gotten cold feet or changed his mind. Then, without preamble, on July 22, he said or seemed to say at a cabinet meeting that he was going to issue an emancipation proclamation.

Why did he take this step? The answer is plain. It was the least he could do under the circumstances, and no president in his position could have done less. Most in fact would have done considerably more, not because of their love for Blacks but because the strategic situation required it. More than that, a proclamation had, from Lincoln's standpoint, a number of tactical advantages. First of all and most important of all, a proclamation, unlike the Second Confiscation Act, was a gesture, not an act. Announcing that you were going to free four million slaves three or fourth months later made you feel good and made others feel good but didn't free anybody or change anything. A proclamation, moreover, had the advantage, from Lincoln's standpoint, of freezing the status quo and making it unnecessary to immediately hire Black soldiers and confiscate Southern mansions. It also provided additional time to make the political and military arrangements that might eliminate the need for any emancipation. And, to extend the argument, if these arrangements failed and he was actually forced to sign the document, he could draft it so that it would not actually free anybody. Best of all, war proclamations, as he never stopped saying later, were *war* proclamations that expired with the war, were of questionable legality and would end up finally in the hands of judges.

Did Lincoln perceive all this? We don't know, and it doesn't matter. What matters historically is not what he perceived but what he did; and what he did historically on the emancipation issue from July 1862 to 1864 followed the assumptions outlined above so closely that this script or one similar to it must have been in his mind or unconscious. Lincoln, for instance, used the deceiving armistice (between Lincoln and liberal Republicans) following his 1862 proclamation to ignore or sidetrack the Confiscation Act and the antislavery initiatives mandated by Congress. Was this instinct, accident, or design? In the same period, Lincoln signed two emancipation proclamations and both were drafted in such a way that they freed no slaves. Was this inadvertence, inattention, or strategy? From 1863 to 1865, Lincoln said privately and publicly that the Emancipation Proclamation was a war measure of doubtful legality and that it would have no force when the war ended. Was this plan or pretext? No matter. Lincoln couldn't have followed the script better if he had written it himself.

No other hypothesis, moreover, explains so fully what he did and didn't do from 1862 to 1864 when the forces accidentally unleashed by his limited tactical moves overwhelmed him and made him assume, at least publicly, the emancipation role he had resisted all his life. Nor does any other hypothesis explain contradictory moves that make no sense otherwise. Why, for example, did he continue to argue for a gradual emancipation plan that contradicted and threatened the Emancipation Proclamation? If Congress had adopted the Lincoln plan, which included a proposed thirteenth amendment, the Emancipation Proclamation, as Ralph Korngold said, would have been negated and it would have been impossible to pass the real Thirteenth Amendment (1955, 179).

Was this inadvertence or design? And how many inadvertencies pointing to the same end do we need before we can call a blueprint a blueprint?

In any case, it is evident that Lincoln was doing more—and less—than what he said he was doing when he told his cabinet on Tuesday, July 22, that he was going to issue an emancipation proclamation freeing the slaves. In appraising this announcement, we have to note first that the July 22 cabinet meeting was not an isolated event, as so many commentators say, but the second part of a two-day discussion on a number of issues, including the colonization of Blacks, the arming of Blacks, and two contradictory emancipation plans. Significantly, the second session—where the Emancipation Proclamation was *not* issued—was considered so uneventful that one of Washington's biggest gossip diarists didn't even note the event in his diary. Even more astonishing, two of the main participants—President Lincoln and Secretary Welles—couldn't remember later whether the meeting took place in July or August or on a Saturday or Tuesday. How explain this? The explanation is simple. The July 22 cabinet meeting is one of the biggest nonevents in American history, marking a spot and a time where nothing happened.

The main evidence of Lincoln defenders is the uncorroborated account painter F. B. Carpenter gave in his book, *Six Months At The White House.* From February 1864 to July 1864, Carpenter lived at the White House while painting a fanciful portrait of the first reading of the Emancipation Proclamation. Certain contemporaries, Mary Todd Lincoln and Herndon among them, warned against accepting Carpenter's account unreservedly. Allan Nevins conceded that the Carpenter account is a secondhand source but said "we must take his record in default of a better" (165).

Nevins is wrong. There is a better record, the two firsthand contemporary accounts by Secretary Chase and Secretary Stanton, which must, under prevailing rules of evidence, be accepted above all other accounts, including the error-ridden account Lincoln reportedly gave Carpenter some twenty months after the event. It is important also to remember that Carpenter didn't make notes at the time and reconstructed Lincoln's words months later from memory. For all that, the Carpenter account has certain points of interest. Notice his art in a detailed and flowing (and uncorroborated) report that would have taxed a court report. Notice also that this is the self-serving statement of a great storyteller, who omitted critical details and emphasized others that were crucial in the developing portrait that *he* was painting of his role in an event he didn't understand or accept or praise until after the event.

"It had got to be midsummer, 1862," Lincoln said, according to Carpenter (20-4.). "Things had gone on from bad to worse, until I felt that we had reached the end of our rope on the plan of operations we had been pursuing; that we had about played our last card, and must change our tactics, or lose the game!"

Go back and read that second sentence, which is one of those marvelous moments in the Lincoln sound stage when he tells the truth despite himself. Analyzing this sentence, Hofstadter said nothing was more revealing of the true Lincoln spirit: Things had gone from bad to worse and *therefore* it was necessary to free the slaves.

Under these circumstances, and, by his own admission, against his will, Lincoln said: "I now determined upon the adoption of the emancipation policy; and, without consultation with, or the knowledge of the Cabinet, I prepared the original draft of the proclamation, and, after much anxious thought, called a Cabinet meeting upon the subject. This was the last of July, or the first part of the month of August, 1862. (The exact date he did not remember.) [The exact date was July 1862]. "This Cabinet meeting took place, I think, upon a Saturday. [The cabinet meeting took place on a Tuesday]."

This was the way Lincoln described the cabinet meeting that occurred in a month and on a day that he didn't really remember:

> All were present, excepting Mr. Blair, the Postmaster-General, who was absent at the opening of the discussion, but came in subsequently. I said to the Cabinet that I had resolved upon this step, and had not called them together to ask their advice, but to

lay the subject-matter of a proclamation before them; suggestions as to which would be in order, after they had heard it read . . . . Various suggestions were offered. Secretary Chase wished the language stronger in reference to the arming of the blacks. [There is nothing in the July 22 document about the arming of the Blacks.] Mr. Blair, after he came in, deprecated the policy, on the ground that it would cost the Administration the fall elections.

Nothing, however, was offered, Lincoln said, that he had not already anticipated until Secretary Seward spoke up.

He said in substance: 'Mr. President, I approve of the proclamation, but I question the expediency of its issue at this juncture. The depression of the public mind, consequent upon our repeated reverses, is so great that I fear the effect of so important a step. It may be viewed as the last measure of an exhausted government, a cry for help; the government stretching forth its hands to Ethiopia, instead of Ethiopia stretching forth her hands to the government.' His idea," said the President, "was that it would be considered our last *shriek*, on the retreat." (This was his *precise* expression.) "'Now,' continued Mr. Seward, 'while I approve the measure, I suggest, sir, that you postpone its issue, until you can give it to the country supported by military success, instead of issuing it, as would be the case now, upon the greatest disasters of the war!" Mr. Lincoln continued: "The wisdom of the view of the Secretary of State struck me with very great force. It was an aspect of the case that, in all my thought upon the subject, I had entirely overlooked. The result was that I put the draft of the proclamation aside, as you do your sketch for a picture, waiting for a victory."

If we examine the self-serving, secondhand Lincoln-Carpenter account closely, we find that it is made up of four germinal themes: 1) The Eroica Theme of a hero who makes a hard decision and takes responsibility for it; 2) The Last Card; 3) The Last Shriek or Ethiopia To The Rescue; 4) Waiting for Godot or McClellan. The only two contemporary reports—and the only two reliable accounts—a memorandum made at the time by Secretary of War Stanton and a diary account by Secretary Chase—do not corroborate 1, 2, 3, or 4.

Here, for example, is the memorandum prepared at the time by Secretary Stanton:

Tuesday, July 22

The President proposes to issue an order declaring that, all slaves in States in rebellion on the . . . day of . . .

The Attorney-General and Stanton are for its immediate promulgation.

Seward against it; argues strongly in favor of cotton and foreign Governments.

Chase silent.

Welles . . .

Seward argues . . . That foreign nations will intervene to prevent the abolition of slavery for sake of cotton. Argues in a long speech against its immediate promulgation. Wants to wait for troops. Wants Halleck here. Wants drum & fife and public spirit. We break up our relations with foreign nations and the production of cotton for sixty years.

Chase . . . thinks it a measure of great danger, and would lead to universal emancipation . . . The measure goes beyond anything I have recommended. (NH 6:128)

The other contemporary document, the diary entry of Secretary Chase, gives the only full account of the meeting and starts on July 21, not July 22. In this diary entry, dated Monday, July 21, 1862, Secretary Chase says he received a notice to attend a cabinet meeting at 10 a.m on July 21 (CD 95-100).

I went at the appointed hour, and found that the President had been profoundly concerned at the present aspect of affairs, and had determined to take some definitive steps in respect to military action and slavery. He had prepared several Orders, the first of which contemplated authority to Commanders to subsist their troops in the hostile territory—the second, authority to

employ Negroes as laborers—the third requiring that both in the
case of property taken and of Negroes employed, accounts
should be kept with such degrees of certainty as would enable
compensation to be made in proper cases—another provided for
the colonization of Negroes in some tropical country.

There was, Chase said, a good deal of discussion on the three
points. In the end, he said, the first order was "universally approved."
The second was approved entirely; and the third was approved by all
except Chase, who doubted "the expediency of attempting to keep
accounts for the benefit of the inhabitants of the rebel States."

> The Secretary of War [then] presented some letters from Genl.
> Hunter, in which he [asked for authorization] to enlist all loyal
> persons without reference to complection. Messrs. Stanton, Seward
> and myself, expressed ourselves in favor of this plan, and no one
> expressed himself against it. (Mr. Blair was not present.) The Pres-
> ident was not prepared to decide the question, but expressed him-
> self as averse to arming Negroes. The whole matter was post-
> poned until tomorrow.

If we dig deeper into the Chase account, several things become
obvious. There was, first of all, no mention of emancipation on the
first day of the meeting, and, secondly, Lincoln didn't on this day or
the next one, according to the only contemporary evidence, go
through the Napoleon routine of announcing that he was in charge
and that he had already made a decision. When the meeting continued on the next day, Tuesday, July 22, Chase said:

> It was unanimously agreed that the Order in respect to Coloniza-
> tion should be dropped; and the others were adopted unani-
> mously . . . .
> The question of arming slaves was then brought up and I advo-
> cated it warmly. The President was unwilling to adopt this mea-
> sure, but proposed to issue a Proclamation, on the basis of the
> Confiscation Bill, calling upon the States to return to their alle-
> giance—warning the rebels the provisions of the Act would have

full force at the expiration of sixty days—adding, on his own part, a declaration of his intention to renew, at the next session of Congress, his recommendation of compensation to States adopting the gradual abolishment of slavery—and proclaiming the emancipation of all slaves within States remaining in insurrection on the first of January, 1863.

This was a mouthful, and an anticlimactic mouthful at that, for the major announcement was tacked on at the end, almost as an afterthought. Chase said he and others were surprised by the proposed proclamation and the subject was discussed pro and con without agreement.

What was the result of the meeting? How did it end? It ended, as almost all bureaucratic meetings end, not with a bang but with a whimper:

> The President determined to publish the first three Orders . . . and to leave the other for some further consideration . . . .

This is a critical eyewitness account and deserves an instant replay, in slow motion if possible. For Chase tells us first that the July 22 meeting continued the dialogue of the preceding day and that it was agreed, apparently without any dissent, to publish the first three orders and to leave the emancipation order for further consideration.

One of the warmest legends of the war recounts in loving detail how Lincoln worked for weeks on the proclamation, sitting in the telegraph office, looking into space, painfully dredging up sentence after sentence. This is a libel on a great writer. The forty-three or so lines he read to the cabinet on July 22 could have been written by any entry-level bureaucrat on his/her lunch hour. Since the first eleven lines quoted the Confiscation Act, which was passed on July 17, it is virtually certain, as Neely and others have said, that the document was cobbled together in the four days between July 18 and July 22. In the remaining lines, Lincoln squared the emancipation circle, offering two diametrically opposed modes of emancipation. One said he would ask Congress to approve the gradual, compensated emancipation plan that Border States representatives had turned down eight days before. The other said he would free all slaves in rebel-held states on January 1.

Here are the lines; let's read them together. The boiler-plate announcement required by the Confiscation Act is in regular type. The twice-rejected compensated emancipation proposal is in italics. The *one sentence* on the emancipation proclamation is in boldface.

In pursuance of the sixth section of the act of congress entitled "An act to suppress insurrection and to punish treason and rebellion, to seize and confiscate property of rebels, and for other purposes" Approved July 17, 1862, and which act, and the Joint Resolution explanatory thereof, are herewith published, I, Abraham Lincoln, President of the United States, do hereby proclaim to, and warn all persons within the contemplation of said sixth section to cease participating in, aiding, countenancing, or abetting the existing rebellion, or any rebellion against the government of the United States, and to return to their proper allegiance to the United States, on pain of the forfeitures and seizures, as within and by said sixth section provided.

And I hereby make known that it is my purpose, upon the next meeting of Congress, to again recommend the adoption of a practical measure for tendering pecuniary aid to the free choice or rejection, of any and all States which may then be recognizing and practically sustaining the authority of the United States, and which may then have voluntarily adopted, or thereafter may voluntarily adopt, gradual abolishment of slavery within such State or States—that the object is to practically restore, thenceforward to be maintain[ed], the constitutional relation between the general government, and each, and all the states, wherein that relation is now suspended, or disturbed; and that, for this object, the war, as it has been, will be, prosecuted. **And, as a fit and necessary military measure for effecting this object, I, as Commander-in-Chief of the Army and Navy of the United States, do order and**

declare that on the first day of January in the year of Our Lord one thousand, eight hundred and sixtythree, all persons held as slaves within any state or states, wherein the constitutional authority of the United States shall not then be practically recognized, submitted to, and maintained, shall then, thenceforward, and forever, be free. (CW 5:336-7)

Generation after generation of Americans have been raised on the poetic image of the heroic Lincoln reluctantly putting the document aside. How many times—many more than I care to remember—have we been charmed—and misled—by the moving story of how the careworn president put away the signed document to await a Union victory that would permit him to fulfill his lifelong pledge to "free" the long-suffering slaves.

Diverted by these and other pleasantries, almost all readers, and not a few historians, have neglected to notice that the major events of this day happened not during the cabinet meeting but before and afterward. For, as John Hope Franklin and others have noted, Lincoln, as usual, was still undecided and still on the fence at the end of the meeting. One of the main reasons he was still undecided was a two-hour conference he held *before* the meeting with Francis Brockholst Cutting, a proslavery New York Democrat who argued strongly in favor of an emancipation proclamation. Cutting told Lincoln that his fears about the Border States were groundless and that "we had already sacrificed too much to the vain attempt to conciliate these people, a majority of whom were at heart disloyal, or not better than neutral . . . ."

Based on a long Cutting letter on this meeting, and other information, some historians say Cutting met with Lincoln for a second time after the cabinet meeting. But a careful reading of the Cutting letter suggests that Stanton, not Cutting, conferred with Lincoln after the cabinet meeting and that Lincoln told Stanton that he had been impressed by Cutting's argument and that he intended to issue the proclamation the next day. Here is the language Cutting used in a letter of understanding to Stanton: "On the afternoon of the same day [July 22] I saw you again, and had the satisfaction to hear that after referring to his conversation with me *he had informed you* it was his intention on the following day to issue his Proclamation."[49]

Not everyone shared Cutting's certainty. Seward, who had less faith in the Last Shriek argument than modern scholars, had sent for reinforcements, which arrived in the nick of time, according to the *New York Tribune's* "Washington Report, "which had an interesting item: "Thurlow Weed is in town?"

Why was Seward's ally, master political operator Thurlow Weed, in town, and how did he know he would be needed that night to hold Lincoln's hand? The only tenable answer is that Weed's ally, Secretary Seward, knew *before* July 22 what Lincoln was going to say on July 22 and that Weed would be needed to scare him out of it with stories of White ethnic rioting and Democratic generals defecting and dominoes falling in Kentucky, Maryland, and Missouri.

Thus it came to pass that Weed, the consummate political fixer, met with Lincoln that night and argued passionately against the proclamation, saying it would accomplish nothing and would cause adverse political, military and diplomatic reactions. Persuaded by the fears of Weed, Seward, and Blair and by fears of his own, Lincoln retreated, and July 23 came and went without a proclamation to make it famous.

The proof of all this—and indisputable proof against the dominant theory of the Lincoln establishment—is that Weed and Cutting ran into each other on the morning of the twenty-third at Willard's Hotel. "After the usual Salutations," Cutting said, "he stated in substance that he had undone in the evening what I had nearly accomplished in the morning; that after further reflexion the President had decided to postpone the Proclamation." Cutting expressed regrets but Weed told him he [Weed] had persuaded Lincoln not to issue the proclamation "because as the war then stood, it could not be enforced in the Rebel States—that it would add to the intensity of their hatred, and might occasion serious disaffection to the Union cause in the border States; that it could work no good and probably would do much harm, and that it was more prudent to wait on events."[50]

To recapitulate, then, on the basis of the only contemporary evidence we have—evidence that destroys the Last Shriek Theory on which almost all scholars based their Proclamation melodrama—Lincoln, responding to unprecedented political and military challenges, decided to float four new departures on emancipation and slaves at cabinet meetings on July 21 and July 22, 1862.

1. On July 21, he proposed several orders, one authorizing commanders to live on the land in hostile territory, the second authorizing commanders to use Blacks as laborers, the third requiring commanders to keep accurate records of confiscated property and slaves, the fourth providing for the colonization of Blacks. The Secretary of War presented a proposal for the utilization of Black troops. Although every cabinet member present approved, Abraham Lincoln balked, saying he was "averse to arming Negroes," and the whole matter was postponed until the next day.

2. Before the continuation of the cabinet meeting on Tuesday, July 22, Lincoln conferred with a prominent Democrat who happened apparently to be in the White House. According to this Democrat, Francis B. Cutting, Lincoln said he was worried about adverse political and military reaction. Cutting said he told Lincoln that his fears were groundless and that a proclamation would save the Union by making it difficult and perhaps impossible for European countries to recognize the Confederacy.

3. At the continued cabinet meeting, Lincoln announced that he intended to renew his compensated emancipation proposal and issue a proclamation freeing Blacks in all states in insurrection on January 1, 1863. Most members of the cabinet approved this new departure, but at least two—Secretary of State Seward and Postmaster Blair—disapproved, citing potential political and military problems.

4. The meeting ended inconclusively, Secretary Chase said, with a decision to publish the first three orders and "to leave the other for some further consideration."

5. After the meeting, Lincoln, if we can believe Cutting, changed his mind for the third time that day, saying that he was going to issue

the proclamation the next day.

6. Lincoln changed his mind for the fourth time that day after a late-night meeting with Seward ally, Thurlow Weed, who told him a proclamation would have disastrous political and military effects.

7. The proclamation was not issued on Wednesday and was not discussed again in cabinet, Welles said, until September. Weed told Cutting on Wednesday morning that he had persuaded Lincoln not to issue the proclamation, citing the usual fears about Border State defections.

Thus, on July 22, 1862, Abraham Lincoln came to the Rubicon and the Mississippi and the Nile—and remained on dry land.

A charming—and absurd—part of the emancipation myth is that Lincoln and his men kept the details of the meeting secret for at least two months. Anybody who knows Washington—the Washington of 1862 or the Washington of 2000—knows that that was impossible. Even before Lincoln held his late-night meeting with Weed, insiders knew that a cabinet meeting had been held and had a good idea of who said what and why. In fact, a *New York Tribune* story, *printed on the day of the cabinet meeting,* told its readers that the president was going to issue important general orders, which, according "to some who have seen these orders," spell "the doom of the peculiar institution."

The *Tribune* told its readers to watch for a forthcoming exclusive on the orders and was embarrassed when Lincoln didn't sign the proclamation that Lincoln or somebody had told Deep Throat—was it Sumner, Stanton, Assistant Secretary of War Peter H. Watson, or General James S. Wadsworth?—that Lincoln was going to sign. *Tribune* Washington correspondent Adams S. Hill told his boss on July 24 "that a part of what Sumner thought would be in the order was omitted, subsequently, and that he was led a little astray by the Presd't" (Gay). In an August 21 "fragment," Hill reported that "Gurowski says that he *knows* that the President had an emancipation proclamation prepared three weeks ago & would have issued it, but for the opposition of Seward & Blair, reinforced by T. Weed. Sumner says substantially the same thing, says that at all the Cabinet meetings where the subject has been under discussion, they two aided by T. W. outside opposed the policy, tooth and nail . . . ."

Despite overwhelming evidence to the contrary, Lincoln specialists still base the Lincoln emancipation myth on the idea that Lincoln and his cabinet kept his proclamation proposal secret for two months. It was no secret. It was all over town. On Friday, August 22, the *New York Tribune* said it had heard the story from so many sources that it could no longer be considered a state secret, adding:

"Two or three weeks ago—the Presdnt laid before his Cabinet a proclamation of Emancipation abolishing Slavery wherever on the first of next December the Rebellion should not be crushed . . . . All but two, Secretary Smith, we believe being absent, approved. Secretary Seward and Postmaster General Blair, however, opposed it with all their might, and the result was that it did not appear . . . ."

In a letter to Massachusetts Governor John A. Andrew, Count Gurowski added additional details, saying Weed had helped change Lincoln's mind. In a note that he made in his diary, Gurowski said:

> *Vulgatior fama est*, that Mr. Lincoln was already raising his hand to sign a stirring proclamation on the question of emancipation; that Stanton was upholding the President's arm that it might not grow weak in the performance of a sacred duty; but that Messrs. Seward and Blair so firmly objected that the President's outstretched hand slowly began to fall back; that to precipitate the mortification, Thurlow Weed was telegraphed; that Thurlow Weed presented to Mr. Lincoln the Medusa-head of Irish riots in the North against the emancipation of slaves in the South; that Mr. Lincoln's mind faltered . . . before such a Chinese shadow, and that thus once more slavery was saved. *Relata refereo.* (1:245)

Three days after the cabinet meeting, on July 25, Lincoln provided the public warning the Confiscation Act required by issuing a proclamation consisting of the first paragraph of his abandoned proclamation. In the process, he himself provided compelling evidence of his continuing opposition to emancipation, for, as the *New York Tribune* noted on July 28, the proclamation on the enforcement of the Confiscation Act didn't even mention the ninth section, which freed the slaves of all rebels, that is to say, practically all slaves, as of July 17. Why—the *Tribune* and abolitionists and Black leaders asked—did Lincoln ignore this revolutionary proclamation?

The answer to that question, as it is to so many other strange happenings in this history, is in the political schizophrenia that makes Lincoln incomprehensible in July 1862. He started the month, as we have seen, by saying on July 1 that "so much of [slavery] as remained after the war will be in precisely the same condition that it was before the war." But all signals changed when Congress gave a clear signal that the revolutionary Confiscation Act was going to pass.

That happened on Saturday, July 12. The next day, July 13, a new Lincoln, a Lincoln that nobody, Welles said, had ever seen before, surfaced with a story nobody had ever heard him tell. It was time, he said, to disturb the institution and "he had about"come to a decision to issue an emancipation proclamation.

The new Lincoln was next seen nine days later at the cabinet meeting where he made substantially the same announcement. Then a strange thing happened. The new Lincoln disappeared and was replaced by the old Lincoln, who continued to say the same things the old Lincoln had been saying for years. It is tempting to deny that the new Lincoln ever existed, especially since there were only two sightings and since the old Lincoln returned—six days after the cabinet meeting—to the same theme he stressed in his meeting with the Border State representatives, telling a Southern White loyalist that "it is a military necessity to have men and money; and we can get neither, in sufficient numbers, or amounts, if we keep from, or drive from, our lines, slaves coming to them." He then went on to corroborate once again Rule Five (page 416) of the Lincoln Rules for the Road, saying that "*Mr. Durant cannot be ignorant of the pressure in this direction; nor of my efforts to hold it within bounds till he, and such as he shall have time to help themselves"* (CW 5:345, italics added).

What was the mood of the Lincoln White House at this critical moment in the war? Did visitors, especially antislavery visitors, get the sense that Lincoln had turned a corner and was heading toward glory? General James S. Wadsworth, who had been "with the President and Stanton every day at the War Department—frequently for five or six hours—during several months," told *New York Tribune* correspondent Adams S. Hill that Lincoln was still committed to the Old Union and was on his way to the other place. "He says," Hill told his managing editor, "that the President is not with us; has no Anti-slavery instincts. He never heard him speak of Anti-slavery men, otherwise than as 'radicals,' 'abolitionists,' and of the 'nigger question,' he frequently speaks." Wadsworth believed at this crucial juncture that if emancipation came at all it would come not from Abraham Lincoln but "from the rebels, or in consequence of their protracting the war" (Rhodes 4:64).

Lincoln himself provided evidence for the Wadsworth view, ending the month as he began it, with a long look backward at his dream of saving the half-slave, half-free Union he loved. In a letter to financier August Belmont, who had forwarded a letter from a disappointed Southern White loyalist, Lincoln said "broken eggs cannot be mended; but Louisiana has nothing to do but to take her place in the Union as it was, barring the already broken eggs. The sooner she does so, the smaller will be the amount of that which will be past mending . . . . If they [Southern Whites] expect in any contingency to ever have the Union as it was, I join with the writer in saying, 'Now is the time'" (CW 5:350-1).

Do you believe that?

A fifty-three old man, a professional politician holding the office of president of the United States, actually said on July 31, 1862, that it was still possible to restore "the Union as it was."

How, after the hundreds of thousands of Union casualties and the Second Confiscation Act and Shiloh and Corinth, could he or anyone else fail to see that the time for the Union as it was, was gone with McClellan and Halleck and the wind?

Lincoln hadn't changed.

There is no evidence that he ever changed. Consider, for example, what he said and did at a cabinet meeting in the first week of August. "There was a good deal of conversation" at this meeting on Sunday, August 3, Secretary Chase wrote, "on the connection of the Slavery question with the rebellion." Chase said he expressed his conviction "for the tenth or twentieth time, that the time for the suppression of the rebellion without interference with slavery had long passed . . . that the bitterness of the conflict had now substantially united the white population of the rebel States against us . . . that the blacks were really the only loyal population worth counting and that, in the Gulf States at least, their right to Freedom ought to be at once recognized, while, in the Border States, the President's plan of Emancipation might be made the basis of the necessary measures for their ultimate enfranchisement . . . ."

Although Chase made a diplomatic bow to "the President's plan" of compensated emancipation in the Border States, and although Seward said he was in favor of any measure that would accomplish "the results [Chase] contemplated, which could be carried into effect without Proclamations," Lincoln rejected the idea of immediate emancipation of Blacks in the Gulf States, saying he was not "satisfied that the time had come for the adoption of such a plan . . ." (CD 105-6).

What is astonishing is that nobody, according to Chase's diary, said a word about Lincoln's proposed emancipation proclamation at the August meeting, if we except Seward's cryptic support of any policy that could be executed "without Proclamations." In the days that followed, Lincoln's proposed emancipation proclamation disappeared from view, like a harpooned whale.

"I do not recollect," Welles said later, "that it was again alluded to in Cabinet until after the battle of Antietam, which took place . . . six weeks later." (WH 845).

21

Lincoln Asks Blacks To Leave America

L INCOLN'S conversion didn't last long. After mentioning emancipation two times on two days in July—July 13 and July 22—Lincoln reversed his field and said in August what he had said before July, that emancipating Blacks would be inexpedient, impolitic and provoking to Kentucky.

Lincoln partisans would say later that Lincoln was playing possum and that he didn't really believe what he said in August, but you couldn't prove it by the men who heard him say it.

Secretary of the Treasury Chase said Lincoln told his cabinet on August 3—twelve days after the July 22 announcement—that he was opposed to emancipation in the Gulf States.

A high-level delegation of Midwesterners said he told them that he would rather resign than use Black soldiers to kill White men.

A Lincoln crony said he told him "frankly" that he was not going to emancipate the slaves.

Cassius Clay of Kentucky said he told him in August what he had told him and everybody else before August, that he couldn't do anything about emancipation because he was scared Kentucky would join the Confederacy or do something else foolish. Clay told the president, as one Kentuckian to another, that he was mistaken and that all Kentuckians who were going to join the Confederacy were already in the Confederacy and that "ten men would not be changed" (RR 303-4). This didn't change Lincoln, who kept on telling his Kentucky stories and opposing antislavery initiatives.

In a fragment of a letter, dated August 21, Adams S. Hill said a certain W.J.A. Fuller told him that the president "entertained" him "with a long argument against emancipation, unburdering his mind without stories [and] combatting F's arguments" (Gay).

Monitoring all this, and collating the information he received from Lincoln insiders, Adam Gurowski told his diary in August 1862 that "the President is indefatigable in his efforts to—save slavery" (1:256).

He was also indefatigable in his efforts to ship Blacks out of the country. Since his first days in office, he had maneuvered to fulfill his Illinois dream of ensuring that Blacks left America "in a body," as the Hebrew children left Egypt. His election gave him an unexampled opportunity to make his private fantasy a public reality, and he worked fervently in 1861 and 1862, trying to organize a national campaign to deport Blacks.

When, largely at his insistence, Congress appropriated money to colonize Blacks freed by the D.C. emancipation act and the confiscation acts, he told Secretary of the Interior Caleb Blood Smith to make a deal with Ambrose W. Thompson, a shady character who said he had a long-term lease on what Lincoln considered a potential Negro paradise on an isthmus in what is now Panama.

To facilitate his plans for the racial cleansing of America, Lincoln created a Black emigration department, without giving it that name, in the Interior Department and employed James Mitchell, an Indiana minister and American Colonization Society activist who had worked with him on colonization issues in Springfield. At Lincoln's direction, or at least with Lincoln's approval, Mitchell prepared a master plan for the final solution of the Black problem, *Letter on the Relation of the White and African Races in the United States, Showing the Necessity of the Colonization of the Latter.* In this official document of the U.S. government, printed by the Government Printing Office and mailed on May 18, 1862, to "His Excellency Abraham Lincoln," Mitchell said that the presence of the Negro race on the North American continent was more dangerous to the peace of the country than the

Civil War. For "terrible as is this civil war between men of kindred race for the dominion of the servant, future history will show that it has been moderate and altogether tolerable when contrasted with a struggle between the black and white race, which, within the next one or two hundred years must sweep over this nation, unless the wise and prudent statesmen of this generation avert it" (3).

The chief danger in the future, Mitchell told Lincoln, was that "we have 4,500,000 persons, who, whilst amongst us, cannot be of us . . ." (4).

Why couldn't they be "of us"?

They were, he said, of a different race, a race that threatens the blood stream of the nation and "is giving to this continent a nation of bastards."

Sex: for Lincoln and for almost all his men, the basic problem was sex. On page after page of his government-sponsored diatribe, Mitchell warns against endangering the purity of White blood by "this repulsive admixture of blood," the "possible admixture of infe-rior blood," attempts to engraft "Negro blood on the population," and attempts "to pour the blood of near five million Africans into the veins of the Republic" (10, 23, 8).

This was a threat, he said, to the White nation and the purity of White blood. It was a threat to "our people, the men of Europe," who constituted "one family, *ordered so of God*, and by him kept com-pact and together through the ages gone" (italics added).

Mitchell saw conspirators everywhere and warned Lincoln against England and France as well as New England idealists who were op-posing efforts to colonize Blacks and who were therefore working together to make the White men of America dilute their blood. He even charged that some Blacks were deliberately using sex for politi-cal reasons, furthering a strategy "predicated on the hope of the col-ored race to rise by the illicit absorption of their blood into the mass of this nation." Time and again, Mitchell said, "has this hope been expressed in our hearing" (5).

What was the solution?

The solution was "perfecting the proposed plans of the [Lincoln] administration" and "the careful and gradual removal of the colored race to some desirable and convenient home" in the tropical lands of South America or Africa. It was necessary to remove all Blacks, for "our republican institutions are not adapted to mixed races and classified people. Our institutions require a homogenous population to rest on as a basis" (24, 26), a view that Lincoln echoed in his "physical difference" theory.

God, Rev. Mitchell said, was in his—and Lincoln's—plan.

"'God ordained in the beginning a separate and distinct subsistence for the great races of men . . . 'when he determined the times before appointed, and the bounds of their habitation'" (25-6).

Mitchell prayed that "a perpetual barrier" would be "reared between us and that land of the mixed races of this continent—Mexico." Then, mixing metaphors and races, he said, "As Abraham and Lot agreed to separate their conflicting retainers and dependents, the one going to the right and the other to the left, so let these two governments agree to divide this continent between the Anglo-American and mixed races," the Anglo-American taking the Northern road, and Africans and mixed races taking Central America, "which nature, in her wisdom, has prepared for them, and which for beauty, fertility, and grandeur of scenery, cannot be equaled on the globe . . ." (26).

The major obstacle to realizing this new Eden was the African-American, a race that "has hardly attained a mental majority" and cannot be expected to rise in a day to the grandeur of the White race which founded empires and laid "the ground work of civil institutions like ours" (25). Mitchell didn't find it necessary to remind Lincoln that it was the Black race, not the White race, which created the foundations of American wealth, and Lincoln made no mention of that fact when he appropriated Mitchell's idea and told a group of Blacks, as we shall see below, that "you should sacrifice something of your present comfort for the purpose of being as grand in that respect as the white people" (CW 5:373).

To make Blacks as grand in that respect as Whites, and to overcome "the natural inertia" of Black critics of colonization, Mitchell told Lincoln he should try, first, to win over "intelligent" Blacks, a plan Lincoln adopted, and to use a little "gentle pressure" which the world would not, he thought, condemn.

What if the "gentle" pressure failed?

Then, he told His Excellency, "there would . . . be more propriety in weighing the requirement of some to remove without consultation, *but not till then*." There is, he wrote, "a growing sentiment in this country which considers the removal of the freed man, without consulting him, '*a moral and military necessity*'—as a measure necessary to the purity of public morals and the peace of the country . . . . But we cannot go further now than suggesting, that the mandatory relation held by the rebel master should escheat to the Federal government in a modified sense, as to enable his proper government and gradual removal to a proper home where he can be independent" (25, italics in original).

What Mitchell was saying here, in plain English, was that the freed slave would become, under his and presumably Lincoln's, colonization plan, a slave "in a modified sense" of the federal government, which could use a "mandatory relation" in shipping him to South America or Africa. In any event, "the peace and prosperity of the country and the permanency of our republican civilization, required a separation of the colored or Negro race from us . . ." which would make America "the light of the world" (27) or, as Lincoln put it later, "the last best, hope of the world."

It would be pleasant to report that Abraham Lincoln read this repulsive mixture of racism and fascism and immediately fired Rev. Mitchell. But instead of firing Mitchell, Lincoln promoted him and gave him the task of rounding up four or five "intelligent" colored men who believed in colonization and who were willing to listen to Abraham Lincoln tell them why it was good for them.

And so, on Thursday, August 14, the Rev. James Mitchell, the man the *New York Tribune* and other papers called America's official "Commissioner of [Black] Emigration," led a group of five Black men into the executive office and introduced them to His Excellency Abraham Lincoln. This was, we are told, the first time in history that African-Americans had been invited to the White House to confer on an official matter. If so, it was an inauspicious occasion, for the president of the United States used this forum to tell native-born Americans of African descent that it was their duty to leave America for racial reasons.

The chairman of the group, the Rev. Edward M. Thomas, gave the game away by saying "they were there by invitation to hear what the Executive had to say." Lincoln, delighted, began his monologue by saying that "a sum of money had been appropriated by Congress, and placed at his disposition for the purpose of aiding the colonization in some country of the people, or a portion of them, of African descent, thereby making it his duty, *as it had for a long time been his inclination*, to favor that cause . . ." (CW 5:370-5, italics added).

Why was this necessary? Lincoln asked, adopting, as Michael Vorenberg said, "the unfortunate tone of a condescending [great White] father scolding ignorant children" (33). Why "should the people of your race be colonized, and where? Why should they leave this country?"

The reason, Lincoln said, going back to the Lincoln-Douglas debate was the "physical difference" between Blacks and Whites.

"You and we," he said, "are different races. We have between us a broader difference than exists between almost any other two races. Whether it is right or wrong I need not discuss, but this physical difference is a great disadvantage to us both, as I think your race suffer very greatly, many of them by living among us, while ours suffer from your presence."

More to the point, Lincoln said, Negroes were the cause of the problem and the war. "But for your race among us there could not be a war, although many men engaged on either side do not care for you one way or the other."

There were two or three moments—no more—in the conflicted and conflicting life of this fascinating and faulty man when he confronted the horror of what racism has done to Blacks and Whites. One was when he told the five African-Americans that "*your race are suffering, in my judgment, the greatest wrong inflicted on any people.*"

Here at long last was a Lincoln analysis. The solution to that national crime, Lincoln critics said, was to wage war on the institutions and people in the North and South, Lincoln among them, who were by acts of omission and commission inflicting "the greatest wrong" ever "inflicted on any people." The solution was for Lincoln to convert himself and others in a lifelong struggle against slavery and segregation and the spirit of slavery and segregation.

But Lincoln had no intention of dealing with racism or even discussing it. He didn't seek the opinions of his visitors. He was simply, he said, presenting a fact: Whites didn't want Blacks in America and therefore Blacks would have to go. "There is an unwillingness on the part of our people, harsh as it may be, for you free colored people to remain with us." The only solution from his standpoint, that is to say, from a White standpoint, was a Black exodus."It is better for us both," he said *twice*, "to be separated."

Lincoln proposed a Black settlement on Central American land, "rich in coal" and asked his visitors to help him find Black settlers "capable of thinking as white men." The interview, as Lincoln anticipated, made national news. There was a headline in the August 15 edition of the *New York Tribune:*

SPEECH OF THE PRESIDENT
He Holds That the White and Black Races
Cannot Dwell Together

This is valuable testimony not only because it takes Lincoln's racial temperature at a critical juncture but also because it provides unassailable evidence against traditionalists who say Lincoln had already decided on an emancipation policy and was simpy waiting for a victory to announce it to the nation. No rational person, to paraphrase Korngold, could possibly believe that the man who made this statement was itching for an opportunity to turn African-Americans loose in America.

This idea, the idea of millions of African-Americans going to South America or Africa and leaving land they had helped develop in the hands of White people, moved Lincoln to poetry, and he asked his visitors "to consider seriously not pertaining to yourselves merely, nor for your race, and ours, for the present time, but as one of the things, if successfully managed, for the good of

mankind—not confined to the present generation, but as

> From age to age descends the lay,
> To millions yet to be,
> Till far its echoes roll away,
> Into eternity.

The response was immediate and explosive. Some Blacks said they had as much right as Abraham Lincoln to live in their native land. Others, more subversive perhaps, certainly more inventive, suggested that the easiest way to solve the problem was to remove the real problem, White people.

Despite the unimpeachable authority of a record that cannot be denied, despite the testimony of cabinet officials and cronies, and the testimony of Abraham Lincoln himself, some historians maintain that Lincoln was trying to fool Northern bigots and prepare the way for emancipation. If so, this was a strange way of going about it. For the effect of all this was to increase the level of racism in America. More than that, and more troubling than that, even today, is the obvious fact that the racism of the commander in chief of Union forces was giving aid and comfort to the enemies of the Union and especially White Northern sympathizers of the Southern cause.

Abolitionists and advocates of a hard war made these and other points in speeches and editorials. The *New York Tribune* said on August 16 that "with all deference to the President, we suggest that before our country begins the arduous, expensive task of exporting to some foreign shore Four Million of her loyal people, she should finish up the little job she has at hand by [exportation] of some thousands of her leading traitors . . . . After they should have been disposed of, we shall think of the expediency of exporting Four Millions of Unionists."

Frederick Douglass attacked Lincoln's logic and his racism, saying that "a horse thief pleading that the existence of the horse is the apology for his theft or a highway man contending that the money in the traveler's pocket is the sole first cause of his robbery are about as much entitled to respect as is the President's reasoning at this point. Lincoln's position didn't surprise Douglass. "Illogical and unfair as Mr. Lincoln's statements are, they are nevertheless quite in keeping with his whole course from the beginning of his administration up to this day, and confirm the painful conviction that though elected as an anti-slavery man by Republican and Abolition voters, Mr. Lincoln is quite a genuine representative of American prejudice and Negro hatred and far more concerned for the preservation of slavery, and the favor of the Border Slave States, than for any sentiment of magnanimity or principle of justice and humanity" (FD 3:268).

Additional and weighty reasons came from Philadelphia Blacks, who told Lincoln that there were strong "pecuniary and political" arguments against his proposal.

Blacks, they said, "have produced much of the wealth of this country" and "we constitute, including our property qualifications, almost the entire wealth of the Cotton States, and make up a large proportion of that of the others."

Therefore:

"We believe that the world would be benefitted by giving the four millions of slaves their freedom, and the lands now possessed by their masters. They have been amply compensated in our labor and the blood of our kinsmen. These masters 'toil not, neither do they spin.' They destroy, they consume, and give to the world in return but a small equivalent. They deprive us of 'life, liberty, and the pursuit of happiness'" (Aptheker 474-5).

Neither Charles Beard nor Karl Marx nor Andrew Brimmer could have improved on that analysis, which didn't, of course, change Lincoln's mind. But Lincoln, who was to the right of almost everybody on this issue, including, one might note, capitalists and plantation owners concerned about the labor supply, was not the only element in the equation. Southern Whites, who hated Lincoln and Blacks, were appalled by his naivete. They knew, if Lincoln didn't, that Blacks were the only people who worked in the South and that the South without Blacks would be a White wilderness.

There was even opposition within Lincoln's official family. Secretary Chase noted in his diary on Friday, August 15: "Saw in '*Republican*' account of interview invited by President with colored people, and his talk to them on Colonization. How much better would be a manly protest against prejudice against color!—and a wise effort to give freemen homes in America!" (CD 112).

The most serious charge against Lincoln came from Douglass and other Blacks who said the president of the United States was fanning the flames of bigotry and inciting acts of violence against Black men and women and their children.

"Mr. Lincoln takes care," Douglass wrote, "in urging his colonization scheme to furnish a weapon to all the ignorant and base, who need only the countenance of men in authority to commit all kinds of violence and outrage upon the colored people of the country." In pressing his suit, Lincoln, Douglass said, showed "all his inconsistencies, his pride of race and blood, his contempt for Negroes and his canting hypocrisy" (FD 3:267).

The same complaint was made by the Blacks of Newtown, Long Island, who held a mass meeting on August 20, 1862, and adopted resolutions which said, in part, that Blacks were at home and that they had "the right to have applied to ourselves those rights named in the Declaration of Independence." Like Douglass, they said that the president of the United States was serving as a cheerleader for "our enemies, who wish to insult and mob us, as we have, since [the publication of his statement], been repeatedly insulted, and told that we must leave the country" (Aptheker 472-3).

Lincoln's colonization campaign coincided with a wave of violent attacks on Blacks. In a report on "Persecution of Negroes," the *New York Tribune* said in an August 6 story that the wave of violence "commenced weeks ago in Cincinnati, Evansville, Ind., and Toledo."

The Toledo violence was "traced directly," the newspaper said, "to the instigation of emissaries from [New York City]." According to the *Tribune* report, the violence was instigated by Democrats and undercover Confederate agents.

"Months ago," the report continued, "when the Rebellion seemed at its last gasp, its partners in the loyal States were secretly impelled to get up a diversion in its favor by instigating riotous assaults on the unarmed and comparatively defenseless Blacks of our Northern cities. In furtherance of this plot, stories were started that thousands of Negroes at Washington, Fortress Monroe, and elsewhere, were being subsisted in idleness at public cost; next, that fugitive slaves were so abundant in Chester County, Pennsylvania, and its vicinity, that they were taking the bread out of the mouths of White laborers by working for ten cents a day . . . ."

The *New York Tribune* and other papers proved that these reports were false, citing, among other evidence, the fact that the labor market was so tight that White laborers could find jobs almost anywhere. Neither facts nor logic stopped the assaults. On Tuesday, August 4, "a serious riot" erupted in South Brooklyn when a mob of White ethnics tried to beat and burn to death Black women and children working at two tobacco factories owned by a certain "Mr. Lorillard."

Taking advantage of the temporary absence of the men, the mob chased the women and children to a top floor, barricaded the door and set the building on fire. The White police showed little or no interest in the attack, which was thwarted at the last minute by the return of the men. The *Tribune* reported on August 6 that the attack was "instigated and carried into effect by Democrats" and that the ringleader was a rum seller.

The wave of attacks got worse after publication of newspaper headlines on the president's proposal for a Black exodus. A week later, in the same area of South Brooklyn, Whites tried to lynch a Black on Furman Street. The leader of this mob, the New York *Tribune* said in an August 21 story, was a man who had deserted from a Brooklyn regiment after the Battle of Bull Run.

"With seemingly no regard for black reaction to this plan" (Vorenberg 34), Lincoln stepped up his high-visibility campaign to send Blacks away, making the White House the bully pit and national center of the colonization movement. Hustlers, promoters, zealots, land developers, international adventurers, and colonizationists from all over the United States made their way to the White House, and Lincoln received them with open arms.

The president, Secretary of the Navy Welles said, was importunate. He "had a belief, amounting almost to conviction that the two races could not dwell together in unity and as equals in their social relations" (WH 840-1).

In August, Lincoln held at least nine White House conferences on the subject. On August 18, Edward M. Thomas, chairman of the Black group which met with Lincoln on August 14, was back with a proposal for a national tour. Lincoln conferred with A.W. Thompson of the Chiriqui/Linconia colony on August 19 and met with M. T. Goswell of the same group on August 20. On August 24, he asked Dr. Orestes Brownson, editor of *Brownson's Review*, to support his colonization plans but was urged to concentrate on emancipation first. In a strange move on the same day, he named Senator Samuel Pomeroy of Kansas commissioner or coordinator of African colonization (LDD 3:133-6).

When, on Thursday, August 28, Central American governments protested the proposed Chiriqui colony, Lincoln and his cabinet backed away temporarily "from the president's plan of sending out a Negro colony this fall." This setback did not deter Lincoln, who pressed forward on other fronts. The *Chicago Tribune* reported on August 29 "that the president does not desire to have the matter abandoned here, and that Senator Pomeroy is yet expected to have some sort of roving commission to make explorations through the tropical regions of the continent, for a suitable locality for starting the proposed Negro colony."

Far from being an anomaly, Lincoln's ethnic cleansing plan was the cornerstone of his military and political agenda and was based on what Randall called a "grand design" for a new White America without slaves—and without Blacks.

In support of this White dream, Lincoln mobilized the State Department, the Interior Department, the Treasury Department, and the Smithsonian Institution. By the end of August, Lincoln's ethnic cleansing plan was the official policy of the Union.

Part Nine

"Let This Cup Pass From Me"

"September 27th. —*Had a call at the* Intelligencer *office from the Honorable Edward Stanly, Military Governor of North Carolina. In a long and interesting conversation Mr. Stanly related to me the substance of several interviews which he had had with the President respecting the Proclamation of Freedom. Mr. Stanly said that the President had stated to him that the proclamation had become a civil necessity to prevent the Radicals from openly embarrassing the government in the conduct of the war. The President expressed the belief that, without the proclamation for which they had been clamoring, the Radicals would take the extreme step in Congress of withholding supplies for carrying on the war—leaving the land in anarchy. Mr. Lincoln said that he had prayed to the Almighty to save him from this necessity, adopting the very language of our Saviour, 'If it be possible, let this cup pass from me,' but the prayer had not been answered.*"

—Diary of editor James C. Welling

On Tuesday last the President brought forward the subject and desired the members of the Cabinet to each take it into serious consideration. He thought a treaty could be made to advantage, and territory secured to which the Negroes could be sent. Thought it essential to provide an asylum for a race which we had emancipated, but which could never be recognized or admitted to be our equals . . . .

—Diary of Secretary of the Navy Gideon Welles

22

Lincoln Tries To Escape History

A

S Union military disasters multiplied, and as more and more people began saying the words *resignation* and *impeachment,* Lincoln tried to hold back the wind and waves of an emancipation tide that had become virtually unstoppable. He would become famous later for telling other people that they couldn't escape history, but what defines him in his year of decision was a quixotic attempt to stop history by deporting Blacks and preventing the immediate and general emancipation of slaves. By late summer of 1862, both goals had become impossibilities, and in pursuing them Lincoln made a series of strategic decisions that imperilled the war and his administration.

What astonishes us after all these years is the carnival of contradictions he embraced.

Instead of strengthening Union military forces, he weakened them by refusing—for racial reasons—to utilize the Black soldiers authorized by Congress.

Instead of strengthening the Republican Party by mobilizing Republicans and potential Republicans, he weakened it by mobilizing conservative Democrats, Border State slaveholders and the allies of Southern slaveholders, all of whom opposed the Republican Party and the war he was waging.

Instead of strengthening his moral and political position by obeying the law, he weakened his moral and political position by ignoring and evading the law.

This was bizarre, by any standard, and caused, as can be imagined, no end of comment by Republican Party leaders and abolitionists, who said openly in 1862 that the president of the United States and the commander in chief of the Army and Navy was impeding the war effort, squandering lives and fortune, and playing into the hands of the enemies of the Union. Senator Trumbull said then and later that "a large number of slaves" could have been emancipated if Lincoln had enforced the Confiscation Act of 1861. "So far as I am advised," he said later, "not a single slave has been set at liberty under it" (Krug 218). According to a *New York Tribune* dispatch of July 16, 1862, conservative Democrat Joseph A. Wright told the Senate that if the president of the United States did his duty under the confiscation act "fifty millions of [rebel] property could be seized within ten days."

The property was not seized in ten days or a thousand days. When the final tally was made, it was discovered that only $129,680 had been collected under the confiscation acts.

"Nobody," Allan Nevins said, "was terrified, and almost nobody hurt" (204).

Why was almost nobody in the Confederacy hurt by the confiscation acts?

The reason is simple. The president of the Union was protecting them. Major historians who adore Lincoln concede this point, saying quite openly and with no sense of concern that Lincoln deliberately violated his oath of office by refusing to take care to see that the laws of the United States were enforced.

Although the law "specifically authorized" Lincoln to use Black soldiers, he was, Donald says, "averse to pursuing so revolutionary a policy" (430).

Although the law authorized Lincoln to use free Blacks and even slaves to increase the power of the army and navy, Lincoln "shrunk," Thomas said, "from using black men to kill white men" (361).

Although the law required the freeing of the slaves of all rebels

and the confiscation of their property, Lincoln had "such large powers to delay or restrict action," Nevins said, ". . . that the act remained
almost a dead letter" (204).

Not only did Lincoln refuse to enforce the confiscation acts and
other antislavery measures, but he also permitted Union officers to
capture and return slaves in open defiance of the revised military
code and congressional acts. This was a dangerous game, for what
Lincoln was doing again, to be blunt about it, was violating the law
and his oath of office. He was doing this for what he considered the
best of reasons, the defense of a conservative racial policy threatened by "radical" demands, but there is no provision in the Constitution that permits a chief executive to execute only those laws that
protect what he considers the true interests of Whites.

Lincoln's reputation rested on his reported honesty and his repeated statements that he supported slavery and the Fugitive Slave
Law because of his respect for the law and the constitutional provisions that reportedly legitimized slavery. But when Congress passed
laws favoring Blacks, Lincoln openly flouted them, leading some
people to say that Lincoln never met a law in favor of slavery that he
didn't like and never met a law against slavery that he didn't oppose
or evade. This at any rate was the chief complaint of Douglass, who
said Lincoln was " scrupulous to the very letter of the law in favor of
slavery, and a perfect latitudinarian as to the discharge of his duties
under a law favoring freedom."

A case in point, he said, was the Second Confiscation Act. "When
Congress . . . made the Emancipation of the slaves of rebels the law
of the land, authorized the President to arm the slaves which should
come within the lines of the Federal army, and thus removed all
technical objections, everybody who attached any importance to the
President's declarations of scrupulous regard for law, looked at once
for a proclamation emancipating the slaves and calling the blacks to
arms. But Mr. Lincoln, formerly so strict and zealous in the obser-
vance of the most atrocious laws which ever disgraced a country,
has not been able yet to muster courage and honesty enough to obey

and execute that grand decision of the people" (FD 3:269).

So much, then, for government of the people when the people, or at least the representatives of the people, mandate emancipation and arming of Black people.

As the hot weeks wore on, and as the number of Union casualties increased, more and more people raised questions about Lincoln's violation of his oath of office. Here again, Douglass, a former slave and spokesman for the slaves, was in the forefront, telling a New York audience on July 4, 1862, that General McClellan was "either a cold blooded Traitor" or "a military impostor," and that his boss, President Lincoln, was either incompetent or an objective traitor. Douglass's bill of indictment against Lincoln was clear and sharp:

1. "He has scornfully rejected the policy of arming the slaves . . . ."

2. "He has steadily refused to proclaim, as he had the constitutional and moral right to proclaim, complete emancipation to all the slaves of rebels who should make their way into the lines of our army."

3. "He has repeatedly interfered with and arrested the anti-slavery policy of some of his most earnest and reliable generals."

4. "He has assigned to the most important positions, generals who are notoriously pro-slavery, and hostile to the party and principles which raised him to power."

5. "He has permitted rebels to recapture their runaway slaves in sight of the capital."

6. "He has allowed General Halleck to openly violate the spirit of a solemn resolution by Congress forbidding the army of the United States to return the fugitive slaves to their cruel masters, and has evidently from the first submitted himself to the guidance of the half loyal slave States . . ." (FD 3:250-6).

One month later, Phillips told a crowd at Abington, Massachusetts, that McClellan was an objective traitor "and almost the same thing may be said of Mr. Lincoln,—that if he had been a traitor, he could not have worked better to strengthen one side, and hazard the success of the other" (PS 450).

The human costs of Lincoln's default were incalculable, as a Union soldier indicated in a letter Sumner read on the floor of the Senate (SW 8:355-6). According to this letter, a slave escaped from his owner and was put to work in a Union camp near Nashville. "His owner came after him while we were camped on the other side of the river," the soldier said, "but the boys hooted him out of camp. The Negro said he would sooner be killed on the spot than go back with his master . . . ."

One day, "while the greater part of the regiment were out on picket, the boy's owner came with two sentinels of the provost guard from the city, and, after chasing the poor frightened boy through the camp several times,—he drawing a knife once, and the sentinel knocking him down with his musket,—they captured and delivered him to his owner, who stood waiting outside the lines. The latter paid the catching sentries fifteen dollars each, and led Henry away with him unmolested, flourishing a pistol at his head as he went."

In the person of the brave Henry—the record, racist as usual, does not give his last name—we catch a glimpse of the human nightmare that engulfed tens of thousands of Blacks who were betrayed and sent back to slavery by Lincoln's troops with or without the express authorization of Lincoln. It has been conservatively estimated that before Lincoln was forced to change this policy some twenty thousand African-Americans were forced back into slavery, not counting, of course, the tens of thousands who remained in slavery because they knew that Lincoln's soldiers would drive them away or return them to their slavemasters.

The most damaging charge against the commander in chief of the Union Army and Navy was that he was impeding the war effort and refusing to organize Black troops, despite congressional authorization, and despite the shortage of White troops. This led to a heated exchange between Lincoln and a delegation of Midwesterners, including two senators, who on August 5, 1862, offered "certain Negro regiments to the president."

"The President," according to a *Chicago Tribune* story of August 6, "replied that he had decided not to arm Negroes . . . . The President was plied with arguments against his decision, and discussion gradually became more fully explained.—"Gentlemen, you have my decision. I have made my mind up deliberately and mean to adhere to it. It embodies my best judgment, and if the people are dissatisfied, I will resign and let Mr. Hamlin try it," to which one of them replied, "I hope in God's name, Mr. President, you will."

The New York Tribune's Horace Greeley didn't ask Lincoln to resign, but he did ask him in a public letter to obey the law. The letter, published in the August 20, 1862, edition of the *New York Tribune,* was called "The Prayer of Twenty Millions." Greeley was in a hurry, and got right down to business, telling Lincoln publicly that "a great proportion" of those who supported you for the presidency and who wanted "the unqualified suppression of the Rebellion" are "sorely disappointed and deeply pained by the policy you seem to be pursuing with regard to the slaves of Rebels."

A great mythology would grow up around this letter and Lincoln's reply. To this day, almost all laypersons and apparently large numbers of historians think that Greeley asked Lincoln to issue an emancipation proclamation and to take other new and revolutionary steps. It comes, therefore, as something of a surprise to learn that the only thing Greeley asked Lincoln to do was to perform his oath of office and to "EXECUTE THE LAWS" of the United States.

The letter is a little long but should be read in its entirety, for it is the most closely reasoned argument against Lincoln's war policies, an argument that has been singularly neglected in American scholarship.

Let us consider Greeley's plea a little further; he is arraigning the president of the United States for failing to perform his constitutional duties and for pursuing a policy that had, he said, needlessly cost lives and money, and was threatening the future of the Union.

What did Greeley want?

"We require of you, as the first servant of the Republic [my italics], *charged especially and preeminently with this duty, that you* EXECUTE THE LAWS [capitals in original]. Most emphatically do we demand that such laws as have been recently enacted, which therefore may fairly be presumed to embody the present will and to be dictated by the present needs of the Republic, and which, after due consideration have received your personal sanction, shall by you be carried into full effect, and that you publicly and decisively instruct your subordinates that such laws exist, that they are binding on all functionaries and citizens, and that they are to be obeyed to the letter."

Closing in and coming to the main point, Greeley said "the twenty million" believed that Lincoln was "strangely and disastrously remiss in the discharge of your official and imperative duty with regard to the emancipating provisions of the new Confiscation Act. Those provisions were designed to fight Slavery with Liberty. They prescribe that men loyal to the Union, and willing to shed their blood in her behalf, shall no longer be held, with the Nation's consent, in bondage to persistent, malignant traitors . . . ."

The problem was not administrative; the problem was strategic. "We think," Greeley said, "you are unduly influenced by the counsels, the representations, the menaces, of certain fossil politicians hailing from the Border Slave States" and "that the Union cause has suffered, and is now suffering immensely, from mistaken deference to Rebel Slavery."

As for specifics:

"We complain that the Confiscation Act which you approved is habitually disregarded by your Generals, and that no word of rebuke for them from you has reached the public ear" (italics added).

"We complain that the officers of your Armies have habitually repelled rather than invited approach of slaves who would have gladly taken the risks of escaping from their Rebel masters to our camps, bringing intelligence often of inestimable value to the Union cause."

"We complain that those who have thus escaped to us, avowing a willingness to do for us whatever might be required, have been brutally and

madly repulsed, and often surrendered to be scourged, maimed and tor-
tured by the ruffian traitors, who pretend to own them."

"We complain that a large proportion of our regular Army officers, with
many of the Volunteers, evince far more solicitude to uphold Slavery than
to put down the Rebellion."

"And finally, we complain that you, Mr. President . . . seem never to
interfere with these atrocities, and never give a direction to your Military
subordinates, which does not appear to have been conceived in the interest
of Slavery rather than Freedom."

As evidence, Greeley cited the fact that "Frémont's Proclamation
and Hunter's Order favoring Emancipation were promptly
annulled by you; while Halleck's No. 3, forbidding fugitives from
Slavery to Rebels to come within his lines—an order as unmilitary
as inhuman, and which received the hearty approbation of every
traitor in America—with scores of like tendency, have never provoked even your remonstrance."

Because of Lincoln's failure to perform his "official and imperative
duty," men and women were dying needlessly, and some of that
blood, Greeley said publicly, might be on Lincoln's hands. There was,
for instance, the recent massacre of "a considerable body of resolute,
able-bodied men," former slaves who had left their plantations and
made their way some thirty miles to New Orleans to the United States
flag and what they believed was freedom.

Did these Black rebels know that they had been freed by the Confiscation Act?

Whether they knew or not, Greeley said, "they reasoned logically
that we could not kill them for deserting the service of their lifelong
oppressors, who had through treason become our implacable enemies. They came to us for liberty and protection, for which they
were willing to render their best service: they met with hostility, cap-
tivity, and murder . . . . They were set upon and maimed, captured
and killed, because they sought the benefit of that act of Congress
which they may not specifically have heard of, but which was none
the less the law of the land . . . *which it was somebody's duty to publish*

far and wide, in order that so many as possible should be impelled to desist from serving Rebels and the Rebellion and come over to the side of the Union. They sought their liberty in strict accordance with the law of the land—they were butchered or reenslaved for so doing by the help of Union soldiers enlisted to fight against Slaveholding Treason. *It was somebody's fault that they were so murdered*—if others shall hereafter suffer in like manner, in default of explicit and public directions to your generals that they are to recognize and obey the confiscation act, the world will lay the blame on you. Whether you will choose to hear it through future History and at the bar of God, I will not judge. I can only hope."

And so:

"I close as I began with the statement that *what an immense majority of the Loyal Millions of your countrymen require of you is a frank, declared, unqualified, ungrudging execution of the laws of the land, more especially the Confiscation Act.* That Act gives freedom to the slaves of Rebels coming within our lines, or whom those lines may at any time inclose—we ask you to render it due obedience by publicly requiring all your subordinates to recognize and obey it" (my italics).

This is a strong letter, devastating in its critique of the personal failure of the president to enforce the law of the land and to prevent the capture and murder of slaves. Apart from its call for obedience to law, it contains an alternative theory of the war and a brilliant critique of Lincoln's Border State strategy and "the seeming subserviency of your policy to the slaveholding, slavery-upholding interest."

Greeley said Lincoln made a disastrous mistake at the beginning of the conflict by not defining opposition to the Union as treason and by not hanging a few rebels. Having permitted the Confederates to consolidate their position, he compounded the original mistake by trying to appease slaveholders. Temporizing with traitors and semi-traitors, trying to bribe them" to behave themselves"and making "fair promises in the hope of disarming their causeless hostility," Greeley said, was naive and counterproductive, for slave-holders, whether they lived in Kentucky or Georgia, were defined by their objective interests as slaveholders and not by sentimental ties to the Union. The duty of the government, Greeley concluded, was "to oppose force to force in a defiant, dauntless spirit. "

Running through all this and informing all this is a subdued but searing indictment of Lincoln for his personal responsibility in the crimes of New Orleans and the crimes of generals, officers, and enlisted men who returned fugitives to slavery. The New Orleans indictment is overwhelming and should be better known:

It was somebody's fault that they were murdered . . . .

Whose fault was it?

And why is this honest, searing, soaring appeal for "obedience to the law of the land" almost universally condemned? The answer is clear: Greeley's letter is a pro-freedom document in favor of the least of these; and support for freedom for the least of these has always been in the minority in the Republic.

Knowing this and knowing that it is shamefully easy to bamboozle the White population on the issue of race, Lincoln ignored the indict-ment—and the massacre of the New Orleans slaves—and pitched his answer on the level of an ultimate abstraction that is more important than the concrete people and values that give the abstraction value. His answer therefore has the formal structure not of a choice between freedom and slavery or of a choice between freedom and concentra-tion camps but of a choice between Negroes and the United States. And how many Whites, if offered that choice in 1862 or 2000, would choose Negroes? In any case, it is necessary to point out here what nobody points out: that *Lincoln said these chilling words eight days after he asked Black people to leave the United States.*

What Lincoln said in 1862 is that if I could save the Union by help-ing all Negroes (all human beings) I would do it; and if I could save the Union by helping some Negroes (human beings) and leaving other human beings in slavery, I would do it; and if I could save the Union without helping any Negro (human being) I would do it.

What I do about Negroes (human beings) I do because I believe that it helps to save the Union; what I forbear, I forbear because I don't believe it would help save the Union.

Is that clear? Or must we transpose the false dichotomies that almost all historians praise and say: If I could save the Union by saving all Whites from concentration camps, I would do it. And if I could save the Union by saving some Whites from concentration camps and leaving others in concentration camps, I would do it. And if I could save the Union by leaving all White people in concentration camps, I would do it. What I do about White people and concentration camps I do because I believe it helps to save this abstraction called Union, an abstraction that is divorced from Whites, Blacks, and time; what I forbear, I forbear because I do not believe it would help this abstraction.

What was this abstraction for which Lincoln was prepared to sacrifice freedom and justice?

It was, Phillips said in a speech printed in the *Liberator*, January 17, 1862, " a Union bought by submission to slavery. It was a Union that meant slavery in the Carolinas, and gags in New York. It was a Union that meant Massachusetts with the right to say so much and only so much, as South Carolina would permit . . . . It was Union whose fundamental conditions violated justice—a Union whose cement was the blood of the slave."

That was the Union, that was the abstraction, for which Lincoln was apparently prepared to sacrifice everything and everybody Black.

Someone will say that that's not fair, that you are loading the dice. Precisely. That's what Lincoln intended to do when he said:

> As to the policy I "seem to be pursuing" as you say, I have not meant to leave any one in doubt.
>
> I would save the Union. I would save it the shortest way under the Constitution. The sooner the national authority can

be restored; the nearer the Union will be "the Union as it was." If there be those who would not save the Union, unless they could at the same time *save* slavery, I do not agree with them. If there be those who would not save the Union unless they could at the same time *destroy* slavery, I do not agree with them. My paramount object in this struggle *is* to save the Union, and is *not* either to save or to destroy slavery. If I could save the Union without freeing *any* slave I would do it, and if I could save it by freeing *all* the slaves I would do it; and if I could save it by freeing some and leaving others alone I would also do that—What I do about slavery, and the colored race, I do because I believe it helps to save the Union; and what I forbear, I forbear because I do *not* believe it would help the Union. (CW 5:388-9, Lincoln's italics)

Having made it clear, once again, that he was prepared to leave some or all of the slaves in slavery, perhaps forever, and that freedom was not his goal, Lincoln—in the Super Bowl of bad faith—pulled out his trusty semicolon and said: "I have here stated my purpose according to my view of *official* duty; and I intend no modification of my oft-expressed *personal* wish that all men every where could be free" (CW 5:389, Lincoln's italics).

Lincoln said here what he never stopped saying, that morality was what advanced the cause of the Union. Phillips criticized this position, saying he was not aware that the servants of this morality had ever named the value or virtue—or person—they would not sacrifice for the Union. The guiding principle of Lincoln and the Union-above-all party—the principle that "everything is to be sacrificed to save the Union— was, he said, "equivocal, and, if unlimited, false" [for] "unqualified, it justifies every crime, and would have prevented every glory of history."

The gospel of this class of Republicans, he added, was "the Constitution, and the slave clause [was] their Sermon on the Mount" (PS 345, 351-2).

It is easy to understand why Lincoln's maneuver worked in 1862, when few people had the supporting documents and the leisure to compare the indictment and the answer. What is not so easy to fathom is why so many people are still playing Lincoln's game. One of the reasons, of course, is that most people have made a choice in history and in their contemporary lives between Lincoln and Greeley. Since their inarticulate major premise is a fundamental agreement with Lincoln's conservative anti-Black policies, they generally refuse to tell their readers that Greeley was asking the president of the United States to enforce the laws of the land. Carl Sandburg, for instance, loved Lincoln's reply but was unaccountably inarticulate in explaining what Greeley wanted. Incredibly, in view of Greeley's detailed complaint, Sandburg said the letter was "a little vague" as to what Greeley wanted Lincoln to do. It "seemed," Sandburg said, that "Greeley wished Lincoln to tell the armies in camp and field that they were fighting against slavery first of all" (1:567).

Other historians take a different approach—and the same approach— mentioning, in passing, two or three Greeley specifics and killing him with adjectives. Basler tells us that Greeley's "Prayer" expressed the opinion "that Lincoln might have dealt the rebellion a staggering blow in its infancy by holding out the threat of emancipation in his 'Inaugural Address' and that a rigid execution of laws passed by Congress—especially the Confiscation measure—would go far toward concluding the war" (1946, 653).

Rigid: this is the word that enlightens us. Why should a historian, why should anybody, expect a president of the United States to enforce *rigid* laws freeing Black people, *rigid* laws that might have ended the war sooner and saved tens of thousands of lives?

It will be said in objection that since the author and other historians express their ideological position in their analyses, Lincoln defenders have the same right. Exactly. I'm for freedom and against slavery in 2000; I'm opposed to people who were for slavery and against freedom in 1863. Everybody in favor of slavery—in 1863 or 2000—hold up his or her hand. Not so fast, the defenders of the faith will say: the issue was not slavery or freedom—the issue was the

Union. All right: everybody in favor of Union *uber alles*—of Union of the American states, of Union of the South African states, of Union of the German states, of Union of the Russian states, choose one—over freedom, hold up his or her hand. Someone will reply that you are being willfully obtuse and that the question here is not the end but the means to that honorable end. But how can anyone fail to see that means and ends are related and that slavery and genocide have never been the means to freedom and humanity?

There is also the mundane matter of strategy. To argue in 1862 in favor of a policy based on a refusal to hit the enemy in his most vulnerable spot by depriving him of his most valuable weapon is to express a secret preference or even a bet in favor of the enemy or the values of the enemy. To argue the same thing one hundred and thirty-five years later, after history has proved that there was no viable alternative, is to commit oneself to the same past and future.

Will it be said, as it usually is, that Lincoln deliberately held up emancipation until the North was prepared to accept it? There are two problems with that theory. The first is Abraham Lincoln, and the second is Abraham Lincoln. First, sudden emancipation, as Lincoln said at Hampton Roads, two months before his death, was never his policy (Stephens 613-4). Secondly, Lincoln himself said he deliberately held up emancipation because he was trying to save slavery in America (CW 6:49).

Lincoln at least had the excuse of not being able to see the outcome, which does not, of course, absolve him of historical responsibility, for a number of his contemporaries, Black and White, chose a different historical path and a different future. In 1864, Lincoln told visitors that the Civil War could not be won without using "the Emancipation lever" and Black soldiers (CW 7:507). Douglass, Tubman, Phillips, Sumner, Stevens, Trumbull, Medill, Julian, Garrison, Wade, Chandler told Lincoln that in 1861, 1862, and 1863. *A historian from Mars would find it curious that all of these men and women are vilified today because they were right historically and because Lincoln was wrong historically.*

Donald tells us that Lincoln's reply received "universal approval"

(369), but he overlooked the almost universal disapproval of slaves and former slaves, who were appalled by words that seem callous and uncaring even today.

There was also widespread disapproval from abolitionists, liberal Republicans, and hard-war advocates, who said Lincoln's professed indifference to the fate of the slaves sounded like the policy of his old nemesis, Stephen Douglas. Four years earlier, during the Illinois debates, Lincoln had denounced Douglas, saying, "No man can say that he does not care if a wrong is voted up or down, he cannot say that he is indifferent as to a wrong; but he must have a choice between the right or wrong." Now Lincoln was saying the same thing, using almost the same language. Douglas had said that he would not endanger the perpetuity of the Union "for all the n——rs that ever existed" (Holzer 1993, 367). Now Lincoln was saying he would not endanger the Union for all the Negroes who ever existed. "The anti-slavery critics of the President insisted," Julian said, "that in thus dealing with slavery as a matter of total indifference he likened himself to Douglas, who had declared that he didn't care whether slavery was voted up or down in the Territories" (221).

The *Chicago Tribune* said in a brilliant analysis on August 26 that Lincoln didn't answer the Greeley questions and didn't seem to understand the law or the situation. "[T]he law declares," the *Tribune* said, "that the slaves of all persons committing rebellious acts *shall* be free whenever inclosed in our military lines" and that "their title to freedom" did not depend on anything Abraham Lincoln said or did, "but solely on the acts of their masters." The "slaves of rebels," the *Tribune* said, "are already free *de jure*. So far as legal rights go the President can neither emancipate nor enslave them." The problem, then, was not to free the slaves of rebels—they had already been declared free by the Second Confiscation Act—the problem was their de facto status, which required the president of the United States to enforce the law.

Another problem here, from the standpoint of methodology, is that Lincoln defenders as usual interpret Lincoln's response in a vacuum, separating the words from the man and the man from the situation and history. One need only reverse that process to understand what was at stake. For when Lincoln wrote the letter, he was hoping for a big Union victory that would have silenced the critics of his emancipation policy. Even as the Greeley controversy raged, Union troops were marching, and Lincoln was going back and forth to the War Department telegraph office, looking for the big victory that would make Greeley and slaves irrelevant. McClellan, Halleck, Buell: a who's who of proslavery Democratic Union generals had beguiled him and failed him. The great hope of the White Man's War in this summer was John Pope, who was talking bad and marching strong, giving Lincoln new hope of a big-bang victory that would smash the Confederacy and put an end to the peevish arguments of Greeley and the "Radicals."

It was Lincoln's habit during big battles to set up shop in the War Department telegraph office, where he could read the reports and ride herd on the results. David H. Bates, manager of the telegraph office, said on many occasions Lincoln stayed in the telegraph office until late at night, and occasionally all night long. "One of these occasions," he said, "was during Pope's short but disastrous campaign, ending in the second battle of Bull Run." Lincoln, according to General Herman Haupt, was in "a state of extreme anxiety" (118-9, 122). Nathaniel Wright Stephenson, one of Lincoln's major academic supporters, says "Lincoln was confident of victory. And after victory would come the new policy, the dissipation of the European stormcloud, the break-up of the vindictive coalition of Jacobins and Abolitionists, the new enthusiasm for the war" (272).

When the news came, it was not of victory but of another disastrous defeat. Confederate troops had slammed into the luckless Pope, driving him back toward Washington, sending his troops reeling in a humiliating replay of the first Bull Run and creating panic and fear in the nation's capital.

Bull Run II, like Bull Run I, like the Peninsular Campaign, triggered the central dynamic of the war, strengthening antislavery forces and increasing the pressure on Lincoln and his aides. This time, however, the pressure rose so high that it almost overwhelmed Lincoln and his beleaguered administration. A disturbed and disturbing picture of conditions in Washington in these days has been handed down to us by Secretary of the Navy Welles, who noted after the September 2 cabinet meeting that "there was a more disturbed and desponding feeling than I have ever witnessed in council..." (WD 105). On September 4, the city was "full of rumors." The next day word came that the Confederates had crossed the Potomac. The bad news continued until September 13: "The country is very desponding, and much disheartened. There is a perceptibly growing distrust of the Administration and of its ability and power to conduct the war (WD 129)."

There then followed the Lincoln Emancipation Dance, made famous by Lincoln specialists choreographing the spastic movements of a man who went forward by going backward and who said yes by saying no. At the height of this dance, in August and September, Lincoln, according to almost all Lincoln biographers, "amused" himself by confusing and confounding "zealots" who besieged the White House with demands that he do, his biographers say, what he fully intended to do. Donald uses the word *game*, telling us that "he often played a kind of game with the numerous visitors who descended on him to urge him to free the slaves. The measures they advocated were precisely those he was attempting to formulate in his document at the War Department" (364). This, of course, begs the question of what Lincoln "was attempting to formulate" and where and when he formulated it and how much of it he was forced to formulate against his will.

This maneuver reaches artistic levels in the hands of a master like Stephenson, who virtually invented the "game" theory:

"If at any time Lincoln was tempted to forget Seward's worldly wisdom, it was when these influential zealots demanded of him *to do the very thing he intended to do* [my italics] . . . ."

What did Lincoln tell these misguided zealots?

"With consummate coolness he gave them no light on his purpose. Instead, he seized the opportunity to 'feel' the country. He played the role of *advocatus diaboli* arguing the case against an emancipation policy"(276).

Nicholas and Hay use the same argument:

"Individuals and delegations came to him [in the summer of 1862] to urge one side or the other of *a decision, which, though already made in his own mind*, forced upon him a reexamination of its justness and its possibilities for good or evil" (6:154, my italics).

J. G. Randall uses it.

"One can only imagine Lincoln's feelings as he heard the delegation urging a proclamation which he had decided to issue . . ." (1957, 157).

Thomas uses it:

"All through the troublous summer, while Lincoln waited for a victory in order to issue the Emancipation Proclamation, he and his cabinet had kept his intentions secret" (342).

Oates uses it:

"Then he engaged in his old habit of quarreling with the very thing he hoped to do" (317).

Oates and other scholars say in all seriousness that Lincoln sat there with the proclamation in his desk drawer and toyed with the "zealots," rebutting their arguments and rehearsing the reasons— Kentucky would go over to the Confederates, fifty thousand soldiers would desert to the Confederates, Negroes were not worth it— why it was inadvisable to issue a proclamation.

Why would Lincoln do this? Why would any serious president condition the public to respond negatively to a policy initiative that would affect the future of the country? If, as the defenders say, honest Abe agreed with the petitioners and was waiting for the right moment to issue the proclamation, why didn't he tell them that their arguments made some sense and that he would give them serious consideration? Why didn't he go further and seize these opportunities to educate the public by emphasizing how important Black laborers and soldiers would be to the Union war effort and how emancipation could shorten the war and save the lives of White men?

Lincoln defenders brush aside these questions and tell us how clever Lincoln was, sitting there with the document, some say the *signed* document, in his drawer, making fools of the sanctimonious "zealots" from Chicago, Boston and elsewhere. But this argument proves too much—and too little. For in reading the record of these exchanges, one is struck by Lincoln's incoherence and painful ambivalence. And if we consult contemporaries who worked with Lincoln, *advocatus diaboli* disappears. Nicolay and Hay worked with Lincoln every day in this hectic summer. What did they see? They saw a man stretched to the limit, anguished, self-tormenting and close to the edge (NH 6:154).

Clearly, he wasn't having any fun. Just as clearly, he was passionately involved in the argument against issuing a proclamation. Perhaps the most damning evidence against the traditional defense is the long personal letter Lincoln crony Leonard Swett wrote to his wife on August 10, detailing a personal discussion he had with Lincoln in the White House. "I have seen him often," he wrote, "and he has told me frankly his opinions. He will issue no proclamation emancipating Negroes. He believes if he should 50,000 troops, armed with our weapons, and in our service, in Kentucky and Tenn. would in a body go over to the enemy. Neither will he accept Negro regiments in the war. He has no confidence, in them as fighting men and says that as much harm would come to us from the fact that we are arming Negroes, as from a general proclamation of freedom."[51]

This is unusually strong evidence from a Lincoln intimate who was told by Lincoln himself in August 1862 that he had no intention of issuing an emancipation proclamation. And this evidence, which has additional weight because it was relayed in a private letter not meant for public dissemination or polemical purposes, returns us to the question we raised earlier: What did Lincoln want to do in the summer of 1862? That question can only be answered by evidence, not only by documentary evidence and the testimony of reliable witnesses but also by the evidence of what Lincoln did.

The prevailing view is that Lincoln was waiting for a victory in order to do what he had always wanted to do. That statement is literally true, but Lincoln defenders beg the question and falsify Lincoln's life by assuming and asserting for ideological reasons that Lincoln was waiting for a victory *in order to* issue an Emancipation Proclamation freeing the slaves immediately. In fact, as we have established by a great deal of evidence, including the evidence of Lincoln's own words and the evidence of his whole life, the last thing in the world Abraham Lincoln wanted to do was to issue a proclamation freeing Blacks generally and immediately in 1862—or any other year. What he wanted in the summer of 1862, as in the summer of 1861, was to end the war without touching slavery. And if that was impossible, he wanted to proceed with the only emancipation plan he ever approved, the presidential plan, to use Chase's words, of gradual compensated emancipation with the approval of the slaveholders.

Must we then abandon the idea that Lincoln was waiting for a victory?

Not yet. For there is truth in that notion, although it is not the truth that traditionalists want to hear. The strongest statement in favor of that view, if we can believe the uncorroborated account of Francis B. Carpenter, came from Lincoln, and that is suggestive. For Lincoln was one of that Civil War cult who had an almost religious belief in a coming big victory that would end the war and bring the Confederate "brethren" back without a revolutionary transformation of slavery. "He was ridden, as most men were," Stephenson said, "by the delusion of one terrific battle that was to end all" (231). In May and June, he waited anxiously for McClellan to storm into Richmond and end all his problems. In August he was in a state of "extreme anxiety" waiting for a Pope victory. In September, waiting for the big battle of Antietam, he was beside himself, "still obsessed with the notion that one great victory would end the war" (Williams 181), sending telegram after telegram, pleading for a decisive victory. Nicolay and Hay said later that Lincoln's "high hope" had been the destruction of Lee's army before it recrossed the Potomac," adding: "His constant entreaty to McClellan, from the time he put him in command of the army up to the day of the battle [of Antietam], was, 'Please do not let him get off without being hurt.'" Lincoln, they said, wanted the rebel army destroyed (NH 145). In a telegram to General McClellan on September 15, two days after he opposed emancipation in a conference with Chicago religious leaders, Lincoln begged McClellan: "Destroy the rebel army if possible" (CW 5:426).

Victory: Lincoln's war was defined by the quest for a big victory. Conventional wisdom says he was waiting for a victory in order to issue the proclamation. What if the opposite were true? What if Abraham Lincoln was waiting, as he had waited since Fort Sumter, for a decisive military victory that would have made it unnecessary to issue the proclamation?

In answering that question, we must keep in mind two critical factors. One is that Lincoln's statement to Carpenter makes no sense from a military and political standpoint. The time to seek additional help, from any standpoint, is not when you need it the least, after a big victory, but when you need it the most. Editor James C. Welling said later that he never really believed "the last shriek" alibi, for "the proclamation could never have come more appropriately than when the military need was greatest" (RR 530). Not only did Welling, Sumner and others tell Lincoln that, but Lincoln himself used the same argument. When Postmaster General Montgomery Blair told Lincoln in March 1862 that he shouldn't ask Border State representatives to approve his gradual emancipation plan until "the army did something further," he said: "That is just the reason why I do not wish to wait. If we should have successes, they may feel and say, the rebellion is crushed and it matters not whether we do anything about this matter" (Segal 164).

A point of primary interest here is that Lincoln told different people he was waiting for different things. Senator Samuel Pomeroy, Lincoln's Black emigration coordinator, told Hill, according to a dispatch of August 25, that Lincoln told him confidentially that he "would emancipate so soon as he was assured that his colonization project would succeed . . ." (Gay). Not only did Lincoln tell different people different things, but he told the same person different things. Having told one person he was waiting on "the voice of the people, "he changed his tune the next morning. "This morning," the informant told Hill on September 1, 1862, "the President was talking about Providence and did not seem to be in as good heart quite as last night" (Gay). It was always a bad sign, informants said, when Lincoln started blaming Providence for the decision he couldn't or wouldn't make.

For Lincoln, then, the word *victory* had the immense psychological advantage of being both true and false, expressing at the same time his real obsession about a victory that would eliminate the need for an emancipation order and his alibi for not issuing an emancipation order. Armed with this word, which was simultaneously wish, decoy, and alibi, he waged a successful do-nothing struggle for more than two months. Forced to act finally after a poetically just event that was half victory and half defeat, he resurrected the word *victory* and made it the centerpiece of the fanciful portrait *he* was painting for painter Francis Carpenter. In this form, it has beguiled and misled battalions of historians, who have overlooked the record and the evidence of his acts.

Lincoln defenders say the situation was so indeterminate and there were so many possibilities and options that it is impossible to prove that Lincoln wouldn't have issued a proclamation if his generals had delivered a knockout victory in the East. But we are not dealing here with an indeterminate situation that could go either way. The Lincoln we are talking about is a *known* quantity, defined by his words and acts, defined precisely by his dread of immediate emancipation; and you have to white out Lincoln's whole life—his opposition to sudden and general emancipation, his fear of Black violence and amalgamation—to believe that *this* Lincoln, the Lincoln who feared "the evils" of immediate emancipation, would have issued an immediate emancipation order if his generals had "destroyed" Robert E. Lee's army.

From this standpoint, it is virtually certain that Lincoln was waiting in the summer of 1862, as he had waited every day since Fort Sumter, for a big victory that would limit the social disruption he feared and make it possible to, as he said, "practically restore" the old Union.

As it happened, events had conspired to arrange the events Lincoln had been dreaming about since Fort Sumter. Lee had crossed the Potomac and was within the crossbars of a larger Union force, which had received a lost copy of his battle plans and knew exactly what he planned to do. If, as Lincoln hoped, McClellan crushed Lee, there would be light at the end of the tunnel and the "Union as of old"—with slavery—would be saved.

Everything—Lincoln's private conversations and his behind-the-scenes maneuvering—suggests that this was his hope if not his plan. For instead of mobilizing public opinion for a projected emancipation proclamation, Lincoln continued to mobilize public opinion against an emancipation proclamation, telling delegation after delegation that a proclamation was impolitic and unwise. It is not an accident that his most passionate statements against emancipation came on the eve of the nonvictory that made him issue the proclamation.

All this time, day after day, in the summer and fall of 1862, the pressure for emancipation kept building, especially in Lincoln's home state of Illinois. On July 4, 1862, the *Chicago Tribune* said, "Let My People Go." Seven days later, Governor Richard Yates asked

Lincoln in an "urgent" public letter, published in the *Tribune* on July 12, 1862, to let Black people fight. Yates told Lincoln that his "conservative policy" had "utterly failed," and that Illinois believed "the time had come for the adoption of more decisive measures," including the "services of *all loyal men*." Lincoln, who was not a formally religious man, told Yates, in so many words, to pray.

Lincoln's neighbors took him at his word, organizing on Sunday evening, September 7, a monster rally of "Christians of all denominations" at Chicago's Bryan Hall, a rally that sent ripples across the prairie, setting Christians in Illinois and Iowa towns to trying to outdo one another. A meeting in Dubuque, Iowa, hailed "the great meeting of Christians in Bryan Hall." In a letter published in the *Chicago Tribune* on September 18, "An Iowan" said that since "the pro-slavery and border State men are continually pouring their views into the President's ears . . . it is high time for the freemen of this section to speak."

The North Illinois Conference of the M.P. Church, representing fifteen hundred members, was of the same mind, resolving, according to a *Chicago Tribune* report of September 18 :

> WHEREAS the convention of Christian men, held in Chicago, requested the co-operation of all Christians in urging upon the President of the United States the immediate emancipation of all the slaves; therefore,
>
> *Resolved*, That we fully coincide with the memorial of said convention; and further, that we urge upon the president a full acknowledgement of the manhood of the colored race, by employing them in whatever way they can best serve the country in this the hour of its peril.

An answering echo came from the Christians of Rockton, Illinois, who spoke 138 years ago against the dominant Lincoln theory that Lincoln couldn't go any faster than the people. The problem, these Christians said in a *Tribune* dispatch, printed on September 19, was not the people, but the president. "The president," the memorial said, "has expressed a willingness to go as fast as the people go. *He does not know how fast we have gone*" (italics added).

The clearest example of this was the delegation of religious leaders from the Land of Lincoln, and the city of Chicago, who asked Lincoln on Saturday, September 13—nine days before he issued the proclamation—to free all slaves (CW 5: 419-25, italics in original). Lincoln's secretaries, Nicolay and Hay, go out of their way to apologize for his language and behavior on that occasion, saying that he was going through "a species of self-torment," "almost a feeling of self-accusation," that "affected his overstrung nerves like so many persecuting inquisitors" (NH 6:154).

Even so, his language was extraordinary. For he went out of his way to disparage not only emancipation but also the slaves, saying he had little faith in Blacks and feared what would happen after emancipation. Suppose, he said, warming to the argument, that the slaves could be "induced by a proclamation of freedom from me to throw themselves upon us, *what should we do with them*? How can we feed and care for such a multitude?" The president conceded that slavery was at the root of the rebellion and that emancipation "would help us in Europe" and "would help *somewhat* at the North . . . [and] weaken the rebels by drawing off their laborers . . . . " But he wasn't sure that "we could do much with the blacks. If we were to arm them, I fear that in a few weeks the arms would be in the hands of the rebels . . . " (423).

Urged by the ministers to lead the country in a war for a new birth of freedom, Lincoln said once again in September 1862 that he was fighting for an old birth of freedom. Using the same language he used in talking to Jessie Benton Frémont and John Hay, he said, "I think you should admit that we already have an important principle to rally and unite the people in the fact that constitutional government is at stake. This is a fundamental idea, going down about as deep as anything."

Reading the record of this conference, one is struck by Lincoln's bad faith. At one point, for example, he blamed Blacks and their allies for the crimes of Confederates, saying, "I am told that when-

ever the rebels take any black prisoners, free or slave, they immediately auction them off! They did so with those they took from a boat
that was aground in the Tennessee river a few days ago. And then *I
am very ungenerously attacked for it*! For instance, when, after the late
battles at and near Bull Run, an expedition went out from Washington under a flag of truce to bury the dead and bring in the wounded,
and the rebels seized the blacks who went along to help and sent
them into slavery, Horace Greeley said in his paper that the Government would probably do nothing about it. What *could* I do?"

Rev. William W. Patton and Rev. John Dempster, who presented
the memorial adopted by a meeting of Chicago Christians of all
denominations, told the president of the United States in so many
words that he should be ashamed of himself. The Confederate violation, they said, was "a gross outrage on a flag of truce, which covers
and protects all over which it waves, and that whatever he could do
if *white* men had been similarly detained he *could* do in this case."

The ministers went on to rebut the president's arguments, point
by point. "We observed (taking up the President's ideas in order)
that good men indeed differed in their opinions on this subject; nevertheless *the truth was somewhere*, and it was a matter of solemn
moment for him to ascertain it . . . ."

Lincoln had observed, as all Lincoln defenders observe, that it was
strange that God had revealed his will on emancipation, "on a point
so connected with my duty," to others and had not revealed it to him.
He said further, in a great line, that if God wanted to send him a message, it was strange that he "sent it in a roundabout route by that
awfully wicked city of Chicago" (RR 335).

In response, the ministers "freely admitted the probability, and
even the certainty, that God would reveal the path of duty to the
President as well as to others, provided he sought to learn it in the
appointed way . . . ."

Lincoln rehearsed his usual argument about emancipation costing
the Union Kentucky and fifty thousand soldiers. The ministers countered that this danger "was greatly diminished," as he himself had

conceded. "But let the desertions be what they might, the increased spirit of the North would replace them two to one. One State alone, if necessary, would compensate the loss, were the whole 50,000 to join the enemy."

Having improved Lincoln's arithmetic, if not his morals, the ministers moved the discussion to a level it never reached at Gettysburg, saying:

"The struggle has gone too far, and cost too much treasure and blood, to allow of a partial settlement. *Let the line be drawn* at the same time *between freedom and slavery,* and between loyalty and treason. *The sooner we know who are our enemies the better"* (italics added).

This eloquent and eminently sane appeal didn't change Lincoln, who continued to argue against an emancipation policy. The heart of his argument was in one paragraph:

"What *good* would a proclamation of emancipation from me do, especially as we are now situated? I do not want to issue a document that the whole world will see must necessarily be inoperative, like the Pope's bull against the comet! Would *my word* [Lincoln's italics] free the slaves, when I cannot even enforce the Constitution in the rebel States?"

The answer clearly lay with the man asking the question. And from the way he asked the question, it was clear that he neither expected nor desired an affirmative answer, which is surprising since he issued a proclamation nine days later that was presumably as inoperative as "the Pope's bull against the comet." Even more surprising is the fact that almost all historians contend that the man who made this statement had already decided to issue such a proclamation. How explain this? The explanation, defenders of the myth say, is plain: Lincoln was lying. (Isn't it curious that so many defenses of honest Abe are based on the assumption that he was lying?) He was, they say, "pretending" to disagree with the very thing he wanted to do.

Why would he do that? He was, we are told, hiding his cards and trying to prepare the public for the proclamation he was going to issue. But that's absurd. How do you prepare the public for an act by arguing against it?

Lincoln's attitude, arguments and body language convinced many that he had no intention on September 13 of issuing an Emancipation Proclamation. And in evaluating his responses, it is important to remember that he believed on September 13 that the war would soon be over. He was so confident, in fact, that he wired General McClellan on September 15 to destroy Lee's army.

James C. Welling said that although Lincoln said he had not definitely decided against a proclamation, "this statement [to the Chicago delegation] only served to bring into bold relief the little faith he then seemed to have in a measure for which, considered as a means to the end proposed by its patrons, he could, with all his meditations, find no good and sufficient reasons"(RR 529).

The strongest evidence against the prevailing theory that Lincoln was waiting for a victory to issue the proclamation is the fact that key members of the cabinet had no idea what Lincoln was trying to do in August and September of 1862. Postmaster General Montgomery Blair, a conservative and a close adviser to the president, said he was mystified by Lincoln's maneuvers. Looking back later, he told Secretary Welles: "I had urged him previously to make the proclamation and a letter of mine will be found in his papers arguing the point, but he had scarcely a week before ridiculed the idea of such a proclamation . . . and I had to support him against Chase and therefore [was] taken aback by this somersault [of ridiculing the proclamation to the Chicago delegation and then signing the document nine days later] at first, and so hesitated; but after sleeping on it I came back to my former position" (W. Smith 186).

Secretary Chase was also mystified, telling his diary on Sunday, September 12 that Lincoln "has yielded so much to the Border State and Negrophobic counsels that he now finds it difficult to arrest his own descent towards the most fatal concessions." Chase added, "He has already separated himself from the great body of the party which elected him; distrusts most those who most represent its spirit; and waits. For what?" (CD 136).

That was the question. And it is curious that latter-day historians claim to know the answer to a question that Chase and Blair, who saw Lincoln almost every day and who participated in the July cabinet meeting, didn't know. Perhaps the most confused and confusing person of all was Abraham Lincoln, who told his cabinet on September 22 that he had decided on September 6—"when the rebel army was at Frederick"— to issue a proclamation that he told the ministers on September 13 would be absurd (CD 150).

There are three possible explanations for this bewildering situation.

First: The only contemporary narrative on this point—the diary entry of Secretary Chase—was correct in its assertion that the July proposal was put off for further discussion, which, according to the diary reports, never happened.

Second: Lincoln had changed his mind and was preparing the public and the cabinet for the *nonappearance* of the document.

Third: Lincoln was waiting, as he later maintained, for a victory, but he was waiting for a victory— the destruction of Lee's army—that would have made it unnecessary to issue the proclamation.

The answer is almost certainly all of the above. And from this standpoint, which is the standpoint of the slaves, the best thing that happened at Antietam was that McClellan fumbled and let Lee escape across the Potomac. This was, as has been well said, "a defeat for both armies," but for the slaves, McClellan's fumble was better than a victory. "McClellan's failure," Sumner said, "did more for the good cause than any argument of persuasion" (SM 108).

Since the proclamation followed Antietam, the tendency is to make the *post hoc, ergo propter hoc* mistake of saying that Antietam was responsible for the proclamation. But a less visible and perhaps even more important factor was pressure from Republican leaders, who upped the ante, threatening, in some cases, to withhold money, men and matériel if Lincoln didn't fire McClellan and strike at the heart of the Confederacy by freeing the slaves.

Even more threatening was the highly irregular meeting of loyal governors called for September 24. Lincoln signed the proclamation two days before the meeting opened, but Lincoln defenders, and even some of the participants, contradict the evidence and common sense by saying the meeting didn't force the proclamation and was not in fact designed to bring pressure on Lincoln. Certain of the participants may have been innocent, although it is hard to believe that any governor could have been *that* innocent, but some of the participants and supporters said clearly that the meeting was designed to pressure and even threaten Lincoln. The *New York Herald* reported on September 17 "on the authority of prominent politicians that the proposed meeting of Northern governors was part of a coordinated Republican plot 'to request President Lincoln to resign, to enable them to carry out their scheme.'" In a confidential letter, Zachariah Chandler, the powerful Michigan senator, told Illinois Senator Lyman Trumbull that "it is *treason rank . . . treason* call it by what name you will, that has caused our late disasters . . . . I fear nothing will ever serve us but *a demand* of the loyal Governors *backed by a threat*, —that a change of policy & men shall *instantly* be made."

What about the president?

"Your President," Chandler wrote, " is unstable as water, if he has as I suspect, been bullied by those traitor Generals [.] how long will it be before he will by them be set aside & a military dictator set up" (Harris 60-1).

A lot of people were talking in these days about pushing Lincoln aside or shaking him up. Governor Andrew, one of the moving forces behind the conference of loyal governors, wrote Gurowski on September 6: "Besides doing my own proper work, I am sadly but firmly trying to help organize some movement, if possible to save the Prest. from the infamy of ruining his country . . . (Pearson 48).

Based on these and other contemporary reports, one gets the impression that matters were more serious in Washington than we have been led to believe. In any case, we ought to give more credence to Lincoln's repeated statements that he couldn't have stopped the proclamation if he had wanted to and that he would have been toppled if he had tried to renege on it. Inversely, we can say that issuing the proclamation dampened a near-revolutionary uproar and probably saved Lincoln's job. Proslavery sources bring this out even more clearly. T. J. Barnett, the lower-level Interior Department official who played a major role in Lincoln's curious proslavery clique, wrote his mentor S. L. M. Barlow on November 18 that "Chase has got the inside track against the predisposition of the President to regard the late elections from a desirable standpoint, by threatening him with a conspiracy among the Radical members of Congress to stop the supplies, and end the war in that way, making him have the responsibility" (Barlow Papers).

James C. Welling, a Washington editor with close White House contacts, was convinced that the proclamation was issued "primarily and chiefly as a political necessity, and took on the character of a military necessity only because the President had been brought to believe that if he did not keep the Radical portion of his party at his back he could not long be sure of keeping an army at the front."

For eighteen months, Welling said, Lincoln had fought a war based on the "Border State theory" of preserving the Union as it was. "But the most active and energetic wing of the Republican Party had become, as the war waxed hotter, more and more hostile to this 'Border State theory of the war,' until, in the end, its fiery and impetuous leaders did not hesitate to threaten him with repudiation as a political chief, and even began in some cases to hint the expediency of withholding supplies for the prosecution of the war, unless the President should remove 'pro-slavery generals' from the command of our armies, and adopt an avowedly antislavery policy in the future conduct of the war. Thus placed between two stools, and liable between them to fall to the ground, he determined at last to plant himself firmly on the stool which promised the surest and safest support" (RR 530-1).

The same analysis with a different metaphor—"between two fires"—was presented by Lincoln's close friend, Henry C. Whitney, who said Lincoln changed because he believed "the extremists at the north would withhold supplies for the government unless he did free the slaves." Men in high quarters, "both excitable persons like Greeley, Phillips and Lovejoy, [but] also imperturbable leaders like Andrew, Curtin and Raymond," had made these threats. So there he was "between two fires. If the Radicals should concentrate their opposition, as appeared inevitable, and withhold supplies, the armies would be disbanded, and the Rebels would occupy Washington; the Confederacy would be acknowledged by foreign powers as a de jure government; and Mr. Lincoln would be a President 'of shreds and patches;' in fact, anarchy would be regnant, or, at least, close at hand" (322).

In "this dire stress of circumstances," Whitney wrote, Lincoln issued the Preliminary Proclamation as a tactical move "to placate the Radicals for the time" and to preserve his political base, "hoping that the Border States would acquiesce in its absolute necessity; and designing to ultimately get the Negroes out of the country; to compensate the Rebels for the loss of their property; and to secure a constitutional amendment to make the proclamation effectual" (323).

Edward Stanly, the proslavery military governor of North Carolina, told Welling that Lincoln had told him pretty much the same thing when he rushed to Washington to offer his resignation in protest against the proclamation. Five days after the proclamation was signed, Welling noted in his diary:

> *September 27th.*—Had a call at the *Intelligencer* office from the Honorable Edward Stanly, Military Governor of North Carolina. In a long and interesting conversation Mr. Stanly related to me the substance of several interviews which he had had with the President respecting the Proclamation of Freedom. Mr. Stanly said that the President had stated to him that the proclamation had become a civil necessity to prevent the Radicals from openly embarrassing the government in the conduct of the war. The President expressed the belief that, without the proclamation for

which they had been clamoring, the Radicals would take the extreme step in Congress of withholding supplies for carrying on the war—leaving the whole land in anarchy. Mr. Lincoln said that he had prayed to the Almighty to save him from this necessity, adopting the very language of our Saviour, 'If it be possible, let this cup pass from me,' but the prayer had not been answered." (RR 532-3)

The slaves, who had a deeper understanding of these matters, said in a great Jubilee that the prayer had been answered, that the answer was in the cup he was forced to drink and the Preliminary Proclamation he was forced to sign. And in evaluating the document he finally issued, one must never forget that in the back of Lincoln's mind, in the back of almost everyone's mind, was the Second Confiscation Act, which had freed the slaves of all rebels on July 17 and which required Lincoln to start confiscating the mansions and land of Southern rebels in sixty days. The sixty-day grace period was going to end in September, and Lincoln was going to have to get off the fence and start emancipating and confiscating. In several public statements and letters, including a September 17 letter which was handed to Lincoln on September 19, reformer Robert Dale Owen told the president that the sixty days would expire on September 23 and that he could make the day memorable by "a Proclamation declaring liberated the slaves of every man then in rebellion or aiding & abetting,—declaring, also, that, under the necessity of self-preservation, the slaves of the loyal are taken by the Government at an appraisement, —private property for public use . . . ." The people, Owen said, "are athirst for decisive action . . . . The 23d of September is *the day.*— nay the eleventh hour" (CP 254-5).

On September 22, *one day before "the eleventh hour,"* Abraham Lincoln signed the relatively conservative Preliminary Proclamation, staying the implementation of the most revolutionary act of confiscation and emancipation ever passed by Congress.

Was this, as we asked before, accident, design, or inadvertence?

In any case, the result—an emancipation document that didn't free anybody—was the same.

Despite what almost everybody says, the document Lincoln issued was not a recycled version of *the one-sentence fragment* that he read in July. Nor was it the document mythologists say he had been hiding in his drawer for two months. Lincoln said that he was staying at the Soldiers' Home, the Camp David of the day, about three miles outside Washington, when he heard that "the advantage was on our side" at the Battle of Antietam—"the news came, I think, on Wednesday." Lincoln said he "finished writing the second draft of the preliminary proclamation; came up on Saturday; called the Cabinet together to hear it, and it was published the following Monday" (Carpenter 22-3). It is strange and significant that Lincoln made so many factual errors (see pages 437-43) in recalling the proclamation. There are, for example, at least four major errors in that short statement. The cabinet was called together on Monday, September 22; the document was published on Tuesday, September 23. There is strong evidence from the president's secretary and a Chase diary entry that Lincoln "rewrote the Proclamation on Sunday morning carefully" after he returned to the White House (CD 149).

Finally, and conclusively, the news came not on Wednesday but on Friday (NH 6:145-6). For although the battle was fought on Wednesday, September 17, Lincoln didn't know until Friday, September 19, that McClellan had missed a sensational opportunity to end the war. When he discovered, "in the forenoon of the 19th," that McClellan had stopped Lee's advance but had let him escape into Virginia, he was disconsolate. Nicolay and Hay, who were there, said he was "glad and thankful for the measure of success which had been achieved, *but the high hope he had entertained of destroying Lee's army before it recrossed the Potomac was baffled*" (NH 6:145-6, italics added). It is scarcely possible, once again, to doubt in the face of this testimony from two of Lincoln's most devoted aides that his main hope in the fall of 1862 was a victory that would have destroyed Lee's army, ending the war and, from our standpoint, eliminating the need for an emancipation proclamation or any other antislavery measure.

What did this all this mean as a practical matter?

It meant that Lincoln had exhausted all avenues of evasion and that the only alternative left was to summon his cabinet and stretch forth his hand to Ethiopia.

Two firsthand reports of the cabinet meeting have come down to us, and both agree that Lincoln finally made his Eroica Declaration, saying that he had made a hard decision without asking anybody's advice and that he was going to accept responsibility for it. What is striking in the diary accounts of Secretary of the Treasury Chase and Secretary of the Navy Welles is that neither Lincoln nor Seward nor anyone else corroborated the dominant Lincoln myth that Seward had persuaded Lincoln to postpone the proclamation in July because it would have seemed like "a last shriek" of help to Blacks and that Lincoln had put the document aside to wait for a victory. Instead, Chase's diary account, corroborated by Welles's diary account, quotes Lincoln as saying, "Several weeks ago, I read to you an Order I had prepared on this subject, which, on account of objections made by some of you, was not issued" (CD 149-52; WD 142-5).

According to the only two contemporary accounts, Lincoln did not repeat to the assembled members of the cabinet the fabled story of how he put the document back into his drawer and waited two months for a victory. Instead of repeating this myth, Lincoln told cabinet members one of the most extraordinary stories in the history of presidential decision-making. The way he told it, he had made a deal with God and had submitted the whole thing to a divine lottery. He remarked, Welles wrote, "that he had made a vow, a covenant, that if God gave us the victory in the approaching battle, he would consider it as an indication of Divine will, and that it was his duty to move forward in the cause of emancipation. It might be thought strange, he said, that he had in this way submitted the disposal of matters *when the way was not clear to his mind what he should do* [my italics]. God had decided in favor of the slaves."

In a later account, in the *Galaxy*, Welles reported that Lincoln said that he often made decisions that way. Whatever account we accept, we would be well advised to take Lincoln's recollections with a grain of salt. He later gave conflicting reasons for issuing the documents, citing most often the more worldly pressures of profane politicians who were threatening to depose him or to withhold men and money to fight the war, but he also said that he had asked God to let this cup pass from him and that God had not answered his prayer.

How did the cabinet members respond to all this?

Most were apparently relieved that Lincoln had gotten off the fence, whether the impulse came from above or below. The only real objection came from Postmaster General Blair, who expressed fears about the impact of the proclamation on the Border States and pro-slavery segments in the Army and the North. Lincoln said he had considered these "dangers," but "the difficulty was as great not to act as to act"(WH 847).

Lincoln invited comments and criticism of the language of the proposed proclamation, which is one of the worst freedom documents in world history. It would have been worse if Secretary Seward, who had strongly opposed the first proclamation, had not offered several suggestions. Lincoln, always equivocal in talking about Black freedom, had written a suspicious phrase which said that the act would be sustained during the service of "the present incumbent." Seward, Chase and others suggested new language which said that the government "will recognize and maintain the freedom" of persons freed by the document.

Lincoln had written that efforts to colonize Blacks would continue. Seward corrected his syntax—and his morals—adding "with their consent."

Neither Seward nor other cabinet members corrected the sinister distinction Lincoln made between the show freedom of the document and "actual freedom."

The heart of the document was in the third and fourth paragraphs, which said:

That on the first day of January in the year of our Lord, one thousand eight hundred and sixty-three, all persons held as slaves within any state, or designated part of a state, the people whereof shall then in rebellion against the United States, shall be then, thenceforward, and forever free; and the executive government of the United States, including the military and naval authority thereof, will recognize and maintain the freedom of such persons, and will do no act or acts to repress such persons, or any of them, in any efforts they may make *for their actual freedom.*

That the executive will, on the first day of January aforesaid, by proclamation, *designate the States, and parts of states,* if any, in which the people thereof respectively, shall then be in rebellion against the United States; and *the fact that any state, or the people thereof shall, on that day be, in good faith represented in the Congress of the United States, by members chosen thereto, at elections wherein a majority of the qualified voters of such state shall have participated, shall, in the absence of strong countervailing testimony, be deemed conclusive evidence that such state and the people thereof, are not then in rebellion against the United States.* (CW 5:434, italics added)

The slaves and their allies were heartened by Lincoln's apparent change of heart; but when they examined the document closely, they discovered that they had been outmaneuvered and that the Preliminary Proclamation was an expression not of Lincoln's desire to free the slaves but of his campaign to save as much slavery as he could. And if we examine the document with the eyes of the slaves, we find a number of disturbing and seldom-explored propositions.

First of all, and most important of all, the Preliminary Proclamation was a bribe that failed. It said first that if Southerners pledged allegiance to the flag, they could keep their slaves. Lincoln, who was always considerate to slaveholders, gave them one hundred days to think about it.

Secondly, as we have seen, the Preliminary Proclamation was issued exactly one day before the expiration of the sixty-day grace period for implementation of the Second Confiscation Act, thereby halting or postponing the most revolutionary emancipation/confiscation event in U.S. history.

Thirdly, it silenced Lincoln's critics for one hundred days and put the emancipation process in Lincoln's hands instead of the hands of congressmen, thereby ensuring a conservative spin for a potentially revolutionary act. This was a brilliant political move. For by issuing the proclamation, Lincoln, like a savvy quarterback who throws up his arm in a pump fake, froze his critics in place and gained time for maneuvers to either end the war without touching slavery or to mobilize support for his favorite program of compensated emancipation and colonization. Richard N. Current said in a hypothetical analysis that supporters of Black liberation thought at first that Lincoln was at long last joining their crusade but were quickly disillusioned "since [it could have been argued that] the proclamation had as its purpose and effect the checking of the Radical program. Having announced in September that he would make a final proclamation the first of the following year, Lincoln had an excuse for disregarding the laws about confiscation and Negro troops . . . " (226).

There is evidence for this view in the document, which is, like all Lincoln productions, praised but not read. Few noticed in the first flush of celebrations and fewer have noticed since then that Lincoln had changed the language of the one-line proclamation he read in July. The July document said he would free "all persons held as slaves within any [rebel] state or states . . . ." The September document said he would free "all persons held as slaves within any [rebel] state, or *designated part of a state* . . ." (my italics). What did this small, significant and sinister change in language mean? It meant that Abraham Lincoln had decided some time between July and September to play an emancipation game. It meant that he knew in September 1862 that he was not going to free any slaves on January 1, 1863. It meant that Abraham Lincoln had deliberately given himself the power to keep in slavery the only slaves he could free. As he told General John A. Dix, the reactionary commander who was re-creating slavery under another name in liberated Virginia, "I left my self at liberty to exempt *parts* of states" (CW 5:476, Lincoln's italics).

The fourth provision, flowing in and out of the first one, made it possible for Southerners to keep their slaves if they organized a government and sent representatives to Congress.

To sum up the discussion so far, then, the evidence points strongly toward four conclusions:

1. That Lincoln under overwhelming military and political pressure decided in late July to issue a proclamation and then changed his mind because of his fears and the fears of Secretary of State Seward, Postmaster General Blair, and political advisor Thurlow Weed.

2. That Lincoln decided to wait for a military victory and/or a political victory, i.e., a North/South compromise on slavery that would make the emancipation proclamation and immediate emancipation unnecessary.

3. That the Preliminary Emancipation Proclamation was issued in September because the rising political fury and the growing strength of antislavery forces threatened his political position and his ability to govern and conduct the war. Gurowski said "the words 'resign,' 'depose,' 'impeach,' were more and more distinct in the popular murmur, and the proclamation was issued" (1:276).

4. That the proclamation was a continuation at a higher level of desperation of the waiting-game strategy he had adopted in July and was designed at least in part to take the steam out of the emancipation movement and to give him one hundred days' grace during which time he could delay enforcing the Confiscation Act and mobilize allies for the gradual emancipation/colonization plan he intended to introduce in December.

Perhaps the most chilling commentary on the document came from Lincoln who told a group of Washingtonians who came to the White House to congratulate him, "I can only trust in God I have made no mistake." [Cries "No mistake—all right; you've made no mistake yet. Go ahead, you're right."] Still doubtful, Lincoln added: "It is now for the country and the world to pass judgment on it, and, may be, take action upon it" (CW 5:438).

That's what he said: "and, may be, take action upon it."

Hearts are not captured, battles are not won, slaves are not freed by that kind of talk, which was the the only kind of talk you could get from Lincoln in the cause of Black freedom. Garrison said the proclamation was a step forward but that "the president can do nothing for freedom in a direct manner, but only by circumlocution and delay" (1979, 114-5). Gurowski said "the proclamation is written in the meanest and the most dry routine style, " adding:

"Nothing for humanity, nothing to humanity."

Gurowski said it was clear "that the writer was not in it either with his heart or with his soul; it is clear that it was done under moral duress, under the throttling pressure of events . . ." (1:278).

The same point was made with equal force by Union General James S. Wadsworth, who said "never a noble subject was more belittled by the form in which it was uttered" (GD 278). Wadsworth missed, according to a Hill letter of September 23, "an earnest human word for Freedom," and noted that the president "spoke often of the slaves as cattle" (Gay).

23

Lincoln Asks Congress To Deport Blacks

L INCOLN read the Preliminary Emancipation Proclamation to his cabinet on Monday, September 22, and it was published on Tuesday, September 23. The next day, Wednesday, September 24, 1862, he convened one of the most sinister cabinet meetings in American history.

The question before this meeting was the ethnic cleansing of the United States by the deportation of native-born African-Americans. Secretary Welles was there, and he told his diary that the president of the United States was insistent; he wanted to send the Negroes away. He "thought it essential to provide an asylum for a race which we had emancipated, but which could never be recognized or admitted to be our equals" (WD 152).

Lincoln had been saying that for years. It was an article of faith to him that emancipation and deportation went together, like firecrackers and July Fourth, and that you couldn't have one without the other.

"Following the preliminary proclamation, and as a part of the plan," Welles said, *"was the question of deporting and colonizing the colored race.* This was a part of the President's scheme, and had occupied his mind some time before the project for emancipation was adopted, although the historians, biographers, and commentators have made slight, if any, allusion to it. The President, however, and a portion of

his Cabinet considered them *inseparable*, and that deportation should accompany and be a part of the emancipation movement" (WH 848-9, italics added).

Congressman Julian, who conferred with Lincoln often as a member of the powerful Joint Committee on the Conduct of the War, used almost the same words, saying that when Lincoln "very reluctantly issued his preliminary proclamation . . . he wished it distinctly understood that the deportation of the slaves was, in his mind, *inseparably connected* with the policy" (RR 61).

The deportation campaign, as we have seen, started before Fort Sumter and moved to a new level in August 1862 with farcical efforts to persuade South American governments to accept Black colonies. When these efforts failed, Lincoln asked the State Department to launch an international effort to persuade England and other colonial powers to sell or lease America space in their colonial possessions.

This was the issue Lincoln presented to his cabinet on the day after he announced in the Preliminary Proclamation that he was going to free Blacks in rebel-held areas in one hundred days "and that the effort to colonize persons of African descent, with their consent, upon this continent, or elsewhere, with the previously obtained consent of the Governments existing there, will be continued" (CW 5:434). Seward, as we have seen, suggested that he add the words "with their consent."

The president and all members of the cabinet, with the exception of Secretary Welles and Secretary Chase, were in favor of deportation, according to firsthand reports. Secretary Seward, who supported Lincoln on most issues, opposed his "colonization scheme" on "the self evident principle that all *natives* of a country have an *equal* right in its soil" (Carpenter 291, italics in original). At least one member of the cabinet, Attorney General Bates, was, according to Welles, in favor of forcible deportation. Welles said in a diary entry added later that the meeting was held on Tuesday, but Chase said in a contemporary entry that the special meeting was held on Wednesday, September 24. Welles said "the President brought forward the subject [of colonization] and desired the members of the Cabinet to each take it into serious consideration."

He thought a treaty could be made to advantage, and territory secured to which the Negroes could be sent . . . . Several governments had signified their willingness to receive them. Mr. Seward said some were willing to take them without expense to us.

Mr. Blair made a long argumentative statement in favor of deportation. It would be necessary to rid the country of its black population, and some place must be found for them. He is strongly for deportation, has given the subject much thought, but yet seems to have no matured system which he can recommend. Mr. Bates was for compulsory deportation. The Negro would not, he said, go voluntarily, had great local attachments but no enterprise or persistency. The President objected unequivocally to compulsion. Their emigration must be voluntary and without expense to themselves. Great Britain, Denmark, and perhaps other powers would take them. (WD 152)

The subject was so important that Lincoln asked his aides to give it further thought and return for a second meeting on Friday, September 26. At that meeting, Welles said, Bates read "a very well prepared paper," urging deportation. "Little was said by anyone else," but the president was "not satisfied," said he wanted a treaty "and territory secured to which the Negroes could be sent" (WD 153, 152).

Following Lincoln's instructions, Secretary of State Seward on September 30 asked the governments of England, France, the Netherlands, and Denmark to help find a place for the Americans Abraham Lincoln considered orphans. At the same time, the government stepped up investigations of possible colonization sites in Surinam, British Guiana, British Honduras, Haiti, Liberia, New Granada, Ecuador, and the Danish Island of St. Croix in the West Indies.

As these international efforts unfolded, Lincoln worked behind the scenes on administration plans to ship Blacks to South America. Final plans for this venture, dubbed "Linconia," by the press, had been announced before the signing of the Preliminary Proclamation and were linked to it. A number of highly placed onlookers said later that they doubted that Lincoln would have signed the proclamation if he had known that the Linconia plans would collapse.

If these plans didn't succeed, it wasn't Black emigration coordinator Pomeroy's fault. In late August, the Kansas senator told the press that he and the first contingent of 500 Black males authorized by President Lincoln would leave for Central America before October 1. One press report said he recruited several persons at the contraband camp in Washington, D. C. The *Chicago Tribune* announced on September 18, four days before the signing of the Preliminary Proclamation, that "the government today completed the arrangements for the settlement of free colored persons in Central America . . . . Senator Pomeroy, who will conduct the expedition, has full powers in the premises. It will start early in October with 500 emigrants, nearly all of them provided with implements of husbandry." On October 11, Pomeroy was in Quincy, Illinois, according to a Browning diary entry, "on the way to New York to embark for New Granada with a colony of blacks" (BD 577).

All systems were go, according to press reports, when Lincoln suddenly cancelled the whole thing, bowing, it was said, to Central American governments who were threatening military action to prevent the settlements. Undaunted, Lincoln and his associates changed directions and announced plans for new Black colonies in of all places, the Amazon.

Throughout all this, and on into the New Year, Lincoln argued for a two-stage process in which the freed slaves would live first in a halfway house of apprenticeship before being colonized. In a late November conference with Democrat T. J. Barnett, he said, according to a Barnett letter of November 30, 1862, that he still thought that "many of them [Blacks] will colonize, and that the South will be compelled to resort to the Apprentice System" (Barlow Papers).

It was during this period, "very close to the new year of 1863," Registrar of the Treasury Lucius E. Chittenden wrote, that rumors swept

Washington of the impending removal of slaves to western Texas. Chittenden said later that he thought the rumors were groundless, but there is evidence, some of it provided by Chittenden, that Lincoln himself was involved in the plan. At any rate, Lincoln, according to Chittenden, came to his office with a provocative question (336-40):

"Do you know any energetic contractor? One who would be willing to take a large contract, attended with some risk?"

Chittenden said he knew a number of contractors who would not be frightened by the magnitude of the task if there was "a fair prospect of profit."

"There will be profit and reputation in the contract I may propose," Lincoln reportedly said. "It is to remove the whole colored race of the slave states into Texas. If you have any acquaintance who would take that contract, I would like to see him."

Chittenden immediately sent a telegram to John Bradley, a Vermont businessman, who was visiting in New York. Bradley, he said, was in his office "when the treasury opened, the morning after I sent the telegram," and was immediately taken to the White House. After the conference with Lincoln, Bradley was optimistic, telling Chittenden that if the president "decides upon this wholesale transfer of the colored race, they will be in Texas within a year." Nothing, however, came of the project, which Lincoln, Chittenden said, later abandoned.

In the same period, Lincoln renewed his buy-and-ship plan, sending to Congress, on December 1, 1862, precisely one month before the scheduled signing of the Emancipation Proclamation, a State of the Union Message that called for three constitutional amendments to complete a *national* plan of gradual compensated emancipation and colonization (CW 5:518-37).

This document, which Basler called one of the greatest statements in human history (1946, 38), is actually one of the most damning documents in human history. There is, to begin with, the fact that Lincoln used the dangerous word *deportation* in an official document for the first time; in fact, he used the word three times. More ominously, Lincoln said he was still committed to an all-White nation with a transitional period of quasi freedom followed by the deportation of the freedmen. This is what he said:

> *Heretofore* colored people, to some extent, have fled north from bondage; and *now*, perhaps, from both bondage and destitution. But if gradual emancipation and deportation be adopted, they will have neither to flee from. Their old masters will give them wages at least until new laborers can be procured; and *the freed men, in turn, will gladly give their labor for the wages till new homes can be found for them, in congenial climes, and with people of their own blood and race.* (CW 5:535-6, italics added)

Here, then, in unexpurgated language, is Lincoln's blueprint for the American future. It's all there, all of it—his gradualism, his racism, his deeply rooted belief that this land was the White man's land—and there is no possibility of understanding him or the Proclamation without an understanding of the official plan for a new White America he unfolded in this State of the Union message. The Proclamation was not his plan. Gettysburg was not his plan. His plan, the only plan he ever had, was the plan he presented in this annual message on Monday, December 1, 1862.

Despite its thrice-repeated calls for deportation of Blacks, despite its passionate plea for a continuation of slavery for thirty-seven years, despite its official projection of the notion of an all-White nation, the whole American cultural structure—historians, curators, writers, editors—has endorsed this message. Donald praised its "Shakespearean cadence" (398). Basler said the message reached" peaks of eloquence unsurpassed in the annals of history," adding: "Perhaps no American living at the time save Walt Whitman ever expressed so large a vision of the future of American democracy . . ." (38-9). Ignoring for the moment the fact that Whitman was as androgynous racially as Lincoln, it can be said that at least four million Blacks and a not inconsiderable number of Whites, notably

Phillips, Stevens, and Sumner, had a far more expansive view of the American future than Lincoln or Whitman ever had. In any case, it's hard to see why anyone would say that a message calling for deportation of Blacks and creation of an all-White nation expressed "a large vision" of the American future.

To gain more insight into this matter, and to understand how badly Basler, Copland and others misread the State of the Union Address of 1862, one need only glance at the three constitutional amendments Lincoln asked the Congress to pass "as permanent constitutional law" one month before he signed the Emancipation Proclamation (CW 5:527-37).

The first amendment, *Lincoln's proposed thirteenth amendment*, called for the ending of slavery, not on January 1, 1863, but by January 1, 1900:

> Every State, wherein slavery now exists, which shall abolish the same therein, at any time, or times, before the first day of January, in the year of our Lord one thousand and nine hundred, shall receive compensation from the United States . . . .

The second amendment, *Lincoln's proposed fourteenth amendment*, discussed *actual* freedom and the compensation to loyal slaveowners.

> All slaves who shall have enjoyed actual [watch that word] freedom by the chances of war, at any time before the end of the rebellion, shall be forever free; but all owners of such who shall not have been disloyal, shall be compensated for them . . . .

The third amendment, *Lincoln's proposed fifteenth amendment*, called for the ethnic cleansing of the United States of America.

> Congress may appropriate money, and otherwise provide, for colonizing free colored persons, with their own consent, at any place or places without the United States.

Anticipating objections, Lincoln said that the gradual emancipation he proposed in this document was better than the immediate emancipation he had threatened in the Preliminary Emancipation. He even used his favorite word, saying that "the time spares both races from the *evils* of sudden derangement" and saves slaves from "the vagrant destitution which must largely attend immediate emancipation in localities where their numbers are very great . . ." (italics added).

As for colonization, Lincoln said, "I cannot make it better known than it already is that I strongly favor colonization."

What about the moral issues surrounding deportation?

Lincoln said his proposed fifteenth amendment related "to the future of the freed people" and that it was a voluntary matter that would come to nothing "unless by the mutual consent of the people to be deported, and the American voters, through their representatives in Congress." He thus pretended to believe, as most of his defenders pretend to believe, that there was no moral difference between a person making an individual decision to emigrate and a country making a collective decision to deport a whole group for racial reasons. And he had to know, as his commissioner of Black emigration had told him, that if American voters made a national decision to deport a group for racial reasons, it would have been easy—in 1862 or 2000— to get the consent by private and public violence and direct and indirect government pressure.

Will someone say in Lincoln's defense that it is harsh to call this ethnic cleansing since Lincoln knew nothing of the twentieth-century horrors of Germany, Bosnia, and Kosovo? But how can any literate person say that since the Slave Trade and the removal of the Indians to the West were the prologues of the twentieth century horrors and since Lincoln volunteered three times for what author Cecil Eby called *"That Disgraceful Affair," the Black Hawk War* "in which a small band of peaceful Sauk Indians, led by the aging Black Hawk, was sacrificed to land greed and political ambition."

Lincoln knew what he was doing, and why, and he begged Congress to accept his *means*: gradual compensated emancipation and deportation."Other *means*," he said, "may succeed; this could not fail. *The way* is plain, peaceful, generous, just—*a way* which, if followed, the world will forever applaud, and God must forever bless (italics added)."

What would happen if Congress refused to accept the God-ordained way, "peaceful, generous, just," of buying slaves over a thirty-seven year period and deporting them to a place "without the United States" in "congenial climes, and with people of their own blood and race"?

We shall lose, Lincoln said, "the last best, hope of earth."

What did Lincoln mean by the phrase everybody praises and nobody questions?

What was "the last best, hope of earth?"

The last best hope of earth was a Union of White people purified and annealed by the deportation of Blacks. It was, as Lincoln said in the Lincoln-Douglas debates, a White asylum for *"free White people everywhere,* the world over—in which Hans and Baptiste and Patrick, and all other men from all the world, may find new homes and better their conditions in life" (CW 3:312, Lincoln's italics). Since almost all Americans pretend to misunderstand Lincoln's meaning, let us repeat once again what he said in the last fourteen lines of the most quoted and least understood presidential message in our history:

"In *giving* freedom to the *slave* [by buying the slaves over a thirty-seven-year period and deporting them to "a congenial clime" with people of their own blood and race] we *assure* freedom to the free [White people], honorable alike in what we give, and what we preserve."

Perhaps the worst thing about this celebrated speech is the bad faith of Lincoln, who does not seem to know who he is and what he has done.

Having tried for nearly eighteen months, by his own words and his own admission, to escape history, and having refused to listen to abolitionists and militant Republicans, he turns the tables and lectures the men who have been telling him for twenty months that he could not escape history. Then, having learned the words, he renounces the action, returning to the ditch he had just climbed out of by trying once again to stop history and the virtually inevitable movement of the juggernaut of immediate emancipation.

Having violated history on all these levels, he makes the unpardonable historical mistake of embracing in the same message two unrealities—ethnic cleansing and the creation of an all-White state—that would be condemned by all subsequent history.

Thus, Abraham Lincoln hoist with his own historical petard.

Trying to escape history, he says that *we* cannot escape history.

Trying to escape immediate emancipation, he calls for a compensated gradual emancipation plan condemned by history and the Border State representatives.

Trying to deny the arithmetic of life, he calls a land inhabited by Native Americans, Africans, Asians, and Europeans "the last best, [White] hope" of a world that was and is overwhelmingly colored.

In denying history on all these levels, and in giving new life to racists and deportationists, Lincoln provided additional proof that the Emancipation Proclamation was not his plan.

The only remaining question is why he decided to oppose the Proclamation so publicly one month before he was scheduled to issue it. We have maintained since the first chapter that this was deliberate and that Lincoln hoped by this initiative to either slow down or disrupt the movement for immediate emancipation. Where is the evidence for this view? One piece of evidence is in the document, and Abraham Lincoln as usual provides it himself, saying seven paragraphs from the end:

"Nor will the war, nor proceedings under the proclamation of September 22, 1862, be stayed because of the *recommendation* of this plan. Its timely *adoption*, I doubt not, would bring restoration and thereby stay both" (CW 5:536, Lincoln's italics).

In what was perhaps the turning point of the American drama, the Thirty-seventh Congress refused to consider Lincoln's gambit, ending the most serious proposal ever made to Congress for the deportation of Blacks. It was too late even then, but this was the last possible chance for a solution by sailing. By rejecting that plan, the Thirty-seventh Congress, unlike Lincoln, confirmed what history had confirmed, that Blacks and Whites were condemned to walk this road together and that the Declaration and the Dream would never have any real meaning until the meaning was real in Black, White, and Red.

In reading the responses to Lincoln's proposal, one is struck by the contempt and condescension expressed by conservatives and liberals. Congressman James A. Garfield said he could hardly believe his ears when he listened to the message and heard no concrete proposal for winning the war. "The President," he said, "goes into what seems to me a most weak and absurd scheme of emancipation in the year of our Lord, 1900, and goes on to say that this scheme will end the rebellion sooner than it can be ended by force, and much cheaper" (T. Smith, 262-3). Lincoln's old friend, Illinois Senator Orville B. Browning, was struck by "the hallucination the President seems to be laboring under that Congress can suppress the rebellion by adopting his plan of compensated emancipation, when if there was no opposition to it, it would require at least four years to have it adopted as he proposes" (BD 591).

Republicans were more amused than enraged by the proposals. Horace Greeley harrumphed in the *New York Tribune* of December 2: "Gradualism, compensation, exportation, if these tubs amuse the whale, let him have them."

There was, as Greeley indicated, an element of farce in all this. For having given himself and the South one hundred days to contemplate the possibilities of a paper proclamation, Lincoln stumbled in the last days of 1862 from improbability to improbability. First, as we have seen, he sent out SOS's to foreign governments in a comic-opera attempt to deport freed slaves and make the problem disappear. Secondly, he proposed a totally impracticable scheme to Congress based on the passage of three constitutional amendments and the appropriation of billions of dollars. Thirdly, he maneuvered behind the scenes in vain attempts to manufacture White Southern governments that could avoid the proclamation and keep their Blacks in slavery. Having specified in the proclamation that Southern areas could avoid emancipation by sending representatives to Congress, he pressed his generals to find "gentlemen of character" who wanted to bring back the Union as it was. Toward this end, Abraham Lincoln sent the following letter to military and civilian authorities in occupied Louisiana:

> Executive Mansion,
> WASHINGTON, OCTOBER 14, 1862
>
> Major General Butler, Governor Shepley, & and [sic] all having military and naval authority under the United States within the S[t]ate of Louisiana.
>
> The bearer of this, Hon. John E. Bouligny, a citizen of Louisiana, goes to that State seeking to have such of the people thereof as desire to avoid the unsatisfactory prospect before them, *and to have peace again upon the old terms* under the constitution of the United States, to manifest such desire by elections of members to the Congress of the United States particularly, and perhaps a legislature, State officers, and United States Senators friendly to their object. I shall be glad for you and each of you, to aid him and all others acting for this object, as much as possible. In all available ways give the people a chance to express their wishes at these elections. Follow forms of law as far as convenient, but at all events get the expression of the largest number of the people possible. All see how such action will connect with, and affect the proclamation of September 22nd. *Of course the men elected should be gentlemen of character willing to swear support to the constitution, as of old,* and known to be above reasonable suspicion of duplicity. (CW 5:462-3, italics added)

If you want to know where Lincoln's head was shortly after he signed the Preliminary Proclamation, and what he really thought about that document, re-read the revealing sentence in which he appealed to White Southerners who wanted to avoid *the unsatisfactory prospect before them* and "to have peace again upon the old terms under the constitution . . . ." The "men elected," he said, "should be *gentlemen* of character [my italics] willing to swear support of the constitution, as of old . . . ." Which constitution was that? It was the pre-Fort Sumter constitution, the one that sanctioned slavery and the hunting and capturing of fugitive slaves.

Avoiding "the unsatisfactory prospect" of freeing Blacks, even symbolically, was close to Lincoln's heart, and he followed up with urgent commands to commanding generals in Tennessee, Arkansas and other occupied areas. In a letter to General Benjamin F. Butler on November 6, Lincoln said he was "anxious to hear" what was being done about the election in Louisiana. Another letter, fifteen days later, said Lincoln was "annoyed" that nothing had been done. He wanted an election held even if it could not be held strictly according to law. "Do not waste a day about it," Lincoln said (CW 5:487, 504-5).

Responding to these and other urgent Lincoln appeals, Union generals created White Lincoln nuclei in liberated areas while practically reestablishing slavery under a name. Historian George Bancroft and abolitionists decried the "sham pacification" on the Eastern Shore of Virginia, where General John A. Dix permitted slaveholders to continue their old ways. "Dix's approach," Thomas and Hyman said, "matched that of Lincoln, whose thinking at this time envisaged no change in race relations in ostensibly loyal areas . . . (243).

If we look closely behind the curtain of events in the last weeks of 1862, one can hardly avoid the view that Lincoln was wholly involved in an agenda that differed markedly from his announced agenda. We know now—and the message he sent to Congress on December 1 proves—that his "whole soul," as crony David Davis reported after conferring with him, was engaged not in the Preliminary Proclamation but in a compensated emancipation/colonization plan that contradicted his proposed emancipation proclamation. There is evidence, moreover, that he seemed to have believed at this crucial moment that the war would soon be over and that he could keep from issuing the Proclamation or minimize its impact. In an unusually perceptive analysis, Donald said that Lincoln, "elated" by the possibility of bringing some of the Confederates states back into union via his "White enclave" plan, and "confident" that Grant and other generals could inflict a series of decisive blows against the Confederacy, "fore-saw the possibility that by January the war might be nearly over and the Union might be restored—but the United States would still be a slaveholding nation" (397).

These and other maneuvers heightened suspicion in Washington, where some people were saying Lincoln would never sign the promised document. Of all those who monitored Lincoln's actions in the last days of 1862, perhaps Congressman Charles Sedgwick understood it best. "Some," he said, "doubt his intention to issue the proclamation of 1st January; I do not. Many assert, more fear, that it will be essentially modified from what is promised. I do not fear this; but what I do fear, is that he will stop with the proclamation and take no active and vigorous measures to insure its efficacy" (Forbes 345-6).

If anything, Sedgwick underestimated the extent of Lincoln's opposition to *his* emancipation policy. For as the New Year deadline approached, Lincoln desperately doubled his anti-emancipation bets, maneuvering behind the scenes in frantic efforts to expand the size of the emancipation-proof White enclaves he was trying to create in liberated areas. Day after day, in the last days of the year, he sent hurry-up telegrams and inquiries to the generals and federal offi-cials who were arranging "show" and sham White elections in Louisiana, Virginia and other liberated areas in order to avoid "the unsatisfactory prospect" of freeing Blacks. On the last day of the year, he told General Dix that he had less than twenty-four hours to create a White-dominated enclave in eastern Virginia, adding:

"Time nearly up."

24

No Hidin' Place

THERE was "no escape." For almost two years, he "had tried various expedients to escape issuing an executive order emancipating the slaves . . . ." But "turn which way he would," this "disturbing element . . . rose up against "him, and now he was confronted with "the last and only alternative" (WH 842).

God knows he didn't want to do it, but "there was no dodging this Negro question any longer" and he had to face it "or in all probability go under" (Carpenter 83-4).

So:

He was "driven"—his word—to it.

Why was he driven to it?

Part of the answer to that question is in a last-minute revolt staged by Senate Republicans, who threatened to bring his government down. This revolt is usually interpreted narrowly as a plot to oust Secretary of State Seward, who was considered the anti-emancipation power behind the throne. But a closer examination reveals the main issue: Abraham Lincoln and his failure to organize and lead a real war.

The leaders of the Senate revolt, which met in secret caucuses on Tuesday, Wednesday and Thursday, December 16, 17 and 18, 1862, lodged five major charges against Lincoln: 1) he lacked firmness,

2) did not lead, 3) listened too much to proslavery advisors, 4)didn't confer with his cabinet, and 5) placed "our armies under the command of officers who did not believe in the policy of the government and had no sympathy with its purposes." A leading Senate moderate, William Pitt Fessenden, told Lincoln to his face that his administration had favored proslavery generals and "that almost every officer known as an anti-slavery man had been disgraced."[52] What moderates, radicals and conservatives said in Congress was echoed by a chorus of critics at every level of the Union. Emerson told his *Journal* that Lincoln never intended to put "radicals into power. When he puts one into office, as Frémont, or Phelps, or Lane, he takes care to neutralize him by a Democrat or a Kentuckian who will thwart him" (457).

Most congressional critics used Seward as a scapegoat, but Senator John Sherman of Ohio told the Senate caucus that the problem was not Seward but Lincoln. "The difficulty," Senator Sherman said, "was with the President himself. He had neither dignity, order, nor firmness."

The next day, according to Browning's *Diary*, Lincoln and Seward were bitterly denounced by a number of senators. "Many speeches were made," Browning wrote, "all expressive of want of confidence in the President and his cabinet. Some of them denouncing the President and expressing a willingness to vote for a resolution asking him to resign" (BD 598-9).

When, on Thursday, December 18, Browning visited the White House, Lincoln called him aside and asked "me if I was at the caucus yesterday. I told him I was and the day before also. Said he 'What do these men want?' I answered "I hardly know Mr. President, but they are exceedingly violent towards the administration, and what we did yesterday [naming a committee to confer with Lincoln on the composition of his cabinet] was the gentlest thing that could be done. We had to do that or worse." Said he "They wish to get rid of me, and I am sometimes half disposed to gratify them." Browning replied that some senators "do wish to get rid of you," and urged Lincoln "to stand firmly at your post." Lincoln said: "We are now on the brink of destruction. It appears to me the Almighty is against us, and I can hardly see a ray of hope" (BD 600).

Lincoln survived by pitting Secretary Chase against Secretary Seward and by promising, implicitly, to change his ways, but one thing was certain at the end of 1862: he had only one option, and that was to sign the promised Emancipation Proclamation.

This was the sense if not the exact language of the message Lincoln gave to a last-minute caller, Judge Benjamin Franklin Thomas of the Massachusetts Supreme Court, who told Browning, according to a diary entry he made on the night of December 31, that "the President was fatally bent upon his course, saying that if he should refuse to issue his proclamation there would be a rebellion in the north, and that a dictator would be placed over his head within the week" (607).

Lincoln went to glory kicking and protesting.

At a last-minute cabinet meeting on Wednesday, December 31, he argued passionately in favor of excluding the only slaves he could free, the slaves in areas held by Union forces in the South. Five cabinet members, including the conservative Seward and ultraconservatives Blair and Bates, told him that this was unfair and possibly unconstitutional, but Lincoln refused to budge. "Without interchanging opinions," Welles noted, the cabinet members "advised that any and all exceptions of fractional parts of any State should be omitted. It was stated that, slavery being the creature of local law, no State where it existed could discriminate in its enactments so as to authorize its continuance in some counties, yet prohibit it in others. There could be no such unequal, sectional legislation in any State" (WH 849).

Postmaster General Montgomery Blair, one of the most conservative members of the cabinet, "spoke of the importance of the proclamation as a state paper, and said that persons in after times, in seeking correct information of the occurrences of those times, would read and wonder why the thirteen parishes and the City of New Orleans in Louisiana, and the counties in Virginia about Norfolk, were excepted from the proclamation; they were in the 'very heart and back of slavery,' and unless there was some good reason which was then unknown to him, he hoped they would not be excepted" (RR 92-3).

Seward, who was widely believed to be unsympathetic to the proclamation, said: "I think so, too; I think they should not be excepted."

Lincoln replied: "Well, upon first view your objections are clearly good; but after I issued the proclamation of September 22, Mr. [John] Bouligny, of Louisiana, then here, came to see me. He was a great invalid, and had scarcely the strength to walk up stairs. He wanted to know of me if these parishes in Louisiana and New Orleans should hold an election, and elect Members of Congress, whether I would not except them from this proclamation. I told him I would."

The question is what came first, the chicken or the Boulignys. For Lincoln said in the Preliminary Proclamation that liberated Southern areas could keep their slaves if they created Boulignys. It follows therefore that Lincoln himself created the Boulignys of the South, and it is ironic that Bouligny was later disqualified because he had run for office under the Confederacy.

Chase submitted a written statement in favor of the half-million or so slaves that Lincoln intended to keep in slavery. There were, he said, two major objections to Lincoln's proposed course: "Such exceptions will impair, in public estimation, the moral effect of the Proclamation," and will practically reestablish slavery in certain areas. "Through the operation of the various acts of Congress, the slaves of disloyal masters in those parts are already enfranchised; and the slaves of loyal masters are practically so. Some of the latter have already commenced paying wages to their laborers, formerly slaves; and it is to be feared that if, by these exceptions, Slavery is practically reestablished in favor of some masters, while abolished by laws and by the necessary effect of military occupation as to others, very serious inconveniences may arise" (CL 350).

Lincoln insisted on "practically" reestablishing slavery in designated areas and in keeping in slavery the only slaves he could have freed on January 1, 1863. Chase continued for more than a year to argue for the freedom of the Blacks Lincoln insisted on keeping in slavery in the document that allegedly freed Blacks.

After the cabinet members dispersed on December 31, a shady opportunist named Bernard Kock slipped into the White House with a contract that called for the colonization of five thousand Blacks on Vache Island off the coast of Haiti at a cost of fifty dollars a head. Koch was by almost all accounts a poseur and charlatan—he called himself "Governor of Ile á Vache"—but he was backed by New York and Boston "capitalists."

On Wednesday night, December 31, 1862, the man who would be hailed on January 1, 1863, as "the great emancipator," read the fine print and signed a contract on behalf of the United States of America to deport American-born citizens of African descent to an island off the coast of Haiti.

This was not, by any means, the end of the night before the Christmas–like celebrations of what one museum exhibit called "the most revolutionary act in American history." And before leaving the White House, one must pause to note "the curious incident" of the dog that didn't bark in the night. Sherlock Holmes, as you remember, made his case in *The Silver Blaze* by proving that if a certain phenomenon had happened the dog would have barked. We can make our case by proving that if Lincoln had expected one of the greatest social upheavals in American history, he and his aides would have barked or, at least, would have done *something* to prepare the people and the armed services. But, astonishingly and revealingly, Lincoln did nothing.

After announcing that he was going to free some four million slaves on January 1, one would have expected a prudent executive to send out a call for tents and blankets and additional flour for bread. But September passed and October, and Lincoln did nothing.

During this time, he sent letter after letter to Union generals, ordering them to organize elections that would make it possible for

Southern areas to avoid emancipating slaves. But in all that time, from September 23 to December 31, he didn't write a single letter telling Union officials to prepare for the forthcoming day of freedom for four million slaves.

Thanksgiving Day passed and Christmas and December 30 and December 31, and still Lincoln did nothing, proving beyond conjecture that he knew on December 31 that he wasn't going to free anybody on January 1.

Part Ten

"Whipped Into...Glory"

[T]he patriots of both Houses, as the exponents of the noble and loftiest aspirations of the American people, whipped in—and this literally, not figuratively—whipped Mr. Lincoln into the glory of having issued the Emancipation Proclamation. The laws promulgated by this dying Congress initiated the Emancipation—generated the Proclamation of the 22d of September, and of January 1st. History will not allow one to wear borrowed plumage.

—Diary of Adam Gurowski

Lincoln became Lincoln because of the Negro . . . .

—Historian Benjamin Quarles

25

Emancipating The Emancipator

W HEN, at last, after the 74,000 nights of American slavery and the four hundred years of the slave trade and the slaughter of tens of millions of Blacks, when, after all this blood, after the blood of Nealee and Nat Turner and John Brown, and after all the compromises, the compromises of 1787 and 1820 and 1850, and after all attempts to evade the issue, including his own, had failed—when, after all this, Abraham Lincoln picked up his pen to sign the thing, he couldn't do it.

It was Thursday, January 1, 1863, and Lincoln was poised before a handful of people in the cabinet room of the White House to sign the promised Emancipation Proclamation. But at the last moment, something in him—was it his conscience, his unconscious, or his fear of what he called the evils of sudden emancipation?—revolted, and when he picked up the pen to do it, his arm trembled so violently that he stopped, overcome suddenly by a superstitious feeling.

He "took a pen," an eyewitness said, "dipped it in ink, moved his hand to the place for the signing, held it a moment and then removed his hand and dropped the pen. After a little hesitation he again took up the pen and went through the same movement as before" (Carpenter 269).

Always superstitious, always on the lookout for supernatural signs, Lincoln paused, awed despite himself. Then a simple explanation came to him: he had, he said, been shaking hands for hours in the New Year's Day reception and it was only natural that his right arm should be paralyzed.

Without being a Freudian analyst and without even being a psychiatrist at all, we have the feeling that the explanation was *too* simple, given Lincoln's deep-seated opposition to sudden and general emancipation and his lifelong fear-fascination with the Black/White thing. But the explanation, whatever its limitations, at least consoled Lincoln, who shook off the spasm and scrawled his name, saying he didn't want the signature to be "tremulous" because people would say "he had some compunctions."[53]

He had "compunctions."

Nothing testifies to this more powerfully than the document itself, which is more often celebrated than read, or lived. Cold, forbidding, with all the passion and eloquence of a real estate deed, the Proclamation doesn't contain a single quotable sentence and doesn't enumerate a single principle hostile to slavery. As a document, it lends weight to the observation of Herndon, who said, "When he freed the slaves, there was no heart in the act" (HW 483).

There wasn't much else in it, either.

For the Emancipation Proclamation didn't, as we have seen, emancipate anybody. Worse, it practically reenslaved some five hundred thousand slaves. On the day after the big signing, Donn Piatt congratulated Secretary of State Seward.

"Yes," Seward replied, "we have let off a puff of wind over an accomplished fact."

"What do you mean, Mr. Seward?" Piatt asked.

"I mean that the Emancipation Proclamation was uttered in the first gun fired at Fort Sumter, and we have been the last to hear it. As it is, we show our sympathy with slavery by emancipating slaves where we cannot reach them, and holding them in bondage where we can set them free" (Piatt 150).

The Proclamation argues so powerfully against itself that the author and other commentators believe it was a ploy by which Lincoln hoped to buy time and forestall a definitive act of liberation. There is evidence, in fact, that he never intended to free the slaves, and that he hoped that events—a stunning Union victory or adoption of his thirty-seven-year gradual emancipation plan—would make the Proclamation moot or enable him to recall it.

Critical opinion is almost unanimous on the limitations of the document that freed all Blacks and freed no Blacks.

Hofstadter said the Proclamation has "all the moral grandeur of a bill of lading" (169).

Randall said "limitations in the famous proclamation itself, with its definite lack of kingdom-come quality, produce a sense of amazement," almost as if "he didn't like his most famous act" (1946, 46).

Count Gurowski, who kept both ears to the ground, concluded that Lincoln had been literally "whipped into the glory," noting in his diary that "the patriots of both Houses [of Congress], as the exponents of the noble and loftiest aspirations of the American people, whipped . . . Mr. Lincoln into the glory of having issued the Emancipation Proclamation. The laws promulgated by this dying Congress initiated the Emancipation—generated the Proclamation of 22d of September, and of January lst . . . " (GD 2: 99-100).

How did Blacks respond to all this?

They were jubilant, of course. How would you respond if you were told that a jolly White man with a beard had signed a document ending your slavery and ensuring that you and your family could live in freedom like other people, with land and a decent house and, at a minimum, a mule? Because of the criminal slave system, most Blacks could not read and even the Blacks—and Whites—who could read didn't understand immediately what few Blacks or Whites understand today, that the Proclamation in and of itself didn't free anybody on January 1, 1863.

Quarles is at his best on this point, telling us that Blacks overlooked the Proclamation's "lack of any exalted sentiment, as if Lincoln's heart were not in it." Nor did they "bother themselves with the proclamation's other language, its 'whereas's" and "to wit's." It was natural, he said, that the Negro's reading of the edict should be selective. "In a document proclaiming liberty, the unfree never bother to read the fine print" (1962, 149).

Although the document had little immediate effect on the masses of slaves, it saved the Union by making it impossible for foreign governments to intervene on the side of the Confederacy. Despite that fact or perhaps because of it, the English government frowned on the whole process, saying in the words of Earl Russell that the Proclamation "professes to emancipate all slaves in places where the United States' authorities cannot, exercising jurisdiction, now make emancipation a reality, but it does not decree emancipation of slaves in any States or parts of States occupied by Federal troops and subject to Federal jurisdiction, and where, therefore, emancipation, if decreed, might have been carried into effect."

The net effect of all this, Russell said, was that Lincoln made slavery "at once legal and illegal," and made "slaves either punishable for running away from their masters, or entitled to be supported and encouraged by so doing, according to the locality of the plantation to which they belong, and the locality in which they may happen to be" (AC 1863, 834).

Englishmen, Americans, Northerners, Southerners, Lincoln friends, Lincoln critics and Lincoln experts, Randall, Hume, Hofstadter, Quarles: almost everyone concedes that Lincoln's Proclamation wasn't much and that it did little if any emancipating. Does this mean that "the greatest moral act of the nineteenth century," to quote one enthusiast, was a fraud? Was it, as so many students have said, a gambit in a White game that had nothing at all to do with freedom? Or was it the earnest, equivocating gesture of an earnest, equivocating man, torn apart by conflicting personal, racial, and political impulses he could neither name, reject, or accept?

To answer these questions, we shall have to begin with a task that almost all Americans shun—we shall have to read one of the most uninspired documents in American history and the only major Lincoln document with not one scintilla of the famous Lincoln panache.

The Proclamation, simply called "A Proclamation," begins by quoting the Preliminary Proclamation of September 22, 1862, and then continues:

> Now, therefore, I, Abraham Lincoln, President of the United States, by virtue of the power in me vested as Commander-in-Chief, of the Army and Navy of the United States in time of actual armed rebellion against authority and government of the United States, and as a fit and necessary war measure for suppressing said rebellion, do, on this first day of January, in the year of our Lord one thousand eight hundred and sixty three, and in accordance with my purpose so to do publicly proclaimed for the full period of one hundred days . . . order and designate as the States and parts of States wherein the people thereof respectively, are this day in rebellion against the United States, the following, towit:
>
> Arkansas, Texas, Louisiana, (except the Parishes of St. Bernard, Plaquemines, Jefferson, St. Johns, St. Charles, St. James [,] Ascension, Assumption, Terrebonne, Lafourche, St. Mary, St. Martin, and Orleans, including the City of New-Orleans) Mississippi, Alabama, Florida, Georgia, South-Carolina, North-Carolina, and Virginia, (except the fortyeight [sic] counties designated as West Virginia, and also the counties of Berkeley, Accomac, Northampton, Elizabeth-City, York, Princess Ann, and Norfolk, including the cities of Norfolk & Portsmouth; and *which excepted parts are, for the present, left precisely as if this proclamation were not issued.*
>
> And by virtue of the power and for the purpose aforesaid, I do order and declare that all persons held as slaves within said designated States, and parts of States, are, and henceforward shall be free; and that the Executive government of the United States, including the military and naval authorities thereof, will recognize and maintain the freedom of said persons.
>
> And I hereby enjoin upon the people so declared to be free to abstain from all violence, unless in necessary self-defence; and I

recommend to them that, in all cases when allowed, they labor faithfully for reasonable wages.

And I further declare and make known, that such persons of suitable condition, will be received into the armed service of the United States to garrison forts, positions, stations, and other places, and to man vessels of all sorts in said service.

And upon this act, sincerely believed to be an act of justice, warranted by the Constitution, upon military necessity, I invoke the considerate judgment of mankind, and the gracious favor of Almighty God. (CW 6:28-30, italics added)

The first thing to notice about this celebrated document is that there is no hallelujah in it. There is no new-birth-of-freedom swagger, no perish-from-the-earth pizzazz. Without even thinking about it, without even giving it a second thought, the allegedly illiterate slaves came up with twenty or so phrases, including "Free At Last!" that circled the globe and even shook the foundation of the Lincoln Memorial when Martin Luther King Jr. quoted it one hundred years later. But the Gettysburg Man, who homered, we are told, out of town in Gettysburg, came up to the plate in the last of the ninth with three men on base and two outs in the World Series of Freedom and struck out semantically and politically. Lincolnians say he missed on purpose, that he was so terrified by the possibility of Black violence and White opposition that he bent over backwards to keep from exciting Blacks and scaring Whites. Even if we allow these considerations, the swing was so inappropriate and missed the ball by such a wide margin that it refers us to the author, who never missed when he was talking about the freedom of White folks but who always sounded like a probation officer when he was talking about the freedom of Black folks.

If someone says in defense that one sentence in the document reaches for the mountaintop and absolves Lincoln of indifference, or worse, I will agree. The only problem is that that sentence—"And upon this act sincerely believed to be an act of justice," etc.—was written by Secretary of the Treasury Chase, who told Lincoln, in so many words, that the "greatest moral act of the nineteenth century" needed a little morality and a little humanity.

It also needed a little emancipating.

For not only did the document fail to free anyone, but it re-enslaved and/or condemned to continued slavery more than a half-million persons. The 556,540 slaves in the Border states of Maryland, Missouri, Delaware and Kentucky were excluded, of course. But the most surprising and damaging omissions were the areas controlled by federal troops, large sections of Tennessee, Louisiana and Virginia, including the cities of New Orleans and Norfolk, "all of which excepted parts," Lincoln said, "are for the present left precisely as if this proclamation were not issued."

This meant that Lincoln, as Treasury Secretary Chase had already told him, was practically reenslaving some 500,000 slaves (87,812 in Louisiana, 33,332 in Virginia, and 275,719 in Tennessee), some of whom were already working for wages and enjoying the first fruits of freedom (CL 350). [54]

The limitations of the document were analyzed with great insight by Horace Greeley who expressed amazement that Lincoln had excepted the 275,000 slaves of Tennessee and the slaves in the lower portion of Louisiana, "two states with more than one hundred thousand of their citizens in open revolt." Over and above that, Greeley said Lincoln had broken faith with the slaves. He had proclaimed unconditionally in September that he would declare free all slaves in states or districts then in rebellion—"not such of them as he should at the set time see fit to liberate." This was unfortunate, Greeley said, adding: "We do most profoundly regret that he has not hewed up to the line chalked by himself."

This, Greeley said, suggested trickery, for *Lincoln could have been a contender*. He could "have stricken the shackles from the limbs of several hundreds of thousands of slaves, and thereby given to those left in bondage to the Rebels an earnest that our failure to reach and liberate them resulted from want of power rather than of will. The exemptions will be seized upon by the Rebels to make the slaves believe that the Unionists are trifling with and duping them—seeking to use them in the contest, but not intending to reward them with liberty."

Greeley published this analysis in the *New York Tribune* on January 3, 1863, and almost nobody since then has quoted it or asked his questions. Why did Lincoln fail to hew "up to the line chalked by himself"? Why did he give ammunition to people, Southern Whites especially, who said that the Proclamation was a trick and that Lincoln was no more interested in Black freedom than Jefferson Davis? More concretely, why did he "free" slaves in Atlanta and Richmond, where he couldn't free them, and leave them in slavery in New Orleans and Norfolk, where he could have freed them.

Lincoln, as we have seen, gave different and conflicting explanations for the exemptions, saying on one occasion that he had promised certain White politicians that he would except New Orleans and large sections of Louisiana and Virginia so loyal Whites could form (White) governments in these areas. To Secretary Chase, who objected to the exceptions and pressed his objections for the next year, Lincoln explained that there was no "military necessity" to free Blacks in areas controlled by Union troops. When Chase told him that learned lawyers and a Southern governor said that military necessity was precisely why the exemptions should be revoked, Lincoln shifted ground and said on Thursday, September 17, 1863, two months before he called for a new birth of freedom at Gettysburg, that freeing the only slaves he could free "should be deferred until after the Fall elections" of 1863 (CD 199).

Lincoln's default had vast implications not only in rebel states but also in the so-called loyal slave states. It was general knowledge that Kentuckians, for example, were selling and reenslaving African-Americans freed by the war and congressional acts There were also repercussions in the North. The *Annual Cyclopaedia* of 1862 reported that the officers of Illinois troops who returned to the state "and brought Negroes with them" were indicted for violating the state law banning Black immigration (752).

Lincoln never stopped plotting against his Proclamation.

He never stopped trying to limit it or to change and soften its potential impact. Seven days after signing the document, he told one of his old Illinois friends, proslavery Democratic general James A. McClernand, that loyal and disloyal slaveholders had nothing to fear and that he was still on their side.

"As to the States not included in [the Proclamation]," he wrote General McClernand on January 8, "they can have their rights in the Union as of old" (CW 6:48).

What did that "as of old" business mean? It meant their "rights" to hold, buy and sell slaves as in the prewar Constitution? What about the slaveowners whose slaves had been "freed" by the Proclamation? "Even the people of the states included," he wrote, "if they choose, need not be hurt by it."

How could Lincoln say, seven days after he signed the Proclamation, that slaveowners in the Confederate states need not be hurt by a Proclamation which declared all slaves in Confederate states, with certain exceptions, free?

"Let them," Lincoln answered, "adopt systems of apprenticeship for the colored people, conforming substantially to the most approved plans of gradual emancipation . . . ."

What did Lincoln mean by "the most approved plans of of gradual emancipation"? He meant the most approved plans he suggested in his Delaware proposal (CW 5:29-30), which would have continued slavery under another name for twenty or even fifty years.

While Lincoln was pressing his recycled apprenticeship plans on this level, he was at the same time using emancipation not to emancipate but to enslave. It is not noted often enough that *Lincoln turned the Emancipation Proclamation on its head and made it the principal instrument for keeping hundreds of thousands of men, women and children in slavery for two more years.* During these three years, from 1863 to 1865, the biggest slaveowner in the United States was Lincoln, who used the Proclamation as a shield to protect himself—and slave-holders—from the rising emancipation waves. It will be said in objection that the half-million or so slaves in occupied Union areas in the South, especially the slaves in occupied Louisiana and Virginia, were the slaves of the United States, but the man who kept them in slavery and who could have emancipated them at any moment was Abraham Lincoln.

Thus, paradoxically, Lincoln fought emancipation with emancipation, presenting the document as a conservative defense against radicals who wanted to go further and emancipate all slaves immediately and confiscate the property of slaveowners. In this guise, the Proclamation became the slaveholders' best friend since it legalized slavery and quasi slavery in Norfolk, New Orleans and other areas where Union generals became de facto overseers, using rifles and bayonets to make Blacks render "faithful" and "respectful" service to former slaveowners.

As if that wasn't enough, the Proclamation became, in Lincoln's hands and in the hands of his generals, its own limit since, as Lincoln never tired of saying, it was a war document of doubtful legality that would self-destruct with the war. This meant of course that the issue would end up in court and would probably lead to decades of litigation, a possibility that didn't seem to disturb Lincoln, who said repeatedly and, as I have said, indiscreetly that the Proclamation was full of legal loopholes.

"Nobody," editor James C. Welling said, "was more quick to perceive or more frank to admit the legal weakness and insufficiency of the Emancipation Proclamation than Mr. Lincoln." Lincoln recognized more than anyone else, Welling said, that the Proclamation "was a frail muniment of title to any slave who should claim to be free by virtue of its vigor alone" (RR 551).

The problem here was that the document didn't deal with the *institution* of slavery and would not have secured the permanent freedom of slaves anywhere, Julian pointed out, "because the *status* of slavery, as it existed under the local laws of the States prior to the war, would have remained the same after the re-establishment of peace. All emancipated slaves found in those States, or returning to them, would have been subject to slavery as before, for the simple reason that no military proclamation could operate to abolish their municipal laws. Nothing short of a constitutional amendment could at once give freedom to our black millions and make their re-enslavement impossible . . ." (RR 63-64).

Lincoln went out of his way to emphasize the limitations of the document. Anyone who doubts this need only read the disturbing language he drafted for the loyalty oath of returning White Southerners, who were required to swear that they would support the Proclamation "so long and so far as not modified or declared void by decision of the Supreme Court" (CW 7:54).

Not content with undermining emancipation on these levels, Lincoln argued publicly against the basic principle of the Proclamation, telling everybody that he was still opposed to the alleged basic principle of the Proclamation—immediate emancipation—and that he still thought gradual emancipation was better for both Blacks and Whites. Not only did he say that but he used the immense resources of the federal government and the Army to support men and parties who were fighting immediate emancipation.

When, several months after he issued the Proclamation, the gradual and immediate emancipation parties clashed in the Border state of Missouri, Lincoln announced his support for the gradual emancipation party and threw his support to a Union general who was opposing militant emancipationists in that state. After conferring with Lincoln at the White House, James Taussig, a militant Missouri leader, reported that Lincoln said that he still favored a gradual emancipation process that contradicted the immediate emancipation principle of the Emancipation Proclamation.

> The President said that the Union men in Missouri who are in favor of *gradual emancipation* represented his views better than

those who are in favor of *immediate emancipation*. In explanation of his views on this subject, the President said that in his speeches he had frequently used as an illustration, the case of a man who had an excrescence on the back of his neck, the removal of which, *in one operation,* would result in the death of the patient, while 'tinkering off by degrees' would preserve life.

Taussig said "he was sorely tempted . . . to reply with the illustration of the dog whose tail was amputated by inches," but restrained himself as Lincoln "announced clearly that, as far as he was at present advised, the radicals in Missouri had no right to consider themselves the exponents of his views on the subject of emancipation in that State" (Raymond 430-1).

Lincoln doubted the wisdom of the Proclamation for months afterward and told Congressman Julian and others that it had "done about as much harm as good" (RR 56). When, on Sunday, January 25, 1863, Lincoln received a group of abolitionists, including Wendell Phillips, he said "he had not expected much from [the proclamation] at first, and consequently had not been disappointed . . . ." The abolitionists urged a strong follow-up campaign, using antislavery generals and governors in the South. Lincoln objected, saying, "Suppose I should put in the South these anti-slavery generals and governors, *what could they do with the slaves that would come to them?"*

The question, and the mind-set it reflected, alarmed the abolitionists. Rev. Moncure D. Conway said later that the group was shocked "that the recent proclaimer of liberty to three millions of Negroes should at that date thus confess that he was putting forward in the South generals and governors who would *not* carry it out in good faith by freeing practically as many as possible of those declared free . . . ." Even more shocking, Lincoln seemed to "be genuinely exercised in mind on so rudimentary a question as to what should be done with a people who had always supported themselves and their masters . . . ."

All this suggested to Conway and the delegation that President Lincoln was indifferent and uninformed and "that the nation, like Issachar of old, was a strong ass between two burthens—slavery in arms, and an administration two years behind the mind of the country . . ." (Segal 240, italics in original).

Still more unmistakable evidence of Lincoln's orientation can be found in his failure to provide equal pay and equal protection for Black soldiers, who were promised thirteen dollars a month, the same pay as White privates, and were insulted with an offer of seven dollars a month. Many Black soldiers refused to accept the seven dollars. When the Massachusetts legislature passed a bill providing the six dollar difference, the state's Black soldiers refused to accept the money, saying they were fighting for a principle, not money.

Pressing that issue, Black and White abolitionists organized a national campaign in favor of Black soldiers, but Lincoln refused to budge. When his conservative attorney general Edward Bates told him that it was his constitutional duty to order equal pay, he sat on the opinion until Congress rebelled. Before Congress rectified Lincoln's error, a brave Black sergeant named William Walker, who participated in a protest against Lincoln's policy, was arrested and charged with mutiny. At his trial, he pleaded in extenuation that "nearly the whole of his regiment acted in like manner as himself," that "when the Regiment stacked arms and refused further duty . . . . I did not then exercise any command over them" and that "I carried my arms and equipment back with me to my company street."

Despite this testimony and pleas from major leaders, including some Union officers, Walker was convicted and sentenced to death. Although Lincoln repeatedly overruled the death sentences of White soldiers, he looked the other way when, on February 29, 1864, at 9 o' clock in the morning, Sergeant William Walker of Company A, South Carolina Volunteers, was "shot to death with musketry" in the presence of his brigade (Berlin 392-4). A biting footnote was added by Massachusetts Governor Andrew, who said that "the Lincoln administration which found no law to pay Walker except as a nondescript or contraband, nevertheless found law enough to shoot him as a soldier" (Pearson 109).

Not a few African-Americans wrote Lincoln to protest his policy,

but he probably didn't see the letters since "nearly every letter written to President Lincoln during the Civil War by an African-American was routinely, often mindlessly, sent on to the War Department's
Bureau of Colored Troops" (Holzer 1998 xv).

Lincoln, as every schoolchild knows, was always writing eloquent letters to the mothers of White soldiers, but it appears from
this and other evidence that it was his policy to ignore the pleas of
Black mothers like Hannah Johnson, who wrote from Buffalo, New
York, to ask the man she addressed as "Excellent Sir" to stand up
"manfully" and retaliate against Confederate officials who were
murdering some captured Black soldiers and selling others into
slavery (Holzer 1998, 97-8)

"My son," Hannah Johnson wrote, "fought at Fort Wagoner but
thank God he was not taken prisoner, as many were I thought of this
thing before I let my boy go but then said Mr. Lincoln will never let
them sell our colored soldiers for slaves, if they do he will get them
back quck he will rettallyate and stop it. Now Mr. Lincoln don't you
think you ought to stop this thing and make them do the same by the
colored men they have lived in idleness all their lives on stolen labor
and made savages of the colored people, but they now are so furious
because they are proving themselves to be men, such as have come
away and got some education. It must not be so. You must put the
rebels to work in State prisons to making shoes and things, if they sell
our colored soldiers, till they let them all go. And give their wounded
the same treatment."

All this, she said, might seem cruel, but "their [is] no other way,
*and a just man must do hard things sometimes, that shew him to be a great
man*" (italics added).

Hannah Johnson, who never went to school and who was the
daughter of a slave who escaped from Louisiana, must have been a
great person to write such truths. All the wisdom of Machiavelli and
Hegel and Malcolm X are in that line, "a *just* man must do hard
things sometimes, that shew him to be a great man." For "what," as
Merleau-Ponty asked, "is a goodness incapable of harshness? What

is a goodness which wants to be goodness? A meek way of ignoring others and ultimately despising them" (217).

Mrs. Johnson had heard through the grapevine that Lincoln was going to take the Emancipation Proclamation back. She begged him not to do it, saying slavery was "wicked" and "a horrible outrage." There "is no sense in it, because a man has lived by robbing all his life and his father before him, should he complain because the stolen things found on him, are taken. Robbing the colored people of their labor is but a small part of the robbery their souls are almost taken, they are made bruits of often." She added, "You know all about this," and closed with an appeal:

"Will you see that the colored men fighting now, are fairly treated. You ought to do this, and do it at once, Not let the thing run along meet it quickly and manfully, and stop this, mean cowardly cruelty."

Lincoln never rose to Hannah Johnson's level, and the atrocities continued, reaching a new low in the history of warfare in the massacre at Fort Pillow, a Union fort near Memphis, Tennessee, which was captured on April 12, 1864, by forces under the command of General Nathan Bedford Forrest:[55]

> Then followed [the Senate report said] a scene of cruelty and murder without a parallel in civilized warfare . . . . The rebels commenced an indiscriminate slaughter, sparing neither age nor sex, white or black, soldier or civilian. The officers and men seemed to vie with each other in the devilish work; men, women, and even children, wherever found, were deliberately shot down, beaten, and hacked with sabres; some of the children not more than ten years old were forced to stand up and face their murderers while being shot; the sick and the wounded were butchered without mercy, the rebels even entering the hospital building and dragging them out to be shot, or killing them as they lay there unable to offer the least resistance."

According to official records, General Forrest and his soldiers slaughtered men, women and children for hours and continued the bloody work the next morning.

> All around were heard cries of "No quarter!" "No quarter!" Kill the damned niggers; shoot them down!" . . . No cruelty which the most fiendish malignity could devise was omitted by these murderers. One white soldier who was wounded in the leg so as to be unable to walk, was made to stand up while his tormentors shot him . . . . a mere child, whom an officer had taken up behind him on his horse, was seen by [Brigadier General James] Chalmers, who at once ordered the officer to put him down and shoot him, which was done . . . . The huts and tents in which many of the wounded had sought shelter were set on fire . . . while the wounded were still in them . . . . One man was deliberately fastened down to the floor of a tent, face upwards, by means of nails driven through his clothing and into the boards under him, so that he could not possibly escape, and then the tent set on fire; another was nailed to the side of a building outside the fort, and then the building set on fire and burned.

Pressured by Blacks and congressional leaders, Lincoln promised retaliation but never did anything. Neither General Forrest nor General Chalmers nor any of their men was ever called to account for "a scene of cruelty and murder without a parallel in civilized warfare."

Having walked a few lines in the shoes of Hannah Johnson and the victims of Fort Pillows, we are now in a position to answer the questions we posed earlier: Was the Emancipation Proclamation a fraud? Was it a gambit in a White game, or was it the earnest, equivocating response of an earnest and equivocating man?

The answer is that it was certainly a fraud to the slaves, who were led to believe, on the basis of erroneous information, that "Father Abraham" had freed them from the slaveowners only to discover that Lincoln had made the former slaveowners their guardians and keepers. In 1864, Douglass denounced "the swindle by which our government claims the respect of mankind for abolishing slavery—at the same time that it is practically re-establishing that hateful system in Louisiana" (FD 3:404). On January 25, 1865, in a speech printed in the *Liberator*, February 10, Douglass said that the system of forced labor inaugurated in Louisiana by General Banks, with Lincoln's approval, "practically enslaves the Negro, and makes the Proclamation of 1863 a mockery and delusion." Phillips echoed the same theme, saying in a letter to the 1864 Cleveland convention opposing Lincoln's renomination that Lincoln's "model of Reconstruction puts the Black race into the hands of the unchanged white race, makes the freedom of the Negro a sham, and perpetuates slavery under a softer name."

Looked at from this perspective and from the perspective of the freedmen who were practically reenslaved or sentenced to two more years of slavery by Lincoln's exemptions, the Proclamation was a gambit in a veritable Super Bowl of White games. On one level, Lincoln was trying to outmaneuver his Republican critics and limit Black emancipation until he could mobilize support for his real plan of compensated emancipation over a thirty- or forty-year period coupled with the deportation of American Blacks. On another level, Lincoln was playing games with England, France and other foreign powers and "moderate" forces in the South, hoping that the flare of the limited proclamation would scare off foreign powers and force Southern "moderates" to come home with their slaves before it was too late.

There was finally—and conclusively—the game plan of Northern industrialists, who were fighting not for Black freedom or, to tell the truth, White freedom, but for the freedom to exploit and develop the American market. Everything indeed suggests that Ralph Bunche was correct when he said that the freeing of the slaves was "only an incident in the violent clash of interests between the industrial North and the agricultural South—a conflict that was resolved in favor of the industrial North. In this struggle the Negro was an innocent pawn" (13).

Was Lincoln a pawn or a player in that game? This question, one of the truly interesting inquiries in Lincoln's history, is outside the range of this essay and cannot detain us here. For whether Lincoln was a pawn or a player, the ultimate result, etched in the stones and whirring machines of contemporary Atlanta, New Orleans, Charlotte, New York and Los Angeles, was that the only people who could really say, "Free at Last!" after the Civil War were Northern industrialists and their allies. That's what Andrew Johnson meant, more or less, when he said that the Emancipation Proclamation freed more White people than Black people.

However we approach the Proclamation, then, whether from the standpoint of Lincoln the colonizationist or Rockefeller the industrialist or Lord Charnwood the English aristocrat, it is plain that Blacks were not its central concern. Must we say then that the Proclamation was useless? Certainly not. For the Proclamation was one of those historical documents that are written not by the authors but by historical men and women who give them a meaning the real authors never intended. From this standpoint, the real emancipation proclamation was written not by Lincoln but by the slaves, who misinterpreted Lincoln and the document into glory. Thus, as Quarles said in a statement that has not yet been understood, Lincoln became Lincoln not because of his deeds but because of the deeds of the slaves he subordinated and tried to deport.

In the days and months following the signing of the Proclamation, the invisible slave telegraph told slaves all over the South that a man named Abraham had issued a document that made them free forever. The message was wrong, but the slaves, who had no way of knowing this, exploded in an unprecedented human upheaval.

There had never been anything quite like it, John Eaton said, a slave population "rising up and leaving its ancient bondage, forsaking its local traditions and all the associations and attractions of the old plantation life, coming garbed in rags or in silks, with feet shod or bleeding, individually or in families and larger groups." Eaton said it was like "the oncoming of cities" (2).

By this circuitous route, and by a veritable carnival of bad faith, we come to a historical irony that literally takes your breath away. For in the end, it was the slave who made the Lincoln of history and not the Lincoln of history who made the slave. It was the slave— going in the thousands and tens of thousands to find President Lincoln's soldiers and singing the praises of a new Father Abraham, like the one in the Bible, who had issued a document "freeing" them forever—it was the slave who created the historical halo around the head of "the great emancipator." And it is shocking to realize that Lincoln, who knew all of this and who knew that the slaves were risking their lives to get closer to a false freedom, did nothing to meet them halfway.

Told once that South Carolina slaves believed he was a magic man who would solve all their problems, Lincoln bolted from his chair and "walked in silence two or three times across the floor," saying finally: "It is a momentous thing to be the instrument, under Providence, of the liberation of a race" of people. (Carpenter 208-9).

In the long sight of history, only two things are more momentous.

One is receiving the key to their dungeon and refusing to use it.

The other is giving the key to their jailers and their enemies.

These considerations lead to a question of critical importance. How do African-American scholars evaluate the Proclamation that, media say, freed their ancestors? The answer is simple, and extremely complicated. For most Black scholars of the last generation supported the traditional view of Lincoln, not out of devotion to myths but out of fear that segregationists and moderates would appropriate the dominant American icon and use him against us. There was also, to tell the truth, a deep-seated ambivalence about the myth and the man. The best evidence here again is the evidence of silence. For since 1865, Whites have produced at least sixteen thousand Lincoln titles, compared with only two or three major books by Blacks, including valuable studies by John Hope Franklin and

Benjamin Quarles, which dealt with particular aspects of Lincoln's life. Surprisingly, and revealingly, no Black felt the need (or the interest) in the nineteenth or the twentieth century to confront the man or the myth in a full-scale biography or study.

"No one has understood better than the educated Negroes," Basler said, "that Lincoln was not, above all other things, the liberator of the colored race. They have honored his name in literature with sparing reference to their freedom. Perhaps they have not found the Emancipation Proclamation a sign to conjure with" (1935, 220).

Or a sign to emancipate with.

When, in the 1950s, I made my first speech on this subject at a Black University, major historians urged caution, saying that although my facts were impeccable, it was dangerous to shake Black Americans' belief in a figure that bound them to America and America to them. I said then, and I have said since, that they were too late, for from Ulysses Grant to George Bush, White Americans have used Lincoln to support the racial and political status quo and to warn Blacks and Whites against Black Frederick Douglasses and White Charles Sumners and Thaddeus Stevenses. In the 1940s, Ralph J. Bunche argued that the Civil War myths, and especially the Great Emancipator myth, were "the controlling factor in determining the political attitudes and activities of Negroes" from 1865 to 1932 and were centrally responsible for "the Negro voter's blind loyalty" to the Republican party for sixty-seven years (14).

Since the 1960s, an increasing number of Blacks have openly criticized these myths. In *Lincoln and the Negro,* published in 1962, Benjamin Quarles gave a generally favorable picture of Lincoln but drew the line at the Emancipation Proclamation, noting the vast disparity between the document and Black perception of the document. "The proclamation," Quarles said, "was an accessory after the fact. Negroes had been making themselves free since the beginning of the war"(148-9, 187).

In 1963, in the centennial of the Emancipation Proclamation, John Hope Franklin, the dean of American historians, noted that the

Proclamation itself is overrated. "At best," he wrote, "it sought to save the Union by freeing *some* of the slaves [Franklin's emphasis]." Franklin said the Proclamation "was another step toward the extension of the ideal of equality . . ." (1980, 153).

In 1967, C. Eric Lincoln noted that the Proclamation "contained no provisions not already provided for by Congress in the Confiscation Act of 1862" (58).

As for "the great emancipator, " Vincent Harding, writing in 1981, said: "In those same times when black men and women saw visions of a new society of equals, and heard voices pressing them against the American Union of white supremacy, Abraham Lincoln was unable to see beyond the limits of his own race, class, and time, and dreamed of a Haitian island and of Central American colonies to rid the country of the constantly accusing, constantly challenging black presence" (236).

White defenders of the Lincoln myth have criticized Black historians for using "Black Power rhetoric" in appraising Lincoln's racial views, overlooking the fact that the central themes of the Black critique can be found in George Washington Williams's *History of the Negro Race In America*, which was published in 1882. Like twentieth-century Black historians, the nineteenth-century Black historian deplored Lincoln's "gradualism" and his "conservative policy." The Civil War veteran was especially disturbed by "the military slave hunt" and Lincoln's attempt over an eighteen-month period to define the Civil War as "a white man's war." As for the Preliminary Emancipation Proclamation, it was, he wrote in 1882, "a harmless measure," riddled with fantasies and contradictions, particularly the idea of buying Blacks and colonizing them in some area outside the United States. The final Emancipation Proclamation was not much better. "Even this proclamation—not a measure of humanity—to save the Union, not the slave—left slaves in many counties and States at the South" (274). Then, in a stylistic leap that almost all Black historians have followed, Williams said that the miracle of 1863 was not Lincoln's poor, hesitant, double-tongued words but the response of the slaves who dragged Lincoln, to vary the words of Count

Gurowski, into glory.

To W.E.B. DuBois, as to Williams, the miracle was not Lincoln but the slaves who exploded in an American Apocalypse. Because of Lincoln's limits and limitations in the document, the first Black Jubilee was limited to pockets in the South and never became general. But it was, for all that, breathtaking. "It was all foolish, bizarre, and tawdry," DuBois wrote, "Gangs of dirty Negroes howling and dancing; poverty-stricken ignorant laborers mistaking war, destruction and revolution for the mystery of the human soul; and yet to these black folk it was the Apocalypse. The magnificent trumpet tones of Hebrew Scripture, transmuted and oddly changed, became a strange new gospel. All that was Beauty, all that was Love, all that was Truth, stood on the top of these mad mornings and sang with the stars (1935, 124).

There had never been a great Black cry like this in the world, and flowing with and out of it came the 200,000 soldiers and 200,000 laborers without whom, Lincoln conceded later, the Union could not have been saved.

Will someone say that all this redounds to the glory of Lincoln? But who cannot see that this had nothing at all to do with the real Lincoln, who neither desired nor intended the consequences and who, in fact, desired and intended opposite consequences? It is sad, moreover, to have to add that Lincoln betrayed the trust of slaves who, lacking reliable information, poured their volcanic hopes and aspirations into, George Washington Williams said, "the significant name of Abraham," "father of the faithful," whom they had known in other venues and climes (275).

What makes this all the more discreditable is that Lincoln knew that the slaves had mistakenly identified him as their Moses. And we catch him at the end appropriating the act he opposed, consciously and not a little dishonestly sitting for and painting his historical portrait, telling artist Francis Carpenter that "as affairs have turned, *it is the central act of my administration, and the great event of the nineteenth century*" (90, italics in original). In the end, then, the deed

Lincoln tried so hard to evade captured him and almost freed him, making him the first creator—and victim—of the myth.

Even as Lincoln basked in the glow of the Emancipation and as the season of Jubilees started, some 450 African-Americans, one-third of them women and children, were being deported, with their consent, we are told, and at Lincoln's direction, to an island off the coast of Haiti to establish the first Lincoln colony. The island, contrary to the tourist literature of the Lincoln administration, was a desolate place full of poisonous insects and snakes, and the whole affair ended, as almost everyone except Lincoln predicted, in a comic-opera disaster, with scores of casualties and the survivors covered with bugs and suffering from various illnesses. On March 20, 1864, three hundred and fifty survivors, minus a hundred or so casualties, returned to the United States on the ship *Marcia C. Day*, ending America's last official attempt to deport African-Americans.

Congressman Stevens and other friends of Black freedom publicly criticized Lincoln's colonization hobbyhorse. In a speech to the House on May 2, 1864, Stevens said colonization was "a salve for the consciences of slaveholders and their advocates. As a means of removing the African from the country it was puerile. All the revenue of the United States would not pay for the transportation of one half their annual increase. The scheme of colonizing them in South America . . . was a very shallow vision. They were averse to removing them from their native land; their forcible expatriation would be as atrocious a crime as stealing them in Africa and reducing them to bondage. Five hundred were lately seduced to go to an island near St. Domingo. Such as have not died in six months have been brought back at our expense. I hope this will be the last of the unwise and cruel schemes of colonization . . . ."[56]

In addition to the Haitian venture, Lincoln also considered plans for settling Blacks in the state of Texas, and a bill was actually introduced in Congress to set aside part of the Lone Star state for Black settlement. There was also talk of colonizing all Blacks in Florida. Nothing came of any of these plans, and it is fascinating to speculate on what would have happened to the Texas oil barons and the Texas Cowboys, not to mention Disney World, if Lincoln had been successful on these fronts.

Lincoln's emigration aide, the Rev. James Mitchell, said the Proclamation "did not change Mr. Lincoln's policy of colonization, nor was it so intended." On August 18, 1863, seven months after the signing of the Proclamation and three months before the Gettysburg Address, Mitchell said he asked Lincoln if he "might say that colonization was still the policy of the Administration." Lincoln replied *twice*, he said, that "I have never thought so much on any subject and arrived at a conclusion so definite as I have in this case, and in after years found myself wrong." Lincoln added that "it would have been much better to separate the races than to have such scenes as those in New York [during the Draft Riots] the other day, where Negroes were hanged to lamp posts."[57]

Another piece of evidence indicating that Lincoln never abandoned his colonization hobby is the letter Attorney General Edward Bates wrote Lincoln on November 30, 1864, shortly after he submitted his letter of resignation. Bates apologized in this letter for having overlooked in the press of his last days in office "the duty to give formal answer *to your [Lincoln's] question concerning your power still to retain the Rev. Mitchell* as your assistant or aid [sic] in the matter of executing the several acts of Congress relating to the emigration or colonizing of the freed Blacks." This letter—Bates told Lincoln that he had the legal right to retain Mitchell despite a congressional decision to embargo colonization funds—provides conclusive proof that Lincoln was still fishing in the troubled waters of colonization four or five months before his death. Mitchell noted later with pride that he served as Lincoln's emigration aide until Lincoln's death. [58]

To this bleak picture one should add in all justice that Lincoln said later that the Proclamation and the arming of Black soldiers constituted the heaviest blows yet against the rebellion. "Abandon all the posts now possessed by black men," he told two visitors on August 19, 1864, "surrender all these advantages to the enemy, & we would be compelled to abandon the war in 3 weeks" (CW 7:507).

The methodological and political implications of this statement are immense. For what Lincoln tells us here in his own words is that his critics were right, and he was wrong. All through the first and second years of the war, all through 1861 and 1862 and the first part of 1863, these men and others, including the so-called vindictives, Ben Wade and Zachariah Chandler, had demanded an emancipation policy and the use of the Black troops, and for two years at least Lincoln had opposed them. Now, in August 1864, he says, without saying it, that Greeley, Douglass, Stevens, Sumner, Trumbull, and Medill were right and that the war cannot be won without an "emancipation lever" and Black soldiers.

To be fair, it should be noted that Lincoln, after a period of vacillation and doubt, helped to win passage of the Thirteenth Amendment, which made the paper freedom of the Proclamation real. In this movement, as in all other forward movements involving Blacks, Lincoln was a follower instead of a leader. For after dissident Republicans nominated John C. Frémont on a platform demanding a Thirteenth Amendment and absolute equality, Lincoln had little or no choice.

Having said all that, it remains to be said that Lincoln continued to fight a strange rearguard action against the Proclamation and the Thirteenth Amendment. Reading the documents of his last days, it is difficult not to feel sorry for him, as he slowly and grudgingly walked toward the future, repeatedly casting nostalgic glances over his shoulder at the lost dream of deportation and the all-White cities on the prairie.

26

Goin' To Gettysburg, Sorry I Can't Take You

IT is customary for assorted historians and Pulitzer Prize-winners to approach the Gettysburg Address on their knees, which is not, all things considered, the best position from which to assess its strengths and weaknesses.

The strengths are obvious: brevity, repetition, parallelism. No less obvious are the weaknesses, the chief of which is that it evades the biggest moral crisis of its time and contains not one word of wisdom on the sociopolitical problems of Lincoln's time or ours.

The speech is pretty, of course, but—hold your breath, I'm going to say something shocking—*it doesn't say anything*, an awkward fact that generations of scholars have managed to hide by talking about Greece instead of South Carolina and by counting antitheses instead of slaves. [59]

It is no accident that the "Sermon on the Mount" of politics doesn't say anything (Hertz 317) and that what it says is false. This was a function of the political choices of the speaker, who made an art of evading moral crises and who sought a rhetorical solution to every political crisis of his life. *It was his art to say nothing eloquently in support of abstract political principles that were true everywhere and nowhere and that he had no intention of doing anything about anywhere.* If you don't believe that, test every high-sounding phrase of his life—"A house divided against itself cannot stand"/"With Malice Toward

None"—against the real challenges of the time and ask yourself if he really believed that and if he ever did anything about the phrase before or after he said it.

To be fair, Lincoln faced an impossible situation at Gettysburg. He had been invited there to say a few words at the dedication of the Gettysburg Cemetery. He was called upon therefore to speak to the ghosts of the Confederate and Union dead—and the ghosts of the millions of slave victims—and to meet the pressing expectations of the living exponents of three major groups: abolitionists and Republican leaders who were calling for a hard war to defeat Confederate traitors; 2) Confederates and ultraconservative Democrats who were fighting to preserve what his friend, Alexander Stephens, called the first government in human history based on the cornerstone of racial superiority and human slavery; and 3) Conservative Democrats and Republicans who were fighting to preserve what Lincoln called "the Union as of old."

How could one speaker satisfy these divergent expectations? How could one speaker commemorate dead soldiers who fought for slavery and dead soldiers who fought for the Union, if not for freedom? And how could a speaker who had fought to preserve slavery and "the Union as of old" and who was trying to organize lily-White governments in the South and deport Blacks satisfy his own schizophrenic expectations?

Lincoln decided, as usual, to say all of the above, and none of the above.

Instead of speaking to somebody, he decided to speak to everybody, and nobody.

Instead of telling Confederate soldiers that it was wrong to fight—and die—for slavery, instead of telling Union soldiers that "as he died to make men holy let us die to make men free," instead of telling everybody, including the speaker, *that the White forefathers blew it*, that the graves of Gettysburg were contained in the Constitution as the plant is contained in the seed, and that it was necessary now to let freedom ring, as King said one hundred years later at his

Memorial, from Stone Mountain in Georgia and "the heightening Alleghenies"—instead of saying all that, *instead of saying something,* Lincoln decided to say nothing, a decision that has delighted generations of interpreters who never stop talking about what he didn't say.

Lincoln didn't say anything.

He didn't mention the biggest media event of the year, the Emancipation Proclamation. He didn't mention the biggest challenge of the century, the challenge of winning the war, freeing the slaves, and creating a democratic South (and North). He didn't mention "the most disgraceful drama ever enacted in America",[60] the New York City Draft Riots, led by anti-Black White ethnics who took over the city three months before Gettysburg and murdered more than a dozen Blacks, hanging some from lamp posts and burning others alive.

Lincoln didn't say a word about the burnings and lynchings in New York City.

He didn't say the word *riot.*

He didn't say the word *Confederate.*

He didn't say the word *South.*

He didn't say the word *slave.*

He didn't say anything—and they have never stopped praising him for *not* saying it.

Lincoln specialists say in all seriousness that Lincoln transcended all particularities at Gettysburg. He *rose,* they say, to a level of abstraction that purged the battle of all gross matter. He *ascended,* they say, to a realm where real things, real issues, real people no longer mattered. He hovered, they say, "far above the carnage," no longer knowing the difference between Union and Confederacy, living and dead. Even the earth, we are told, was etherealized.

This, of course, is religion, and we have no right to interfere with communion. The only thing we know for sure is that although Lincoln may not have known the difference between blue and gray on

November 19, 1863, he knew the difference between Black and White.

The proof is that when he descended from the platform he knew the difference between William Johnson, the Black servant he called *boy,* and Postmaster General Montgomery Blair, who wanted to deport all Blacks.

The proof is that his first major act after he descended gave the vote in reconstructed Southern areas to Whites and denied it to Blacks, including Black soldiers who were fighting for the Union.

Gettysburg, in short, was a discourse of the unreal, by the unreal, for the unreal. Wills says that Lincoln volatilized everything (37)—the battle, the soldiers, the blood, the screams, the curses, the rotting bodies, the manure—"as the product of an experiment *testing* whether a government can maintain the *proposition* of equality." Since none of "the fathers," least of all Washington, Jefferson or Madison, had ever tested that proposition *or had ever conceived of testing it,* and since Lincoln had never tested it or conceived of testing it, this was an experiment testing whether something that had never existed could be maintained.

The problem, however, is deeper down. For by etherealizing everything, traditional analyses etherealize Lincoln, giving us an ideal speaker saying ideal words about ideal soldiers who fought an ideal war for ideal reasons, and who bled and died and rotted for real.

It was—again—no accident that Lincoln didn't take the slaves and the cause of concrete freedom to Gettysburg. Ever since his Illinois days, he had opposed equal rights and concrete freedom for Blacks in America, and he was engaged in the days before the speech in an increasingly acrimonious struggle with liberal Republicans on the future of freedom in America. Would the new America be half Black and half White? Would it be a Red/Black/White/Brown/Yellow rainbow or would it be the last best White hope of Lincoln's and Jefferson's and Madison's dream?

Before Gettysburg and after Gettysburg, Lincoln opposed government of *all* the people. There is no evidence anywhere that he ever believed in government of Black people, White people, Brown people, and Red people. Even as he jotted down notes for the big Gettysburg speech, he was maneuvering frantically to keep the Black majority from participating in the government of the White people he was organizing in Louisiana. On November 5, fourteen days before the speech, he told General Nathaniel Banks that he would not be opposed to a "reasonable temporary arrangement" of quasi slavery (CW 7:1-2). On the same day, New Orleans Blacks asked Lincoln and his hand-picked Louisiana commander to do something about the Declaration of Independence and government of the people in America.

"Your petitioners," they said to Lincoln's Louisiana commander, "further respectfully represent that over and above" the rights proclaimed in the Declaration, they were army veterans and citizens "who were paying their taxes on assessments of more than nine millions of dollars." In consideration of these facts, "as true and as clear as the sun which lights this great continent; in consideration of the services already performed, and still to be rendered by them to their common country, they humbly beseech your Excellency to cast your eyes upon a loyal population, awaiting with confidence and dignity the proclamation of those inalienable rights which belong to the condition of citizens of the great American republic" (AC 1863, 591-2).

Here, fourteen days before he said the words that "changed American democracy," was a plea that Lincoln should have carried to Gettysburg. But Lincoln cast his eyes in the opposite direction and paid no heed to the "government of the people" that was *perishing from his earth*, when he left Washington on Wednesday, November 18, in an entourage weighed down with the most conservative members of his cabinet: Secretary of State Seward, who had initially opposed the Emancipation Proclamation; Secretary of Interior John P. Usher, who wanted to deport Blacks; and Postmaster General Blair, who also wanted to deport Blacks.

It is a curious fact that nobody in Lincoln's official party, including Lincoln, believed in equal rights—and that nobody has said it before. It is a also curious that none of the leaders of the equal rights struggle– neither Sumner nor Trumbull nor Lovejoy nor Stevens nor Chase–

accompanied Lincoln.

Gettysburg watchers say all cabinet members were invited but that the two most liberal members, Secretary Chase and Secretary Stanton, decided to stay at home. According to a story that Lincoln told later at a cabinet meeting, Stevens was asked where the president and secretary of state were going.

"To Gettysburg," he said.

"But where are Stanton and Chase?" the man asked.

"At home, at work," was the reply. "Let the dead bury the dead" (Carpenter 38).

Stevens undoubtedly included among the living dead District of Columbia Marshal Ward Hill Lamon, who had distinguished himself by filling the D.C. jail with fugitive slaves. To the disgust of a number of congressional leaders, Lamon, the man Lincoln called "my particular friend," had been named master of ceremonies at Gettysburg. Thus, shortly after 2 p.m., on Thursday afternoon, November 19, 1863, after the big main speech by Edward Everett, "a slavecatcher," in Gurowski's words (GD 1:33), introduced the president of the United States to make the speech which, enthusiastic Lincoln specialists say, created or helped create modern America.

Before analyzing the speech, let us note first that the major problem with the Gettysburg Address is not the address itself but the fallacies of the interpreters, who make a fetish out of it and pretend that they can interpret it without reference to the speaker and his situation and the situation of his audience. Having divorced the word from the speech and the speech from the speaker and the speaker from the situation, they give us word-things which interpret themselves and mean the same thing in Greece or South Carolina in 1863 or 2000. This is ungenerous to the Union veterans who died there for the Union, or something, and it distorts the speech which must be interpreted first in terms of the personal and political projects of the speaker, in terms of who he was and what he wanted.

Who was the clean-up speaker at Gettysburg?

He was a fifty-four-year-old man who opposed equal rights for Blacks.

What did he want?

He wanted to win the war, bring the Southern [White] brethren home, deport the slaves, and create an all-White nation. He was, in other words, a *project* supporting certain social forces and wanting certain things. And every word he said at Gettysburg was colored and defined by who he was, what he wanted to do in the Gettysburg world and what he was, in fact, doing in that world.

Even as he spoke, even as he said the word *liberty* and the words *all men are created equal,* he was scheming to deny liberty and equal rights to Black people in Louisiana, South Carolina and other Southern states.

The critical issue facing Lincoln in the Gettysburg season was the issue he didn't mention at Gettysburg—race. In the days preceding the speech, and the days that followed, he spent most of his time preparing his second major proclamation of the year, a proclamation of amnesty that made it unmistakably clear that he was in favor of a reconstruction of the White people, by the White people, for the White people. Although the second proclamation contradicted everything he planned to say at Gettysburg, he was, Barton said, "very happy about his Amnesty Proclamation" and considered it "one of his dearest achievements" (1950, 97, 100).

There was additionally the question of the spreading emancipation movement in Missouri, where pro-emancipation forces had repudiated his gradual emancipation/colonization plans and were moving toward the immediate emancipation he opposed and feared. On September 30, a big delegation from Kansas and Missouri descended on the White House and demanded immediate emancipation in Missouri. Lincoln rejected their plea, saying he was still in favor of a gradual emancipation that contradicted what he allegedly did in the Emancipation Proclamation.

No less pressing were nagging questions about the emancipation that never happened. On September 17, two months before Gettysburg, the Gettysburg orator refused, despite pleas from Secretary Chase to revoke his exemptions of the only slaves he could have freed in 1863, the slaves in liberated Southern areas.

Holding center stage in all this, overshadowing all and judging all, Lincoln especially, was the honored guest nobody invited to Gettysburg—the African-American slave. Even as the four-car Gettysburg Special sped across the Maryland countryside, the reality everybody tried to forget—then and now—intruded on Lincoln's aesthetic contemplations in the person of Wayne MacVeagh, a prominent Pennsylvania lawyer, who "pitched into" Lincoln and "told him some truths" about his reactionary policy in Missouri. During the train trip and afterward, John W. Forney criticized the political orientation of Postmaster General Blair, a key member of the Lincoln entourage and a devout believer in Black deportation (Hay 119-20).

The unwanted guest followed Lincoln into his private chambers. For like Thomas Jefferson, who drafted the Declaration of Independence attended by a favorite Black servant, Lincoln drafted part of the Gettysburg Address attended by William Johnson, a favorite Black servant. It is eerie—and significant—how often history and the American heart arrange for a Black witness—and a Black negation—of its dearest moments. Thus, "between nine and ten" on the night before the big speech, Lincoln went to his upstairs room in the home of Judge David Wills, "accompanied only by his colored servant, William [sic]," and completed or polished one of the final drafts (Barton 1950, 64).

Before and after the speech, which allegedly defined democracy in America, Wendell Phillips and others said publicly that racism made it impossible for the man who made the speech to conceive of a democratic state in the United States of America. Speaking one month after Gettysburg, Phillips denounced Lincoln's amnesty plan and said, according to a *Liberator* report of January 1, 1864, that Lincoln was a bigot whose conditioning made it impossible for him to look at Blacks the same way he looked at Whites.

"Mr. Lincoln," Phillips said, "is anti-slavery. He doesn't believe in a nation half slave and half free. But he is a colonizationist, and he doesn't believe in a nation half black and half white. Hence prejudice makes it impossible for him to do justice to the Negro." Pursuing the same theme in a second speech, printed in the *Liberator* on February 5, 1864, Phillips said Lincoln "does not recognize the Negro as a man; he does not remember the Negro as a soldier; he does not blot out races; he does not forget them; he does not tell of rights, he talks of benefits."

Viewed from this vantage point, which is also the vantage point of the slave, the fundamental problem of the Gettysburg Address is that Abraham Lincoln didn't mean a word he said.

Not a word?

Not a word if we understand that an isolated word means nothing in and of itself and that the word of discourse is not the isolated word but the sentence and the speech that give it meaning. *Fourscore,* for example, or, to be less archaic, eighty. What does that mean? Eighty eggs? Eighty Confederates? Eighty slaves? The word means nothing standing alone. Nor does *and* or *seven* or *ago*. But if we put them all together, we get a famous first sentence, a famous first *word*, that starts with biological confusion and ends in political fantasy.

> Four score and seven years ago our fathers brought forth on this continent, a new nation, conceived in Liberty, and dedicated to the proposition that all men are created equal.

Abraham Lincoln didn't believe that.

No discerning person believes that Abraham Lincoln believed on November 19, 1863, that George Washington and Thomas Jefferson believed on July 4, 1776, that they were conceiving a nation dedicated to the proposition that the slaves at Monticello and Mount Vernon were equal to George Washington and Thomas Jefferson in the same way that George Washington and Thomas Jefferson were equal to George III.

So much for the first word.

The second word—"testing whether that nation, or any nation so conceived and so dedicated, can long endure"—raises profound problems of physical and philosophical science. How could a thing that had never existed, and which did not exist on November 19, 1863, not to pursue the matter further, endure? Wendell Phillips, among others, was contemptuous of careless thinkers who said the Civil War was a test of democracy. "Democracy," Phillips said, "[had] never been on trial," for the simple reason that the United States of America had never been a democracy, even for White people. "Except in our Northern State Governments," Phillips said in a speech, printed in the January 1, 1862, *Liberator*, "we have never had a democracy in this country. We have had an attempt at a free government, an attempt at free institutions, poisoned, tainted, conditioned on toleration of the system of slavery."

In this effort, no one had made a bigger effort to harmonize slavery and freedom, and no one perhaps had been more tainted and conditioned by the effort than Lincoln.

What about the last word, the celebrated statement about government of the people, by the people, for the people? The first thing to notice in dealing with that phrase is that Lincoln probably borrowed it, as he borrowed so many of his great phrases. I say that not to criticize him, for no rational person believes anybody can make a speech, even a speech of 268 or 272 words, without borrowing from somebody. That's not the problem—the problem is that Lincoln misquoted Theodore Parker, who called for "a democracy, that is, a government of all the people, by all the people, for all the people." Only Lincoln could turn a revolutionary slogan into a conservative slogan and become an immortal by eliminating the dangerous word *all*.

And he didn't even believe that.

On November 19, 1863, there were 412,320 Blacks and 291,300 Whites in the state of South Carolina.

Did Lincoln believe on November 19, 1863, in government of the people et cetera in South Carolina?

No.

Did Lincoln believe on November 19, 1863, that it was the duty of

White people to create "a new birth of freedom" in South Carolina by giving the vote to the Black majority?

No.

Did Lincoln believe that it would *ever* be possible to create a government of the people et cetera with the Black majority and the White minority of South Carolina?

No.

If he didn't believe that, what in the world did Abraham Lincoln (and his apologists) think he was doing and saying at Gettysburg? The answer is shocking: *he was just rapping,* celebrating something that had never existed before men and women who had never believed in it and who would have stoned him to death if he or anybody else had seriously suggested that they should either live or die for it.

In a satirical take-off on people like Lincoln who were always talking about their "fathers," Frederick Douglass asked, "Who were your daddies?" And why are you relying on them to justify what they did not do and what you are not doing for freedom? (FD 2:208).

From Douglass's standpoint, and from the standpoint of the slave, the big Gettysburgh question was who were Lincoln's daddies, the ones who did all that conceiving, without, it is to be noted, the benefit of mothers? Were they the direct ancestors of Americans living in 1863, or were they the spiritual ancestors who founded the country? Were they, to be quite precise, the Revolutionary War soldiers, including the five thousand Black soldiers, who seized the prize? Or were "the fathers," to use Lincoln's words, the men who wrote the words and signed the papers that named the prize? And where did the fathers do all of that conceiving? Was it in Independence Hall or was it perhaps on Bunker Hill, where Prince Hall and other Brothers did some conceiving of their own?

Lincoln, who had an Oedipal problem bigger than the Washington Monument and who was always adopting fathers and abandoning fathers, favored the founding few but was never clear on their actual identity, saying at Cooper Institute that "our fathers" were the 115 who created the Constitution and its amendments and saying, or seeming to say, at Gettysburg that they were the fifty-six who signed the Declaration of Independence. Arithmetic apart, it's possible, as Charles B. Strozier said, to interpret Lincoln's idealization of the White founding fathers—the words *the fathers* and *our fathers* were mantras to him—as an attempt to work out a personal problem and "to establish paternal surrogates" (55-7).

Whatever the number of the fathers and wherever they conceived, they were, in Lincoln's view, White fathers who conceived for Whites, making it possible for all immigrants from Europe to become their blood descendants by identifying spiritually with the words of the Declaration of Independence. This was a controlling element in Lincoln's philosophy and requires a critical reading of his July 10, 1858, speech on the meaning of the July Fourth. Going to Chicago and going back to the Revolutionary generation, he said "we find a race of men living in that day whom we claim as our fathers and grandfathers; they were iron men, they fought for the principle that they were contending for . . . ."

Besides these men, "descended by blood," Lincoln said, "from our ancestors," we have "among us perhaps half our people who are not descendants at all of these men . . . ."

Who were the new descendants?

They were, Lincoln answered, *"men who who have come from Europe—German, Irish, French and Scandinavian—men that have come from Europe themselves, or whose ancestors have come hither and settled here, finding themselves our equals in all things.* If they look back through this history to trace their connection with those days by blood, they find they have none . . . but when they look through that old Declaration of Independence they find that those old men say that 'We hold these truths to be self-evident, that all men are created equal,' and then they feel that that moral sentiment taught in that day evidences their relation to those men, that it is the father of all moral principle in them, and that they have a right to claim it as though they were blood of the blood, and flesh of the flesh of the men who wrote that Declaration, (loud and long continued applause) and so they are" (CW 2:499-500, italics added).

If the biology in this incredible statement seems fanciful and foreboding, and if you are unable to understand how White men who came to America after the Revolution, and *only* White men who came to America after the Revolution, can ingest the Declaration of Independence host and become blood descendants of the Revolutionary fathers, the problem is in that strange mishmash of blood, race and mythology that Lincoln concocted to explain and explain away a document that instantly and magically made all White men from Europe equal partners and celebrants of a political sacrament that instantly and magically subordinated and excluded all men who didn't come from Europe.

What Lincoln expressed here above all was the White humanism that defined and limited the Declaration of Independence and the French Declaration of Man that preceded it. For in his haste to color his dream white, he identified free White people everywhere with man in opposition to the other species, nonWhite people everywhere, free and otherwise. Since the overwhelming majority of the people in the world, then and now, were nonWhite, this racist humanism made Lincoln and Lincoln's limited and truncated minority the enemy of Humanity.

It follows from all this—and this is the point we want to make—that when Abraham Lincoln said "our fathers" at Gettysburg he was not talking about the fathers, spiritual or biological, of all Americans. It follows further that Lincoln knew that the nation the White fathers brought forth was conceived not in liberty but in political sin and a fatal compromise between slavery and freedom.

If the fathers were ignorant of the terms of the conception, some of the mothers weren't, for it was during the golden age that Lincoln praised and mythologized at Gettysburg that Abigail Adams told her husband, John, that "it always appeared a most iniquitous scheme to me to fight ourselves for what we are daily robbing and plundering from those who have as good a right to freedom as we have " (24).

Unquestionably; and it was during the same period that Benjamin Banneker, *a forefather that Lincoln excluded*, sent a letter to Thomas Jefferson, calling him and other White fathers to account for the betrayal of the Revolution, saying:

> Look back, I entreat you and remember how 'pitiable' it is to reflect that although you were so fully convinced of the benevolence of the Father of Mankind, and of his equal and impartial distribution of these rights and privileges, which he hath conferred upon them, that you should at the same time counteract his mercies, in detaining by fraud and violence, so numerous a part of my brethren under groaning captivity and cruel oppression, that you should at the same time be found guilty of that most criminal act, which you professedly detested in others . . . . (Aptheker 24-6)

Speaking thus of fraud and violence and accusing Jefferson and the White forefathers of criminal culpability, one of the fathers, a rejected father, calls us back to a desecrated shrine and makes us all witnesses to a national tragedy perpetrated by a small and ruthless minority. For the awkward fact is that the famous "We the People" preamble, as Supreme Court Justice Thurgood Marshall pointed out, didn't even apply to the vast majority of the American people at that time—women of all races, African-Americans, Hispanic Americans, Native Americans, and Lincoln's real fathers, poor and propertyless Whites, many of whom were semi-slaves called indentured servants.

The same indictment, the same crimes, and the same implicit criticism of Lincoln's golden age inform Frederick Douglass's July 4, 1852, oration at Rochester, New York, an oration many Blacks consider the greatest of all Fourth of July speeches.

Speaking sixty-one years after Banneker wrote his letter and eleven years before Lincoln went to Gettysburg, Douglass was pitiless in his denunciation of the crime Lincoln called a blessing.

The theme of the speech was hypocrisy:

What to the American slave, is your 4th of July? I answer; a day that reveals to him, more than all other days in the year, the gross injustice and cruelty to which he is the constant victim. To him, your celebration is a sham; your boasted liberty, an unholy license; your national greatness, swelling vanity; your sounds of rejoicing are empty and heartless; your denunciation of tyrants, brass fronted impudence; your shouts of liberty and equality, hollow mockery; your prayers and hymns, your sermons and thanksgivings, with all your religious parade and solemnity, are, to Him, mere bombast, fraud, deception, impiety, and hypocrisy—a thin veil to cover up crimes which would disgrace a nation of savages . . . .

Douglass went on to add words that are all too familiar to anthropologists studying the Jefferson/Madison/Clay/Lincoln genus.

You invite to your shores fugitives of oppression from abroad, honor them with banquets, greet them with ovations, cheer them, toast them, salute them, protect them, and pour out your money to them like water; but the fugitives from your own land you advertise, hunt, arrest, shoot, and kill. You glory in your refinement and your universal education; yet you maintain a system as barbarous and dreadful as ever stained the character of a nation—a system begun in avarice, supported in pride, and perpetuated in cruelty . . . . (FD 2:181-204)

Here, then, in graphic detail, are Mount Vernon, Monticello, and the Gettysburg Address turned upside down and viewed from the perspective of the slave, who experienced a nation conceived not in liberty but in compromise and hypocrisy and whose testimony is unimpeachable because it is written in blood.

The details of this compromise were well-known to Lincoln, who said in the Lincoln-Douglas debates and at Cooper's Institute that the nation was conceived in compromise because "the fathers" were forced by "the necessities" to make a temporary deal with the devil.

Lincoln went further and said in *his* July Fourth speech in Chicago that this compromise was not only necessary but good, for—you remember the words—"we could not get *our* constitution unless we permitted *them* to remain in slavery" (CW 2:501, italics added).

It was in the context of Lincoln's statement that "a house divided against itself cannot stand," that historian John Hope Franklin asked in another great July the Fourth speech, "Who divided this house?"

The answer, Dr. Franklin told an audience at the Chicago Historical Society on July 4, 1990, was that the house was divided in large part by Lincoln's "fathers."

Who divided this house?

> The house was divided by George Washington, who was at least as diligent in maintaining control over his wealthy wife's slaves as he was in prosecuting the war against Britain. It was divided by Thomas Jefferson, who not only graciously acquiesced in the deletion of the antislavery clause from the Declaration of Independence but also pleaded unsuccessfully with his protégé, Edward Coles, not to set his slaves free and migrate to Illinois but to remain in Virginia and uphold the institution of slavery.

Who divided this house?

> The house was divided by James Madison, the author of the Constitution, who was not only responsible for the style in which slavery was written into the document, but who also helped enact the laws of the first and second Congresses that respectively barred African-Americans from becoming naturalized citizens and prevented them from becoming members of the United States militia.

Who divided this house?

> It was divided by all the other slaveholders and their accessories, who believed in the obscene incongruity that they could establish a prosperous social order from the exploitation of a

labor force without its consent and with no thought of just compensation for it . . . .

The house was divided, Franklin said, by a cast of millions:

> The house was divided by the . . . nonslaveholding leaders at the Constitutional Convention, and in subsequent years by those whose fears, like those of Benjamin Franklin, seemed to be limited to the possible Africanization of the country if too many Africans were imported . . . .

The house was also divided, in Franklin's view, by the abolitionists, who were, from his standpoint, a negative catalyst White and who, from my standpoint, were a positive catalyst who drove Southerners mad and made it impossible to create a permanent compromise between slavery and freedom.

This brilliant analysis throws new light on the last part of the first sentence, "dedicated to the proposition that all men are created equal," and brings us to the center of the piece. For Lincoln at Gettysburg was America at its best—and worst. Here, give or take a face or a date, was Thomas Jefferson, attended by a favorite slave, writing the Declaration of Independence. Here was Woodrow Wilson segregating the toilets in Washington, D.C., and setting out to make the world safe for democracy. Here was Nobel Laureate William Faulkner saying that man would prevail and promising to go out into the streets and shoot Black men and women to keep Mississippi safe for White folks. Cotton Mather in Salem, Sheriff Clark at Selma, Custer at Little Big Horn, LBJ in the Vietnam quagmire, Ronald Reagan in the White city on the hill: they were all there in spirit at Gettysburg, where Abraham Lincoln carried the American sin, the dissociation of word and reality, of affirmation and act, of principle and practice, to its highest pinnacle.

This political schizophrenia defined and defines the White founding fathers and all those, Lincoln foremost among them, who followed and follow in their path. The White fathers' dilemma was obvious: They were murdering and robbing Indians and Blacks, and they were in love with words that condemned people who murdered and robbed Indians and Blacks. The solution to this dilemma was clear: they had to give up the words or the murders and robberies. But since they couldn't—or wouldn't—live without the slaves or the Indians' land or the pretty words, they split themselves and reality into two parts, cutting the words off from reality and telling themselves and others that principles were one thing and practice was another and that there was nothing in the Bible or the Declaration of Independence or the Constitution that required White men to respect the rights of Blacks or Indians or women.

In that way or some other way, reality was made safe for the word, and the master of Monticello was able to read his books in peace and to sleep at night, secure in the knowledge that the cabalistic words, *all men are created equal*, were safe in a dry, white place above the blood of the massacres and plantations, and that they didn't require him or anybody else to do anything to make them real. Finally, in one of the most extraordinary moral reversals in history, *the dilemma itself became a confirming grace,* and men congratulated themselves on their high ideals and the difficulty of making them real in a world of Indians and African-Americans.

But we must take care here. For if we are not careful, we will fall into the ditch of the Lincolns and Myrdals and Gettysburg Address worshippers, who attribute real and magical power to the words of the Declaration. There are even men and women who have put forward the astounding theory that Lincoln invented America, or something, by saying 268 or 272 words at Gettysburg. To see the danger of that kind of talk, one need only read Oliver Cromwell Cox's cutting critique of Gunnar Myrdal's *American Dilemma.* Myrdal, like modern-day worshippers of this political religion, attributed magical properties to the so-called "American Creed" and postulated an "American Dilemma," saying or seeming to say that the greatness of America, which is "continuously struggling for its soul," is that it has a high-minded political creed that it has never obeyed. "In principle,"

Myrdal said, "the Negro problem was settled long ago . . ." (24). To which Cox replied: "Indeed, speaking abstractly, we may conclude similarly that all the major social problems of the Christian world were solved 'in principle' by the opening words of the Lord's Prayer—to say nothing of the whole Sermon on the Mount" (510).

The problem with Myrdal's and by extension Lincoln's romantic and mystical approach to the magic words of the Declaration is that it ignores material and economic determinants. Lincoln would have been better advised to pay more attention to his cynical forefather, James Madison, who said: "Wherever there is an interest and power to do wrong, wrong will be done" (qtd. in Cox 514).

The forefathers had an interest to do wrong. They had the power to do wrong. And wrong was done, especially by Lincoln's fathers. And it is preposterous to suggest, as some have suggested, that one man saying two or three hundred words can change the history of a nation. History is not changed by men saying words; history is changed by men working, fighting, struggling. What changed American history was not the speech made at Gettysburg but the series of events that sent Lincoln to Gettysburg, *a series of events that Abraham Lincoln fought every step of the way.*

To tell the truth, America was reinvented not by Lincoln but against Lincoln. It was reinvented not by his acts but by the acts he opposed. It was reinvented not by the words he said at Gettysburg but by the event-words of the Civil War, by the event-words of Nat Turner and John Brown and the abolitionists, by the emancipating acts of the Thirty-seventh Congress, by the Thirteenth, Fourteenth and Fifteenth amendments, by the sacrifices of Union veterans, including the two hundred thousand Blacks without whom the prize could not have been won, by the Black Freedom Movement, which continued the process of emancipation in the twentieth century that Lincoln tried to stop in the nineteenth.

In the process of reinventing America, *a process that is going on right now*, the men and women who opposed Lincoln and Lincoln's ideas, most notably Republican leaders like Sumner, Stevens and Phillips, and Black protestants like Douglass, W.E.B. DuBois, Thurgood Marshall and Martin Luther King Jr., were more important than Abraham Lincoln. This is what DuBois helps us to understand in *The Gift of Black Folk (138-9*, italics added*):*

> [I]t was the rise and growth among the slaves of a determination to be a free and an active part of American democracy that forced American democracy continually to look into the depths . . . . This great vision of the black man was, of course, at first the vision of the few, as visions always are, but it was always there; it grew continuously and it developed quickly from wish to active determination. *One cannot think of democracy in America or in the modern world without reference to the American Negro* . . . . The democracy established in America in the eighteenth century was not, and was not designed to be, a democracy of the masses of men and it was thus singularly easy for people to fail to see the incongruity of democracy and slavery. It was the Negro himself who forced the consideration of this incongruity, who made emancipation inevitable and made the modern world at least consider if not wholly accept the idea of a democracy including men of all races and colors.

This democracy was not conceived, as Lincoln erroneously believed, four score or even eight score years ago. On the contrary, *it has not yet been conceived*, which is another way of saying, to continue what the *New York Herald* called Lincoln's "obstetric analogies," that it is a multiple, many-colored, many-fathered, many-mothered birth that evolved and is still evolving.

It was precisely because of "the evolving nature of the Constitution" that Supreme Court Justice Thurgood Marshall refused to take part in the hoopla of the 1987 Bicentennial celebration, saying: [61]

> I cannot accept this invitation, for I do not believe that the meaning of the Constitution was forever "fixed" at the Philadelphia

Convention. *Nor do I think the wisdom, foresight, and sense of justice exhibited by the framers particularly profound.* To the contrary, the government they devised was defective from the start, requiring several amendments, a civil war, and momentous social transformations to attain the system of constitutional government, and its respect for the individual freedoms and human rights we hold as fundamental today. When contemporary Americans cite "The Constitution," they invoke a concept that is vastly different from what the Framers barely began to construct two centuries ago. (Italics added)

Justice Marshall added pointedly:

"We the People" no longer enslave, but the credit does not belong to the framers. It belongs to those who refused to acquiesce in outdated notions of "liberty," "justice," and "equality," and who strived to better them.

Nor does the credit belong to Lincoln or his political godfather, Thomas Jefferson, who passed the torch and his advocacy of gradual emancipation and deportation of (other people's) slaves on to Henry Clay, the Kentucky slaveholder who was Lincoln's hero and "beau ideal of a statesman."

Perhaps the most important fact about the Gettysburg Address is the one most often overlooked: Lincoln's rendering of the phrase, "conceived in liberty and dedicated to the proposition that all men are created equal" was based on the opportunistic idealism Clay devised to explain why Whites could believe in the Declaration of Independence and continue to enslave and oppress Blacks.

The Mendenhall, Indiana, speech in which Clay discovered the $E = mc^2$ of racism was a sacred text to Lincoln who never tired of quoting what Clay told the Black and White petitioners who asked him to free his slaves. The way Lincoln told it, the indignant Clay answered:

And what is the foundation of this appeal to me in Indiana, to liberate the slaves under my care [nice touch] in Kentucky? It is a general declaration in the act announcing to the world the inde-

pendence of the thirteen American colonies, that all men are created equal. Now, as an abstract principle, there is no doubt of
the truth of that declaration, and it is desirable, in the original con-
struction of society, and in organized societies, to keep it in view
as a great fundamental principle. But, then, I apprehend that in no
society that ever did exist, or ever shall be formed, was or can the
equality asserted among the members of the human race be practically enforced and carried out.[62]

This clever—and duplicitous—defense of holding slaves was
canonical scripture to the "great emancipator," making it possible
for him to believe in the Declaration of Independence as an abstract
ideal which didn't have to be realized in the real world of slave
states, Negroes, and Indians. Speaking at the seventh Joint Lincoln-
Douglas debate in Alton, Illinois, on October 15, 1858, Lincoln noted
that "Mr. Clay says . . . that we cannot practically apply [the phrase
"all men are created equal"] in all cases, and he illustrates by bringing forward the case of females, minors, insane, culprits, and so on,
but he says that it is true as an abstract principle, and it is desirable
in the formation of new societies, and even in organized societies,
that it should be constantly kept in view as an abstract principle"
(Holzer 1993, 346-7).

Did you catch that phrase? *And so on.* Females, minors, insane,
culprits, Negroes, Indians, and so on.

That's cute.

Even cuter is the distinction Clay and Lincoln made between "new
societies," where it might be possible to realize the Declaration, and
"old States" like America, where he and Clay said it was impossible to
realize it, and the further distinction they made between the real Declaration and the abstract Declaration of Independence which did not
grant political and civil rights to any concrete colored person anywhere in America.

What did this mean concretely?

Listen!

Lincoln is explaining it to the multitudes at Alton:

Now, then, the principle that I had insisted upon, and all the principle that I have insisted upon, from the Declaration of Independence, as applicable to this discussion and this canvas, is in relation to laying the foundation of new societies. I have never sought to apply this principle to those old States where slavery exists for the purpose of abolishing slavery in those States. It is nothing but gross perversion to assume that I have brought forth the Declaration of Independence to ask that Missouri shall free her slaves. (Holzer 348)

Never.

Abraham Lincoln never sought in the Lincoln-Douglas debates or the Gettysburg Address or the Second Inaugural or in the White House to apply the principles of the Declaration to any concrete slave or any concrete Negro in any existing American state.

For Lincoln, then, and for his mentors, Jefferson and Clay, the Declaration of Independence didn't require men (and women) to do anything. It didn't require Clay (or Jefferson) to free his slaves. It didn't require Lincoln to fight for the emancipation of slaves in the "old States" or for equal rights for Blacks in Illinois. On the contrary, according to the Lincoln/Clay doctrine, reverence for the Declaration of Independence and for the Constitution required Lincoln to support slavery in the old states.

This analysis enables us to understand better what Lincoln was doing at Gettysburg. For although he followed his usual practice of saying the mantra words of the Declaration, the last thing in the world he and his listeners expected or desired in 1863 was a new birth of freedom that would have included equality (political, economic and cultural) for African-Americans and Native Americans.

The situation Lincoln faced in November 1863 was clear and pressing: The logic of war and the intransigence of White Southerners, not Lincoln's purposes and plans, was going to bring about a situation that he considered worse even than slavery itself—the immediate freeing of four million Blacks in a land he, Clay and Thomas Jefferson considered the White man's land. The new Black citizens would constitute a majority in some Southern states and an overwhelming presence in others. Before Lincoln went up to Gettysburg and after he came down from Gettysburg, he didn't have a single rational idea about how to deal with that new birth of freedom.

To be sure, Lincoln talked vaguely and disturbingly about a "probationary period," controlled by the former masters, which would gradually permit the two races "to live themselves out of their old relations to each other." On August 5, 1863, some three months before he discovered a new birth of freedom at Gettysburg, he told Nathaniel Banks, the commanding general in Louisiana, that he was in favor of "some practical system by which the two races could gradually [how that man loved that word] live themselves out of their old relations to each other . . ." (CW 6:365). In other words, Lincoln wanted the slaves to pay the price of gradually "living themselves out of their old relation" in an apprenticeship system that would have inevitably meant the continuation of slavery under another name.

Clearly and lamentably, the new birth of freedom Lincoln invoked at Gettysburg was a White variation on an old theme. And if you want to know how little Gettysburg really meant, you will have to follow the Lincoln method and pose some hard questions.

Did the Gettysburg orator believe that African-American men and Native American men—he didn't say anything about women—were equal to White men with no *ifs, ands,* and *buts* on the day he said the word at the cemetery in Gettysburg?

The answer is no.

The proof is everything he said and did before he spoke at Gettysburg and everything he said and did after he spoke at Gettysburg.

Did Lincoln believe on November 19, 1863, that it would be possible to achieve equality in America for African-Americans and Native Americans, not to mention poor Whites, with all deliberate speed?

Same answer, same proof.

Was Lincoln committing himself on this day to a crusade for the far-off goal of equality in America for Blacks, and was he asking his audience and the widows of the White Northern and Southern brothers who died there to join him in that crusade?

Same answer, and same proof, with the understanding that crusades for Black rights were not Lincoln's style.

Never.

Never in his whole life did Abraham Lincoln ask any White to grant any Black equal rights in the United States of America.

Someone will say in objection that there must have been two Gettysburg addresses, for you obviously didn't read the Gettysburg Address that other historians read.

There was only one, but we read it with different eyes, with, one might almost say, White and Black eyes or, perhaps, slavemaster and slave eyes. In any case, the central message of Gettysburg is so clear that it is hard to miss with anyone's eyes. And objectors will be horrified to learn that Lincoln's most sympathetic Gettysburg interpreter, Garry Wills, and I agree on two key points: 1) the Gettysburg Address had nothing to do with Blacks or equal rights; 2) the Gettysburg address evaded the biggest issues of the time. If you doubt my word, read what Wills said on page 90: "The 'great task' mentioned in the Address is not emancipation but the preservation of self-government. We assume, today, that self-government includes self-rule by blacks as well as whites; but at the time of his appearance at Gettysburg Lincoln was not advocating, even eventually, the suffrage for African Americans. The Gettysburg Address, for all its artistry and eloquence, does not directly address the prickliest issues of its historic moment."

Or of any historic moment since the Slave Trade.

And what we learn from Lincoln's failure at Gettysburg and elsewhere is that principles commit us to nothing and that saying words with no intention of doing anything about them is a mystification that hides men and women from themselves and diverts them from their true tasks. At certain moments—and slavery was one of those moments—professing with no intention of practicing is an instrument of oppression and a mask and accomplice of violence.

If you like feel-good words and if you have no interest in slaves, slavemasters, oppression, and liberation, there is much to admire in the Gettysburg Address, especially the inner sentences—"we can not dedicate—we can not dedicate—we can not consecrate—we can not hallow this ground." But there's no point in praising the document's aesthetic values, its thirteen alliterations and two antitheses, unless you are a professor who wants to teach students and politicians how to alliterate and equivocate. And I have always found it ominous that there is not a single concrete image in the whole speech, not a single concrete Confederate or Union soldier, not a single concrete slave or concrete slavemaster, not a single drop of red blood or Black hope, in contrast, say, with the speech of Jesus, which was always full of salt, bread, wolves and sheep, generations of vipers, and dens of thieves.

It will be said in rebuttal that the inner sentences redeem the speech. But how can anyone fail to see that the inner sentences are linked to the outer sentences and the larger questions that Lincoln refused to face in 1861, 1862, 1863, 1864, and 1865?

It is for us the living, rather, to be dedicated here to the unfinished work which they who fought here have thus far so nobly advanced.

What work?

Was Lincoln calling the assembled White people to "the unfinished work" of freeing the slaves and making the Declaration of Independence real in South Carolina, Washington, D.C., and Springfield, Illinois?

Come off it.

You know Lincoln had no interest in that. Nothing he said at Gettysburg—not a word—was said in the interest of Black people. Every thing he said at Gettysburg—every word—was a word addressed to White people about White people for White people.

For more than two years, abolitionists and congressional leaders had begged Lincoln to define the war as a war to fulfill the unfulfilled pledges of the Declaration. For more than two years, he had maintained with heat and passion that the Civil War was a White man's war and that the Negro, as he put it, had nothing to do with it. The central idea of the war, as he told Congress, Jessie Frémont, John Hay, and various delegations, was to make self-government safe for White folks. And it was this idea, the idea of ensuring that White people could continue to vote for White people—and to subordinate Black people—that Lincoln took to Gettysburg and that generations of Americans, Black and White, have been celebrating since 1863.

Thus, once again, quotation doth make oppressors of us all.

There is a final, defining postscript to this story. For although Lincoln didn't carry African-Americans and their interests to Gettysburg, he did carry one African-American, a man named William Johnson, who worked in the Treasury Department as a messenger and moonlighted as Lincoln's personal servant.[63] Lincoln had "induced Johnson to leave Springfield and accompany him to Washington" as a bodyguard and personal servant. When Lincoln was stricken with chicken pox immediately after making the Gettysburg Address, Johnson probably nursed him and almost certainly provided the towel treatment he required on his way back to Washington.

Before long, Johnson himself contracted the disease, which was sweeping through Washington. Lincoln said later that he didn't think that he gave Johnson the disease, but nobody could be sure. The president survived, but Johnson, who was probably the only African-American close enough to actually hear the Gettysburg Address, died.

Did Lincoln learn anything from his death?

No.

Although Lincoln arranged the funeral, probably with funds

Johnson entrusted to him, and although he was kind to him the way segregation-time White Southerners were kind to a favorite Negro, he never said a word in favor of the human rights of William Johnson and never excluded him from his widely publicized views that it was necessary to deport William Johnson and his kind.

Basler said Lincoln treated Johnson like a man, but he was wrong. Although Johnson was a massive man getting on in age, Lincoln called him *boy*. On March 7, 1861, Lincoln sat down in the "Executive Mansion" and wrote the following "To Whom It May Concern" letter:

> William Johnson, *a colored boy,* and bearer of this, has been with me about twelve months; and has been, so far, as I believe, honest, faithful, sober, industrious, and handy as a servant (CW 4:277, italics added).

Did Lincoln learn anything from Johnson's life and death?
No.

After William Johnson—who was probably the last casualty of Gettysburg—was buried in Arlington, another Johnson, Solomon James Johnson, a Union veteran, succeeded William Johnson as Lincoln's personal servant and was recommended by Lincoln for a job in the Treasury department. The letter of recommendation for the twenty-two-year-old man said:

> *This boy* says he knows Secretary Chase, and would like to have the place made vacant by William Johnson's death. I believe *he is a good boy* and I should be glad for him to have the place if it is still vacant. (CW 7:156, my italics)

Not a word.
Didn't I tell you? He didn't mean a word he said.

Part Eleven

With Malice Toward Some

To trust to the tender mercies of their former masters and to the protection of State legislation, without giving them any voice in making the laws, is simply to turn them over to the torture of their enemies. To turn them loose unaided and unprotected is wholesale murder.

—Congressman Thaddeus Stevens

There stands the Negro man naked, homeless; he does not own a handful of dust; he has no education; he has no roof to shelter him . . . . That man made the South a paradise, and when it was done, he shouldered his musket with us, and saved it to the nation. Look at him! The gratitude of republics! Disfranchised, naked, homeless, poor, we give him back to the white man who hates him, to dictate the terms of his existence! . . . The Negro has earned land, education, rights. Before we leave him, we ought to leave him on his own soil, in his own house, with the right to the ballot, and the school-house within reach.

— Abolitionist Wendell Phillips

27

Reconstruction Of The White People, For The White People, By The White People

L INCOLN spoke at Gettysburg on Thursday, November 19, 1863. When, nineteen days later, he unveiled his own postwar plan, he made it clear that *all* meant the same thing to him that it had always meant: all White people.

Thus, in his Proclamation of Amnesty and Reconstruction, issued on Tuesday, December 8, 1863, Lincoln became the first American president to explicitly draw the color line by officially defining a national program based on the exclusion of Black voters.

It can be said in Lincoln's defense, of course, that the White founding fathers were the real fathers of the color line, but a different point is involved here. For the slavery that condemned the Compromise of 1787 made it possible for the White founding fathers to hide behind state's rights and the three-fifths of other persons language they wrote in the Constitution. This, however, didn't stop Black founding fathers from voting in several of the original states, and nobody told North Carolina that it had to disenfranchise Blacks.

The Civil War changed the three-fifths dance and made it necessary for a president to issue an official order defining the racial space of new persons who had been defined legally as citizens by events and an ultraconservative attorney general. But the language that served George Washington would not serve the presidents of a country without slavery. What was needed now was language that included all Whites and excluded all Blacks in states like South Carolina and Louisiana where most of the people were Black.

Abraham Lincoln led the way in 1863 by proposing a *national* policy of reconstructing a Southern state as soon as one-tenth of the male voters of 1860 took a *future* loyalty oath and organized a government that renounced slavery. Lincoln didn't say a word about race, but every word he said was a race word. In a classic formulation, followed by subsequent Jim Crow regimes, Lincoln grandfathered all Whites in and grandfathered all Blacks out. For as everyone knew, there were no Black voters in Confederate states in 1860 when it was a criminal offense for a Black man to present himself at the polling place.

What about the slaves, who constituted a majority of the population in South Carolina, Mississippi, and probably Louisiana?

There were no *rights* for them or any other Blacks in the Lincoln plan.

For them and for their children, it was not yet Jubilee.

Not for them the brave words of Gettysburg and the Second Inaugural.

Not for them the rockets red glare.

Fondly as they hoped, fervently as they prayed, the scourge was not going to pass away, not, however, because of God but because of the default of men, his servant Abraham foremost among them.

It was this Lincoln—not the Lincoln who went up to Gettysburg—who proposed a probationary period of apprenticeship or de facto serfdom, declaring in this second proclamation that "any provision which may be adopted by such State governments in relation to the freed people of such State, which shall recognize and declare their permanent freedom, provide for their education, and which may yet be consistent, as a temporary arrangement, with their present condition as a laboring, landless, and homeless class, will not be objected to by the national Executive" (CW 7:55). Concerning which there is this further to be said: To assume a fact—to assume that the freedmen would be a laboring, landless and homeless class—is, especially if you have the power to change it, to acquiesce in that fact.

Not only did Lincoln acquiesce in the fact, he helped to create it, saying in the State of the Union Message that he sent to Congress on the same day:

> The proposed acquiescence of the national Executive in any reasonable temporary State arrangement for the freed people is made with the view of possibly modifying the confusion and destitution which must, at best, attend all classes by a total revolution of labor throughout whole States. It is hoped that the already deeply afflicted people in those States may be somewhat more ready to give up the cause of their affliction, if, to this extent, this vital matter be left to themselves . . . . (CW 7:51)

Was there no limit to Lincoln's insensitivity to Black humiliation and pain? Was there no limit to what he was prepared to do in order to keep from facing racism and himself? Apparently not, for what he says here with the acquiescence and or approval of almost all writers is that he was willing to let unreconstructed White Southerners and defiant Confederate veterans deal with Blacks *in their own way,* even if they created an apprenticeship system of serfdom and a Jim Crow system denying Blacks the rights and privileges of United States citizens.

This was mind-boggling. To turn the unprotected former slaves over to unreconstructed slaveowners and Confederates who hated them and feared them and blamed them for their defeat was more than malice to some—it was a license for murder or mayhem. What makes this paragraph almost unbearable in its insensitivity is that Lincoln doesn't seem to see Blacks and does not seem to realize that the "deeply afflicted people" in the South were *not* the former slaveowners but the former slaves and that the causes of their affliction were the former slaveowners to whom he proposed to leave "the vital matter" of Black freedom.

In the same message, incidentally, Lincoln said once again that he had struggled for a long time to preserve slavery in the United States. "[F]or a long time," he said, "it had been hoped that the rebellion could be suppressed without resorting to it [emancipation] as a military measure" (CW 7:49). It had been hoped by whom? By Abraham Lincoln, of course, who signalled once again in December 1863 that the Emancipation Proclamation was not his program. Secretary Chase, the only proBlack voice in the cabinet, deplored the lily-White suffrage provision and the proposed apprenticeship plans, but Lincoln ignored him.

All this had momentous consequences, for the time for imposing a lasting solution to the race problem was at the end of the war when the opposition was weak and disorganized. The South at this plastic moment was dazed by the trauma of defeat. Most Confederate leaders expected imprisonment, confiscation, perhaps even banishment. Expecting the worst, they were willing to give up many things in order to keep some things. If ever there was a moment for imposing a lasting solution to the race problem, this was it. But Lincoln and his successor dawdled, and the moment passed. When the Confederates realized that the North was divided and unsure, hope returned. And with hope came a revival of the spirit of rebellion. Thaddeus Stevens and other liberal leaders pointed out later that this was one of the greatest political blunders in American history.

Good intentions and rhetoric apart, it would not be ungenerous to say that Lincoln never understood the nature of the struggle and never committed himself to a democratic South or a democratic America. This was evident in the way he conducted the war, in his unwillingness, even at Gettysburg, to invoke the dynamic of democracy as a fighting faith. It was evident, too, in his attempt to make peace by collaborating with the forces that caused the war. He didn't see in the concluded struggle new and immense possibilities. He thought of a Union preserved instead of a Union to be created. And if the cancer of slavery and segregation is still circulating in the bloodstream of America, it is in part because Lincoln and his successor didn't deal with that cancer at what was perhaps the last opportunity to cut it out at the roots.

Lincoln's postwar policy, as every TV commentator knows, was based on the maxim, "with malice toward none; with charity for all," which was an excellent sentiment, sound as Second Corinthians, but containing not one ounce of wisdom about what to do in a historical situation where you are forced to choose between irreconcilable interests. The interests of the former slaveholders and the interests of the former slaves were irreconcilable in the postwar South. The former slaveholders wanted to keep Blacks in slavery or as close to slavery as possible, and the former slaves wanted the same rights as the former slaveholders, including the land they had worked for centuries.

These interests were mutually exclusive and were complicated by the fact that the defeated slaveowners hated the former slaves, considered them responsible for their defeat, and were prepared to slaughter a generation to make their point. There was no way, under these circumstances, that you could be charitable to both groups, any more than you could be charitable to both Afrikaners and Africans in pre-Mandela South Africa, any more than you could be charitable to both wolves and sheep in an unfenced field. It was necessary to choose, and a refusal to choose was a choice for the stronger interest, was, in fact, a choice for the wolves.

Lincoln's rhetorical flourish masked, as usual, a real historical choice. In the postwar South, as in the prewar South, he deliberately chose the interests of Whites and former slaveholders over the interests of Blacks and former slaves. His malice toward none was charity to the former slaveholders and malice toward the former slaves, and the choices he made were actionable, legally and morally. For one thing, he was required by his oath and by the Articles of War to protect United States soldiers. It was a criminal offense, punishable by impeachment, for the president of the United States and the commander in chief of the armed forces to knowingly and willingly deliver his former soldiers to sworn enemies they had helped defeat.

Lincoln said once that he would be "damned in time & in eternity" if he returned the brave Black soldiers of Port Hudson and Olustee to slavery (CW 7:507), but he didn't apply the same strict criterion to the Lincoln who practically restored slavery in liberated Louisiana and put the brave warriors of Port Hudson under the de facto control of former Confederates who hated them and who were determined to punish them for picking up the gun against slavery.

And in appraising Lincoln's default, one must remember that when Whites violently overthrew the Republican governments in the South, they declared war on Black Union veterans, who were shot down in daylight, lynched, and burned slowly over open fires because they had fought for a country that didn't have the decency to demand safeguards for them in the peace that couldn't have been won without their help. Looking back on the casualties of the Second Civil War, the one that overthrew Reconstruction and the Fourteenth and Fifteenth amendments, one of the survivors, Albion Tourgee, said that "of the slain, there were enough to furnish forth a battlefield . . . all killed with deliberation, overwhelmed by numbers, roused from slumber at the murk midnight, in the hall of public assembly, upon the river-bank, on the lonely wood-roads, in simulation of the public execution,—shot, stabbed, hanged, drowned, mutilated beyond description, tortured beyond conception."

And the wounded?

"Ah!" Tourgee said, "the wounded in this silent warfare were more thousands than those who groaned on the slopes of Gettysburg" (251-2).

There was only one way to prevent this slaughter and to reconstruct the South humanely, and that was for Lincoln and his successor to use overwhelming pressure overwhelmingly for a number of years. Democracy in the South for the next one hundred years at least was impossible without this imperative. Certain leaders, Stevens, Phillips, Douglass, and Sumner above all, called for action on this level, but Lincoln balked, not only because he lacked the will to deal with the political imperatives but also because he was committed to the opposite of democracy in the South.

Despite what he said at Gettysburg, his real plan was to create a forced labor system under another name and to restore the same social system that caused the war. If Southern White people were prepared to make minimum bows to the new order, he was prepared to let them do what they wanted with Blacks if they didn't do it too brutally and too publicly. What was his plan? His plan, crony Henry C. Whitney said, was "to restore to the South the role of the leading social and political classes" (133)—that is to say, as Lincoln said repeatedly, "the gentlemen of character" who started the war and created the plantation system.

This again was malice toward some. For to deprive Blacks of the political weapons they needed to defend themselves, and to turn them over to embittered White Southerners was murder socially, psychologically and, in thousands on thousands of cases, physically. "We have turned, or are about to turn, loose four million slaves without a hut to shelter them or a cent in their pockets," Stevens said. "The infernal laws of slavery have prevented them from acquiring an education, understanding the common laws of contract, or of managing the ordinary business of life. This Congress is bound to provide for them until they can take care of themselves." The reverse, Stevens said, was too horrible to contemplate. To free Blacks without land, "to trust to the tender mercies of their former masters and to the protection of State legislation, without giving them any voice in making the laws, is simply to turn them over to the torture of their enemies. *To turn them loose unaided and unprotected is wholesale murder* [italics added]."[64]

The same message, and the same warning, was delivered by Phillips, who said in a Boston speech, published in the *Liberator* on February 5, 1864: "There stands the Negro man naked, homeless; he does not own a handful of dust; he has no education; he has no roof to shelter him . . . . That man made the South a paradise, and when it was done, he shouldered his musket with us, and saved it to the nation. Look at him! The gratitude of republics! Disfranchised, naked, homeless, poor, we give him back to the white man who hates him, to dictate the terms of his existence! The Negro has earned land, education, rights. Before we leave him, we ought to leave him on his own soil, in his own house, with the right to the ballot, and the schoolhouse within reach."

Louisiana leaders, including Black Union veterans, appealed to Lincoln and his commanders to no avail. Francis E. Dumas, a brilliant and wealthy Union veteran who had outfitted and captained a Union company at his own expense, told Lincoln's Louisiana commander, according to a *Liberator* report of February 17, 1865, "We have earned the malignant hate of every White man in this city [New Orleans] to save you; give us the ballot to protect ourselves before you withdraw the U.S. cannon."

No one can say that Lincoln wasn't warned.

But having struggled from 1861 to 1863, by his own admission, to keep from touching the institution of slavery, he struggled from 1863 to 1865 to keep from touching the social system that caused the war. What about slavery? As in the first days of the war, he wanted to touch slavery least of all and last of all. He said everywhere that he would not reenslave the minority of slaves who had enjoyed *actual* freedom. This statement, which sounds so noble and which is universally praised by Lincolnians, assumes a different and more sinister aspect if we look at it more closely. For what Lincoln said clearly here was that the overwhelming majority of slaves who had not enjoyed *actual* freedom could, as far as he was concerned, be kept in slavery or quasi slavery, depending on the whims of the court.

The only problem, from his standpoint and the standpoint of slaveowners, was the Thirteenth Amendment. It was not certain at this time that it would be ratified, and it was, unfortunately, Lincoln's death, and not his life, that speeded ratification. But whether ratified or not, Lincoln wanted to soften the blow by making it gradual. How could you ratify a constitutional amendment gradually? One way, as Lincoln suggested below, was to ratify it "prospectively." Another way was to use the devices all colonial powers use and that Lincoln repeatedly recommended: transitional periods of apprenticeship and slavery under the new names of serfdom or sharecropping.

Appalled by Lincoln's naïveté or what comes down to the same thing, his indifference or cynicism, liberal Republicans and abolitionists called for social, political and economic transformation. Lincoln defenders say these White men hated "the South"—they mean the *White* South—which is still saying too much since Stevens and Phillips only demanded sanctions for big slaveholders and the leaders of a war that had cost billions of dollars and more than a half million casualties. What Stevens proposed to do was to punish "belligerent traitors" by confiscating their property, "both as a punishment for their crimes and to pay the loyal men who have been robbed by the rebels . . . to increase the pensions of our wounded soldiers" and to provide reparations for the freedmen.[65]

Like the conveners of the Nuremberg Trials, he also wanted to "inflict salutary punishments to prevent future civil wars and to punish the criminals" who, he said, fought an "unjust war," based, as in World War II, on a theory of racial supremacy; who "deliberately starved to death sixty thousand prisoners of war; who shot or reduced to bondage all captives soldiers of the colored race; who sought to burn our cities through secret agents . . . . "

Confederates denied these charges, but there is evidence, cited even by Abraham Lincoln, of atrocities against Black soldiers. Phillips and others, including Secretary of War Stanton, made the same charges about the systematic starvation of Union soldiers. It is fashionable today to vilify Stevens for demanding punishment for war crimes. Few analysts note that Stevens was not alone, and that some members of Lincoln's official family said the same thing. Attorney General James Speed, a prominent Kentuckian, told Lincoln that traitors "ought to be hung" (HI 476). Both White House secretaries believed Robert E. Lee "should have been shot" (Neely 1982, 225).

Confronting the whole issue of punishment for treason and war crimes, Fawn M. Brodie said that "a provocative comparative study could be made of the difference in the severity of the terms imposed upon the ex-Confederates and those imposed by the United States upon enemies defeated in foreign wars. After World War II, for example, America alone held 950,000 denazification trials in Germany" (404)—compared with zero de-Confederate trials in the United States.

Stevens said he had no malice against Southern Whites. He was interested, he said, in the seventy thousand "aristocrats" out of a population of six million, who owned "about three hundred and ninety million acres of land out of the five hundred million in the Confederate states."[66] The problem, he said, was not the people; the problem was a system, and there was no possibility of creating democratic institutions and democratic people if that system was not destroyed by breaking up the big plantations and distributing the land to poor Blacks and poor Whites.

None knew this better than former slave Sojourner Truth, who called for land reform and federal subsidies integrated into a comprehensive plan of a magnitude never attempted in this country. "America," she said, "owes to my people some of the dividends. She can afford to pay, and she must pay. I shall make them understand that there is a debt to the Negro people which they never can repay. At least then, they must make amends" (Fauset 162).

What was at stake here, in modern terms, was reparations for the victims of history's greatest crime, the four hundred-year ordeal of the slave trade and the two hundred-year ordeal of slavery. The whole economic empire of the West, including the gold that made capitalism possible and the capital that financed the western movement, all of it, the docks and streets of Boston and New Orleans and Charleston, the books and finery of Monticello and Mount Vernon, Wall Street and Canal Street and Scarlet O'Hara's house, the one in the movies and the manors on Peachtree Street, all of it was founded on the blood and bones of the slaves. When Phillips thought of the enormity of the crime and the staggering debt owed African-Americans, he was overcome with horror and remorse. "This nation," he said in a Boston speech, reprinted in the *Liberator*, February 5, 1864, "owes the Negro not merely freedom; it owes him land, and it owes him education also. It is a debt which will disgrace us before the people if we do not pay it," a debt, he said, that required "not charity but justice—absolute, immediate, unmixed justice . . . ."

Even the word *justice* was inadequate to describe an open account unprecedented in world history. " I hate the term justice to the Negro," Phillips said, "There is not wealth enough in all the North to compensate this generation—much less the claim it has as heir to those who have gone before . . . . There is not [enough] wealth in the nation to give him his rights. The whole nation on its knees could not give him his rights . . . . We are not rich enough to give the Negro his rights. For two hundred years he has redeemed twenty states from savagery and barbarism. Every house built upon its surface his labor constructed. Every dollar dug from the soil was got by the toil of the Negro . . . . Agriculture, cities, roads, factories, funded capital—all were made by and belong to the Negro."

That's what Douglass meant when he said, "The white people of this country can never do too much for us. If they should put a schoolhouse at every crossroads of the South, supply each with a teacher . . . they would not cancel the debt contracted by the long years of slavery and suffering of this people" (FD 4:225).

Stevens made all this concrete and captured the imagination of the slaves with a notion that was immortalized in the phrase, "Forty Acres of Land and A Mule." Going back to the Thirty-seventh Congress and to the act Lincoln undermined and later sabotaged, he introduced resolutions providing for the immediate enforcement of the Confiscation Act of July 1862.

The resolutions provided that the land seized should be distributed among slaves who had been liberated by the war and constitutional amendments, and who were living on said land on the 4th of March, 1861, or since; "to each male person who is the head of a family, forty acres; to each adult male, whether head of a family or not, forty acres; to each widow who is head of a family, forty acres; to be held by them in fee-simple, but to be inalienable for next ten years after they become seized thereof . . . ."[67]

What Stevens said in Congress was said differently, but no less eloquently, by hundreds of thousands of Blacks. No one, at any rate, said it better, either in Congress or in the fields, than a certain Ed. D. Jennings of Flange County, Virginia, who sent the following letter to Lincoln on July 22, 1864 (Holzer 1998, 135):

Dr. Sir

Some reckon and others guess. But what I wish to know is this. what do you mean to do, with us Col [ore]d. population are we to suffer and our enemies reap or can we *Reap* now. I was brought up a farmer and if I can have a hut in my own native land and a little help that will suffice me, then I have a family you *know* well do the best you can, and oblige yr obt Servant

Ed. D. Jennings

Jennings's proposal and others of similar depth failed, as I have said elsewhere (1967, 56-8), because most Republicans, Lincoln foremost among them, had no intention of transforming American society. They never intended to give Blacks any more power than was necessary to check Southern planters. They recoiled instinctively from measures that would have given Blacks a measure of the economic security still denied the White workers of the North. They had never admitted the full logic of the democratic idea for poor Whites; it was unthinkable that they would countenance it for poor Blacks, especially since wholesale confiscation of property in the South would have set a bad example for the restless workers of the North and West.

Stevens and his colleagues based their struggle on the Declaration of Independence, which Lincoln reportedly loved but never talked about in concrete struggles. In a great speech, more pertinent and more concrete than the Gettysburg Address, Stevens denounced

Lincoln's successor, Andrew Johnson, and other politicians who supported White supremacy:[68]

> Demagogues of all parties, even some in high authority, gravely shout, 'This is the white man's government.' What is implied by this? That one race of men are to have the exclusive right to rule this nation, and to exercise all acts of sovereignty, while all other races and nations and colors are to be their subjects, and have no voice in making the laws and choosing the rulers by whom they are to be governed . . . .

This, Stevens said, was a monstrous proposition:

> Our fathers repudiated the whole doctrine of the legal superiority of families or races, and proclaimed the equality of men before the law. Upon that they created a revolution and built a Republic. They were prevented by slavery from perfecting the superstructure whose foundation they had thus broadly laid . . . .

Lincoln said at Gettysburg that the task before the nation was a rededication to what the White fathers had done four score and seven years ago. Stevens, with a larger vision and a bigger heart, said the task before the nation was a rededication to what the White fathers had *not* done fourscore and seven years ago. Now was the time, he said, "to complete their work."

> If this Republic is not now made to stand on their great principles, it has no honest foundation, and the Father of all men will still shake it to its center. If we have not yet been sufficiently scourged for our national sin to teach us to do justice to all God's creatures, without distinction of race or color, we must expect the still more heavy vengeance of an offended Father . . . .

Thus, in conclusion:

> This is not "a white man's Government," in the exclusive sense in which it is used. To say so is political blasphemy, for it violates the fundamental principles of our gospel of liberty. This is man's

Government, the Government of all men alike; not that all men will have equal power and sway within it. Accidental circumstances, natural and acquired endowment and ability, will vary their fortunes. But equal rights to all the privileges of the Government is innate in every immortal being, no matter what the shape or color of the tabernacle which it inhabits . . . .

"I insist," Sumner said, "echoing Stevens, that the rebel States shall not come back except on the footing of the Decltn of Indep. with all persons equal before the law, & govt. founded on the consent of the governed. In other words there shall be no discrimination on account of color. If *all* Whites vote, then must all blacks; but there shall be no limitation of suffrage for one more than the other" (SL 273).

Certain people, Lincoln among them, professed to be horrified by the idea of enfranchising people who were largely illiterate because the South, with America's and Lincoln's support, had made it a crime for them to read. "It is sometimes said," Sumner told a correspondent, 'what—let the freedmen yesterday a slave vote?' I am inclined to think that there is more harm in refusing than in conceding the franchise. It is said that they are as intelligent as the Irish just arrived." It was also said that the freedmen were as intelligent, perhaps more intelligent, than the great mass of poor Whites, who had also been denied education by slaveholding Whites. John Eaton told the president and others in 1863 that "many more among them [the freedmen] have learned to read and write than among the whites" (105).

The question before Lincoln, however, was not a question of books—the freedmen were at least as literate as Lincoln's mother and father—but a question of power and principle. "Without the votes of African-Americans, Sumner said, it would be impossible to establish stable governments in the South. "Without them, the old enemy will reappear," coalesce with White reaction in the North and postpone, perhaps forever, "the day of tranquility" and hope. Now was the time to do what the White fathers failed to do. "The Declaration of Indep. has pledges which have never been redeemed. We must redeem them, at least as regards the rebel states which have fallen under our jurisdiction" (SL 273).

Like Sumner, and unlike Lincoln, Phillips took his stand on the Declaration of Independence. "The long promise of seventy years," he said, "is to be fulfilled" (442), not in rhetoric but in land, homes, and ballots. This meant to Phillips and Sumner a new South—and a New North—with no racial barriers in churches, cemeteries, schools, transportation vehicles, cemeteries.

The polar white images in this dialogue were again Lincoln and Phillips. As in the first days of the conflict, as at Gettysburg, Lincoln refused to define Reconstruction in terms of the concrete issues of making all men equal in America. The problem here, a problem overlooked in the literature, was not technical; the problem was that Lincoln refused to treat Blacks as human beings with inalienable rights.

Phillips, in contrast, said Reconstruction was a God-given opportunity to realize the Declaration of Independence in Louisiana and Springfield, Illinois. What he called for in a speech to the Massachusetts Anti-Slavery Society, published in the *Liberator* on February 10, 1865, was a rainbow society with Black and White senators, generals and presidents—"a government color-blind; no distinction of race in the camp or the Senate; the Negro entitled to vote and to be voted for; to fight with rifle in hand or to order the battle with stars on his shoulders; stars and office for the heart, brain and hand, that can win and wield them; this is at once justice, fair play, magnanimity and necessity, and the only pathway to safety and empire."

Negrophobia, Phillips said, had almost destroyed the United States of America. God had sent the war to lift the country out of that rut, and he wanted, he said in another speech, printed in the May 29, 1863, *Liberator,* to greet and celebrate "the triumph in which all tongues, all races, and all creeds, mingle their prayers and offerings to a common liberty and a common God."

We are a long way here from the *ifs, ands,* and *buts* of the Lincolns. This is the terrain of the real emancipators. To contrast Phillips's and

Lincoln's programs is to understand the real issues of the war and the Reconstruction.

Lincoln talked about benefits; Phillips talked about rights.

Lincoln offered handouts; Phillips demanded justice.

Lincoln dreamed of an all-White nation; Phillips said he despised a nation resting its claim on the blood of one race and called for the immediate fulfillment of the Declaration of Independence the White founding fathers had betrayed.

Perhaps the most revealing aspects of this story is that Lincoln talked repeatedly and abstractly about the Declaration of Independence in 1858 but said little or nothing about it during the concrete struggles of the war and Reconstruction. In 1861, after Fort Sumter, he only mentioned the Declaration two times, according to the index tally in *The Collected Works.* In 1862, he only mentioned the Declaration once. In 1863, he only mentioned the Declaration once—at Gettysburg. In 1864, and 1865, *he didn't mention the Declaration at all.*

What all this meant strategically was played out in the last days of Lincoln's life in the state of Louisiana, which was, in a manner of speaking, Lincoln's last Gettysburg, since it almost certainly had a Black majority at that moment and was a perfect venue to talk about government of the people, et cetera, et cetera.

New Orleans and surrounding areas, as you will recall, was captured early in the war and was controlled by Union generals and bureaucrats. The area had a large and articulate Black middle class and a relatively large number of Black Union veterans. Despite these demographics and despite what he said at Gettysburg, Lincoln chose Louisiana as a test case for his Reconstruction program, which required participation by ten percent of the White males of the prewar electorate to the exclusion—by Lincoln's specific order—of a majority of the population. As early as January 30, 1863, twenty-nine days after the signing of the Emancipation Proclamation, General Nathaniel Banks established—with Lincoln's consent—a forced labor system which brought back slavery under another name. In a general order, issued from his headquarters, he said "all the conditions of continuous and faithful service, respectful deportment, correct discipline and perfect subordination shall be enforced on the part of the Negroes by the officers of the Government."[69]

In Louisiana, as in Missouri, two major White groups with different agendas competed for transitional power. As in Missouri, as in Maryland, as in Washington, D.C., Lincoln backed the most conservative and the most racist group, telegraphing at the end, as at the beginning, the color of his orientation and the color of his desire.

Appalled by Lincoln's policy, Blacks and their White allies demanded power safeguards for freedmen, including the right to vote and govern. On November 5, 1863, fourteen days before Lincoln's Gettysburg Address, the free Blacks of New Orleans held a mass meeting and sent a petition to Lincoln's military governor, saying: "That they are natives of Louisiana and citizens of the United States . . . that a large portion of them are owners of real estate [and] that many of them are engaged in the pursuits of commerce and industry, while others are employed as artisans in various trades . . . . . " The Black petitioners said their forefathers had fought with Andrew Jackson in the War of 1812 and that they had been among the first to respond to the call to defend the city from the Confederates, "having raised the first regiment in the short space of forty-eight hours."

In consideration of these facts, "in consideration of the services already performed, and still to be rendered by them to their common country," they asked for ballots and the rights of citizens.

"We are men," they said, "treat us as such."

On March 12, 1864, two Blacks, engineer Jean Baptiste Roudanez and wine merchant Arnold Bertonneau, carried the petition to the White House and asked "that the right of suffrage may be extended not only to natives of Louisiana of African descent, born free, but also to all others, whether born slave or free, especially those who have vindicated their right to vote by bearing arms, subject only to such qualifications as shall equally affect the white and colored citizens."

Lincoln rejected the petition, ignoring the fact that Bertonneau had served as a captain in the Union Army, and saying, according to Colonel John Forney: "I regret gentlemen, that you are not able to secure all your rights, and that circumstances will not permit the government to confer them upon you" (Carpenter 267). In a fuller report on this meeting, published in the *New Orleans Era* (qtd. in Cox 95, italics added), Lincoln said that in matters of this kind—Black citizenship and Black suffrage—he acted not on moral grounds but on the grounds of political necessity. The *New Orleans Era* report said:

> In their interview with President Lincoln, he declined to act upon their petition, taking the ground that *having the restoration of the Union paramount to all other questions,* he would do nothing that would hinder that consummation, or omit anything that would accomplish it. *He told them that, therefore, he did nothing in matters of this kind upon moral grounds, but solely upon political necessities.* Their petition asking to become citizens and voters being placed solely on moral grounds, did not furnish him with any inducements to accede to their wishes, but that he would do so whenever they could show that such accession would be necessary to the readmission of Louisiana as a State in the Union.

In this statement, as in so many others, Lincoln was less than honest, for he knew that Congress was not going to admit Louisiana if it didn't make some gesture toward the recognition of the rights of the freedmen. So, having made that statement for show, he picked up his pen the next day and urged a *gesture,* saying to Michael Hahn, the newly elected White governor of Lincoln's White state:

> I barely suggest for your private consideration, whether some of the colored people may not be let in—as, for instance, the very intelligent, and especially those who have fought gallantly in our ranks. (CW 7:243)

To make sure Hahn got the message, Lincoln added: "But this is only a suggestion, not to the public, but to you alone."

"Barely suggest," "for your private consideration," "the very intelligent," "let in," favors and not rights: thus speaks the faint-hearted White in a direct collision between White rights and Black rights. These, moreover, were private sentiments, not public acts; and they were expressed in an extremely hesitant manner at that. Lincoln didn't require fair or equal treatment for the freedmen. He didn't make any demands at all. Reconstruction, Lincoln style, was going to be Reconstruction of the White people, by the White people, for the White people.

On February 22, 1864, Lincoln's Louisiana commander, General Nathaniel P. Banks, held a state election, with Lincoln's consent, based—you won't believe this—on the prewar slave state constitution. The electorate was confined to "free White males" who had taken the Lincoln oath pledging future loyalty. White Union soldiers could also vote. What about the Black Union soldiers, the heroes of Port Hudson and other battles? They were barred from the election because of their race. So were the ten thousand free Blacks in New Orleans, many of whom were literate, some of whom were wealthy.

Michael Hahn, who ran a racist campaign based on his opposition to Black citizenship and Black voting, and who was supported by General Banks and, presumably Abraham Lincoln, won the election and was immediately anointed by Lincoln in a letter addressed to "His Excellency, Governor Michael Hahn."

Not waiting for a response from Hahn, Lincoln authorized another quickie White-only election, based again on the slave constitution, for members of a constitutional convention. The convention, dominated by conservatives, passed, under military pressure, a resolution banning slavery but balked at demands for Black suffrage, voting overwhelmingly for a provision which said "the legislature shall never pass an act authorizing Negroes to vote, or, to immigrate into this state under any pretense whatever."

Pressured by Banks, the members passed a vague resolution which permitted but did not require the legislature to extend the suffrage to "such persons, citizens of the United States, as by military service, by taxation to support the government, or intellectual fitness, may be deemed entitled thereto." To no one's surprise, the legislature decided that neither intelligent Blacks nor well-to-do Blacks nor Union veterans were entitled to vote. Joe Gray Taylor, the authority on *Louisiana Reconstructed*, said the convention "had no intention of giving the vote to any Negro," and that it was "a safe assumption that a legislature elected by white Louisianians would never do so" (47-8). Shall we go further and say that it is a safe assumption that Abraham Lincoln knew that a legislature elected by unreconstructed White Louisianians was not going to give Blacks the suffrage without overwhelming pressure applied overwhelmingly?

The signs were there for all to see, but Lincoln ignored them and went to his death saying that he believed—preposterously—that the Louisiana constitution was one of the best constitutions ever written.

There is such a big difference between the "new birth" of freedom of Gettysburg and the old-boy Southern White male orientation of the Lincoln reconstruction plan that one is tempted to seek an explanation in other realms. Was Lincoln perhaps misinformed? Or was he forced into this historical cul-de-sac by generals and major economic interests? The answer to these questions is no. Lincoln was not misinformed. He was not being manipulated by generals and reactionaries. On the contrary, Lincoln himself was doing the manipulating, trying, despite clear warnings and pleas from Blacks and congressional leaders, to create majorities based on the prewar White male population.

If Lincoln was set in his purpose, so were Sumner and other congressional leaders. When the Senate was asked to recognize Lincoln's lily-White Louisiana government, Sumner objected, calling for equal rights, including the ballot, for all citizens in the reconstructed states. In the February 1865 debate, Sumner insisted that the first step was crucial and that "a first false step" would be fatal to the cause of freedom in America (SM, 222). As for Lincoln's Louisiana government, he said it was "a mere seven months' abortion, begotten by the bayonet, in criminal conjunction with the spirit of caste, and born before its time, rickety, unformed, unfinished, whose continued existence will be a burden, a reproach, and a wrong" (SW 12:190-1).

Denounced by other senators, including Lyman Trumbull, for his uncompromising approach, Sumner used every parliamentary device, including filibustering, to block the bill. Pierce said later that Sumner almost singlehandedly established the principle of Black suffrage. If Lincoln's plan "had prevailed for Louisiana and the other rebel States," he said, "it would have resulted in the permanent exclusion of the colored people from the suffrage in all the old slave States" (SM 227). DuBois said the fight Sumner waged in February 1865 against Lincoln's Reconstruction Plan was "his greatest parliamentary contest and with his triumph, the cause of Negro suffrage was won" (162).

Sumner's defeat of Lincoln's lily-White Reconstruction plan is important not only because it marks the real beginning of the never-concluded struggle to emancipate Blacks but also because it throws new light on a recurring problem of White leadership, which has tended, from the post-Revolutionary Thermidor of Thomas Jefferson to the Freedom Movement Thermidor of the 1970s, to abandon the struggle for Black rights—and for equal rights in America—as the struggle becomes more radical and comes closer and closer to threatening the cornerstone of White supremacy. At that point, which I call the Garrison Fault, there is always a struggle between paternalistic dispensers of what Phillips called soup and old clothes and radical humanitarians of whatever name who demand equality and freedom.

The imminent collapse of the Confederacy in the winter of 1864 and the spring of 1865 brought these tendencies to the forefront not only in Congress, where Lyman Trumbull defected and opposed Sumner's call for equal rights in Louisiana, but also in the Abolitionist Movement, where men like William Lloyd Garrison backed away from the radical implications of Black suffrage.

Backed by Douglass and most of the Black and female abolitionists,

Phillips seized the reins from the faltering Garrison, saying that the genius of American institutions is that no group is safe without the political and economic means to defend itself. Sumner made the same point in his exemplary struggle against Lincoln, saying more than one hundred years before the Rehnquist Supreme Court, that equality is found not in any pretended equivalent nor in any future promise but in absolute and de facto equality in the here and now. Sumner regrettably met his own Garrison Fault in the liberal Republican movement of 1872, which called, among other things, for a withdrawal of federal troops from the South and a (White) North/South reconciliation.

Perhaps the best way to write the history of the 1860s—and the 1960s—is from the standpoint of the 1870s and the reformers who defected to the Liberal Republican movement—Greeley, Sumner, Trumbull, Carl Schurz, even Horace White—and the Democratic Party—Davis and Logan. There was, to be sure, cause for just complaints against Grant and the corruption of the period, but history is a hard taskmaster, and it should have been clear to the defectors that there was no way out of the traditional Republican Party, as Douglass said, that did not lead to the abandonment of equal rights and the crucifixion of the Black people of the South.

Thaddeus Stevens seems to have glimpsed more clearly than any other leader of the time the dangers that freedom and Black liberation faced. And when it became clear that Congress was not prepared to transform the South economically and politically, he rose in the House on June 13, 1866, and announced that the dream was stillborn. He was seventy-four years old then, and he had been long in the field, tilling. In his youth, in his manhood, in his old age, he had "fondly dreamed that when any fortunate chance should have broken up for a while the foundations of our institutions, and released us from obligations the most tyrannical that ever man imposed in the name of freedom, "that American institutions would be so remodeled "as to have freed them from every vestige of human oppression, of inequality of rights, of recognized degradation of the poor, and the superior caste of the rich. He had hoped, in short, that "no distinction would be tolerated in this purified Republic but what arose from merit and conduct." But, alas, he said, this "bright dream has vanished like the baseless fabric of a vision. I find that we shall be obliged to be content with patching up the worst portions of the ancient edifice, and leaving it, in many of its parts, to be swept through by the tempests, the frosts, and the storms of despotism."[70]

28

The Last Lincoln

SOPHISTICATED Lincoln specialists concede everything you say. Yes, they say, Lincoln was a racist *in contemporary terms.* Yes, he voted for Jim Crow laws and made demagogic speeches. Yes, he tried to save slavery, deport all Blacks and create an all-White nation.

Having conceded all that, they stake everything on their last-ditch defense, saying that almost everything critics say about Lincoln is true but that *he changed.* He was, they say, *moving in the direction* of equality at his death. Did you catch the qualification? He was not moving toward equality—he was moving *in the direction* of equality.

We see what is involved here. The proponents of this theory would have us believe that Lincoln, transformed and ennobled by the war between White Brothers, disenthralled himself, to use his word, and moved to higher ground. Don't believe a word of it! There is no evidence anywhere that Lincoln moved of his own volition in any direction save the direction of White supremacy. Even when he was *forced* in his last speech to make one of his patented rhetorical retreats, he studiously and steadfastly refused to recognize Black people and Black Union soldiers as human beings. Nor did he ever say in this life that Black people or even Black Union soldiers had any political or economic rights in Louisiana, or Illinois for that matter, that White people were bound to respect.

Lincoln didn't change.

"The weight of evidence and logic," Fredrickson said," seems to support the hypothesis that Lincoln died with the same basic views on black-white relations that he had held tenaciously throughout his public life" (58). That was also the conclusion of Lincoln authority Roy P. Basler, who said that "he never contemplated with any degree of satisfaction the prospect of a free Negro race living in the same country as a free white race" (1935, 210-1).

Anyone who doubts this need only consult the seven defining events of his last days. The first event was the abortive peace conference at Hampton Roads, Virginia, on Friday, February 3, two months before Lincoln's death. Lincoln and Secretary of State Seward represented the United States at this conference while Confederate Vice President Alexander H. Stephens, Confederate Senator R.M.T. Hunter and Confederate Assistant Secretary of War John A. Campbell represented the Confederacy.

The two groups met for four hours on the steamer *River Queen*, anchored at Hampton Roads near Fortress Monroe.

According to the ground rules, there was to be "no clerk or secretary—no writing or record of anything that is said," but the Confederate representatives either wrote on their cuffs or made notes immediately afterward. We are forced, therefore, to see the event largely through their eyes, although Lincoln later corroborated some of their main points.

The men knew one another and admired and respected one another. The meeting began therefore in a spirit of camaraderie with a lot of talk about the good old [White] days and the fate of old friends. Lincoln, who had served in the Thirtieth Congress with Stephens, never got around to asking his old friend what he meant when he made that infamous speech, saying that the Confederacy was founded on the cornerstone of slavery and inequality.

The Confederacy, at that point, was on the verge of defeat, and Stephens tried to muddy the water by saying that the North and the South should stop all this foolish disputing over slaves and join hands and wage a war of conquest in South America. Lincoln, to his eternal credit, demurred, saying, as he said repeatedly, that no substantial question could be decided until the South laid down its arms and returned to the Union.

That, of course, raised the billion-dollar question: slavery. Stephens asked "what effect the Proclamation would have upon the *entire* (my italics) Black population."

> Mr. Lincoln said, that was a judicial question. How the Courts would decide it, he did not know, and could give no answer. His own opinion was, that as the Proclamation was a *war measure* [emphasis in original], and would have effect only from its being an exercise of the war power, as soon as the war ceased, it would be inoperative for the future. It would be held to apply only to such slaves as had come under its operation while it was in active exercise. This was his individual opinion, but the Courts might decide the other way, and hold that it effectually emancipated all the slaves in the States to which it applied at the time. So far as he was concerned, he should leave it to the Courts to decide. He never would change or modify the terms of the Proclamation in the slightest particular. (610-1)

The Confederate representatives asked, in effect, if they could make a deal. Seward, flirting with treason, suggested that "if the Confederate States would . . . abandon the war, they could of themselves defeat this [Thirteenth] amendment [and keep their slaves], by voting it down as members of the Union" (612).

Instead of reproving his secretary of state and saying that he could not listen to such talk, Lincoln made a wild suggestion of his own, saying that the Confederates could soften the blow by ratifying the amendment *prospectively* and keeping their slaves for five more years.

Sympathetic Lincoln historians have suggested that Lincoln meant five more months, a defense that makes no sense, especially since Lincoln made *prospective* suggestions to other people. In any case, this, in Stephens's words, is what Lincoln said:

> Stephens, if I were in Georgia . . . I'll tell you what I would do, if I
> were in your place: I would go home and get the Governor of the
> State to call the Legislature together, and get them to recall all the
> State troops from the war; elect Senators and Members to Congress,
> and ratify this Constitutional Amendment *prospectively*, so as to
> take effect—say in five years. (614, emphasis in original)

Lincoln said he had researched the matter and that such a ratification would be valid. He said that whatever happened in the war slavery was doomed and "the best course, it seems to me, for your public men to pursue, would be to adopt such a policy as will avoid, as far as possible, the *evils* of immediate emancipation" (italics added).

When the Confederate representatives asked about Trumbull's Confiscation acts, Lincoln confirmed the worst fears of Trumbull and other congressional leaders, saying that "their enforcement was left entirely with him," and that they had nothing to fear on that score.

Throughout the conference, if we can believe Stephens's words, Lincoln was apologetic about slavery and his role in issuing the proclamation. He said again—*this was two months before his death*— that he had *never* been in favor of immediate emancipation of Blacks, not even by the states. He spoke again of the "many evils attending" immediate emancipation and suggested, as he had suggested on other occasions, a system of apprenticeship (CW 6:365).

It has been said, of course, that Stephens's account cannot be relied on. Apart from the fact that Lincoln verified parts of it, the phrase about the "many evils attending" immediate emancipation is a Lincoln DNA that would identify him anywhere.

Here, then, two months before his death, are the last defining words of Abraham Lincoln on slavery and emancipation:

> He then went into a prolonged course of remarks about the
> Proclamation. He said it was not his intention in the beginning to
> interfere with Slavery in the States; that he never would have
> done it, if he had not been compelled by necessity to do it, to

maintain the Union; that the subject presented many difficult and perplexing questions to him; that he had hesitated for some time, and had resorted to this measure, only when driven to it by public necessity; that he had been in favor of the General Government prohibiting the extension of Slavery into the Territories, but did not think that that Government possessed power over the subject in the States, except as a war measure; and that he had always himself been in favor of emancipation, but not immediate emancipation, even by the States. Many evils attending this appeared to him. (613-4)

The Confederates professed to be greatly concerned about what would happen to the freed slaves. Hunter, according to Lincoln, "said, substantially, that the slaves, always accustomed to an overseer, and to work upon compulsion, suddenly freed, as they would be if the South should consent to peace on the basis of the 'Emancipation Proclamation,' would precipitate not only themselves but the entire Southern society into irremediable ruin. No work would be done, nothing would be cultivated, and both blacks and whites would starve!'"

Since nobody in the South except Blacks had worked for the last two centuries, and since Blacks were primarily responsible for creating the wealth of the South and for keeping Southern Whites from starving, there was madness and unintended humor in Hunter's complaint. But Lincoln, in his reply, overlooked these inconsistencies and said he was reminded of the story" of a man out in Illinois, by the name of Case, who undertook, a few years ago, to raise a very large herd of hogs":

> It was a great trouble to *feed* them, and how to get around this was a puzzle to him. At length he hit on the plan of planting an immense field of potatoes, and, when they were sufficiently grown, he turned the whole herd into the field, and let them have full swing, thus saving not only the labor of feeding the hogs, but also that of digging the potatoes. Charmed with his sagacity, he

stood one day leaning against the fence, counting his hogs, when a neighbor came alone. 'Well, well,' said he, 'Mr. Case, this is all very fine. Your hogs are doing very well just now, but you know out here in Illinois the frost comes early, and the ground freezes a foot deep. Then what are they going to do?' This was a view of the matter that Mr. Case had not taken into account. Butchering-time for hogs was 'way on in December or January. He scratched his head, and at length stammered. 'Well, it may come pretty hard on their *snouts*, but I don't see but that it will be 'root, hog, or die!'" (Carpenter 210-1)

This was all very well for hogs and freed slaves, but slavehold-ers, in Lincoln's view, deserved more consideration, probably be-cause their snouts were more delicate. At any rate, on February 5, 1865, two days after he told the hog story, Lincoln again opposed the principles of the Emancipation Proclamation and the Thirteenth Amendment, suggesting to his cabinet that the United States pay the virtually defeated Southern states $400,000,000 if they returned to the Union and ratified the Thirteenth Amendment by July 1, 1865. Liberal, conservative and moderate members of the cabinet unanimously opposed the proposal. Abraham Lincoln, according to eyewitnesses, withdrew the plan and said mournfully, "You are all opposed to me" (RR 98).

Two months later, and three days before his death, Lincoln again—the third event—expressed dissatisfaction with *his* Proclamation, telling an unreconstructed Confederate, W. C. Bibbs of Montgomery, Alabama, that he did not intend to "hurt the hair of the head of a sin-gle man in the South [he meant a single *White* man in the South] if it can possibly be avoided."

"Mr. Lincoln," Bibb asked Lincoln on Wednesday, April 12, three days before his death, "what do you propose to do in relation to the slave property?"

"I am individually," Lincoln replied, according to Bibb, "willing to grant either gradual emancipation, say, running through twenty years, or compensated emancipation at the option of the Southern [White] people; but there are certain amendments to the Constitution now before the people for their adoption or rejection, and I have no power to do anything at present; but if it should so happen that I could control it such would be my policy" (qtd. in Sandburg 1939, 4:239).

Since Lincoln could no longer control the process, he cast about for other alternatives, summoning General Benjamin F. Butler to the White House shortly before his death and inquiring—the fourth event—about the possibility of "sending the Blacks away." According to Butler's reminiscences (903-7), which have been questioned by some scholars, Lincoln asked: "But what shall we do with the Negroes after they are free? I can hardly believe that the South and North can live in peace, unless we get rid of the Negroes. Certainly they cannot if we don't get rid of the Negroes whom we have armed and disciplined and who have fought with us . . . . I believe it would be better to export them all to some fertile country with a good climate, which they could have to themselves . . . . If these black soldiers of ours go back to the South I am afraid that they will be but little better off with their masters than they were before, and yet they will be free men. I fear a race war, and it will be at least a guerrilla war because we have taught these men how to fight . . . ."

What, then, was to be done?

"I wish," Lincoln said to Butler, "you would carefully examine the question and give me your views upon it and go into the figures, as you did before in some degree, so as to show whether the Negroes can be exported . . . ."

Butler came back two days later with a sobering story. "Mr. President, I have gone very carefully over my calculations as to the power of the country to export the Negroes of the South, and I assure you that, using all your naval vessels and all the merchant marine fit to cross the seas with safety, it will be impossible for you to transport to the nearest place fit for them . . . half as fast as Negro children will be born here."

Scores of historians have spent countless hours trying to discredit Butler and his story. But since it is impossible to prove a negative, and since, as other historians have pointed out, Butler's account is "full and circumstantial" and there was no reason for him to lie, these efforts have proved fruitless. More to the point, Lincoln said the same thing about colonization and his fear of Black violence to others (see page 615). Based on these and other factors, some scholars, Ludwell H. Johnson (68) and Herman Belz (282) among them, have concluded that there is no reason to doubt the Butler account. "If Butler's recollection is substantially correct, as it appears to be," George Fredrickson said, "then one can only conclude that Lincoln continued to his dying day to deny the possibility of racial harmony and equality in the United States and persisted in regarding colonization as the only real alternative to perpetual race conflict" (57).

Lincoln, who betrayed the trust of the slaves so often and on so many levels, mocking their dreams with dialect stories and "darky" jokes and maneuvering behind the scenes to keep them in slavery and in need, never approached the Moses hope that covered Southern fields, like dew. But in one electric moment, never again repeated, he gave a glimpse of what he could have meant to the slaves and the sons and daughters of slaves. That was the moment in the Second Inaugural Address when he spoke with the tongue of the seers of Slave Row, saying: "Fondly do we hope—fervently do we pray—that this mighty scourge of war may speedily pass away. Yet, if God wills that it continue, until all the wealth piled by the bondman's two hundred and fifty years of unrequited toil shall be sunk, and until every drop of blood drawn with the lash, shall be paid by another drawn with the sword, as was said three thousand years ago, so still it must be said 'the judgments of the Lord, are true and righteous altogether' "(CW 8:333).

From this great (rhetorical) height, Lincoln descended to the valley of his strange and unremitting struggle to protect the White body politic (and himself) from the rising and threatening Black masses—and the righteous judgment of the Lord. And his last public speech—the sixth defining event in the last days of Lincoln—provides further and powerful evidence that the last Lincoln was the real Lincoln and the only Lincoln. In that speech on Tuesday, April 11, 1865, four days before his death, he again defended his plan for a lily-White reconstruction. Noting that his Louisiana Reconstruction plan was "unsatisfactory" to some because it denied the elective franchise "to the colored man," Lincoln said "I would myself prefer that it were now conferred *on the very intelligent* [Blacks], and on those who serve our cause as soldiers"(CW 8:403, my italics).

There he was, then, standing on the edge of glory, arguing publicly for invidious distinctions between Blacks and Whites, oblivious to the fact that if the franchise had been confined to "very intelligent Whites" this nation would have perished from the earth long ago.

Based on this confession, new-age Lincoln scholars have constructed an elaborate defense which claims that Lincoln was "moving in the direction of" equality when he was assassinated. What is the evidence for this theory, which assumes and confirms my thesis that he hadn't moved far?

The evidence is that Lincoln was so Machiavellian or so maladroit in expressing himself that he gave different people different ideas about what he wanted, thereby creating a window of confusion that his field commanders could have exploited to put some loyal Black citizens on the Reconstruction suffrage rolls in Louisiana.

Here, once again, we find one of the great fallacies of Lincolnography, which tells us that honest Abraham Lincoln spoke with a forked tongue the better to fool the bigots. But this argument proves too little and too much, for Lincoln said repeatedly in the beginning, middle and end of his career that he, as much as any other White man, believed in White supremacy and that Blacks should be denied equal rights because of their inferiority. The forked-tongue argument is based, moreover, on a dubious theory of leadership, which says that one leads not by defining a policy and clearly articulating it, but by not leading and by saying two different things at the same time.

This is what a contemporary columnist meant when she wrote in the August 1, 1999, *Chicago Tribune*—LESSONS FROM ABE—that George W. Bush and other contemporary Republican and Democratic leaders reminded her of Abe Lincoln, who, taught us, she said, "the virtues of vagueness" and that "waffling does not always equal intellectual cowardice." But her argument, based, she said, on Garry Wills's argument that Lincoln "calibrated what he had to say about slavery according to his audience" (92), ignores historical coordinates and the incontestable fact that waffling is always intellectual cowardice, or worse, at a historic moment when men and women are being brutalized and murdered in concentration camps and on slave plantations. As for the comparison with Bush and the condemnation of "confrontational rhetoric," we are reminded once again that history knows its own and that Abraham Lincoln is praised *today* not because he was a reformer or a radical but because he was *not* a reformer or radical.

The summit of waffling leadership, according to the new school, occurred when Lincoln wrote the letter we have already examined to the Lincoln-approved White governor of Louisiana, "barely suggesting" for his "private consideration" whether very intelligent Blacks and Union veterans might "be let in" (CW 7:243) as voters. The operational words here are *let in;* Lincoln, even in a private letter, was not talking about a right—he was talking about a favor, a gratuity. Although Lincoln asked the governor not to make the letter public, proponents of this theory contend that he proved his good faith and his love of Black people by suggesting sotto voce to various people that they could pass this letter around to build public support for a Jim Crow suffrage.

This is clearly insufficient. First, and definitively, Lincoln did not in this letter or any other communication demand or require participation by Black voters, intelligent or otherwise. In the second place, Lincoln accepted and defended to his death the racist Louisiana government that rejected all suggestions and disenfranchised at least half the Louisiana population, including his Black soldiers. What is truly astonishing, however, is that the defenders do not recognize that the defense is an indictment of Lincoln and the defense. For if Lincoln had duplicated that timid letter and distributed it to every White voter in America, it would not have changed the fact that the letter itself called for invidious and racist distinctions between Black voters, who were required to be "very intelligent," and White voters, who could vote even if they were "very ignorant."

One of the strongest arguments against the *moving in the direction of defense* is the man cited most often to justify it, Lincoln's Louisiana commander Nathaniel Banks, who knew as well as Lincoln's modern defenders that the Louisiana plan was not going to fly unless he could find a way to qualify enough Blacks to satisfy congressional critics without endangering the numerical superiority of Louisiana Whites. To that end, Banks came up with the mad idea of turning a certain number of Black men into White men. He even found a federal judge who was willing to rule that any Black with "a majority of White blood" was a White man. But the plan went awry at the last moment, primarily because light-skinned Louisiana Blacks refused to dissociate themselves from the Black population (AC 1864, 480).

Lincoln moved during his last public speech, but he didn't move in the direction of equality. Former Treasury Secretary Chase, who was then chief justice, noted with approval that Lincoln had moved away from the apprenticeship idea he and others had opposed more than a year. But Chase and others regretted that Lincoln in April 1865 was "not yet ready for universal or at least equal suffrage" (CD 66).

Most contemporary scholars defend Lincoln on this point, primarily because they believe in 2000 that it would have been wrong in 1863 to give votes to the freedmen, who constituted the majority of the population in South Carolina and Mississippi and at least one-half of the population in Louisiana. This contemporary defenses ignores the fact that the freedmen, who had been violently denied the right to read and write, with Lincoln's practical approval, were at least as intelligent as the recent White immigrants.

Furthermore, and on a deeper level, the Louisiana defense assumes that Lincoln could not express himself, ignoring the fact that he *always* expressed himself clearly and unambiguously when he was pushing conservative and proslavery policies he favored. He was, for example, unmistakably clear and *demanding* in outlining a Reconstruction program based on the participation and the votes of former Confederates and former Confederate soldiers. Who cannot see that the reason he was not equally clear in demanding Black suffrage is that he was opposed to general Black suffrage?

In any case, Lincoln said repeatedly and clearly that he was in favor of a Jim Crow suffrage. Lincoln's great friend, Ward Hill Lamon, said Lincoln was adamant about reconstructing Southern governments on the basis of "the qualified voters" before secession. Secretary Chase, "alone of all the Cabinet," Lamon reported, objected to Lincoln's Proclamation of Amnesty, suggesting that the language be changed to read "instead of 'qualified voters,' 'citizens of the State.'" Lincoln refused to make the change. Why did he refuse? The answer, according to Lamon's recollections, was that the attorney general had ruled that Negroes born in the United States were citizens of the United States, "and if the phrase 'one-tenth of the qualified voters . . . were changed to 'one-tenth of the citizens,' the organization might have been legally composed entirely of colored men." Lincoln was determined to prevent that. He was "set in his purpose that the restored governments in the seceded States should be organized by the 'qualified [White] voters' of those States before secession was attempted, and Mr. Chase had to submit to the inevitable" (1911, 240-1).

Lincoln pressed the same view in a White House conference on December 18, 1864, with his hand-picked Louisiana commander, General Nathaniel Banks, and Postmaster General Blair on Congressman James Ashley's proposed Reconstruction bill. "The President," Hay wrote, "had been reading [the Ashley bill] carefully & said that he liked it with the exception of one or two things which he thought rather calculated to conceal a feature which might be objectionable to some" (244-5).

What were these objectionable features?

"The first," Lincoln said, "was that under the provisions of that bill Negroes would be made jurors & voters under the temporary governments."

"Yes," said Banks, "with Lincoln's concurrence, "that is to be stricken out and the qualification 'white mail [sic] citizens of the U.S.' is to be restored. What you refer to would be a fatal objection to the Bill. It would simply throw the Government into the hands of the blacks, as the white people under that arrangement would refuse to vote" (Hay 244-5).

The second "objectionable" feature, Lincoln said, was "the declaration that all persons heretofore held in slavery are declared free," an objection that proves once again the central thesis of this book. For if Lincoln had already emancipated Blacks, why would he object on any ground in December 1864 to a bill that proposed to emancipate Blacks.

Two other points are crucial and revealing. The first is that Lincoln returns here, four months before his death, to issues he had been pressing for almost a generation—the issue of Black suffrage, which he had opposed since 1836, and the issue of Blacks serving on juries, which he had opposed implicitly as an upholder of the Illinois status quo and explicitly in the Lincoln-Douglas debates of 1858.

But enough of these word games. For in the end, as in the beginning, the best evidence of what Abraham Lincoln thought is Abraham Lincoln himself. Let us once again and finally, forsaking all others, pose the final questions to The Last Lincoln:

Q. Did Abraham Lincoln believe in April 1865 that African-Americans were entitled to the same rights as other Americans with no *ifs*, *ands*, and *buts?*

A. No. The proof is the evidence cited to prove that he was moving—everything he said and did on Reconstruction, including his Proclamation of Amnesty, his last speech, and his last cabinet meeting.

Q. Did he believe in April 1865 that Black Union soldiers and

Black Americans were entitled to the same rights and privileges as Confederate soldiers and Confederate supporters who signed the oath of amnesty?

A. No. Same proof.

Q. Did Lincoln believe in April 1865 in a Jim Crow system which defined Blacks as second-class citizens and denied them the basic rights of citizenship?

A. Yes. Same proof plus the additional proof of the Jim Crow system of politics, civil rights, and forced labor created in Louisiana under his leadership and defended by him at his last cabinet meeting.

Q. Lincoln said in his last public speech on April 11—four days before his tragic death—that "I would myself prefer that it were *now* (my italics) conferred on the very intelligent, and on those who serve our cause as soldiers" (CW 8:403) Did he suggest at any time and under any circumstance that the suffrage be confined to very intelligent Whites?

A. No.

Q. Did he also make invidious distinctions between Black Union soldiers and White Confederate soldiers?

A. Yes. White Confederate soldiers who fought to destroy the Union and who signed the *future* loyalty oath were empowered under the Lincoln-approved plan to vote in the Louisiana elections of 1864. Black Union soldiers, without whom the Union could not have been preserved, could not vote in the Lincoln-approved Louisiana elections of 1864.

It was this Lincoln, the *last* Lincoln, who defined himself for the last time at the last cabinet meeting on the last full day of his life. At this meeting, which lasted from 11 a.m. to 2 p.m. on Friday, April 14, 1865, Lincoln vehemently defended the lily-White Louisiana government, saying that the Louisiana constitution, which disenfranchised his soldiers and most of the people of the state, was "one of the best constitutions that had ever been formed." He was disturbed by the attacks of Sumner and others who had rejected the Louisiana representatives. Welles, who was there and who reported the conversation in the *Galaxy* magazine of April 1872, quoted Lincoln as saying, "These humanitarians break down all State rights and constitutional rights. Had the Louisianians inserted the Negro in their Constitution, and had that instrument been in all other respects the same, Mr. Sumner, he said, would never have excepted to that Constitution."

He never did get a chance to tell us, and now we will never know, why he chose to define himself on the last full day of his life as an anti-humanitarian, but the statement is on record and is consistent with the record he made on the issues of race, equality, emancipation, and Black freedom from 1836 to 1865.

Lincoln didn't change.

He believed until his death that the Negro was the Other, the inferior, the subhuman, who had to be—Lincoln said it was a NECESSITY—subordinated, enslaved, quarantined to protect the sexual, social, political, and economic interests of Whites. Everything he did in his last one hundred days, everything he said, even the speeches his defenders are always praising, was based on this racist idea, which defined his life, his politics, and his Gettysburgs.

Lincoln's assassination and the aggressive dissemination of the "Massa Linkun myth" pushed the real Lincoln with his real limitations into the background, and African-Americans were soon pooling their pennies to erect a monument to the mythical emancipator. When, on April 14, 1876, this monument was unveiled, Frederick Douglass punctured the myths and looked frankly at the man, praising his growth and criticizing his limitations.

> Truth [Douglass said] is proper and beautiful at all times and in all places, and it is never more proper and beautiful in any case than when speaking of a great public man whose example is likely to be commended for honor and imitation long after his departure to the solemn shades, the silent continent of eternity. It must be admitted, truth compels me to admit, even here

in the presence of the monument we have erected to his memory, Abraham Lincoln was not, in the fullest sense of the word, either our man or our model. *In his interests, in his associations, in his habits of thought, and in his prejudices, he was a white man. He was preeminently the white man's President, entirely devoted to the welfare of white men.* (FD 4:312, italics added)

Speaking thus of interests and passion and public acts, Douglass, who knew Lincoln well, sounded the discordant notes of a national, not a personal tragedy. For, in the final analysis, Lincoln must be seen as the embodiment, not the transcendence, of the American Tradition of racism. In his inability to rise above that tradition, Lincoln, often called "the noblest of all Americans," holds up a flawed mirror to the American soul. And one honors him today, not by gazing fixedly at a flawed image, not by hiding warts and excrescences, but by seeing oneself in the reflected ambivalences of a life which calls us to transcendence, not imitation.

It turns out, then, that Lincoln spoke good words in a bad cause when he asked Congress to buy the slaves and deport them, blandly observing, "*We* cannot escape history." Saying this, the great emancipator who refused the role of the great emancipator was judging himself and everybody who chooses himself by choosing for or against Lincoln. For nobody, neither Lincoln nor Robert E. Lee nor Nathan Bedford Forrest, can escape history, which judges us prospectively, giving our acts their true meaning based on the meaning those acts acquire objectively in an unfolding history process.

From this standpoint, we draw our portrait in history by what we do and what we fail to do in history, which has an infallible accounting system and which will, Lincoln said, judging himself, "light us down in honor or dishonor to the latest generation." This, in fact, is the only power the powerless have in history, the power to say to the powerful and the comfortable that if you take a stand in history against us and against history, history will never forget or forgive you.

That's why Lincoln still has something to say to us negatively. For although the language and the political parties have changed, the

Lincolns, Stevenses, Sumners, Douglasses, Tubmans, and Lees are still with us, and the situation has not changed since the time people were forced to choose between slavery and freedom.

This means, among other things, that a choice for or against Lincoln today is a choice for or against a certain kind of politics. It is a choice for or against masters, slaves, fugitive slave laws, moderates, and militants. Above all else, it is a choice for or against slavery, the slavery that defined George Washington, Thomas Jefferson, and Abraham Lincoln and the slavery that is still walking the streets of America.

Lincoln was right against Lincoln.

We cannot escape history.

We—Thomas Jefferson, Abraham Lincoln, John Jones, John Brown, Wendell Phillips, Thaddeus Stevens, Charles Sumner, Woodrow Wilson, Carl Sandburg, James G. Randall, Stephen Oates, Calvin Fairbanks, William Walker, Jane Doe, John Doe, Lerone Bennett Jr., researchers, scholars, authors, critics, readers—are responsible for what we did and did not do and for the choices *we* made, and the choices *we* are making, in our history between humanity and White supremacy, freedom and oppression, truth and lies.

Notes

1. Among Carl Sandburg's best-known works are the multivolumed *Prairie Years* and *War Years*; Lindsay's poem, "Abraham Lincoln Walks at Midnight," is in *The Poetry of Vachel Lindsay*, 1:169, edited by Dennis Camp. Martin Luther King Jr. invoked the broken promise of emancipation in his "I Have A Dream" speech at the March on Washington in August 1963 but was critical of the great emancipator myth. See his *Where Do We Go From Here?* 77-9; Copland's *Lincoln Portrait*.

2. David B. Davis to Leonard Swett, Davis Papers, Nov. 26, 1862, Illinois State Historical Library (hereafter ISHL).

3. Appletons' *Annual Cyclopaedia* (hereafter AC) 1863 reported that the Emancipation Proclamation only applied to slaves in Confederate-held areas—where Lincoln did not have the power to free them. The Proclamation did not apply to the 429,396 slaves in the "loyal" slave states of Kentucky, Maryland, Missouri, and Delaware, and left in slavery the 402,863 slaves in Union-controlled areas Lincoln could have freed: 275,719 in Tennessee, 87,812 in Louisiana, and 39,332 in Virginia. The AC estimate was based on the 1860 Census and did not take into consideration population growth and the large number of slaves who flocked to Union-controlled areas in Tennessee, Louisiana, and Virginia. I have therefore used a conservative estimate of 500,000 for the number of slaves Lincoln could have freed and deliberately did not free.

4. The letters and dispatches of *New York Tribune* Washington correspondent Adams S. Hill to his supervisor, managing editor Sidney Howard Gay, are a valuable and often overlooked source of information on Lincoln and the Lincoln White House. The letters (hereafter cited as Gay) are in the Gay MSS in Butler Library, Columbia University. The Wadsworth letter cited was listed by the historian James F. Rhodes (4:64), who said that Hill "kindly placed at my disposal" his private correspondence.

5. T. J. Barnett to S. L. M. Barlow, Nov. 30, 1862, Barlow Papers, Huntington Library. Lincoln played an interesting and perhaps double game with a provocative group of Democratic moles, including T. J. Barnett, a lower-level Interior Department worker who conferred with Lincoln often and reported regularly to Democratic powerhouse S. L.M. Barlow, an intimate of General McClellan.

6. *Reasons Against the Re-nomination of Abraham Lincoln, Adopted February 15, 1864, by a Republican Meeting at Davenport, Iowa,* pamphlet in the Huntington Library.

7. Almost all scholars believe the Wadsworth letter is a forgery. The undated

Lincoln letter was purportedly written to General James S. Wadsworth, who was killed in the Battle of the Wilderness, May 5-7, 1864, and who could not therefore verify or deny the letter. The letter surfaced first in the *New York Tribune* of Sept. 26, 1865, which quoted a self-serving account that reportedly appeared in the *Southern Advocate* of September 18, 1865, and which reportedly favored "universal amnesty" for former Confederates and "universal suffrage" for Blacks." Twenty-eight years later, in January 1893, the letter appeared in *Scribner's* magazine with new Lincoln lines—and the only Lincoln lines in existence—on "civil and political equality" for Blacks: "The restoration of the Rebel States to the United States must rest upon the principle of civil and political equality of both races; and it must be sealed by general amnesty" (CW 7:102). Despite the suspicious circumstances surrounding the letter—neither the *Southern Advocate* nor the original letter has been found and the lines on civil and political equality do not appear in either newspaper account—the editors of *The Collected Works* (CW 7:101-2.) said the letter "seems to be genuine" and "is closely in keeping with views Lincoln expressed elsewhere . . . ." In support of that conclusion, the editor quotes an undated Lincoln fragment which said absolutely nothing about universal suffrage or civil and political equality (CW 6:410-1). In fact, as almost everyone admits, the quotation contradicts the words and spirit of everything Lincoln said and did from 1836 to 1865, especially his opposition to Black suffrage and "civil and political equality" in the Lincoln-Douglas debates and his active opposition to universal suffrage and civil and political equality in Louisiana in the last days of his life. See Ludwell H. Johnson, "Lincoln and Equal Rights for Negroes: The Authenticity of the Wadsworth Letter."

8. See CW 3:81. This statement, which almost every schoolchild knows, is, like so many Lincoln statements, a myth. There is no evidence that Lincoln ever said it, which is poetic justice, since the manipulation of the Lincoln myth proves that you *can* fool all the American people, save one or two, all the time.

9. *Journal of the House of Representatives at the Second Session of the Ninth General Assembly, State of Illinois, 236,* Jan. 5, 1836, hereafter *House Journal.*

10. *Congressional Globe,* 40th Cong., 1st sess., March 19, 1967: 207.

11. *Journal of Negro History,* 37 (July 1952): 449.

12. *Civil War Times Illustrated,* Dec. 1995, named the following books, in this order: *Collected Works of Abraham Lincoln,* edited by Roy P. Basler; *Lincoln* by David H. Donald; *Lincoln Day by Day,* edited by Earl S. Miers; *Herndon's Lincoln* by William H. Herndon and Jesse Weik; *Lincoln and the Economics of the American Dream* by Gabor Boritt; *Lincoln the President* by J.G. Randall; *Abraham Lincoln* by Benjamin Thomas; *The Fate of Liberty* by Mark E. Neely Jr; *Prelude to Greatness* by Don E. Fehrenbacher; *Abraham Lincoln* by John G. Nicolay and John Hay.

13. Donald 633-4; Fehrenbacher 1987, 106; See also Fredrickson 39-58.

14. Jaffa, "Lincoln, the Emancipator," in Fehrenbacher 1970, 149, italics added.

15. Charles H. Ray To E. B. Washburne, Dec. 12, 1854, Washburne Papers, Library of Congress (LC).

16. Herndon (HW) 10-11; NH 1:21; Beveridge 1:11-2; Sandburg *Prairie* 1:26-7; Thomas 4-5.

17. HW 54; Holland 31-2; Whitney 309; Beveridge 88.

18. I have followed Harris's standard work, *The History of Negro Servitude in Illinois.*

Except where otherwise indicated, quotations are from this book. See also Gertz 1963; Cole 225-9.

19. "Negro Merchant's Career Recalled by Ottley," by Roi Ottley, *Chicago Tribune*, July 24, 1955, John Jones File, Chicago Historical Society.

20. ibid. See also Jones *Black Laws*; Bontemps and Conroy 43-52; Charles A. Gliozzo, "John Jones, A Study of a Black Chicagoan," *Illinois Historical Journal* 80 (Autumn 1987): 177-88.

21. See Quarles 1962, 26-8; and Washington 189-93.

22. *House Journal*, 12th General Assembly, Dec. 30, 1840: 164

23. I have relied here on the excellent summary in Eric Foner's study, *Free Soil, Free Labor, Free Men* 281-95.

24. Randall said "Lincoln's efforts toward colonization would make a long story and a dismal one" (1945-55, 2:139). Hofstadter said "the alternative idea of colonizizing the Negroes abroad was and always had been pathetic" (167).

25. See also *The Papers of Henry Clay*, 6:92.

26. *Congressional Globe*, 31st Cong., 1st sess., Feb. 20, 1850: 141-3.

27. ibid., 30th Cong., 2d sess., Dec. 21, 1848: 83-4.

28. ibid., Dec. 27: 107.

29. ibid., Jan. 10, 1849: 212

30. Eastman and other Illinois antislavery leaders are overlooked by almost all scholars. All Eastman quotes except where otherwise indicated are from the Glassman study.

31. See Weik 1897; Beveridge 1:392-7; Duff 130-49. See also Matson file in the Herndon-Weik Collection, LC.

32. Randall 1945-55, 1:24; Basler 1946, 42; White 19.

33. Lincoln borrowed the phrase "the human family" from the infamous chief Justice Roger Taneyand later used it without quotes. Taney, who said in the Dred Scott decision that members of the Black human family had no rights in America that members of the White human family were bound to respect, obviously didn't believe in the human family. Nor did Lincoln, who denied that he wanted "a Nigger wife" and who repeatedly denounced intermarriage and the mixing of the blood of the Black and White races.

34. *Official Records of the War of Rebellion* (hereafter OR), 2d ser., vol. 1, 753.

35. ibid., 778.

36. Barlow Papers, Nov. 30, 1862.

37. OR, 760.

38. ibid., 761-2.

39. There are several versions of the story. The only difference is that the expurgated versions delete the word *damn*. See Angle 1950, 51-2; Hertz 327-8; Seitz 332-3.

40. Pierce to Herndon, Sept. 15, 1889, Herndon-Weik Collection, LC. The last word in the sentence is not entirely clear and has been rendered as *lines* and *lives*. I believe the word *lives* captures the sense and meaning of the conversation.

41. Medill to Lincoln, Feb. 9, 1862, Lincoln MSS, LC.

42. Medill to Washburne, April 12, 1864, Washburne Papers, LC.

43. *Reasons Against the Re-nomination 6*.

44. Schurz to Lincoln, Nov. 8, 1862, Lincoln MSS, LC; CW 5:493-5.

45. *Globe*, 37th Cong., special sess., Aug. 2, 1861: 414-5.

46. White to David Davis, Sep. 14, 1861, Davis Papers, ISHL.

47. Globe, 37th Cong., 2d sess., Jan. 22, 1862: 440-1.

48. *Liberator*, Oct. 10, 1862 ; Gay, July 9, 1862.

49. F.B. Cutting to Stanton, Feb. 20, 1867, Stanton Papers, LC.

50. ibid.

51. Leonard Swett to Laura Swett, Aug. 10, 1862, Davis Papers, ISHL.

52. Fessenden 1:231-6; BD 596-604.

53. Seward 151. See also Carpenter 87, 269-70.

54. AC 1863 said "the gross number" the Proclamation recognized as slaves in the Border States, Tennessee, and liberated areas was 832,259 (835). This, of course, was an approximation based no doubt on the last census and did not include the large number of slaves who had flocked to New Orleans and other Union-held areas. See note 3.

55. U.S. Senate, Joint Committee on the Conduct of the War, *Fort Pillow Massacre*, 38th Cong., 1st sess., May 5, 1864: 1-7.

56. *Globe*, 38th Cong., 1st sess., May 2, 1864: 2042.

57. James Mitchell interview, *St. Louis Daily Globe Democrat*, August 26, 1894.

58. Bates to Lincoln, Nov. 30, 1864, Lincoln MSS, LC; Mitchell, op cit.

59. I am again using the word *pretty* here as a technical term to signify a rhetorical use of perfumed words that is so deeply ingrained it takes the place of assertion about reality and, in the mouths of a Lincoln or a Jefferson, becomes reality.

60. *Harper's Pictorial History of the Civil War: Contemporary Accounts and Illustrations*, May 1866: 650.

61. "Remarks of Thurgood Marshall," May 6, 1987.

62. Holzer 1993, 346; See also Clay Papers, Vol. 9: 778-9.

63. I have followed the factual outline of Basler's interesting essay, "Did President Lincoln Give The Smallpox to William H. Johnson?" The conclusion, of course, is my own. See also Washington 130-6.

64. Qtd. in Woodley 474; see also *Globe*, 39th Cong., lst sess., Dec. 18, 1865: 74.

65. *Globe*, 40th Cong., 1st sess., March 19, 1867, 203-6.

66. ibid., 206.

67. ibid., 203.

68. ibid. Dec. 18, 1865: 74-5.

69. OR, lst ser., vol. 15, 667-8.

70. *Globe*, 39th Cong., lst sess., June 13, 1866: 3148.

Works Cited

Adams, Abigail. *Letters of Mrs. Adams, the Wife of John Adams.* Edited by Charles Francis Adams. Boston, 1841.

Angle, Paul M., ed. 1930. *New Letters and Papers of Lincoln.* New York.

———, ed. 1950. *Abraham Lincoln By Some Men Who Knew Him.* Chicago.

Appletons' Annual Cyclopaedia. New York. 1861-65. (Cited as AC.)

Aptheker, Herbert, ed. *A Documentary History of the Negro People in the United States.* Vol. 1. New York, 1951.

Bancroft, George. 1866. *Memorial Address on the Life and Character of Abraham Lincoln.* Washington.

———. 1908. *The Life and Letters of George Bancroft.* Edited by Mark Anthony de Wolfe Howe. Vol. 2. New York.

Arnold, Isaac N. *The Life of Abraham Lincoln.* Chicago, 1885.

Barton, William E. 1925. *Life of Abraham Lincoln.* Vol. 1. Indianapolis.

———. 1950. *Lincoln at Gettysburg.* New York.

Basler, Roy P. 1935. *The Lincoln Legend.* Boston.

———, ed. 1946. *Abraham Lincoln: His Speeches and Writings.* Cleveland.

———, ed. 1953-55. *The Collected Works of Abraham Lincoln.* 11 vols. New Brunswick (Cited as CW.)

———. 1972. "Did President Lincoln Give the Smallpox to William H. Johnson?" *Huntington Library Quarterly* 35 (May 1972): 279-84.

Bates, David Homer. *Lincoln in the Telegraph Office.* New York, 1939.

Bates, Edward. *The Diary of Edward Bates, 1859-1866.* Edited by Howard K. Beale. Vol. 1. Washington, 1933.

Baxter, Maurice G. *Orville H. Browning, Lincoln's Friend and Critic.* Bloomington, 1975.

Belz, Herman. *Reconstructing the Union.* Ithaca, 1969.

Bennett, Lerone Jr. 1961. *Before the Mayflower.* 6th ed. Chicago, 1995.

———. 1967. *Black Power U.S.A., The Human Side of Reconstruction, 1867-1877.* Chicago.

———. 1968. *Pioneers in Protest.* Chicago.

———. 1975. *The Shaping of Black America.* Chicago.

———. 1968. "Was Abe Lincoln A White Supremacist?" *Ebony* (February 1968): 35-8, 40, 42.

Berlin, Ira. *Freedom: A Documentary History of Emancipation.* Series II. Cambridge, 1982.

Berwanger, Eugene H. *The Frontier Against Slavery.* Urbana, 1967.

Beveridge, Albert J. *Abraham Lincoln, 1809-1858.* 2 vols. Boston, 1928.

Bontemps, Arna, ed. *Golden Slippers.* New York, 1941.

Bontemps, Arna, and Jack Conroy. *They Seek a City.* New York, 1945.

Boritt, Gabor S. *Lincoln and the Economics of the American Dream.* Urbana, 1978.

Bradford, Sarah H. *Harriet, The Moses of Her People.* Auburn, 1897.

Brodie, Fawn M. *Thaddeus Stevens, Scourge of the South.* New York, 1959.

Brooks, Noah. 1895. *Washington in Lincoln's Time.* New York.

———. 1967. *Mr. Lincoln's Washington: Selections from the Writings of Noah Brooks.* Edited by P. J. Staudenraus. South Brunswick.

Browning, Orville H. *The Diary of Orville Hickman Browning.* Vol. 1. Edited by Theodore C. Pease and James G. Randall. Springfield, 1925. (Cited as BD.)

Bunche, Ralph J. *The Political Status of the Negro in the Age of FDR.* Edited by Dewey W. Grantham. Chicago, 1973.

Burlingame, Michael, ed. *An Oral History of Abraham Lincoln: John G. Nicolay's Interviews and Essays.* Carbondale, 1996.

Butler, Benjamin F. *Butler's Book.* Boston, 1892.

Cain, Marvin R. *Lincoln's Attorney General: Edward Bates of Missouri.* Columbia, 1965.

Capers, Gerald. *Occupied City: New Orleans Under the Federals.* Frankfurt, 1965.

Carpenter, F. B. *Six Months at the White House with Abraham Lincoln.* New York, 1866.

Chase, Salmon P. 1903. *Diary and Correspondence of Salmon P. Chase. In American Historical Association Annual Report, 1902. Vol 2.* Washington.

———. 1954. *Inside Lincoln's Cabinet: the Civil War Diaries of Salmon P. Chase.* Edited by David Donald. New York. (Cited as CD.)

———. 1993. *The Salmon P. Chase Papers*. Vol. 3. Edited by John Niven. Kent. (Cited as CP.)

Charnwood, Lord. *Abraham Lincoln*. New York, 1917.

Chittenden, Lucius E. *Recollections of President Lincoln and his Administration*. New York, 1891.

Clarke, Grace Julian. *George W. Julian*. Indianapolis, 1923.

Clay, Henry. *The Papers of Henry Clay*. Edited by James F. Hopkins, Mary W. M. Hargreaves, R. Seager and M. P. Hay. Vols. 6 and 9. Lexington, 1959-.

Cole, Arthur Charles. *The Centennial History of Illinois: The Era of the Civil War*. Vol. 3. Springfield, 1919.

Copland, Aaron. *Lincoln Portrait, for speaker and orchestra*. New York, 1943.

Cox, Oliver C. *Caste, Class, and Race*. New York, 1948.

Cornish, Dudley Taylor. *The Sable Army: Negro Troops in the Union Army, 1861-1865*. New York, 1956.

Current, Richard N. *The Lincoln Nobody Knows*. New York, 1958.

Curry, Leonard P. *Blueprint for Modern America: Nonmilitary Legislation of the First Civil War Congress*. Nashville, 1968.

Dahlgren, John A. *Memoir of John A. Dahlgren*. By Madeleine Dahlgren. Boston, 1882.

Delaney, Martin R. *The Condition, Elevation, Emigration, and Destiny of the Colored People of the United States*. Philadelphia, 1852.

Donald, David H. *Lincoln*. New York, 1995.

Douglass, Frederick. *The Life and Writings of Frederick Douglass*. Edited by Philip S. Foner. 4 vols. New York, 1955. (Cited as FD.)

DuBois, W.E.B. 1924. *The Gift of Black Folk*. Boston.

———. 1935. *Black Reconstruction*. New York.

Duff, John J. *A. Lincoln: Prairie Lawyer*. New York, 1960.

Dumond, Dwight L. *Antislavery*. Ann Arbor, 1961.

Eaton, John. *Grant, Lincoln and the Freedmen*. New York, 1907.

Emerson, Ken. *Doo-dah! Stephen Foster and the Rise of American Popular Culture*. New York, 1997.

Emerson, Ralph Waldo. *Journals of Ralph Waldo Emerson*. Vol. 2. Edited by E.W. Emerson and W.E. Forbes. Boston, 1913.

Fauset, Arthur Huff. *Sojourner Truth*. Chapel Hill, 1938.

Fehrenbacher, Don E. 1962. *Prelude to Greatness: Lincoln in the 1850's*. Stanford.

———. 1987. *Lincoln in Text and Context*.

———, ed. 1970. *The Leadership of Abraham Lincoln*. New York.

Fessenden, Francis. *Life and Public Services of William Pitt Fessenden*. Vol. 1. Boston, 1907.

Fischer, LeRoy H. *Lincoln's Gadfly, Adam Gurowski*. Norman, 1964.

Foner, Eric. *Free Soil, Free Labor, Free Men*. New York, 1970.

Foner, Philip S., ed. *The Life and Writings of Frederick Douglass*. 4 vols. New York, 1950-55. (Cited as FD.)

Foner, Philip S. and George F. Walker, eds. *Proceedings of the Black State Conventions, 1840-1865*. Philadelphia, 1980.

Forbes, John Murray. *Letters and Recollections of John Murray Forbes*. Edited by Sarah Forbes Hughes. Boston, 1899.

Franklin, John Hope. 1963. *The Emancipation Proclamation*. New York, 1963.

———. 1990. "Who Divided This House?" An Address at the Chicago Historical Society, July 4, 1990, printed in *Chicago History*, Fall and Winter, 1990-91.

Fredrickson, George M. "A Man but Not a Brother: Abraham Lincoln and Racial Equality," *Journal of Southern History* 41 (February 1975): 39-58.

Frémont, Jessie Benton. *The Letters of Jessie Benton Frémont*. Edited by Pamela Herr and Mary Lee Spence. Urbana, 1993.

Garfield, James A. *The Life and Letters of James Abram Garfield,* by Theodore Clarke Smith. Vol. 1. New Haven, 1925.

Garrison, William L. 1831. *An Address Delivered Before the Free People of Color of Philadelphia and Other Cities*. Boston.

———. 1894. *William L. Garrison*. Edited by W. P. Garrison and F. L Garrison. 4 vols. Boston.

———. 1979. *The Letters of William L. Garrison*. Edited by Walter M. Merrill. Vol. 5. Cambridge.

Gertz, Elmer. *1945. Joe Medill's War*. Chicago, 1945.

———. 1963. "The Black Laws of Illinois," *Journal of the Illinois State Historical Society* 56 (Autumn 1963).

Glassman, Paula. "Zebina Eastman: Chicago Abolitionist." Master's thesis, University of Chicago, 1968.

Grover, Leonard. "Lincoln's Interest in the Theater," *Century* (April 1909): 943-50.

Gurowski, Adam. *Diary*. 3 vols. 1862-1866. Reprint: New York, 1968. (Cited as AG.)

Harding, Vincent. *There Is a River*. New York, 1981.

Harris, N. Dwight. *The History of Negro Servitude in Illinois and the Slavery Agitation in that State.* Chicago, 1904.

Harris, Wilmer C. *Public Life of Zachariah Chandler.* Chicago, 1917.

Hay, John. *Lincoln and the Civil War; in the Diaries and Letters of John Hay.* Edited by Tyler Dennett. New York, 1939.

Hegel, G. W. F. *The Phenomenology of Mind.* Translated by J. B. Baillie. London, 1964.

Herndon, William H., and Jessie W. Weik. 1930. *Life of Lincoln.* Introduction and Notes by Paul M. Angle. Reprint: Cleveland, 1949. (Cited as HW.)

———. 1938. *The Hidden Lincoln: From the Letters and Papers of William H. Herndon.* Edited by Emanuel Hertz. New York. (Cited as HH.)

———. 1998. *Herndon's Informants.* Edited by Douglass L.Wilson and Rodney O. Davis. Urbana. (Cited as HI.)

Hertz, Emanuel. *Lincoln Talks.* New York, 1939.

Hofstadter, Richard. *The American Political Tradition.* New York, 1974.

Holland, J. G. *Life of Abraham Lincoln.* Springfield, 1866.

Holzer, Harold, ed. 1993. *The Lincoln-Douglas Debates.* New York.

———, ed. 1998. *The Lincoln Mailbag.* Carbondale.

Hook, Sidney. *The Hero In History.* Boston, 1943.

Howard, Robert P. *Illinois: A History of the Prairie State.* Grand Rapids, 1972.

Howard, Victor B., *Black Liberation in Kentucky.* Lexington, 1983.

Hume, John F. *The Abolitionists.* New York, 1905.

Jaffa, Harry V. "Lincoln, the Emancipator." In *The Leadership of Abraham Lincoln.* Edited by Don. E. Fehrenbacher. New York, 1970.

Jefferson, Thomas. 1899. *The Writings of Thomas Jefferson.* Vol. 10. Edited by Paul L. Ford. New York.

———. 1950-.*The Papers of Thomas Jefferson.* Edited by Julian P. Boyd. Vol. 10. Princeton.

Johannsen, Robert W. *Lincoln, the South and Slavery.* Baton Rouge, 1991.

Johnson, Ludwell. "Lincoln and Equal Rights: The Authenticity of the Wadsworth Letter," *Journal of Southern History* 32 (Sept. 1966): 83-7.

Jones, Edgar DeWitt. *The Influence of Henry Clay Upon Abraham Lincoln.* Lexington, 1952.

Jones, James P. *Black Jack: John A. Logan and Southern Illinois in the Civil War Era.* Tallahassee, 1967.

Jones, John. *The Black Laws of Illinois and A Few Reasons Why They Should Be Repealed*. Chicago, 1864.

Julian, George W. *Political Recollections*. Chicago, 1884.

Keckley, Elizabeth. *Behind the Scenes: Thirty Years a Slave, and Four Years in the White House*. 1868. Reprint: New York, 1968.

King, Martin Luther Jr. 1967. *Where Do We Go From Here?* Boston, 1967.

————. 1993. *I Have A Dream*. San Francisco.

Kinsley, Philip. *The Chicago Tribune: Its First 100 Years*. Vol. 1. New York, 1943.

Korngold, Ralph. 1950. *Two Friends of Man: The Story of William Lloyd Garrison and Wendell Phillips and Their Relationship with Abraham Lincoln*. Boston, 1950.

————. 1955. *Thaddeus Stevens*. New York.

Krug, Mark. *Lyman Trumbull: Conservative Radical*. New York, 1965.

Lair, John. *Songs Lincoln Loved*. New York, 1954.

Lamon, Ward H. 1872. *The Life of Abraham Lincoln*. Boston.

————. 1895. *Recollections of Abraham Lincoln 1847-1865*. Edited by Dorothy Lamon Teillard. Washington.

Lester, Charles Edward. *Life and Public Service of Charles Sumner*. 1874.

Lincoln, Abraham. *The Collected Works of Abraham Lincoln*. Edited by Roy P. Basler. 9 vols. New Brunswick, 1953-55. (Cited as CW.)

Lincoln, C. Eric. *The Negro Pilgrimage in America*. New York, 1967.

Linder, Usher F. *Reminiscences of the Early Bench and Bar of Illinois*. Chicago, 1879.

Lindsay, Vachel. "Abraham Lincoln Walks At Midnight." In *The Poetry of Vachel Lindsay*. Vol. 1. Edited by Dennis Camp. Peoria, 1984.

Lott, Eric. *Blackface Minstrelsy and the American Working Class*. New York, 1993.

Luthin, Reinhard H. *The Real Abraham Lincoln*. Englewood Cliffs, 1960.

McCaul, Robert L. *The Black Struggle for Public Schooling in Nineteenth-Century Illinois*. Carbondale, 1987.

McClure, A. L. *Abraham Lincoln and Men of War-Times*. Philadelphia, 1892.

McColley, Robert. *Slavery and Jeffersonian Virginia*. 2d ed. Urbana, 1973.

McCoy, Drew R. *The Last of the Fathers: James Madison and the Republican Legacy*. New York, 1989.

McPherson, Edward. *Political History of the United States of America During the Great Rebellion*. 1876.

McPherson, James M. 1964. *The Struggle for Equality: Abolitionists and the*

Negro in the Civil War and Reconstruction. Princeton.

———. 1965. *The Negro's Civil War.* New York.

Mann, Charles W. "The Chicago Common Council and the Fugitive Slave Law of 1850." An Address Read Before the Chicago Historical Society, January 29, 1903.

Magdol, Edward. *Owen Lovejoy: Abolitionist in Congress.* New Brunswick, 1967.

Marshall, Thurgood. "Remarks of Thurgood Marshall at the Annual Seminar of the San Francisco Patent and Trademark Law Association," Maui, Hawaii, May 6, 1987. Mimeographed.

Martyn, Carlos. *Wendell Phillips, the Agitator.* New York, 1890.

Mearns, David C., ed. *The Lincoln Papers.* Vol. 1. Garden City, 1948.

Merleau-Ponty, Maurice. *Signs.* Translated by Richard McCleary. Evanston, 1964.

Miers, Earl Schenck, ed. *Lincoln Day by Day: A Chronology, 1809-1865.* 3 vols. Dayton, 1991.

Mitgang, Herbert. *The Letters of Carl Sandburg.* New York, 1968.

Monaghan, Jay. *The Man Who Elected Lincoln.* Indianapolis, 1956.

Myrdal, Gunnar. *An American Dilemma.* New York, 1944.

Neely, Mark E., Jr. 1982. *The Abraham Lincoln Encyclopedia.* New York.

———. 1993. *The Last Best Hope of Earth: Abraham Lincoln and the Promise of America.* Cambridge.

Nevins, Allan. *The War for the Union.* Vol. 2. New York, 1960.

Nicolay, Helen. *Personal Traits of Abraham Lincoln.* New York, 1939.

Nicolay, John G. *An Oral History of Abraham Lincoln.* Edited by Michael Burlingame. Carbondale, 1996.

Nicolay, John G., and John Hay. *Abraham Lincoln: A History.* 10 vols. New York, 1890. (Cited as NH.)

Niven, John. 1973. *Gideon Welles.* Baton Rouge.

———. 1995. *Salmon P. Chase.* New York.

Northup, Solomon. *Narrative of Solomon Northup.* Auburn, 1853.

Oates, Stephen B. *With Malice Toward None: The Life of Abraham Lincoln.* New York, 1977.

Oberholtzer, Ellis P. *Abraham Lincoln.* Philadelphia, 1904.

O'Brien, Conor Cruise. *The Long Affair: Thomas Jefferson and the French Revolution.* Chicago, 1996.

Official Records of the Union and Confederate Armies, The War of the Rebellion. Washington, 1880-1901. (Cited as OR.)

Payne, Daniel A. *Recollections of Seventy Years.* 1888. Reprint: New York, 1968.

Pearson, Henry Greenleaf. *The Life of John A. Andrew.* Vol. 2. Boston, 1904.

Peterson, Merrill D. *Lincoln in American Memory.* New York, 1994.

Phillips, Wendell. *Speeches, Lectures and Addresses.* First Series. Edited by Theodore C. Pease. Boston, 1891. (Cited as PS.)

Piatt, Donn. *Memories of the Men Who Saved the Union.* New York, 1887.

Porter, Horace. *Campaigning With Grant.* New York, 1897.

Quarles, Benjamin. 1948. *Frederick Douglass.* Washington.

————. 1962. *Lincoln and the Negro.* New York.

————. 1964. *The Negro in the Making of America.* New York.

Randall, J.G. 1945-55. *Lincoln, the President.* 4 vols. New York.

————. 1946. *Lincoln and the South.* Baton Rouge.

————. 1947. *Lincoln, the Liberal Statesman.* New York.

————. 1957. *Mr. Lincoln.* Edited by Richard N. Current. New York.

Raymond, Henry. *Life and Public Services of Abraham Lincoln.* New York, 1865.

Reasons Against the Re-nomination of Abraham Lincoln. Resolutions adopted February 15, 1864, by Republican meeting, Davenport, Iowa. Pamphlet in Huntington Library.

Remini, Robert V. *Henry Clay.* New York, 1991.

Rhodes, James F. *History of the United States from the Compromise of 1850.* Vol. 4. New York, 1910.

Rice, Allen Thorndike, ed. *Reminiscences of Abraham Lincoln by Distinguished Men of his Time.* 1888. Reprint: New York, 1971.

Riddle, Donald W. *Congressman Abraham Lincoln.* Westport, 1979.

Sandburg, Carl. 1926. *Abraham Lincoln: The Prairie Years.* 2 vols. New York.

————. 1939. *Abraham Lincoln: The War Years.* 4 vols. New York.

————. 1968. *The Letters of Carl Sandburg.* Edited by Herbert Mitgang. New York.

Scheips, Paul J. "Lincoln and The Chiriqui Colonization Project." *Journal of Negro History* 37 (July 1952): 418-53.

Searcher, Victor. *Lincoln's Journey to Greatness.* Philadelphia, 1960.

Segal, Charles M., ed. *Conversations with Lincoln.* New York, 1961.

Sherwin, Oscar. *Prophet of Liberty: The Life and Times of Wendell Phillips.* New York, 1958.

Siebert, Wilbur H. *The Underground Railway from Slavery to Freedom.* New York, 1898.

Seitz, Don C. *Lincoln the Politician.* New York, 1931.

Seward, William H. *Seward at Washington as Senator and Secretary of State,* by Frederick W. Seward. Vol. 2. New York, 1891.

Simon, Paul. *Lincoln's Preparation for Greatness.* Norman, 1965.

Sinkler, George. *The Racial Attitudes of American Presidents.* Garden City, 1972.

Smith, Theodore Clarke. *The Life and Letters of James Abram Garfield.* New Haven, 1925.

Smith, William E. *The Francis Preston Blair Family in Politics.* Vol. 2. New York, 1933.

Sparks, Edwin E. *The Lincoln-Douglas Debates of 1858.* Springfield, 1908.

Speed, Joshua F. *Reminiscences of Abraham Lincoln and Notes of a Visit to California.* Louisville, 1884.

Stampp, Kenneth M. *The Era of Reconstruction.* New York, 1965.

Stephens, Alexander. *A Constitutional View of the Late War Between The States.* Vol. 2. Philadelphia, 1870.

Stephenson, Nathaniel W. *Lincoln.* Indianapolis, 1922.

Steward, Austin. *Twenty-Two Years a Slave.* Rochester, 1857.

Stewart, James Brewer. *Wendell Phillips.* Baton Rouge, 1986.

Still, William. *The Underground Railroad.* Philadelphia, 1879.

Strozier, Charles B. *Lincoln's Quest for Union.* New York, 1982.

Sumner, Charles. 1883. *His Complete Works.* 20 vols. Boston. (Cited as SW.)

———. 1893. *Memoir and Letters of Charles Sumner 1873-93.* By Edward L. Pierce. Vol. 4. Boston. (Cited as SM.)

———. 1990. *The Selected Letters of Charles Sumner.* Edited by Beverly Wilson Palmer. Vol. 2. Boston. (Cited as SL.)

Thomas, Benjamin P. 1934. *Lincoln's New Salem.* Springfield.

———. 1952. *Abraham Lincoln: A Biography.* New York.

Thomas, Benjamin P. and Harold M. Hyman. *Stanton: The Life and Times of Lincoln's Secretary of War.* New York, 1962.

Tourgee, Albion W. *A Fool's Errand.* New York, 1961.

Townsend, William H. *Lincoln and the Bluegrass.* Lexington, 1955.

Trefousse, Hans L. *The Radical Republicans.* Baton Rouge, 1968.

Truth, Sojourner. *Narrative of Sojourner Truth.* Boston, 1850.

Villard, Henry. *Lincoln on the Eve of '61.* Edited by Harold G. and Oswald

Garrison Villard. New York, 1941.

    Vorenberg, Michael. "Abraham Lincoln and the Politics of Black Colonization," *Journal of the Abraham Lincoln Association* 14 (1993): 23-45

Washington, John E. *They Knew Lincoln.* New York, 1942.

Weik, Jesse W. 1922. *The Real Lincoln.* Boston.

———. 1897. "Lincoln and the Matson Negroes," *Arena* 17 (April): 752-8.

Welles, Gideon. 1911. *Diary of Gideon Wells.* Vol. 1. New York. (Cited as WD).

———. 1872a. "Lincoln and Johnson," *Galaxy* (April 1872): 521-32.

———. 1872b. "The History of Emancipation," *Galaxy* (December 1872): 838-51. (Cited as WH.)

White, Horace. 1913. *The Life of Lyman Trumbull.* New York, 1913.

———. 1914. *"The Lincoln and Douglas Debates: An Address Before the Chicago Historical Society,"* February 17, 1914.

Whitney, Henry C. *Life on the Circuit with Lincoln.* Boston, 1892.

Williams, George Washington. *History of the Negro Race In America.* Vol. 2. New York, 1883.

Williams, Thomas Harry. *Lincoln and the Radicals.* Madison, 1941.

Wills, Garry. *Lincoln at Gettysburg.* New York, 1992.

Wilson, Edmund. *Patriotic Gore.* New York, 1962.

Wilson, Rufus Rockwell. *Intimate Memories of Lincoln.* Elmira, 1945.

Woodley, Thomas Frederick. *Thaddeus Stevens.* Harrisburg, 1934.

Woodson, Carter G. *The Negro in Our History.* Washington, 1947.

Zall, P.M., ed. *Abe Lincoln Laughing.* Berkeley, 1982.

Zilversmit, Arthur. 1971. *Lincoln on Black and White.* Belmont, 1971.

———. 1980. "Lincoln , the Hopeless Racist? A Great Emancipator, no, but no racist either." *Chicago Sun-Times*, Feb. 12, 1980.

Index

ment and reparations, 595-6, 598
—speeches: First Inaugural, 339-40; Second Inaugural, 41, 268, 379-80, 617; State of the Union addresses, 28, 376, 379-80, 385, 513-9, 589; last speech, 82-3, 618, 620

LINCOLN MYTH, THE:

—general, 42, 128; as defense of contemporary ideologies and institutions, 42, 137, 139-40, 481-2, 619, 625, 626; defining structure of American identity, 114; "great emancipator," 6, 30, 45, 114, 549-50, 625; AL as mythmaker, 51-55, 74, 117; a mirror, 114, 625; post-assassination *reversus*, 117-9; a secular religion, 114; and slavery, 254-6; and terror, 128-9; used to mystify Blacks and Whites, 42, 549-50
—academic default, 142; the American Analytic, 360; de facto acceptance of slavery, 142; fallacy of detached data, 63-4, 76, 127; fallacy of the isolated quote, 124-7, 252; moral default, 282-5; the pedagogy of silence, 121-4; perspective of liberation, 39-41; perspective of status quo, 39-40, 137-9; scholarly anxiety, 131; trained blindness, 116-7
—defenders of the faith, 209; anticipatory absolution, 122-123; appropriating acts Lincoln opposed, 29-30, 53, 55; auteur school, 122; begging the question, 121; the Bogart school, 129-31, 211; the consent theory, 142; the Constitution alibi, 247-8, 260-3, 281-2, 471; "everybody was a racist," 134-5; exclusion of testimony of Black and White critics, 120, 141, 142; "the good racist," 133, 134; "the tentative racist," 132, 134; "flogging the vindictives," 407, 408; "moving in the direction of " equality, 610, 617, 618
Lincoln, Mary Todd, wife, 55, 68, 71, 75, 94, 110, 169, 171, 436

Lincoln, Robert Todd, son, 51, 258
Lincoln Day by Day, 116-7, 130, 227
Lincoln, C. Eric, 550
Linder, Usher F., 68, 202, 280
Lindsay, Vachel, 7, 39
Logan, John A., 187, 609
Logan, Stephen T., 69
Louisiana, 31, 163, 376, 450, 520, 522; Blacks in, 560, 594, 603-4; Emancipation Proclamation exemptions, 12-3, 525-7, 535, 537-8, 540, 562-3; population, 343, 354; Reconstruction in, 82, 119, 122, 131, 137, 190, 197, 319, 520, 522, 547, 559-60, 562, 579, 588, 591-2, 594, 601, 602-7, 617, 619-24
Lovejoy, Elijah P., 57, 70, 85, 123, 202, 280, 322
Lovejoy, Owen, 192, 199-201, 273, 322, 364, 402, 432, 500, 560
Luthin, Reinhard H., 68, 214
McClellan, George B., 14, 32, 48, 139, 344, 364, 366, 374-5, 377, 379, 414, 419, 425, 433, 438, 472, 484, 488, 489, 491, 496, 497, 502
McClernand, J. A., 538
McColley, Robert, 7
Madison, James, 47, 149, 223, 308, 369, 433, 559, 569-71, 573
Magdol, Edward, 200, 322
Mann, Charles W., 288
Marshall, Thurgood, 51, 135, 569, 574, 575
Martyn, Carlos, 396
Matheny, James H., 199, 205
Matteson, J. A., 228
Matson case, the, 278-82
Mays, Benjamin E., 361
Medill Joseph M., 118, 120, 399, 431, 482, 555; on Civil War, 365, 394, 399, 431; on AL, 362-3, 364-5, 366, 377-8
Merleau-Ponty, Maurice, 120, 309, 320, 544-5
Minstrel shows, 74, 87, 90-95, 134, 176, 191; patronized by AL, 90, 94, 95;

Speed, James, 284, 595
Speed, Joshua Fry, 45, 68, 74, 102, 171, 248, 255, 259, 285
Stampp, Kenneth, 43
Stanly, Edward, 468, 500
Stanton, Edwin M., 101, 348, 364, 420, 423, 425, 436, 438, 439, 440, 444, 446, 448, 560, 595
Stephens, Alexander H., 4, 72, 222, 338, 341-2, 365, 375, 557, 611-4, 626
Stephenson, Nathaniel W., 15, 44, 100, 110, 294, 417, 484, 485
Stevens, Thaddeus, 24, 44, 198, 212-3, 284, 343, 349, 350, 405; compared with AL, 198, 212-3, 235, 404, 405; criticized, 284; evaluated, 23-4, 78-9, 349, 369-70, 555, 574; as leader, 235, 432; on Civil War, 368, 372-3, 393-5, 599 ; on colonization, 553; on Declaration of Independence, 394-6; on emancipation, 373, 393-4, 395; on "40 acres and a mule," 404, 597-8; on AL, 50, 119; on punishment and reparations, 284, 406, 595-6; on racism, 64, 599, 600; on Reconstruction, 590, 592, 593, 595-6, 597-8, 599-600, 608-9
Stevenson, Adlai, 114
Strozier, Charles B., 52, 135, 566
Sumner, Charles, 321, 554, 560, 626; career, 24, 27, 30, 44, 212-3, 273, 343, 349, 350, 403, 404-5, 420, 431; compared with Lincoln, 198-9, 212-3, 273, 404, 405; evaluated, 78-9, 349, 369-70, 401, 402, 482, 514-5, 550, 555, 574-5; as a leader, 350, 402, 404-8; on Black suffrage, 600-1, 606-7; on the Civil War, 41, 365, 368, 372, 379-80; on emancipation, 24, 400, 447; on Lincoln, 30, 102, 142, 362, 363, 370, 372, 379; on Reconstruction, 592, 606-7, 624; and slavery, 473
Stuart, John T., 170, 172, 205
Swett, Leonard, 27, 73, 74, 84, 170, 487
Taussig, James, 541

Thirteenth Amendment, 8, 19, 26-30, 54, 201, 221, 340-1, 361, 392, 404, 421, 435, 515, 518, 555, 574, 594, 612, 614, 615
Thirty-seventh Congress, 21, 347, 372, 390-2, 395, 397, 401, 402, 411, 518, 574, 597; Joint Committee on Conduct of the War, 24, 393, 404, 468, 499, 500, 510; confiscation acts, 18, 392, 453, 470, 471, 612; First Confiscation Act, 25, 372, 392, 404, 418, 421, 424, 427, 440, 597; Second Confiscation Act, 11, 12, 25, 245, 425, 430, 434, 448, 449, 450, 471, 483, 501, 506; started emancipation process, 390-3
Thomas, Benjamin, 110, 124, 137, 160, 161, 194, 470, 471, 486, 525
Thompson, Ambrose W., 382, 453
Tourgee, Albion W., 406, 592
Townsend, William H., 259, 260
Trefousse, Hans L., 23
Truth, Sojourner, 109, 141, 394, 596
Trumbull, Lyman, 208, 362, 402, 498; 607; career, 27, 294-7, 304; compared with AL, 25, 135, 294-7, 392-3; as a leader, 27, 30, 402, 404, 410, 433, 482, 555, 607, 608, 613; on Lincoln, 119, 361, 363-4, 470
Tubman, Harriet, 15, 39, 58, 149, 253, 287, 349, 364, 366, 368, 394, 482
Turner, Nat, 58, 166, 201, 253, 272, 352, 358, 531, 574, 353
Underground Railroad, 56, 190, 273, 275, 292, 293
Usher, John P., 560
Van Buren, Martin, 99, 116, 204-6
Villard, Henry, 5
Vorenberg, Michael, 457, 464
Wade, Benjamin, 23, 199, 402, 404, 406, 407, 429, 432, 482, 554
Wadsworth, James S., 14, 43, 431, 447, 450, 508
Walker, David, 58, 352, 433
Walker, William, 31, 543
Was Abe Lincoln A White Supremacist? 42